EVERYDAY ARGUMENTS

A Guide to Writing and Reading

Effective Arguments

KATHERINE J. MAYBERRY
Rochester Institute of Technology

Longman

New York • San Francisco • Boston
London • Toronto • Sydney • Tokyo • Singapore • Madrid
Mexico City • Munich • Paris • Cape Town • Hong Kong • Montreal

Senior Vice President/Publisher: Joseph Opiela
Acquisitions Editor: Susan Kunchandy
Executive Marketing Manager: Carlise Paulson
Supplements Editor: Donna Campion
Project Coordination, Text Design, and Electronic Page Makeup: Pre-Press
    Company, Inc.
Cover Designer/Manager: John Callahan
Senior Manufacturing Buyer: Dennis J. Para
Printer and Binder: The Maple-Vail Book Manufacturing Group, Inc.
Cover Printer: Lehigh Press, Inc.

For permission to use copyrighted material, grateful acknowledgment is made to the
copyright holders on pages 419–421, which are hereby made part of this copyright page.

Mayberry, Katherine J., 1950–
    Everyday arguments : with readings / Katherine J. Mayberry.—1st ed.
       p. cm.
    Includes index.
    ISBN 0-321-01193-7
       1. English language—Rhetoric. 2. Persuasion (Rhetoric). 3. College readers. 4. Report
writing. I. Title.

PE1431 .M39 2001
808'.0427—dc21

                                                                    2001038118

Please visit our website at http://www.ablongman.com

ISBN 0-321-01193-7

10 9 8 7 6 5 4 3 2 1—MA—04–03–02–01

Brief Contents

Detailed Contents

Preface

Everyday Arguments is a spin-off of the popular *For Argument's Sake,* first published in 1988 and now in its fourth edition. *For Argument's Sake* is a practical, easy to follow rhetoric text that teaches students to write effective arguments. Over the years, users of *For Argument's Sake* have expressed the desire for a single volume combining the common-sense approach of the rhetoric with a comprehensive collection of readings that illustrate the principles and practices contained in the rhetoric, as well as the critical link between writing and *reading* arguments. *Everyday Arguments* is the response to this request.

Part I of *Everyday Arguments* is the latest version of the rhetoric. Updates include expansion of the Toulmin method of argument, discussions of the role of computer research in argument formation, more student writing samples, and references to the readings contained in Part II.

Part II contains over 35 examples of written arguments. This anthology is gathered from the kinds of writing most of us read every day. These arguments are contemporary and varied; each one illustrates practices and principles taught in Part I. From a Web site for men with eating disorders to the side panel of a cereal box to a prize-winning article in *Sports Illustrated,* these writing samples demonstrate the central premise of the rhetoric: that most of the writing and reading we do in our daily lives falls under the heading of argument. By helping students become critical readers of argument, they likewise contribute to their becoming effective argument writers.

ORGANIZATION

Part I

Part I of *Everyday Arguments* is organized around the three major phases of argument writing: focusing, supporting, and reviewing. Chapters 1 through 5 discuss how to bring a developing argument into focus, including finding and focusing a claim, identifying and accommodating the audience, and understanding the relationship between claim and support. Chapters 6 through 9 show students how to support the four different classes of argument (arguments of fact, cause, evaluation, and recommendation). And Chapters 10 through 12 present the reviewing activities necessary to refine and polish an argument: considering image and style, composing openings and closings, and revising and editing the argument draft.

These three writing phases are presented in the order students typically follow when composing arguments, but there are of course perfectly acceptable and effective exceptions to the typical. The order presented is meant to guide, not prescribe. Further, the sequential presentation of these writing phases is not meant to contradict the received wisdom about the recursive nature of good writing; in the real practice of writing, changes made in one phase lead to changes in the others.

SPECIAL FEATURES OF PART I

The discussion of dissonance in Chapter 2 is unique to argument texts. The question of what moves people to write arguments is a critical one for students that can lead them to make a greater personal investment in their own writing.

The treatment of formal and informal logic also is unique to argument texts. In this book, they are introduced at the point in the argument process where they are most useful: the development and evaluation of the arguments' support. Too often, argument texts include the theory of logic and examples of informal fallacies without addressing how they are useful in the actual writing process. Chapter 5 presents both formal and informal logic as practical tools for creating reasonable arguments.

The inclusion of an entire chapter on style and image (Chapter 10) enriches the traditional view of argument, which sometimes seems to suggest that effective arguments have more to do with formulas and principles than with using language fairly and effectively. Here, a writer's style—the image he or she projects through the writing—is a fundamental component of argument, not just a lucky accident of talent.

Everyday Arguments contains many examples that today's college students can relate to, plus examples from diverse academic and career areas. This range of applications helps students see the importance of writing effective arguments not only in college courses, but also in their post-college careers.

Because improvement in writing comes only with practice, the emphasis in all the activities in Part I is on *writing*. Each chapter gives students many opportunities to practice what they are learning by writing (and rewriting) full and partial arguments.

Part II

The readings in Part II of *Everyday Arguments* are divided into six topic areas: "Today's College Student"; "The Internet"; "Sports"; "Work"; "Diet"; and "Reading Popular Culture." By design, these are not the typical subjects of traditional argument anthologies, which tend to focus on abstract issues—such as capital punishment or euthanasia—and the classical canon of arguments addressing them.

These six topic areas were selected to engage students' attention, and demonstrate the importance of regular critical reading and critical writing.

Each topic area begins with an introduction, including a discussion of the importance of critical reading on that topic. The first argument in each section is accompanied by a detailed commentary that serves as a model for the attentive, critical reading of argument. Following each reading is a set of discussion questions and suggestions for writing.

SPECIAL FEATURES OF PART II

The arguments contained in Part II of *Everyday Arguments* are representative of the reading we do on a daily basis, so students can see the immediate usefulness of the writing and reading skills they are learning. The arguments are also drawn from a wide range of contexts—newspapers, Web sites, magazines (from the *New Yorker* to *Wired*), and books. The variety of sources gives students many opportunities to study the effect of context and audience on written argument.

The discussion questions following each argument encourage collaboration among students and are closely tied to the contents of Part I. The suggestions for writing following the discussion questions are directed toward students of all ages, backgrounds, and majors, with an emphasis on the stages of composition. Part II is in continuing conversation with Part I, repeatedly demonstrating the connection between principle and practice. Part II of *Everyday Arguments* maintains the same highly practical, student-friendly, writing-intensive approach to learning how to compose an argument.

SUPPLEMENTS

An Instructor's Manual is available to adopters of *Everyday Arguments*. Please contact your local Longman sales representative for further information. A companion Web site is also available to users of *Everyday Arguments*. Visit us at *www.ablongman.com/mayberry* to find additional Web resources for instructors and students.

ACKNOWLEDGMENTS

Everyday Arguments, like *For Argument's Sake,* remains closely tied to the vision I shared with Robert E. Golden when we began the first edition of *For Argument's Sake* more than 15 years ago. In addition to Dr. Golden and the many people who contributed to the success of later editions of *For Argument's Sake,* I have a new group of extremely helpful individuals to thank. A number of people have served as readers and editors of the manuscript, both from Longman and from a variety of colleges and universities. Among the Longman folks are Susan Kunchandy, Anne Smith, Lynn Huddon, and Rebecca Gilpin. Readers outside Longman include: Larry

Beason, Eastern Washington University; Bill Bolin, Texas A and M University; Michael A. Bryson, Roosevelt University; Theresa Conefrey, University of Hawaii; David Fabish, Cerritos College; Anthony C. Gargano, Long Beach City College; Billie S. Hara, Texas Wesleyan University; Will Hochman, University of Southern Colorado; John Jablonski, Ferris State University; Catherine Carr Lee, University of Texas–Dallas; Janet Lockhart, Chemeketa Community College; and Jennifer W. Spirko, North Carolina State University. I am grateful as well to Peggy L. Richards from the University of Akron, who helped with the identification of new student essays in Part I and other key revisions.

PART I

WRITING ARGUMENTS

1

An Introduction to Argument

AN EXTENDED DEFINITION

If you grew up with siblings, or if you and your parents had a particularly stormy relationship during your adolescence, you may think you know all there is to know about argument. And you may be right, if you understand the word *argument* to mean a verbal battle where reason is absent and agreement rarely reached. A teenager engaged in this kind of argument with her mother might proceed as follows:

> Mom, I don't believe you! You are so unfair! Why can't I stay out 'til three? You never let me do anything fun. None of my friends has a curfew. How do you think it feels to be the only one who has to leave a party early? Everybody thinks it's ridiculous, and I bet they're all really glad they don't have you for a mother.

The unpleasant and usually unproductive practice illustrated in this example is not the subject of this book. In fact, the kind of argument focused on in these pages is almost the exact opposite of the preceding illustration. Of concern here is the formal, traditional meaning of *argument:* the process of establishing, through the presentation of appropriate evidence, the certainty or likelihood of a particular point or position (what we call the *claim*).

Another daughter, using the principles of traditional argument, might make the following case about her curfew:

> Mom, I would really like to stay at this party tonight until it's over. I know you have a problem with my being out late, and I understand you're concerned about my welfare. But I'm eighteen now, I'll be leaving for college next month, and maybe it's time you let me start testing my own judgment. You and I both know I'm not going to do anything stupid, and I

would really like to get some practice making my own decisions about my comings and goings.

While there is no guarantee that Daughter 2 would succeed with such an argument, it *is* a reasonable argument. Daughter 2 is acknowledging her mother's chief concerns and citing a sensible reason for lifting the curfew: she needs some practice at being grown up while still in the safety of her home environment. Daughter 1, on the other hand, has a lot to learn about making her point successfully; indeed, she commits about every foul imaginable in reasonable argument, including insulting her mother, irrelevantly and probably inaccurately appealing to crowd behavior ("None of my friends has a curfew"), and failing to offer any sensible reason why her mother should change her mind.

Daughter 2's request is an oral argument, and the subject of this book is written argument; yet the principles and practices are essentially the same. The objective of each is to gain agreement about a point through the use of reasonable evidence. When you think about it, much of the writing you will do in college and in your careers following college falls under this definition. Research papers, lab reports, literary interpretations, case studies—all these forms of writing seek to convince an audience (your professor) of the reasonableness of certain conclusions. All these forms of writing, as well as application letters, instructional manuals, and corporate annual reports, are built around the simple objective of making a point.

An argument, whether written or oral, is different from an opinion. An *opinion* is based not so much on evidence as on belief, intuition, or emotion. Argument, on the other hand, is a position supported by clear thinking and reasonable evidence, with a secure connection to solid facts. While arguments rarely prove a conclusion to be absolutely true, they do demonstrate the probability of that conclusion. Opinions tend to be expressions of personal taste that have not been tested by the application of reasonable principles. Your opinion may be that history is a more interesting subject than literature, or that yellow is prettier than red, but these remain only opinions until they are thoughtfully and fully justified.

Effective arguments are ethical as well as reasonable. They make their points openly and honestly, avoiding underhanded methods and false promises, and seeking to remove ambiguity rather than exploit it. We make arguments in order to advance a reasonable position, not to trick a reader into serving our self-interest. As writers of ethical arguments, we recognize the influence that skilled writing can exert over credulous or ignorant readers, and we are committed to exercising that influence reasonably and responsibly.

Of course, what constitutes a reasonable and responsible argument is sometimes up for grabs. When they argue, people disagree about basic assumptions, beliefs, and values, and those disagreements affect their understanding of what is reasonable. Daughter 2 in the previous example is working from the assumption that children should be encouraged to behave maturely. This seemingly inarguable assumption leads her to the conclusion that she should be allowed to exercise her own judgment about curfew. But perhaps her mother believes it is a parent's responsibility to protect her child from harm—another seemingly inarguable assumption. This reasonable assumption leads her to conclude that she cannot put her child at risk by lifting her curfew. Both daughter and mother are being reasonable, but their differing beliefs take them in two very different directions.

So this book will not be able to define what constitutes a reasonable argument for every writer, every audience, and every occasion. But it can introduce you to some concepts, processes, and tools that will help you make informed and effective decisions about how to construct your own arguments. This is the purpose of the first half of the book. The second half of the book—a collection of the "real-world arguments" we all encounter daily—will illustrate how writers actually apply the principles and practices of formal argument. And the many writing samples included at the end of most chapters will demonstrate how the principles and practices of formal argument carry over into a wide variety of writing contexts.

THE CLASSES OF ARGUMENT

Once you begin paying attention to the writing you do for school and work, you will notice how frequently your assignments fit within the definition of argument. You may also notice that the claims, or propositions, of these arguments tend to fall into certain patterns. Papers in economics or history courses may tend to concentrate on identifying the causes of certain events, whereas lab reports in biology or physics focus on describing a particular process and interpreting its results. In fact, argument can be divided into four classes: (1) factual arguments, (2) causal arguments, (3) evaluations, and (4) recommendations. These classes are distinguished both by the type of claim being argued and the degree of agreement expected from the reader.

Factual arguments try to convince an audience that a certain condition or event actually exists or has existed. Factual arguments, though they sound quite simple, are the most ambitious type of argument, for they try to convince readers of the truth or factuality of a claim. Those laboratory reports from biology or physics are examples of factual arguments, and their purpose is to convince their reader (usually a professor) that certain steps were taken and certain things actually happened.

Causal arguments—often found within those economics or history papers—try to convince readers that one event or condition caused another or is likely to cause another in the future. A paper identifying the complex economic reasons for the 1987 stock market crash would be a causal argument. Causal arguments can only rarely claim truth or certainty; most are judged successful if they establish a certain cause or future effect as *probable*.

Evaluations, or **evaluative** arguments, make value judgments. The film critics Roger Ebert and Richard Roeper are in the business of oral evaluations, as they share their judgments about the quality of recent films with their television audience. Because evaluations are often tied up in personal tastes and opinions, they are the hardest of all arguments to make successfully; nevertheless, they *can* be reasonable and effective.

Finally, **recommendations,** as their name suggests, try to get readers to *do* something, to follow a suggested course of action. While the other three classes of arguments aim for armchair agreement, most recommendations want the reader's agreement to be translated into action.

This book will take up the principles and practices of each argument class in isolation from the others, but you should realize from the outset that many of the writing assignments you will do for this course, for other courses, and on the job will *combine* these classes. In fact, the most common type of argument is the combined, or *hybrid,* argument.

ARGUMENT THROUGH IMAGE

An argument's success depends on many things: the clarity and exactness of its claim, the appropriateness and adequacy of its supporting evidence, and the particular *image* it projects. Image is the total impression a reader gets by reading your writing, and it is composed of a number of elements. Among these is the writing *style,* which consists of word choice, sentence length and structure, and the writer's tone of voice. Other elements of image include grammar, punctuation, neatness of the page, and quality of graphics. Together, these elements compose an overall impression of the writer and the work that will influence the reader's final acceptance or rejection of the argument. A positive image will help to secure the reader's confidence, respect, and attention; a negative image inevitably gets in the way of the agreement that all arguments seek from their readers.

Consider the example of an application letter for a job. Let's say that you are the head of the work-study program at your college, the person responsible for placing students in campus jobs. You have whittled the pool of applicants for the desirable job of dean's assistant down to two applicants: Jon Marshall and Becky Quinn. Both students have comparable academic qualifications, and both have been highly recommended by faculty and former employers. Becky's application letter is a well-organized, neatly typed business letter that carefully lists and develops Becky's qualifications for the job. Jon's letter also contains his qualifications, but it is filled with misspellings and faulty punctuation, it addresses you by your first name, and it has a grease spot on the upper-right corner. All other things being equal, which candidate is likely to have the edge? Which image better argues the writer's suitability for the job?

THE ARGUMENT PROCESS

It is one thing to recognize the prevalence of argument in the writing you do but quite another actually to create effective written arguments. While this book contains no single blueprint or recipe for writing effective arguments, it will suggest a practical process, as well as theoretical principles, that will help you reach the desired product of an effective written argument. Unless you are extraordinarily gifted—one of those rare students who can produce a perfectly acceptable essay in a single sitting—your writing process will consist of at least three broad stages: forming the argument, supporting the argument, and reviewing the argument.

In order to explain and illustrate these stages, we have created the hypothetical case of Rob Wade, a journalism major with the ambition of becoming a radio sports announcer—the Vin Sculley of the twenty-first century. In this age of high-tech video, you may find Rob's ambition a bit old-fashioned, but it is based on his belief that television is ruining sports for the American public. After watching the television coverage of the 1998 Winter Olympics in Nagano, Japan, and the 1997 World Series between the Florida Marlins and the Cleveland Indians, Rob's convictions have grown so powerful that he feels compelled to communicate them to a large audience. He decides to kill two birds with one stone: his professor has assigned a "Letter to the Editor" as part of his journalism portfolio, and Rob plans to use this requirement to communicate his strong disapproval of television sports coverage. Let's watch how Rob moves through the three stages of argument composition as he creates his letter.

Forming the Argument

Forming your argument consists of discovering a motive for writing, identifying an audience to address, and discovering and sharpening the point or points to be argued.

Most successful arguments originate in the writer's strong personal interest, which often includes a desire to change the status quo. The origin of Rob's letter to the editor, his *motive* for writing it, is his long and growing discomfort with television sports coverage. He is disappointed in this coverage, angry at how it packages sports for the public; the desire to communicate these feelings and to remedy the harm he sees being done are powerful motives that will energize his writing.

Once Rob has decided to act on these motives, he needs to think seriously about where he would like his letter to be published—in the school newspaper, the city newspaper, the *New York Times,* or *Sports Illustrated*? This decision must be made before he begins writing; otherwise he will lack the necessary sense of audience. *Audience* is an inescapable consideration in writing, yet writers often underestimate its importance, forgetting that argument always consists of one person addressing another person, or a group of people. In Rob's case, a letter to the editor of the school newspaper, whose readers consist largely of young men and women in their late teens and early twenties, would be very different from a letter to the editor of *Sports Illustrated,* whose readers are typically educated males of all ages. Also, *Sports Illustrated* will be more selective in choosing which letters to publish than the school paper is likely to be. Regardless of where Rob decides to send his letter, his argument will gain focus and immediacy if he has a clear sense that he is writing to a particular audience, with particular backgrounds, expectations, values, and beliefs.

Rob also must be clear from the outset about the exact point or points he plans to argue. Sure, he knows he wants to attack television sports coverage, but he will soon find that such a goal is too vague and too emotional to inform what must be a clear and reasonable argument. Before he starts writing, he'll need to compose a clearly focused statement of the point or points he wants his readers to agree with. In most arguments, such a statement is a one- to three-sentence summary of the argument's conclusion—called the *claim*. Some claims come to writers early and easily in the writing process, whereas others are the result of considerable reading, thinking, and narrowing. Though Rob knows generally what he wants to write about, it will take him some time to develop a claim that will interest his readers, that will be clear, and that he can reasonably support.

After more thinking than he had anticipated, Rob finally comes up with the following as his working claim: "While television coverage of sporting events allows us to be armchair spectators of exciting athletic contests that we would otherwise never see, we are paying a price for the convenience of this coverage. For what we are watching from our comfortable vantage point is glossy, high-tech artifice, not *real* sports."

Supporting the Claim

Having identified his claim and his audience, Rob now must decide how to support that claim. An argument's *support* is all the material that turns a tentative claim into a justified conclusion. Support is the most important component of argument. Without adequate and suitable support, a claim remains merely a hunch or an opinion; with appropriate support, it becomes a sound and credible conclusion.

At the very least, Rob can support his claim through his own viewing experience, which is, after all, what led him to the claim. But he's pretty sure that one person's experience is not enough to support an argument, so he knows he has some work to do. Identifying the class of his argument will help Rob select appropriate support, because certain kinds of support tend to apply to certain classes of argument. After careful consideration of his claim, and a thorough review of the four classes to which it might belong, he decides that his claim introduces an evaluative argument: it is making a negative judgment about the quality of television sports coverage.

This identification will help him, but there is more to selecting support than matching it to the class of the argument he is making. Rob will also need to ensure that the relationship between his claim and its support will be *reasonable,* that it will accord with the principles of formal and informal logic. So he will review carefully the material in Chapter 5 of this book, which presents these principles.

Reviewing the Argument

The product of these three steps—identifying an audience, composing a claim, and selecting appropriate support—will be a first version, or *draft*, of Rob's argument. As a journalism major, Rob has a fair amount of writing experience; he knows how difficult it is to evaluate your own writing, particularly when you have no distance from it. So, as he always tries to do, he puts his first draft away for a couple of days, so that when he returns to it, he has a fresh perspective that allows him to see problems in style and organization and reasoning that he hadn't noticed two days ago.

While getting distance from his argument will help to freshen his perspective, there is no fresher perspective than that of a second party who is unfamiliar with the work. In his writing classes, Rob has learned how well the process of "peer reviewing" works. As the name suggests, peer review is getting a friend or classmate or coworker to read your writing before you submit it to your professor, or, in Rob's case, for publication review. Peer review works best when you ask your reviewers to consider certain questions as they read. In the case of Rob's argument, these questions might be listed as follows: Does the argument effectively address its intended audience? Is its claim completely clear, and does it stick to that claim throughout? Is the supporting material reasonable and relevant to the claim? Does the argument project a positive image of its writer? Does the argument convince its audience? Friendly readers of your writing can identify problems and suggest solutions that you yourself are too close to the writing to see. Peer review is not cheating; it is not the same thing as getting someone else's answers to a calculus test. Peer review is a perfectly acceptable form of collaboration, providing an invaluable supplement to the writing process that the writer alone simply cannot supply: a *reader's* perspective. As a college student, Rob is lucky to have plenty of reader perspectives to call on. And his experience tells him that he would be foolish to ignore them, that without this collaboration, the revision process might become nothing more than superficial editing for spelling, punctuation, and grammatical errors. While editing is a necessary part of the review process, it is the final "spit-and-polish" step; revising often entails significant changes.

One addition that Rob will make to the first draft during the revision process is composing an introduction and conclusion. Like many writers, he finds it difficult to write interesting and representative introductions right out of the gate; the problem is partly psychological (first paragraphs are always the hardest) and partly practical (he won't know the exact content of the argument until he has finished a first draft). Likewise, it makes little sense to labor over a conclusion if the content of the first draft is going to be changed substantially during the revision process.

CONCLUSION

Having provided an extended definition of argument and a brief overview of the writing process, let's proceed to a detailed description of the steps involved in creating effective written argument, the reasoning principles that inform effective argument, and the special elements and requirements of each of the four classes of argument.

SUMMARY

An Introduction to Argument

- Written argument attempts to convince the reader of the writer's point of view, using reasonable and ethical methods. Most effective writing contains some form of argument.

- The *image* projected by the argument is the overall impression the writer makes on the reader. Image is created through writing style; correct spelling, punctuation, and grammar; and the physical appearance of the document.

- Argument can be divided into four classes: arguments of fact, cause, evaluation, and recommendation.

- While the process of argument composition varies from writer to writer, most writers follow these three stages: (1) forming an argument, which can consist of discovering a motive for writing and identifying an audience to address, discovering and sharpening a position, and developing an appropriate style; (2) supporting the argument; and (3) reviewing the argument, which can include considering the image projected by your argument, making substantial additions or deletions to a first draft, and adding an introduction and conclusion.

SUGGESTIONS FOR WRITING (1.1)

1. If you are planning on finding a summer job or a part-time job while in school, you will probably need to write a letter of application to your prospective employer. Give yourself some practice by writing a one-page letter of application for a real or made-up job. Try following a sequence like the following:

   Paragraph 1: State the position desired and your primary qualification for it.

   Paragraph 2: Expand on the primary qualification.

   Paragraph 3 and following: Develop other qualifications for the job.

   Concluding paragraph: State your willingness to answer questions and be available for an interview.

   Before writing, be sure to identify to yourself the needs and expectations of your reader—that is, your prospective employer. Then be sure your letter addresses these needs and expectations through such elements as the content of the letter, its level of formality, and the overall image projected by the letter.

2. Find an editorial in your local newspaper or on-line. With two or three classmates, analyze your responses to the editorial. Do all members of the group find the argument convincing? Why or why not? Do your disagreements reveal anything about your different concerns and values as readers? What im-

age is projected by the editorial? Does the image appeal to all members of your group? Why or why not? Are there ways that the editorial could be changed to be effective for all members of your group?

3. With a small group of your classmates, review an essay examination that one of you has written recently. As a group, identify the expectations of the professor giving the exam. To what extent do the claim, the support, and the overall image of this one essay meet these expectations? As a group, rewrite the essay so that all of these considerations are met.

2

Where Writing Begins: Motives and Audience

Most of us write because we have to, not because we want to. As a college student, you write a research paper because your political science professor has assigned it; a sales rep writes a monthly report because her boss requires it; a mother writes a note explaining her son's absence from school because school policy insists on it. Yet the best writing, the kind we read voluntarily and the kind that endures over centuries, springs from some source other than mere necessity. And even when necessity drives great writing, other motives are also at work. Shakespeare wrote *Hamlet* to make a living, Dickens wrote *David Copperfield* to feed his many children, but these writers were surely inspired by some motive beyond making money.

MOTIVES FOR WRITING

What are these other motives for writing? They are powerful intellectual and emotional drives of enormous variety—from the desire to create a lasting record of some important experience (think of Anne Frank's *Diary of a Young Girl*), to the yearning to express love or joy (a common motive for music through the ages from Renaissance musicians to Tracy Chapman), to the need to disagree strongly or even complain (Harriet Beecher Stowe's *Uncle Tom's Cabin* was written from a deep disagreement with the institution of American slavery). One common motive for writing, especially for writing arguments, is our drive to resolve personal dissonance. *Dissonance* is actually a musical term meaning an inharmonious arrangement of tones that the listener wants resolved into harmony.

On a more general level, the term *dissonance* suggests tension or uneasiness. It is a good word for describing the mismatch between the way we want life to be and the way it is. Dissonance drove the angry voice of the prophets in the Old Testament, the determined defiance of the Declaration of Independence, and the heartfelt challenges in the *Communist Manifesto*. Driven by intense dissatisfaction with the way things were, the writers sought a resolution of this tension by expressing it in writing.

The Value of Dissonance

The principle of dissonance is a useful starting point whenever you are at a loss to discover an argument worth making. If you find yourself doing nothing but staring at a blank page when you are supposed to be writing a ten-page paper for an English composition class, try asking yourself the following questions: "What really bothers me? What do I wish were different? What could be done to improve the situation?" The cause of the dissonance may be anything from parking problems on campus, to the status of women in large corporations, to the chemistry professor you don't understand.

If you begin the process of forming your argument by identifying a cause of dissonance, you will find both a subject to write about and a position to take on that subject (i.e., a claim). Because this position comes from your own interests and experience, developing it into an argument will be interesting to you, and if it's interesting to you, it's likely to be lively and interesting to your reader.

Let's assume that in an English composition class, you are asked to write about the impact of technology on education. An obvious position to take would be that the computer and associated technologies like educational CD-ROMs and the World Wide Web enhance the learning process for children and young adults. A solid position, certainly, but a bit predictable: probably 90 percent of your class will take this or a similar position. Plus, though you know it's a defensible position, it's not one that you find particularly exciting. So put that tentative claim on a back burner, and take some time to probe the general topic for personal dissonance. What discomforts, uneasiness, or inconveniences have you experienced from the new educational technology? Perhaps you were an avid reader as a child, someone who treasured the physical properties of books—the texture of the pages, the shape and heft of the volumes, the warm look of a filled bookshelf. As you think about it, you realize that as amazing as educational technology is, it threatens the reader's important physical relationship to books, to tangible texts. Reading about the Byzantine Empire or cell mitosis from a computer screen just isn't the same as learning about them from a volume taken down from your living-room shelf. This could be the beginning of an interesting argument about the losses incurred when screens replace pages, when electronic texts make the comforting tangibility of books obsolete.

This approach has a number of advantages. First, it promises to be different, unusual. In writing, an unusual approach, as long as it is intelligent and not merely eccentric, is often effective: it gets people's attention. Second, working from dissonance lets you get to the core of your discomfort by discovering reasons for it. Turning an opinion into an argument is a great way to challenge and define your unexamined views. And finally, focusing on problems is more useful and productive than ignoring them; neither you nor your readers can improve a situation until you have identified and accounted for its problems.

Don't take this advice to mean that you should turn every writing assignment into an occasion for complaining. Searching for dissonance should help you learn to be a critical and discerning thinker, not a cynic or whiner. And one of the hallmarks of a discerning thinker is the ability to recognize value where it exists: a student writing on the disadvantages of educational technology should acknowledge its obvious positive impacts. To pretend that they don't exist will only make the argument seem nearsighted and unfair. Of course, sometimes balance and fairness are not appropriate; the Declaration of Independence would be much less effective if it presented a balanced view of the British government. But extreme situations calling for one-sided appeals are relatively rare.

Writing Arguments That Are Meaningful to You

Of course, not every writing assignment will allow you to call on your own feelings and opinions; sometimes you are required to write about topics that simply don't interest you. Yet there are ways to make even those assignments more relevant to your interests and experience. The next time you find yourself working with an uninspiring assignment, try these three suggestions for making that assignment more meaningful to you:

1. *Search for the most interesting facets of the assignment*. If you must write on the American Civil War—a topic that holds little interest for you—try to find one aspect of the war that is at least potentially more meaningful to you than any other. You may need to do some research, but your time is well spent if you get excited about the topic. If you are interested in medicine, for example, why not write about the medical treatment of the wounded during the war?

2. *Don't lie*. Express only those opinions you honestly believe in. If you are unsure of your claim despite your best efforts to become comfortable with it, don't hesitate to use qualifiers such as *perhaps, probably, usually,* or *likely*. Never be lukewarm when you can be hot or cold, but don't take a position simply for the sake of taking it. A qualified claim, such as "Athletes who train with professional coaches usually perform better than athletes who do not," is preferable to the unqualified statement "Athletes who train with professional coaches perform better than athletes who do not" because there are bound to be some exceptions to this rule.

3. *Don't be pompous*. You don't want your writing to be too informal and colloquial, but you also don't want to sound like someone you're not—like your professor or boss, for instance, or the Rhodes scholar teaching assistant. Good writing is always genuine writing.

These suggestions apply to any assigned writing, from a monthly sales report to a memo on improvements in office procedures, to a lab report, to an anthropology research paper. You may not have chosen to do the writing in the first place, but energy spent making the project your own will result in a more lively and credible argument.

ACTIVITIES (2.1)

1. Look at the last four things you have written: letters, e-mail, reports, essays, memos, and so on. What were your reasons for writing them? How many of them were not written out of choice? Would these have been better if you had tried to write about what is important to you? Adjust the topic of one of these to make it more meaningful to you, and then rewrite it following the suggestions presented in the preceding part of the chapter.

2. List four aspects of your life or of the world around you that you wish were different. From these four aspects, derive tentative topics for essays.

THE IMPORTANCE OF AUDIENCE

When you prepare writing assignments for a college professor, you are usually writing for an audience of one: a professor who is a specialist in the subject of the paper, who has certain expectations of the paper, and who is obliged to read it carefully. Having such a predictable audience is actually a luxury to students, freeing them from one of the most important steps in argument formation: identifying the audience. But in most of the writing you will do outside an academic setting, you won't be able to ignore this step. Written argument assumes a relationship between a writer and a reader: the writer speaks and the reader listens and reacts. As a writer, your first and most basic goal is simply to engage your audience—to get their attention. Taking the time before you write to consider your audience will help you avoid boring or offending or confusing them. Considering your audience will also add focus and purpose to your writing: you will write with an imaginary "reader over your shoulder," as poet Robert Graves put it, which is vastly preferable to writing into a void.

Audience consideration is important to all writing, but particularly to arguments. Since the purpose of all arguments is to convince someone of something, knowing who that "someone" is is crucial. An argument seeking to convince college students of the need for a tuition hike would proceed very differently from an argument seeking to convince the school's board of trustees of the same claim.

Developing an accurate sense of audience depends in part on experience, but you can sharpen this sensitivity by considering the following questions each time you prepare to write: *Who* is the audience? *Why* will the audience read your argument? *What* should the audience be able to do after reading your argument? You should try to keep the answers to these questions in mind not only as you form the argument, but also as you write it.

Who Is the Audience?

Sometimes this question will be answered in terms of specific individuals (my supervisor, my prospective employer). More frequently, it is answered in terms of categories or groups of readers (readers of a certain magazine, users of a certain product, students in a particular class).

Having identified your audience, you will want to consider how familiar they are with the subject matter. Readers usually know much less than writers about the topic at hand; even readers in the same organization with similar education and experience may be unfamiliar with the subject matter of your report. With this in mind, consider where you might provide background information, what terminology you might define, what difficult concepts you might explain or illustrate. No matter how convincing your argument is, if it baffles its readers it's not going to succeed. Most readers, if they have any choice in the matter, will stop reading a difficult argument before they will struggle through its unfamiliar language and concepts. If you don't know how much your audience is likely to know, or if they have different levels of knowledge, you are better off providing too much explanation than too little. Most people prefer feeling superior to feeling ignorant.

Finally, audience identification also includes considering your readers' probable disposition to your claim. Are they likely to be friendly or hostile to your position? The answer to this question will influence a number of your argument strategies. For example, if you expect your audience to be hostile to your claim, you might give them credit for their views at the outset. In recommending an expensive federal crime prevention program to an audience already frustrated by the cost of crime to taxpayers, acknowledging and legitimizing that frustration may help to neutralize their hostility: "There is something wildly unjust about living in fear of crime *and* having to pay for that crime as well." Once you have conceded that your audience probably won't want to pay more to prevent crime, you could proceed to argue for a new crime bill that, while temporarily costly, offers an excellent chance of reducing crime and its costs to the taxpayer. Telling the audience that they are selfish or pigheaded or shortsighted will not gain you much agreement, but expressing a genuine understanding of their frustration may convince them that your motives and theirs are essentially the same.

When you know that someone in your audience holds a view completely different from your claim, or even when you know that there is a good counterargument to your position, you may need to include a *refutation* of that opposing argument. (Refutations are discussed in Chapter 4, under "Addressing the Counterargument.") Even if you don't refute such a counterargument directly, acknowledging that you are aware of its existence can convince your audience that you have taken time to learn about the issue.

If you are confident that your audience shares your views, your work will be easier, but don't let yourself become sloppy, or you may lose the agreement you started with. To guard against triteness and predictability, try playing devil's advocate (appearing to support the opposing view), or expressing your central claim outrageously, or reminding your audience of the dangers of knee-jerk responses.

If you have no idea how your audience might respond to your claim, perhaps you can get some information about their general beliefs and values, which you can then appeal to in the course of your argument. Some arguments—particularly evaluations and recommendations—depend on successful appeals to readers' values and beliefs. An argument written for the *New Left Journal* recommending the recitation of the Pledge of Allegiance in public schools will succeed only if it appeals to a value held by the *Journal's* politically liberal readers. These readers will not be moved by a "Your country: love it or leave it" approach. But if your claim rests on the principle of free choice, arguing that every student should have the choice of saying the pledge, your argument may succeed with this difficult audience.

In considering these questions about your audience—who they are and what they know, think, and believe—you are considering audience psychology. But it is important that you understand your reasons for doing so. You are not going to the trouble to understand your audience so that you can manipulate them through underhanded, unreasonable, unethical methods. Rather, you are giving your good argument the best chance at success by trying to ensure that the audience will approach it fairly and reasonably.

ACTIVITIES (2.2)

1. Examine a copy of *four* of the following and try to identify the probable audience for each. Estimate the level of education and the kinds of occupations each audience would probably have.

   Example: *Publications of the Modern Language Association* (PMLA). Level of education: usually at least some graduate education. Occupations: primarily graduate students in English or foreign language and literature and college-level instructors in these subjects.
   a. The *Wall Street Journal*
   b. *Time* magazine
   c. *Cosmopolitan*
   d. *People* magazine
   e. The *New England Journal of Medicine*
   f. *Popular Mechanics*
   g. *Soldier of Fortune* magazine
   h. Online "Instructor's Manual" for the Apple Macintosh computer (or some other personal computer)
   i. *Mad* magazine
   j. The *New York Times*

2. The following passage is from a brochure on how employees can use statistics to improve the quality of their organization's products. The intended audience for this brochure is company employees with a seventh-grade reading level and no previous knowledge of statistics. How well does this passage communicate with its intended audience? If you believe the passage would be difficult for its intended audience, rewrite it so that it addresses its audience more appropriately.

   Quality can be best maintained by preventive action in advance of complete tool wear or predictable machine maintenance. If we check characteristics of parts on a sampling basis as they are produced, it is better than sorting through a bin of hundreds of parts looking for the defective parts and then trying to determine which parts can be salvaged.

   Collecting and analyzing data on current operations is essential in supplier and company plants. By studying the data, the causes of defects for each main quality characteristic can be investigated and determined. Appropriate solutions, including redesign or reprocessing, can be developed.

Once problems are identified, a decision can be made whether to analyze past data, to collect new information, or a combination of both.

Why Will the Audience Read the Argument?

Readers can be divided into two broad groups: those who *have* to read the argument (a professor, a supervisor, etc.) and those who are free to read or not read,
depending on the argument's appeal (think of the fickle magazine browsing you
do in waiting rooms). As part of your preliminary consideration of audience, it
pays to determine why your audience will read your argument—because they
have to or because they want to?

If your readers are a captive audience—if they have no choice about reading
your argument—you are not freed from making your writing interesting and engaging. In fact, the captive audience puts considerable pressure on the writer to
be engaging. The professor with piles of student compositions to read, or admissions committee members with hundreds of application essays to evaluate, are
likely to be bored and irritable by the time they come to your composition or essay. Knowing this, you should put more, not less, effort into getting and keeping
their attention. In some cases, this may mean getting to the critical issues quickly
and directly, or it may mean taking care to follow directions exactly, or putting a
unique spin on your argument that will distinguish it from all the others your audience has to read.

When your audience is a purely voluntary one—readers of popular magazines,
for example—they may not approach your work bored and irritable, but they are
under no obligation to read further than your title if they don't find your argument
interesting. Writers who write for daily or weekly periodicals are continually looking for "hooks" that will attract their readers to subjects that are already quite familiar. For example, in the Summer Olympics of 1996, Kerri Strugs's courageous
vault landing received a landslide of positive attention from the international press.
Patricia Dalton, a weekly columnist, wrote one of the hundreds of articles on the
Kerri Strugs "moment." But she distinguished her article from the rest by opening
with a very different take on Strugs's moment of valor: "I wanted to shout to the
millions of kids watching [Kerri's heroics] on TV two weeks ago: This might not be
good for Kerri—and it certainly isn't good for you." A position so different from the
popular one was far more likely to get and keep the reader's attention than one that
took the more predictable route of praise and applause.

ACTIVITIES (2.3)

The following audiences are likely either to be uninterested in or hostile to the following claims. Working with two or three students in your class, rewrite the
claims, and add whatever additional sentences would help to engage audience
attention. Be prepared to justify your changes to the rest of the class.

1. Parents of a college student: Tuition must be increased.
2. A social worker: Because of budget cuts, your caseload will increase.

3. An African-American woman: Affirmative action results in reverse discrimination.
4. An inner-city high school principal: Metal detectors are unconstitutional.
5. A software specialist: Our society looks at too many screens.

What Should the Audience Be Able to Do After Reading the Argument?

All arguments want something from their readers. At the very least, they want to convince their readers that the claim and its supporting material constitute a reasonable position, even though readers may not agree with it completely. Many arguments are more ambitious, looking for their readers' full agreement, which may mean changing readers' minds. The most ambitious arguments want not only full agreement from their readers, but also action taken on the basis of this full agreement. What you expect from your audience will influence the nature and extent of your supporting material as well as the overall tone of your argument.

For example, if you were trying to convince an audience that fraternity term paper files on your campus are a problem, you would argue why and to what extent they are a problem. But if you wanted your audience to take action to solve this problem, your argument would need to include specific steps to be taken, such as applying pressure on fraternity councils, setting up a more rigorous honor code for students, and encouraging faculty to change term paper assignments yearly. Including these steps means convincing your audience that they are likely to be effective: fraternity councils will monitor the problem more carefully if they are in danger of losing campus support; term paper files will be useless if assignments are not repeated from year to year; and so on. Arguments that seek to inspire the reader to action should be specific about the action proposed, show the connection between the claim and the proposed action, and convince the reader that the action will lead, or at least will probably lead, to the desired changes.

The expectations you have of your readers should also influence your argument's tone. If you want to convince gently, the tone can be mild: "Members of the International Students Club need to consider an alternative to their international banquet for raising money for travel." If you intend to exhort, the tone should be more forceful, as in Winston Churchill's famous address to the British people in their darkest days of World War II: "We shall fight on the beaches, we shall fight on the landing grounds, we shall fight in the fields and in the streets, we shall fight in the hills." If you want to command (in which case, you are no longer seeking reader agreement), you can afford to be very blunt: "No smoking is allowed in this computer room."

ACTIVITIES (2.4)

For which of the following occasions should the argument spell out the actions it wishes its readers to take? Why?

1. **Claim:** The flood of no-fat and low-fat packaged foods is turning a generation of kids into low-fat anorexics.
   Audience: High school dietitian.

2. **Claim:** Our college needs wireless computer capability.
   Audience: President or "Information" Administrator of your college.

3. **Claim:** The new mandatory bicycle helmet law is an infringement of personal liberty, depriving the citizen of his or her right of self-determination.
   Audience: Listeners of a local call-in talk show.

4. **Claim:** Bicycle helmets should be made mandatory in this state, just like motorcycle helmets.
   Audience: Your state legislature representative.

5. **Claim:** While I have had some academic difficulties over the past year, my commitment to receiving a college degree and my newfound understanding of study strategies will contribute to my eventual academic success, if only you will agree to waive my suspension.
   Audience: Dean of your college.

SUMMARY

Where Writing Begins

- Dissonance—the mismatch between the way we want life to be and the way it is—is a motive for effective arguments.

- When you write, try to write about what is important to you, expressing only those opinions you honestly believe in and avoiding pomposity.

- Before you write, consider these three questions:

  –*Who* is the audience?

  –*Why* will the audience read the argument?

  –*What* should the audience be able to do after reading the argument?

SUGGESTIONS FOR WRITING (2.5)

1. From your list of topics from the second activity in Activity (2.1) at the end of the first section of this chapter, "Motives for Writing," select one of the topics and write a two- to three-page essay proposing a solution to the problem that bothers you.

2. Write a letter to your parents asking them for something you know they won't want to give you—for example, a raise in your allowance, a charge card, or a round-trip ticket to Europe. What steps can you take to neutralize the objections you know they are going to have?

3. Examine the last report or essay you wrote, and answer the following questions: Who was your audience? Why would they read what you wrote? What did you expect them to do after they finished reading? How well does that report or essay, when viewed in light of these questions, communicate with its intended audience? What changes would you make?

4. To recognize how audience affects the tone and content of an argument, write an informal evaluation of one of your current professors for your student e-mail conference system; then write a one-page evaluation of that instructor for the instructor himself or herself.

5. Attend a lecture or speech sponsored by your college or university. Then write a letter to the speaker evaluating her or his sensitivity to the audience.

ILLUSTRATIVE ARGUMENTS IN PART II: WHERE WRITING BEGINS

3

The Claim

You've discovered a subject and motive for your argument, and you've considered some key questions about your audience. Now you are ready to begin focusing your argument. Focusing—clearly defining the center and extent of your argument— occurs throughout the writing process, from discovering a motive to revising a final draft. This chapter concerns an early and critical stage in the focusing process: formulating, modifying, and positioning your argument's claim.

While some writers compose their claims before they begin writing, others let their claims evolve during an exploratory first draft, clarifying and modifying as they write. You can experiment with the sequence that works best for you, but regardless of how and when you reach your claim, your argument is not focused until you can summarize its principal point within a few sentences.

HOW CLAIMS WORK

An argument's claim is a short summary of its central point or points. All arguments have at least one claim; some longer arguments have more than one. Usually, the claim is stated directly, but sometimes, it is only implied by its supporting material. Regardless of where and whether it appears in an argument, the claim shapes and moves the argument, giving it structure and energy.

Claims can be short and tightly packed, as in the statement "America's youth are entirely apolitical," or they can be long and intricate, reflecting the argument's structure as well as its main points: "Because a capitalist system rewards aggressiveness, competitiveness, and intelligence, it is an almost perfect economic extension of Darwinism. In a capitalist society, the 'fittest' get rich; the unfit stay poor."

Crystal-clear claims are extremely useful to readers. All readers, whatever their levels of interest, knowledge, and intelligence, approach an unfamiliar manuscript clueless about its content and direction. An unequivocal, succinct statement of an argument's chief point or points alerts them to the argument's goal and prepares them to understand the relationship between the parts and the whole.

Good claims also help readers evaluate an argument. Knowing the proposition to be argued, they are equipped to judge how successfully it has been made. A claim such as "Television coverage of the O.J. Simpson trial turned our already tarnished criminal justice system into no more than a serial plot for a tabloid news show" provides a benchmark against which readers can judge the supporting argument. On the other hand, a claim such as "The O.J. Simpson trial was a joke" is too vague, too unfocused, to serve as a useful benchmark.

While claims can be discovered or changed at virtually any point in the writing process, you will probably find that formulating a tentative working claim early in the process is quite helpful. Such a preliminary claim will help you determine the kinds of supporting evidence you will need, will guide your argument's organization and direction, and will keep you from darting off on tangents.

Finding a Claim

Many student writers are insecure about their ability to come up with a position worth arguing. But even experienced, mature writers with a wealth of experience and opinions often have to work to find a claim. For inexperienced and experienced writers alike, claims tend to evolve gradually from reading and thinking (at both the conscious and the unconscious levels) about the subject or from personal discomfort with a particular situation or issue.

On occasion, however, the process of developing a claim can be short-circuited. In many college classes, particularly introductory ones, claims are actually assigned. Students in English composition courses, for example, are often assigned a particular thesis (claim) to develop ("Write a two-page essay supporting your view of the effectiveness of student orientation at this college"). And essay exams offer students at least the foundation of a claim. For example, the question "Was dropping the atom bomb in 1945 on Hiroshima and Nagasaki necessary to achieve Japan's surrender? Support your answer with specific reasons" dictates the form, though not the content, of the claim that will begin the essay: "Dropping the bomb was/was not necessary, for the following reasons."

And some writers do come to their work with their main point firmly in mind. But what usually happens to these seemingly lucky folks is that this main point gets modified, changed, and sometimes even reversed as they go about the business of developing and supporting it. And this is as it should be; clinging to a claim that clearly needs modifying can doom an argument at the outset. So if you find yourself passionately attached to a particular position at the beginning of the writing process, try to treat that position as a starting point, a tentative claim that will guide your research and thinking, not a commandment set in stone.

Some assignment topics cause problems because they are too vague. A literature student assigned a fifteen-page analysis of the early poetry of William

Wordsworth will set out with little focus or sense of direction. A new employee asked to evaluate the product quality and cost-effectiveness of a particular supplier would probably be equally adrift.

How do such writers move from vague assignments like these to working claims that will give the developing argument some direction and discipline? There are many answers to this question, because coming up with a claim—indeed, the entire writing process—is a highly idiosyncratic business. Some writers logically deduce claims from the evidence, in Sherlock Holmes fashion, whereas others discover them unexpectedly while daydreaming or jogging or listening to music. Claims can be slowly and painfully dredged from the earth, or they can come like lightning from the sky.

When you find yourself doing more dredging than you'd like, consider the following suggestions:

1. Don't press to arrive at a claim prematurely. More time is wasted following up a forced, dead-end claim that eventually has to be scrapped than in thinking, reading, and taking notes as preparation for deciding exactly what your position is going to be.

2. Instead of rushing the claim during the preliminary research phase (and research can mean nothing more than tapping the contents of your own brain without ever opening a book), concentrate on gradually narrowing your topic. For example, if you're preparing to write a paper on the poetry of Wordsworth, your reading and thinking might lead you originally (and accidentally) in the direction of thematic content, then to the narrower concern of images of nature, then still more narrowly to the recollection of nature as an inspiration to poetry. By the time you have gathered material on this focused subject, you will not be far from imposing a particular point of view on the subject. This point of view on a focused topic will be your claim, which might be something like "Wordsworth as a poet was inspired by nature, but nature sifted through memory, not nature as it is immediately perceived." While you may have accumulated a lot of seemingly useless notes along the way, you should be saved the agony of distorting your paper to fit an unworkable claim you have discovered with too little consideration. As you are closing in on a claim, keep in mind that good claims are rarely too narrow, and that poor ones are often too broad.

3. In the early stages of writing, don't spend too much time polishing and refining your claim. At this stage, a claim needs a narrow topic and the expression of a definite attitude toward that topic. A good working claim could be no more than "Smoking in public places is harmful to everyone." Later, after the first draft, you can refine and shine, adding a summary of supporting reasons if necessary.

4. Today's computer technology offers valuable tools for narrowing a broad topic to a focused position. Most libraries have moved their card catalogs to computer databases and are now adding electronic catalogs and major bibliographic indexes stored in CD-ROMs. You will probably also have access to the Internet, which contains not only databases, but huge volumes of information in various

forms. (Chapter 6 will discuss resource materials and steps to help evaluate credible sources.) Whether we are looking for books or articles, we get at the information we want through *keywords* or *descriptors*—words or brief phrases that describe our subject. Searching for information by keyword can give you good ideas for narrowing your topic.

Say you're planning to write an evaluative essay on the films of Stephen King, and you search several film indexes (e.g., *Film Research: A Critical Bibliography* or *Film Review Annual*), using *King, Stephen* as your descriptor. You get close to a hundred "hits" through this search, and you notice that many of the sources have to do with King's novels as well as his films. You become interested in the whole question of adaptation, so you search other film indexes using narrower descriptors like *King, Stephen, and adaptations* or, even more narrowly, *The Shining*. Through this early search for sources, you have imposed considerably more focus on your initial, broad topic—a focus that would soon lead to a working claim like "The true genius of Stephen King is in his ability to adapt the printed page to the medium of film."

Keeping Your Working Claim Flexible

As you proceed with a rough draft that works from a tentative claim, you may discover that the preliminary claim needs modification. Perhaps the thinking and research you have done on the subject have made you realize that your claim does not apply as widely as you thought, and that there are significant exceptions to your position. Be flexible enough to accept these discoveries and change your claim accordingly. Writing is not simply the recording of previously established thoughts but also a way of clarifying your thoughts, of discovering if what you meant to say can be said in a coherent and defensible way. If possible, take advantage of the guidance offered by a thoughtful claim, while remaining open to those discoveries to which writing and thinking can lead you.

Let's say you begin the composition process with a claim that arises fairly easily out of your own strong opinions about the issue of affirmative action. Your preliminary or working claim is "Jobs should be given to the most qualified applicant, not to the most qualified minority applicant. To reject the best candidate on the grounds of his or her majority status is unjust and inequitable." This claim statement not only summarizes your position toward affirmative action but also points to the main support for that position—that affirmative action is unjust and inequitable. In order to argue this evaluative claim convincingly, to convince your audience that one's minority or majority status is irrelevant to considerations of merit, you will need to demonstrate the injustices of affirmative action.

So far, so good. Even though you aren't personally aware of a wide range of cases, it should be easy to come up with examples of the basic unfairness of affirmative action. In the course of your reading, however, you keep coming up against the stubborn argument that majority candidates are often more qualified for jobs and educational opportunities because they are more educationally and economically privileged than members of minority groups. To reward the most qualified, this argument continues, is to perpetuate this tradition of unequal opportunity. You find this position persuasive and reasonable, though it doesn't change your central view that qualifications, not race, should determine one's success in the job market. Gradually, you realize that this is a more complicated issue than you had recognized; a hard-line position is not completely defensible.

You consider ignoring the counterargument and sticking to your original claim, but you conclude that your argument will actually be stronger if it reflects the ethical complexity of the issue and your awareness of the unfair advantage long given to the majority group. So you rewrite your working claim to read:

> In the United States, all men (and women) may be *created* equal, but for many, that birthright of equality is fleeting at best. Few would argue that, where women and minorities are concerned, inequality in economic and educational opportunity has been our national tradition. The affirmative action legislation of the 1960s was designed to redress the harms resulting from this indefensible tradition. Impeccable in its intent, affirmative action has been problematic in application: hiring on the basis of race and gender with secondary consideration to qualifications does not solve the problem of inequity; it merely changes the victims.

This new working claim is richer and more balanced than the first, reflecting your new understanding of the issue as well as your continuing disagreement with affirmative action laws.

The primary lesson to be learned from this example is that working claims should be seen as starting points, not as immutable conclusions; the thinking and writing processes will inevitably influence the starting point of an argument, shaping and modifying and in some cases even reversing the original position. Your final argument will benefit if you remain flexible about the original claim; always be prepared to alter it in the face of contrary evidence or new ideas.

ACTIVITIES (3.1)

1. With a small group of your classmates, select three of the following topics to work with. For each selected topic, work together to narrow the topic to one that could be written about in a seven- to ten-page essay. From this narrower topic, derive a working claim for this paper. Remember that the working claim is the claim with which you would begin to write the essay, though it might be refined or changed as you write.

   Example topic: The risks of cigarette smoking.
   Narrower topic: The health effects of cigarette smoking in public places.
   Working claim: Cigarette smoking in public places is harmful to everyone.
   a. Japanese automobiles
   b. The voucher system
   c. Women's rights
   d. College education
   e. Television
   f. Unemployment

g. Presidential elections
h. New York City
i. Careers
j. Popular music

2. With one of your classmates, agree on a very broad topic of interest to you both, for example, professional basketball, computer games, or a certain actor. Then conduct independent computer searches on the subject, progressively focusing it (and focusing your keywords) as you get a sense of the information available. When you have reached a focused topic that could be argued about in a five-page paper, compare that topic with your classmate's. How similar or different are the two? Retrace the evolution of your keywords for each other.

Positioning the Claim

Another important decision you'll have to make about your claim is where to place it in your argument. You can make this decision before, during, or even after your first draft, but whenever you make it, it's one that requires careful thought. Different placements will have different effects on your audience, in some cases influencing their ultimate acceptance of your argument. As long as you base your decision on audience consideration and the intended function of the claim, you can put the claim almost anywhere. There are two main points to consider in positioning your claim: first, what is the function of your claim? second, what is your audience's probable disposition toward your argument?

Claim Stated Up Front

Stating your claim within the first couple of paragraphs makes sense

- if your argument is complicated or the subject matter is unfamiliar to readers (an up-front claim will let your readers know what's coming)
- if your audience is likely to be comfortable with your argument (so that its claim will not alienate them at the outset)
- if your claim is particularly engaging, curious, or intriguing (an up-front claim will lure readers into your argument)

The following excerpt from an article on fund-raising in higher education, where the claim (in italics) appears after a brief introduction, illustrates the second and third of these conditions. Readers of the *New York Times* (where this article appeared) are not likely to object to the article's claim, though they may be intrigued by the argument's redefinition of the traditional practice of fund-raising.

As the last mortarboards are flung like Frisbees into the air and the last speaker winds up a peroration on endings and beginnings, at least one campus office marches on into summer on an unending mission: raising money.

The task is ancient but the tools get more modern all the time. Colleges and universities, long seen as aloof from the commercial crush of life, are increasingly willing to pull out all the stops in getting alumni to give.

It's still called fund-raising—or development or even institutional ad-vancement. But it's getting to look a lot like marketing. ("Some Schools Won't Take No for an Answer," Janny Scott, the *New York Times,* June 19, 1994, section E, p. 3; emphasis added)

Claim Stated at the End of the Argument

Delaying your claim until the end of the argument can be effective

- when your audience may find the claim objectionable (readers who accept a claim's support as reasonable before they know precisely what the claim is may be less hostile to that claim once it is stated)
- when your evidence builds directly and inevitably toward your claim, which can then serve as your argument's conclusion

Let's say you write for your school newspaper. An example of the first instance would be your editorial recommending stricter enforcement of quiet hours in the dorm—a position that may not be welcome to all student readers. In this case, you can first present all the problems associated with the nightly bedlam in the dorms. Once you have established the seriousness of the problem, you can conclude the argument with your recommendation for stricter quiet hours. Having been con-vinced of the seriousness of the problems, your readers will be more likely to ac-cept the final claim as necessary and logical.

Or to exemplify the second case, if you were reviewing a film for your news-paper, you might choose to describe various elements of the film first—acting, plot, cinematography—before summarizing these remarks with the inevitable statement of the central claim: "Find the time to see this film."

Unstated Claim in an Argument

You may choose to omit an explicit statement of your claim in situations like the following:

- when your readers will see red at your claim (because it is so bold or so objectionable) regardless of where you place it
- when the claim is very, very obvious
- when stating your claim will oversimplify your argument
- when stating your claim will break the momentum or shape of your argument

A wise mother might use this strategy in a letter counseling her college-age son to hit the books. She knows that outright directions won't work, but she might tell a story that implicitly makes her point—a story about an uncle who frittered away his college opportunities and always regretted it. She does not end her letter with the point "Don't be like Uncle Jake"; that would be too obvious, too heavy-handed. Instead, she lets her narrative speak for itself.

A word of caution, however, about omitting claims: make sure that you have a very good reason for using this tactic, and that the point or points of your argu-ment are absolutely clear without being stated.

ACTIVITIES (3.2)

1. Read the following essays included at the end of Chapters 7 and 9: "I, Too, Am a Good Parent" (7); and "The Side Effects of Affirmative Action" (9). In a discussion with three or four classmates, identify the central claims and consider the reasons for their placement in each essay.

CLASSIFYING YOUR CLAIM

Once you have come up with a claim—even a tentative one—you'll need to identify the class it belongs to. Knowing at the outset of a first draft that you are working with a factual, causal, or evaluative claim or with a recommendation will simplify the gathering and presentation of support, since each class uses different kinds and arrangements of support. Recognizing your claim's class requires familiarity with the characteristics and functions of each class. The following section offers a full discussion of the different categories and examples of claims from each.

Factual Claims

The purpose of *factual claims* is to convince an audience that a certain statement is factual—that a given condition or phenomenon exists or has existed. The fact can be as basic as "Despite appearances, the sun is the center of our solar system, not the earth," or as unfamiliar as "In 1993, 65,091,168 people flew in and out of Chicago's O'Hare Airport." Writers of arguments introduced by factual claims attempt to convince their readers that their claims are true, although perhaps not true forever and under all circumstances (in the Middle Ages it was a "fact" that the earth was the center of the solar system).

Perhaps you find the idea of arguing facts a contradiction in terms; to you, facts are unchanging statements about reality, not provisional statements requiring support and verification. If it's a fact, why argue it? But a statement becomes factual only if it is accompanied by evidence that makes it extremely probable to its particular audience. Because facts become the cornerstones of so much of what we know and expect of the world, we cannot afford to accept them on faith. In short, factual claims must be supported carefully.

Facts are crucial to argument; indeed, it is hard to imagine an argument succeeding if it doesn't include some facts. In the arguments you write in college and beyond, facts will play three roles:

1. They will sometimes appear as an argument's central claim, as in a laboratory report claiming that "The addition of sulfur to the compound created sulfuric acid."
2. They will function as support for other claims. A general claim such as "All the teachers in the Child's Play Day Care Center have experience working with preschool children" would be supported by facts about the specific experience of each teacher.

3. They will serve as examples or illustrations of difficult, unfamiliar, or abstract ideas. Suppose you're writing an essay on photosynthesis for an audience unfamiliar with the process. You might follow the scientific definition of the term ("the formation of carbohydrates in living plants from water and carbon dioxide, by the action of sunlight on the chlorophyll"— *Webster's New World Dictionary*) by the more familiar description of the yearly cycle of a cherry tree.

The four types of facts that will figure most commonly in your arguments are (1) common knowledge facts, (2) personally experienced facts, (3) facts reported by others, and (4) factual generalizations.

1. **Common knowledge facts** are so widely acknowledged as true that they require no support or proof beyond mere statement.

   Examples: Men cannot bear children.

   Opposite poles attract.

2. **Personally experienced facts** are the events, observations, and conditions that you have personally experienced.

   Example: I have taken countless history courses in my life, and I have never had a teacher who excited me about the subject.

3. **Facts reported by others** are those that you have learned from second- or third-party sources. A second-party source is the person who ascertained the fact. A third-party source is the person or document reporting facts ascertained by someone else.

   Examples: "The 'man shortage' and the 'infertility epidemic' are not the price of [women's] liberation; in fact, they do not even exist" (Susan Faludi, *Backlash,* xviii; second-party source).

   "The mental health data . . . are consistent and overwhelming: The suicide rate of single men is twice as high as that of married men" (Faludi, 17; third-party source).

4. **Factual generalizations** claim that an assertion is true for a large number of subjects or over a long period of time. Factual generalizations can be common knowledge facts, personally experienced facts, or facts reported by others.

   Examples: Most of my friends are interested in sports.

   In 1995, 14.9 percent of American children lived in blended families" (*World Almanac,* 1995, 962).

All factual claims are stated as definite and unequivocal assertions, as in the following examples:

- New York City is the banking center of the United States. (The claim makes a quantifiable assertion that can be verified by a survey of the number of banks and banking transactions in major American cities.)

- Our solar system is approximately five-billion years old. (While no individual can verify this claim through firsthand experience or knowledge, it represents the consensus of experts on the subject and can be documented in this way.)
- Steel radial tires last longer than tires made with nylon. (Again, this claim can be verified, though the process may be tedious and time-consuming.)
- Most of my friends are involved in intramural sports. (A statement of fact that can be supported, if necessary, by a listing of the number of friends who are involved and not involved in intramural sports.)

ACTIVITIES (3.3)

1. For each of the factual propositions in the following list, identify the category or categories of fact (common knowledge, personal experience, second- or third-party, generalization) in which the proposition belongs.

   Example: The Cuban Missile Crisis occurred in October of 1962. Second- or third-party for most students; personal experience for older people.
   a. The disappearance of former Teamsters Union leader Jimmy Hoffa is still unexplained.
   b. The risk of getting cancer is decreased by a high-fiber diet.
   c. My communications professor routinely missed her 8:00 class.
   d. Alaska is the largest state in the United States.
   e. An apple a day keeps the doctor away.
   f. I get better grades on the papers I take the time to revise.
   g. Severe air pollution is dangerous for people suffering from lung disease.
   h. Women under age 30 have better driving records than men under age 30.
   i. In Italy, people take more time to enjoy life than we do in the United States.

Causal Claims

Causal claims propose a causal connection between two events or conditions. They can argue that A caused B or, more speculatively, that A may cause B at some future time. Statements such as "The violence represented in movies and television has numbed us to the horrors of violence in the real world" or "High consumer spending will lead to greater inflation" are examples of causal claims.

It is human nature to be curious about cause. We watch the careers of prominent public figures and wonder about the reasons for their spectacular successes and failures. We reflect on a tragedy like the Holocaust and demand to know how such a thing could happen. We look for the reasons behind events to assure ourselves that the world is governed by certain rules, not merely by random chance. We also learn by discovering cause. Knowing what caused the crash of TWA Flight 800 off the south shore of Long Island in the summer of 1996 gives us a reasonable chance of preventing a similar event in the future. And you can be sure that George W. Bush did whatever he could to reproduce those factors that led to Bill Clinton's successive elections.

Just as we are given to discovering cause, we are also fascinated by predicting *effects.* Stockbrokers must be skilled in this form of causal argument, as they try to enhance the interests of their clients by predicting market activity. Doctors practicing *preventive* medicine are also in the business of predicting probable effects: they tell their patients to reduce dietary fat in order to prevent a future heart attack, or to exercise regularly to maintain bone density. And in business and industry, the long-term health of a corporation often depends on the accurate prediction of future trends. Eastman Kodak, for example, with its enormously successful business of traditional photographic products, had to determine the probable future of those products in the face of electronic imaging.

Under carefully controlled scientific conditions, it is possible to identify cause and even to predict effect with so much certainty that the causality can be established as *factual.* Researchers have determined that smoking increases the risk of lung cancer and that lobar pneumonia is caused by pneumococcus bacteria. But in the causal arguments that most of us make, arguments concerning human behavior—our actions, our successes and failures, our relations with others—certainty is impossible to reach. In these more speculative arguments, the best we can hope for is to establish *probable* cause or effect convincingly.

But because a claim cannot be proven with certainty doesn't mean it isn't worth arguing; if we always waited for certainty before acting, our progress would be slow. An argument that establishes probable cause or effect *can* be a reasonable basis for decisions or actions. In fact, probability is the goal of most of the arguments we write. But even probability isn't easy to achieve; in many cases, it calls for more skill than establishing certainty in factual arguments.

Causal claims are easy to spot because they (1) often contain words indicating causality—*cause, produce, effect, consequence*—and/or (2) involve the relationship between two phenomena occurring at different points in time. The following are examples of causal claims:

- According to social critic Neil Postman, technology is causing the surrender of American culture. (The word *caused* is a dead giveaway of a causal argument.)
- If Sally had written a better résumé, she might have landed that job. (An early event—Sally's poor résumé—caused a later one, her failure to land the job.)
- A balanced budget promises a stable government. (The claim proposes a close causal relationship between a balanced budget and a stable government. The verb *promises* indicates cause.)
- Increasing numbers of two-career families have contributed to the rising divorce rate. (*Contributed to* suggests a causal relationship between the two facts.)

ACTIVITIES (3.4)

1. Look back at the distinction between factual and probable causes. For which of the following causal claims could you establish a factual cause—one that

few people would dispute? For which could you establish only a probable cause—one for which you would have to argue?

a. If Abraham Lincoln had not been assassinated, he could have lessened the bitterness between the North and the South after the war.
b. The widespread use of computers in business and industry will increase total employment, not decrease it.
c. If it had not snowed, Ohio State could have defeated Michigan in that football game.
d. In most automobiles, failure to change the oil at regular intervals will damage the engine.
e. The decline in the percentage of the population attending organized religious activities has caused the rise in the crime rate in the past 40 years.
f. The use of seat belts decreases the number of fatalities in automobile accidents.
g. If newlyweds had more realistic expectations about marriage, there would be a decline in the divorce rate.
h. The children of the affluent would be happier if they had to do more for themselves.
i. Some cold medicines cause drowsiness.
j. The existence of nuclear weapons has prevented the outbreak of World War III.

2. Write a claim for a causal argument for one of the following; then make a list of all the reasons you can think of that would convince a reader of the cause or effect you identify. Describe these reasons in a paragraph.
   a. The cause of a particular war
   b. A team's victory or loss in a certain game
   c. A change in some aspect of the government's social or economic policy
   d. A change in exercise or dietary behavior
   e. The cause of a person's career success or failure

   Example of (c): "There would be fewer homeless people if the federal government increased its aid to cities."
   Reasons: Money could be used for low-income housing. Money could be used for training programs that would give the poor a means of self-support. Other countries that give substantial aid to cities do not have the problem with the homeless that we do.

Evaluations

When we argue an evaluation, we are proposing our personal judgment of the value of a work of art, a policy, a person, an action, even another evaluation. No doubt you often find yourself making informal pronouncements of personal taste: "Your tie is ugly," "That restaurant serves the best chicken wings in town," "I enjoy playing basketball more than playing tennis." These pronouncements are so purely subjective, so clearly a matter of personal preference, that there is little point in trying to argue them reasonably. We are all inclined to pass judgment on what we observe, and frequently we don't much care whether these judgments are taken seriously.

But sometimes we do care about the impact of these judgments; sometimes we want our opinions to influence others. In these cases, we must understand how to argue judgments of value. And many value judgments, even those originating as unconsidered personal opinion, *can* be convincingly argued. Claims such as "Pornography is an offense to all women" or "The government was mistaken in trading weapons for hostages," if they are serious, carefully considered judgments, can be developed into meaningful arguments.

Evaluations are probably the hardest of all arguments to argue successfully. Not only do they originate in the writer's personal value system, they also speak to his or her readers' equally personal, passionately held, and often unexamined values. Changing someone's mind about an opinion or judgment is an uphill struggle, so your goals in arguing evaluations should be rather modest: to gain your audience's sympathy toward a conclusion that you have reached through responsible and reasonable evidence rather than to change the mind of everyone who reads your argument.

An important variant of the evaluative claim is the *interpretive* claim. Interpretations are *explanatory* evaluations of a person, event, or object: "Dreams of beautiful gardens often suggest a state of profound satisfaction in the dreamer" or "Will's domineering and self-centered style is an expression of his profound insecurity." Neither of these examples is simply factual or descriptive; each reveals something unexpected beneath the visible surface of behavior. Interpretive claims surpass mere opinion only when they are supported by facts and reasoned argument. Reasonable, intelligent people may differ in their interpretation of a person or a situation, but not all interpretations are equally plausible or illuminating. To argue, for example, that Hamlet's actions are the symptoms of gout, when there is no evidence to support that view, is an example of poor interpretation.

The following statements are examples of claims introducing evaluative arguments:

- Many people do not realize that Herman Melville, the author of *Moby Dick,* was also an accomplished poet. (Evaluative claims often contain descriptive modifiers, like *accomplished* in this example.)
- Former president Jimmy Carter may not have been a great president, but he was an honorable one.
- Mary's constant chatter is an attempt to keep people from abandoning her. (An interpretive claim, in that it offers a beneath-the-surface explanation of Mary's behavior. Like many interpretive claims, this one contains causal elements, but what distinguishes it as primarily interpretive is the identification of a *coincidence* between visible and hidden phenomena.)
- For my money, soccer players are the most gifted of all athletes. (*Gifted* is a subjective term: it not only means different things to different people, but it also cannot be conclusively verified. Claims including superlative or comparative adjectives are likely to be evaluative claims.)
- "Human memory is a marvelous but fallacious instrument." (Primo Levi, *The Drowned and the Saved.*) (This claim makes two judgments about memory.)

ACTIVITIES (3.5)

1. Write claims for evaluative arguments for the following subjects.

   Example subject: Theft of library books
   Example claim: Stealing library books is not only a criminal act; it is a serious trespass against the ideals of community.
   a. Political campaign spending
   b. Computer games
   c. Pass-fail grading
   d. A particular television show
   e. Distance Learning courses
   f. Your composition instructor
   g. Rap music
   h. Television sports coverage

2. Give an example of an interpretive claim for the following topics.

   Example of topic (a): The cinematic revival of Shakespeare is an expression of *fin de siècle* anxiety.
   a. The significance of a play, movie, or short story
   b. The importance of a contemporary political figure
   c. The meaning of a current trend in fashion
   d. The attitude of students at your college toward their future careers
   e. The attitude of young Americans toward religion

Recommendations

A common goal of argument is to convince an audience that existing circumstances need to be changed. Some *recommendations* seek only to gain an audience's agreement with an idea or a decision, but others have a more practical (and ambitious) purpose: they try to convince their audience to take a particular action or, more modestly, to convince an audience that a particular action should be taken by others. As a student in English composition, you might write a paper for your instructor arguing that the legal drinking age should be lowered, or you might make that same argument in a letter to your congressional representative with the hope of getting him or her to take action. A lab technician might write a memo to her supervisor suggesting the purchase of new equipment. Or the chairperson of the history department might write to the dean requesting an adjustment in faculty salaries. All of these arguments would be recommendations.

All recommendations are concerned with the future, with what should be done at a later time, but they also imply a judgment about present conditions. Writers propose change because of dissatisfaction with an existing situation. Early in arguing a recommendation, you'll need to determine whether you want to concentrate on the current problem or on the improvements resulting from your recommendation; in some recommendations, you'll emphasize both.

- The main goal of recommendations emphasizing *present* conditions is to demonstrate the problems in the current situation. Because these recommendations argue *that* something needs to be done rather than *what* exactly that something is, they usually don't discuss a proposed change in any detail.

- The main goal of recommendations emphasizing the *future* is to present a plan for change and to demonstrate that it is feasible and likely to produce the desired effects.
- Recommendations with *equal* emphasis on present and future argue the problems of the current situation *and* the likely effects of the proposed change.

You may have noticed that recommendations are hybrid, or combination, claims with elements of both causal and evaluative arguments. That is exactly right. When proposing that an existing situation be changed, you are at least implying a negative judgment of that situation. And implied in the changes you recommend is a positive evaluation of those changes. Furthermore, you will support the recommendation itself through an argument of effect—demonstrating the positive future effects of the change.

Because arguments of recommendation argue for an action not currently in effect, words such as *should, would, must, ought, needs to be, will* or *might* typically introduce these arguments. The following are some sample claims for arguments of recommendation:

- We need more emphasis on science and math in our schools to prepare the next generation for a world of international economic competition. (The claim proposes a *change* in the current curriculum.)
- In order to attract more nontraditional students, this university must review and revise its course offerings. (Again, this claim calls for a change in an existing situation—a change that will have positive effects in the future.)
- If this company is to regain financial health, it must divest itself of all divisions not directly connected to its traditional core business. (The words *must divest* identify this claim as a recommendation—a suggestion for a particular action is being made.)
- Take back the night. (A trenchant recommendation expressed in the imperative mode. In the word *back*, the command implies making a change in an existing situation.)

ACTIVITIES (3.6)

1. For the following situations, write two claims of recommendation, one focusing on current conditions and one on the results of recommended improvements.

   Example: Taking a typing course
   Claim with a focus on current conditions: I need to take a typing course because I can't use the word processor required in my English composition course.

Claim with a focus on future improvements: I need to take a typing course so that I will be ready for the day when every office has its own word processor.
a. Replacing a television
b. Requesting a new strict policy on noise in a dormitory
c. Advocating a freeze on the research for and manufacturing of nuclear weapons
d. Purchasing a new car to replace your or your family's current one
e. Increasing the number of police in the most dangerous sections of a city

2. Read the two recommendations at the end of Chapter 9. As you read, consider whether these recommendations emphasize the present, the future, or both. See how well your ideas match up with those of a group of your classmates.

Combination Claims

A brief look at any essay anthology may persuade you that "real" claims in "real" arguments don't always fit neatly into the four categories presented in this chapter. But your experience of writing *and* reading arguments will persuade you that all arguments contain claims that fulfill one or more of these four functions.

In some cases, you will need to recast claims mentally to decide what kinds of arguments they are. For example, the famous claim "The only thing we have to fear is fear itself," which is a forceful, lively claim needing no revision, can be translated to mean "We should beware of the dangers of fear"—a recommendation based on an argument of effect identifying the negative consequences of fear. The claim itself need not be rewritten; having identified the category of the recast version of the claim, you can proceed to support the original claim.

Often, as the preceding example demonstrates, the context of a claim will help you categorize it. This quotation about fear is taken from President Franklin Delano Roosevelt's first inaugural address in 1933, during the heart of the Great Depression, when fear about the future pervaded America. In this context, Roosevelt's remark is part of a broad recommendation to the American people to regain their confidence and to begin to plan for the future with new hope. In a less urgent context, "The only thing we have to fear is fear itself" might be a causal claim meaning "The experience of fear is dangerous because it builds on itself."

If you are arguing a claim that doesn't seem to fit into any of the categories discussed here, and you can't seem to recast it mentally, ask yourself some questions about the function of the argument that will support the claim. For example, is the claim verifiable? If not, it is not factual. Does it make an unverifiable judgment about something or someone? If so, it is probably evaluative. Does it propose a course of action? If so, it is a recommendation. Does it account for or predict a particular phenomenon? Then it is a causal argument.

Some claims actually contain two propositions to be argued, as in the sentence "Acts of terrorism are serious offenses against human freedom and should meet with deadly retaliation." The first claim is the *evaluation* that acts of terrorism are serious offenses, and the second is the *recommendation* that they should meet with deadly retaliation. In supporting this double claim, you would have to defend the value judgment about terrorism before moving on to the second assertion, the recommendation. Ideally, both claims should be defended, though writers frequently assume that their audience agrees with them on the most basic points—that terrorism is abhorrent, for example—and concentrate on one or two more arguable points, such as the need for deadly retaliation.

While space constraints may require this kind of corner cutting, be careful not to assume too much about your audience's position. A writer dealing with the controversial topic of terrorism should at least *consider* whether terrorism is always completely unjustified, even if she doesn't address this question in her essay.

Often, a factual claim is combined with one of the other three kinds of claims. When this is the case, as in the statement "The rise in the divorce rate in the last 30 years may increase the divorce rate in the next generation," you must establish the accuracy of your facts (the rise in the divorce rate) before you go on to speculate about the possible effects of this fact. So, too, with the statement "The flight of business and industry from the Northeast to the Sun Belt will eventually have a damaging effect on the quality of public education in the Northeast." First, the flight of business and industry must be established as a fact, probably through outside research; then the long-term causal argument can be made.

The following are examples of combination claims:

- The recent rise in interest rates may contribute to higher inflation. (This statement combines a factual assertion about rising interest rates, which can very quickly be supported, with a causal argument predicting the effect of the higher rates. This second claim would be the focus of your argument.)
- No nation is truly free that does not offer its citizens equal opportunity in education and employment. (This statement combines a causal argument—lack of equal opportunity results in an unfree nation—with an evaluation judging the degree of a nation's freedom.)
- If the candidate wants to win votes, he must convince constituents that his reputation for moral laxness is undeserved. (This statement combines a recommendation that the candidate make his case to his constituents and a causal argument that making this case will win him their votes.)
- While men seem to be driven to success by a fear of failure, women are made comfortable with failure by their fear of success. (This breathtaking generalization combines interpretation—identifying hidden motives for behavior—with elements of a factual argument. The writer will have to present *many* instances of these gender-linked phenomena in order to warrant the generality of the claim.)

ACTIVITIES (3.7)

Into which of the four main argument types or combination of types do the following belong? Be prepared to support your answer.

Example: Automobiles should be designed so that they get a minimum of 30 miles per gallon of gasoline.

Type of argument: Recommendation

1. Excessive consumption of alcohol can lead to many illnesses.
2. Honesty is the best policy.
3. Cutting defense spending will create a safer world.
4. Tariffs on imports merely raise prices for domestic consumers.
5. Alley cats are a public nuisance in this neighborhood.
6. Politics is the art of the possible.
7. An improved sewer system would solve these flood drainage problems.
8. America should protect its domestic industries with tariffs and quotas.
9. Without a belief in God, life has no meaning.
10. Obesity can help cause heart disease.

SUMMARY

The Claim

- Claims help readers to understand and evaluate arguments, and they help you, the writer, to generate the direction and content of your arguments.

- If you have difficulty coming up with a working claim, you probably need to do more thinking and reading about your topic. When you are knowledgeable enough, a claim should come to you.

- Always be prepared to modify a working claim to fit with new ideas and information.

- Claims can be placed virtually anywhere in an argument. The most effective placement depends on the nature of your argument and its probable reception by your readers.

- *Factual claims* seek to convince an audience that a given object or condition exists or has existed. The four kinds of facts are common knowledge facts, facts experienced by you, facts reported by others, and factual generalizations.

- *Causal claims* assert that one event or condition produces or helps to produce another event or condition. In claiming *cause,* we look for what produced a past or current event or condition. In claiming *effect,* we predict a future occurrence on the basis of certain current or intended circumstances.

- *Evaluations* make a value judgment of a person, activity, or object.

- *Recommendations* argue for a particular course of action in order to change existing circumstances. Recommendations can focus on present conditions, future effects, or a combination of both.

- Some arguments work from claims that combine elements of the four classes.

SUGGESTIONS FOR WRITING (3.8)

1. Read an argumentative essay (hardcopy or online) in a magazine like the *Atlantic Monthly* or the *New York Times Magazine,* and write a one- to two-page essay on what kind of argument it is and why. Be sure to give your instructor a copy of the argumentative essay you are analyzing.
2. Select a familiar document, such as Martin Luther King, Jr.'s "I Have a Dream" speech, Lincoln's Gettysburg Address, the Declaration of Independence, or a famous Shakespearean soliloquy, and identify the class or classes of argument it represents. In a one- to two-page letter to your instructor, support your identification. (Texts of each of the suggested sample documents are available online.) Be sure to give your instructor a copy of the document you are analyzing.
3. Find the lyrics to your favorite song, probably available online, and determine whether or not an argument exists. Support your reasoning in an e-mail message to one of your classmates. Be sure to provide your instructor with both a copy of the lyrics and your response.

ILLUSTRATIVE ARGUMENTS IN PART II: THE CLAIM

4

An Argument's Support

Now that you have a working claim and a good idea about the kind of argument it summarizes, you are ready to begin supporting that claim. The body of your argument, the material that will convert your claim into a conclusion, is your presentation of support. Broadly defined, an argument's support is all the material you insert into your argument to strengthen the probability (and in some cases, truth) of your claim. To argue your claim successfully, you must know how to select appropriate support for your particular claim, how to determine how much support is necessary, and how to arrange that support in the most convincing way.

Once you have a working claim, you will probably find that you have some ideas for supporting it. The more your claim emerges from your experience of dissonance and from your own interests, the more likely you are to have solid support ready at hand, though you will have to do *some* research on even the most familiar topics. On the other hand, regardless of how much research goes into them, claims having no connection with your own experiences, interest, or knowledge will be more difficult to support.

Let's say that you are worried about your grandmother, who, although healthy, is growing increasingly depressed and withdrawn. You know from talking with her that she feels useless, ignored, and aimless. Your concern makes you angry about the way our society treats its older citizens, and you decide to let this concern and anger fuel an argument about age discrimination. Your grandmother's experience has given you a number of specific examples of age discrimination and its effects. Some of these examples will help to support the claim "American society, for all its public attention to human rights, is guilty of systematically depriving its senior citizens of countless 'inalienable' rights." But you know that in order to argue such a far-reaching claim convincingly, you will need to find support beyond your personal observations.

Since different classes of arguments often require different kinds of support, knowing the class of argument that your claim belongs to will help you know what kinds of additional support to look for. Chapters 6 through 9 discuss these specific requirements. There are also more general types of support, not specifically associated with a particular class, that you will want to be familiar with. And you will need to determine how much support will be enough and how to arrange that support strategically. These generic supporting tactics are treated in this chapter.

SOME VARIETIES OF SUPPORT

It is useful to think of supporting material as separate units or building blocks that strengthen a claim in different ways and to different degrees. What follows is a discussion of some of the generic varieties of support commonly used to strengthen arguments.

Secondary Claims

All claims, regardless of their class, are supported by further claims, which will require their own support. Sometimes these *secondary* claims will belong to the same class as the main claim, sometimes to a different class. If you were arguing the factual claim "Students in my major are more interested in learning marketable skills than in truly educating themselves," you would need to support your fairly general claim with individual examples of this phenomenon. You probably would cite conversations in which individual students had expressed this preference to you and/or perhaps a survey asking students in your major to rank their educational priorities. In both cases, you are supporting your main claim with a secondary factual claim, which will itself need to be verified.

A recommendation claiming "This university should offer a pass-fail grading option to its students" may include as support the secondary *causal* argument "Removing the traditional evaluative system of letter grades will facilitate learning by reducing pressure." While not the chief point of this argument, this secondary causal claim still needs to be supported. One way to support it is through a third, *factual* claim. Perhaps the writer has access to a survey taken at another university that offers the pass-fail option, and this survey demonstrates a positive student response to the option. Or maybe the writer has friends at other schools who have spoken favorably about their pass-fail grading policy. Whether these responses are gathered through a large survey or individual conversations, they are facts that will strengthen the secondary claim (provided they are responsibly obtained and accurately reported).

As these examples illustrate, eventually all main claims will come to rest on factual claims that are supported by observations, examples, statistics, studies, and so forth. While some arguments depend more heavily on facts than others, no argument is likely to be convincing if it doesn't at some point refer to verified factual claims. In the previous example, the factual generalization about learning goals is supported by secondary factual claims: the expressed preferences of other students in your major and/or a survey of student learning goals. In the second example, a recommendation ultimately comes to rest on a secondary factual claim: positive student response to the pass-fail option. As you will see in Chapter 6, these fundamental factual claims would be supported by the writer's assurance that they have been gathered, interpreted, and reported responsibly.

ACTIVITIES (4.1)

Supply secondary claims that would support the following main claims of arguments. In each case, identify the class of the secondary and primary claims.

1. The *Boles GRE Study Guide* is an excellent tutorial for students preparing to take the GRE.
2. Television newscasting influences how Americans think about social and political issues.
3. In my high school, food abuse was a far bigger problem than alcohol or drug abuse.
4. Dostoyevsky's *Crime and Punishment* is a ponderous novel of sin and redemption.
5. If we really want to eradicate racism, we must institute within the primary grades curricula that honor diversity.

Comparisons

You can support some claims by citing a comparable claim that has already gained wide acceptance. Note, however, that this supporting strategy will work only if the two claims are truly comparable, not just vaguely similar. In an argument predicting financial difficulties for a new snowboard store in your town mall, you might cite the failure of the three other stores that have rented the same space. Or if you are arguing against proposed cuts in state money for scholarships, you may cite what another state has done to avoid reducing its education budget. This comparison will work only if the fiscal situation of the state you refer to is truly comparable to that of your state. In order to know this, you will have to get considerable information on each and probably present that information in the argument itself.

Appeals to Authority

You can support any claim by referring to a similar view held by a recognized authority in the field. You could support an evaluative argument claiming that Michael Jordan is the most talented professional basketball player in the game today by quoting Charles Barkley pronouncing the same judgment (of course, Barkley has to have made this pronouncement—you can't make it up). Just be sure that the person whose judgment you cite *is* an established expert in the subject of your argument. Even though Barkley is a sports celebrity, his fame does not make him an expert on investment strategies or health care.

Appeals to Audience Needs and Values

Remember the emphasis of Chapter 2 on audience consideration, including an identification of audience needs and values? You can convert this preliminary identification into explicit support for your argument. Obviously, audiences will be more accepting of arguments that they see as likely to satisfy their needs or affirm their values. Many arguments presume these needs and values without referring to them explicitly. But you can strengthen some arguments by directly addressing these considerations, particularly when the match between claim and audience needs or values is not obvious. For example, a recommendation addressed to the administration of your college proposing a change from a trimester to a semester calendar should identify precisely how the change would benefit the administration—perhaps in the form of increased enrollment, higher student satisfaction, or long-term savings.

ACTIVITIES (4.2)

Get together with a small group of your classmates and discuss which methods of support (comparison, appeal to authority, appeal to audience needs and values) could be effectively applied to the following claims:

1. The costs of statewide and national political campaigns will discourage all but the rich from running for office.
2. The study of homosexuality is (is not) appropriate in a college course.
3. Using e-mail to keep in touch with friends who have gone off to other colleges is better than making telephone calls.
4. Parents should recognize how they risk their children's intellectual development by parking them in front of a television.
5. The widespread use of antidepressant drugs has revolutionized the psychotherapeutic community.

Addressing the Counterargument

A defining feature of argument is that its claim or claims are subject to disagreement: they are arguable. Thus, any claim you argue should be capable of evoking a *counterargument*—a position different from and often directly opposed to your claim. Just as you must carefully consider certain questions about your audience before you begin arguing, you must also identify the probable counterargument or arguments. Though this statement may seem counterintuitive, your arguments will be strengthened by your acknowledgment of their most powerful counterarguments. Why? For one thing, it is entirely possible that your readers are aware of the counterargument and even convinced by it. In stating and rebutting this position, you are dealing head on with the opposing view. Second, even if your readers aren't familiar with the alternative view, identifying it in your own argument will contribute to your image as a responsible and well-informed thinker.

The following are approaches to dealing with your argument's counterargument:

- You can omit direct reference to the counterargument when it is a weak position or likely to be unfamiliar to your audience. But note that omission does not mean ignorance: you should keep even the weakest counterargument in mind while you are writing, if for no other reason than that a reader may raise it.
- You can acknowledge or identify the counterargument without directly refuting it. This technique shows your readers that you are aware of the complexity of the issue and the legitimacy of other positions; it gives the impression that you are reasonable and broad-minded. In the following example, Margaret Whitney includes a brief acknowledgment of some predictable objections to her claim that competitive athletics are good for girls:

I am not suggesting that participation in sports is the answer for all young women. It is not easy—the losing, jealousy, raw competition and intense personal criticism of performance.

And I don't wish to imply that the sports scene is a morality play either. Girls' sports can be funny. You can't forget that out on that field are a bunch of people who know the meaning of the word cute. During one game, I noticed that Ann had a blue ribbon tied on her ponytail, and it dawned on me that every girl on the team had an identical bow. Somehow I can't picture the Celtics gathered in the locker room of the Boston Garden agreeing to wear the same color sweatbands.

Whitney has chosen not to refute these objections, probably because of the relative brevity of her argument, but her identification of the objections does suggest that she is reasonable and flexible.

- You should identify and directly refute an opposing position in the following situations:
  –When you know your audience holds that position.
  –When you know a credible, often-cited countercase exists, regardless of whether your audience subscribes to that position.
  –If it is vital to your argument to project a broad-minded, well-balanced image.

The full text of Martin Luther King, Jr.'s 1963 "Letter from Birmingham Jail" appears on multiple Web sites, including "The Martin Luther King, Jr. Papers Project at Stanford University." Some of the links reveal the various rhetorical strategies that King uses to develop his response to criticism by Alabama clergy of his program of nonviolent resistance to racial segregation. The following excerpt from paragraph eight of his letter is an example of direct refutation:

You may well ask, "Why direct action? Why sit-ins, marches, and so forth? Isn't negotiation a better path?" You are quite right in calling for negotiation. Indeed, this is the very purpose of direct action. Nonviolent direct action seeks to create such a crisis and foster such a tension that a community which has constantly refused to negotiate is forced to confront the issue. It seeks so to dramatize the issue that it can no longer be ignored. My citing the creation of tension as part of the work of the nonviolent resister may sound rather shocking. But I must confess I am not afraid of the word "tension." I have earnestly opposed violent tension, but there is a type of constructive, nonviolent tension which is necessary for growth. Just as Socrates felt that it was necessary to create a tension in the mind so that individuals could rise from the bondage of myths and half truths to the unfettered realm of creative analysis and objective appraisal, so must we see the need for nonviolent gadflies to create the kind of tension in society that will help men rise from the dark depths of prejudice and racism to the majestic heights of understanding and brotherhood.

Notice how King identifies the opposition's position and even concedes them a point (they're correct in calling for negotiations) before he refutes their position and moves to an idealistic statement of his own. This pattern of statement-concession-refutation is typical of effective refutations, though you have to be careful not to give away too much in the concession.

Direct refutations should be thoughtfully placed in your argument. If your audience appears to be firmly committed to an opposing position, you're not likely to convince them of the error of their views at the outset. On the other hand, readers without strongly held views are less likely to be swayed by a counterargument if it follows an impressive array of support for your claim. But if you include your refutation as the final piece of support, remember that it may linger in your reader's mind for some time, so make it as strong and convincing as possible. And finally, some very powerful arguments are exclusively refutations of opposing positions; these arguments gain form, precision, and intensity from the position they are opposing.

ARRANGING YOUR ARGUMENT'S SUPPORT

Having accumulated support for your claim, you now have to consider the best way to arrange it in your argument. You can make strong support even stronger by arranging it to have the most powerful impact on your readers. Once again, audience consideration is key: your decisions about the organization of your argument's support should be based on your readers' familiarity with the subject, their ability to follow the path of your argument, and their probable disposition toward your claim.

It helps to think of your support as separate units that can be moved around within your argument. In an essay claiming that "The Student Activities Board should bring Matchbox 20 to campus," the units of support could be listed as follows:

1. A survey shows that Matchbox 20 is the most popular performing group with students at your college.

2. The college would increase student satisfaction by showing their willingness to please students.
3. Ticket sales would be brisk and therefore would substantially offset the cost of bringing the band to campus.
4. In a letter to the *Chronicle of Higher Education,* the vice president of student affairs at a college in the adjoining state praised Matchbox 20 for their entertainment ability. "This is a band that any school should be proud to host," the letter concluded.
5. The band has a solid reputation for being professional and audience-appropriate.
6. Bringing such a popular band to campus would increase the college's community visibility.
7. Student enrollment would increase as a result of bringing Matchbox 20 to campus.

A good general principle is that the *strongest* support should be presented first, so that you gain some early agreement from your readers. If possible, you should also save an effective supporting point for the end of your argument; it will leave your readers with a positive final impression. In the preceding list, the strongest argument may be Argument 2, particularly if the college in question is, like most schools in today's competitive higher-education environment, extremely concerned about student satisfaction. Argument 6, a secondary causal claim, is likely to be persuasive to the Student Activities Board as well, since community visibility is always a plus to college administrators.

What constitutes strong support? To some extent, this will depend on your audience. A credulous, inexperienced group and a cynical or expert audience will be convinced by different points. However, relevant factual support (figures, examples, and statistics, as in Argument 1) is usually very strong, whereas highly speculative arguments (predicted effects with a remote chance of being realized) are weaker; for example, Argument 7 would be extremely difficult to predict convincingly and probably should be omitted altogether. Citing expert opinion, as in Argument 4, is usually effective, provided your expert is credible and his or her support is documented. In Argument 4, does the opinion of a vice president for student affairs qualify as expert in this context? Does she have an obvious bias that might weaken her statement? How respectable a publication is the *Chronicle of Higher Education?* Are your school and hers comparable?

Sometimes you have little choice about the arrangement of your support. Scientific experiments dictate a certain organization, as do causal chains, where Cause A must be discussed before Cause B, Cause B before Cause C, and so on. In these cases, you'll need to make sure that all supporting arguments are strong and that they fit tightly together, because one weak link can destroy the entire argument.

ACTIVITIES (4.3)

1. The following argument, written by student Sharon Bidwell, contains a number of varieties of supporting material. Pretend that you are the editor of your

school newspaper and have decided to print Sharon's letter. In a two-page letter to Sharon, comment on the effectiveness of her choice and arrangement of support.

The administration's decision not to allow Dr. Fasciano and his white supremacist group to participate in a roundtable discussion with the students on our campus is clearly an act of censorship and should not be tolerated in a country that prides itself on free thought and expression. Censorship, as defined by the *Encyclopaedia Britannica,* is "the suppression or prohibition of speech or writing that is condemned as subversive to the common good." It is obvious that the administration is making a selective decision of what the "common good" is for the students of this campus.

There is no doubt that the administration has legitimate concerns that need to be addressed. First of all, Mr. Fasciano's visit will raise some eyebrows among those who make regular contributions to the university. Second, Mr. Fasciano's visit is likely to set off active protests which have the capacity to seriously disrupt the campus and even threaten the safety and security of the students.

Despite these very real risks, the administration must make it known that this university supports the Constitution of the United States—namely, the First Amendment—and does not bow to pressure when it comes to suppressing free speech. To paraphrase John Milton in his *Areopagitica* of 1644, we must allow that free and open encounter in which truth may indeed prevail over error.

The argument against censorship has been made by many who fought hard against it—against anything, in fact, that interferes with self-development and self-fulfillment. For example, in his first inaugural address, Thomas Jefferson addressed the necessity of free dissent: "If there be any among us who would wish to dissolve this Union or to change its republican form, let them stand undisturbed as monuments of the safety with which error of opinion may be tolerated where reason is left free to combat it."

The administration must give the students the freedom to be the best guarantors of quality and fairness. We rely on these institutions of higher learning to *teach* future generations by allowing them to choose *freely* and make difficult decisions. For those who oppose Mr. Fasciano and his views, let there be an open forum with a free exchange of ideas. Our forefathers fought for this privilege. Let's not let them down.

DEFINITIONS

Obviously, readers can't agree (or reasonably disagree) with what they don't understand. Clarity is the result of many different elements in written argument: precision of ideas in the writer's mind, an understanding of the relationship among these ideas, careful organization of claim and supporting material, clear transitions among parts of the argument, reliance on the conventions of grammar and punctuation, and comprehensible, unambiguous language. It is this final element—the clarity of your language—that concerns us here. Ideally, writers of argument would use only those words that they knew their readers would understand. But arguments can't always rely on simple language, and even the simplest words mean different things to different people. This is where *definition* comes in: the careful delineation of the intended meaning of a potentially troublesome word or term.

Knowing when and how to define terms is critical to successful argument. Because effective and strategic definition strengthen any argument by making it more accessible to readers, it can be viewed as a form of support. In some cases, definition moves from its clarifying supporting function to that of a secondary claim, where the writer must convince the reader to understand a term in a particular way before the central claim can be argued. Sometimes definition of a key term is so crucial and controversial that it becomes a central claim in itself.

When to Define

You should plan on defining the following types of language in your arguments:

- *Unfamiliar terminology.* Any specialized or unusual terms that may be unfamiliar to your readers must be explained. If, for example, you aren't sure whether your readers will have heard of "Maxwell's Demon," or a "net revenue model," or "dysthymic disorder," provide a clear definition.

  Unfamiliar terminology includes *jargon* (specialized vocabulary and idioms). Generally speaking, jargon should be avoided, but there are times when it is the best language for the job. If you must use phrases like "the dialogic principle of feminist discourse," don't assume that everyone in your audience will know precisely what you mean; provide a definition.

- *Nonspecific language.* In general, avoid vague, fuzzy terms, particularly in statements of evaluation and measurement. If you claim, "The Dave Matthews Band is the most popular band in contemporary music," consider how little this statement tells the reader about the nature and extent of that popularity. Popularity based on CD sales? Popularity based on money earned? On concert attendance? And popularity with whom? Certainly they are not the most popular band with people over 65. A more specific statement, such as "The Dave Matthews Band has sold more CDs in the last year than any other contemporary band" is far more useful to the reader.

  And when you use nonspecific words like *poor, excellent, large, grand,* or *considerable,* make sure you explain the meaning of your modifier as precisely as possible.

- *Abstract terms.* While you should try to make your writing as concrete as possible, sometimes you can't avoid using abstract terms in argument, especially in evaluations. The problem with abstractions is that they can be understood in different ways; that is, they can be *ambiguous.* If you must use a term like *popular,* or *talented,* or *conservative,* be sure to pin down explicitly your understanding of the term. While your readers may not agree with your definition, at least they will understand how you intend to use the word and will judge the success of your argument within those parameters.

- *Controversial terms.* Some terms have been at the center of heated public debate for so long that they are emotionally and politically loaded. Their meaning is ambiguous—that is, it can be interpreted in more than one way—and people tend to argue over which interpretation is correct. *Euthanasia* and *gay marriage* are examples of such controversial terms; how one defines them often determines one's position toward them. When you use such terms in your arguments, you will almost certainly need to clarify what you mean by them.

Sometimes such terms are so controversial that your definition, because it implies a position on the subject, becomes the point of the argument. Consider, for example, an essay on doctor-assisted suicide: a carefully delineated definition of what the practice *is* (or is not)—the prescription of lethal amounts of medication to a dying patient at the patient's request, for example—would take you a long way in an argument supporting the practice.

Or, consider the implications of denying or justifying gay marriages in terms of the "Defense of Marriage Act," which is what student Doug Edwards did when Hawaii seemed about to authorize gay marriages (see Chapter 8). Later, the Vermont legislature removed the religious issue of the "sanctity" of marriage from the debate by legalizing same-sex civil unions, and perhaps redefined "gay marriage" as a result.

Types of Definitions

Terms requiring clarification can be defined briefly or extensively, depending on the needs of your audience and the importance of the term to your argument. The four types of definition you will most commonly use as support for your argument are the shorthand definition, the sentence definition, the extended definition, and the stipulative definition.

Writers often resort to *shorthand* definitions when the term in question requires only a quick explanation. A shorthand definition substitutes a familiar term for an unfamiliar one, as in the following example: "Acetylsalicylic acid (aspirin) is an effective medicine for most headaches."

A *sentence* definition, similar to a dictionary definition but written as a grammatical sentence, consists of the term to be defined (the *species*), the general category to which it belongs (the *genus*), and those characteristics that distinguish it from all other members of that general category (the *differentiae*). A sentence definition has the following structure:

SPECIES = GENUS + DIFFERENTIAE

An example of this form of definition is "A heifer [species] is a young cow [genus] that has not borne a calf [differentiae]."

An *extended* definition includes this basic sentence definition *and* any additional material that would help a reader understand the term being defined. The following are strategies for extending a sentence definition.

Evolution of Definition. Sometimes an understanding of the historical development of a word's usage will illuminate its richness for readers. The word *queer,* for example, means strange or out of the ordinary. Thus it was eventually coined as a derogatory term for a male homosexual. Recently homosexuals have embraced the term, converting it from a slur to a compliment. There is now an academic field called Queer Studies.

Comparison. Readers can gain a better understanding of a term if it is compared to something with which they are familiar. An argument that needs to define the term *docudrama* might explain that a docudrama is similar to a movie, except the events depicted are based in fact.

Example. Offering specific examples of unfamiliar terms is an excellent way to explain them. To define what a *haiku* is, for example, you would almost certainly present an example or two.

Definition by Negation. Sometimes you can explain a term by telling your reader what it is not, what it should not be confused with. For example, at the beginning of this textbook, we defined the term *argument* by distinguishing it from *opinion,* a term often mistaken as being synonymous with argument.

Etymological Definition. Providing the etymology of a word—the meanings of its original roots—can also help to explain its meaning. The word *misogynist,* for example, derives from the Greek *miso,* meaning "hate," and *gyne,* meaning "woman."

Definition by Description. Unfamiliar or abstract terms can often be explained or introduced by a physical or figurative description. If you were defining a Phillips screw, you might explain what the screw looks like. Or in defining contrapuntal music, you could describe the sound: the listener hears two distinct melodies going on at exactly the same time.

Functional Definition. You can explain some unfamiliar terms by telling readers what the object or person does or how it operates. It would be helpful for a reader unfamiliar with the meaning of *provost* to learn what duties that academic officer performs. Functional definitions are particularly helpful in explaining unfamiliar *objects* such as tools. After describing the appearance of a particular drill bit, for example, you could explain what that particular bit is used for or how it is used.

The following extended definition of "poetry," from Laurence Perrine's *Sound and Sense,* contains many of these strategies of extended definition:

> Between poetry and other forms of imaginative literature there is no sharp distinction. You may have been taught to believe that poetry can be recognized by the arrangement of its lines on the page or by its use of rime [*sic*] and meter. Such superficial tests are almost worthless. The Book of Job in the Bible and Melville's *Moby Dick* are highly poetical, but

the familiar verse that begins: "Thirty days hath September, April, June, and November . . ." is not. The difference between poetry and other literature is one only of degree. Poetry is the most condensed and concentrated form of literature, saying most in the fewest number of words. It is language whose individual lines, either because of their own brilliance or because they focus so powerfully on what has gone before, have a higher voltage than most language has. It is language that grows frequently incandescent, giving off both light and heat.

This definition uses a sentence definition ("Poetry is the most condensed and concentrated form of literature"), a definition by negation (indicating what poetry is *not*: poetry has little to do with line arrangement or rhyme or meter), comparison ("Between poetry and other forms of imaginative literature there is no sharp distinction"), and figurative description ("It is language that grows frequently incandescent, giving off both light and heat").

Stipulative definitions *argue* that a particular definition should be assigned to a term. In other words, a stipulative definition argues a claim about meaning. While all definitions can be seen as claims, in that they propose meaning, and meaning is never fixed, the types of explanatory definitions discussed so far record meanings that most audiences would agree on. Stipulative definitions, on the other hand, argue for a particular meaning rather than record a consensual one. Sometimes stipulative definitions are made for convenience and clarity: "When we use the term *argument,* we are referring only to its primary meaning of demonstrating the reasonableness of a proposition." In this example, the writer is clarifying, not arguing.

But extended stipulative definitions are often fully developed arguments supporting an arguable, often controversial, claim about meaning. Think of the often-repeated argument "Abortion is murder." This short sentence definition opens a Pandora's box of controversies about meaning. First, there is likely to be disagreement over the meaning of the term *murder* in this context. The dictionary tells us that murder is the "unlawful and malicious or premeditated killing of one human being by another" *(Webster's New World Dictionary of the American Language).* But abortion is not illegal, so an antiabortion argument would have to reject this definition and stipulate its own. Or to open another controversy: is the fetus a "human being"? Is there consensus about the meaning of this term? Clearly not: a pro-choice advocate would want to restrict or stipulate the meaning of *human being.* Through your stipulated definitions of *abortion, murder,* and *human being,* you are actually arguing your position on the issue of abortion.

Extended stipulative definitions are essentially interpretive arguments: in proposing a restricted, possibly unusual, definition of a concept, you are arguing a particular interpretation or understanding that is suggested and supported by the context of the argument. Stipulative definitions can be supported through a variety of supporting methods. One of the most useful is an argument of effect—that is, demonstrating the positive effects of adopting your particular definition of the term. For example, if you were proposing a new definition of the word *minor* as a way of making a case for lowering the legal drinking age ("The traditional definition of *minor* as someone under the age of 21 leaves out those 18–20 year olds who are considered old enough to die for their country, to get married, and to terminate their education"), you might introduce a supporting argument of effect that money could be saved if police didn't have to enforce the current drinking age. Or if you were arguing that education is a lifelong process, you might base your argument on a stipulative definition of *education,* supporting that definition through the secondary causal argument of the positive consequences that education, so defined, can lead to.

Chapter 10 of this book, "Writing and Image," begins with a stipulative definition of the word *image* as applied to written argument. This definition serves more of a clarifying than an argumentative purpose, but it does make the claim that despite the largely negative popular understanding of the term, a writer's "image" is positive and important.

ACTIVITIES (4.4)

1. Examine an extended definition in an online encyclopedia, reference guide, or textbook, and write a one- to two-page essay that describes what elements (sentence definition, examples, history of the object or concept being defined, comparison or contrast, and so on) have been included in the definition, and speculate on why they have been included. Are there other elements you believe should have been included to help the definition? Are there any elements that could have been omitted?

2. Write your own stipulative definition of *beauty, murder,* or *friendship.* Compare your definition with those of your classmates who define the same term.

S U M M A R Y

An Argument's Support

- An argument's support is all the material that transforms your working claim into a reasonable conclusion. Knowing the class of the argument you are making will help you determine the appropriate support, but there are some generic varieties of support that can be used to strengthen any class of argument. These are

  – secondary claims

  – comparisons

  – appeals to authority

  – appeals to audience needs and values

  – addressing the counterargument

  – defining key terms

- When possible, arrange your support to have the greatest impact on your readers, with strong support placed at the beginning and end of your argument.

- Any terms in your claim or the body of your argument likely to be unfamiliar to your readers should be defined by a sentence definition, an extended definition, or a shorthand definition.

- Stipulative definitions, which restrict the meaning of a term to one of the term's possible meanings, can be used to clarify an argument or to make an interpretive argument.

SUGGESTIONS FOR WRITING (4.5)

1. Write a claim that comes out of a position or belief you hold strongly (about a political issue, a policy at your university, or your relationship to your family, for example). Identify the category of your claim, and make a list of all the points you can think of to support your claim. Give your list to a classmate and see if he or she can add any supporting reasons you haven't thought of.
2. Write a two- to three-page extended definition of some concept or object, making sure your definition includes a formal sentence definition. Your instructor may have suggestions for this assignment, but other suggestions include entropy, eugenics, amber, ecosystem, and e-commerce.

ILLUSTRATIVE ARGUMENTS IN PART II: AN ARGUMENT'S SUPPORT

5

Making Reasonable Arguments: Formal and Informal Logic

In Chapters 6 through 9, you will learn the most appropriate supporting methods for each class of claim. But before you begin working at the specific levels of claim and support, you should have some understanding of the principles of logic. The primary definition of the term *logic* is "the science of correct reasoning." The many and complicated rules of formal logic do, in fact, make up an intricate mathematical system that yields absolutely right and absolutely wrong answers. But this system does not dominate the fuzzier province of written argument, where variations in context, occasion, audience, and purpose make absolute conclusions exceedingly rare. Nevertheless, the fundamental principles of formal logic and their less formal derivatives do have their use in written argument: they are excellent tools for testing the reasonableness of the relationship between claim and support, for measuring the probability of an argument's conclusion. Think of it this way: you can't write successful arguments without some familiarity with logic, but this familiarity will not ensure that your arguments will be successful.

FORMAL LOGIC

The principles of formal logic were identified by the Greek philosopher Aristotle (384–322 B.C.). Today, almost 2,500 years later, these principles continue to influence what we mean by *reasonable* thinking. Just as children learn to speak their native language unaware of its underlying linguistic and grammatical principles, so we learn to think reasonably with little understanding of those complex principles informing reasonable thought. At some point in their education, children must learn the rules of grammar in order to refine their language skills; similarly, as educated adults and certainly as writers of argument, we must become familiar with the principles of logic to refine our reasoning skills.

Formal logic comes in two broad varieties: induction and deduction. *Induction,* or inductive reasoning, involves reasoning from observed evidence (the support) to a general statement (the claim or conclusion). *Deduction,* or deductive reasoning, involves reasoning from premises (assertions accepted as true or probable) to a conclusion or claim.

Induction:

> **Observed evidence:** In the 20 years I've lived in New York State, warm weather has begun every year between March and May.
>
> **General statement:** In New York State, warm weather begins between March and May.

Deduction:

> **Premise:** All human beings are mortal.
> **Premise:** Jane is a human being.
> **Conclusion:** Jane is mortal.

In the first example, notice the movement from specific examples (every spring for 20 years) to a very general assertion. But notice also that the specific examples suggest only that the general assertion is likely or probable, not necessarily true. The move from specific examples to a general conclusion is often referred to as the *inductive leap,* a term which underlines the large gap between the truth of the individual instances and the truth of the generalized conclusion.

In the deductive example, on the other hand, the statement that Jane is mortal is *necessarily true* if the premises preceding it are true. If certain conditions are met, deductive arguments *can* lead to necessary, or absolute, conclusions. But the "if" is a big one; in reality, the principles of deduction will enhance the reasonableness of your argument, but they will rarely ensure its absolute truth.

As you'll see in the next four chapters, some logical principles are more useful with one kind of argument than with another. The remainder of this chapter offers a general introduction to the principles themselves.

Induction

In inductive reasoning, we make generalizations on the basis of individual instances. For example, if you observed repeated instances of male students dominating class discussion, you might conclude that at your school, male students participate in class more than female students. Your conclusion is useful not because it represents the absolute truth, which of course it doesn't (there are exceptions to any generalization), but because it summarizes a set of similar events that you have observed. Inductive reasoning comes naturally to all of us, whether we're highly trained in Aristotelian logic or don't know the difference between a reasoned argument and a shouting match.

But the process does carry risks. For one thing, irresponsible induction can lead to harmful misconceptions. There is a world of difference between the conclusion "Male political science majors at Miller College tend to dominate class discussion" and one claiming "Men are more skillful speakers than women." You can avoid making irresponsible conclusions if you heed the following three cautions: (1) be sure you have *enough* individual examples to warrant the conclusion (your experience in one political science class is not enough to warrant even the preceding first conclusion); (2) provide the context of your examples and conclusion—in this case, your observations of students in a particular major at a particular college; and (3) always qualify your conclusion by using verbs or modifiers that limit the degree of certainty you're insisting on ("Male students often dominate class discussion").

A second risk of inductive reasoning concerns the use to which we put its conclusions. Inductive conclusions are safest if they are used *descriptively,* as a way of summarizing a set of observations or facts ("Male political science majors at Miller tend to dominate class discussion"). But induction is more commonly used to *predict* events or behavior. Many of the predictions we make on the basis of induction are perfectly harmless. If you know that the shopping mall is usually crowded on Saturday afternoons, your decision to shop Saturday morning is a harmless and quite useful prediction based on inductive reasoning. But predictive inductive reasoning can lead to harmful stereotypes. It may be true that women in your major do not participate in class discussion, but if you assume, on the basis of these limited observations, that all the women you associate with will be quiet and unassertive, your false conclusion may put you in personal and political hot water.

Responsible inductive reasoning depends in large measure on recognizing and arguing factual claims, since induction involves supporting a general claim by individual factual instances. For this reason, a full discussion of induction is reserved for Chapter 6, "Arguing Facts."

Deduction

The basic form of the deductive argument is the *syllogism:* a three-part argument consisting of a *major premise* (a premise is an assertion or proposition), a *minor premise,* and a *conclusion.* The earlier sample of deductive reasoning is a classic example of a syllogism:

> **Major premise:** All human beings are mortal.
> **Minor premise:** Jane is a human being.
> **Conclusion:** Jane is mortal.

This syllogism is an example of thinking in terms of classes. The major premise establishes two classes—a larger one of mortal beings and a smaller one of human beings—and it asserts that the smaller class belongs in the larger. The minor premise establishes that a still smaller class—in this case, one individual (Jane)—belongs in the smaller class of the major premise. From there it necessarily follows that Jane will also be a member of the largest class, mortal beings. The syllogism can also be displayed visually.

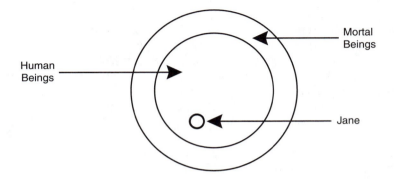

Thinking in terms of classes can be misleading if the process is done incorrectly. Examine the following syllogism:

> **Major premise:** All Catholics believe in the sanctity of human life.
> **Minor premise:** Jane believes in the sanctity of human life.
> **Conclusion:** Jane is a Catholic.

At first glance this argument may seem plausible, but as the diagram below shows, the argument is seriously flawed because the minor premise puts Jane in the larger group of those who believe in the sanctity of life but not in the smaller group of those who are Catholics. All the argument can really tell us is that Jane and Catholics share this one trait. They may differ in everything else.

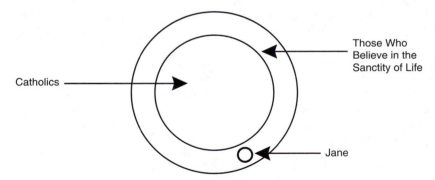

This sample syllogism leads us to an important distinction in deductive reasoning: the distinction between validity and truth. A syllogism is *valid* when it's set up correctly, according to the rules of formal logic. You can look these rules up in a logic textbook, but in many cases, you can tell when a syllogism doesn't follow them correctly because, as in the case of Jane's religious persuasion, you recognize instinctively that the conclusion doesn't make sense. On the other hand, a syllogism is *true* only if its premises are true. The syllogism about Jane's mortality is both valid and true. But consider the following syllogism:

All women are feminists.
Jane is a woman.
Jane is a feminist.

Clearly, the generalization that *all* women are feminists is untrue; so, though the relationship between premises (support) and conclusion (claim) is valid, the conclusion is untrue because it works from a false premise. On the other hand, while the premises of the syllogism about Jane's religion are true, the syllogism is not valid because the relationship between premises and conclusion is incorrect.

Deductive arguments that are both true and valid are *sound.* Deductive arguments that are untrue, invalid, or both are *unsound.* Whether reading or writing arguments, you'll need to be on guard against the seductions of the valid argument built on false premises, and of the invalid argument luring you with the truth of its premises or conclusion.

Conditional Syllogism.   The conditional syllogism, sometimes referred to as the *if-then syllogism,* takes the following form:

If John drops the glass on the sidewalk, then the glass breaks.

John drops the glass on the sidewalk.

The glass breaks.

This syllogism is valid, and if its premises are true, it is also sound.

With conditional syllogisms, however, you need to watch out for a very common error, usually called *affirming the consequent,* where the "then" clause of the major premise is turned into an affirmative statement in the minor premise:

If John drops the glass on the sidewalk, then the glass breaks.

The glass breaks.

John drops the glass on the sidewalk.

The argument is invalid because the major premise merely claims that John's dropping the glass causes it to break; it does not exclude other ways of breaking the glass, such as hitting it with a hammer. Given this major premise, we cannot conclude that John has dropped the glass simply because the glass is broken.

Disjunctive Syllogism.   The disjunctive, or "either-or," syllogism takes the following form:

Either the doctor gave the patient oxygen or the patient died.

The patient did not die.

The doctor gave the patient oxygen.

Note that this argument is invalid if the alternative is affirmed—that is, if it turns out to be true—rather than denied, or declared untrue, as in the preceding example:

> Either the doctor gave the patient oxygen or the patient died.
>
> The patient died.
>
> The doctor did not give the patient oxygen.

The major premise merely asserts that we can assume that the first alternative occurred because the second one didn't. (In other words, if the doctor hadn't given the patient oxygen, the patient would surely have died.) But if the second one, the patient's dying, did occur, we can't turn around and assume that the doctor failed to give the patient oxygen. Again, the patient could have died from a number of other causes even if the doctor did his "duty."

Making Use of Deduction in Written Arguments. For writers of argument, classical logic offers a good way of "checking your work." Familiarity with the basic principles of deductive reasoning will probably not help you *create* arguments, but it will help you test the reasonableness of your claim and support once they are composed. Of course, the writing and thinking we do every day do not come packaged in classical syllogistic form, so that detecting sound and unsound reasoning is a little more difficult than in the preceding examples. But with a little practice, you can become adept at recasting your claim and support into the syllogistic model.

Let's say you are writing an argument claiming, "Your name does not determine your destiny." You plan to offer the following support for your claim: (1) students with common names receive higher grades than students with unusual names, but there could other issues operating here; (2) studies of prisoners reveal half of the inmates in prisons undergoing psychiatric evaluations have uncommon names; and (3) many successful people have unusual names. To determine whether your claim and support are logical, you'll need to work with each supporting claim separately, finding the place it would occupy in a formal syllogism that concludes, "Your name does not determine your destiny."

So where would your first supporting claim be placed? Because it's fairly specific, it is likely to be a minor premise, since minor premises of syllogisms are almost always more specific than major premises. You now have an incomplete syllogism that looks like this:

> **Major premise: ?**
> **Minor premise:** Students with common names receive higher grades than students with uncommon names, but there could be other reasons involved.
> **Conclusion:** Therefore, your name does not determine your destiny.

The syllogistic formula requires that the major premise establish a larger class of which the class in the minor premise is a subset. Here, the major premise would read something like "Your name does not determine your destiny." Now the syllogism looks like this:

> **Major premise:** Your name does not determine your destiny.
> **Minor premise:** A study showed teachers gave students with common names higher grades than students with uncommon names, but there could be other reasons involved.
> **Conclusion:** Therefore, your name does not determine your destiny.

You don't have to state the major premise in your argument, but it is extremely helpful to know what it is so that you can determine whether that assumption—and its relationship to the rest of the argument—is reasonable.

To determine its reasonableness, you test the validity and soundness of the syllogism. The syllogism is valid: the internal relationship among premises and conclusion is deductively proper. But its soundness (the truth of the premises) is another question. Let's take the minor premise first. You would need considerable evidence of incidences where names have been studied to support this premise. One or two examples of names and their co-relations do not justify the premise. But if you can find examples where names do or do not consistently lead to success, and illustrate this through factual support and perhaps a comparison based on character names in a novel, the premise could be accepted as true. (Chapter 6 will discuss the principles of support for factual claims like this one.)

The major premise is much more problematic. At the very least, it is debatable. Some might say that it is indefensible, since it asks readers to accept as universally applicable a single notion related to a complex problem. Even if the premise is true, its truth is too controversial to be assumed; it must be justified through a careful secondary argument.

The incomplete syllogism discussed above (the one lacking a major premise) is an *enthymeme*—a form of syllogism common to spoken and written arguments, where presenting all components of the syllogism may be tedious for the audience. An enthymeme is a rhetorical syllogism that implicitly relies on an audience's existing beliefs to support the conclusion. Enthymemes are not inferior syllogisms; their very incompleteness helps to convince. An audience that helps to complete the argument will have a stake in it and thus will be more likely to accept it. But as in the case above, the writer must have good reason to believe that the audience will accept the premise provided. As you will see in Chapters 8 and 9, this process of uncovering the syllogism or enthymeme of an argument can be particularly useful when arguing evaluations and recommendations.

ACTIVITIES (5.1)

1. Identify the major premise of the following incomplete syllogisms, as in the following example.

   Conclusion: My physics professor is a skilled teacher.

Minor premise: My physics professor knows her physics thoroughly, uses imaginative examples, is concerned that her students learn, and is an excellent speaker.

Major premise: A skilled teacher knows his or her subject matter thoroughly and can present it imaginatively, is concerned that students learn, and speaks clearly and compellingly.

a. **Minor premise:** Mack's résumé was poorly written.
   Conclusion: Mack did not get the job because his résumé was poorly written.

b. **Minor premise:** Jessie made faces at the refs behind their backs, cursed members of the other team, and refused to congratulate them on their victory.
   Conclusion: Jessie is a poor sport.

c. **Minor premise:** Professor Callahan constantly interrupts his students.
   Conclusion: Professor Callahan does not respect his students.

d. **Minor premise:** Young people of today do not value family or community.
   Conclusion: Our young people will not grow up to be good citizens.

e. **Minor premise:** Bill Clinton is a master of the art of compromise.
   Conclusion: Bill Clinton is a fine statesman.

f. **Minor premise:** There is no way I can write my final research paper for this class.
   Conclusion: I will not pass this class.

2. With a small group of your classmates, discuss the extent to which the major and minor premises of three of the preceding syllogisms would need to be argued.

3. Examine an essay you wrote recently and present its major argument as a syllogism. What are the argument's major premise, minor premise, and conclusion? Are any of these components implicit rather than explicit in your essay? Is the syllogism sound and valid?

THE TOULMIN MODEL:
A MODERN VARIANT OF FORMAL LOGIC

Formal deductive reasoning yields necessary or certain conclusions, yet written arguments about our complex, provisional, and messy world rarely presume to discover absolute truth. It is in this mismatch between the goals of formal reasoning and those of written argument that the limitations of deduction are exposed. The fact is that most of the arguments we judge to be worth making are worth making *because* they are arguable, because they admit the possibility of more than one reasonable position. Few people waste time, for example, arguing about whether the sun will come up tomorrow, but they do argue about whether the problem of ozone depletion in the atmosphere warrants strict regulation of pollutants.

Recognizing the limitations of Aristotelian logic for practical rhetoric, the twentieth-century philosopher Stephen Toulmin identified and formalized a slightly different relationship between an argument's claim and its support. Toulmin's model is a useful way to judge the reasonableness of many of the arguments you construct.

According to the Toulmin model, a claim is linked to its support through what is called a *warrant*. A claim's warrant indicates how one gets from factual support (which Toulmin calls *data*) to the claim. It is the general belief, convention, or principle that permits the data to support the claim.

Suppose you were proposing that your college major institute a junior-year-abroad program. You have a number of supporting reasons for this claim: the program will attract students to the major; it will be an invaluable educational experience for students; it will allow the department to establish important international connections. The Toulmin model requires that each supporting reason be linked to the claim through some assumption or principle acceptable to the audience. Using the last support cited, a diagram of this argument would look like this:

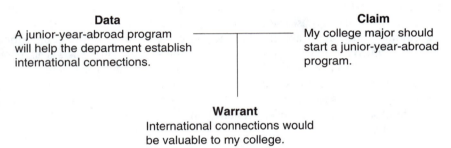

Data
A junior-year-abroad program will help the department establish international connections.

Claim
My college major should start a junior-year-abroad program.

Warrant
International connections would be valuable to my college.

We can identify an argument's warrant (which is not always stated explicitly in the argument itself) by asking, "What is it about the data that allows me to reach the claim?" In this case, it is the *value* of international connections that makes the claim desirable. Just as major premises are sometimes left unstated in real arguments, warrants are sometimes only implied. If you have any reason to suspect that your audience will not accept the warrant as generally true or at least reasonable, you will have to support it with what Toulmin calls *backing*. In this case, one backing for the warrant might be identification of the benefits of international connections in a world where more and more college graduates will be working for international organizations.

A fifth element of the Toulmin model, which makes the concept particularly useful to written argument, is the *qualifier*. The qualifier is a word or words that modify or qualify the claim. In our example, that qualifier is the word *should*, a word that makes the recommendation less strong than *must*, but more strong than *might want to consider*. Unlike the syllogism, the Toulmin paradigm gives the writer room to entertain claims that are less than necessary or certain. Adding the backing and the qualifier to our example, we come up with the following diagram:

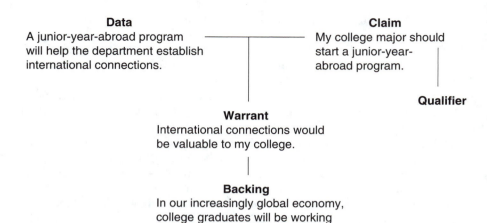

Data
A junior-year-abroad program will help the department establish international connections.

Claim
My college major should start a junior-year-abroad program.

Qualifier

Warrant
International connections would be valuable to my college.

Backing
In our increasingly global economy, college graduates will be working for international organizations.

Applying Toulmin's model to your own arguments can help you flush out the assumptions that generate your claim and evaluate their reasonableness. You may find that this model is most useful in making recommendations (as in the preceding example) and causal arguments. The most useful point in the composition process at which to apply both the Toulmin and the Aristotelian models is after you have formulated a claim and collected some support. Fitting these elements into one or the other paradigm will help tell you what is missing, what needs further support, and what is patently unreasonable. Don't *begin* the argument process by trying to fit ideas into the models; this will only frustrate your thinking and limit your inventiveness.

ACTIVITIES (5.2)

1. Identify the unstated warrants for each of the following pairs of claim and support.
   a. **Claim:** Secondary smoke is harmful.
      Support (or data): The Surgeon General's report on smoking establishes this.
   b. **Claim:** Celebrities who stand trial for capital crimes are not likely to get fair trials.
      Support (or data): The media focus unrelentingly on celebrity suspects.
   c. **Claim:** If you have the flu, you should stay at home.
      Support (or data): This year's strain of the flu is highly contagious.
   d. **Claim:** Writing is a dying art.
      Support (or data): My freshman students don't know the difference between an independent clause and Santa Claus.
   e. **Claim:** Mick is an unorthodox runner.
      Support (or data): Mick holds his arms high when he runs, and his heels never touch the ground.

2. Which of the previously supplied warrants would require some backing in order to be acceptable to readers? What kind of backing might you supply?

INFORMAL FALLACIES

Unfortunately, even when we pay careful attention to the logical principles discussed in this chapter, our reasoning can still go awry through any of a number of *informal* fallacies. Like the principles of formal logic, informal fallacies usually involve a faulty relationship between an argument's claim and its support. Familiarity with these flaws in reasoning is especially useful during the revision stage, when, with these fallacies in mind, you examine the relationship between your claim and its support. Since an inclusive list of these fallacies is a very long one—as inexhaustible as human inventiveness—included here are only those fallacies that frequently turn up in student writing. For each fallacy, the category or categories of argument in which it is most likely to occur are also indicated.

Ad Hominem Argument

An *ad hominem* argument is against the arguer (Latin *ad hominem* means "to the man") rather than against the argument: "Smith's argument against increasing taxes on the rich is worthless because he himself is rich." This fallacy, which substitutes irrelevant judgments of an individual for reasonable evaluations of an issue, is most likely to occur in evaluative arguments.

Ad Populum Argument

Ad populum is Latin for "to the people." One commits the *ad populum* fallacy when supporting a claim by referring to popular opinion or behavior to justify it. A teenager trying to convince her parents to remove her curfew because "everybody else's parents have done it" is attempting to convince her parents through an appeal to popular behavior rather than to reason. This fallacy is a corruption of the legitimate tactic of appealing to established authorities to strengthen a claim.

Circular Argument

A circular argument (also known as *begging the question*) is one in which the claim is already contained in the support: "John did not succeed on the track team [the claim] because he did not do well in track events [the support]." In this example, "did not do well in track events" really only restates "did not succeed on the track team"; it adds no new information about *why* John didn't succeed. Another common version of circular argument, or begging the question, assumes what has to be proven, as in the statement "This film should be banned because it contains immoral scenes." This claim requires a definition of *immoral* and evidence that the film meets this definition. Lacking such material, the claim begs the question of the immorality of the film. Evaluative, interpretive, and causal arguments seem to be particularly subject to this fallacy. One giveaway that your argument is circular is that your supporting statements repeat a key term from your claim.

Distraction

Distraction is bringing in irrelevant points to distract attention from the issue being argued: "Sure I cheated on my income taxes, but I've never broken any other laws." It is also known as the *red herring,* from the practice of dragging a dead herring across a trail to distract hunting dogs from the scent of their prey. Distraction is frequently used to deflect unfavorable evaluations.

Either-Or Argument

The either-or argument is setting up two extreme positions as the only alternatives and denying any possible middle ground: "The painting is either a masterpiece or trash." The painting could be something in between. Also known as *bifurcation* or the *fallacy of the excluded middle,* this fallacy can occur in any category of argument, though it is probably most frequent in evaluations (as in the claim about the painting) or in recommendations, where extreme solutions are sometimes seen as the only options: "Either we build a new computer facility or we give up on using computers at this school."

Emotive Language

The fallacy of emotive language involves making a case through slanted, value-laden language rather than through reasonable support, as in the statement "Smelling blood, the media will attack and destroy any candidate with a newsworthy weak spot." This claim, in its implicit identification of the media with carnivorous beasts, presumes a value judgment about the media that the claim does not justify. Writers of argument should try to refrain from using prejudicial language, at least until their claims have been reasonably made. Emotive or slanted language can be used in any kind of argument, but it is most common in evaluative arguments.

False Analogy

The false analogy supports a claim by comparing its subject to something not *essentially* similar: "Offering courses in gay and lesbian theory is no more defensible than teaching pedophilia or necrophilia." While both sides of the comparison refer to noncustomary sexual preference, there are more *differences* between gay theory and pedophilia than there are similarities, and comparing them attempts to prejudice the reader against gay and lesbian theory. As pointed out in Chapter 10, analogies can be useful in generating and illuminating arguments, but they can never prove a point. Just as legitimate comparison can be used to support any kind of argument (see Chapter 4), analogies can be misused in all of the four classes of argument. If you find that you have introduced an analogy to *support* rather than explain or illuminate a claim, you have probably committed this fallacy.

Hasty Generalization

Basically a misuse of the inductive method, hasty generalization consists of a general claim based on an insufficient sample: "Young professional people tend to be self-centered and materialistic. My friends Eric and Melanie certainly are." This fallacy typically occurs in factual arguments and in the supposedly factual support for evaluative statements about entire groups of people: "Women are sentimental"; "Asian-American students are good in mathematics."

Non Sequitur

A *non sequitur* claims a logical relationship between a conclusion and a premise where none exists: "Henry should make a good governor because he is tall and handsome." *Non sequitur* in Latin means "it does not follow"; *non sequitur* reasoning is behind almost all fallacies. The term is really a generic one that has been specifically applied to cases where the relationship between a premise and a conclusion is seriously askew. The term is also used to cover some fallacies in causal analysis: "I performed poorly on that speech because I wore my green tie rather than my red one." This is an example of our next fallacy—*post hoc, ergo propter hoc. Non sequitur* reasoning can occur in any category of argument.

Post Hoc, Ergo Propter Hoc

Post hoc, ergo proper hoc is Latin, meaning "after this, therefore because of this." It means claiming that because one event preceded another, it must have caused the subsequent event to occur: "I performed poorly on that speech because I wore my green tie rather than my red one." This fallacy is at the root of much superstition, as in the case of a pitcher who carries a red handkerchief with him whenever he pitches because he had one with him the day of his no-hitter. It is a serious risk in any causal analysis, and a writer can guard against it by following the principles of causal reasoning presented in Chapter 7.

Slippery Slope

Designating a first and a last step in a causal chain, when the intervening steps have not occurred, constitutes the slippery slope fallacy: "I didn't get the first job I interviewed for, so I guess I'd better forget about a career as an engineer." In this simple example, the speaker creates a worst-case scenario (forgetting about engineering) based on a series of events that has not yet occurred and will not necessarily occur, that is, repeated failure to be hired in engineering jobs. This fallacy appears most commonly in arguments of effect, usually when the writer wishes to prove that the consequences of a particular action are likely to be negative.

Strawperson Argument

A strawperson argument involves attacking a view similar to but not identical with that of an opponent: "How long will America tolerate softheaded opponents of gun control who want only criminals to have guns?" Advocates of gun control vary in their views, but they do not want only criminals to have guns. The adjective *softheaded* is an example of emotive language; in this sentence, it is designed to arouse a particular emotional response. Negative loaded terms are frequent in strawperson arguments. This fallacy is a common but misguided tactic of evaluative arguments.

You can improve your ability to analyze your own and others' arguments by familiarizing yourself with the kinds of fallacies previously defined, but you need to remember that what is considered "correct" thinking depends on your context. What may be incorrect in one context may be perfectly acceptable in another: *ad hominem* arguments are frowned on in academic writing (though they do occur), but they are perfectly acceptable in a court of law, where questioning and at least implicitly attacking witnesses' backgrounds and motives are frequently practiced. In addition, some of these fallacies are only a slight step off the path of correct reasoning. For example, there is nothing inherently fallacious about either-or reasoning, but this kind of reasoning goes wrong when either-or alternatives lead to excluding other, real possibilities.

ACTIVITIES (5.3)

Identify the informal fallacies committed in the sentences that follow. Select from the following list:

ad hominem argument	false analogy
ad populum argument	hasty generalization
circular argument	*non sequitur*
distraction	*post hoc, ergo propter hoc*
either-or argument	slippery slope
emotive language	strawperson argument

1. Legalized abortion puts us only a step away from legalizing murders of anyone we deem undesirable or inconvenient.

2. If you can't beat them, join them.

3. I strongly disagree with your proposal to allow women to join fraternities. Fraternities are men-only clubs.

4. Those traitorous, draft-dodging youths who preferred deserting their country to serving it should never have been granted amnesty.

5. Discrimination should be fought on every front—whether it's practiced against members of a certain race, a certain sex, or those who bear arms.

6. I spent two weeks at a military academy and realized that private school is just not for me.

7. It is unfair to penalize Eastman Kodak for harming the environment when it has been such a strong supporter of the local economy.

8. *Supercop* had the highest ratings of any television movie. Clearly it was a superior film.

9. Tom Hanks is a brilliant comedian; he should leave heavy drama alone.

10. Opponents of the Equal Rights Amendment believe that women should stay barefoot and pregnant.

SUMMARY

Making Reasonable Arguments: Formal and Informal Logic

- Understanding the principles of formal logic will help you link claim and support reasonably.

- The principles of inductive logic—moving from specific instances to general conclusions—are important to all writers of argument and are particularly applicable to factual arguments.

- The syllogistic formula, common to most deductive reasoning, can be applied to an argument's claim and support as a way of determining the reasonableness of their connection.

- The Toulmin model of claim-warrant-backing is particularly useful to writers of argument, as it does not make absolute certainty a requirement of the claim.

- Informal fallacies are any of those errors in reasoning that can undermine the credibility of a claim. The best time to consider the possibility of informal fallacies is during the revision process.

The following article by Leslie Knowlton (*Psychiatric Times,* XII, 9, September 1995) contains a number of claims supported in a variety of ways. One important claim is Knowlton's explanation for the lower incidence of eating disorders in males as compared to females. The reasonableness of this causal claim can be tested by applying the Toulmin method. Placed within the Toulmin structure, the assertion that fewer men than women experience eating disorders would be the claim, and the data would be that men are subjected to less social reinforcement of thinness than women. As is often the case, the warrant—that principle linking claim and data—is unstated, but it would read something like "social reinforcements influence behavior."

EATING DISORDERS IN MALES

LESLIE KNOWLTON

About 7 million women across the country suffer from eating disorders including anorexia nervosa and bulimia and, as a result, most research into those two diseases has been conducted on females. However, as many as a million men may also struggle with the diseases.

One of the nation's leading researchers on eating disorders is Arnold E. Andersen, M.D., a professor of psychiatry in the University of Iowa College of Medicine. In addition to his academic and clinical work—some of it conducted as director of the Eating and Weight Disorders Clinic at Johns Hopkins—Andersen has edited a book of studies, *Males with Eating Disorders* (Brunner/Mazel 1990), and is writing another for families faced with the problem. His most current research project involves tracing and comparing the development of attitudes about body shape and weight among fifth- and sixth-grade males and females in the United States and India.

Speaking by telephone, Andersen said that despite being mentioned among the first case presentations in the English language three centuries ago, males with eating disorders have been "relatively ignored, neglected, dismissed because of statistical infrequency or legislated out of existence by theoretical dogma."

"There's a need to improve our recognition of eating disorders in males and to provide more adequate treatment," he said. "In addition, the category of males with eating disorders presents intellectual challenges regarding the etiology and mechanism for this gender-divergent abnormality of human-motivated behavior."

Andersen said that although the disorders look the same for men and women, the paths for getting there are quite different.

"The twin spotlights of empirical scientific studies and broad clinical experience can be brought to focus on either the similarities or the dissimilarities between males and females with eating disorders," said Andersen. "When individuals are very ill, suffering from emaciation or abnormal electrolytes and other medical complications, they appear very similar and require similar treatment."

But as patients become medically more healthy and the symptoms are "deconstructed," the individual life story behind each patient unfolds to reveal differences between the sexes in predisposition, course and onset, Andersen explained.

"We have to go back to where the roots are formed and look at gender diversity," he said.

For example, while women who develop eating disorders *feel* fat before they begin dieting, they typically are near average weight, whereas the majority of men who develop the diseases actually *are* medically overweight. Males with eating disorders are also more likely than women to have alcohol-related conditions and obsessional features.

Also, whereas women are concerned predominately with weight, men are concerned with shape and muscle definition. Additionally, more males than females diet in relationship to athletic achievement or slimming to please a homosexual lover.

"More men who develop anorexia or bulimia were seriously teased as overweight children," Andersen said, adding that about 21 percent of males with eating disorders are gay.

Finally, more men diet to prevent medical consequences of being overweight than do females, said Andersen.

So why do fewer males than females develop full-blown eating disorders?

Andersen said definitive answers are not available, but sociocultural influences have a lot to do with it.

"There's clearly less general reinforcement for slimness and dieting for males than for females, with only 10 percent as many articles and advertisements promoting dieting in magazines read by young males as compared to those read by young females," he said, referring to a study he conducted. "But when subgroups of males are exposed to situations requiring weight loss—such as occurs with wrestlers, swimmers, runners and jockeys—then a substantial increase in the behaviors of self-starvation and/or bulimic symptomatology follows, suggesting that behavioral reinforcement, not gender, is the crucial element."

Therefore, he continued, there's an apparent "dose-response" relationship between the amount of sociocultural reinforcement for thinness and the probability of developing an eating disorder, with the intermediate variable being dieting behavior.

"The process of transition from a normal behavior such as dieting, which is not in itself abnormal, into a fixed illness meeting *DSM-IV* criteria for an eating disorder has not yet been well-defined," he said. "But it probably involves a transition from psychosocial to biomedical mechanisms."

Andersen said men who develop eating disorders can generally be divided into three groups: those in whom the onset was preadolescent, those in whom it was adolescent or young adult and those in whom it was adult. As in females, most male onset is adolescent.

While diagnostic criteria for anorexia and bulimia in men are similar to that in women, doctors often are less likely to think of making a diagnosis of eating disorders in males than in females. Likewise, the patient and his family and friends may not recognize it.

One reason anorexia may elude diagnosis in men more than in women is that men don't experience the on-off phenomenon of loss of menstrual periods, which can alert professionals and others to the problem, Andersen said. Rather, testosterone is gradually reduced, with an accompanying decline in libido and sexual performance.

Binge eating disorder may go unrecognized in males because an overeating male is less likely to provoke attention than an overeating female.

"And men are hesitant to seek medical attention for a disorder they fear will be seen as a girl's disorder or a gay guy's disease," Andersen said.

Source: *Psychiatric Times*, XII, 9 September 1995

SUGGESTIONS FOR WRITING (5.4)

1. Pay attention to the informal conversations and discussions of your friends. Start a list of all the generalizations you hear them make. Then write a one- to two-page letter to your friends telling them what information and evidence they would need to support their generalizations reasonably.

2. Focus on three advertisements you see repeatedly on television or in print. Write a one-page essay on each advertisement, discussing your application of the syllogistic and Toulmin models. How would the advertisement look within the format of each model? What premises or warrants are only implied? Are those claims true? What would have to be argued in order to make the advertisement more reasonable? Finally, rewrite the ad so that it conforms to the principles of deduction and the Toulmin model.

ILLUSTRATIVE ARGUMENTS IN PART II: MAKING REASONABLE ARGUMENTS

6

Arguing Facts

An argument's claim can be supported in a number of ways—some common to all arguments, some particular to specific classes. As is mentioned in Chapter 4, one common form of support for a claim is another claim. For example, if you were arguing that students graduating from your major have had trouble finding jobs, you could support that claim with job placement figures for students in your major, and/or with anecdotes about the employment woes of your friends. In both cases, you would be supporting a central factual claim by further factual assertions.

But take a slightly more complicated example. Suppose that in arguing the claim "First-time DWI offenders should have their driver's licenses revoked" (a claim of recommendation), you cite as support the secondary claim "The threat of license revocation would deter many from driving while intoxicated." This secondary claim is causal (predicting the *effect* of the change) and would require support appropriate to causal arguments. Among others, one piece of support you might use for this secondary causal claim is a factual assertion about the effectiveness of similar laws in other states.

There are two points to be taken from these examples: first, arguments almost always consist of a central claim supported by secondary claims, which themselves must be argued appropriately; second, sooner or later, all argumentative claims will come to rest on factual assertions. Because so many of the assertions we consider factual are themselves debatable, the facts holding up your arguments are not necessarily bedrock. Furthermore, even gathering the most reliable facts available seldom means that you will arrive at absolute truth. But some factual assertions are more solid than others, and it is the purpose of this chapter to show you what constitutes a reliable factual assertion or claim.

WHAT IS A FACT?

The New College Edition of *The American Heritage Dictionary* defines a fact as "Something known with certainty." According to this definition, a fact is a statement that is known to be true and about which there can be no debate or doubt. Assertions like "My physics teacher is a woman," "George Washington was the first president of the United States," and "Human beings are mortal" would fall under this definition; they are inarguable, unambiguous, proven facts that in most arguments would require no support beyond their simple assertion. Facts like these often come from your own experience or have been confirmed by your experience; sometimes they fall under the heading of "common knowledge." In any event, they can be accepted as indisputable.

But what about statements like "Beta-carotene is a carcinogen," "Secondary smoke is not harmful," or "The FDA-established minimum daily nutritional requirements are inadequate"? While these claims are stated as if they are known with certainty, careful readers might hesitate to call them indisputable. For one thing, they come from fields in which most of us are comparatively ignorant; we lack the expertise to judge their accuracy. Second, anyone who reads the newspaper regularly knows that these are the kinds of "facts" that seem always to be retired or revised when new evidence or new research methods emerge. Indeed, each of these statements is a correction of an earlier assertion that claimed to prove the opposite: beta-carotene was for years thought to be cancer-inhibiting; the known dangers of secondary cigarette smoke have just recently been moderated; and millions of perfectly healthy people have based their diets on the minimum daily requirements suggested by the FDA.

Assertions like these fall more properly under the dictionary's secondary definition of *fact:* "Something asserted as certain." Such statements are made in good faith, based on the best available evidence, and stated with conviction, but they are the findings of incomplete and ongoing research in comparatively dynamic fields and thus are always subject to revision and correction as newer, more inclusive, more reliable evidence is gathered. In other words, such factual assertions are *believed* to be certain, but not *known* with certainty; they are more like state-of-the-art educated guesses.

Finally, there is the assertion that is stated with certainty, dressed up as factual, and credited to a seemingly impeccable source, but that is nonetheless utterly preposterous. Some of these impostor facts are easy to detect; we know never to trust anything we read in the *National Enquirer,* for instance. But in more cases than we'd like to admit—particularly with the rush by the media to be the first on the scene— these preposterous facts can sneak right by you without your even suspecting that they are unreliable. You may find yourself particularly vulnerable to accepting (and circulating) false facts if they will strengthen your own argument.

The more your argument relies on the first and second type of facts, the more solid it will be. Your job in presenting facts supporting your argument's claim will be to convince your readers of their truth or likelihood, to convince them, that is, that your supporting facts are "known with certainty" or "are based on the best available evidence." The principles that follow should help you with this crucial job.

SUPPORTING FACTS REPORTED BY PRIMARY AND SECONDARY SOURCES

Most of the arguments you will write will depend on facts you find in your reading and research. Sometimes these facts will be reported by what are called primary sources, sometimes by secondary sources. A primary source is the individual or group that determined the fact in the first place—for example, a manager reporting that sales declined 5 percent in the last quarter or a research oncologist summarizing the findings of her study on cancer remissions in a medical journal. A secondary source is the person or document reporting facts discovered by someone else—for example, a biology textbook describing some little-known facts about Darwin's work on the HMS *Beagle,* or a member of an electronic listserv summarizing information heard at a professional conference.

Electronic listservs are e-mail discussion groups set up to cover specific educational and technical topics, among others. If you want to know more details about Darwin's work in this area, you can use your favorite search engine (*AltaVista, Metacrawler,* etc.) to find listserv groups that might cover this topic. One provider, L-Soft (http://www.lsoft.com), reveals a group that might be perfect for your needs. The listserv is hosted by St. John's University and gives you a description of the topics they cover:

> The Darwin-Med list (Darwin/Evolution Medicine mailing list) is a [sic] open discussion list for anyone interested in a Darwinian/evolutionary perspective on medicine, mainly people who have read "Why We Get Sick" (British edition: "Evolution and Healing") By Randolph M. Nesse & George C. Williams.

Most listservs, like the Darwin-Med list, allow you to look at their archives to see whether or not the subject you are interested in has been covered. If not, but you feel the group is where you can find answers, then you can subscribe to the list and join the discussion. If you do sign up, be sure to save the instructions for having your name removed from the list in the event that you do not want to continue to receive mail from this list after you have completed your research. You will also need to know how to cite the listserv in your list of references if you use any information you obtain from the list.

Because reliable facts are critical to successful arguments and because so many of the statements paraded as facts are unreliable, you'll want to be extremely discriminating about selecting facts from primary and secondary sources, recognizing that whenever you include a fact in your argument, you are tacitly saying to your audience, "I believe this to be a trustworthy statement." When your sources are printed texts (e.g., books, journals, newspapers), you have some assurance that the factual material has been reviewed by someone, though this assurance does not relieve you of responsibility for further evaluating the reliability of your source. But when your material comes from the Internet, that assurance may be completely missing. For both print and electronic sources, there *are* certain steps you can, and should, take to assure yourself—and thus your audience—that the facts you're presenting are relatively trustworthy.

Evaluating Print Sources

The first thing to look at when evaluating print sources is the identity of the author. Books and journal articles are almost always published under the author's name. If you are familiar with the author and know he or she is an acknowledged expert with a proven track record in the field, you have some assurance that the facts you wish to cite are reliable. You are probably safe trusting the facts given out by your college career counselor on postgraduate career opportunities, or facts about astronomy contained in an article by the noted astronomer Carl Sagan, because both have established professional reputations. But you should be wary of advice on the stock market obtained from a staff writer of your school paper. It's not that information obtained from nonexperts can't be reliable, but you should always be skeptical of these sources.

If you're not familiar with the author of the facts in question, it often pays to do a little digging. Your library has a number of professional biographical dictionaries either in its reference section or on-line. It pays to spend a little time looking up the author's qualifications. One thing to consider is the objectivity of your author. If Tiger Woods writes that Nike makes the best running shoe in the world, accept that pronouncement with a good dose of suspicion.

If you can't discover anything about the reliability of the author, or if the author isn't identified (as often happens in reference books, magazines, and editorials), consider the reputation of the publisher. Most university presses, for example, are considered careful reviewers of the material they publish, and certain journals and periodicals have established a reputation for accuracy. The publisher's good reputation will not ensure that the material in question is accurate, but it does make the odds of accuracy relatively high. Certainly a report found in the *Wall Street Journal* is more credible than one found in *Star* magazine or the *National Enquirer*. If you don't know anything about the reliability of your source's publisher, ask a professor in the field.

You also want to be sure to check the date of your source's publication. While a book on Abraham Lincoln dated 1966 might not be considered outdated, a 1966 book on computer technology would be barely worth reading, unless you were doing a historical survey of the field.

Evaluating Electronic Sources

The huge growth in electronically accessible information is both a blessing and a curse to writers who must work with reliable facts. On the one hand, finding information has never been easier. Hundreds, even thousands, of sources on a given topic are available with a few keystrokes. But the sheer volume of information can make us lazier and less effective researchers. Furthermore, because anyone with the proper equipment can post information on the Internet, there is a lot more unreliable information on-line than between the pages of a book or journal that has gone through some kind of review process (The article "'Vonnegut Speech' Circulates on Net" at the end of this chapter shows how quickly misinformation can circulate on the Internet).

For the most part, evaluating electronic sources isn't all that different from evaluating print sources. Begin by trying to determine the author's reliability—again, through biographical dictionaries or perhaps the *National Dictionary of Addresses and Telephone Numbers*. While you're on the Internet, try a search through the World Wide Web using the author's name as your keyword; you may find some useful information on his or her reputation.

Checking the electronic address of your source gives you some generic information about its origin and thus at least a hint of its reliability. *Edu* means it comes from an educational institution; *gov* is a governmental organization; *org* is a nonprofit organization; and *com* is a commercial organization.

Make sure to check the date of the material if it's available. Much of the material on the Internet has the virtue of being very current, but in quickly moving fields, information may become out-of-date in a matter of days.

If you read useful factual information on a listserv, try communicating with the author (whose name and e-mail address are included on the listserv posting) to get information about the sources of his or her information. Or if you find nonattributed information on a Web site, try following up some of the related "links" on the site; these may lead you to the background you need on the sources of the Web site material.

Citing the Source in Your Text

Another way to support the primary and secondary facts you present is to cite their source within your argument. Providing the source is not only a courtesy to readers who may want to examine the subject in more depth, but also avoids the possibility of plagiarism. Including the source assures your readers that your argument is a responsible one—that your facts are not fabricated for the sake of argument but come from legitimate sources. Failure to cite the sources of the facts on which your claim rests will weaken your argument considerably.

In most cases, your citation of a source will take the form of a footnote, an endnote, or, increasingly, inclusion of the work in a "Works Cited" list at the end of your argument. The subject matter of your argument, and the discipline you are writing for, will determine which citation form you should follow. For example, many education programs require students to follow *The Chicago Manual of Style* footnote format, whereas sociology will probably rely on *The Publication of the American Psychological Association*, more commonly known as APA. Many English professors insist on MLA, the Modern Language Association's format, whereas some may require APA. Scientific notation and documentation procedures can vary widely, so you should ask your instructor which format he or she wants you to follow if it is not specified in the assignment.

You can find models of these forms in most college writing handbooks, CD-ROM handbooks like *Take Note*, and on-line through your library and many college writing lab pages. Purdue, Washington State University, North Carolina State University, and Dakota State University are only a few of the universities who have published their OWLs (Online Writing Lab) and made them available to the public through the Internet.

In addition to a footnote or bibliographic reference, you can also include a brief reference to your source within the text of your argument. For example, "According to the *Oxford English Dictionary,* the word *flick* at one time meant 'thief.'" In this case, the source would also appear in a works cited or bibliography section at the end of the argument.

If your readers are not likely to be familiar with your source, you may want to provide credentials briefly within your text. For example, "In his book *The Mismeasure of Man,* Stephen Jay Gould, the noted Harvard paleontologist and popularizer of science, argues that the results of standardized intelligence tests can be misleading and also misused by those in power."

A note on citing electronic sources: works on the Internet are copyrighted, so you must give full citations (including the Web address and the path, or URL, needed to obtain the file).

ACTIVITIES (6.1)

Write a one-page analysis of the credibility of two of the following passages. Consider the issues of expertise, bias, and currency of facts. You may need to do some research on the credentials of the author or of the publication in which the passage appeared.

1. Mailer had the most developed sense of image; if not, he would have been a figure of deficiency, for people had been regarding him by his public image since he was twenty-five years old. He had in fact learned to live in the sarcophagus of his image—at night, in his sleep, he might dart out, and paint improvements on the sarcophagus. During the day, while he was helpless, newspapermen and other assorted bravos of the media and literary world would carve ugly pictures on the living tomb of his legend. Of necessity, part of Mailer's remaining funds of sensitivity went right into the war of supporting his image and working for it. (Norman Mailer. *The Armies of the Night.* New York: Signet Books, 1968. 15–16.)

2. Chow chow, powerful NONSPORTING DOG; shoulder height, 18–20 in. (45.7–50.8 cm); weight, 50–60 lb (22.7–27.2 kg). Its coat has a soft, wooly underlayer and a dense, straight topcoat that stands out from the body. It may be any solid color and is the only breed with a black tongue. A hunting dog in China 2,000 years ago, it was brought to England in the 18th cent. (*Concise Columbia Encyclopedia.* New York: Columbia University Press, 1983. 168.)

3. A SPECTER is haunting Europe—the specter of communism. All the powers of the old Europe have entered into a holy alliance to exorcise this specter: Pope and Czar, Metternich and Guizot, French Radicals and German police spies. (Karl Marx and Friedrich Engels. *The Communist Manifesto.* Ed. Samuel H. Beer. New York: Appleton-Century-Crofts, 1955. 8. Originally published in 1848.)

4. Many devices have been used in the attempted measurement of interests. The interest inventory is the most important of these both from the standpoint of the number of counselors using them and the number of investigators working with them. The inventory approach consists of the comparison of likes and dislikes of individuals through questionnaire items. Since the individual

is asked to estimate his feeling, the method may be said to be subjective. A complete discussion of interest inventories is given by Fryer [Douglas Fryer. *The Measurement of Interests*. New York: Henry Holt, 1931]. (Harry J. Older. "An Objective Test of Vocational Interests." *Journal of Applied Psychology*. 28, 1944: 99.)

5. People who have a good sense of humor *suffer less constipation, acid stomach and sensitivity to cold* than those who don't get the joke, according to a study presented at the American Psychosomatic Society annual meeting. ("Medical Flash." *Self*. July 1994: 59.)

6. In a report presented to the House of Representatives, Marnie S. Shaul, the Director of Education, Workforce, and Income Security Issues noted that voucher school programs have not been "rigorously evaluated" to determine whether or not the programs are achieving what they claim they can achieve for students. (U.S. General Accounting Office. *At-Risk Youth: School-Community Collaborations Focus on Improving Student Outcomes*. Washington, GAO-01-66. Oct. 2000. Accessed 02 Jan. 2001. Available: http://www.gao.gov/)

SUPPORTING PERSONALLY EXPERIENCED FACTS

Sometimes you'll need to support a fact obtained through your own experience or observation rather than from a second- or third-party source. Personally experienced facts are supported by a credible and objective description of the experience or observation.

Describing the Experience

Let's say you are writing a report for a psychology class on phobias and you want to demonstrate how extreme and irrational phobic behavior can be. As evidence for this position, you cite your observations of a friend who is terrified to fly: "Traveling with a friend on a short domestic flight, I observed firsthand what phobic panic looks like." Because this statement suggests extreme behavior, it requires a careful and accurate description of the panic as support: the pallor, the tremors, the hysteria you observed in your friend. (At this point, we are not talking about explaining or interpreting the fact, but about presenting it in such a way that your reader will accept that it happened.)

The principle holds in more complicated contexts. Take the scientific laboratory reports that are written in all lab courses from ninth grade through graduate school. The writer's basic purpose in these assignments—to report an experience in the lab—is achieved through a careful, detailed description of the steps followed and the results obtained.

Establishing Your Own Credibility

Writers of argument must appear credible to their readers, projecting an image that inspires confidence and trust. This requirement applies to all components of

your argument, but it is particularly relevant to the presentation of personally experienced facts. Since you, the writer, are usually the sole support of a personally
experienced fact, you must give your readers no reason to mistrust your description of the experience.

If your readers have any reason to suspect that your description is dishonest
or inaccurate, your argument is going to fail. For example, if you referred to your
85-year-old grandmother as support for an argument against mandatory retire-
ment, citing her daily five-mile runs, her ability to bench-press 300 pounds, and
her current prize-winning research on recombinant DNA, your readers would be
very suspicious of such obvious exaggeration, and your credibility as an observer
would be seriously questioned.

In presenting facts derived from personal experience, you must also guard
against the inevitability of your own bias. Without realizing it, we often see only
what we want to see and ignore what is convenient to ignore. Ask two politicians
on opposing sides of an issue their perceptions of a stormy meeting and you will
almost certainly get two very different stories about what happened. They are not
necessarily trying to falsify evidence, but their biases color their perceptions. In
some contexts, such as sportswriting about the hometown team or essays on the
opinion page of the newspaper, readers expect and even welcome a certain bias,
but they tend to reject open manifestations of it in other contexts, such as front-
page news, academic projects, or business reports. One way to avoid excessive personal bias when you report facts you have observed is to ask yourself whether a
person making a different claim would have observed the same things; if the answer is no, you should aim for more neutrality in your description. Another way to
guard against the possibility of bias in reporting fact is to consult other people
who observed or experienced the same event to ensure that your view is essentially a shared one. If it is not, you must consider whether your own bias accounts
for the difference.

SUPPORTING FACTUAL GENERALIZATIONS

Any claim, regardless of the class it falls into, can be stated as a *generalization*.
For example, the factual claim *"People* magazine and *USA Today* use much the
same format as television news shows" becomes a factual generalization when the
communications scholar Neil Postman tells us that "the total information environment begins to mirror television." Similarly, the claim "Frank is a successful
sales representative because his father was also a good sales representative" (introducing a limited causal argument with an element of evaluation) can be extended
to the following generalization: "Successful salespeople tend to have other good
salespeople in their families."

To support any generalization, you need to apply two sets of principles. First,
you must convince your readers that your original claims about *People* and *USA
Today* or about Frank and his father are plausible—that significant similarities do
exist between the television news show *20/20* and *People* magazine, or that there
is a demonstrable *causal* connection between a father and a son who are both

sales reps. How you support your claim will depend on the category to which it belongs. The first example is a largely factual claim, and the second is a causal claim.

Second, you must show that your generalization is reasonable—that what you've observed about Frank and his father can be plausibly applied to salespeople and their children all over the world. We will use factual generalizations to illustrate this second principle, but it applies to all categories of argument.

Applying the Principles of Induction

All generalizations, even the most informal and sweeping, begin on a specific level. We see something a few times and assume that it happens frequently or even all the time. That is, we move from specific observations to general conclusions; from the particular, we infer the general. In traditional logic, this process by which we assume the widespread existence of particular instances is called *induction*. Conclusions drawn by inductive reasoning are always somewhat risky because they are based on incomplete evidence. You assume that because you have never seen or heard of a flying cat, no such creature exists, yet unless you have seen every cat that ever existed, your claim "There is no such thing as a flying cat" has made a rather staggering leap from the particular to the universal. Yet these leaps are the nature of induction.

Support for a generalization consists of identifying a number of specific, verified instances or examples. If you claim, for example, that American films increasingly show the dangers of casual sexual relationships, you will have to cite individual films to support your claim. Or if you write, "Many young American novelists find universities a supportive and economically secure place to work," you will need to point to specific examples. If the generalization is a factual generalization, the specific examples will be individual facts, which in some cases may need verification. What makes a factual generalization "factual" is not the absolute truth of the generalization, which can never be proven, but its foundation in singular factual instances.

The most credible generalizations are those supported by the most, and best, examples. You cannot reasonably conclude that all algebra teachers are women if your experience is limited to one or two teachers, but you can reasonably conclude that many teenagers like rap music if you have known hundreds of teenagers in many different settings who like rap. In supporting generalizations, you need to know how many examples are enough, whether they are representative of all the available evidence, and which examples to include. Unfortunately, no simple formula exists that answers these questions, but the following general rules of thumb are helpful.

How Many Examples Are Enough?   First, the more sweeping your claim, the more examples you will need. You can position a generalization at any point along a continuum of frequency: "*Some* business majors are good in math"; "*Many* business majors are good in math"; "*All* business majors are good in math." Although the word *some* does constitute a generalization, it is a very limited generalization, a safe one to make if you don't have abundant evidence. To support "some," you need only a handful of examples. "Many" requires more than a handful of examples, certainly, but is far easier to prove than "all." In fact, absolute statements using words like *all, everyone, never,* or *always* should be avoided in written argument unless every constituent in the group referred to can be accounted for. Otherwise, the claims these words make are too grandiose to be credible. The following passage supports its factual generalization with carefully chosen examples:

> A number of fraternity members on this campus contradict the broad and usually unflattering stereotypes circulated about "brothers." While I am not a fraternity member myself, I know a number of members well, and none of them fits the popular image of the beer-swilling, women-chasing party boy. For instance, my friend Judd, a dean's list electrical engineering major and obviously a dedicated student, says that fraternity living gives him the supportive environment he needs to excel in a difficult major. Two of my roommates from freshman year who have joined fraternities have become respected student leaders: Brad is vice president of Student Council, and Kelly is the student representative to Faculty Council. Both Brad and Kelly are well-rounded, academically successful students. Finally, I know that the entire pledge class of one campus chapter received the mayor's commendation for public service for their renovation of an inner-city recreation center. Of course, there will always be individuals who confirm the stereotype, but my observations question its widespread applicability.

In this passage, three examples, the last involving a large group of individuals, are presented to support the claim that few fraternity members fit the campus stereotype. In a more formal academic argument, we would probably insist on more rigorous, less personally observed evidence, but we would very likely accept these examples as adequate in a short, informal essay. As a general rule, three is a good number of examples for a short essay, since one or two examples may seem to be merely exceptions, whereas four or more would become tedious.

The less familiar your readers are with your subject matter, the more specific examples you should supply. If your readers are very comfortable and familiar with your topic, they will often accept sensible generalizations that are only minimally supported. If you refer in an internal business report to the "widespread problems with our new computer system," those familiar with the problem will accept the reference and not demand that it be supported. But a reader unfamiliar with this problem may demand evidence that the problem really exists. Of course, some readers unfamiliar with your subject area will accept dubious generalizations simply because they don't know any better. If these readers are misled, however, some of them will probably eventually learn that you were wrong in your generalizations, and they will then suspect your reliability in other situations, even when you are correct in your claims.

Do Your Examples Represent the Evidence Fairly?   In selecting which evidence for your generalization to include in your argument, you should make sure that the examples you choose fairly represent all the available examples, including the ones you omitted. Imagine, for example, that you support the statement "Fraternity hazing is obsolete on our campus" with examples of changes in the rules and practices of the three largest fraternities, but in the course of your research, you discover that there are significant exceptions to this generalization. You are misrepresenting the evidence if you fail to tell your readers about these exceptions. True, you may have provided enough examples to satisfy your readers, but you are misleading them by excluding the contradictory evidence. The best way around this problem is to qualify the claim in such a way that the evidence you omit is not contradictory. If you rewrite the claim as "Instances of fraternity hazing on our campus have decreased significantly in the last ten years," your three examples will perfectly support the claim, and the omitted evidence will no longer be contradictory.

Is Your Conclusion Too Broad for Your Examples?   Inductive reasoning always requires that the breadth of your conclusion match the breadth of your supporting evidence. If your generalized claim is very broad ("Art majors are the most politically liberal of all college students"), it must be based on proportionately broad examples—in this case, instances taken from a number of different colleges in different areas of the country that offer majors in art. If your claim is more limited ("Art majors at my college are the most politically liberal students"), you are justified in citing examples taken only from your college.

But even in this second, narrower case, you still must guard against generalizing on the basis of instances drawn from too narrow a context. If the art students at your school come from all over the country, yet you use as examples only those who come from the New York City area, your support is not broad enough to justify your conclusion. You will either need to limit your claim further ("Art majors from the New York City area are the most politically liberal students at my college") or to collect examples drawn from a broader geographic group.

ACTIVITIES (6.2)

1. The following conclusions are generalizations derived through inductive reasoning. What kinds of examples, and how many, would you need to make each one plausible?
   a. Most librarians are women.
   b. High school librarians tend to be women.
   c. In my experience, librarians have been pretty evenly divided between men and women.
   d. I have attended two major universities and have been struck by the number of librarians who are women.
   e. Library science departments tend to attract more women students than men.

2. Write a generalization that is adequately supported by the examples listed for each of the following cases.
   a. John, Susan, and Jim prefer chocolate ice cream, whereas Jane prefers strawberry, and Henry prefers vanilla.

    b. Last Saturday night I sat alone at a showing of the new film *Anxious Hours,* and I saw no line for the film when I walked by the theater just before show time on Sunday.

    c. It is January 15 here in Minnesota, and so far this winter, we have had two snowfalls that just covered the ground and then disappeared.

    d. There were 25 Mercedes-Benz automobiles parked in the lot the night of my high school reunion, and as I recall, there were only about 70 students in my graduating class.

    e. When I returned from winter break to my classes here in Vermont, I noticed that Jack, Jeff, Mary, Matthew, Carrie, and Megan all had deep tans.

STATISTICS

Statistics are derived from the practice of drawing conclusions about a large number on the basis of a limited number of instances. Statistics are factual information compiled and reported numerically. The following are examples of statistical claims:

- Thirty percent of the American people believe a woman should never be president.
- The unemployment rate is 11 percent.
- One-quarter of all bridges in this state need repair.

In our world, statistics are an inevitable and integral part of our lives. We judge the quality of our manufactured products and of many of our services through statistics; we constantly encounter statistics on the health of our economy, our educational system, our sex lives, our souls. We tend to suspect claims that lack statistical support, and we use statistics in virtually every field in our society, from weather forecasting to managing baseball teams. But these general conclusions inferred from a limited number of instances are reliable only if the original process of information gathering was conducted according to certain principles. Whether you are conducting your own statistical studies as support for your argument or citing statistics obtained from other sources, you must be sure of the following:

1. The smaller group surveyed (or *sample,* as statisticians refer to it) must be *known.* If you read that eight out of ten women think they are overweight, but no reference is made to the source of the survey or who or how many were surveyed, you should not accept or use the figure. For all you know, only ten women were questioned, and they were picked from a list obtained from a weight reduction clinic. Every cited study should be identified and the sample group defined. Without such information, the figures are suspect.

2. The sample must be *sufficient,* or sufficiently large, in order for you to accept the conclusion drawn from that sample. That both of your roommates prefer classical music to rock does not justify the conclusion that classical music is more popular with college students; you need a much larger sample. Trained statisticians sometimes use small samples, but only under very specific conditions and with very specific mathematical models. Our inability to evaluate the use of these statistical for-

mulas makes it hard for us to judge whether statistics are actually being used correctly. In such cases, it's important to learn as much as you can about the context of the studies and the methods by which the samples were gathered before relying on the figures completely. For example, researchers often critique each other's studies, and their analyses provide valuable information about the reliability of the results.

3. The sample must be *representative*. If a figure is given about the political inclinations of all Californians, the sample surveyed must represent a cross section of the population. If the 2,000 people questioned all have incomes of $40,000 and up, or if they're all over the age of 45, your sample is slanted and not representative of the variety of the population as a whole. Professional polling organizations like Gallup and Harris (groups hired to identify the preferences of large populations based on small samples) choose either a representative or a random sample. A *representative sample* is one that guarantees in advance that the sample will reflect the major characteristics of the population—for example, that the sample will have a percentage of Californians earning over $40,000 that is equal or nearly equal to the percentage of Californians earning over that figure in the total population. In a *random sample* on political attitudes in California, every adult Californian would stand an equal chance of being questioned. When chosen randomly, in 95 out of 100 cases, a sample group of 1,500 people will be within 3 percentage points of duplicating the answers of the entire adult population. In evaluating the usefulness of any poll, you should know the method by which the sample was selected.

When you include in your argument statistics obtained from other sources, not only must you test them for the preceding three principles, you must also be certain they satisfy the requirements of second- or third-party facts. The source should have a reputation for expertise in the field and for objectivity, and the figures themselves should be recent. It is unwise to accept as support for your own argument any statistical data not credited to an authoritative source. If you cannot identify the instrument, individual, or organization through which these facts were obtained, chances are good that those facts are not reliable.

When using statistics in your argument, you also need to be aware of the variety of terms used to report large figures and of the way these terms influence the impact of the figures. A study on high school literacy could report its findings on extracurricular reading habits in a number of ways. It could say that out of 500 high school seniors surveyed, *100* had read at least one unassigned novel in the last year, or the same fact could be reported as *20 percent* of the students. Of those 100 readers, one could report the *average* number (or *mean*) of novels read (the total number of novels read divided by the 100 readers), the *mode* (the number of novels most frequently read by individual students), or the *median* (the midpoint of the range of frequency of novels read). The mean, mode, and median for this sample of students follow:

	Students	Novels Read	Total Novels
	25	4	100
	10	3	30
	45	2	90
	20	1	20
Total	100		240

Average = 2.4 novels (total number of novels read divided by total number of students)

Mode = 2 novels (the most common number)

Median = 2 novels (the midpoint of the list of number of novels read according to the frequency of the number. Imagine the 100 students standing in a line, starting with all of those who read four novels, then those who read three, then two, and so on. The midpoint of this line of 100 would occur in the group of students who had read two novels.)

Statistics can be powerful tools in argument, but again, it is crucial to realize that they cannot *prove* claims; they can only *support* their likelihood. A recent poll indicating teenage hostility toward adult society is not proof that it was a teenager who attacked your English teacher or even that the students in a particular high school have hostile feelings toward their parents. It merely indicates that out of a sample of so many teenagers a certain percentage indicated feelings of hostility toward the adult generation. Responsibly gathered statistics are not suspect, but the use to which we put these figures may be.

You should also be restrained in your use of statistics; if scattered profusely throughout a written text, they have a deadening effect on the audience. Often, a visual display of statistics in a chart or a table is more valuable to your audience than a verbal summary; graphic representations can clarify the meaning of the statistics and reinforce their significance. With statistics, it is easy to lose track not only of the "big picture" but also of any picture at all, and visual displays can give the reader the necessary perspective.

ACTIVITIES (6.3)

1. For two of the following statements based on statistics, discuss with a small group of your classmates the kind of information necessary to ensure the statement's reliability.
   a. Over 50 percent of the doctors surveyed in a nationwide study recommend Brand A medicine over any of the leading competitors.
   b. Brand C: the best built truck in America, according to a survey of truck owners.
   c. Over 60 percent of all Americans favor the president's plan for peace, whereas 85 percent oppose Senator Flag's call for more offensive weapons.
   d. Despite competition from television and VCRs, moviegoing is still popular in America. When asked how much they enjoyed going to the movies, 88 percent of moviegoers responded that they enjoyed moviegoing a great deal.
   e. A survey of leading economic forecasters indicates that a mild recession will occur in the next six months.

2. Conduct a survey of some of your classmates or of some friends. Ask them one or two questions that can be summarized in statistics, such as how many hours they studied last week. Compute the mean, mode, and median of these statistics. Write a one-page description of the results of your survey, and also present this information in visual form. Also state how representative you believe this group is of some larger, similar group, such as all students who studied last week.

SUMMARY

Arguing Facts

- All arguments rely on factual claims, either as their primary claim or as a form of support for the primary claim.

- To support facts reported by others, you must be satisfied of their accuracy and provide in your argument a brief reference to the source of the fact.

- To support facts founded on your own experience, you must describe the experience accurately and clearly and establish your own credibility through a responsible, objective, and accurate rendering of the experience.

- To support a factual generalization, you must cite a number of the verified facts that have led you to the general conclusion. The more sweeping the generalization, the more examples you will need to cite. If your readers are likely to be unfamiliar with the subject matter, you should provide several examples as evidence. The examples cited must be typical of all the evidence discovered. The breadth of the examples cited must match the breadth of the generalization.

- Statistics can effectively support arguments, provided they are not overused and their significance is made clear.

- When including a statistical generalization, you must be satisfied of its reliability. It is reliable if the sample cited is known, sufficient, and representative.

- You must be aware of the exact meaning of the terms used to report statistical conclusions, particularly *average, median,* and *mode.*

TWO SAMPLE FACTUAL ARGUMENTS

The following analytical report was written by a student in a "Tools For Engineering" course. Unlike most lab reports, it is primarily a factual generalization. The hypothesis in paragraph 1 is the unsupported claim, which, by the final paragraph, has been converted into a supported conclusion. The writer supports his claim by reporting analytical facts: the procedure he followed and its observed results. Through his attention to detail, his fully developed discussion of the graphics supplied, and adherence to the conventional lab report format, he implicitly demonstrates that he is a reliable reporter.

Advantages of Matlab

Purpose: To discuss the ability to create and run scripts by Matlab. The programmable nature of this application makes it ideal for engineering and many of its repetitively analyzed functions. It combines the power of mathematical software such as Maple or Mathematica with the programming advantages of a language such as C++.

Discussion: An application of this inherent advantage is one working with the function:

$$y = px^2 + qe^{x/5} + r\ln[x]$$

By creating a function that asks for input values of the constants $(p, q,$ and $r)$, one can quickly compare different cases with four plots.

One of the features of such a function that both scientists and engineers would be interested in is that of curve fitting. When scientific data is collected, scientists often try to summarize their results by noticing characteristics such as linearity in their results. Microsoft Excel's charting includes curve fitting options that aid in deciding if a set of data is best fit by a linear, quadratic, logarithmic, or exponential type of curve. This Matlab script gives you a similar advantage.

The supplied constants that best test this and their graphs follow:

Case 1: The values of $p = 1$, $q = 0$, and $r = 0$ yield an equation proportional to the quadratic and produce the graph of:

Case 2: The values of $p = 0$, $q = 1$, and $r = 0$ yield an equation proportional to an exponential curve and produce the graph of:

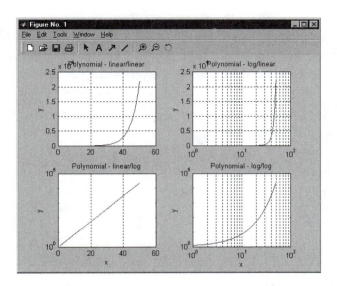

Case 3: The values of $p = 0$, $q = 0$, and $r = 1$ yield an equation proportional to the logarithmic curve and produce the graph of:

When analyzing these graphs, one needs to note the nature of each of the four subplots. The upper left gives the straightforward linear graphical representation. The upper right offers a graph with an x scale that is exponential. This is characteristic of a logarithm. The lower left is reversed; this time the independent variable remains unaltered while the dependent variable is exponential. This is characteristic of an exponential function. The last plot, the one appearing in the lower-right corner, is exponential on both axes. This plot would be useful to see overall trends of a function.

Applying this information to the three cases allows us to see how each set of data could be fitted. For the graph produced by *Case One* data, the most linear is the third graph. This indicates that the function is neither exponential nor logarithmic. Inspection of the component producing the data verifies this. *Case Two*'s data is most linear in the lower-left subplot. This would indicate that it would be best fit by an exponential function. Once again, inspection verifies this. In regard to the *Case Three* data, the most linear graph is the upper-right graph. This means that the data would be best fit by a logarithmic function, which is again verified.

Conclusion: Matlab has many applications and the ease of creating functions is one of its greatest. Although only three cases need to be considered in this instance, sometimes the best cases are not always apparent. They can only become apparent after trying several different values and inspecting the results. Because of the repetition involved, the ability to create a function to quickly reproduce your results for different values is a highly powerful feature with innumerable applications.

"VONNEGUT SPEECH" CIRCULATES ON NET

DAN MITCHELL

A copy of Kurt Vonnegut Jr.'s recent MIT commencement address made heavy email rotation on Friday. The characteristically pithy, funny, thoughtful speech was passed from friend to friend stamped with such comments as "worth a read" and "check this out—it's great."

And it *was* great. Trouble is, it wasn't Vonnegut's. "Kurt Vonnegut Jr. had never given a commencement address at MIT," said Robert Sales, associate director of the school's news office.

It turns out the "speech" was actually a column penned by the *Chicago Tribune*'s Mary Schmich. The column ran on 1 June—five days before UN Secretary General Kofi Annan delivered the actual commencement address at MIT. That speech "was a lot longer and maybe not as clever" as the purported Vonnegut address, Sales said.

Much of Schmich's column—which consists of advice for graduates—sounds like stuff Vonnegut might say: "Don't be reckless with other people's hearts. Don't put up with people who are reckless with yours. . . . Remember compliments you receive. Forget the insults. If you succeed in doing this, tell me how. . . . Keep your old love letters. Throw away your old bank statements. . . . Do one thing every day that scares you."

Nobody—least of all Schmich—can figure out why Vonnegut's name was slapped onto her column. "Some prankster apparently decided it would be funny. Why is it funny? If you can figure that out, you're a genius," she said Monday.

Perhaps the act itself wasn't funny, but some of the fallout has been. First of all, there's the fact that (ahem) Wired News ran part of the column as its Quote of the Day on Friday. Also, Schmich says she's gotten as much attention from the incident as just about anything she's written. "My email's just flooded with messages," she says. And she says she's actually been accused of plagiarizing Vonnegut—and vice versa. On Friday, she managed to reach Vonnegut, who, Schmich says, said the whole thing is "spooky."

In her column on Monday, Schmich writes that she wrote the piece "one Friday afternoon while high on coffee and M&Ms." And, she insisted, "It was not art."

In part, Schmich blames the "cyberswamp" of the Internet for all the trouble. "At newspapers, things like this have to go through a barrier before they go out to the world," she said. But on the Net "anybody can put anybody's name on anything."

Nonetheless, she added, "No one involved in this did anything bad, except the person who started it."

SUGGESTIONS FOR WRITING (6.4)

1. Write a two- to three-page essay supporting a fact that runs counter to popular opinion. This fact can come from your own experience, from your studies in college, or from your general knowledge. Examples of such surprising facts

are "Despite predictions to the contrary, the increasing use of computers has created more new jobs than it has eliminated existing ones"; "Milk does not always do a body good." This surprising fact can be about yourself, your family, your friends, your hometown, your college, your job, your major, or whatever else comes to mind.

2. Stereotypes are misleading factual generalizations that make the false claim that all members of a group have a certain trait: "The English people have stiff upper lips in times of crisis"; "American men like to watch football." Take a prevalent stereotype and analyze to what degree the stereotype is true and how the stereotype is misleading. Make sure the stereotype is one you can deal with in a three- to four-page essay, such as "Engineering students of my college don't get involved in extracurricular activities." You don't have to do a statistical survey to gather data for this essay, but you should carefully examine and present examples to support your claim.

3. Analyze either a newspaper or a television news show for examples of bias or misleading generalizations (for the television news show, you may have to videotape the show so that you can view it two or three times). How objective is the reporting of the news? Are there any examples of misleading generalizations? What kind of news is *not* included? Write a two- to three-page essay addressing these questions.

ILLUSTRATIVE ARGUMENTS IN PART II: ARGUING FACTS

7

Arguing Cause

The goal of causal argument is to establish a probable cause or effect for a given condition. A claim arguing "Many teenagers abuse alcohol because they are desperately disappointed by their 'real lives'" will establish the *cause* of teen alcohol abuse, whereas the claim "Today's generation of college students will be far more successful in marriage than their parents have been" argues the *effect* of certain conditions. In order to convince your readers that the cause or effect you argue is reasonable, you must have a good understanding of the nature of causality and of the processes used to determine and report causes and effects. Written causal arguments are essentially reports of the process the writer followed to determine causes or effects.

The first part of this chapter concentrates on arguments of *cause:* arguments that identify and support the cause or causes of an existing situation. As you'll see in the last part of the chapter, the principles and processes involved in arguments of cause are identical to those you'll rely on when you write arguments of *effect* (arguments predicting the probable future effects of an existing situation).

DETERMINING CAUSE

Any single effect is the consequence of a number of causes—some powerful and direct, others less influential but still contributing. For this reason, arguing cause usually involves more than isolating *the* single cause of a given effect: most extended causal arguments discover and support those causes most useful to the context, purpose, and audience of your argument. If your goal is to give as full a causal explanation as possible for the effect in question, you will identify and support a number of causes, both direct and indirect. But if the point of your argument is to assign responsibility, you will address only the most immediate causes (such as who did what, regardless of why). If the purpose of your argument is to instruct, or if you want some future action taken or avoided on the basis of the causality you demonstrate in a comparable situation, you are likely to emphasize both the immediate and the more remote causes of the current situation. For example, if you wish to improve your GPA, you might try to reproduce as many of the habits of a successful student friend as you can: careful budgeting of time, keeping up with assignments, regular class attendance, and so on.

Brainstorming for Possible Causes

Whether or not you begin with a particular causal claim in mind, it is a good idea to begin the argument process by listing all the facts and conditions you can think of that seem to be causally linked to the effect you are explaining. Depending on your subject, this list may come from your own thinking and brainstorming and/or from any reading and research you might do. The list should include as many facts or conditions you can think of that seem even remotely connected to the effect. The next step will be to apply your knowledge of causal principles to this working list in order to identify the most influential causes.

Let's assume you are arguing the reasons for the high student dropout rate at your college. Part of your argument will consist of a discussion of individual cases: why particular people you know decided to leave school. You know one student (we'll call her Emma) who explains her plans to drop out of school by saying, "I just don't like college." But you know this is not a satisfactory explanation. Why doesn't she like college? What events and conditions have made her unhappy enough to make this extreme decision? So, in a couple of long conversations, you press Emma further, and you talk with some of the people who know her well. The result of these discussions is a list of more specific possible reasons for her decision.

For one thing, Emma's grades have not been very good. Though her grades were good in high school, Emma can't seem to pull her GPA above a 2.0. It's clear to you from talking to her that she's the kind of person who expects a lot from herself, so her undistinguished grades have to be a blow to her self-esteem. It makes sense that she would want to leave a place where she doesn't feel good about herself. You also learn that Emma is the first person in her family to go to college, and her parents have made many sacrifices to give her every educational advantage. Their ambition for Emma puts a lot of pressure on her, which has probably made it even harder for her to relax and do her best. And Emma's family situation has worked against her in another way: it offers no close role models to emulate, no family tradition of academic success. Add to these factors Emma's crazy roommate and their closet-size room, and you begin to wonder how Emma lasted through the first semester.

Your examination of the situation has identified a number of possible causes for Emma's decisions—all much more specific and useful than her vague claim that she doesn't like college. Some of the possible causes on your list seem directly influential, like her mediocre grades, their blow to her self-esteem, and her crazy roommate; others are more remote, like her parents' lack of a college degree. But you conclude that, one way or another, each of these factors may have influenced Emma's decision.

Only a thorough investigation like the one you have conducted will yield a full explanation of the causes of a particular effect. The next step is to determine more precisely the relative influence of each point in this cluster of causes, and in order to take this step, you must know something about the causal properties of the different points on your list.

ACTIVITIES (7.1)

1. For the following effects, brainstorm a list of possible causes:
   a. The popularity of John Grisham's novels
   b. The success of Japanese products in the American market
   c. The popularity of disaster movies
   d. An increase (or decrease) in the size of the student body at your school
   e. The popularity of a particular major at your school

Necessary and Sufficient Causes

Understanding the concepts *necessary cause* and *sufficient cause* will help you identify which of the causes from your original list are likely to have been most influential in bringing about the effect you are explaining. To qualify as a cause for a given effect, a causal candidate *must* satisfy the conditions of a necessary or sufficient cause, or both. If it does not, it is not a direct cause of the effect, though it may well have contributed to the effect in some way.

A *necessary* cause is a cause without which the effect could not have taken place. One cannot get typhus without the introduction of a rickettsia, or gram-negative microorganism, into the bloodstream. This rickettsia is necessary to the contraction of the disease. Thus you can be certain that anyone who has contracted typhus has been infected by this particular microorganism. But while introduction of the rickettsia is necessary to the contraction of typhus, it doesn't guarantee that the disease will result. People with a vigorous immune system or those who have been inoculated against typhus will be safe from the disease.

Necessary causes are usually easy to identify: if we know the effect, we know that certain causes or conditions had to be operating. To use a nonscientific example, if you had not parked your car next to a construction site, it would not have been hit by falling debris. Parking your car in that spot was necessary to the effect. In the case of Emma, the cause necessary to her withdrawing from college is her unhappiness there. Presumably, if she were happy and liked college, she would stay.

Sometimes identifying the necessary cause will not be particularly helpful in your attempt to explain an effect. Necessary causes can seem like redundant restatements of the effect itself: the necessary cause of a company's filing for bankruptcy is that it ran out of money, but that doesn't tell us very much about the significant factors that led to the bankruptcy filing. In the case of Emma's planned withdrawal from college, the necessary cause—her unhappiness with college—

does not shed much light on the question of the student dropout rate. In order to understand her decision, we have to work backward from the necessary cause, identifying those factors that set it up.

Sufficient causes, on the other hand, are always helpful in causal analyses. A sufficient cause is one that by itself is capable of producing a particular effect. A person's decision to join a health club can have a number of sufficient causes: for example, winning a year's membership in a raffle, wanting to meet new people, or wanting to become physically fit. Any one of these motives would be enough to prompt an individual to join a health club, but none of them *has* to exist for that decision to be made; that is, they are all sufficient to the effect, but not necessary. In Emma's case, a number of sufficient causes are operating: her poor self-esteem, her crazy roommate, and her distaste for dormitory life. Any one of these might have been enough to prompt her decision, but none of them was necessary to that decision.

Sometimes a single cause combines the properties of necessity and sufficiency. The example of the rickettsia demonstrates this combination. Not only *must* one be infected with that microorganism to contract typhus (the necessary cause), but this infection is by itself enough to cause the disease (the sufficient cause). For every effect, we can expect at least one necessary cause and any number of sufficient causes.

In determining which factors on your initial list have been most influential, you need to identify those that are necessary and those that are sufficient. Unless you are writing a full causal analysis, you will usually find yourself concentrating on the sufficient causes for the effect in question.

Identifying Sufficient Causes

The ability to identify a factor as causally sufficient depends on your good sense and your personal experience of causality. There is no rule or formula to follow in isolating sufficient causes, yet most of us have little difficulty answering the question "Is this factor by itself sufficient to have caused this effect?"

When your subject involves human behavior as either cause or effect, there is a useful test you should apply to those factors you think are sufficient. Actions performed by an individual or group are linked to their causes by some commonly accepted principle or motivator of human behavior. If you argue, for example, that a sluggish economy is a cause of the increased popularity of taped movie rentals, you are accounting for a particular human behavior: the rental of taped movies. Your claim is a simple claim of cause, with a fact at the causal end and an action (also a fact) at the effect end.

Sluggish economy   Increase in movie rentals
(cause)   (effect)

This causal proposition is plausible only if its two sides are linked by some acceptable motive. Why would people rent more movies for home viewing in a sluggish economy? What motive or need would urge them to react to a particular condition with a particular behavior? In this case, a linking motivation is easy to identify: in tight times, people need to economize, and it is considerably cheaper to watch

rented movies at home than to pay high prices in a theater. The cause and the resulting behavior can be linked by a motivation that everyone can understand and
identify with:

Sluggish economy.................Increase in movie rentals
{Desire to economize in tight times}

Identifying this motivation doesn't tell you whether this is the only sufficient
cause, but it will reassure you that the link between this cause and the effect is
plausible. If you can supply no such motivation between cause and effect, your
theory is probably not plausible, and it's time to look for another cause.

Applying the Toulmin Model

The Toulmin model discussed in Chapter 5 is particularly useful when you are
composing causal arguments. Indeed, the relationship just presented among
possible cause, existing effect, and linking principle fits perfectly into Toulmin's
data-claim-warrant formula. Here is the example about increased movie rentals
translated into the Toulmin model:

In this case, the warrant is that general behavioral principle that connects
the cause, which is placed in the data position, and the effect, which is placed
under "claim" (even though the actual claim of the argument is the causal relationship between data and claim). When you are trying to identify sufficient
causes for a particular effect, you may find it useful to apply the Toulmin model
to your cause and effect, making sure that you can provide a warrant that would
be widely acceptable to your readers. Remember that in many cases, the warrant
will not be acceptable without further support, or what Toulmin calls *backing*.
In those cases, the warrant and its backing will need to be provided explicitly in
the argument. If the warrant does seem immediately acceptable, it need not be
stated outright.

ACTIVITIES (7.2)

1. With three or four other students, study the following effects and possible
   causes. For each effect, which of the possible causes, if any, do you think
   are necessary? Which would you class as sufficient? Make sure you can defend your choices.
   a. **Effect:** John's car accident.
      Possible causes: John was driving at night on a poorly lit road; the road
      was wet from rain; John had taken a very difficult exam that morning;
      John was driving ten miles per hour over the speed limit.
   b. **Effect:** The dramatic increase in the use of VCRs in the last few years.
      Possible causes: The cost of VCRs is now at an affordable level for most
      Americans; videotapes of films are increasingly available; viewers can
      choose what films they will watch with the VCR; many Americans have a
      large amount of leisure time available.
   c. **Effect:** The decline in oil and gasoline prices in the mid 1980s.
      Possible causes: On the average, cars were more fuel-efficient than they
      had been ten years before; there was a growing awareness that petroleum

was a nonrenewable resource; the oil-exporting countries were producing more oil than the world consumed.

d. **Effect:** Louise's winning of an award for the best violin recital at the music festival.

   Possible causes: Louise practices the violin three hours each day; Louise's parents found the city's best violin teacher for her when she was five; from a very early age, it was obvious that Louise was talented musically; Louise prefers Mozart to any other composer.

e. **Effect:** Charles's favorite hobby is cross-country skiing.

   Possible causes: Charles wants to stay in shape, and cross-country skiing is very good for the cardiovascular system; he likes winter and being out-of-doors; he is on a tight budget and cannot afford downhill skiing this year; he was once injured while downhill skiing; in high school, he won prizes in cross-country ski races.

2. For each following pair below, place the cause and the effect within the Toulmin model and supply a warrant that links the data and the claim acceptably. For which warrants should you also supply backing? What would that backing be?

   a. **Cause:** Increased leisure time
      Effect: More participation in sports like skiing and windsurfing
   b. **Cause:** Fifteen percent increase in tuition
      Effect: Decrease in enrollment
   c. **Cause:** Special incentives that reduce the price of automobiles
      Effect: Higher automobile sales
   d. **Cause:** More women receiving professional degrees
      Effect: A rise in the average age of women having first children
   e. **Cause:** The banning of a book
      Effect: Increased demand for the book

DISTINGUISHING AMONG SUFFICIENT CAUSES

Sometimes, in analyzing causes, you will discover a number of possible sufficient causes for an effect and not know which were actually operating. In these cases, you will need other methods for determining probable cause. The following strategies were formulated by the nineteenth-century philosopher John Stuart Mill to determine cause in such situations. While Mill was looking for ways to establish cause with scientific certainty, his methods are also very useful in situations where certainty is unreachable.

Method of Agreement

The method of agreement is useful when you are investigating the cause of *two or more* similar effects. In these instances, you determine what the sets of events preceding each effect have in common; you are looking for a single sufficient cause that operated in all these similar cases.

If you were investigating the reason or reasons for the success of the five best-selling hardbound books of the year, you would list all the factors that might have contributed to the success of each book—that is, the significant characteristics of each. If all the books center on the subject of personal relationships in the 1990s, you could safely identify subject matter as a leading cause of the books' success. Sometimes you will not discover a factor common to all your effects; perhaps the five best-sellers have no single common characteristic, so that a number of sufficient causes are operating in these instances.

Method of Difference

Mill's method of difference can be used to determine why two essentially similar situations turned out very differently. If you want to know why one self-help book succeeded while another failed, why one calculus class with Professor Jones was interesting while another was boring, or why the Confederate army lost the battle of Gettysburg but won the battles of Bull Run, you can apply the difference method by looking for the factor present in one case but absent in the other. If the only difference between your two calculus classes with Professor Jones was that the subject matter of the second class was more advanced, that could well be the reason for your unhappiness in the second class.

This method will work only when you are examining truly similar situations that share a number of common factors. If you were trying to account for the difference between your career choice and that of one of your grandparents, the situations would be too dissimilar for the method of difference to tell you anything; your grandparents faced an entirely different range of career choices than you did.

Method of Proportional Correlation

The method of proportional correlation is useful in determining the cause of an effect that is continuing and varied: the movement of the Dow-Jones industrial average, the increase and occasional decrease in the gross national product, the enrollment of college students in certain kinds of majors. In trying to identify possible causes of such measurable trends, you should look for conditions preceding the trends that vary and persist proportionally. In considering the reasons for the rise in the divorce rate since the 1960s, you might discover that there has been a congruent increase in the number of two-income families over the same time period—that is, that there has been an increase in the number of married women who are economically self-sustaining. This increasing economic independence of women is a plausible explanation of the increased divorce rate if it satisfies the following three conditions: (1) if it is truly independent of the effect (not a result of the same cause); (2) if the two trends, with all their fluctuations, are truly proportional; and (3) if the cause and effect are plausibly linked by an accepted behavioral principle—in this case, the principle or motive of independence or self-reliance. If these three conditions are satisfied, we would accept that the economic independence of wives is a sufficient cause of divorce.

ACTIVITIES (7.3)

1. Take a group of at least three of your classmates or friends who share a common trait, such as their academic major, a hobby, or some other favorite activity, and try to determine what sufficient cause made each member of the group have this trait. Try to find a common sufficient cause for the entire group, but be prepared to end up with different sufficient causes if a common cause does not reveal itself. Write a one- to two-page essay describing the results of your investigation.

2. Compare two classes you have taken sometime in your education, one that you liked and one that you disliked. The two classes should be as similar as possible in subject matter and level of difficulty. What made the one class likable, while the other was not? Write a one- to two-page essay addressing this question.

3. For the next week, compare fluctuations in two phenomena that you believe may be related, such as the weather and attendance at one of your classes. Make a chart comparing the movement of these two phenomena, and then see if any proportional correlation exists between the two. If there is such a correlation, ask yourself if the two are the result of the same cause and if some plausible behavioral principle links the two. Write a one- to two-page analysis of your study. Be sure to give your instructor the chart you have created.

CAUSAL CHAINS

Some effects are best understood in terms of a directly related series of causes, like links in a single chain, or a row of sequentially falling dominoes. In these cases, identifying the entire chain of causes is far more useful than isolating those causes that are closest to the effect, or isolating the more remote cause that originally set the chain in motion.

If someone told you that closed captioning of television shows (where subtitles can be seen on specially equipped televisions) is a result of the rubella epidemic in the United States during the 1960s, you might initially reject the connection as utterly implausible. What you have been given is the first cause and the final effect in a causal chain; if the links in the causal chain are filled in, the connection is reasonable. In the 1960s, there *was* a widespread outbreak of rubella, or German measles (at the time, there was no rubella inoculation). Rubella is a relatively harmless disease except to the fetuses of pregnant women; babies whose mothers contract rubella during pregnancy often suffer birth defects, one of which is deafness. Because of the epidemic, huge numbers of babies were born deaf. In the last 30 years, as these children have grown, we have seen increased sensitivity to the needs of the hearing-impaired, one of the most notable being the media's provision of closed captioning for television. With all the links in the chain identified, the causal connection between a common virus and closed captioning is no longer implausible, though there were other factors at work, including the increasing emphasis on the rights of the handicapped in the last 30 years.

The constellation leading to Emma's planned withdrawal from college contains a causal chain. Beginning with her decision to withdraw, we can move straight back as far as her parents' lack of a college education. The chain works as follows: Emma plans to withdraw from college because she doesn't like it. She doesn't like it because she feels low self-esteem in this setting. This low self-esteem is a result of poor grades, which at least in part have been caused by the enormous pressure she has been under to do well. This pressure comes from her parents, who, because they have never been to college, desperately want Emma to be the first in the family to get a college degree. Not all of the points in the constellation we identified earlier appear in this chain. So while the chain explains much about the evolution of Emma's decision, it does not explain everything, just as the chain linking the rubella epidemic with closed captioning is not the fullest possible explanation of the situation.

CONTRIBUTING FACTORS

In analyzing causes, we occasionally find a circumstance that is neither necessary nor sufficient yet is somehow relevant. This type of circumstance is labeled a *contributing factor*. If Kathy continues to jog even when she is run-down and then catches a virus, her jogging is not a sufficient cause of her illness; the presence of the virus without sufficient antibodies to combat it is the sufficient cause. Nor is the jogging a necessary cause, since she might have gotten the virus even without jogging. Yet her pushing herself while not feeling "100 percent" certainly didn't help and may have made her more susceptible to disease. In this case, we can label the jogging as a probable contributing factor.

Emma's situation contains at least one contributing factor: her lack of a close role model. Clearly, this factor is not necessary to the effect, nor is it sufficiently influential to have caused her decision to withdraw. Yet it has made a bad situation worse, depriving Emma of any positive example from which to take heart. Contributing factors are present in most complicated situations; if your goal is a thorough analysis of cause, you need to take contributing factors into account.

ACTIVITIES (7.4)

1. For two of the following causes and remote effects, find a plausible causal chain that links the cause with the remote effect.
   a. **Cause:** The rise of industrialization
      Effect: The growth of the conservation movement
   b. **Cause:** The invention of gunpowder
      Effect: The decline of knighthood
   c. **Cause:** Jane's high absenteeism in third grade
      Effect: Jane's difficulty with cursive writing
   d. **Cause:** The invention of printing
      Effect: The growth of democracy in Europe and America
   e. **Cause:** Jack's love of parties
      Effect: Jack's becoming the mayor of his city

2. In Activities (7.2), review the clusters of causes presented in Number 1 and identify possible contributing factors for each cluster.

SUMMARY

Determining Cause

- Because causality is always multifaceted, keep your mind open to all possibilities early in your causal investigations.

- The ultimate purpose of your argument (to explain, instruct, or designate responsibility) will determine which causes you will concentrate on in your argument.

- To determine the most influential causes for your effect, you need to be able to identify the necessary and sufficient causes. A *necessary cause* is a cause without which the effect could not have occurred; a *sufficient cause* is one that by itself is capable of producing the effect.

- Where human behavior is concerned, sufficient causes must be linked to their effect through an assumable motive.

- When you have a number of potential sufficient causes for an effect, use the following methods to determine the most probable cause or causes: the method of *agreement,* which will help you determine the cause of similar effects; the method of *difference,* which will help you determine why two similar situations turned out differently; the method of *proportional correlation,* which will help you determine the cause of an effect that varies over time.

- Some effects are best explained by a chain of causes, often originating at a time remote from the effect.

- Thorough causal arguments may also identify *contributing factors* to the effect—circumstances that are neither necessary nor sufficient causes but do play a role in creating an event or condition.

SUPPORTING CAUSAL CLAIMS

You support most causal claims by (1) establishing the factuality of the effect(s) and cause(s) you present; (2) identifying, sometimes only implicitly, an acceptable motive in arguments involving human action; (3) in some cases, describing the process that helped you validate a causal candidate (method of difference, agreement, or proportional correlation); and (4) qualifying the degree of certainty your argument claims.

Establishing Factuality

Facts are the foundations of causal argument. While in most causal arguments you will write, the causal relationship you propose between two events will rarely be certain and verifiable, there can be no room to doubt the certainty of the events you are linking; they *must* be true if your argument is to be meaningful and plausible. If you exaggerate, understate, or misstate the effect, your identification of cause is useless; you are explaining something that didn't actually occur.

If an article in a campus newspaper claims that the firing of a popular hockey coach has resulted in lower student attendance at home hockey games, the reporter needs to be absolutely sure that (1) the coach *was* fired (perhaps this is only a campus rumor and the coach got a job offer elsewhere) and (2) student attendance at home games really has declined since the coach's departure. Both cause and effect need to be presented and, if necessary, supported as individual factual claims before their causal relationship can be explored (see Chapter 6 for supporting factual claims).

Identifying an Acceptable Motivation

When you're dealing with human behavior as either cause or effect, your argument should suggest a common human motive. If a generally acceptable linking motive is obvious, you probably won't need to identify it explicitly. For example, if you are arguing that a decrease in DWI arrests is a consequence of tougher DWI laws, you don't have to point to people's unwillingness to risk the new penalites as the linking motivator between cause and effect; it is so obvious that it can merely be implied.

But let's take a more complicated example: an argument accounting for the increased divorce rate since the 1960s by a proportional rise in two-career families. Here, you would want to state the motive linking the proposed cause and effect, because it may not be immediately obvious to your readers: women who have some degree of financial independence and employment security are more likely to leave unhappy marriages than women who are financially dependent on their spouses. If the motive you identify may not be immediately acceptable to your audience, you will have to provide some backing for it.

There is a tendency among student writers to omit identifying the linking motivation when they should include it; that is, they find obvious what may not be so obvious to their readers. So if you have any doubt about whether or not to include this explanation in your argument, go ahead and provide it. It is usually better to err on the side of too much information than too little.

Describing the Process of Validation

In arguments where John Stuart Mill's processes of determination have been useful to you, you can support your claim by reporting in your argument how the method was applied. You don't need to use the formal terms *method of agreement* and so on, but you should provide a summary, a kind of narrative of your investigation.

If you were to identify the reasons for the failure of four different food conces-sion stands at your school, you would make use of the method of agreement, be-cause you are looking for a single explanation common to the closing of all four operations. Your report of the process might read something like this:

> Between 1996 and 2000, four different concession stands have been opened in the foyer of the Student Union. Not one of these stands was able to draw enough customers to keep operating; each closed within five months of its opening.
>
> The stands had little in common. One was run by students from the hotel program and sold gourmet coffee and pastries; one was a national fast-food franchise; one was a "mom-and-pop" frozen yogurt stand; and the fourth was a minideli operated by campus food services. Prices at the gourmet coffee stand were slightly on the high side, so when it failed, it was replaced by the inexpensive fast-food stand. Frozen yogurt from the yogurt stand was competitively priced, and it was the only frozen yogurt available on campus. Finally, the deli offered the most choice to cus-tomers, with food ranging from sandwiches to chips to pasta salads to drinks.
>
> The stands operated at different times of the day: the coffee stand in the mornings between 7 A.M. and 11 A.M.; the fast-food concession between 11 A.M. and 2 P.M.; the yogurt stand in the afternoons from 1 to 5; and the deli between 11 A.M. and 3 P.M.
>
> In short, campus food services tried very hard to learn from its mis-takes, trying to eliminate every reason for failure. But the one factor common to all four concerns that they did not address was *location*. All were set up in exactly the same spot in the foyer of the Student Union. The thinking was that since this space saw more daytime student traffic than anywhere else on campus, food sales would be brisk. But the prob-lem with this particular space in the union is that it is very close to the student-faculty cafeteria (on the same floor and open during lunchtime), and to the large student snack bar (in the basement of the union and open for lunch and dinner). It is reasonable to conclude that the food market in this heavily trafficked building was already saturated; if food services wants to make a success of the "portable food" idea, it will have to locate the next food stand in another area of campus.

As indicated in the preceding section on determining cause, some of Mill's methods of determination carry particular risks that you'll want to avoid. The dif-ference method, for example, is reliable only if the effects you examine are truly comparable. And when using the method of proportional correlation, you'll need to be sure that the trends you identify are independent—that is, that they are neither effects of another cause nor mutually contributing (for example, bad tempers caus-ing quarrels and quarrels exacerbating bad tempers).

It's a good idea when supporting your causal argument to point out that your use of a particular method of determination has avoided the associated pitfalls. For example, if you use the difference method to determine why you like golf but your friend with similar athletic ability and experience in golf does not, you should demonstrate that the apparent differences between you and your friend—family background, interest in other sports—are not significant in terms of your argument.

Qualifying Your Argument

Since certainty is rare in causal arguments, you must not mislead your reader and thereby undermine your own credibility by claiming more certainty for your argument than is warranted by its support. You have a wide range of words indicating degrees of causality to choose from, so make sure you use language that accurately reflects your level of certainty. If you are very certain about your causal proposition, you can use such definite words as the following:

necessitated

caused

resulted in

attributable to

produced

created

brought about

was responsible for

But use these words with caution. Without qualifiers like "may have," "probably," "seems to have," and so on, they claim a certainty that may be difficult to document.

The words listed in the following group also indicate causality, but a causality that is clearly qualified:

contributed to

is associated with

is a function of

facilitated

enabled

influenced

increased

decreased

improved

You are better off using words such as these when the causality you propose is not certain. By using such terms, you are both indicating causality and admitting *some* degree of uncertainty.

ACTIVITIES (7.5)

For two of the following examples, write a paragraph on each indicating what would be needed to make the causal argument more convincing. This additional material may include establishing facts, reporting the process of determination, describing motives, demonstrating the independence of two elements in a proportional correlation, or adding qualifying language, though other steps may also be necessary to make the argument credible.

1. Bill's alleged cheating on the exam was certainly a result of his low grades early in the semester and his desire to be accepted into a reputable law school.
2. Police report the arrest of Hubert Midas, the oil and gas billionaire, for shoplifting a thirty-five-dollar shirt from a downtown department store. Midas must have forgotten to pay for the shirt.
3. As more women have entered the workforce, the number of families without children has risen proportionally. The increasing number of women in the workforce has caused this rise in childless families.
4. Without Martin Luther King, Jr.'s charismatic personality, the civil rights movement of the 1960s would not have had the impact it did.
5. The Roman Empire fell because of the moral decadence of many of its citizens.

SUMMARY

Supporting Causal Claims

- To support a cause, you must establish the factuality of cause and effect; identify an acceptable motivation in cases where human actions are at least part of the cause; usually report how you determined the causes; if necessary, qualify your assertions about the certainty of your argument.

ARGUING EFFECTS

Because arguments of effect are concerned with the future, with events that haven't yet occurred, their claim to certainty is even less absolute than arguments of cause. Even the most carefully constructed argument of effect, one firmly grounded in the principles of causality and in experience in the relevant field, can go awry. We have only to look at the accuracy rate of weather forecasters and political analysts to recognize how frequently the future refuses to cooperate with our plans for it. But if executed carefully and according to certain principles, arguments of effect *can* be reasonable and convincing, serving as useful guidelines for many courses of action.

Claims of arguments of effect can be stated in a number of ways, as in the following:

1. If John continues to drink heavily and drive, it's only a matter of time before he will have a serious accident.

2. The number of high school graduates will continue to decline for the next five years, then begin to stabilize.

3. I will not see a woman president in my lifetime.

4. Consumers are so comfortable with certain companies that they will buy almost anything carrying those companies' logos.

While they may seem quite different, these four claims share certain features common to all arguments of effect. Most obviously, all predict that something will happen in the future (or in the case of the third claim, that something will not happen). Claims 1 and 4—John's heavy drinking, and brand appeal—also identify a causal relationship between a current condition and a future event. Claims 2 and 3 don't identify a current condition that will lead to the effect the writer predicts. In order to make them qualify as arguments of effect rather than mere assertions, the writer will have to identify current conditions that might lead to these effects and claim that the conditions and effects are causally linked. For Claim 2, those conditions could be certain demographic trends that have persisted over time; for Claim 3, those conditions could be the conservative disposition of most voters, or perhaps a poll indicating strong opposition to a woman president among teenagers and young voters. These current conditions and trends set the ground for an argument of effect. An argument of effect demonstrates that the existence of these conditions and trends is enough to cause a particular future effect. Lacking identified causes, these kinds of claims are nothing more than random predictions, similar to the bizarre predictions on the covers of the sensational magazines found in supermarkets: "Psychic Foresees Economic Collapse Following Landing of Martians on White House Lawn!"

Determining and Supporting a Probable Effect

The processes of determining and supporting a probable effect overlap considerably. If you identify a future effect through sound methods, the best supporting strategy will be to report these methods, which we discuss in the following paragraphs.

Applying the Principles of Causality. To argue an effect, you need to identify a sufficient cause for the effect and prove that this cause exists or could exist. Are the causes that are currently operating (or that might be set in place) enough to bring about the effect? If you can identify an existing sufficient cause or causes for the effect, your prediction is probably a good one.

Let's take the case of a publishing house editor trying to decide whether to publish a book submitted to her on personal relationships. The editor will accept the book if she thinks it will sell well; her job is to decide whether current circumstances will make the book a best-seller. In other words, the projected effect is excellent sales. The circumstances operating are as follows: the market for books on this topic has been very strong; the writer has written popular books on this subject before; the book itself, in the view of this experienced editor, is interesting, original, and provocative. An analysis of these circumstances reveals that all are sufficient causes; in the absence of the other two, one cause alone would be sufficient to create the effect. The editor's experience with bookselling makes her a good judge of the sufficiency of these causes. She also knows how important these three circumstances are because she has seen them again and again. In projecting any effect, the arguer must understand the principles of the subject matter.

Missing from this list of current circumstances is a necessary cause, one that has to operate in order for the effect to occur. The absence of a necessary cause does not make the projected effect implausible; often it is the sufficient causes that create the necessary cause. In this example, the necessary cause of high sales would simply be that people buy the book, and they will buy the book in the presence of one or more of these sufficient causes.

Causal Chains.   In some situations, you can argue a future effect by revealing a chain of causes that plausibly connects Cause A with Future Effect D. To demonstrate the connection between a past or present cause and a future effect, you need to make a series of arguments of effect; if A is the remote cause and D the predicted effect, you will argue that A will cause B, which will cause C, which finally will cause D.

The field of economics often uses causal chains as a basis for future action. A classic example is the Federal Reserve Bank's setting of interest rates on money it lends to banks, which in turn affects the interest rates banks and other financial institutions charge customers on mortgages and other loans and the interest they pay to customers for savings and other deposits. One key step the Federal Reserve Bank can take to reduce consumer spending is to raise its interest rates, which means the banks will raise their rates, and customers will find that it costs more to get a mortgage on a house, to finance a car loan, or to buy other items on credit. Faced with these rising costs, consumers will decide to spend less. Also, because these same banks are now paying more interest for deposits, consumers have an incentive to save rather than spend—another reason why they will reduce spending. Visually, the causal chain looks like this:

(A) higher government interest rates➤(B) higher bank interest rates➤
(C) lower consumer spending

This causal chain can be extended, since lower consumer spending may lead to a lower inflation rate or to less importing of consumer goods from other countries. With causal chains, however, the greater the length of the chain, the less predictable become the effects.

Sometimes causal chains simply don't work the way they are supposed to. When Prohibition became law in 1919, its proponents predicted that alcohol consumption would decrease and along with it a host of evils, including crime, broken homes, and absenteeism from work. They did not foresee a roaring 14 years of speakeasies, bathtub gin, and bootleg whiskey before Prohibition was abolished in 1933. Especially when trying to predict human behavior through elaborate causal chains, you should always keep in mind the adage about the road to hell being paved with good intentions.

Comparable Situations.   You can also determine the probable future result of current conditions by examining comparable situations in which this cause and effect have already occurred. In trying to raise the educational standards of American primary and secondary schools, teachers, school administrators, and government policymakers look to the experience of other countries. The average scores of students from some other industrialized countries are higher than the average scores of American students on certain standardized achievement tests in areas such as math and science. In some of these countries, notably Japan, children spend much more of the year in school, and the schools introduce rigorous academic material earlier in the student's academic career. Some proponents of reform argue that the same methods used here will improve students' performance.

This comparison method will work only if the situations being compared are *significantly* similar. In arguing that the United States should follow Japan's example, advocates of these changes also need to look carefully at what each country expects from its schools and how these expectations relate to the general culture. What seems comparable at first may turn out to be more complicated on closer inspection, since the American and Japanese cultures have very different expectations about the role of the individual in society.

The more comparable the situations you find, the more convincing your argument of effect will be. If you can demonstrate that a certain cause has had the same result over and over again, and that the current conditions you are considering are truly similar to these other causes, your identification of effect will be well supported.

ACTIVITIES (7.6)

1. For two of the following actions, project two effects that might be caused by the action. State whether the action would be necessary or sufficient to the effect.
   Example action: Graduating *summa cum laude.*
   Possible effects: Being accepted into a prestigious graduate school (sufficient); receiving eight job offers (sufficient).
   a. Getting an A in a course
   b. Arranging a date with someone you don't know
   c. Reducing the danger of theft at your college or in your community
   d. Finding a good place to live
   e. Being stopped by the police for speeding

2. Write a two- to three-page essay describing a causal chain for some area or activity with which you are familiar (for example, gaining or losing weight, saving money, raising your grades).

3. For the following five predictions, cite a truly comparable activity or situation that can be used to support your prediction.
   Example: Extending the academic year in primary and secondary education in the United States. A comparable situation could be the long academic year in Japan, to support the prediction of higher test scores for American students.
   a. Being governor of a state
   b. Student success in graduate school
   c. Decreasing alcohol consumption at fraternity parties at your school
   d. Being removed from academic probation
   e. Making the varsity lacrosse team

SUMMARY

Determining and Arguing a Probable Effect

- To argue an effect, you need to identify a sufficient cause for the effect and prove that this cause exists or could exist.

- You can argue that a certain effect is likely if you can create a causal chain that demonstrates how you move from one cause to an effect that is the cause of the next effect, and so forth. The longer your chain, however, the less likely it is that the chain will perform as predicted.

- You can demonstrate that an effect is likely in a situation if you can prove that a similar situation produced a similar effect.

TWO SAMPLE CAUSAL ARGUMENTS

The following argument is a sample of causal analysis. Based on an essay written by college student Michele Statt, the essay considers possible causes of the recent growth of student interest in liberal arts majors. The essay is not an elaborate and definitive causal argument, but it is a good example of an exploration of the possible causes of an interesting phenomenon (note the qualification of Michele's causal claims). As you study the essay, see if you can locate where Michele establishes the factuality of her cause and effect. Does she report on a process of determination used to test her main cause? What is it? Do you find any reference to a common human motivation?

THE NEW INTEREST IN THE LIBERAL ARTS

In 1978, only 443 students were enrolled in liberal arts majors at my college. Today, with the recent establishment of new liberal arts majors, 604 students are enrolled in these majors. (In the same period, the total enrollment at my college has decreased by 40 students.) Many other schools have also reported that interest in liberal arts majors has been increasing. According to Michael Useem, Director of Boston University's Center for Applied Social Science, across the nation "the proportion of baccalaureate degrees in the liberal arts in 1986 was the largest in four years, and the proportion of first-year college students reporting an interest in a liberal arts major in 1987 was the highest in 10 years" (46).

Several causes may have influenced this increase in interest. Many students entering college are unsure of their career choice and gravitate to the liberal arts because such programs typically do not insist on early declaration of a major. Even if the undecided student then chooses to pursue a major outside the liberal arts, she will find that her liberal arts courses can be applied to her new major. However, having started in the liberal arts, she is likely to find a liberal arts major that appeals to her.

Another cause probably associated with this increase is the growing emphasis on career training within the liberal arts majors themselves. At my college the liberal arts majors include such programs as economics, school psychology, criminal justice, and communications—all of which include a significant element of career preparation that appeals to today's college students. Several of these programs at my college are relatively new. Their existence as additional options for students certainly helps to explain the growth in liberal arts enrollment here.

Liberal arts enrollment, however, has been increasing throughout the country, even at institutions that have not added many new liberal arts programs. The central cause of this growth is very likely the increasing demand for liberal arts majors in the job market. Michael Useem's article, based on research supported by the Corporate Council on the Liberal Arts and the President's Committee on the Arts and Humanities, states that since the early 1980s, many business leaders have stressed the importance of the liberal arts as preparation for a career in business (46). Useem received responses to his survey from 535 large and mid-sized American corporations. The results indicated that corporations do indeed hire liberal arts graduates, with 44 percent of the respondents recruiting liberal arts graduates on campus and 47 percent hiring such students for internships and cooperative education programs; 29 percent reported other efforts to recruit liberal arts graduates, and 61 percent have created programs to train liberal arts graduates for jobs in their corporations (47).

Students are becoming aware of this demand for liberal arts graduates. I chose my field of communication both because of my interest in it and because I was aware of job possibilities after graduation. Twelve students that I talked to said that career preparation was one of the two major causes of their choosing a liberal arts major, the other being their interest in the subject. These results are hardly scientific proof, but they are another piece of evidence demonstrating the importance of the job market in rising liberal arts enrollments.

Useem's study also notes that although many companies hire liberal arts graduates, they are often looking for accomplishments in addition to a liberal arts major, including campus or community involvement and a good grade point average. Another important requirement of most of these corporations was exposure to business courses or experience in business before graduation (47-48, 50-51). The increasing emphasis on career training in at least some liberal arts majors undoubtedly enhances the attractiveness of these majors to employers.

Ten or fifteen years ago, many college students felt that they were forced to make a choice between a liberal arts major or preparing themselves for a career. Because they wanted to find a good job, some of these students chose a program outside of the liberal arts even when they really preferred a liberal arts major. Today's students are more fortunate. They know that in choosing a liberal arts major, they can also prepare themselves for their future after college.

WORKS CITED

Useem, Michael. "The Corporate View of Liberal Arts."
    Journal of Career Planning and Employment. (Summer
    1988): 46-51.

The following argument, "I, Too, Am a Good Parent," combines elements of a causal argument and a recommendation. The author, Dorsett Bennett, claims that the continuing custom of granting child custody to the mother is a result of the prejudice of older male judges who continue to dominate the courts. Is the cause Bennett identifies necessary or sufficient? Is it adequately supported by facts and examples? Do you find any further causal arguments embedded in the essay? What are they?

I, TOO, AM A GOOD PARENT

Dads Should Not Be Discriminated Against

DORSETT BENNETT

Divorce is a fact of modern life. A great number of people simply decide that they do not wish to stay married to their spouse. A divorce is not a tremendously difficult situation unless there are minor children born to the couple. If there are no minor children you simply divide the assets and debts. But you cannot divide a child. The child needs to be placed with the appropriate parent.

In my own case, my former wife chose not to remain married to me. That is her right and I do not fault her decision. My problem is that I do not believe it is her right to deny me the privilege of raising our children. Some fathers want to go to the parent/teacher conferences, school plays, carnivals, and to help their kids with homework. I have always looked forward to participating on a daily basis in my children's lives. I can no longer enjoy that privilege— the children live with their mother, who has moved to a northern Midwest state.

I tried so hard to gain custody of my children. I believe the evidence is uncontradicted as to what an excellent father (and more important, parent) I am. My ex-wife is a fairly good mother, but unbiased opinions unanimously agreed I was the better parent. Testimonials were videotaped from witnesses who could not attend the out-of-state custody hearing. I choose to be a fa-

ther. When I was 3 years old, my own father left my family. While I've loved my father for many years, I did and still do reject his parental pattern.

A couple of centuries ago, a father and mother might have shared equally in the care and raising of children above the age of infancy. But with the coming of the Industrial Revolution the father went to work during the day, leaving the full-time care of the young to the mother, who stayed at home. It was easier to decide who should get child custody under those circumstances. That would be true today even if the mother were put into the position of working outside the home after the divorce.

Now, a majority of married mothers are in the workplace—often because the family needs the second income to survive. With the advent of the working mother, we have also seen a change in child care. Not only have we seen an increase in third-party caregivers; there is a decided difference in how fathers interact with their children. Fathers are even starting to help raise their children. I admit that in a great many families there is an uneven distribution of child-care responsibilities. But there are fathers who do as much to raise the children as the mother, and there are many examples where men are full-time parents.

But, because we have this past history of the mother being the principal child caregiver, the mother has almost always been favored in any contested child-custody case. The law of every state is replete with decisions showing that the mother is the favored custodial parent. The changes in our lifestyles are now being reflected in our laws. In most, if not all, states, the legislature has recognized the change in childcare responsibilities and enacted legislation that is gender blind. The statutes that deal with child custody now say that the children should be placed with the parent whose care and control of the child will be in the child's best interest.

This legislation is enlightened and correct. Society has changed. We no longer bring up our children as we did years ago. But it is still necessary to have someone make the choice in the child's best interest if the parents are divorcing and cannot agree on who takes care of the kids. So we have judges to make that enormous decision.

The state legislature can pass laws that say neither parent is favored because of their gender. But it is judges who make the ultimate choice. And those judges are usually *older males* who practiced law during the time when mothers were the favored guardians under the law. These same judges mostly come from a background where mothers stayed home and were the primary caregivers. By training and by personal experience they have a strong natural bias in favor of the mother in a child-custody case. That belief is regressive and fails to acknowledge the changed realities of our present way of life. Someone must be appointed to render a decision when parents cannot agree. I would ask that those judges who make these critical decisions re-examine their attitudes

and prejudices against placing children with fathers.

After the videotaped testimony was completed, one of my lawyers said he had "never seen a father put together a better custody case." "But," he asked me, "can you prove she is unfit?" A father should not be placed in the position of having to prove the mother is unfit in order to gain custody. He should not have to prove that she has two heads, participates in child sacrifice, or eats live snakes. The father should only have to prove that he is the more suitable parent.

Fathers should not be discriminated against as I was. It took me three years to get a trial on the merits in the Minnesota court. And Minnesota has a law directing its courts to give a high priority to child-custody cases. What was even worse was that the judge seemed to ignore the overwhelming weight of the evidence and granted custody to my ex-wife. At the trial, her argument was, "I am their mother." Other than that statement she hardly put on a case. Being the mother of the children was apparently deemed enough to outweigh evidence that all the witnesses who knew us both felt I was the better parent; that those witnesses who knew only me said what an excellent parent I was; that our children's behavior always improved dramatically after spending time with me; that my daughter wished to live with me; and that I had a better child-custody evaluation than my wife.

So I say to the trial judges who decide these cases: "Become part of the solution to this dilemma of child custody. Don't remain part of the problem." It is too late for me. If this backward way of thinking is changed, then perhaps it won't be too late for other fathers who should have custody of their children.

Source: *Newsweek*, July 4, 1994.

SUGGESTIONS FOR WRITING (7.7)

1. Write an essay describing the necessary and sufficient causes for a major event in your life. Be sure to indicate to the reader how you determined that

these causes were operating. Make the essay as long as necessary to describe fully the causes of this event.

2. Analyze at least three persons or organizations that share major common traits, and determine what similar causes, if any, made them the way they are. As examples, you could analyze successful or unsuccessful teams in some sport, or successful or unsuccessful television shows. Report your analysis in an essay of approximately four pages.

3. Analyze two persons or situations that share significant traits but that have ended up differing in some major way. What caused this major difference? For this essay, you might analyze why you and a close friend or a sibling chose different colleges or majors or why you performed differently in two similar classes. Report your analysis in an essay of approximately four pages.

4. Examine two trends that you believe may be causally related to see if there is any proportional correlation between them. An example might be the national crime rate and the national unemployment rate, or the national unemployment rate and the inflation rate. If you expect to find a correlation and you do not, speculate on why the correlation is not present. For the most current information available, your library will probably have the *Statistical Abstracts of the United States* in database format, but you may also be able to retrieve any government statistical data you may need through the Web site at http://www.census.gov/statab/www/. Report your analysis in an essay of approximately four pages.

5. Fewer and fewer college students are completing bachelor's degrees in the traditional four-year period. Do some research at your own institution, and find out the average time students are taking to graduate. Then write a four- to five-page essay that explores possible causes of this phenomenon. Make sure that the causes you suggest originate in the same time period as the effect.

ILLUSTRATIVE ARGUMENTS IN PART II: ARGUING CAUSE

8

Arguing Evaluations

EVALUATIVE SUBJECTS AND TERMS

All evaluations include a subject to be judged and an evaluative term that is applied to the subject. In the claim "John is a good writer," *John* is the subject, and *good writer* is the evaluative term; in "Tracy Chapman is a gifted musician," *Tracy Chapman* is the subject and *gifted musician* the evaluative term. Some evaluative claims include only partial evaluative terms, but their context should suggest the missing parts. In the claim "Capital punishment is immoral," the full evaluative term is *immoral act,* and in "Rembrandt was a master," the evaluative term is *master painter.*

To make a successful evaluative argument, you need to lay some careful groundwork. First, you must define the evaluative term. In the claim "John is a good writer," where *good writer* could mean different things to different people, you'll want to specify your understanding of the term. In many cases, you can do this by a shorthand definition: "John is a good writer; he communicates ideas clearly and gracefully" (see Chapter 4 for a discussion of shorthand definitions). This definition establishes clarity and grace in the communication as the criteria by which John's writing will be judged.

Sometimes evaluations are expressed negatively, as in "John is a poor writer," or "The instructions for this camera are useless." A negative evaluation can either imply its opposite as the standard of judgment or establish a definition of the negative term itself. The writer of the claim "William Faulkner's *Fable* is a failed novel" could work from a definition of *successful novel,* showing how this novel falls short of that definition, or could establish criteria for the term *failed novel* and apply those to the subject.

The second piece of groundwork necessary to most successful evaluations is gaining your readers' agreement about your definition of the evaluative term. If your readers' understanding of the criteria for good writing do not agree with yours, however clearly you have presented them, your argument won't get very far. Perhaps they agree that John's writing is clear and graceful, but because their understanding of good writing includes rich ideas and original expression, they will never be convinced by your argument that John is a good writer. In this situation, and in many evaluations, you will need to argue the definition of your evaluative term, convincing your readers that the criteria by which you define the term are reasonable and complete. Only then can you proceed to the heart of your evaluation: demonstrating the match between your subject and your evaluative term.

ACTIVITIES (8.1)

1. What is the evaluative term (implied or stated) in the following assertions?
   a. Mark Twain's *Adventures of Huckleberry Finn* is an American classic.
   b. When Roger Bannister broke the four-minute mile barrier in 1954, he accomplished one of the greatest athletic feats of this century.
   c. Calvin Coolidge was a mediocre president.
   d. Calculators are a real boon to mathematics students.
   e. The terrible losses in wars in the twentieth century show the bankruptcy of nations' using war as an extension of foreign policy.
2. Write a paragraph giving a brief definition of one of the evaluative terms you identified in Activity 1.

ESTABLISHING THE DEFINITION OF THE EVALUATIVE TERM

How much space and energy you devote to establishing your term's definition will depend on your audience and the nature of the term. There is so little dispute about some terms that an extensive definition is unnecessary—an honest bank teller, for example, or a reliable car. And in cases where you are very confident about your readers' values, about what is important to them and why, you may not need to argue or even propose a definition. A doctor writing to other doctors about the unprofessional behavior of a certain physician could probably assume agreement among her readers about the definition of unprofessional behavior. But when the following conditions apply, you should define your evaluative term and argue its definition:

- When your audience consists of people with expertise and/or values different from yours
- When your definition of the evaluative term is unconventional or controversial
- When there are different definitions of the term

Whether or not you define the evaluative term explicitly, remember that very vague or inflated evaluations are usually harder to argue than those that are limited and precise. It would be far easier to convince an audience that "Indigo Girls are ingenious lyricists" than that "Indigo Girls are the best songwriters ever."

Presenting the Definition

In most cases, the actual definition of the term can be stated quite briefly, usually as part of or directly following the claim: "Alison is the ideal management trainee: she is intelligent, ambitious, congenial, and hardworking"; "In his highly original and influential reflections on the American spirit, reflections that affected common citizens as well as fellow philosophers, Ralph Waldo Emerson proved himself to be a great thinker."

When defining an evaluative term, you are proposing a *stipulative* definition—a definition that restricts the understanding of a term to a particular meaning appropriate to your context. (See Chapter 4 for a full discussion of definition.) In the argument about John's writing skills, the definition of good writing as the clear and graceful communication of ideas is stipulative: it asks readers to accept this particular and limited definition of the term for the context of this argument. In most cases, your definition will take the shorthand, sentence form identified in Chapter 4, although if the term is very difficult, you might want to provide an extended definition.

As in all definitions, the explanation you offer must be clear and precise. Your definition will be useless if it offers only broad or abstract generalizations. If you write, "The brilliance of the film *Citizen Kane* lies in its wonderful structure," but you fail to define *wonderful structure,* you will leave readers guessing. Try also to avoid definitions that include highly subjective terms. If you define a "talented soprano" as one whose voice is beautiful at all points in her vocal range, you have not done much to clarify the evaluative term. What is beautiful to one listener may be mediocre, or heavy, or thin to another; "beautiful" is a measurement that frequently provokes disagreement. So if you wish the term to be useful, define it by offering comparatively objective standards, like fullness, or clarity, or fluidity. While these, too, are subjective terms, they are more precise and are less a matter of personal taste than a term like *beautiful.*

The following are three examples of promising opening definitions; each is clear, precise, and informative.

- A good argument is one that directly identifies its central proposition; supports that proposition with reasonable, relevant, and concrete evidence; and admits the possibility of alternative points of view.
- A dedicated mother devotes herself to her children because she knows she should; a good mother devotes herself to her children because she can't imagine doing otherwise.
- A good education will prepare a student not only for a career but for a fulfilling life outside a career. As important as careers are in our lives, they do not and should not occupy all of our time and energy. The well-educated person is the one who can view life outside work with zest, knowing that there are many other interests aside from a career.

While the qualities included in your proposed definition should be as clear and precise as possible, the very nature of evaluations will not always allow you to avoid subjective terms. In the last of the three preceding examples, the term *fulfilling life* is inherently subjective, yet it is not meaningless. There are certain qualities and activities we can identify that constitute a fulfilling life, including having friends, having hobbies or other recreational interests, and being curious about the past, the future, and the world. It may not be easy to measure each of these qualities or activities precisely, but they do exist, and they can be gauged on some comparative scale.

ACTIVITIES (8.2)

Using the preceding definitions as a model, give a brief but useful definition of the following. After you have written your definitions, compare them with the definitions written by two other students in your class. How much agreement is there among your definitions? How do you account for the differences that exist?

1. A safe automobile
2. An inspiring professor
3. An honest politician
4. A natural athlete
5. The perfect roommate

Arguing the Definition

Based on your assessment of their backgrounds, needs, and values, you may conclude that your readers will not automatically agree with your definition of the evaluative term. In such cases, you have one more job before you move to the evaluation per se: to *argue* that your definition is just, that the criteria you have assigned to a term such as *necessary war, master craftsman,* or *inspired teacher* are reasonable and complete. You can argue the justness of your definition using any of the methods for supporting definitions presented in Chapter 4, including appeal to assumed values, identification of effect, appeal to authority, and comparison.

To illustrate the application of these methods, let's work with the following example: as a branch manager for a local bank, you are asked to write a formal evaluation of three new management trainees. Your reader will be the bank's vice president of personnel. There is no fixed evaluation form or criteria to work from; *you* must decide which qualities constitute promising performance in a new trainee. The qualities you settle on (in unranked order) are (1) honesty, (2) the ability to foresee the consequences of decisions, (3) attention to detail, and (4) courtesy to customers. Because you have created this list, you will need to justify it, however briefly, to the vice president. Your justification for each item on the list could use the following methods of argument:

- *Honesty:* appeal to assumed value. You wouldn't have to say much about this quality. For obvious reasons, bankers place a premium on honesty in their employees.
- *Ability to foresee the consequences of decisions:* identification of effect. This criterion may not be as obvious as the first, but bankers must base decisions about lending money, setting interest rates, and making investments on the probable consequences of these decisions. You could briefly point out the positive results of having this ability and the negative results of lacking it.

- *Attention to detail:* appeal to assumed value. Like honesty, the importance of this quality doesn't have to be argued to bankers.
- *Courtesy to customers:* identification of effect. You can easily demonstrate that good customer relations lead to good business. For many bankers, this criterion would be an assumed value.

You can buttress these criteria with other support. To bolster the third criterion, attention to detail, you might cite recognized authorities who stress this quality and the grave risks banks run when they hire employees who lack it. To support the fourth criterion, courtesy to customers, you might use the method of comparison, pointing to the success of a competing bank that stresses good customer relations.

If you can make a reasonable argument for your definition of the evaluative term, your readers are likely to accept the qualities you cite. But they may still object to your definition on the basis of omission: your definition is acceptable as far as it goes, but you have omitted one quality critical to them. Without the inclusion of that quality, they cannot accept your evaluation of the subject. So, in formulating your definition, try to anticipate the reactions of your readers; if they are likely to be concerned about the omission of a certain quality, you must explain why you chose to omit it. Any of the methods previously identified will help you make this explanation. For example, you could justify your omission of a knowledge of computer programming as a criterion for judging trainees by using the identification of effect, pointing out that few bank employees do any programming anyway and that it is cheaper and more efficient to hire outside programming experts when they are needed. In this case, you are pointing out that no bad effects are caused by these trainees' inexperience with programming.

Ranking the Qualities in Your Definition

In some evaluative arguments, it is not enough to establish a list of qualities constituting your evaluative term; often you will need to indicate the relative importance of these qualities by ranking them. Ranking is almost always necessary in evaluations of multiple subjects. If you are evaluating four models of home coffee brewers, for example, you might establish the following qualities as essential: reasonable price, good-tasting coffee, a quick-brew cycle, and an automatic timer. A reader may agree with each of these qualities yet disagree with your final choice of brewer. The reason for the disagreement would be that you and your reader rank the four qualities differently. If a quick-brew cycle is most important to you but least important to your reader, he or she will not accept your final evaluation of the three machines.

In some evaluations, particularly those that are likely to directly affect your reader, you may have to justify the relative value you place on each quality. If you are evaluating dormitory life as a valuable freshman experience, you will let your readers (incoming freshmen) know which of the criteria you cite is most important and which is least important. Suppose you rank the qualities as follows: (1) quiet study atmosphere, (2) good social opportunities, (3) proximity to campus, and (4) comfortable surroundings. You could argue the importance of the first quality, a quiet study atmosphere, by a number of familiar methods: appeals to value or authority, comparison, or identification of effect. Regardless of the method you choose, you must be able to demonstrate that without a quiet study atmosphere, one that allows students to work hard and succeed academically, all of the other qualities are meaningless. If a student flunks out of school the first year, the other three qualities will have been useless. Thus the first quality is the most important because, in your view, it is the *essential* quality.

ACTIVITIES (8.3)

For one of the following subjects, list in order of importance the criteria you would include in its definition. Compare your definition with your classmates' criteria, and based on any disagreement you find, write a two-page essay justifying your selection and ranking of the criteria.

1. A college or university
2. A musical concert
3. A campus newspaper
4. A church or synagogue
5. A textbook for a college course

ARGUING THE EVALUATION

Having laid the necessary foundation for a successful evaluation, you're ready to make the evaluative argument.

The evaluation itself will be largely *factual.* By verifying data and presenting concrete examples, you will argue that your subject possesses the criteria you have cited. Establishing this match is especially important when your subject is a service—a travel agency, a long-distance phone service—or a functional object, such as a coffee brewer or a pickup truck. In these cases, where the evaluative term is defined by objectively measurable qualities (for example, speed, efficiency, accuracy, and price), your job is to verify the existence of those qualities in your subject.

Suppose you were evaluating portable MP3 players. For college preparation, your grandparents offered to purchase a portable CD player in the $150 price range. You don't want to take all of your CDs to your dorm room because you won't have enough storage space, and you are worried about some of your favorites disappearing. Your computer has enough memory to store your CDs and a good speaker system, so you really don't need a portable CD player, but you would like to have a stable MP3 player that will allow you to listen to music while you are in the library or walking to class. You see an ad for a *Walkme3* that is comparable in price to the CD player your grandparents suggested. You don't want to hurt their feelings because they thought they were being "hip" by offering to purchase the CD player, and they are not completely "up" on computers. So you prepare an evaluation to show them how the MP3 player will benefit you and provide you with the listening pleasure that they want you to have. Your evaluation will be convincing if the MP3 player will be better for you than a CD player. You evaluate the Euphony *Walkme3* as a *good portable MP3 player*. Your evaluation will be convincing as long as you can establish the following three facts: the suggested retail price of the *Walkme3* is below $150; it offers good quality sound; it holds a reasonable number of songs.

These facts can be convincingly established through reference to your own experience, provided you present yourself as reliable and objective. (Other supporting sources—the experience of friends or impartial analyses of the *Walkme3* found in consumer guides—could be referred to as well.) You could cite the actual price of the *Walkme3* at three local stores to verify the first fact. The second, which is the most subjective, can be verified by your physical description of the *Walkme3*'s sound quality—full tones, adjustable balance treble and bass levels, clear reproduction of the original CDs—a description of what you require for your listening pleasure. The third fact can also be established by reference to the number of songs you want to be able to select. "When I'm studying at home in my own room, I like familiar classical music that doesn't interfere with my reading. But when I'm walking around, I like a wide variety, including folk, rock, alternative, and even heavy metal on occasion. I need enough storage space for at least three hours of listening, and the Walkme3 provides four hours of storage." As with all factual arguments, the key to success in arguing evaluations is to cite reliable and authoritative experience and observations and to include specific, concrete examples of general statements.

Not all evaluations are as neat and objective as the preceding example. Let's look at a very different example involving more subjective measurement and see how the principles of factual argument apply. This evaluation argues that your friend Ellen knows how to be a good friend: she respects her friends, accepting and loving them for who they are, and she expects the same treatment from them. Because the definition included in the claim is not a standard definition of friendship, it requires some preliminary support (see the preceding section on "Arguing the Definition").

Once supported, the definition must be applied to the subject, your friend Ellen. The quality of respecting others—a key criterion of your evaluative term—cannot be measured as objectively or established as definitively as the price of a radio or the fuel efficiency of an automobile. Yet general agreement exists about what constitutes respectful behavior: it is attentive, considerate, accepting behavior. The best way to demonstrate the applicability of the quality to your subject is through specific examples illustrating such behavior. As in any factual argument, you must *describe* the experience faithfully and objectively. Because you want to establish that Ellen's respectful treatment of her friends is habitual, not occasional, you should cite a number of examples.

Beyond citing the examples, you might also need to point out what is respectful in the examples cited, particularly if your readers might interpret the behavior differently. But in general, the more concrete and immediate your presentation of examples, the less explicit commentary you will need.

Testing Your Evaluation Through the Syllogism

A good evaluative claim falls very neatly into the basic syllogistic model presented in Chapter 5. Once you have come up with your claim, you can test its reasonableness and completeness by rewriting it in syllogistic terms. The definition of the evaluative term will be the major premise, the application of the defining criteria will be the minor premise, and the claim itself will be the conclusion. The preceding example regarding Ellen's friendship would compose the following syllogism:

> **Major premise:** A good friend respects her friends, accepts them and loves them for who they are, and expects the same treatment from them.
> **Minor premise:** Ellen respects me, accepts me and loves me for who I am, and expects the same from me.
> **Conclusion:** Ellen is a good friend.

The major premise establishes characteristics that constitute friendship; the minor premise applies those same characteristics to Ellen; and the conclusion makes a very specific claim derived from the relationship between the two premises. This syllogism tells us that the claim is valid, but we can accept it as true as well only if the two premises are also true. If the major premise (the definition of friendship) does not appear to be immediately acceptable, it will have to be argued in the ways we have suggested. Similarly the truth (or probability) of the minor premise may have to be established through a factual argument that provides examples of Ellen's behavior toward you. While you may not be able to *prove* the absolute truth of both premises, you can strengthen them by providing appropriate support, thus moving the entire argument much closer to a position of soundness.

ACTIVITIES (8.4)

Working from the definitions you created for Activity (8.2), compose a specific claim from each. Then turn the definition and the claim into a syllogism. To what extent would the major and minor premises of each syllogism need further support?

FURTHER METHODS OF SUPPORTING EVALUATIONS

Definition and factual argument are central to evaluations, but there are other ways to support these arguments. The tactics that follow can be used along with definition and factual arguments or by themselves.

Identification of Effect

Since an action, policy, or object is generally considered valuable if its effects are valuable, a good way to support evaluations is by identifying the positive effects of the subject. Freedom of speech is good because it encourages the widest exchange of ideas, which is more likely to lead to the truth or to solutions to problems. Child abuse is bad because it causes physical and mental anguish in children. Of course, such a causal support of evaluations will work only if it accords with the principles of causality discussed in Chapter 7, and if your audience agrees with your assessment of the effect. If you anticipate any disagreement from your audience, you'll need to argue, if only briefly, your evaluation of the effect.

Appeal to Authority

You can support any evaluation by appealing to the similar judgment of a recognized authority. If Chris Evert has publicly expressed her admiration for the tennis game of Martina Hingis, this statement would be effective support for your argument that Hingis is the finest tennis player on the women's tour. Just be sure, when you cite the judgment of an expert, that that person truly qualifies as an authority on this particular subject.

Comparison

You can often support your evaluation by showing similarities between your subject and one that your audience is likely to evaluate in the same way. For example, many feminists have supported their arguments against sexual discrimination by comparing it to racial discrimination. The two forms of discrimination are similar in many ways: both base inequitable treatment on irrelevant and immutable characteristics—race and gender. An audience that would object to racial discrimination would, when the similarities were pointed out, be likely to object to sexual discrimination as well. But as with any comparative argument, make sure the similarities between the two subjects are essential, not peripheral.

ACTIVITIES (8.5)

With a small group of your classmates, identify which kinds of support (factual argument, identification of effect, appeal to authority, comparison) would be most appropriate for two of the following evaluative claims. Discuss your reasons for choosing each form of support.

1. Shakespeare is one of the world's greatest writers.
2. Mercedes-Benz makes many of the world's best cars.
3. Failure to build a water treatment plant for the city would be a serious mistake.
4. Strato Airlines has the best customer service record of any airline in America.
5. Military involvements by major powers in small countries are usually unwise in terms of lives lost, money wasted, and the increased suspicion of other small countries.

THE VARIETIES OF EVALUATIONS

By now, you realize that different kinds of evaluations demand different kinds of support. While there are no hard-and-fast rules in this area, if you can identify the *kind* of evaluation you're arguing, you'll have a better sense of how to support it. Evaluations usually fall into one of three main categories: ethical, aesthetic, or functional. Included in this section is a fourth subclass as well: the interpretation. Strictly speaking, interpretations are not evaluative arguments, but since they are argued in much the same way as evaluations, they are addressed here.

Ethical Evaluations

The word *ethical* is one of those terms that we all understand in a vague way yet might be hard pressed to define precisely. To avoid confusion, consider the following definition: *ethical* describes behavior that conforms to an ideal code of moral principles—principles of right and wrong, good and evil. That code may be derived from any number of cultures: religious, professional, national, or political.

All of us operate within many cultures: we are members of families, communities, organizations, religions, professions, and nations. Each one of these cultures has its own set of ethical standards. For example, among the many ethical principles of Judaism and Christianity are the Ten Commandments. As United States citizens, we are subject to other standards of conduct, such as those recorded in the Constitution—including the Bill of Rights—and the Declaration of Independence. Your college also operates by certain standards that it expects its members to follow: respect for school property, respect for faculty, and academic honesty. In most cultures, these standards are formally recorded, but in some instances they remain implicit. There also exist certain ethical ideals common to virtually all cultures—ideals such as fair play, kindness, and respect for others.

Because individuals are tied to a number of different cultures, clashes between standards are inevitable. Some pacifist groups, for example, see a clash between the religious commandment "Thou shall not kill" and the government's standard that citizens must be prepared to defend their country in time of war. Sometimes conflicts occur between standards of the same culture. Such clashes are commonplace in law. What happens, for example, when the right of free speech collides with the right of a person to be free from libel? Free speech cannot mean that someone has a right to say anything about another person, regardless of how untrue or harmful it is. On the other hand, protection from libel cannot mean protection from the truth being told about mistakes or misdeeds, particularly when they have some impact on the public. Throughout our history, the courts have struggled to find a balance between these two competing claims, sometimes slightly favoring one value, sometimes the other, but always denying that either value can have absolute sway over the other.

Defining the Evaluative Term in Ethical Arguments.   Whenever you evaluate a subject in terms of right or wrong conduct, you'll be appealing to certain ethical values or standards that you believe your audience holds. When asserting that "Hitler was an evil man," or "Ms. Mead is an honorable lawyer," or "The coach used unfair tactics," you are assuming that your readers both *understand* what you mean by the evaluative term and *agree* with that meaning. As in all evaluations, if you have reason to doubt your readers' understanding of the term, you'll have to define it, and if you're uncertain about their agreement with the definition, you'll have to support it.

The Argument in Ethical Evaluations.   Most ethical arguments concentrate on demonstrating what is unethical or immoral about the subject being evaluated.

At the center of these evaluations, then, is a factual argument. In arguing that Hitler was evil, your focus would be on documenting the behavior you identify as evil, and on demonstrating that your evaluative term fits the examples you are citing.

You can also strengthen your evaluation through other supporting methods, including comparison (Hitler was as bad as or worse than certain other dictators) or identification of effect (in addition to all of the bad he did in his life, the war Hitler started led to the division of Europe into two opposing camps, or to a pervasive sense of victimization among Jews of later generations).

ACTIVITIES (8.6)

Using one of the following evaluative assertions (from Activities 8.5) as your claim, write a two-page "Letter to the Editor" of your local city newspaper. Or create your own claim derived from a current local or national controversy.

1. Shakespeare is one of the world's greatest writers.
2. Mercedes-Benz makes many of the world's best cars.
3. Failure to build a water treatment plant for the city would be a serious mistake.
4. Strato Airlines has the best customer service record of any airline in America.

Aesthetic Evaluations

Writing a convincing evaluation of a work of art—a poem, an opera, a painting— is not as futile a task as many believe, provided you understand the goals of such an argument. Just as personal tastes in clothes or food are usually immune to reasonable argument, aesthetic preferences—liking Chopin's music and despising Mahler's—are often too much matters of personal taste to be arguable. There is much truth in the Latin saying *De gustibus non est disputandum:* there is no arguing about taste. Nevertheless, while changing aesthetic tastes or opinions is difficult, it is possible and often useful to convince an audience to *appreciate* the strengths or weaknesses of a work of art by giving them a greater understanding of it. A successful aesthetic evaluation may not convince a reader to like Rubens or to dislike Lichtenstein, but it will at least give a reader reasons for approving of or objecting to a work.

All artistic fields have their own sets of standards for excellence, standards about which there is surprising conformity among experts in the field. Most literary critics, for example, would agree on the standards for a successful short story: coherence of the story, careful selection of detail, avoidance of digression, an interesting style. When critics disagree, and of course they do so regularly, they usually disagree not about identified standards of excellence but about the application of those standards. Often such disagreements are matters of a personal preference for one kind of artist over another. Even professional critics are not immune to the influence of their personal tastes.

When you argue an aesthetic evaluation, you should work from standards currently accepted within the field, though you may not have to do more than briefly or implicitly refer to them. Your evaluation is likely to fail if you ignore these standards, or if you try to effect an overnight revolution in them. Like ethical standards, aesthetic standards usually change gradually, though there have been periods of revolutionary change, as occurred in artistic tastes in the early twentieth century.

Usually, then, your chief task is to demonstrate that these standards apply (or don't apply) to your subject. This demonstration consists of careful description and concrete examples, as in the following excerpt from an essay on the famous comedians the Marx Brothers ("From Sweet Anarchy to Stupid Pet Tricks"). In this excerpt, Mark Edmundson gives a description and examples from a particular scene in a Marx Brothers film and then presents his criteria for rich "antiestablishment comedy."

Groucho always rebels against his own success. When it seems that Trentino might treat him on equal terms, as a gentleman, Groucho stages an imagined encounter between himself and the Sylvanian ambassador that ends in disaster. "I'll be only too happy," Groucho pledges in most statesmanlike tones, "to meet Ambassador Trentino and offer him, on behalf of my country, the right hand of good fellowship." But then, Groucho worries, maybe the ambassador will snub him (stranger things have happened). "A fine thing that'll be! I hold out my hand and he refuses to accept it! That'll add a lot to my prestige, won't it? Me, the head of a country, snubbed by a foreign ambassador! Who does he think he is that he can come here and make a sap out of me in front of all my people?" Then, rising to a boil, "Think of it! I hold out my hand and that hyena refuses to accept it! . . . He'll never get away with it, I tell you! . . . He'll never get away with it."

Enter Trentino, looking haughty. Groucho, raging now, "So! You refuse to shake hands with me, eh?" Groucho slaps Trentino with his gloves. This means war!

It's Groucho's contempt for his own high-mindedness and posing—"I'll be happy to meet Ambassador Trentino and offer him the right hand," blah, blah, blah—that sends him into a spin. Groucho was about to act decorously, something for which he cannot forgive himself. As his predecessor Thoreau put it, "What demon possessed me that I behaved so well?"

Our current outsider comics—Roseanne, Eddie Murphy, Martin Lawrence—attack incessantly, and they sometimes score. But what they don't generally do is what Groucho does so superbly, turn the lens back, dramatize their own flaws. The richness of Groucho's antiestablishment comedy is that it compels us not only to challenge social hypocrisy but to consider our own. And it's that double vision, it seems to me, that helps make Groucho and the Marx Brothers as indispensable now as they were in the 1930s.

Edmundson's chief measure of the success of antiestablishment comedians is what he calls their "double vision," their ability to "turn the lens back, dramatize their own flaws." With the criterion clearly identified, the reader can discover it easily in the detailed description of the film scene.

As with all arguments, when composing an aesthetic evaluation, be sure to consider your readers' level of knowledge—both of the subject being evaluated and of the field in general (comedy, tragedy, jazz, autobiographies, etc.). Edmundson assumes that his readers are familiar with Marx Brothers' films, but he also reviews individual scenes in some detail to ensure that his points are made. In cases where your subject and your evaluative criteria may be less familiar to your audience, you may want to offer not only a careful description of the subject, but also a lucid explanation of the criteria. People often fail to appreciate what they don't understand, so if your evaluation can teach them about the standards of a particular field, it will have a better chance of convincing them that your subject meets (or fails to meet) those standards.

Another useful tactic when arguing a positive evaluation to an inexperienced audience is to relate your subject to one with which they are more familiar. If, for example, you want to convince an audience familiar with and appreciative of modern abstract art that the art of ancient Egypt is also interesting, you might point out the similarities between the two: "Although they are widely separated in time, modern abstract art and ancient Egyptian art both concentrate on the essence of a person or object, not the surface appearance." In taking this approach, you are borrowing from your readers' appreciation of modern abstract art, shining its positive light onto the subject of your evaluation.

ACTIVITIES (8.7)

For each of the following forms of art or entertainment, list at least three standards by which you would judge the quality of a specific work of this type. Then, for one of the categories, write a two- to three-page essay demonstrating how a specific work of that type does or does not fit your standards of excellence. (You should make these standards explicit in your essay.)

1. An action film
2. A mystery novel
3. A jazz recording
4. A portrait photograph
5. An abstract painting

Functional Evaluations

Functional evaluations stand a better chance of changing readers' minds than do ethical and aesthetic evaluations. It is easier to convince a reader that her views about turbo engine cars are inaccurate than that her views about abortion are wrong. While people do form sentimental attachments to objects and machines, they can usually be convinced that however powerful that attachment, it has nothing to do with the subject's actual performance; an audience's preconceptions about performance quality are less matters of cultural values and personal tastes than of practical experience, assumptions, or hearsay.

Functional evaluations always work from a definition of ideal standards: like evaluating MP3s, you can't demonstrate that Sony makes an excellent CD player without some criteria for measuring the player's performance. Some functional evaluations require an explicit presentation of evaluative criteria and some can safely assume reader familiarity with the relevant criteria. Certainly, if your criteria are unusual or innovative ("The most important feature of a car for me is that it *look* good"), you'll have to state them explicitly and argue their relevance and completeness (using any of the methods discussed earlier in this chapter).

Sometimes functional evaluations work best from a ranked list of criteria. For example, a lawn mower can be evaluated in terms of safety features, cost, and noise, but the three criteria may not be equally important. To justify your evaluation, you should explain and support the relative weights you've assigned to each criterion.

Any of the other supporting methods discussed earlier in this chapter (identification of effect, appeal to authority, comparison) can also be used in a performance evaluation. Of these, the most valuable is identification of effect. "Virginia Wensel is a good violin teacher" because she has produced a number of fine players; "My college provides an excellent education" because 85 percent of its graduates go on to graduate school. In each case, the subject is judged in terms of its positive effects. Note that sometimes the effect you identify as an evaluative criterion must be argued. Why, for example, does acceptance into graduate school mean you have received an excellent undergraduate education?

If the effect you are citing has already occurred, your support will be a factual argument. In arguing that "Virginia Wensel is a good violin teacher," you would cite the number of fine players she has produced and briefly support your positive judgment of those players. In other cases, where the effect has not yet occurred, your argument is necessarily more speculative: "Based on the evidence we have, this car is likely to give you years of reliable service."

ACTIVITIES (8.8)

List in ranked order at least three standards by which you would judge the performance of the following. Then, for one of the categories, write a two- to three-page essay demonstrating how well one person or object in that category meets your standards of performance.

1. An automobile for a family with three small children
2. A president of a college or university
3. A personal computer
4. A United States senator
5. A college reference librarian

Interpretations

The purpose of an interpretation is to disclose the meaning of a particular subject—often a meaning not immediately obvious to a casual observer or reader. At some time or other, all students must practice interpretive arguments in literature classes. The following are examples of possible claims for literary interpretations: "Beneath the apparently modest and conventional surface of Christina Rossetti's lyrics lie fiery manifestoes of independence and rebellion"; "In placing the last scene of *Tess of the d'Urbervilles* at Stonehenge, Thomas Hardy reminds us that Tess is a pagan, not a Christian, heroine." But interpretations are not solely the province of literature; we make interpretive arguments all the time about the behavior of people we know ("Paul says he craves a close relationship with a woman, but it's easy to see he's terrified of intimacy") and about the productions of popular culture ("Television advertisements are selling one thing: sex").

Interpretations are often paired with explanatory causal arguments. In claiming that "Hamlet's indecisiveness is a symptom of his unresolved Oedipal complex," we are really making two claims, both of which propose an increased understanding of the play *Hamlet*. First, we are identifying the *cause* of Hamlet's indecisive behavior (his unresolved Oedipal complex), and second, we are claiming that an unresolved Oedipal complex can be discovered within Hamlet's character. Now, if you've read the play, you know that Shakespeare is never explicit about the oddities of Hamlet's relationship with his mother. No character ever says to Hamlet, "Oh Hamlet, cast thy infantile and possessive love of thy mother off." But keen readers who recognize some of the telltale symptoms of the Oedipal complex detect one in Hamlet's words and actions. And that detection is the interpretive argument: the demonstration of meaning beneath the surface. You will remember that causal claims are always somewhat speculative; this brand of causal claim is even more so, because the cause it identifies is interpretive, not factual.

Interpretations can imply a positive or a negative evaluation, but they are not evaluations per se. Nevertheless, the processes for arguing the two are very similar. The subject of an interpretive argument is the visible surface we wish to understand or explore further; it is the behavior, data, or event that openly exists for all to observe. The interpretive term is the summarized explanation of the reality beneath the visible surface. In the interpretive claim "The current baseball cap craze among boys expresses their rejection of tradition and authority," the subject is *current baseball cap craze among boys,* and the interpretive term is *rejection of tradition and authority.*

As in evaluations, your central task in interpretive arguments is to demonstrate a match between the subject and the interpretive term. But also as in evaluations, you will need to lay some groundwork. Most solid interpretations satisfy the following requirements: (1) the interpretive term is clearly defined; (2) the interpretive term and the subject are matched—that is, demonstrated to be equivalent or coincident; and (3) evidence is supplied to support the interpretation.

Defining the Interpretive Term. Like evaluative arguments, interpretations work from assumptions about definition—about what elements make up a certain condition or reality. In interpretations, we are stating that X (the subject) is Y (the interpretation). To prove or support this assertion, we must define Y in such a way that it restates X or restate X in such a way that it coincides with Y. In the interpretive claim "Television news broadcasting is no longer news; it is entertainment," we must demonstrate the coincidence of our definition of entertainment on the one hand with what we see of television news on the other.

In the following passage, we see a similar assertion of coincidence, where Sigmund Freud equates literature (the subject) with the play of children:

> Now the writer does the same as the child at play; he creates a world of phantasy which he takes very seriously; that is, he invests it with a great deal of affect, while separating it sharply from reality. Language has preserved this relationship between children's play and poetic creation. It designates certain kinds of imaginative creation, concerned with tangible objects and capable of representation, as "plays"; the people who present them are called "players."

The first step in assembling an interpretive argument is to consider whether to define the interpretive term and argue your definition. As with evaluative arguments, you should define the term if you are using it in an unusual or controversial way, and you should justify that definition if you think your audience is likely to object to it. In the first example, the term *entertainment* probably should be defined, as it is a very broad and even subjective term. You might define the term as "any brief, self-contained, sensually pleasing performance that amuses but does not challenge." If your audience is likely to disagree with this definition, you will have to support it with the methods discussed in the preceding section titled "Arguing the Definition" in this chapter.

Of course, you can work from an unstated definition, provided your argument clearly reveals the elements of that definition. The following example illustrates this tactic:

> Much of television news broadcasting is no longer news; it is entertainment. Most local and national news broadcasts, news shows like *60 Minutes* and *20/20*, and even public television news are putting out slick, superficial performances that are usually neither challenging nor controversial, but that capture huge audience shares.

Here the definition of entertainment is contained in the characterization of television news.

Extensive interpretations of a series of events or continuing behavior work somewhat differently, though the basic principles are the same. In these cases—for example, an interpretation of a character's actions in a novel or of quarterly stock market activity—the subjects are usually explained in terms of a coherent and preestablished theory, system of thought, or belief. Instead of demonstrating the coincidence or equivalence of the subject and a single concept (like children's play or entertainment), these more ambitious interpretations reveal the existence of a series of related concepts—an entire system—behind the visible activity of the subject. The system identified could be Christianity, Marxism, Jungian psychology, feminism, Freudian drive theory, capitalism, semiotics—virtually any set of facts or principles logically connected to form a coherent view of the world.

Examples of this kind of systematic interpretation are especially prevalent in artistic and literary interpretations, though they are not limited to these contexts. A feminist interpretation of a literary figure like Emily Dickinson would work from a thorough understanding of feminist theory. The interpretation might explain Dickinson's poems in terms of the tension between her vocation as a poet and the very different expectations that nineteenth-century society had for women.

However compelling such an interpretation, readers are not likely to be swayed if they strongly object to the interpretive system—to the Freudian, or Marxist, or feminist model of human behavior. Even if the construct used to explain the subject is not formally named, the principles contained in that construct must seem at least plausible to your readers. If you interpret modern American history on the basis of tensions and conflicts between different social and economic classes, your readers may not give your interpretation fair consideration if they are opposed to this set of principles. On the other hand, a good interpretation often helps readers gain sympathy for a philosophy or point of view they were previously hostile to or ignorant of. When you write interpretations, you should be sensitive to your audience's beliefs and prepared at least to acknowledge their probable objections as you proceed. In doing so, you may convince some hostile readers, bringing them to accept not only your interpretation but also at least some aspects of your underlying point of view.

Establishing Coincidence.   All interpretations must demonstrate coincidence between the subject and the interpretive term. *Coincidence* in this context can mean equivalence (as in "Television news is the same as entertainment"), substitution ("Although marriage looks like a romantic partnership, it is often a formalization of female dependence"), or revelation ("Behind Jack's warmth and friendliness is a cold and impenetrable shield of defenses"). The challenge of interpretations is in demonstrating these coincidences.

When the interpretive term is concrete, this task is comparatively easy. We recognize such concepts as entertainment or economic dependence; they are verifiable. Once we agree on the meaning of the term, a simple factual argument will demonstrate the applicability of the term to the subject. If we know what economic dependence is, we can detect it in a relationship with little difficulty or little guesswork, provided we have the necessary facts.

But what about detecting a "cold and impenetrable shield of defenses" in an acquaintance? There is no sure way to verify the existence of such a "shield," so how do we argue its existence? Remember in Chapter 7 on causal arguments the principle of a generally accepted link between cause and effect? Just as a cause and its effect must be linked by some acceptable motivational principle that agrees with human experience and observation, so must the interpretation (the less visible reality) relate to the subject (the visible reality) according to an acknowledged principle of experience.

Let's take the case of Jack's misleading warmth and friendliness. Basically we want to demonstrate that his apparent friendliness is an expression of his need to protect himself. First, we'll have to recast the subject or the interpretive term so that the two are shown to be equivalent. We can do this by elaborating on the friendliness: "Jack is as friendly to a grocery clerk as he is to a lifelong friend. He is completely indiscriminate in how he relates to people. This may be good for the grocery clerk, who enjoys Jack's friendly manner, but not so good for the friend, who, in fact, has never gotten to know Jack any better than the grocery clerk has," and so forth. Having established the coincidence or equivalence of this brand of friendliness and defensiveness, you'll want to assure yourself (and your readers, if necessary) that the equivalence you cite agrees with the principles of human behavior that we generally accept: indiscriminate behavior (even friendliness) often expresses its opposite.

Documenting the Interpretation. Interpretations need documentation, or evidence. As well as explaining your subject through an acceptable principle of experience, you'll have to document your claim through examples taken from your subject. Different arguments will provide different kinds of evidence, so it is difficult to generalize about the best kind of evidence. In literature papers, professors are looking for examples from the literary work that support the claim. For example, in a paper arguing, "Behind Othello's seeming self-confidence is a collection of debilitating insecurities," the student would need to cite a number of passages in the play that suggest these insecurities. In the student paper at the end of this chapter, an interpretation of popular media, the writer documents his interpretation of a magazine ad by carefully describing the visual details of the ad.

The Possibility of Multiple Interpretations. Most subjects lend themselves to a number of different interpretations, and these interpretations are not necessarily mutually exclusive. Widely varied and equally convincing interpretations of Shakespeare's *Hamlet* have been written through the centuries; it is a testament to the brilliance of the play that it can accommodate so many different readings. Because of the likelihood of multiple interpretations of any subject, try to resist adopting a dogmatic and inflexible tone in your arguments. You don't need to constantly acknowledge the possibility of other interpretations, nor should you present your own interpretation too tentatively; on the other hand, don't lay out your argument as if it were immutable, inarguable dogma.

ACTIVITIES (8.9)

1. Write a brief interpretation (approximately one page) of a recent event. Your interpretation should include the interpretive term, the kind of coincidence, and the supporting evidence. Then write a second interpretation of the same event, again including all the necessary elements of an interpretation. Give both essays to a classmate to read, and then discuss with him or her which is the most plausible interpretation and why. Some possible events: a recent election, a political scandal, a friend's recent success or failure in some endeavor, an athletic contest.

2. Find in a magazine an interpretation of a film that you have seen recently. Many magazines that offer movie reviews and criticisms can be found on-line: *Boxoffice, Entertainment Weekly, Premiere, Film Journal, FilmMaker: The Magazine of Independent Film, Shock Cinema, MovieMaker,* and *Beatdown: British Film Magazine* are just a few. Be sure to support your argument with concrete references to the film itself. (Give your instructor a copy of the magazine review whether you found the review on-line or in hardcopy.)

SUMMARY

Arguing Evaluations

- All evaluations include a subject to be judged and an evaluative term applied to the subject.

- Before you argue the evaluation, consider whether your readers will recognize and accept your definition of the evaluative term. When their acceptance seems questionable, you'll want to argue your particular definition. Definitions can be argued by appeals to assumed reader values, appeals to authority, identification of effect, and comparison. When evaluating more than one subject against a single set of criteria, you may have to rank the criteria and justify that ranking.

- Applying the syllogistic model to your evaluative claim can help you test its reasonableness.

- Evaluations are made in ethical, aesthetic, or functional terms. *Ethical* evaluations focus on applying the ethical standard (evaluative term) to the subject, or on arguing a stipulative definition of that standard. *Aesthetic* evaluations typically work from standards currently accepted within the field, demonstrating their applicability to your subject. *Functional* evaluations typically work from a number of ranked criteria in terms of which the subject is measured.

- *Interpretations* closely resemble evaluations in structure. They establish coincidence or equivalence between the subject and the interpretive term by linking them through an acknowledged principle of experience.

SAMPLE ETHICAL EVALUATION

The following essay on homosexual marriages, written by college student Douglas Edwards, is an example of an ethical evaluation. (A version of this essay appeared in the September 4, 1997, issue of The University of Akron's student newspaper, *The Buchtelite*.) After carefully reading the argument, collaborate with a small group of your classmates in answering the questions following the essay.

CRITICALLY ANALYZING THE DEFENSE OF MARRIAGE ACT:

A MATTER OF LOVE

One in ten people is gay or lesbian (Marcus 8). When
the United States passed the Defense of Marriage Act, the
government violated the rights of approximately 25 million
Americans ("United States"). Succumbing to myths and
stereotypes about homosexuals, politicians denied gays and
lesbians federal recognition of marriage. However, they
were denying the ultimate expression of commitment. The
Defense of Marriage Act violates the Constitution and
basic human rights and must be overturned.

Introduced by Georgia Representative Bob Barr, the
Defense of Marriage Act gives federal recognition to
heterosexual marriages only and allows a state to refuse
to recognize a homosexual marriage conducted in another
state ("Defense"). However, before we examine this law, we
must address certain popular and erroneous beliefs about
homosexuals. No one chooses homosexuality just as no one
chooses heterosexuality (Marcus 9). Both are natural
tendencies with origins scientists do not understand. As
author Eric Marcus explains:

> Homosexual people come in all shapes and sizes and
> from all walks of life, just like heterosexual
> people do. Some are single, and some are involved
> in long-term, loving relationships with same-sex
> partners . . . Homosexual people are a part of
> every community and every family, which means that
> everyone knows someone who is homosexual. (1-2)

Throughout history, homosexuality and marriage have
been discussed in virtually every culture. The ancient
Greeks saw homosexual love as normal and acceptable.
Although virtually every Christian or Jewish religion
condemns homosexuality and/or homosexual acts, literally
or loosely interpreting the Bible does not support
fundamentalists' arguments. According to Baptist minister
and Plummer Professor of Christian Morals at Harvard,

Peter J. Gomes, Leviticus 18:19-23 and Leviticus 20:10-16
ban homosexual acts *and* tattoos, eating raw meat, wearing
garments made of two types of yarn, planting two different
seeds in the same field, and sexual intercourse during a
woman's menstrual period. The Gospels do not mention
homosexuality, and St. Paul condemned lust and sensuality
in anyone (Marcus 132). Homosexuality and AIDS educator
Ann Northrup asks if marriage's purpose is children,
should sterile couples be denied marriage (17)? Before
the Civil War, blacks could not marry since that made them
" . . . less marketable" (Troy). Psychologist Dr. Evelyn
Hooker demonstrated in the 1950s that heterosexual and
homosexual men were not different psychologically, and the
American Psychiatric Association does not consider
homosexuality a mental illness (Marcus 11-12).

Based on the previously mentioned stereotypes
and false beliefs, the Defense of Marriage Act is
unconstitutional. Bound by the Constitution's "full faith
and credit," states must honor other states' contracts,
including marriage. A federal marriage license does not
exist; the federal government recognizes marriages in all
50 states. Adoption, marriage, and divorce are all under
the states' jurisdiction, and only 34 have dealt with same-
sex marriage ("Defense . . . Fact Sheet"). However, a
recent court case may allow same-sex marriages in Hawaii.
The following is from a <u>Los Angeles Times</u> article:

> In his opinion, Hawaii Circuit Judge Kevin S.C.
> Chang said that the state had failed to prove it
> had a compelling interest in preventing such
> marriages. He issued an injunction to prevent the
> State Department of Health from denying licenses
> solely because applicants are of the same sex,
> basing his reasoning on the equal protection
> clause of the state constitution ("Hawaii . . .").
> Since the federal government will not recognize
> these marriages, a complicated state and federal
> tax network will result causing numerous problems.

> If a married couple moved to another state, their
> marriage may suddenly not exist ("Defense . . .
> Fact Sheet").

Obviously, gays want federal recognition of their
marriages for dignity and respect. However, there are many
financial benefits. Married couples in most states have
legal rights to be on their spouses' insurance and pension
plans, to receive special tax exemptions, to receive
Social Security benefits, and to be the legal "next
of kin." There have been many stories in which gays'
long-term partners could not visit their lovers in the
hospital, make decisions regarding medical care, or become
legal guardians of incapacitated loved ones since the
government did not recognize their relationships (Marcus
83). This is not to suggest that gays are motivated
by financial gains, but these are practical issues that
heterosexuals take for granted. Fortunately, companies
such as IBM, Microsoft, American Express, and Walt Disney
grant benefits to their gay employees' partners, and
other corporations are following their lead (Jones).
These businesses realize that sexual orientation is not
connected with employee performance. Some claim that
gays should not be given special privileges. However,
if heterosexuals can marry but gays cannot, then
heterosexuals are receiving special privileges.

Some politicians suggest that homosexual marriage is
a pressing national priority, but many Americans disagree.
In a Mellman Group poll, only 13% said passing the Defense
of Marriage act was an "important priority"; 73% believe
the nation faced more pressing issues. 37% of Americans
support the law, and only 27% of the public believes gay
marriages threaten families ("Defense . . . Poll"). In a
nation faced with mounting crime and an out-of-control
budget, certainly gay marriages—acts of love—do not
deserve national scrutiny. In a <u>Los Angeles Times</u> article
describing the Hawaiian court decision allowing same-sex
marriages, the author said, "Conservative opponents

condemned the opinion as an outrageous example of a court thumbing its nose at public opinion" ("Hawaii"). However, as mentioned earlier, America does not consider this to be an important issue, and popular opinion is not always right. Slavery was popular in the South, but the public opinion certainly was not correct.

National Gay and Lesbian Task Force Executive Director Melinda Paras says, "While they would have us believe that they seek to 'preserve legalized, traditional marriage,' the truth is that they seek to impose their own narrow agenda on every American by playing on people's real fears and concerns about the changing American family" ("NGLTF"). It is understandable that many people fear gays and they hope this legislation will force them to "not choose this lifestyle"; negative stereotypes instigate prejudice. However, gays do not choose their attractions; someone cannot make a homosexual straight just as a person cannot make a heterosexual gay (Marcus 13). People cannot understand what they do not know; since one out of every 10 people is gay, we all know a gay person, whether we realize it or not. Does Congress want gay people to marry into heterosexual relationships that eventually result in divorces, displaced children, and declining family values? Biracial marriage was illegal in some areas of the United States until a 1967 Supreme Court ruling (Marcus 85), but biracial marriage certainly was not evil or sinful.

Executive Director Barry Wick of the South Dakota Gay, Lesbian, and Bisexual Federation, called the Defense of Marriage Act "patently offensive to anyone who remembers the miscegenation laws of the South that banned inter-racial marriage" (Dunlap). When two gay people commit to each other, it is a *natural* expression of their love as it is when African Americans love white Americans. Denying gays marriage will not force them into isolation; it invigorates their civil rights movement. America's family values need serious examination since heterosexuals can marry and divorce without limitation, yet committed, gay couples cannot receive federal recognition.

The Constitution guarantees life, liberty, and the pursuit of happiness with no exceptions for homosexuals. By banning federal recognition of gay marriages, the U.S. government demonstrated that it focuses on fiction, not fact. Love will prevail; homosexuals will continue to share their lives together. However, heterosexual love should not be given a higher status; every couple deserves the right to solidify their relationship with marriage.

WORKS CITED

"Defense of Marriage Act." n. pag. Online. Internet. 25 Nov. 1996.

   <http://www.hrc.org/issues/leg/doma/billtext.html>.

"Defense of Marriage Act—Fact Sheet." n. pag. Online. Internet. 25 Nov. 1996.

   <http://www.hrc.org/issues/leg/doma/factsheet.html>.

"Defense of Marriage Act—Poll." n. pag. Online. Internet. 25 Nov. 1996.

   HTTP://www.hrc.org/issues/leg/doma/polling.html.

Dunlap, David W. "Some States Trying to Stop Gay Marriages Before They Start." The New York Times. (14 March, 95) n. pag. Online. Internet. 3 Dec. 1996.

   <http://www.cs.cmu.edu/afs/cs.cmu.edu/user/scotts/ domesticpartners/NYTimes-Same-sex-couples.txt>.

"Hawaii Judge ends ban on gay marriages." Los Angeles Times. Rpt. in The Plain Dealer. 4 Dec. 1996: 1A, 28A.

Jones, Del. "IBM gives gay/lesbian partners health benefits." USA Today. 20 Sept. 1996: 10A.

Marcus, Eric. "Is It A Choice?" San Francisco: Harper Collins, 1993.

"NGLTF Condemns Federal Anti-Marriage Legislation." National Gay and Lesbian Task Force. n. pag. Online. Internet. 25 Nov. 1996.

<http://www.ngltf.org/news/release.cfm?releaseID=205>.

Troy, David C. "Baltimore & the Fifteenth Amendment, May
    19, 1870." <u>Celebrating Rights and Responsibilities</u>.
    n. pag. Online. Internet. 3 Dec. 1996. Available
    <http://www.toad.net/~dave/project/>.

"United States." <u>Microsoft Encarta</u> n. pag. CD-ROM. 1995

DISCUSSION QUESTIONS

1. What are the subject and evaluative term of Doug's argument?
2. Why do you think he provides a definition of the evaluative term?
3. Through what methods does Doug support his evaluation? Are these effective? Why or why not?
4. Identify and discuss the placement of the argument's claim.

SAMPLE INTERPRETATION

The following is an essay by first-year student Kevin Maloney on "Reading Popular Culture." Read it through carefully, then answer the questions that follow the essay. Compare your answers with those of your classmates.

READING POPULAR CULTURE

Hidden within the productions of popular culture are quiet endorsements of specific values or attitudes. Such attitudes are projected not only in print, but in music, advertisements, and television programs. Just as it is important to be able to read the written word, it is also vital to know how to read these other forms of expression. Being unable to recognize the sometimes hidden messages of these forms of expression is like being in a foreign country where you don't speak the language. In both cases, you can easily fall prey to individuals eager to take advantage of your ignorance, to manipulate you into doing what they want you to do.

Often, the skill of discovering the values or attitudes promoted in popular culture involves nothing more than stepping back and seeing "the big picture," recognizing what is really pretty obvious. Take, for example, the popular sitcom *Seinfeld*. It is possible to

watch and enjoy this show week after week without
realizing how it is dominated by sexually promiscuous
behavior. On a recent episode, Jerry Seinfeld pursued a
female gymnast. His goal was to see if sex with a gymnast
was more exciting and varied than with someone less
physically flexible. Within a week's time, he was sleeping
with the gymnast and joking about their sexual encounters.
By the end of the show, he had broken up with her, merely
because the sex wasn't really all that different.

Elaine, another character on the program, seems to
have new sexual partners almost every episode. Since she
can always find some very superficial reason to break up
with them—she doesn't like one guy's name, another gets a
haircut—none of these relationships lasts. But in show
after show, she persists in her search for "the one."

None of the characters in the show disapprove of
Jerry's and Elaine's promiscuity. In fact, their behavior
is often the source of delight and envy for their friends,
some of whom, like George, try to emulate it. I have
watched the show regularly for at least three years, and I
realize that I have never seen sex presented as anything
other than a joke. The program never explicitly says that
viewers should lead a promiscuous life, but that lifestyle
is repeated again and again. And this is one way that
cultural values are constructed and instilled—through
repeated themes and behavior in television programming
(George and Trimbur 228). Whenever a behavior—in the case
of Seinfeld, sexual promiscuity—is repeated, the viewer is
asked to accept it as a norm.

Television is not the only form of popular culture
that promotes promiscuity as a norm. Magazine advertising
does the same. As Jean Kilbourne says, these ads "sell a
great deal more than products" (152).

Take the example of an ad from a recent computer
magazine. A scantily clad woman stands in the middle of
the page, her perfect body more prominent than anything
else in the ad. She is wearing spotted, tight-fitting

pants; her skin-tight T-shirt bares most of her abdomen; her shirt is covered by suggestive fishnet mesh; and a navel ring adorns her trim stomach. Apparently the waitress in this diner, she wears a pair of in-line skates and holds a tray. Everything about this woman suggests available sexuality.

And why is this ad set in a diner with a waitress as its focal point? The answers to these questions don't have much to do with computers, but they do have a lot to do with sex. As a waitress, the woman's job is to bring her customers what they want, and her dress suggests that this means anything. The table closest to the camera has partially empty cups sitting on it; clearly other customers have dined here before. And if they left something in their cups, they must have left satisfied— another instance of the advertisement's sexual insinuations. The text beneath the photograph tells us "Monday's Chef's Special" is "the obvious choice." What this woman can bring you is obviously what you want. And the sexual innuendoes go on and on.

Popular music also frequently contains implicit endorsements of sexual promiscuity. The words are often camouflaged by a good beat, a nice voice, and interesting harmonies, but their message is there.

Pop singer Bruce Springsteen has a song called "Secret Garden." The title suggests something pure and natural, but take a look at the lyrics: "She'll let you in her house if you come knocking late at night. She'll let you in her mouth if the words you say are right." Apparently these lyrics are about a woman who will engage in oral sex if the man sweet-talks her. The next line is "If you pay the price she'll let you deep inside." Again, sex is the reward for saying the right words to a woman. Later in the song, we hear "She'll let you into the parts of herself that'll bring you down." What is remarkable about these lyrics is how clearly they refer to promiscuous sex; you don't have to be a Houdini of interpretation to understand their meaning.

Some might say that such sexually promiscuous TV characters, sexually suggestive computer ads, and sexually symbolic song lyrics may represent promiscuous behavior, but they don't necessarily promote it. Yet the more behaviors and images are repeated in popular culture, the more "normal" they begin to seem. If we don't stop to recognize and evaluate these repeated behaviors and images, we will find ourselves influenced by their sheer volume. Without even realizing it, we may feel it's all right to repeat them in our own lives. So let's learn the language of cultural manipulation so we can avoid being its victim.

WORKS CITED

George, Dianna, and John Trimbur, Eds. "Introduction to
    Television Culture." Reading Culture: Contexts for
    Critical Reading and Writing. New York: Harper, 1995.
    228-29.

Kilbourne, Jean. "Beauty...and the Beast of Advertising."
    Reading Culture: Contexts for Critical Reading and
    Writing. Ed. Dianna George and John Trimbur. New
    York: Harper, 1995. 152-54.

Springsteen, Bruce. "Secret Garden" Bruce Springsteen:
    Greatest Hits. Recording. Columbia, 1995.

DISCUSSION QUESTIONS

1. What is Kevin interpreting in this essay, and what is his interpretive term?
2. Do you agree with Kevin's decision about providing an explicit definition of the interpretive term?
3. Kevin does not address the possibility that the *Seinfeld* show is satirical, that it presents certain shallow and irresponsible behaviors to criticize or poke fun at them. With a group of your classmates who know the show, consider this possibility and how it would affect Kevin's argument.
4. Discuss the evidence offered as support of the claim. Is it relevant and sufficient? Are you convinced by the argument?

SUGGESTIONS FOR WRITING (8.10)

1. Write a two- to three-page evaluation of a course you have taken or are taking in college. Your evaluation will be primarily a functional evaluation, one of the crucial questions being whether the course actually achieves its intended goals.

2. Write a three- to four-page argument for or against a subject that requires evaluation—i.e., sexual harassment policies, ethnicity issues, Distance Learning, or even euthanasia—based on your reading of the sample student paper at the end of the section on evaluation. Have you established a clear definition? What about the other supporting arguments? Are there other arguments for the stand you have taken or do you have what you believe are more powerful arguments against it?

3. Write a combination interpretation and evaluation (three to four pages) of a recent artistic or entertainment event you enjoyed: a film, play, novel, concert, or something similar. Your evaluation will be primarily aesthetic, but it may be ethical as well.

ILLUSTRATIVE ARGUMENTS IN PART II: ARGUING EVALUATIONS

9

Arguing
Recommendations

At one time or another, most of us—whether student, professional, or concerned citizen—will have to argue a *recommendation* (sometimes called a *proposal*). A recommendation is a written request for change of some sort: cable TV in the dorms, paternity leave in a company, or a new major in a university. Recommendations vary in format from a simple one-page letter to an elaborate minivolume with strictly prescribed components. But despite the many variations in format, all recommendations argue for change.

Recommendations are the hybrids of argument, drawing on the principles and practices of factual, causal, and evaluative arguments. So, for the most part, writing a successful recommendation is a question of applying what you have already learned about the different kinds of argument and their support.

All recommendations establish a current situation (how things are now) and a probable future situation (how they would be if the change were instituted). In other words, recommendations rely on arguments of fact and arguments of effect. How central either type of argument is to your recommendation will depend on the emphasis demanded by the particular situation.

If you focus on the current situation, which usually means showing that things have gotten so bad that change must be considered, much of your argument will be factual. Let's say you want to impress the authorities with the inadequacy of parking facilities at your commuter campus. You figure it's up to them to come up with the answer to the problem, but you know they won't do it without being convinced that a serious problem *does* exist. In this case, your recommendation would begin with a factual argument that establishes exactly what the current situation is.

But if you are the contractor asked to submit a proposal for new parking lots, your focus will be on the future effects of your particular plan and predicting its ability to solve the current problem. In this case, the recommendation will be largely causal, establishing the probable effects of the implemented recommendation.

Regardless of their emphases, all recommendations also make evaluative arguments; they include a judgment of the current situation (the parking situation is inadequate or unfair) and/or an evaluation of the proposed change (parking will be more available, more convenient, etc.).

AUDIENCE NEEDS AND VALUES

By now you've learned how important it is when making any kind of argument to know as much about your audience as possible. Nowhere is this knowledge more critical than in writing recommendations. Most recommendations asks readers to *do* something, not merely to give their armchair agreement to a claim. Human nature being what it is, people are more likely to take action if there is a possibility that the action will benefit them in some way. Thus, a powerful way to support any recommendation is to appeal to the needs, values, and desires that you have identified in your readers. Making such an appeal means paying particular attention to the early stage of audience consideration: who is your audience? what are their needs and values likely to be regarding your claim? can you responsibly appeal to these in your recommendation? Luckily, it is usually fairly easy to answer these questions when you're preparing a recommendation, because in most cases, you're addressing a very specific audience (often a single individual).

For example, suppose your favorite professor is denied tenure, and you and a number of other students write a letter to the dean arguing for a reconsideration of the decision. What kinds of appeals would most likely move the dean? To answer the question, you have to know what the dean's priorities and responsibilities are, which, in fact, you're never thought about. In speaking with faculty members, you learn that your dean is determined to enhance the academic reputation of the college as a way of attracting and retaining good students. Knowing this, you're not going to get far arguing that Professor Morris be granted tenure because he's a good shortstop on the faculty-student softball team or an easy grader. You'll need to find a way to demonstrate just how valuable Professor Morris is to students in the *classroom,* perhaps including testimonials from students.

Though you'll always need to be aware of the needs and values of your readers, you will rarely identify them explicitly in the recommendation. In the case of Professor Morris's tenure, you will identify the positive effects on students of granting him tenure, but you probably won't need to identify which of the dean's needs or priorities will be addressed by this action. Provided your assumption about these priorities is correct, you can trust her to recognize that the change you are proposing would satisfy them.

When Your Values Differ from Assumed Reader Values

Recommendations actually work with two sets of values: the reader's *and* the writer's. While a successful recommendation must appeal to the appropriate reader values, it will originate in values held by the writer. Indeed, most recommendations are born in the writer's experience of *dissonance,* that sense of mismatch between one's values and a current situation (see Chapter 2).

Often the values that move you to recommend a certain change will be the same as those that will move your reader to accept your recommendation. But sometimes writer and reader values do not coincide. Usually, as long as the two values or sets of values are somehow related and not directly opposed, their lack of coincidence will not weaken your recommendation. But you do need to be aware of the difference between them.

Suppose you are a commuter student who takes the city bus to get to campus each day. This term, you have an 8 A.M. class, the early bus from your stop has been overcrowded and unreliable, and you have been late to class a number of times. You decide to write a letter to the local transit authority recommending improvements in bus service. Your letter derives from your own experience of dissonance—your frustration at not making it to class on time—and it seeks to satisfy your rights to good service as a paying customer (your needs and values).

But you realize that these values are not necessarily going to move your audience—the transit authority—to make the necessary improvements to the service. The manager of customer service may not care much about your rights as a paying customer, but he does care about the value of *customer satisfaction*. No business, even one that holds a virtual monopoly, as most transit authorities do, can afford to ignore the importance of customer satisfaction.

In this example, the values of customer rights and customer satisfaction are not identical, but they can comfortably coexist in the recommendation because they are not in conflict, and they are *causally* connected: if your rights are being served, you will be satisfied.

Your letter to the transit authority might look like this:

Mr. Brian Rose
Manager, Customer Service
Metro Transit Authority
Collegetown, USA

Dear Mr. Rose:

I am writing to complain about the quality of the morning bus service on Bus 15, which runs from Main and Winton to the community college. By the time the bus scheduled to stop at 7:21 A.M. gets to the stop at Main and Winton, it is usually late (in October, by an average of 15 minutes) and always overcrowded, with standing room only. Two days in October (the ninth and the fifteenth) the bus was so crowded that some people could not get on at all. I have tried to take the 7:04 bus, but the situation is essentially the same, and I cannot take a later bus because I have an 8:00 A.M. class at the college.

I and a number of others who rely on bus service are very unhappy. We are being cheated of the service we deserve, given the high fares we pay, and we would like some action taken to improve the situation. I am enclosing with this letter a petition signed by eight other students who depend on Bus 15 to get them to campus.

Now that you are aware of this problem, I hope you will take action to correct it. I look forward to hearing from you about what that action might be.

Very truly yours,

Patrick Booth

This letter has a good chance of influencing its reader because the values from which it is written and the values to which it appeals are related and compatible. In cases where there is clear conflict between your values and your readers', you must search for other values to appeal to. You couldn't convince an audience of cigarette smokers that cigarette sales should be restricted because smoking is, as you believe, a stinking, filthy habit. But you might make some headway with an argument citing the risks of secondary smoke to loved ones—a risk that might concern even the most committed of smokers.

ACTIVITIES (9.1)

1. In each of the following cases, the value cited to win the audience's acceptance of the recommendation is not appropriate. With a small group of your classmates, identify alternative values that are more appropriate. Then discuss your list with the entire class.
   Sample recommendation: A longer school year for elementary and secondary students
   Audience: Elementary and secondary teachers
   Inappropriate value: More work from teachers
   Alternative value: A greater opportunity to ensure students' mastery of skills
   a. **Recommendation:** Earlier closing of a college cafeteria
      Audience: College students
      Inappropriate value: Shorter hours and fewer headaches for cafeteria staff
   b. **Recommendation:** A new federal tax on gasoline
      Audience: Truck drivers
      Inappropriate value: Reduced reliance on trucks for transporting goods
   c. **Recommendation:** A curfew for everybody under the age of 16
      Audience: Those under 16
      Inappropriate value: Those under 16 can't be trusted
   d. **Recommendation:** A law requiring motorcyclists to wear helmets
      Audience: Motorcyclists
      Inappropriate value: Reduced claims against insurance companies and therefore increased profits for insurance companies
   e. **Recommendation:** A shorter work week
      Audience: Employers
      Inappropriate value: More leisure time for employees
2. With the same small group of classmates, identify values that would be shared by the following pairs, or that would be compatible.
   Example: Republicans and Democrats
   Common value: Concern for the national interest—the country as a whole
   a. Planners of a new highway; homeowners whose property is in the path of the new highway
   b. Managers of a company; workers on strike against that company

c. Parents planning to take away a child's allowance as punishment for bad behavior; the child in question
d. Planners of a large rock concert; neighborhood groups opposed to the concert because of noise
e. Proponents of legislation restricting the use of handguns; opponents of this legislation

RECOMMENDATIONS EMPHASIZING THE PRESENT

Some recommendations, like Patrick Booth's letter to the transit authority, concentrate on problems in a current situation, leaving a detailed proposal for change to another argument. The goal of such arguments is to demonstrate more *that* something needs to be done than *what* exactly that something is.

To accept this kind of recommendation, your readers need an accurate and, usually, detailed picture of the current situation. They must grasp the situation as it is before they can agree or disagree with your evaluation of it. Recommendations emphasizing the present usually open with a factual argument.

Establishing the Current Situation

Patrick's letter to the transit authority does a good job establishing the current situation through facts and figures that Patrick collected: the average tardiness of the bus, the number of times the bus had to leave customers behind, and so on. Establishing these details is critical to the recommendation for a couple of reasons. First, readers are likely to take exact figures more seriously than irate vagueness. Exaggerations like "Huge numbers of people are regularly prevented from riding the 7:21 bus" are far less effective than exact figures.

Second, misrepresenting the facts, whether intentionally to strengthen your case or negligently through sloppy research, will be detected. The recipient of any recommendation is going to investigate the situation before taking action, and if the results of that investigation differ substantially from your figures, your recommendation will have reached a dead end.

Evaluating the Current Situation

All recommendations contain some evaluative elements. In recommendations emphasizing the present, the subject of the evaluation is the current situation. If you have a good understanding of your audience and their needs and values, you probably won't need to write a full-blown evaluation complete with a defined evaluative term. The transit authority letter, for example, doesn't require an explicit judgment of the situation presented. Any reader, whether an official of the transit authority or an occasional passenger, will recognize that the conditions described are undesirable. You could point to this fact for rhetorical emphasis, but the judgment is implicit within the factual presentation.

Sometimes your recommendation will be addressed to readers who may not immediately recognize the problems in the current situation. In these cases, you'd be wise to identify *what* is wrong by providing a clear and limited evaluative term. For example, a professor's schedule of assignments on a syllabus is unfair to students or hopelessly unrealistic. You can then proceed to match the subject (the syllabus) with the evaluative term according to the suggestions in Chapter 8, remembering the importance of considering audience needs and values.

Applying the Toulmin Model

The Toulmin logical model is especially useful when you're composing a recommendation. Placing your claim and support in the Toulmin paradigm (see Chapter 5) will help you detect any weaknesses of reasoning or wording in your argument and will suggest the secondary claims you'll need to support the central claim. Assume that an outside consultant, hired to analyze the employee benefits package of Quick-Stop Copy (the current situation), recommends that the company provide a benefits package more competitive with those of comparable companies (central claim). The consultant's recommendation would fit into the Toulmin model as follows:

Remember that in the Toulmin model, the warrant is equivalent to the major premise in a syllogism; it is the general statement about a class that enables the data (or the minor premise in a syllogism) to justify the claim (or conclusion in a syllogism). As noted in Chapter 5, sometimes both data and warrant need further support. Indeed, one of the virtues of the Toulmin system is that once you have stated your argument in its terms, you can recognize what further support (backing) your argument will need. In this example, you realize that the argument will need a breakdown of facts and figures to back the data (i.e., how the Quick-Stop package actually compares with those of other companies). And you should recognize as well that the warrant will need further backing if it is not self-evident to the reader that companies should have competitive benefits packages. Depending on the reader's point of view, the consultant may want to strengthen the warrant by supporting it with a secondary argument of effect—that is, demonstrating the negative results of the inferior benefits package to employees and to the company.

ACTIVITIES (9.2)

1. For two of the following current situations, what kind of facts would be necessary to convince readers that some change is necessary? Make a list of all the kinds of factual evidence you can think of.
   a. Traffic at an intersection
   b. Someone's physical appearance
   c. A friend's choice of career
   d. A company's health care benefits
   e. The local court system
2. Using the material you developed for Activity 1, create two claims of recommendation. Then state your argument in terms of the Toulmin model, indicating what additional support or backing is necessary.

RECOMMENDATIONS EMPHASIZING THE FUTURE

When your recommendation emphasizes the probable future effects of its proposed changes, you'll have to move beyond the current problems and the general claim that something must be done; you'll also have to identify, reasonably and convincingly, *what* that something is. A recommendation emphasizing the future will be effective if it can demonstrate (1) that your proposal is likely to produce desirable effects and (2) that the proposal is feasible.

Presenting the Recommendation

The recommendation itself—the proposed plan for change—must be crystal clear. Obviously, readers can't agree with a plan they don't understand. Some situations will call for a rather general recommendation, leaving the details to others, whereas in other cases, particularly when you have some responsibility for implementing the plan, a detailed recommendation will be necessary.

Kate Quill is a second-year student at Carlson College, a small liberal arts college in Maine. Carlson has operated on a trimester calendar for years, with three ten-week terms per academic year. It is common knowledge at Carlson that many students are unhappy with the trimester system: they feel rushed and overworked by the short terms. Kate and a number of her friends think it's time to do something about this dissatisfaction, so they decide to write a letter to the college administration recommending that a committee of faculty and students look at alternatives to the trimester calendar. The letter they write, which follows, is an example of a *general* recommendation emphasizing the future.

Dr. Dale Hill
President, Carlson College
Carlson, Maine

Dear Dr. Hill:

It should be no surprise to you that students feel considerable dissatisfaction with the trimester calendar used at Carlson. Faculty report that students have complained about the excessively fast pace of courses for years. Given this long history of dissatisfaction, we feel it is time for a formal examination of alternative calendars. Such an analysis should determine once and for all whether our current trimester calendar is the best system for Carlson.

We recommend that you put together a calendar committee consisting of students, faculty, and administration to conduct such an examination. This group could research the calendars used by comparable institutions, determining the advantages and disadvantages of each case. If the committee concludes that our current system is the best, we believe that the current level of student dissatisfaction would be reduced. Similarly, if a different calendar more suitable to Carlson were discovered and implemented, students would be much happier.

Any of the students signing this letter would be eager to serve on such a committee. We appreciate your time in considering this proposal.

Very truly yours,

Kate Quill and Carlson Students

Let's assume that President Hill has been hearing complaints about the trimesters for years and decides, on reading this letter, to take its recommendation seriously. After consulting with the deans and vice presidents, the president decides to constitute a "blue ribbon" committee to investigate the calendar issue. While Kate's recommendation was appropriately general (it's not a student's job to dictate details to a college president), the review process President Hill recommends to the chairperson of the Calendar Committee must be detailed and specific. This letter might read as follows:

Professor Rachel Eisenberg
Chair, Calendar Committee
Department of English
Carlson College

Dear Rachel:

Thank you for agreeing to serve as chair of the Calendar Committee. As you know, the calendar issue is extremely controversial; it is my hope that under your competent leadership the committee will put to rest once and for all the question of what calendar is the most appropriate for Carlson.

It is not my intention to direct the committee's work, but I hope you will allow a few suggestions about process and objectives:

- It will be critical to your deliberations to identify and verify the most common student complaints about our trimester system and the most common faculty complaints. This information can be obtained through survey instruments and through individual or group interviews.
- When exploring the alternative calendars currently used by other colleges, you should try to select schools whose size and mission are closely comparable to Carlson's.
- Please do not forget to factor in the budgetary implications of the various alternatives. While our primary concern should be with the quality of the education we deliver, an extremely costly calendar implementation could actually jeopardize our educational quality.
- While the final action taken on the basis of your report will be determined by the Carlson Board of Trustees, it would be helpful if the report included a ranking of the alternative calendars.
- The format and style of the final report I leave up to the committee, but bear in mind that it will be distributed to a number of different campus groups, so brevity and readability will be important.

Again, I thank you for agreeing to take on this challenging and important task. If there is any way that my office can help the work of the committee, don't hesitate to let me know.

Very truly yours,

Dale Hill

President

The preceding examples illustrate only two possibilities; recommendations can be more or less detailed than the second example. Generally, the more concrete your recommendation, the more effective it will be, provided your plan reflects a sound understanding of the operations of the group that will implement it. But there are times when a great deal of detail is inappropriate. Most editorials make recommendations without much detail; most politicians give few details in their speeches to general audiences. In deciding how much detail to include, be sure to consider your audience's capacity for and interest in the details, as well as their proposed role in carrying out the recommendation.

ACTIVITIES (9.3)

1. The following sample recommendations are extremely general. The writers have given no indication of how they expect their plans to be implemented. For each, provide at least three specific recommendations that will help an audience understand how the plans can be carried out. If you like, instead of working with the claims provided, create your own general recommendations (the kind that might come out of a conversation with friends), and then provide more specific recommendations for each.
   Example: We need a city with cleaner air.
   Specific recommendations: (1) Encouragement of "park-and-ride" lots for commuters to decrease automobile traffic, (2) tighter inspection standards for automobiles' exhaust emission systems, and (3) restrictions on the burning of leaves and trash.
   After you have made this list of recommendations, write a short essay (250–500 words) briefly explaining each of the recommendations and how they relate to the general recommendation.
   a. Our college needs more school spirit.
   b. Americans need to be more tolerant of racial and ethnic diversity.
   c. Adolescents must be made more aware of the dangers of alcohol.
   d. American industry needs to put more emphasis on the quality of its products.
   e. Students and professors must learn to see each other as human beings.

2. In your student or local newspaper, find an example of a recommendation that you think is good, but that is too general to be implemented. Write a letter to the editor suggesting specific ways that the recommendation might be developed further.

Arguing the Effects of Your Recommendation

Recommendations with future emphasis always identify and evaluate the probable effects of the proposed plan. Identifying probable effects will take the form of an *argument of effect* and will follow the steps presented in Chapter 7. This part of your recommendation will be strong if you can show that the proposed changes (the causes) are related to the results you predict (the effects) through established causal principles.

In the example of the Carlson College calendar, the Calendar Committee might predict the following short causal chain: converting to a semester calendar (cause) will give students more classroom contact with their faculty (first effect), which in turn is likely to make students feel more satisfied with their college experience (second effect). Readers would be likely to accept the first causal link: a semester course meets something like 45 hours per term, whereas a trimester course meets approximately 30 hours per term. Unless faculty use the additional time showing films and bringing in guest lecturers, the increase in hours will result in increased contact with faculty.

To support the second link in the chain, the committee needs to identify a linking behavioral principle. In this case, the principle linking increased student-faculty contact and student satisfaction has to be spelled out explicitly. That principle might be stated as follows: young people go to college to receive an education and to become adults; faculty not only provide that education but offer a new brand of adult relationship based on mature, intellectual foundations. Thus, substantial contact with faculty will meet a primary objective of many students. The committee report might also want to support this second effect in the chain by citing existing higher education studies that have discovered this connection between student-faculty contact and student satisfaction.

ACTIVITIES (9.4)

With a small group of your classmates, discuss the likelihood of the projected results of the following three recommendations. Have one student write up the reasons for your judgment of each. Submit this write-up to your instructor.

1. **Recommendation:** Increase the price of tickets to films at the college theater from $2.00 to $2.50.
   Projected results: No significant decline in attendance; more revenue from tickets to allow the theater to rent better films, which will eventually lead to higher attendance.

2. **Recommendation:** Allow students to take one course pass-fail.
   Projected results: Students will feel under less pressure about grades and more willing to take tough courses; the students will work just as hard in the courses they take pass-fail as they would have if they had taken the course for a regular grade.

3. **Recommendation:** Increase school taxes to subsidize new athletic facilities at the high school.
   Projected results: Greater community involvement in and identification with high school athletic teams; improvement in high school image; increased student enrollment.

Judging Effects in Terms of Assumed Needs and Values

In developing your recommendation, you will probably identify several probable effects, only some of which will meet the needs and values of your readers. Suppose you support your recommendation to faculty of a pass-fail grading option by predicting the effect of students' doing less work in their courses. Such an effect isn't likely to appeal to faculty values. This does not mean that you should deny the effect if it seems probable, but at the same time, there is no reason to emphasize it.

You may not always have to evaluate the probable effects explicitly nor identify the needs and values that those effects will satisfy. But at a minimum, you must be aware of the values that the probable effects of your implemented recommendation will satisfy.

When Some Effects Are Undesirable.   Few recommendations can promise exclusively positive results. But as long as the desirable effects outweigh the undesirable ones, your recommendation is worth making. When you know that along with the positive effects there may be some less desirable repercussions, you should acknowledge them in your argument. Provided you can demonstrate that the negative effects are less significant than the positive ones, you will not weaken your argument by mentioning them. In fact, an argument that acknowledges and measures its own weaknesses is usually more effective than one that fails to admit what any intelligent reader will recognize.

If you are on a committee recommending the building of a new expressway, you should admit that the building of the new expressway, whatever its ultimate advantages, will cause inconveniences. This is a more effective and responsible approach than ignoring altogether the obvious negative consequences of your recommendation. You will enhance your credibility by admitting what many people will know or suspect anyway.

Implementation.   To be successful, your recommendation must pass one further test: it must be feasible. Even the most brilliant recommendation will be rejected if its implementation is fraught with difficulties. While a detailed implementation plan is not required of all recommendations, some indication of the feasibility of your plan will strengthen your argument. At the least, you must provide a general indication that the recommendation *is* feasible. There is no point in advancing a recommendation that your audience will see as totally impractical, regardless of how desirable the results might be. Sometimes, your audience will expect a very detailed implementation plan, including a list of activities and the name of the person responsible for each activity, the dates for beginning and completing each activity, and the likely costs of each activity.

A crucial element of a general or detailed implementation plan is an analysis of costs. Many great ideas born in the heat of inspiration have failed to materialize because of a lack of cold cash; programs that many judge worthwhile (such as human exploration of Mars) have been delayed because of their expense. Whenever you present a proposal and outline its benefits, you also need to project its costs as accurately as you can. Remember that these costs often include not only the expense of constructing a new building or starting a new program but also the continuing costs once the proposal is a reality. Your community may need a new and larger airport, or a new bus service for the elderly, or new day care facilities, but once these are established, there may be additional costs of keeping the services going from day to day. The new and larger airport, for example, may need more employees to maintain it and may cost more to heat and cool than the old one did. These continuing expenses are easy to overlook or to minimize; the great temptation in making a recommendation that you believe in strongly is to overstate the benefits and understate the costs.

You need to fight this temptation, remembering that some of your readers will be expecting just such a miscalculation.

People tend to accept recommendations that can be implemented within existing systems more readily than those requiring radical changes. Most of us are reluctant to make major changes on the strength of what *might* happen, however convincingly the probabilities are argued. Other things being equal, people usually prefer the least disruptive course of action.

On the other hand, sometimes existing structures need to be shaken up and disruptive measures taken. Much of our world, including the very existence of this country, is a result of radical changes. You should at least consider whether a drastic change will not be more effective ultimately and easier to implement than a piecemeal one. Sometimes piecemeal recommendations are like putting money into an old car that is going to break down anyway, or like eighteenth-century Americans hoping King George III and the British government would see the error of their ways. One test here, though a difficult one, is whether the piecemeal changes will improve the situation enough to justify the time and cost of the changes: the old car may not be worth keeping; on balance, it was easier to leave King George than to reform him.

Applying the Toulmin Model

The Toulmin model will help you evaluate the reasonableness and completeness of recommendations emphasizing the future. Applying the Toulmin format to the Carlson College example, we get a look at what kinds of secondary arguments the recommendation calls for.

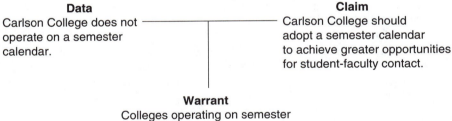

Data
Carlson College does not operate on a semester calendar.

Claim
Carlson College should adopt a semester calendar to achieve greater opportunities for student-faculty contact.

Warrant
Colleges operating on semester calendars provide the most opportunities for student-faculty contact.

Laying the recommendation out this way shows us what additional support the argument will need. The data in this case will need minimal backing (all the readers will accept it as true), but the warrant is clearly not self-evident and thus calls for backing. Depending on your assessment of the readers' needs, that backing may follow at least two directions. On the one hand, you'll probably want to support the generalization with a secondary factual argument that compares the number of student-faculty contact hours in semester and trimester systems: "Students at Rusk College, which operates on a semester system, meet in class with their course faculty four hours per week for fourteen weeks, as opposed to Carlson's three hours per week for ten weeks."

A second issue raised by the warrant is the unstated assumption that student-faculty contact is a good thing. If you think your readers need to be convinced of this assumption, then you'll want to provide a secondary evaluative and/or causal argument demonstrating the positive elements and results of student-faculty contact. Here, you can resort to anecdotal evidence, but your best bet is to cite some of those higher education studies demonstrating the merits of this contact.

ACTIVITIES (9.5)

1. The following are recommendations that many believe are good ideas. For at least two of these claims, make a list of possible drawbacks to the recommendation that the writer would need to admit. Compare your list with those of some of your classmates. If you like, you may come up with your own recommendations—changes you would like to see occur—and consider the possible drawbacks.
   a. Sending astronauts to explore Mars
   b. Passing elementary and secondary students from one grade to another only after they have passed strict competency tests
   c. Prohibiting smoking in all public facilities
   d. Increasing the school year by an average of one month for all elementary and secondary schoolchildren
   e. Abolishing fraternities and sororities on your campus

2. Prepare an implementation plan for some change you would like to make in your own life, such as studying harder, learning a new sport or hobby, or exploring a possible career. Your implementation plan should include the sequence of activities you will undertake, the dates you plan to begin and end each activity, and the costs, if any, of the project. See the recommendation report "A Proposal for a Computer Facility in Marshall Dormitory" at the end of this chapter for a sample implementation plan.

3. Derive a claim of recommendation from three issues that you feel strongly about. Then place each claim within the Toulmin model, providing data and warrant. For each claim, where will you need additional backing? On the basis of your answer to this question, prepare an outline of a four- to five-page paper that would argue this recommendation.
   Example: Our staggering divorce rate suggests that a course in marriage and relationships should be mandatory for all high school students.

RECOMMENDATIONS THAT CONSIDER PRESENT AND FUTURE

The two types of recommendations we have discussed rarely occur in pure form; many recommendations contain some discussion of both the current situation and the future possibilities. Obviously, such recommendations combine the strategies discussed in this chapter: they present and evaluate the current situation, lay out the recommendation, and finally identify and evaluate the probable results of the recommendation. Because these arguments consider what currently exists and what could exist, they provide the groundwork for a useful comparative evaluation. After you have examined both the present and future elements of your argument, you may wish to compare the two explicitly—to demonstrate that the probable effects will be preferable to the current situation. If you have an accurate grasp of your audience's needs and values, you should be able to make this comparison effectively.

SUMMARY

Arguing Recommendations

- Recommendations emphasizing present conditions include the following:
  - A presentation of the current situation, policy, and or practice (a factual argument).
  - An evaluation of this situation in terms of the values and needs important to your audience. The judgment expressed and the value appealed to may be stated or implied.
  - When applicable, a presentation of the existing effects (causal argument) and a judgment of these effects.
  - When applicable, a presentation of the probable future effects (argument of effect) and a judgment of these effects.

- Applying the Toulmin model will help you identify the supporting secondary claims your argument will need to make.

- Recommendations emphasizing the future include the following:
  - Presentation of the recommendation. The degree of detail in this presentation is usually dictated by your degree of responsibility for implementing the recommendation.
  - Identification of probable effects of your recommendation if it is implemented.
  - Evaluation of these effects (both desirable and undesirable) in terms of audience needs and values.
  - In some cases, a suggested implementation plan and an analysis of costs.

    Whether or not you include such a plan, those recommendations requiring minor changes to existing structures are generally more acceptable, though not necessarily more valuable, than those requiring radical restructuring.

- Recommendations considering present and future include the following:
  - Presentation and evaluation of the current situation.
  - Presentation of the recommendation.

– Identification and evaluation of the probable results of the recommendation.

– In many cases, a demonstration that the probable effects of the implemented recommendation will be preferable to the current situation.

TWO SAMPLE RECOMMENDATIONS

The following sample recommendation report considers both the current situation and probable results of its implementation. The report is an example of what a student might include in a recommendation for a computer room in the dormitory. The format of the report, outlined here, is one of several possible formats for a recommendation report:

I. STATEMENT OF PROBLEM
II. STATEMENT OF RECOMMENDATION
III. ADVANTAGES OF RECOMMENDATION
IV. DISADVANTAGES OF RECOMMENDATION
V. COSTS AND IMPLEMENTATION PLAN

Many organizations and many professors have a preferred format for such reports; you would be wise to check whether there are such preferred formats before you begin to write this kind of report either at work or for a class.

This recommendation is briefer and more general than many. If a report with the same proposal were prepared by the university's office of computing, it would undoubtedly include more detail on the scheduling of the project, the nature of the renovations, and the kind of equipment that would be purchased. But a recommendation like this one—proposed by a student to an administrator—need not include an implementation plan (although some suggestions about implementation might impress the audience with how carefully the writer has thought about her recommendation).

```
A PROPOSAL FOR A COMPUTER FACILITY IN MARSHALL DORMITORY

                      Prepared for

                   Dr. Hector Martinez,

        Assistant Vice President for Student Life

                   by Elaine Weston,

       Chair, Marshall Dormitory Student Committee

                  February 13, 1998

                  Statement of Problem
```

Currently many students living in Marshall Dormitory have difficulty getting access to a computer. The college's main computer facility is located over a mile away on the other end of campus, and that facility is often overcrowded; many students find that they can use a computer only after

eleven at night or before ten in the morning. Some students
bring their own computers with them to college, but not all
students here can afford their own computers. I surveyed all
students living on the third floor of Marshall and found
that only 25 percent had their own computers, while another
50 percent said they use computers frequently for course
work. Of this 50 percent, 45 percent said that they have
sometimes found it hard to get access to one of the
college's computers, and 35 percent frequently had this
problem. Clearly, this lack of access to needed computers is
a serious problem for Marshall students. When I spoke with
Helen Borshoff, the Vice President for Computing, she
confirmed the severity of the problem and said that her
organization is trying to deal with the problem within the
constraints of its limited resources.

RECOMMENDATION

We recommend that the Office of Student Life work
with the Office of Computing to convert the student lounge
at the west end of the second floor of Marshall into a
computer facility equipped with seven PCs connected to the
central campus computer system and three printers: our
discussions with the Office of Computing indicate that the
number of computers and printers is the maximum that would
fit into the amount of space available and that this range
of equipment would be most appropriate for student needs.
Since the need for more computers and more access to
computers is so pressing, we recommend that the necessary
renovations take place this summer so that the facility
will be ready by the beginning of the next academic year
on September 6, 1998.

ADVANTAGES OF RECOMMENDATION

If our recommendation is implemented, students who
live in Marshall will be able to use college-owned
computers without having to go all the way to the college
facility. There will also be more computers available than

there are now, and students without the means to buy their own computers will be at less of a disadvantage than they currently are. For students, then, there are significant educational advantages if this proposal is implemented.

For the administration, there are several other advantages as well. Construction of this facility will alleviate at least some of the overwhelming pressure on the main computer facility. Since the space for this new facility already exists, renovating this space will be less costly than adding new space somewhere on campus. This new facility will also show the administration's concern about increasing student access to computers, and it will therefore help to reduce the growing tension between students and administrators over this issue.

DISADVANTAGES OF RECOMMENDATION

Our recommendation does have some disadvantages. Probably the most significant is the security risk of having a small facility so far removed from the central computer facility, which means that it would not make financial sense to have someone on duty to guard the equipment. Another disadvantage is that some space devoted to student relaxation would be taken and used for another purpose. The placing of a computer facility in a dormitory also raises some new policy questions for the college, including whether only students in the dormitory can use the facility, or whether the facility would be open to all students of the college.

These disadvantages are real, but they can be dealt with. The Vice President for Computing assures us that new electronic security devices reduce the need for security personnel. In a poll taken two weeks ago, the Marshall students indicated that they preferred to see the current lounge converted into a computer facility, with 68 percent expressing this preference, 18 percent opposing it, and 14 percent expressing no opinion. Finally, while this proposal does raise some new questions of policy, these

questions must be addressed at some point in the near
future anyway, as computers and computer facilities become
more pervasive in the college.

COSTS AND IMPLEMENTATION PLAN

The following is a tentative and very general outline
of the costs of the project as well as an implementation
plan. These will have to be refined by the Offices of Student
Life and Computing as they begin to work on the project. The
Vice President for Computing has assured us, however, that
the costs and implementation plan we have outlined here seem
reasonable. On her advice, we have not included personnel
costs for the time of administrators, since these costs are
difficult to calculate and are not usually included in the
budgets for small projects of this kind.

Activity	Dates	Costs
Initial planning with students, Student Life, and Computing administrators	March	—
Work requests for construction; orders for equipment	April	—
Renovation of lounge	June–July	$15,000
Installation of security devices	Early August	$ 3,000
Purchase and installation of computer equipment	Late August	$30,000
Total initial costs		$48,000
Ongoing costs; maintenance of equipment		$ 3,000 per year

The following recommendation is a more general argument than the preceding
formal proposal, but like the preceding argument, its central claim calls for a new
course of action.

THE SIDE EFFECTS OF AFFIRMATIVE ACTION

PAMELA J. HSU

In the 1960s, the civil rights move-ment said people could not be denied things like employment based on race. In the 1970s, affirmative action injected women and minorties into the workplace. In the 1980s, diversity programs stressed appreciating differences among all people. But are we starting to see some negative side effects in the 1990s?

During the past several decades, many programs have promoted the education and employment of women and minorities. Minority scholarships are readily available in just about every field. And most corporations track hiring, retention, and promotion of women and minorities, and aim to improve performance in these areas.

As a 24-year-old Chinese woman, I benefit from these programs. I received a generous minority internship/scholarship package from a major corporation one summer during college. When I applied to graduate school, one university offered me a fellowship specifically for minorities entering that particular field of study.

I know that these opportunities have provided a boost in my career. I appreciate them. But there are times when I wish I could have competed against everyone else. I believe my ability would have made me at least a strong contender against all applicants.

I know we have not reached that ideal scenario. I realize that problems still exist and that economic and social conditions prevent some children from getting any chance at all. But we need to look at some of the actions taken in the name of fighting discrimination and promoting diversity to see if they are solving these problems—or just creating different ones.

I'm noticing a growing number of white males who say they are now being discriminated against. I'm talking about the professor who warns his white male students that a particular graduate program may be diffi-cult to get into because they are favoring women and minority candidates. I'm talking about a former employer who ran a department one person short for months, even though many applied for the job, because the position had to be filled by a minority. There's a difference between fairness and force fitting.

Daniel J. Boorstin, the Pulitzer Prize-winning historian and best-selling author, said it best: "We must give everybody a fresh start and not try to compensate for past injustices by creating present injustices."

A growing number of groups are voluntarily segregating themselves from others to preserve ethnic identity. Just take a look at the average college campus, and you'll find Greek houses for minorities and organized student groups for just about every ethnic population. But some may be developing blanket beliefs about their own ethnic group. I've heard that you aren't being true to yourself if you "act" white or you aren't really happy if you've assimilated. The fact that I'm Chinese in blood and American in behavior rubs some people the wrong way. They dub me a Twinkie—yellow on the outside but white on the inside.

I was raised to assimilate, and I don't regret that. Just because I live an American lifestyle doesn't make me any less Chinese. It's ironic that groups which intend to promote an appreciation of their culture among others sometimes fail to reciprocate the respect among their own.

Competition between minority groups may be breeding another problem. One minority group complains that a university gave such-and-such group this much money, and how come they didn't get the same? Columnist William Raspberry pointed out that more students these days search for "discrimination nuggets" because if they find enough of them, they can trade in at the administration building for an ethnic sensitivity course or a minority student center.

It's time to step back and refocus on our ultimate goal. The idea that minority status equals money needs to change. Financial assistance should be available for those who need a chance. Ethnic groups should preserve traditions but not alienate those who do things differently. Sharing traditions with other people and encouraging those who are interested to get more involved—even if they do not belong to that ethnic group—would truly promote diversity.

Source: *Detroit News*, Sunday, 22 May 1994.

SUGGESTIONS FOR WRITING (9.6)

1. Following the form of the first sample recommendation, write a recommendation report to improve some aspect of your college or university. Possible areas for improvement include dormitories or apartments, the library, the call for more on-line courses, requiring faculty and students to use laptop computers for class work, the curriculum in your major, or the food service. Make your recommendation as realistic as possible by interviewing people with some responsibility for that area. From these people, you should try to learn why the situation exists in its current form and how feasible your recommendation is as well as to get some sense of the costs of the project. The length of this report will vary with the complexity of the problem and your recommendation, though it might be wise to limit yourself to a maximum of approximately ten pages.

2. Almost every community has its share of white elephants: elaborate projects or expensive buildings that ultimately had to be abandoned or converted to some alternative use because their cost greatly exceeded their benefit to the community. Look for a white elephant in your community and analyze why the project never met its original intentions. Your professor can help you get started. You will almost certainly have to consult the local newspapers and then perhaps the local archives. Since your time is limited and there may be a great deal of documentation, you might have to restrict your research to newspaper accounts of what happened and why. As with Suggestion 1, the maximum length should be approximately ten pages.

3. Working from the outline you prepared for Activity (9.5.3), write a four- to five-page general recommendation emphasizing the future (along the lines of the preceding Hsu sample above). Be sure to include and support all the secondary claims suggested by the Toulmin model.

ILLUSTRATIVE ARGUMENTS IN PART II: ARGUING RECOMMENDATIONS

10

Writing and Image

In our contemporary society of sound bites and spin doctors, the concept of *image* has developed something of a negative flavor, suggesting superficiality and deceit. Public personalities pay a great deal of money to have distinctive images packaged and popularized—images that may bring them enormous success but that bear little relationship to the real people behind them.

This book uses the term *image* differently and more positively, to suggest the ways in which writing honestly reflects to the reader the kind of person the writer is. In successful arguments, writers project an image of intelligence, probity, and trustworthiness. There is nothing false or superficial about this kind of image: these qualities cannot be created out of thin air; they must be true *reflections* of the writer and thus are developed over time and through experience. But whenever you write, you should strive to project such an image, while also being aware that this image will need to be slightly adjusted to fit the context of a given argument.

Image consists of many elements. Most obviously, the quality of the argument itself—its intelligence, honesty, and accuracy—will impress your readers. But image is projected on a smaller scale as well—by your argument's word choice, sentence construction, and figures of speech; by its spelling, punctuation, and physical format; even by its *sound*.

This chapter focuses on some of the conscious choices you'll be making about your image as a writer of argument—choices about voice, diction, metaphor and analogy, emotive language, and the sound of your prose. As you'll see in this chapter, the choices you make will vary from one argument to the next, depending on your subject, your purpose, and your audience.

THE ROLE OF VOICE

A writer's *voice* is the role that he or she takes for a particular occasion, almost like an actor taking a part in a new play. To many inexperienced writers, voice suggests insincerity or fakery, but all of us continually "play" different roles. We behave one way in a classroom, another way playing basketball; we talk to our parents in one way and to our friends in another. Voice is simply the written manifestation of this adaptability.

The following simple example demonstrates the variability of voice:

```
Dear Mr. Jones:

At the suggestion of Ms. Hawkins, I am writing to inquire
about an opening as an electrical engineer in your firm.
```

```
Dear Mom and Dad:

Hi and help! You won't believe this but I'm broke again.
Boy, were my textbooks expensive this quarter!
```

The same student wrote both of these openings and was completely sincere in both cases but the voices differ markedly. In the first case, the student was formal, polite, and restrained. In the second, she was informal and very direct. In cases like these, the choice of a particular voice seems natural; the student did not spend much time or effort choosing these voices. But you can improve your writing by being conscious of the available choices and using them effectively. One crucial choice is between the formal and the informal voices—the voices of the first and second letters, respectively. Using an informal voice in a formal situation may have disastrous effects. What would happen to our student if she wrote to Mr. Jones (whom she presumably does not know) in the following manner?

```
Dear Mr. Jones:

Hi and help! I ran into somebody Hawkins—I forget her
first name—and she says you've got jobs. Boy, do I need
one!
```

The Importance of Ethos

As the Greek philosopher Aristotle noted, a major element of a successful image is the *ethos* projected by the writer. The ethos is the impression of the writer's character that the reader gets; a positive ethos is one reflecting sincerity and trustworthiness. Readers are likely to accept arguments written by someone who comes across as honest, upright, and unselfish; they will distrust the claims of one known to be dishonest or selfish, or whose voice suggests these traits. So, in your own arguments, try to write from the most principled, unselfish part of yourself. And try not to emulate the ethos projected by the angry writer of the following letter to his campus newspaper:

> The grading policies of this college are rotten, just like everything else here at State. How can the administration put a student on probation for failing a course outside of his major? That's just outrageous. When I got an F in physics, they put me on probation even though I received at least a C in the courses in my major. I didn't want to take physics anyway, and the professor really stunk. Now I'm not eligible to play basketball! When are we students going to force the administration to get rid of this stupid policy?

The reasoning in this letter has many weaknesses, but the writer's failure to establish a respectable ethos also destroys its effectiveness. He presents himself as lacking balance (is *everything* at State rotten?) and as concerned only about himself (what about the effect of the probation policy on others?). Almost all readers, including fellow students, would dismiss this letter as the howl of outrage that it is; certainly they would not be likely to join forces with the writer in an attempt to change school policy.

When Aristotle urged writers of argument to establish an effective ethos, he was not urging hypocrisy. In creating an ethos, you will present your best side, but this side is still part of you; it is not wholly fabricated. Our outraged student in the preceding example is doubtless capable of balance and concern for others. Before writing that letter, he should have given himself the time to move from outrage to a broader perspective, using his anger to inspire dissonance but recognizing that hurt feelings and the impulse to dodge responsibility don't advance arguments.

A writer's ethos can be enhanced by the confidence with which his ideas are expressed. You should always appear confident about your claims, though not more confident than their support warrants. A credible ethos finds a balance between dogmatism and apology. Readers suspect writers, such as our angry student, who make sweeping claims (everything at State is rotten) and writers who make forceful statements that they can't possibly support ("the governor is the dumbest woman in the state"). On the other hand, readers will also suspect arguments that seem too wishy-washy: "I think it is probably true that this policy may lead us in the wrong direction."

Let's take a look at how the disgruntled student might create an ethos that works *for,* rather than *against,* him.

> After a painful experience with the academic probation policy here at State, I have concluded that the college should consider revising it. The policy states that any student whose grades fall below a C average will be placed on probation, so that that student will be ineligible for many extracurricular activities. The policy appears reasonable, but its effect is to place too much emphasis on courses outside a student's major. Many students, including three of my acquaintances, have found themselves ineligible to participate in extracurricular activities even though they were doing solid

work in their majors. I now find myself in a similar situation, being ineligible to play basketball yet earning grades of C or higher in my major.

Here, the student comes across as someone who is honest about his own situation and also concerned for others, someone who allows for an apparently reasonable opposing view while remaining firm in his own.

ACTIVITIES (10.1)

1. Write a one-page letter to your parents or a friend asking for a loan to help with college expenses. Then write a letter to your college's financial aid office asking for the same loan. With two to three of your classmates, make a list of the differences in the two letters.

2. Go back to Chapter 8 and reread Kevin Maloney's essay "Reading Popular Culture." In a one- to two-page essay, characterize the argument's ethos. Your instructor may want to devote some class time to a discussion of the effectiveness of Maloney's ethos.

THE VIRTUES AND LIMITATIONS OF PLAIN WRITING

Most writing teachers and most writing textbooks encourage students to make their writing clear and straightforward, without distracting embellishments. Perhaps the most famous advocate of this plain style was British writer George Orwell, who formulated the following six stylistic rules in one of the most famous essays about writing style, "Politics and the English Language":

(i) Never use a metaphor, simile, or other figure of speech which you are used to seeing in print.

(ii) Never use a long word where a short one will do.

(iii) If it is possible to cut a word out, always cut it out.

(iv) Never use the passive where you can use the active.

(v) Never use a foreign phrase, a scientific word or a jargon word if you can think of any everyday English equivalent.

(vi) Break any of these rules sooner than say anything outright barbarous.

The plain style Orwell urges arose as a reaction against the bloated and often dishonest prose of modern bureaucratic society, where military first strikes are called "anticipatory retaliations," visual materials in school curricula become "integrated systems learning designs," and simple sentences and direct expression disappear behind clouds of vague pomposity: "Please contact my secretary about an appointment regarding the project slippages in implementing the new on-line system." The writer could have said, "Please see me about the delays in starting the new on-line system," but to too many writers today, the first version seems more official, more important. A plain style of writing is an antidote to this swollen prose.

But plain writing carries its own risks, as Orwell notes in his sixth rule. Writers who use the plain style exclusively risk prose that is clear but undistinguished, serviceable but dull. To help you avoid this extreme, here are some friendly amendments to Orwell's rules:

    (i) Don't be afraid to use metaphors, similes, or other figures of speech, provided they are not overworked.

    (ii) When a long word is the best one, use it.

    (iii) Use long sentences for variety and when they best suit your needs.

    (iv) Dare to try something different.

    (v) Break any of these rules rather than confuse your reader.

The following passage from Annie Dillard's book *The Writing Life* is a good sample of writing that succeeds by going beyond the plain style. The marginal annotations mark instances of enriched prose.

Effective exaggeration—dare to be different

Varied sentence length

Inventive language

Ironic humor

It should surprise no one that the life of the writer—such as it is—is colorless to the point of sensory deprivation. Many writers do little else but sit in small rooms recalling the real world. This explains why so many books describe the author's childhood. A writer's childhood may well have been the occasion of his only firsthand experience. Writers read literary biography, and surround themselves with other writers, deliberately to enforce in themselves the ludicrous notion that a reasonable option for occupying yourself on the planet until your life span plays itself out is sitting in a small room for the duration, in the company of pieces of paper.

FIGURES OF SPEECH

A figure of speech involves a "turn" on the literal use of words, or using words to suggest something related to but different from their literal meaning. Two of the most common figures of speech are *metaphor* and *analogy*. A metaphor is an implicit comparison of two unlike subjects so that some aspects of one (usually concrete and familiar) illuminate aspects of the other (usually more abstract or unfamiliar). "The twilight of her career" is a metaphor comparing something concrete and familiar, the end of a day, to something more abstract, in this case the end of someone's career. "Global village" is another metaphor, where the abstract concept of the globe or world (the entire population of the earth) is compared to the more familiar and concrete idea of a village. A *simile,* a variant of a metaphor, is an explicit comparison, where the two subjects are linked by *like* or *as:* "Falling in love is like getting caught in a warm spring rain."

Analogy is like metaphor in that dissimilar subjects are compared, but in analogy, the comparison is usually extended through several points. The "global village" becomes an analogy when the world is compared to a village in several respects—for example, the need for certain agreed-upon laws and the importance of communication and cooperation among those in the community.

The following passage by historian Barbara Tuchman shows the value of metaphor in argument. In the first paragraph of "History as Mirror," Tuchman compares history to a mirror reflecting our own image:

> At a time when everyone's mind is on the explosions of the moment, it might seem obtuse of me to discuss the fourteenth century. But I think a backward look at that disordered, violent, bewildered, disintegrating and calamity-prone age can be consoling and possibly instructive in a time of similar disarray. Reflected in a six-hundred-year-old mirror, a more revealing image of ourselves and our species might be seen than is visible in the clutter of circumstances under our noses.

Tuchman could not have made her point about history so succinctly without this metaphor. What aspects of history are clarified through its comparison to a mirror?

The following passage by psychoanalyst Carl Jung contains an effective use of analogy. Here Jung describes the collective mind of twentieth-century humanity through the analogy of a building:

> We have to describe and to explain a building the upper story of which was erected in the nineteenth century; the ground-floor dates from the sixteenth century, and a careful examination of the masonry discloses the fact that it was reconstructed from a dwelling-tower of the eleventh century. In the cellar we discover Roman foundation walls, and under the cellar a filled-in cave, in the floor of which stone tools are found and remnants of glacial fauna in the layers below. That would be a sort of picture of our mental structure.

Of course, Jung could have described the characteristics of the mind in more abstract language, but his description would have been less memorable than this picture of a house with a buried cave underneath. This example demonstrates how analogies crystallize abstract ideas into a sharp picture that both clarifies the ideas and makes them memorable.

Metaphors can also be valuable means of discovery—doors that lead you to important ideas and arguments. We are all naturally disposed to notice correspondences, to see the threads of similarity that unify experience. We have all had the experience of being spontaneously struck by similarities between two seemingly different subjects. Usually our minds hit on such a comparison because it is apt, because it contains a truth that we may not consciously recognize. On close examination, these correspondences or metaphors that come to us may reveal important truths about both subjects and may generate and even structure a theory or argument. When the noted computer scientist Edward Fredkin was struck by the correspondences between the operation of computers and the operation of the universe, he followed up that metaphor, creating a controversial but intriguing theory of digital physics from the implications of a seemingly simple metaphor.

Like Fredkin and others, you should be alive to the generating power of your natural metaphor-making tendency, letting it work for you in the ideas you develop and the arguments you write.

Some Cautions About Figures of Speech

Metaphors, similes, and analogies can illuminate and generate ideas, but they can't prove a point; they offer clarification, not evidence. (See Chapter 5 for a discussion of false analogy as an informal fallacy.) Calling the world a village doesn't prove the need for world government. Ultimately all analogies break down if pursued too far; the two subjects of an analogy are, finally, *different* subjects. The world may be a village, but it is a village with more than five billion inhabitants, speaking thousands of different languages and following countless different customs and beliefs. Some village!

Analogies are risky if people take them too literally, as they did the "domino theory" analogy in the 1960s and 1970s. The domino analogy compared countries in Southeast Asia to a row of dominoes. When dominoes are placed on their ends in a row, they will fall down one by one if the first in the series is pushed. According to the domino theory, these countries would fall to communism in the same manner. The domino theory was a major reason for American involvement in Vietnam; American strategists believed that the fall of South Vietnam to the communists would lead to communist control of all of Southeast Asia and perhaps all of Asia. South Vietnam and some other parts of Southeast Asia are now communist, but other countries in Southeast Asia are not and do not seem to be in any danger of falling under such control. The domino theory may not always be this faulty, yet the theory cannot become an excuse for failing to analyze the particular complexities of a specific situation. Real countries are always more complicated than dominoes.

ACTIVITIES (10.2)

1. For one of the following analogies, write a one-page essay analyzing how the analogy illuminates aspects of the situation and how it does not. Our discussion of the "domino theory" in the previous section is one example of this kind of analysis.
   a. Sexual politics
   b. The family of humanity
   c. The game of life
   d. The war of ideas
   e. The corporate ladder

2. Write a paragraph that develops an analogy. You may use one of the analogies in Activity 1, provided it is not the one you used in that exercise. The paragraph by Carl Jung previously cited is one model for this kind of development.

3. Read a classmate's paragraph from Activity 2 while he or she reads yours. Evaluate the effectiveness of the analogy, and discuss your evaluation with your partner.

CONNOTATIVE LANGUAGE AND SLANTING

Good writers must be aware not only of the *denotations* of words but of their *connotations* as well. The denotation of a word is its explicit meaning, its dictionary definition; the connotation of a word is the meaning or meanings suggested by the word, the word's emotional associations. The denotation of the words *apple pie* is a baked food made with apples. In our society, the connotations of "apple pie" are family life, patriotism, and innocence. Writers of arguments need to be sensitive to the connotations of words and to use these connotations appropriately. A writer urging the development of a suburban tract of land for offices and factories is more likely to succeed by describing it as a "high-tech park" than as an "industrial development area"; the term *high-tech* has a certain vogue, while *"industrial development"* smells of factory smokestacks. And have you noticed how frequently suburban office complexes are called something like Corporate Woods, even when there are few trees anywhere in sight? Beyond a certain point, words used for their connotative value cease to have any meaning at all; there are very few woods in Corporate Woods and nothing fresh in "lemony fresh" soap or in "fresh frozen" juice. And what is so natural about many of the products that advertise themselves as "naturally delicious"? Connotation is an inescapable element of argument, but it should not be used without regard to denotation. Some advertising disregards denotation and gets away with it, but most readers demand higher standards for other kinds of written arguments.

Writers are often tempted to use not only connotation but also blatantly emotional terms as illegitimate supports for their arguments. Suppose you were arguing for a new recreation center on your campus. You might refer to the necessity of having a place "where students can use their free time constructively, letting off the frustrations and pressures caused by rigorous scholastic demands." Here you are portraying students and their needs in a positive way: we tend to respect anyone subjected to "rigorous scholastic demands." But if you were arguing against the recreation center, you could completely alter this impression by using words with negative connotations: "Do our spoiled and spoon-fed students really need another service catering to their already well-satisfied needs?" The respectable students of the first argument have become the undeserving parasites of the second. Words like *spoiled, spoon-fed,* and *catering* are negative words, and their application to the students in question affects a reader's impression of the issue. The words used *slant* the argument, even in the absence of sound evidence. As a writer of responsible arguments, *you* must not fall into the trap of letting such language suggest conclusions your argument does not support.

The temptation to slant is probably strongest in arguments of ethical evaluation; of all the arguments you write, these are the most personal, the most self-revealing, and thus the most important to you. For these reasons, they may tempt you to resort to irrational means to convince your audience. You are not likely to invest high emotional stakes in arguing that four-wheel-drive cars are superior to other kinds of cars, but you can be passionately committed to an argument for or against capital punishment or abortion. Slanting, while almost unavoidable in such cases, must not become a substitute for sound support of your argument.

(See Chapter 5 for a discussion of "Emotive Language" and "Circular Argument" as informal fallacies.)

ACTIVITIES (10.3)

With one other student in your class, select a subject to describe. Each of you should then write a description of that subject—one favorable, one unfavorable. Some possible topics are: city life, a particular television show, a book you both have read. Before you write your descriptions, agree on certain qualities to refer to in your descriptions.

THE MUSIC OF LANGUAGE

Any writer who ignores the importance of *sound* in argument is overlooking a valuable tool. We all know the power of advertising's jingles and catch phrases, which linger in our minds even when we wish they wouldn't. Less obvious but powerfully convincing is prose that holds our attention because of a fresh and pleasing combination of sounds. Such prose contains euphony and rhythm.

Euphony, a term that comes from Greek roots meaning "good sound," is a pleasing combination of sounds. We usually think of euphony as a characteristic of poetry or some kinds of prose fiction, but it can and should be present in written arguments as well. Euphony, of course, depends on the ear of the reader or listener, but ears can be trained to become sensitive to this quality of prose, just as we learn to be sensitive to different qualities of music.

Rhythm is a recognizable pattern of sounds through time. In prose, rhythmical units are often divided by grammatical pauses such as commas or periods, though a rhythmical break may also occur at some other place where we would pause to catch our breath if we were reading aloud. "I came, I saw, I conquered" is a simple example of prose rhythm, with three short, rhythmical units divided by commas. All of us have a rhythm to our prose just as we have a rhythm to our breathing or walking, and this rhythm varies with the situation, just as our walking rhythm does. Good prose writers learn to know their prose rhythms, to develop them as they gain experience in writing, and to recognize and use the appropriate rhythm for a specific purpose.

The following passage is from Jeff Greenfield's "The Black and White Truth About Basketball." Note Greenfield's sensitivity to euphony and rhythm:

> Basketball is a struggle for the edge: the half step with which to cut around the defender for a layup, the half second of freedom with which to release a jump shot, the instant a head turns allowing a pass to a teammate breaking for the basket. It is an arena for the subtlest of skills: the head fake, the shoulder fake, the shift of body weight to the right and the sudden cut to the left. Deception is crucial to success; and to young men who have learned early and painfully that life is a battle for survival, basketball is one of the few pursuits in which the weapon of deception is a legitimate tactic rather than a source of trouble.

For one thing, this passage makes effective use of the stylistic element of paral-lelism. Parallelism is the principle that equivalent thoughts demand equivalent expression. Notice how the actions described in the first and second sentences are presented in the same grammatical form: a noun modified by a verbal phrase ("the half step with which to cut around the defender for a layup, the half second of freedom with which to release a jump shot"). In addition to the grammatical par-allelism within each of these sentences, Greenfield has made the two sentences parallel to each other: in each, two shorter phrases are followed by a third, longer phrase.

As well as parallelism, Greenfield also makes use of repetition ("half step" and "half second"; "the head fake" and "the shoulder fake") and opposition ("the shift of body weight to the *right* and the sudden cut to the *left*"). The overall effect of these strategies is one of balance—a rhetorical balance that nicely mirrors the physical balance of the intricate choreography of basketball.

The sound of your prose *will* affect how readers react to your argument, even if they are not conscious of the role sound plays in written prose and even if they have not developed the skill to create sound-pleasing prose themselves. As the rhetorician Kenneth Burke has noted, audiences tend to identify with skilled speakers and writers and are likely to be carried along simply by the very structure of the prose. A solid argument that is also aurally effective is hard to beat.

ACTIVITIES (10.4)

Read the following passages and choose the one whose prose style you find most memorable or striking. Write a one- to two-page evaluative argument demonstrat-ing what is effective about the style and why.

1. You know how it is, you want to look and you don't want to look. I can re-member the strange feelings I had when I was a kid looking at war pho-tographs in *Life*, the ones that showed dead people or a lot of dead people lying close together in a field or a street, often touching, seeming to hold each other. Even when the picture was sharp and cleanly defined, something wasn't clear at all, something repressed that monitored the images and with-held their essential information. It may have legitimized my fascination, let-ting me look for as long as I wanted; I didn't have a language for it then, but I remember now the shame I felt, like looking at first porn, all the porn in the world. (Michael Herr. *Dispatches*. London: Picador, 1978. 23.)

2. Commercial exploitation and growing population demands will speed de-struction of rain forests as well as oceans, grasslands, lakes, and wetlands. *Pleading ignorance of these vital and fragile ecosystems can only spell global disaster. What can you do?*

    You can accept this invitation to support World Wildlife Fund. *We have a plan for survival. We need your help to make it succeed.* (Letter from the World Wildlife Fund. World Wildlife Fund, 1987. 1.)

3. The stars awaken a certain reverence, because though always present, they are inaccessible; but all natural objects make a kindred impression, when the mind is open to their influence. Nature never wears a mean appear-ance. Neither does the wisest man extort her secret, and lose his curiosity

by finding out all her perfection. Nature never became a toy to a wise spirit. The flowers, the animals, the mountains, reflected the wisdom of his best hour, as much as they had delighted the simplicity of his childhood. (Ralph Waldo Emerson. "Nature." *Essays and Lectures.* Ed. Joel Porte. New York: Library of America, 1983. 9.)

4. Many adults carry high school around with them always. It is a unique, eccentric, and insulated social system, a pressure cooker where teenagers rush from one class to another, shoved into close quarters with twenty-five or thirty others their age they may love, hate, care little about, or hardly know at all. It has its own norms, rituals, vocabulary, and even its own way to tell time— not by the minute and hour but, as sociologist Edgar Friedenberg has pointed out, by periods. As the setting for the adolescent search for identity, high school is, Kurt Vonnegut wrote, "closer to the core of the American experience than anything else I can think of." There is life after high school, but what we do as adults is powerfully shaped by those years. (Myra and David Sadker. *Failing at Fairness: How America's Schools Cheat Girls.* New York: Scribner's, 1994. 99.)

5. Yes, Virginia, there is a Santa Claus. He exists as certainly as love and generosity and devotion exist, and you know that they abound and give your life its highest beauty and joy. Alas! how dreary would be the world if there were no Santa Claus. It would be as dreary as if there were no Virginias. There would be no child-like faith then, no poetry, no romance to make tolerable this existence. We should have no enjoyment, except in sense and sight. The eternal life with which childhood fills the world would be extinguished. (Francis Pharcellus Church. *New York Sun,* 1897.)

SUMMARY

Writing and Image

- The image you project through your writing is the result of a number of conscious choices you make about your style, your voice, and your use of language.

- You should write clearly, but you should also use various strategies to enrich your prose, including metaphors, similes, and other figures of speech, as well as long words and sentences when appropriate. In general, dare to try something different.

- Metaphor and analogy are valuable for illuminating and generating an argument, but they can never prove a point.

- You must be sensitive to the connotations of words, but you must defend your position with adequate support, not merely with connotation or open slanting.

- You should be sensitive to, and use, euphony and rhythm in your prose.

SUGGESTIONS FOR WRITING (10.5)

1. Write a one-page description of a friend for another friend. Then rewrite the description as a speech describing your friend at a ceremony where he or she will be receiving an award. Have a classmate read both versions and identify the stylistic details of each version.

2. Choose a famous brief essay or speech such as Kennedy's Inaugural Address, Lincoln's Gettysburg Address, or Martin Luther King, Jr.'s "I Have a Dream." Each of these speeches and many others can be found on-line reproduced by reliable sources. Using this essay or speech as a model, try to capture some of the spirit of the original while using your own words and ideas on some topic of your choice in a two- to three-page essay. Pay particular attention to frequently recurring patterns of sentences, and try to use some similar patterns in your own essay. (Give your instructor a copy of the speech you select as a model.)

ILLUSTRATIVE ARGUMENTS IN PART II: WRITING AND IMAGE

11

Introductions
and Conclusions

Because your argument's introduction and conclusion are the first and last impression you will make on your readers, they require careful attention. Conclusions—whether a general closing or a specialized summary—are, of course, almost always composed late in the writing process, when you know exactly what it is your argument has concluded. Some writers compose introductions before they write the actual argument, but many delay until the last stage of the first draft, when they know more clearly what is to be introduced. This chapter discusses the importance of effective openings and closings and makes some suggestions for writing them.

INTRODUCTIONS

Because it is your readers' initial experience with your argument, your introduction must be particularly appealing to them. Regardless of what form your introduction takes, it is the hook that draws your readers into your argument.

The style and content of your introduction will be influenced by your argument's context (the occasion and audience for which it is written) and by its length, tone, and level of complexity. But no matter how you choose to open your argument, the basic purpose of any introduction is the same: to engage your readers. Usually an introduction succeeds in engaging readers if it is clear and inviting. Of these two features, clarity—the precise and accurate expression of carefully considered ideas—is probably the easiest to achieve, though for many writers it comes only with careful thought and considerable revision. To be inviting, your introduction must stimulate your readers' interest, as well as arouse their curiosity about the rest of the argument. Since being inviting is, for most of us, a learned skill, we offer some strategies for writing engaging introductions.

Strategies for General Introductions

Introduction by Narrative. Writers of "general interest" arguments (nontechnical arguments intended for a broad audience) often gain their readers' attention by opening their essay with a specific anecdote or short narrative. This kind of opening engages readers in two ways: first, in its narrative approach, it satisfies our delight in being told a story, and second, it gains our interest by its *particularity*—its details about people, places, and events that give readers a firm footing as they enter an unknown text. An essay entitled "Boring from Within," by English professor Wayne C. Booth, begins with the following paragraph:

> Last week I had for about the hundredth time an experience that always disturbs me. Riding on a train, I found myself talking with my seat-mate, who asked me what I did for a living. "I teach English." Do you have any trouble predicting his response? His face fell, and he groaned, "Oh, dear, I'll have to watch my language." In my experience there are only two other possible reactions. The first is even less inspiring: "I hated English in school; it was my worst subject." The second, so rare as to make an honest English teacher almost burst into tears of gratitude when it occurs, is an animated conversation about literature, or ideas, or the American language—the kind of conversation that shows a continuing respect for "English" as something more than being sure about *who* and *whom, lie* and *lay*.

Booth's essay, addressed to high school English teachers, goes on to identify the ways in which English is mis-taught and to suggest alternative teaching methods. As a renowned college professor addressing high school teachers about the problems of high school instruction, Booth must be careful not to alienate his audience by coming across as superior or critical. He does this in part by opening the essay (initially an oral address) with this personal anecdote, which immediately, but tacitly, says "I am one of you." As well as disarming his audience with the personal references, Booth captures their attention with the simultaneous specificity and universality of effective narrative.

Introduction by Generalization. Good introductions can also begin with a strong, unambiguous generalization related to the readers' experiences, as in the following opening paragraph of an article by David Brown published in a medical society journal:

> Few honorable professions have as much inherent hostility toward one another as medicine and journalism. Ask a doctor to describe journalists and you are likely to hear adjectives such as "negative," "sensationalistic," and "superficial." Ask a journalist about doctors, and you will probably hear about "arrogance," "paternalism," and "jargon."

Broad statements such as this should be limited and developed in succeeding sentences or a succeeding paragraph. In the second paragraph of this essay, the writer both justifies and develops the generalization made in the first paragraph.

> The descriptions are the common stereotypes and not wholly inaccurate, for the two professions occupy distant worlds. Physicians are schooled in confidence and collegiality; journalists seek to make knowledge public. Physicians speak the language of science; journalists are largely ignorant of science. Physicians inhabit a world of contingencies and caveats; journalists inhabit a world where time and audience require simplification. Physicians are used to getting their way; journalists are used to getting their story.

This paragraph's development of the idea contained in the initial paragraph is echoed by the writer's syntax (the arrangement of his words): the last four sentences, neatly divided by semicolons into opposing clauses, emphasize the focus on this professional opposition.

Introduction by Quotation.   Some introductions begin with quotations that are eventually connected to the topic of the essay. While perhaps overused and overtaught, this technique *does* work if practiced thoughtfully. The writer using an opening quotation must be sure that it can be made to apply to the subject in an interesting way, and that the quotation is interesting, provocative, or well written (preferably all three). The following paragraph in an essay by Marilyn Yalom is a successful example of this technique:

> When Robert Browning wrote his famous lines "Grow old along with me!/The best is yet to be,/The last of life, for which the first was made," he was undoubtedly not thinking about women. The poet's Victorian optimism is difficult enough to reconcile with the realities of old age for men, and virtually impossible when we consider the condition of older women in the nineteenth century.

As in the article about the antagonism between the medical and journalistic professions, the initial statement here is immediately explained and developed in the succeeding sentence. Here, in fact, the explanatory sentence is also the claim of this essay on the older woman in Victorian England and America.

Other Types of Introductions.   There are a number of other strategies for making arguments inviting to your readers: startling statistics, a brief historical survey of the topic (which can have the same charm as the narrative introduction), a particularly startling or shocking statement (provided, of course, that it is relevant to the content of your argument), and even a direct announcement of the argument's subject (as in "This is an article about bad writing"). Any of these tactics will work as long as it connects in some way with the body of the argument.

Introductions in Professional Writing

Introductions written in a professional context according to established formats don't need to be as inviting as the previous examples, largely because readers of professional reports usually don't have much choice about whether or not to read a given report. Rather than trying to engage their readers, on-the-job writers are concerned about serving the needs of a known audience who will make some use of the report. In these cases, introductions are successful if they accurately represent the report's content. Company policy often dictates the form of a preliminary summary: some companies require an initial outline, others an abstract, still others a summary reflecting both organization and content. When the form is not dictated, the most useful is a simple summary of organization and content.

Take as an example an analysis of problems in customer relations assigned to a customer service representative of a local grocery chain. In her report, the representative first identifies, describes, and documents the different conditions she has found to be damaging to good customer relations: inadequate customer check-cashing privileges, a time-consuming refund policy, impolite carryout personnel, and inaccurate advertising of sale prices. She then estimates the loss of business resulting from each problem. Finally, she recommends possible solutions to the problems she has identified. Her report is clearly written and organized, but it is also lengthy and somewhat complex; it needs an introduction that will prepare its readers not only for the content of the report but also for the arrangement of its material. The preliminary summary will prepare readers for the sequence of the argument's main points, and it will serve as a useful reference should the readers become confused while reading the full report.

Our customer service representative introduces her report with the following preliminary summary:

> This report examines the recent quarterly decline in business at the seven Goodbelly stores. It attributes this loss of revenue to at least four remediable problems in the area of customer relations: (1) inadequate check-cashing privileges, (2) a time-consuming refund policy, (3) lack of concern for customers by carryout personnel, and (4) inaccurate advertising of sale prices. It is estimated that these difficulties may have cost Goodbelly's as much as $300,000 in revenue in the past three months. This report concludes by recommending specific personnel and policy measures to be taken to ease these difficulties and to regain the lost business.

Without being painstakingly mechanical, this brief paragraph identifies the central claim of the report (that the decline in revenue is due to poor customer relations) and prepares the reader for the organization and content of the argument. While an introduction such as this one may not engage a reader who has neither an interest in nor an obligation to the company, its concise and accurate representation of the report's content will be extremely useful to the obligated reader.

General Suggestions About Introductions

Finally, you may find these general suggestions about writing introductions useful:

1. Try writing your introduction *after* you've written your first draft. Often, there's no point in agonizing over a preliminary summary for a professional report or a catchy introduction for a general interest argument before you know

exactly how the argument is going to evolve. Even if you're working from a detailed outline, your organization and content will change as you compose.

2. On those rare occasions when a catchy opening sentence or paragraph comes to you early, giving you a hold on the overall structure, tone, and style of your argument, don't let this opening get away!

3. Don't make your introduction too long. Even the most interesting, captivating introduction is going to seem silly if it's twice as long as the argument itself. The turbot, a variety of anglerfish, has a head that takes up half of its total body length and is one of the silliest looking fish on the planet. Don't follow its example.

4. Make sure your introduction is truly representative of the entire argument. If you are writing a preliminary summary, be sure all the main points of the argument are covered in the introduction. In a less formal argument, don't let your desire to be engaging lure you into writing an introduction that is stylistically or tonally inconsistent with the rest of the argument. In short, the opening paragraph should never look as if it has been tacked on merely to attract reader interest, with no thought about its relationship to what follows. Rather, it should resemble an operatic overture, beautiful in its own right, but always preparing its audience for what is to follow.

ACTIVITIES (11.1)

1. For one of the following writing tasks, write two different introductory paragraphs using two of the tactics discussed in the preceding section: narrative, generalization, quotation, startling statistics, a brief historical survey, a startling statement, or an outright announcement of claim. Then write a two- to three-sentence description of the different effects of the two introductions.
   a. An essay on a relative whom you admire
   b. An essay on a law or policy of the federal government that you strongly support or oppose
   c. An essay on your favorite food
   d. An editorial in your local newspaper opposing teenage curfew
   e. A report to your supervisor (or a parent or a friend) explaining why you have failed to accomplish all the goals you set for yourself six months ago
2. For one of the arguments you have already written for this class, write (or rewrite) an introductory paragraph following the suggestions offered in the preceding discussion.
3. Working on a different argument written for this course, compose an opening paragraph that begins at a general level and ends with the argument's claim.

CONCLUSIONS

Once you have selected and presented the best possible support for your argument, you may feel that you have nothing more to say on the subject. But you're not finished yet. Until you have provided a final closing, a conclusion that rounds out your argument, your argument is incomplete. Most readers need to feel closure in all kinds of writing: letters, imaginative literature, and arguments.

Conclusions are not always easy to write, particularly because by the time we get around to thinking about writing an ending, we're often tired of the whole project. But you don't need to be a master rhetorician to write an effective ending. A conclusion that is direct, precise, and appropriate to the occasion will do the job just fine. Depending on the context, it can be as short as a paragraph or as long as a chapter.

Types of Conclusions

Arguments can have three basic types of conclusions: the findings or results of an investigation, a recommendation or set of recommendations, or a more general closing reflecting on the argument or raising other considerations related to the central claim.

Findings.   The findings or results conclusion usually ends an argument of fact, such as the reporting of a scientific experiment or a case study. Some causal arguments, such as certain historical studies, may also end with findings or results. Actually, these findings are the argument's claim, which may be given in general form early in the argument and then with more detail at the end, or they may be given only at the end. The following paragraph (the second-to-last paragraph of an essay titled "Particle Accelerators Test Cosmological Theory") exemplifies the findings type of conclusion:

> Preliminary results from the machines indicate that there are at most five families of elementary particles. David B. Cline of the University of California at Los Angeles and the University of Wisconsin at Madison . . . has shown that the lifetime of the $Z°$ boson [a subatomic particle] is approximately what one would expect with just three families. Experimental uncertainties, however, allow for two additional kinds of neutrinos [another subatomic particle] and hence two additional families. . . . For the first time accelerators are counting neutrino types and getting a small number, one that was predicted by cosmological theory.

Recommendation.   Not surprisingly, recommendations typically conclude arguments of recommendation. Their purpose is to tell readers exactly what the argument expects of them. If the findings conclusion tells readers what they should *know*, the recommendation conclusion tells them what they should *do*. An example of this type of conclusion is found at the end of "A Proposal for a Computer Facility in Marshall Dormitory" in Chapter 9 of this book. The proposal ends with a "Costs and Implementation Plan" section that spells out in some detail the actions that need to be taken. In this proposal, the more general recommendations came earlier, so ending with more specific steps is a suitable way to conclude. In many other cases, the most appropriate conclusion is a general recommendation, as in this last paragraph from an essay titled "U.S. Economic Growth":

Only if we increase investment in both capital and technology in all sectors of the U.S. economy (particularly manufacturing) and improve the quality of labor at all levels can the American standard of living rise at an acceptable rate. In the present highly competitive world market, the U.S. has some historically demonstrated advantages, but it must take the longer view and pursue those seemingly trivial increases of a few tenths of a percentage point in growth rate each year.

General Closing.   The general closing is what we usually think of when we think of conclusions. This type of conclusion can work in several ways: it can move from the specific argument to a statement of the argument's broader significance, it can suggest future directions for research, or it can raise related issues. The general closing suggests a movement *onward* (where we go from here) or a movement *outward* (how this specific argument relates to other arguments), though the emphasis in any case will vary between these two elements.

The following paragraph (the closing of Mike Messner's "Sports and the Politics of Inequality") exemplifies a conclusion that moves to a consideration of an argument's broader significance:

If this discussion of sports and inequality seems to make contradictory points, it is because sports plays a contradictory role in the larger politics of inequality. On an ideological level, sports strengthens and legitimates class and ethnic inequalities in society while simultaneously providing cultural space where ideologies supporting inequalities can be challenged and debunked. And for participants, sports offers a place where class and ethnic antagonisms and prejudices can be destructively played out *and* it can offer a space where participants can experience transcendent moments of play which are relatively free from the larger social inequities. In this space, it is possible to discover ourselves and each other as human beings. What all this means is that the role sports will play in the politics of inequality will be determined by "how we play the game," both individually and collectively.

The final paragraph of "Particle Accelerators Test Cosmological Theory" (cited previously) demonstrates the concluding strategy of pointing to new directions and future possibilities:

The next step promises to be even more exciting. As new accelerators are completed and begin producing more data with fewer uncertainties, the cosmological limit of three or at most four families will be checked with extreme accuracy. . . . The machines will probe the early universe with an effectiveness that no telescope will ever match.

A conclusion that raises related issues is found in the last two paragraphs of George Orwell's famous essay "Politics and the English Language." Throughout most of the essay, Orwell gives examples of bad English. But toward the end of the essay, he suggests connections between corrupt language and corrupt political systems. The final paragraph addresses this connection directly:

One ought to recognize that the present political chaos is connected with the decay of language, and that one can probably bring about some improvement by starting at the verbal end. If you simplify your English, you are freed from the worst follies of orthodoxy. You cannot speak any of the necessary dialects, and when you make a stupid remark its stupidity will be obvious, even to yourself. Political language—and with variations this is true of all political parties, from Conservatives to Anarchists—is designed to make lies sound truthful and murder respectable, and to give an appearance of solidity to pure wind. One cannot change this all in a moment, but one can at least change one's own habits, and from time to time one can even, if one jeers loudly enough, send some *melting pot, acid test, veritable inferno,* or other lump of verbal refuse—into the dustbin where it belongs.

A conclusion can contain more than one of the three basic types described previously. The second-to-last paragraph of "Particle Accelerators Test Cosmological Theory" presents the results of the research, whereas the very last paragraph presents a statement on the future directions of this research. A results or recommendation conclusion may be supplemented with a more general conclusion that opens the argument outward.

A word of caution about all conclusions: the conclusion must not lie outside the boundaries of what you can legitimately claim in your argument. You should not, for example, turn an argument about the weakness of a certain school's curriculum into a conclusion uniformly condemning all schools, though your conclusion may suggest that the case you have examined is not an isolated one. In other words, don't overgeneralize from the evidence you used to support your argument. Nor should you use your conclusion as the place to launch a whole new argument or to make claims that do not have some basis in what has preceded.

SUMMARIES

A conclusion is different from a *summary,* which is a restatement of the main points of your argument. Most short or medium-length arguments (five hundred to five thousand words) do not require a summary; final summaries are typically found in very long essays, in essays with difficult subject matter, or in books. This book, for example, uses sentence summaries at the end of each chapter to stress certain key points to an audience new to much of this material.

Writers of arguments sometimes provide a summary of the basic points *preceding* the argument. Such summaries are usually either separate from or at the very beginning of the argument. Typically they take one of two forms: the *abstract,* often used in academic or technical research, and the *executive summary,* often used in business reports and proposals.

An abstract is a summary, typically in paragraph form, that states the essential points of the essay so that readers can grasp these points without having to read the essay; in other words, the good abstract can stand alone, being meaningful by itself. If the readers read only the abstract, they will of course miss much of the argument, especially its support, but they will at least know what the argument's main claims are. With the flood of information confronting us all, abstracts have the obvious value of helping us decide what research needs further investigation and what can be left alone.

The following summary by King-Kok Cheung of her essay on Alice Walker's *Color Purple* and Maxine Hong Kingston's *Woman Warrior* is a good example of an abstract for academic writing:

> *The Color Purple* and *The Woman Warrior* exhibit parallel narrative strategies. The respectively black and Chinese American protagonists work their way from speechlessness to eloquence by breaking through the constraints of sex, race, and language. The heroines turn to masculine figures for guidance, to female models for inspiration, and to native idioms for stylistic innovation. Initially unable to speak, they develop distinctive voices by registering their own unspoken grief on paper and, more important, by recording and emulating the voices of women from their respective ethnic communities. Through these testimonies, each written in a bicultural language, Walker and Kingston reveal the obstacles and resources peculiar to minority women. Subverting patriarchal literary traditions by reclaiming a mother tongue that carries a rich oral tradition (of which women are guardians) the authors artfully coordinate the tasks of breaking silence, acknowledging female influence, and redefining while preserving ethnic characteristics.

Here is an example of an abstract introducing a technical argument, "Cutting into Cholesterol," written by Bruce P. Kinosian and John M. Eisenberg:

> We performed an analysis of the cost-effectiveness of treating individuals with significantly elevated levels of total serum cholesterol (>6.85 mmol/L [>265 mg/dL]), comparing treatment with three alternative agents: cholestyramine resin, colestipol, and oat bran (a soluble fiber). We simulated a program for lowering cholesterol levels that was similar to that of the Coronary Primary Prevention Trial, and then used the outcomes of the trial to calculate the incremental cost per year of life saved (YOLS) from the perspective of society. Our findings suggest that the cost per YOLS ranges from $117,400 (cholestyramine resin packets) to $70,900 (colestipol packets) and $17,800 (oat bran). Using bulk drug reduces the cost per YOLS to $65,100 (cholestyramine resin) and $63,900 (colestipol). Targeting bulk colestipol treatment only to smokers has a cost per YOLS of $47,010; the incremental cost of treating nonsmokers would be $89,600 per additional YOLS. Although pharmacologic therapy has substantial costs, it may be more cost-effective when low-cost forms are applied to particular high-risk groups, such as smokers. However, a broad public health approach to lowered cholesterol levels by additional dietary modification, such as with soluble fiber, may be preferred to a medically oriented campaign that focuses on drug therapy.

Executive summaries are often longer than abstracts, though they should not usually be longer than a page. Like abstracts, they give the main points of an argument, but they may also contain some background on why the report was written and on the scope of the original study. If the executive summary is of a recommendation report, the major recommendation should be included in it. Like abstracts, executive summaries should be written to stand alone; readers should be able to get the major points of the report without referring to the report itself.

The following is a sample executive summary with a format that might be used by a group auditing the overall effectiveness of a university computer center:

> The audit completed a review of the Johnston Computer Center in February 1994. The Johnston Computer Center is one of three academic computing centers at the university and contains terminals and microcomputers for up to 200 on-site users, with access also available for up to 50 off-site users, so that it is second largest of such centers at the university.
>
> The objectives of our review were to determine whether present and planned center operations are fulfilling user needs and are in compliance with university policies and procedures for computer security.
>
> In our opinion, the center's operation is satisfactory in meeting the needs of its users and in using its internal resources to meet these needs, but unsatisfactory in meeting security policies and procedures.
>
> Our survey of Johnston Computer Center users indicated that user satisfaction is high and that center personnel are responsive to user needs. While system response time has deteriorated in the last six months because of an unexpected increase in user demand, center management has addressed this problem by encouraging users to use the system during nonpeak hours and by recommending a hardware upgrade to the Vice President for Systems and Computing.
>
> Our review of security showed that unauthorized users could gain access to and change another user's files. Since the center's computers are not directly connected to the university's administrative computers, which do contain other security safeguards, the university does not face a risk to its financial and personnel records because of these deficiencies. The student and faculty academic files contained in the center's computers are at risk, however. The center has reported three instances of tampering in the last six months. Center management is eager to address this problem but will need additional resources to purchase software and to obtain the necessary technical assistance.

Executive summaries have become increasingly common as business executives and other managers find themselves confronted with an overwhelming number of reports to read. The executive summary allows readers to decide if they want to read further, or if the summary alone provides enough information. Unlike abstracts, which are often intended for a specialist audience, executive summaries usually have a nonspecialist audience of higher managers who may be very far removed from the technical details of the report. The executive summary should allow for the audience's lack of familiarity with these details by avoiding specialized vocabulary whenever possible and by defining any specialized terms that are used. In other words, executive summaries demand great attention to the readers' needs and great precision in wording. Typically they are written after the report is finished, when the writer knows all its twists and turns.

ACTIVITIES (11.2)

1. Return to an argument you have written for this course, and write two different conclusions for it: first, a general closing, and second, a conclusion restating the argument's findings or results. Give your argument and these two conclusions to a classmate to read; discuss with him or her which of the two conclusions seems more appropriate to its context.
2. Find a different argument from the one you used in Activity 1, and write a 250-word abstract (one double-spaced page) of the argument.

SUMMARY

Introductions and Conclusions

- The context of your argument will influence the style, content, and length of your introduction, but all introductions should be clear, engaging, and appropriate to the occasion.

- Some useful tactics for general introductions are:
  - Introduction by narrative
  - Introduction by generalization
  - Introduction by quotation

- Introductions of arguments in formal, professional writing should be precisely representative of the content of the report.

- Conclusions are usually one of three basic types: findings or results, a recommendation or set of recommendations, or a general closing. Which type of conclusion you use depends on the type of argument. Findings or results typically conclude reports of scientific experiments or case studies. Recommendations conclude recommendation reports. General closings are used for other types of arguments, especially interpretations and evaluations. The general closing has three subtypes: a statement of significance, suggested directions for research, and a raising of related issues.

- Do not confuse a conclusion with a summary. A summary is a restatement of the main points of your argument. There are three types of summaries: the ending summary, the abstract, and the executive summary. Ending summaries are typically found in books and in very complex or very long essays or reports. Abstracts and executive summaries are typically found at the beginning of or separate from the arguments on which they are based. Readers should be able to understand an abstract or an executive summary without referring to the report or essay on which it is based.

SUGGESTIONS FOR WRITING (11.3)

1. Locate a section of a newspaper or magazine that presents several editorial or opinion essays. The Sunday *New York Times* op-ed page is an excellent source; your local Sunday paper may have its own version. Or, if you choose a reputable newspaper or magazine resource on-line, note that you need to select their op-ed section for your articles. (This is one exercise that might be easier to conduct using hardcopy because all of the op-ed pieces can usually be found on one or two pages of your newspaper of choice.) Examine the types of conclusions used for three pieces, and write an essay of two to three pages describing the type of each conclusion, its effect on readers, and its overall effectiveness. Which of the three do you find the most effective? Why? Be sure to give your instructor a copy of the op-ed articles you use for this assignment.

2. Write a one-paragraph executive summary using one of your last papers, making sure that your readers will be able to understand the summary without reading the paper. When you hand in this assignment, give your instructor both the summary and the paper on which it is based.

ILLUSTRATIVE ARGUMENTS IN PART II: OPENINGS AND CLOSINGS

12

Revising

Finally, you've finished your argument. It has an introduction and a conclusion, a claim and appropriate support, and you're ready to hand it over to your instructor with a sigh of relief.

But not so fast. You've certainly earned a break—writing is hard work—but if you want your paper to be as good as it can be, you've got to find the time and the energy for another crucial step in the writing process: revising.

Revising your argument means stepping back from it and seeing it whole. As the word's Latin roots (*re*—"again," and *visere*—"to look at") indicate, to revise is to see again, to have a new vision of the entire work. Sometimes this new vision leads to dramatic changes in any part of the argument, though the more attention you pay to the content and organization of your argument as you're writing the first draft, the fewer the major changes you will need to make (yes, that paper you've just finished is a only a first draft, not a finished argument). But even the most carefully composed first draft will require some changes. So, if you're not in the habit, it's time to make a practice of allowing plenty of time and attention for revision. It will pay off. Some people revise *as* they write, adjusting earlier parts of the argument to fit better with what they've just written or are about to write. This is a perfectly good practice that can save you time later on, but it shouldn't take the place of the revising process outlined in this chapter.

WRITING A FIRST DRAFT, REVISING, AND EDITING

Don't confuse revising with editing. Editing is a careful check of the spelling, grammar, punctuation, and overall consistency of a manuscript. Revising, as noted, is a more profound look at the argument's entire content, shape, and style.

Revising involves considerable judgment on your part, because questions about claim, support, and style rarely have simple right or wrong answers. On the other hand, most questions about editing do have right or wrong answers; there are only so many ways to spell a word or to punctuate a sentence correctly.

Writing your first draft, revising, and editing require different attitudes and use somewhat different skills. Writing the first draft requires energy and egoism to keep you going through the bumpy parts; revising calls for detachment and reflection; and editing demands close attention to detail. Attempting a "perfect" first draft is actually one of the most dangerous and laborious ways to write. It is dangerous because you will lack the necessary distance to judge the quality of your argument, and laborious because you are trying to combine these three separate tasks. To some extent, of course, revising and editing occur during the writing of any draft; we all make minor changes in wording, organization, and mechanics even in the early stage of writing, and sometimes we decide on major changes as we write. Inserting these changes then makes sense, but you still need to set aside time for revising and editing, making each your major preoccupation in a separate review of the manuscript.

Many college students feel that they don't have time for anything but a first draft; in fact, they usually do. Students of roughly equal ability and with roughly the same amount of time available work in amazingly different ways, some finishing their work with plenty of time to spare, others doing everything at the last minute. Most students who claim that they were forced to write their papers just before the due date mean that writing the paper was not their highest priority and they could get motivated to write it only by the pressure of a deadline. Especially with word processing, writers who write a first draft, leave it for a while, and then revise it, do not spend any more time writing than those who try to write just one polished draft.

SOME SUGGESTIONS FOR SUCCESSFUL REVISING

Offered here are some suggestions aimed at making your revising stage as effective as possible. These suggestions are based on years of writing experience, but they are only suggestions, not ironclad rules.

Suggestion 1: Give Yourself Some Breathing Space

After you've finished your first draft, give yourself some time—at least 24 hours—before you begin the revising process. This "breathing space" gives you some distance from your work, which you will need in order to review it objectively. And it gives your unconscious an opportunity to mull over the material, so that when you return to the argument, you'll find you have fresh ideas about how to make it more effective. You've probably had the experience of rereading a graded paper and wondering how you could have missed the problems that seem so obvious to you now (and that were far too obvious to your instructor). Putting some distance between first draft and the revision gives you an opportunity to gain this fresh perspective, and to put it to use *before* your paper is graded.

Suggestion 2: Avoid the Red Pen

As you're reviewing your first draft, avoid the lure of the red pen or typing in any changes if you are reading from the screen—the temptation to make small editorial changes before you have reread and assimilated the argument as a whole. Reread with your hands tied behind your back (figuratively, that is), and you'll get a much better sense of how the draft works as a whole.

Suggestion 3: Review Your Original Purpose and Audience

In writing your first draft, you've been intent on coming up with the right word and composing individual sentences. It's easy at this level to lose touch with your original purpose and intended audience. So an important question to ask yourself as you're rereading and revising is whether you've fulfilled your original purpose for your intended audience (of course, your original purpose and audience may have changed during the first draft, but that should be your conscious choice, not an accident).

It can be helpful to review your argument pretending that you're one of its intended readers. From this perspective, you can ask yourself: do I understand the purpose and claim of this argument? are the vocabulary and specialized terms clear to me? is the argument meaningful to me? am I convinced by the argument?

Suggestion 4: Review Your Organization

In reviewing the effectiveness of your argument, you'll need to consider not only your purpose and audience, but also the overall organization of what you've written, making sure that the parts fit together well and are logically sequenced, that nothing crucial is omitted, and that the structure is lean, with a minimum of repetition. If it's hard to keep the organization in mind, try reproducing it in outline form, as in the following model. Remember, you're outlining what you actually wrote, not what you intended to write. If you actually wrote your draft from an outline, don't look at it until you have completed this new one.

    I. Introduction (if appropriate)
   II. Claim (if appropriate)
  III. Supporting arguments:
      A.
      B.
      C.
      D.
   IV. Conclusion or summary (if appropriate)

If you have trouble constructing this new outline, your argument probably has organizational problems that need attention.

This is also a good time to review the effectiveness of your claim and your introduction. Ask yourself these questions: if I have an explicit claim, is it clearly stated? If it is implied, will my readers recognize it? does my introduction prepare my readers for what follows? should it be more interesting?

Suggestion 5: Review Your Argument's Coherence

Even the most carefully organized argument will puzzle readers if the relationship between its parts is not indicated in some way. In certain professions and businesses, standard formats include headings like "Introduction," "The Problem," "History," and so on. But such headings are inappropriate in many settings. You can make the elements of your argument *coherent*—establish their relationship to one another and to the whole—by using simple transitional words and expressions that indicate the nature of the relationship.

Words like *therefore, thus, so*, and *consequently* identify a conclusion and its evidence. Words like *but, however*, and *on the other hand* indicate exceptions to a stated point. You can alert your reader to the introduction of each new piece of support by using indicators such as *first . . . , second . . . , and furthermore, and finally*. Transitional words and expressions such as these are enormously useful to readers of arguments, particularly when the argument is long or elaborate. They help readers understand how one statement or section that may otherwise seem a digression or an irrelevancy relates to what has gone before or what might come later.

As well as using such brief signposts, you can also be quite direct about the role of different parts of your argument. Public speakers are often very explicit about the function of crucial parts of their speeches: "Let me give you two reasons why this land should be developed," or "To conclude, I'd like to remind you of a few lines by Walt Whitman." Such obvious signs are crucial when there is no written text for an audience to follow and ponder. But indicators such as these can be used in written argument as well, especially when the parts are many and complex.

Suggestion 6: Review Your Style

The revising stage is the time to consider the effectiveness of your argument's style: its tone, word choice, and general treatment of the reader. As discussed in Chapter 10, style is a crucial component of argument, often playing a major role in convincing or alienating readers. Poor style is just as damaging to an argument as a vague or unsupported claim; an effective style is just as convincing as compelling evidence. And while you're considering your style, think about the ethos projected by your argument: does the argument reflect a writer who is fair, open-minded, and appropriately confident?

This is also a good time to ask yourself if you have followed Orwell's rules for clarity, along with the friendly amendments offered in Chapter 10. Finally, check your draft to see if you have (1) used connotation effectively, (2) avoided slanting,

(3) used metaphor and analogy effectively, and (4) paid attention to the sounds of words. Some of these questions will naturally occur during your consideration of claim (if you have one) and the organization of its support, as well as during your review of audience and purpose.

Suggestion 7: Review Your Argument for Faulty Reasoning

Chapter 5 introduced some basic principles of logic that will help you set up a reasonable argument. The "informal fallacies" presented there are most easily detected during the revision stage. As a final step in reviewing your argument, read it through to detect any unwitting fallacies, paying special attention to those that are particularly common in the kind of argument you've written.

Suggestion 8: Use a Word Processor

Fortunately (some students would say unfortunately), revising may lead to a drastic overhaul of your argument. But if you want your argument to be as good as it can be, you won't ignore the opportunity to make these major changes. Most students now write their papers on computers, which make large- and small-scale revising much easier than any other method. If you're one of those few people who have resisted the move to computers, we strongly urge you to make the change. With a computer and a good word-processing program, you can switch entire sections of a draft around with ease; change words swiftly and even "globally," so that one word replaces another throughout an entire essay; and make corrections with no trace of erasures or correction fluid. Virtually all campuses have computer labs for their students, which save the expense of purchasing your own computer. And while a computer will not make you a better writer, it will give you the chance to make yourself a better writer. So get wired!

ACTIVITIES (12.1)

1. Write an outline of a paper or a draft of a paper that you have written for this class, using the format given in Suggestion 4. Then exchange this paper or draft with one of your classmates, while keeping your outline. Now prepare an outline of your classmate's paper, again using the same format, and then exchange outlines with your classmate. Compare your classmate's outline with your own. Do the two outlines agree on what the claim is and what the supporting arguments are? If there are disagreements, discuss these with your classmate. Find out why he or she saw your argument working in a different way than you did. Remember that if there is disagreement, you cannot simply assume that your classmate is wrong and you are correct: the purpose of your argument is to convince the reader, not yourself. After this discussion, make a list of the changes or possible changes you would make in your paper in the next draft.
2. Have a classmate read a clean copy of one of the papers you have written for this course. Ask him or her to write a one-page description of the overall

image reflected in that paper and a one-page evaluation of that image. Do the same for a paper written by your classmate.

SUMMARY

Revising

- You should plan to spend separate portions of time writing a draft, revising, and editing.

- Allow breathing space between writing a draft and revising it. In your first review of the draft, concentrate on how the draft works as a whole.

- In revising, review your original purpose and audience, your organization, the adequacy and logic of your support, and your style.

- Knowing the principles of logic is a significant help in reviewing your draft.

- Using a word processor makes revising much easier.

AN EXAMPLE OF REVISION

Having read your manuscript all the way through at least once, and preferably twice, you are now ready to make major changes if they are needed. By avoiding the red pen until you have reviewed the entire manuscript, you are more likely to recognize the need for such major changes, and less likely to get lost in grieving over minor errors.

The following sample student essay is a good example of how to correct major problems in an argument. What follows is the first draft of the essay, along with the student's notes for revision, which he wrote in the margins during a second and third reading of the draft.

> When we think about computers, we usually think about how helpful they are to us: they enable us to process huge amounts of data, prepare large written documents with an ease undreamt of even twenty years ago, and by acting as the "brains" of robots, help us perform dangerous or monotonous tasks. But we often fail to think of the negative side of computers, including the threat they pose to our privacy. Also, in many cases, computers are replacing human labor in factories and offices.

Drop-this idea not followed up ‖

> One thing computers are used for is to store information about people. These computers contain databases, which are collections of

discrete data that are divided into fields, such as age, sex, income, and place of residence. A user of a database can pull information out of the database on everyone who fits a category made up of some or all of these fields, such as every male between thirty and forty who earns between thirty and fifty thousand dollars a year and lives in Florida. An example of a database is the Internal Revenue Service's database, which contains basic information on tax returns along with demographic information on those who pay taxes. Other databases contain credit histories. If you have someone's Social Security number, you can find out just about anything you want about that person. Not just anybody can do this, but there are already too many people who can.

overstated →

A separate point, not related to ¶. Also, I have no proof.

wordy, vague ←

As if it isn't bad enough to have someone go through all the information about you in one database, databases can even be linked to other databases because of the increased networking power of computers today. Having this ability leads to the potential problem of wrong information being kept on a person (especially if no written records are kept). Computers do fail, but the most important reason why a database would contain wrong information about someone would be because someone typed in incorrect information. If the police used computer databases to keep track of criminal records without having another record of them on paper somewhere, anyone could input harmful data on innocent people that could cause them a great deal of misery.

Too many separate ideas in this ¶: networking, human error, lack of paper copies. These need separate treatment.

If the major problem with the accuracy of information in databases is human error, then perhaps new forms of electronic entry of data will eliminate some of these errors. Our phone bills are one example of a completely electronic system. But these phone bills can tell someone who wants to know all the people we called and when we called them. Our phone companies could be recording everything we say as well.

No evidence. Statement undermines my credibility.

In our society, privacy is regarded as a right—a right that is being threatened by the

Ideas need development. Is situation hopeless?

increasing use of databases to maintain large amounts of information on all of us. A number of privacy bills have been passed but are almost useless because they are so hard to enforce. Violating someone's privacy is hard to detect, and successfully prosecuting someone for this offense is harder still.

Not relevant to what I've written. ————

Computers are enormously valuable tools, but they can be misused to violate privacy and to manipulate people. We have a population ex-plosion today, and yet we replace people with computers. We must carefully examine the role of computers in our society and learn to con-trol them before they control us.

Is this conclusion justified by what I've written?

First drafts (and final drafts, for that matter) are never perfect, as our student has recognized on rereading his. Here is a list of the problems that his review has discovered:

1. *Claim.* I have a combination claim focusing on the privacy issue and the issue of computers replacing human labor, but I do nothing with the second is-sue. I should drop the second issue and concentrate on the first.

2. *Organization.* My ideas aren't clearly presented and organized, especially in the third paragraph, which talks about the three separate ideas of networking, human data-entry errors, and lack of paper or "hardcopy" backups. All of my para-graphs must be clearly tied to the privacy threat.

3. *Support.* I don't really support my argument because I talk a lot about the threat of invasion of privacy but give no actual cases. I need to distinguish clearly between the potential for abuse and actual cases. Is there a real possibility of abuse? Also, my conclusion about humans controlling computers before they con-trol us isn't warranted by what I've written, since I've offered no suggestions for controlling computers.

4. *Style.* I undermine my credibility with sweeping statements like "If you have someone's Social Security number, you can find out just about anything you want about that person." Some of my writing could be much tighter, including wordy expressions like "As if it isn't bad enough to have someone go through all the information about you in one database . . ."

In his second draft, the student carefully attended to this list, ending up with a much stronger version of the paper. After completing his research, he was able to add authoritative support and documented references, going beyond supposition.

When we think about computers, we usually think
about how helpful they are to us: they enable us to process huge amounts of data, prepare large written documents
with an ease undreamt of even 20 years ago, and by acting
as the "brains" of robots, help us perform dangerous or
monotonous tasks. But we often fail to think of the
negative side of computers, including the threat they
pose to our own privacy. This threat may not seem
immediate, but it is growing with the increasing power
of computers, and so far society has done little to deal
with it (Roszak 181).

One thing computers are used for is to store information about people. Computers often use databases, which are
collections of discrete data that are divided into fields,
such as age, sex, income, and place of residence. A user of
a database can pull information out of the database on
everyone who fits a category made up of some or all of these
fields, such as every male between 30 and 40 who earns between 30 and 50 thousand dollars a year and lives in
Florida. An example of a database is the Internal Revenue
Service's database, which contains basic information on tax
returns along with demographic information on those who pay
taxes. Other databases contain our credit histories, our
history of contributions to a specific organization, our
personnel records with our employers, and a variety of other
information. Businesses and other organizations already use
this information to bombard us with targeted advertising
through the mail; the information could be used to monitor
our opinions and activities (Roszak 182–87).

Databases can be made even more powerful by being
linked to other databases through networking. The increasing capabilities of network systems raise the possibility
of a wide variety of information on us being shared by numerous databases. Such information on specific individuals
would be a boon to marketers trying to find target audiences, but individuals could end up with their records of
contributions to an organization in the hands of the IRS,

or their IRS files in their employers' personnel records, without their even knowing it.

So far at least, cases of deliberate abuse or manipulation of databases to violate an individual's privacy have been relatively rare. Far greater problems have arisen because of errors in the entry of data in databases, with such undesirable results as individuals' receiving bad credit ratings because of erroneous reports of unpaid bills or even some cases of innocent individuals' being denied government jobs because their names appeared on computer lists of people belonging to subversive organizations (Sherman 344). The risk of these kinds of errors may increase with increasing use of the "online" entry of data into computers, where a paper copy (called a hardcopy in computerese) of the transaction is not necessary, so that no trace is left outside the computer system of the source of the error. These errors threaten our privacy, because this supposedly "private" information may mislead others, damage our reputation, and enormously complicate our lives. Common sense suggests that with the increasing amount of "private" data being kept on all of us, the likelihood of harmful errors also increases.

Most such errors are caused by human mistakes, but even computers can develop "glitches." Furthermore, even errorless electronically-entered data can pose threats to our privacy. Our phone bills are one example of a completely electronic system which is almost always error-free. Yet these phone bills can tell someone who wants to know all the people we called and when we called them. The information may be accurate, but in the wrong hands, it can be seriously misused.

In our society, privacy is regarded as a right—a right that is being threatened by the increasing use of databases to maintain large amounts of information on all of us. A number of computer privacy laws have been enacted in the last 20 years, including the Medical Computer Crimes Act of 1984, the Cable Communications Policy Act of

1984, the Financial Privacy Act of 1978, the Fair Credit
Reporting Act of 1974, and the Family Educational Rights
and Privacy Act of 1974 (Organization for Economic Co-operation and Development 22). One aspect of all these laws
is the protection of individuals from unwarranted use of
data about them. But violating someone's privacy is hard
to detect, and successfully prosecuting someone for this
offense is harder still.

Nevertheless, protecting individual privacy against
the threat posed by large databases is not a hopeless
cause. The growing list of computer privacy laws indicates that the public is not blind to the threats posed
by computers, though much needs to be done to make these
laws meaningful. Even consumers can help, by insisting
that their names not be sent to others when they subscribe to a magazine or join an organization. Faced with
such insistence and the possibility of losing customers
or members, many groups will stop sharing these lists.

Computers are enormously valuable tools, but they can
be misused to violate our privacy. While the threat to our
privacy is real, the situation is not yet severe. We still
have the time to control this threat before the threat begins to control us.

                        WORKS CITED

Organization for Economic Co-operation and Development
        (OECD). *Computer-Related Crime: Analysis of Legal
        Policy. Information on Computer Communications Policy*
        10. Paris: OECD, 1986.
Roszak, Theodore. *The Cult of Information: The Folklore of
        Computers and the True Art of Thinking.* New York:
        Pantheon, 1986.
Sherman, Barrie. *The New Revolution: The Impact of
        Computers on Society.* Chichester, UK: Wiley, 1985.

Having read this second version carefully, do you think the student has solved the
problems he noted in his list? Do you see further changes that he might wish to
make before handing the paper in to his instructor?

ACTIVITIES (12.2)

Read the following draft of a student's essay (actually a composite of several essays), and make a list of what you feel the major revisions need to be. Compare your list with those of your classmates; then revise the essay in accordance with your list. Compare your revision with some of those done by your classmates.

STUDENT GOVERNMENT: WHY NO ONE CARES

Being an engineering student here at High Tech, I have very little free time. My time is entirely devoted to academics. Occasionally I will have a few hours free on the weekend, but then I work part time at odd jobs. Tuition here is very high.

I am one of many busy students here who simply doesn't have the time to take an interest in student government. This same fact is true for most of us. Most of us don't even know one person who is in student government and could not tell you what student government actually does.

We are very ignorant about student government and what role we can play in it. Speaking for myself, even if I saw posters announcing a meeting about student government, I would not attend. Most of my fellow students would not either. What can just one student do? None of us has much of a voice in how things are run. The administration really runs the show here at High Tech, not the students. I believe that if the student government started putting up more posters and getting out more publicity about its activities, students would be more interested in its activities even if they did not attend them.

It is a whole lot simpler to just ignore what's going on and to assume that the student government is looking out for our interests than to take the trouble to get involved. Besides, life isn't all that bad around here, so why should we spend a lot of time and effort trying to improve a situation most of us already find satisfactory? By the time we solved some problem, we would be ready to graduate anyway.

SUGGESTIONS FOR WRITING (12.3)

1. Revise a paper you wrote earlier in this course, following the advice outlined in this chapter. Make a list of the major differences between the original paper and your new version, and indicate very briefly why you made these changes.

2. For this assignment, the class should be divided into groups of three or four. Each group will collectively write a three- to four-page paper (750 to 1,000 words) on the general question "What are the three things that infuriate me most about this campus?" Each group will brainstorm ideas that lead it to a working claim for an evaluative paper concerning student life at your school. From this working claim, the group will compose an outline; then each student will write a particular section of the paper. When the first draft is written, the group will discuss it and each student will revise his or her own section. Finally, the group will discuss this second draft and choose one student to prepare and edit a final version consistent in style and tone.

3. Write a description of the steps you typically follow when writing arguments. Start with the step of coming up with ideas and move through writing the first draft to whatever steps you take before you arrive at a final edited version. How efficient is this typical process in terms of time spent? How effective is it in helping you compose a convincing argument? Do you think the process can be improved so that you can write better arguments in a reasonable amount of time? Give the description to your instructor for comments and suggestions.

4. If you selected activity number one in this section, write a complete paper incorporating your resources. Be sure to give your instructor copies of your resource materials along with your first draft and notes you made concerning the draft.

PART II

READINGS

Athletic coaches know the value of practice drills that require players to switch positions. In soccer and basketball, a player will be a more effective dribbler if he practices stealing the ball. A tennis player will hit more ace serves if she practices receiving against a powerful server. The principle applies equally to writing arguments, where a writer attempts to convince a reader of an arguable position. While writer and reader are not exactly opponents, they are, like server and receiver, engaged in a transitive act where the action of one affects the reaction of the other.

Part II of *Everyday Arguments* is based upon the premise that careful reading contributes to successful writing. "Reading" in this context means a great deal more than scanning for the main ideas—what in a novel we would call the plot. A careful reader of argument moves well beyond content comprehension to an analysis of *technique*—how structure, logic, evidence, and style enhance or detract from the reasonableness of the claim. The readings that follow offer you abundant examples of how the strategies of argument laid out in Part I are actually applied in the real-life arguments that people write every day. A wide range of writers is represented in these readings—some famous, others unknown. Likewise, the forms and contexts of these arguments vary widely—from the formal and methodical to the casual and off-hand. But all the selections in this section share the defining characteristics of argument: they promote a position with the intent of convincing an audience through reasonable methods.

The commentaries accompanying the first argument of every unit are detailed analyses of the argument technique. The discussion questions following every argument will guide you in making your own careful analyses—a critical skill if you want to become a truly effective writer. And the suggestions for writing following each reading will give you the opportunity to experiment with the techniques you've analyzed and to engage with the subject matter and claims you've read.

The readings are divided into six subject units, which address such contemporary topics as today's college students, sports, popular culture, the Internet, the diet industry, and the world of work. These topics may at first sight not appear to be the stuff of argument, and they certainly are different from the subject areas typically addressed in writing anthologies. But each satisfies criteria that are critical for arguments designed as practical illustrations of the do's (and sometimes don'ts) of written argument. First, all six units revolve around subjects that are part of the air that today's college students breathe. You can scarcely pick up a newspaper, have a conversation with a friend, or turn on the television without confronting one of these topics. And while as such, they may seem too unexceptional to inspire model arguments, they model one of the central claims of this book: that argument informs virtually all of the writing we encounter—regardless of its subject, its writer, or its audience.

There is another important reason for this particular choice of subject areas. Because they surround us on a daily basis, we tend not to subject them to the same rigorous analysis and interrogation that we might apply to a supreme court decision on affirmative action or a call to action by a renowned world leader. But precisely because of their *dailiness*, these are the arguments that we must scrutinize, taking care to question and challenge the seemingly harmless claims that, if uncritically accepted, form cultural values that will serve only the organizations and individuals that make them, not the general population that unthinkingly accepts them. So these readings ask you to develop the habit of examining *how* the claims of our society are made, to accept or reject them on the basis of the principles of reasonable argument presented in the first half of this book. As in the sports analogy above, you have to be a critical reader of argument to be an effective writer of argument, and there's no better place to start reading critically than these popular issues that daily clamor for our acceptance but sometimes evade our careful scrutiny.

13

Today's College Student

INTRODUCTION

Had this book been written 10 years ago, it would have been much easier to generalize about "today's college student," who at that time tended to be U.S.-born, unmarried, largely middle-class, 18–22 years old, and enrolled in college full time. Recently, this "typical" student has been joined by very different populations of students—adults, single parents, citizens of different countries, part-time students, and students from a wider range of ethnic and economic backgrounds. While responsible generalizations—inductive arguments—about the subgroups comprising today's more diverse student population are still possible, the days of all-encompassing generalizations are past.

Because you are all automatic experts on "today's college student," and because induction plays such an important element in written argument, a set of inductive arguments describing you and your fellow students seems like an excellent place for this argument anthology to begin. The selections that follow—all of which use the inductive method to some degree—don't cover all the major populations of college students, but they do describe at least a representative sampling: the traditional 18–22-year-old full-time undergraduates, adult female students (a quickly growing segment of the undergraduate student population), underprivileged students, and others. The arguments contained here come from an equally diverse set of vantage points—from education specialists, students, professors, and reporters. If you were to write your own, all-inclusive description of today's college student, these arguments would give you much, though certainly not all, of the material you would need.

As you read these arguments, be mindful of the mistakes to which generalizations are prey: insufficiently limited claims; inadequate supporting data; and unsubstantiated facts, to name a few. You may find yourself being particularly critical of those arguments that describe the group to which you belong; it can be an unsettling experience to hear yourself described without having had any opportunity to contribute to or approve that description. The suggestions for writing after each argument will give you ample opportunity to formulate and argue your responses to these essays.

RETREAT FROM INTIMACY

ARTHUR LEVINE AND JEANETTE S. CURETON

Arthur Levine, Ph.D., is one of the nation's top experts on college students. For 30 years, he has been studying and writing on the topic, winning in the process a host of prestigious awards for his work. When Hope and Fear Collide *(1998), from which this essay is taken, is a follow-up to his 1980 study of college students,* When Dreams and Heroes Died. *Levine is currently president and professor of education at Teachers College, Columbia University.*

Jeanette S. Cureton has collaborated with Levine on a number of higher education studies. She holds an M.A.T. from Johns Hopkins and a Master's in Education from Harvard. Her career in higher education research has provided her a wide view of college and university campuses across the country.

COMMENTARY

This argument uses an introductory strategy similar to the one illustrated in the essay by David Brown in Chapter 11. It is a breathtaking generalization that captures readers' attention simply by virtue of its magnitude. Generalizations like these are engaging in part because readers automatically see them as dares that they could win: "I dare you to prove this," we say to the writer.

The essay is a combination factual and causal argument. The opening sentence does double duty: not only is it an attention-grabbing opener, it is also the argument's opening claim—a factual generalization that is then broken down into general examples, which in turn are supported through data and supporting quotations from experts. Just as outlining your own arguments after they are written can help you judge their organizational strengths and weaknesses, performing the same exercise with other people's arguments is an excellent way to judge the reasonableness of that argument's evolution. An outline of the opening factual argument might look like this:

Claim #1: "Today's students are frightened" (factual generalization)

A. Example 1: "They are afraid of getting hurt" (supporting factual generalization) (Par. 1)
    1–3: Supporting data (Par. 1)
B. Example 2: "Students are also frightened about their economic prospects"(Par. 2)
    1–5: Supporting data (Par. 2)

C. Example 3: "Relationships were another source of concern for students" (Par. 3)

1–x: Supporting data (Par. 3–5)

D. Summary: "The bottom line is that students are coming to college overwhelmed and more damaged than those of previous years" (Par. 6)

   1. Supporting data (Par. 6)

   2. Supporting expert opinions (Par. 6)

Once the authors have established the reasonableness of their original factual claim, they introduce the central causal claim of the essay: "The effect of the accumulated fears and hurts that students have experienced is to divide and isolate them" (Par. 7). Par. 8 and 9 support this claim through citing linking behavioral principles: the effect (isolation) is linked to the cause (fear) through such universal human behaviors as withdrawal and escape.

In order for this causal claim to be credible, further support is necessary. First, we need verification of the effect (the first section of the argument has amply verified the cause). And second, because this is a causal generalization, we need evidence that the isolation is a widespread phenomenon.

Both verifications are offered in the second section of the argument, "Having Fun?" Like much of the factual support in this essay, the verifications come in the form of data obtained through interviews and surveys of college students and student affairs professionals. In this case, that data is presented in tabular form (Tables 5.2 and 5.3). Supplementing the tables are quoted statements from students interviewed for the study (Par. 13).

The final three paragraphs turn to a concluding causal argument proposing three reasons for the increased social isolation of college students: the high numbers of students working while attending school (Par. 14); conforming to "a national trend of disengagement" (Par. 15); and the "wiring" of dorm rooms. Each of these proposed causes is amply documented by a variety of strategies.

Overall, the argument by Levine and Cureton is a solid, well-documented inductive argument. The writing, while not stylistically memorable, is clear and serviceable; the organization is sensible and easy to follow. Stylistic moderation and structural predictability are appropriate to an argument that makes such vast and ambitious claims.

RETREAT FROM INTIMACY

Fear and Pain

1   Today's students are frightened. They are afraid of getting hurt. Nearly half of all undergraduates (46 percent) worry about becoming victims of violent crime. Among women the proportion is even higher (54 percent) (Undergraduate Survey, 1993). We asked a female junior on a suburban campus in an affluent area why she was afraid. She could not think of any incidents that had occurred on her campus. Instead, she told us the college had recently introduced emergency phones,

stronger outdoor lighting, and nighttime escort services. For her, cause and prevention were the same thing. Both fueled her fears.

2 Students were also frightened about their economic prospects. Many have had financially unstable lives. More than one-fifth (21 percent) of the undergraduates surveyed reported the ultimate instability: someone who helped pay their tuition had been unemployed during their college years (Undergraduate Survey, 1993). The students saw their own economic futures as uncertain too. They told us over and over again that they were worried about whether they could pay their college tuition. In an age in which students are taking average loans of $3,210 per year at two-year colleges and $4,790 per year at four-year colleges (U.S. Department of Education, 1996c), three college students out of every ten are uncertain whether they have enough money to complete college; this is more than a 50 percent increase since 1976. In fact, only 25 percent of undergraduates were confident of having sufficient funds to pay for college (Table 5.1). They were equally frightened about whether they would be able to repay their college loans, whether they could find a decent job after college, and whether they could afford a home and a family—or would have to move back home with their parents.

3 Relationships were another source of concern for students. Nearly one-third of all college freshmen (30 percent) grew up with one or no parent (Sax, Astin, Korn, and Mahoney, 1996). Even those students who lived with both parents usually experienced divorce up close by seeing it in the lives of their friends and neighbors. These students often told us of unhappy relationships between their own parents. The result is that current undergraduates worry a great deal about divorce. As one dean of students put it: "They want a nurturing and caring environment. They want security. They don't want divorce to happen to them." They are desperate to have only one marriage, and they want it to be happy. They don't know whether this is possible anymore.

4 Again and again, deans of students reported on the growing rate of dysfunctional families among their students. They talked of violence; instability; blended families; and emotional, sexual, and financial problems. As one dean put it, "It's hard to send a student home, when home is the problem."

5 In interviews, students alluded to such difficulties, often very subtly. Others were more concrete, particularly in regard to the feeling of not having a home. Startlingly, 27 percent of the students surveyed had moved four or more times while growing up; 16 percent had moved more than five times. Among students of color, the proportions were even higher, 36 percent and 20 percent respectively (Undergraduate Survey, 1993). For these students, there were frequently no roots, no sense of place, and no strong relationships. They yearned deeply for all of these things but feared they would never have them.

Table 5.1. Student concern about ability to finance a college education: 1976, 1993.

Financial concern	Percentage reporting	
	1976	1993
Confident they will have sufficient funds	38	25
Probably will have enough funds	43	45
Not sure they will have enough funds to complete college	19	30

Source: Undergraduate Surveys (1976, 1993).

6   The bottom line is that students are coming to college overwhelmed and more damaged than those of previous years. Six out of ten chief student affairs officers (60 percent) reported that undergraduates are using psychological counseling services in record numbers and for longer periods of time than in the past; this is true at 69 percent of four-year schools and 52 percent of two-year colleges. Eating disorders are up at 58 percent of the institutions surveyed. Classroom disruption increased at a startling 44 percent of colleges, drug abuse at 42 percent, alcohol abuse at 35 percent of campuses. Gambling has grown at 25 percent of the institutions, and suicide attempts have risen at 23 percent (Student Affairs Survey, 1997). Deans of students concluded:

> "Students carry more baggage to college today."
>
> "Dealing with more developmentally delayed or disabled students."
>
> "Much more time devoted to emotionally-ill students."
>
> "We deal with a greater number of dysfunctional students and dysfunctional family situations."
>
> "Dealing with more psychopathology among students of all levels and all backgrounds."
>
> "Students bring more nonacademic-related issues. We are becoming a secondary social service agency."
>
> "I spend more time dealing with student discipline, stalking, harassment, and domestic violence."
>
> "Students expect the community to respond to their needs—to make 'right' their personal problems and those of society at large." (Student Affairs Survey, 1997)

7   The effect of the accumulated fears and hurts that students have experienced is to divide and isolate them. Undergraduates have developed a lifeboat mentality of sorts. It is as if each student is alone in a boat in a terrible storm, far from any harbor. The boat is taking on water and believed to be in imminent danger of sinking. Under these circumstances, there is but one alternative; each student must single-mindedly bail. Conditions are so bad that no one has time to care for others who may also be foundering. No distractions are permitted. The pressure is enormous and unremitting.

8   This situation has resulted in a generation often too busy or too tired to have a social life. It has produced students who fear intimacy in relationships. Withdrawal is easier and less dangerous than engagement. It has led to undergraduates who want things to be different; escaping from the campus physically and from life via a bottle are both popular.

9   Social life is an area in which student fears loom larger than their hopes. Their behavior differs in this realm from that in the political arena. Though fears and doubts about politics, politicians, and government are extremely high, students have chosen to engage, albeit through the local and more informal approach of community service. In part, the reason stated for their involvement is that they had no choice; they had to embrace the political agenda or it would engulf them. In contrast, a social life is viewed by undergraduates as optional. To be intimately involved is a higher-stakes game than politics. It presents a far greater potential for getting hurt, for adding to one's burden, or for personal failure.

Having Fun?

10   We asked students what they did for fun. We had asked the same question in the prior study, but this time the answers were very different (Table 5.2).

11   We also asked the same question of deans of students, who responded similarly regarding the most popular activities but tended to give greater preference to more wholesome pursuits (Table 5.3).

12   With many students, the question drew a wide-eyed stare or a look of bemusement, as

Table 5.2.   What college students do for fun, according to students: 1979, 1993.

Activities	Percentage of students reporting	
	1979	1993
Drinking	77	63
Clubs and bars	—	59
Off-campus	—	52
Parties	38	41
Sports and intramurals	54	33
No social life, commuter	27	30
Theater	—	26
Music	27	22
Movies	27	22
Concerts	12	22
Fraternities and sororities	19	15
Study	—	21
Travel and trips	8	11
Dances	58	11
Drugs	54	[a]
Sleep	—	11
Residence hall activities	19	—
Cards, backgammon	12	—
Running	12	—

[a]Students talked about drugs regularly, but most often in the negative, saying drug use on campus was less popular than alcohol use.
Source: Campus Site Visits (1979, 1993).

Table 5.3   What students do for fun, according to deans of students: 1997.

Activities	Percentage of deans reporting		
	Two-year schools	Four-year schools	Total
Party	17	52	34
Sports	48	51	50
Drink	9	50	29
Socialize	39	36	37
Games	30	15	23
Video	13	30	21
Outdoor	13	24	18
Comedy or other entertainment	22	7	15
Clubs	13	16	14
Music	9	15	12
Greek	—	9	5
Date	—	2	7

Source: Student Affairs Survey (1997).

if to ask the interviewer, What are you talking about? What planet do you come from? On nearly one-third of the campuses (30 percent) at which we conducted focus group interviews, students said they had no social life. This is only a small increase (27 percent) from the earlier study, but for the first time students (11 percent) listed "sleeping" as a form of recreation. The students at the University of Colorado who selected "tired" as the best adjective to describe their generation apparently knew what they were talking about.

13 Studying was another leisure activity making a first-time appearance on the fun list. It was cited on more than one-fifth of the campuses (21 percent). Undergraduates told us again and again:

"I don't have a social life."
"There is no free time."
"My whole life is juggling."
"Study, that's all we ever do."
"I'm always behind. I never catch up."
"I feel run down."
"People's lives are dictated by their jobs."
"The high cost means I have to work forty to fifty hours per week, and it's killing me. Sometimes I fall asleep in class."

14 For many undergraduates, "life is just work, school, and home." There may be time to gulp the coffee, but there is absolutely "no time to smell the coffee." This is no surprise given the dramatic rise in the proportion of students who work while attending college (now about 60 percent) or the growing percentage who are working full-time (currently 24 percent overall and as high as 39 percent at two-year colleges) (Undergraduate Survey, 1993). During the 1990s, 71 percent of the colleges surveyed reported increases in the proportion of students working while attending college (Student Affairs Survey, 1997). The increase in part-time attenders and students with families is also a factor. Today almost one in five college students (18 percent) has dependent children (Undergraduate Survey, 1993). With all the demands on their time, something has got to give. They have elected to sacrifice social life.

But not all of the retreat from social life 15 is time-based. Chief student affairs officers describe students more often as loners than in the past. Requests for single dormitory rooms have skyrocketed. The thought of having a roommate is less appealing than it once was. Perhaps this desire to withdraw simply mirrors the national trend of disengagement from groups that once connected individuals with a broad swath of other people who shared similar interests. Across the country we are losing our "social capital"—the networks and norms of society—as civic organizations once as commonplace and popular as the Boy Scouts and local bowling leagues have suffered huge declines in membership; so laments Robert Putnam in his thought-provoking essay "Bowling Alone" (1995).

Similarly, group activities that once con- 16 nected students on college campuses are losing their appeal and are becoming more individualized. For instance, the venue for television watching has moved from the lounge to the dorm room. Film viewing has shifted from the theater to the home VCR. As one student put it, these days dormitory rooms come "fully loaded." A dean of students said he was worried about wiring; can it support the electronic menagerie behind each residence hall door? Equally important is whether college can afford to support financially the needed upgrades in wiring, cable, and other technological infrastructure demanded and expected by current undergraduates. Student rooms have microwaves, televisions, VCRs, computers, CD players, tape decks, phones, answering machines, refrigerators, coffee makers, and who knows what else. The dean said, "Everything is right there." He could not imagine a reason, other than eating or attending class, why a student would need to leave his or her room.

That is the point. Increasingly, students 17 are living their lives in ways that allow them not to venture out.

Source: Arthur Levine and Jeanette S. Cureton, "Retreat From Intimacy," in *When Hope and Fear Collide: A Portrait of Today's College Student.* Jossey-Bass, 1998 pp. 93–101.

DISCUSSION QUESTIONS

1. After carefully reading this argument at least twice, work through it with a classmate and see if you can identify any unsupported claims. Then compare your findings with other pairs in your class. Does the existence of these inadequately supported claims (if you found any) weaken the credibility of the argument? Could the claims have been documented?

2. The authors do not provide any lists of the questions that were asked in their surveys and interviews. Yet the wording of such questions can influence the answers obtained. With a small group of your classmates, compose two lists of interview questions that you would ask a group of students at your school about a well-defined topic—for example, the food in the cafeteria, entertainment on campus, parking facilities, and so on. In the first list, try to keep the wording as neutral as possible; in the second, create "leading" questions that attempt to get at predetermined answers.

3. Conduct two sets of interviews of the rest of your class with these questions. How different are the answers? How do these differences reflect upon the authors' decision to omit their interview and survey questions from the text?

4. Levine and Cureton do not identify their intended audience. Based upon this part of their argument, how would you identify that audience? What clues have you based your identification on? What, if anything, do you think the authors want their audience to do as a result of reading the argument?

5. The authors present their data in a number of ways: as part of the text, in tabular form, and as quotations from interviews. Which of these formats do you find most effective? Could all the data have been presented in a single format? What would the effect have been?

SUGGESTIONS FOR WRITING (13.1)

1. College campuses today may be more troubled by alcohol abuse than Levine and Cureton suggest was true in the mid-'90s. Using your own school as subject, write a three- to five-page causal analysis of this phenomenon. Remember to establish the factuality of your effect and cause(s). Assume that the readers of this argument are your student peers.

2. Write a letter to your college president recommending steps to alleviate the drinking problem on your campus. If you are not aware of such a problem, select another one and write a letter to your president recommending solutions.

3. Using the other students in this class as a sample, create two surveys designed to determine what these students do "for fun." In the first, provide open-ended questions that one half of the class must answer without prompts. In the second, provide a list of alternative activities that the other half must choose from. Compare the results of the two surveys.

   Write a two-page causal analysis speculating on the reasons for the different responses.

4. While Levine and Cureton may be experts on the topic of today's college student, they write from an outside perspective. Those of you who belong to the generation they describe have first-hand experience that the authors cannot claim. Based upon your familiarity with your college peers, write a five-page argument assessing the accuracy of Levine and Cureton's claims. The support for the generalizations you make may be personally experienced facts, but be sure to supply enough of these to make your generalizations credible.

TALKIN' BOUT MY GENERATION

LIZ CROTEAU

Liz Croteau wrote this opinion piece in 1998 when she was a college junior at the Rochester Institute of Technology. This argument was printed in the annual "Opinion" edition of the RIT student magazine, the Reporter.

Similar to Levine and Cureton, Croteau views her generation as "afraid to care, fearful for our futures." And like them, she offers explanations.

1   My generation. We are called cynical, apathetic, lazy. We are freakish in our tastes in clothing and music and accessories. We are pierced and tattooed, heroin-chic and goth, with brightly-colored hair and skimpy, baggy, grungy clothing. Generation X . . . no name, no hope, no voice except to whine.

2   Perhaps it is just one more whine from the masses, but I object. Yes, we are a generation afraid to care, fearful for our futures, and saturated by media and hype. But why?

3   We are the latchkey generation. We lost both parents to the Big '80s world of earn, earn, earn to spend, spend, spend; orphans of the corporate machine. We are the children of "Just say no," "Just do it," "Not me, not now," and were told we wanted our MTV. We learned to read with Big Bird and SchoolHouse Rock taught us the rest. If a parent read to us, it was likely a nice, quick, Little Golden Book to get us through the night and get them back to the grind.

4   As we grew, we were educated amidst controversy and tension. The wall fell before many of us figured out why we were supposed to hate Communism. Our teachers tried to teach us and make us safe while not discussing masturbation, homosexuality, a score of banned books, AIDS, STD's, or anything that might not be "politically correct." Our math scores lagged behind the now-fearsome Japanese economic machine. We were pressured to succeed, but still be part of the kinder, gentler nation.

5   We were told to care about the environment, even though the corporations still tear down rain forests and pour sludge into the rivers. We were told to recycle, even though most of the recycled materials still wind up in the landfills. We were told honesty was the best policy as we learned about Watergate, CIA cover-ups, Irangate, Whitewater, and the various and sundry sexual, financial, and moral transgressions of our politicians.

6   We were told to keep up with current events, though they hurtled at us at ever-increasing speeds in ever-shortening sound bites. Bosnia, Serbia, the two hundred countries that used to be the USSR . . . a swiftly changing planet that destroyed our sense of the world's geography that most of us didn't learn anyway. Communism fell, then began to pick itself up again. Mother Russia gave way to Red China as our political nemesis,

even though we have no qualms about buying China's goods.

7   The apathy that the older generation senses is not willful; it is for our own emotional protection from a world we were thrown to, unprotected and unguided. The cynicism is our response to our media-drenched world that taught us, from our first steps on Sesame Street, that though it may be a beautiful day in the neighborhood, McGruff wants you not to talk to strangers because sometimes they don't have your best interests at heart. We distrust authority, because we have seen the lies and the double-talk from day one on our baby-sitter's television screen.

8   Perhaps blaming the inattention of the last generation for the angst of this one is just another sign of my times. Or, perhaps, the desire to call it as we see it is our most fearsome trait. In a world of Watergates and Irangates, whitewash and Whitewater, and "do as I say not as I do" rhetoric, honesty is something our elders might like to see . . . X'ed out.

Source: Liz Croteau, "Talkin' Bout My Generation," in *Reporter Magazine*, Rochester Institute of Technology, Rochester, New York, 1998, pp. 15–16.

DISCUSSION QUESTIONS

1. Liz Croteau's essay appears under the heading "Opinion." Does it also qualify as an *argument*? Why or why not?

2. This essay's first paragraph makes good use of the aural qualities discussed in Chapter 10. With a few students in your class, conduct an aural analysis of the introduction, using the analysis in Chapter 10 as a model.

3. Croteau appoints herself as a spokesperson for her generation. Compare her credibility with that of Levine and Cureton, who write from an outsider perspective.

4. The author addresses an audience of her peers. How would the tone, content, and references have worked with a different audience—say her parents' generation, for example?

SUGGESTIONS FOR WRITING (13.2)

1. Write a two- to three-page argument agreeing or disagreeing with Croteau's generational portrait. Support your own generalizations with personally experienced facts.

2. Compose a one-page "Opinion" essay characterizing your parents' generation. Have a classmate circle the claims that would require support in a fully developed argument. If you are an adult student (over the age of 25) characterize your own generation.

3. For each general characteristic made in Suggestion #2, compose a list of speculative causes for these effects. What kind of support would you need for these causal claims?

4. Most colleges and universities make their student publications available online, usually with an archiving function. Examine the weekly student newspaper of three schools (excluding your own), and write an evaluation of one of them (three to four pages). The evaluative term is up to you, but be sure it is sufficiently limited, clear, and, if necessary, defined. For example, if you claimed that "Paper X regularly demonstrates first-rate reporting," you would need to provide a very clear definition of "first-rate reporting."

SUPER EGOS

PETER FRANCESE

This essay appeared in August of 1997 in a marketing research magazine called Mar-keting Tools. Peter Francese is a market analyst for Dow Jones & Co. In other words, he is in the business of making and relying on highly generalized portraits of large groups of people. Here, Francese interprets results from a national survey of college freshmen.

1   For all the fretting about self-esteem that marked their high school years, today's college sopho-mores feel pretty good about them-selves. Nearly 58 percent of last year's incoming freshmen rated themselves "above average" or "highest 10 percent" in academic ability, compared to 31 percent of incoming freshmen in 1971, ac-cording to a 1996 survey con-ducted by the UCLA Higher Educa-tion Research Institute. A majority of 1996 freshmen (54 percent) also expressed above-average levels of intellectual self-confidence, com-pared to only 35 percent in 1971.

2   UCLA researchers have been surveying college freshmen annu-ally for 31 years, and they have never before recorded such across-the-board high levels of self-confidence. Specifically, last year's freshmen gave themselves unprece-dented high marks for their abili-ties in leadership, public speaking, mathematics, artistic endeavors, and writing.

All the Children Are Above Average

The UCLA study has noted a hefty increase in the number of "A" students over the past 30 years.

(Freshman reporting "A" averages in high school by percent)

1996

1986

1976

1966

0%　5%　10%　15%　20%　25%　30%　35%

Source: UCLA Higher Education Research Institute

3   This uncommon aplomb may be based on uncommonly good grades. Nearly one-third (31.5 percent) told UCLA researchers that they had "A" averages in high school, more than twice the number that reported top grades in 1966. The 1996 report attrib-utes the increase to "grade inflation," a po-lite term for what happens when teachers feel pressured to bestow an "A" on B-plus work.

4   What is remarkable about this study is the disconnection between what freshmen said and the reality of their lives in college. Last year's freshmen also set a record for frequently or occasionally oversleeping and missing class or an appointment (34 per-cent, compared to 19 percent in 1968). Nev-ertheless, half of the 1996 respondents (49 percent) expect to make at least a "B" aver-age, and two-thirds (66 percent) plan to go

to graduate school. It appears that these students feel a sense of entitlement to good grades and a place in graduate school regardless of the amount of effort they expend during their undergraduate careers.

5   The gap between self-image and reality has profound implications for the service sector. First, some college graduates are going to be very disappointed to find that employers demand a lot more from them than their teachers and professors. Second, many employers are going to find it hard to sustain high performance with entry-level managers who may be more focused on nurturing their egos than on taking care of customers.

The contrast between image and reality also suggests problems for the market research industry. When researchers ask for customer input on a product or service, will they get the true picture, or nice words to make them feel good about themselves?   6

Source: Peter Francese, "Super Egos," in *Marketing Tools,* 1997, p. 64.

DISCUSSION QUESTIONS

1. In Par. 4, Francese makes the following interpretive claim: "It appears that these students feel a sense of entitlement to good grades and a place in graduate school regardless of the amount of effort they expend during their undergraduate careers." Identify the support for this claim and discuss with your classmates whether this support is sufficient.

2. Identify the causal claims of this argument and discuss the adequacy of their support.

3. Search the World Wide Web for information on Francese and the work he does. Do his credentials qualify him to interpret this UCLA data?

4. How helpful is the graphic included in Francese's article? Would the point have been made as clearly without it? Are there other facts that would have been clarified by a similar chart?

SUGGESTIONS FOR WRITING (13.3)

1. Make a copy of this article. Then go over it as if you are the professor and Francese is one of your students who has written an assigned factual argument about trends in college grades. Identify all the strengths and weaknesses of the essay, provide comments and questions, and give the paper a grade.

2. Working with a small group of your classmates, create a one-page survey for your class designed to identify a) their musical preferences; b) their post-graduation ambitions; or c) their political persuasion. Ask the class to fill out the survey and to identify their age, gender, and ethnicity. Then write a one- to two-page argument in which you make generalizations about your findings including patterns of responses in certain subpopulations. Conclude the essay with speculations about causes for the survey results. Attach the survey and tabulated results to your argument.

3. Consider possible alternative interpretations of the contradictory data cited in Par. 4. In a one-page outline, identify how you would support this interpretation—that is, what kind of support, how much, in what order?

4. Francese is clearly writing about traditional-aged college students. In a two-page argument, compare Francese's characterization of these students with your own characterization of working adult students.

WHO IS A TEACHER?

CELESTE M. CONDIT

You may be used to hearing your fellow students complain about their treatment by professors, but it may surprise you to hear this writer, a college professor, complain about her treatment by students. Celeste Condit, Professor of Communications at the University of Georgia, is a seasoned teacher whose experience has led her to some less than favorable generalizations about her students.

Clearly originating in the author's experience of dissonance, this argument was written for an audience of other professors. Even for this audience, however, the claims are provocative and unexpected.

Who Is a Teacher?

1   In any speaking situation (and teaching is invariably a speaking situation), all speakers arrive with and develop what classical rhetoricians called "ethos." One's ethos is one's perceived character or persona. It is who the audience thinks you are. Ethos is derived from social roles, personal appearance, voice quality, management of language, selection of reasons, and a complex amalgam of expectations and behavioral interactions. It strongly influences both the nature of the affective relations between speaker and audience and the persuasiveness of the message that the speaker offers.

2   Those who wish to impose cutting edge theories on teaching practices generally presume a certain kind of ethos for the teacher. They presume that the teacher is powerful, probably excessively powerful, and that the teacher has high credibility with the students. They worry that the teacher's power and credibility will cow the students and take away the students' ability to find their own identity or develop their own "voice." In this version of the ivory tower, the professor is in control. Even when the professor decides to "share power" and engage in a collaborative model of teaching, it is the professor who makes that decision. Moreover, this teacher is a rational animal. The teacher rationally and thoughtfully matches theory to practice. Even when the professor decides to abdicate authority and engage in dialogue, this is only a strategy. It is still the teacher, in conversation with other theorists, who decides what rationally devised "theory" is to be presented (or embodied) in the classroom.

3   I do not live in this theoretical university. When teaching undergraduates, I often feel less like a confident, rational professor than a battered woman who cannot escape a bad marriage. For me, undergraduate teaching is not a matter of thoughtful direction of delicate student minds, but more like a desperate attempt to make a relationship work while the other party maneuvers energetically and angrily to shell me. The regnant theories of teaching thus fail me, and call me to search for some alternatives.

4   To reach for these alternatives requires that I share with you some of my experiences from the classroom. To some extent, these experiences are grounded in gendered experience. To a large extent, however, these gendered experiences raise a more general set of issues about the power of the teacher. Unfortunately, like most

members of most oppressed groups, I am not good at drawing the line between those experiences—it is all too easy to see all trauma as gendered. So I will leave it to the men to say which experiences they share. Before I begin, I want to mention that the teaching experiences I describe below will appear very bleak, and that they do not constitute an accurate picture of all of my teaching experience—there are many joyful moments in teaching. However, it is important to attend to the bad side of teaching, and I have had too many of these bad experiences at the University of Georgia, a large Southern "research" university, named by *Money* magazine as one of the "best buys" in the nation.

5   When I came to teach at Georgia, I came to an entirely new set of experiences of teaching. One of the most shocking elements of that experience was the repeated nonverbal behaviors of male students. Most notably, whenever they wanted me to change their grade or give them an "excused absence," they would put their arms around my shoulders or place their hands on my knee. The first time this happened to me, in the middle of a classroom, with other students milling around, I was so stunned I could not react other than by shrugging and backing away. Later, I was to get angry and tell them not to touch me, for which I was verbally accosted. Later still, I learned to give them a quiet, unthreatening explanation about nonverbal behavior and professional gender norms. But as I watched the world around me, I discovered that this mannerism was a routine way in which white Southern males exhibit their dominance over females. Because it was so routine, there was no way (other than submission) that I could react to this behavior without being labeled a "bitch." In the worst cases, that label is overtly used; a female colleague of mine has even been chased by a male student down the hall yelling at her for assigning him a low grade. I myself have been physically threatened \and have had to ask for the protection of campus police.

6   These are the clearest examples of male control in the classroom to which I can point, but they are not the only type of control that is exercised, and probably not the most important one; gender manifests itself in a variety of ways. On a regular basis, male students challenge not only my arguments, but my right to tell them what to do. It is difficult to describe the nonverbal behaviors by which these challenges are made. It is a glare, a lifted chin, a defiance. Occasionally these gestures break out into verbal form, as with the eighteen-year-old who told me (a middle-aged full professor), "you have to earn my respect." The control is also issued in other ways. Male students talk more, and they make it very difficult for me to address female students and raise issues that I perceive are more salient for female students.

7   When I walk into the classroom each quarter, I dread the new term, for I know that, each time, I am going to have to go through a battle establishing my authority; and in classrooms with a hundred students, authority is a necessity. This is not the game I came to the role of teacher to play. It is not the role that my feminist theory would have me play. But I have learned that I am forced to play it, or I cannot be a teacher here. I am now fairly good at waging this battle. I do not lose very often anymore, but I am sapped, and I flinch from teaching undergraduates so that I can avoid these battles.

8   I believe that this "battle of the sexes" that plays itself out in the South is merely an extreme form of something that goes on in most classrooms in America. To put it bluntly, students are not our pawns. They are not sheep that we decide to teach "actively" or "passively." They are highly motivated, highly skilled, and enormously self-interested people who feel themselves forced to share a classroom with us, often against their desires, and they intend to minimize the pain we cause them, and sometimes to maximize the pain they inflict on us.

9   The ethos of "student" has probably always contained more resistance to teach-

ers than our formal theorizing has recognized. The records show that students at Georgia were throwing things at professors and spitting in classrooms and skipping classes in the nineteenth century, and of course demonstrations against the authority of the university were common and loud in the sixties even in the South. However, there are a variety of institutional factors that seem to enhance this power in our own era.

10   The first institutional support for student power is the use and character of teaching evaluations. Let me say first that I believe that students have a right to give anonymous feedback, and, except in exceptional circumstances, I tend to get high teaching evaluations numerically. However, I do this *not* by being a good teacher, but by catering to the prejudices of the students and avoiding irritating their prickly tempers. Nonetheless, I have been attacked in the "open-ended comments" on teaching evaluations, and my younger female peers are even more prone to punishment via this means. Repeatedly, women-oriented content (it needn't be "feminist") garners the ire of male students. They readily report on teaching evaluations that one is "too feminist" or is "biased." This is not in any way an objective evaluation. Even by introducing two or three speeches by women and another two or three speeches by blacks, a female teacher in a speech class can earn this sobriquet on her evaluations. "Too feminist" means simply that one expresses the view that women speakers have had special problems and were historically silenced. It does not mean that one enacts the speaking style or values and arguments of Andrea Dworkin. In other words, for these students, any equality is too much equality.

11   In my experience, male colleagues do not take this kind of abuse. If they do teach feminist content, they are not suspected of being a "biased special interest" (my geologist husband gleefully calls all dinosaurs "she" in his class, and students never complain about his feminism). If males teach conservative content instead of objective or liberal (as in the "liberal arts") content, this is taken as "natural" or "objective" and so not commented on. But even if men do receive political attacks for their perspectives, note two things. First, the point is the same. *Students are exercising enormous power in controlling what is taught in the classroom.* Second, the uses to which these comments are put by administrators are different. Female teachers have their raises and promotions threatened by these comments. Department heads put these comments into year end evaluations as signs of failures of teaching. (I am reporting actual incidents here, not engaging in general hand wringing.) I do not believe the same happens for men. (This may be hand wringing.)

This problem is even greater for female   12 graduate students. I have now had to counsel a parade of female graduate students who received bad course evaluations. In every case, I have gone to observe their teaching in the classroom, only to find them well organized, well prepared, and giving substantive lectures. In each case, the students saw the women as "biased" and "unfair." I believe they did so primarily because of the women's gender. The graduate supervisor, in one case, commented that *he* never had problems with this. Students never challenged his politics. But of course, he fit the profile of a "professor" and its gender expectations, and he sported relatively conservative politics. Judging from his reactions to my graduate students' comprehensive examination papers, I do not think that he is any less biased in the classroom, but he certainly is perceived as less biased. The minute a woman instructor walks into a Southern classroom in pants and short hair she is branded as outside the bounds of the normal—a liberal, a feminist, or a dyke. There is little she can do to dispute that automatic rejection. Male professors have to work a little harder to earn that kind of rejection.

So what happens to the female graduate   13 students? I counsel them to learn to "perform objectivity" for their students, and to drop all the examples that matter to them and their female students. I teach them to lie low, hide themselves and their interests and politics until they become full professors and can tolerate the salary hits. In other words, the vocal, white, male, upper-middle-class undergraduate students get their way.

14   The misuse of teaching evaluations is, unfortunately, not the sole factor in this battering of the college teacher. There are higher administrative structures that participate in this game as well. One notes first the reward structure of the university. Our university takes great pride in the fact that it "takes teaching seriously," but this means only that it rewards those teachers who please students. Good teaching, in my view, requires a lot of hard work focused on writing and speaking exchanges that require extensive feedback (i.e., lots of time outside the classroom). This kind of good teaching, however, is in no way recognized by the institution. Moreover, many students resent both the time they have to put into such assignments and the fact that your feedback to them inevitably asks them to improve (and therefore implies that they are not perfect just as they are). Thus the university definition of good teaching as catering to the lowest common denominator among student pleasure represents a double whammy to the would-be good teacher. Your salary is imperiled and no awards are forthcoming if you do not soothe the students, and if you do teach well, this will take time away from your research responsibilities, and you will be further imperiled.

15   All these problems are further exacerbated by the fact that administrations across the country are pushing for larger and larger classes. The battles of one professor against thirty-five are magnified tenfold when it becomes one professor against the anonymous hundred. Here the culture of student resistance becomes enormously powerful. It makes it impossible to run a democratic classroom or an active one. Students, when told to think and argue, break out into the chaos of a mob, and the instructor is chastised for "losing control of the classroom." The culture of resistance enabled in this environment has taught students to challenge every grade structure and every administrative decision of a professor as "unfair" (where fair is defined as "not to my advantage").

16   Finally, there are "staff" functions, those efforts to "improve teaching," that also batter the (woman) teacher. When faced with the task of teaching classes exceeding a hundred students I diligently began to attend the "large lecture discussion group" on campus. In only a few sessions I learned my lesson. If one admits, before such a body, that one has any type of difficulty teaching, one is immediately attacked for one's bad teaching. One is "at fault." There are no systemic problems, no basic gender difficulties, no bad students. There are only bad teachers. The purpose of these groups is to share successes, which means that elderly male business professors sit around and tell everyone about their wonderful models and many successes, as they bid against each other for this year's teaching awards.

17   By now it should be clear that I see the professor who would well and truly teach as being required to respond to a powerful student culture, and I see a variety of university structures complicit in enhancing student power over teachers. I see female instructors as particularly vulnerable to this power, but I recognize that the same forces are at work against male instructors (they simply have a few more tools to deal with the problems). To some extent, we are all Doonesbury's Professor Deadmon.

Source: Celeste M. Condit, "Theory, Practice, and the Battered (Woman) Teacher," in *Teaching What You're Not: Identity Politics in Higher Education*, Katherine J. Mayberry, ed. New York University Press, 1996, pp. 156–162.

DISCUSSION QUESTIONS

1. Into what class or classes of argument does Condit's essay fall? Identify the central claim or claims.

2. Condit's arrangement of supporting arguments is thoughtful and effective. After carefully reading the argument at least twice, prepare an outline that reflects the kind of support used and its arrangement (use Chapter 4 as a reference for the varieties of support).

3. With a group of your classmates, make a list of changes you would make in the tone, language, and style of this essay if its audience were male college students.

4. Because so much of her argument relies on personal experience, it is critical that Condit project a balanced, objective image. To what extent is she successful in portraying herself in this way?

5. Condit's argument contains much more modest generalizations than some of the other essays in this unit. But even modest generalizations must be warranted by specific examples. Discuss with your classmates the degree to which the writer's general conclusions are credible and reasonable.

SUGGESTIONS FOR WRITING (13.4)

1. Using your own experience and observations as support, write a three- to four-page argument in support or contradiction of Condit's argument about student behavior.

2. Write a letter to Professor Condit recommending, from the student's point of view, strategies she might develop to ease the difficulties she has experienced with students.

3. In Par. 14, Condit offers the following definition of "good teaching": "Good teaching, in my view, requires a lot of hard work focused on writing and speaking exchanges that require extensive feedback (i.e., lots of time outside the classroom)." Create your own extended definition of "good teaching" (approximately two to three pages).

4. Write a general portrait of college professors at your school. Assume that your audience is the upper administration (i.e., president, provost, deans) of the institution. You may limit your support to your own experience and the experiences reported by your acquaintances, but be sure the support is adequate to support the breadth of the claim(s).

A LOST MOMENT RECAPTURED

SARA RIMER

As Sara Rimer demonstrates in this article from the New York Times *(January 9, 2000), the 18–22-year-old post-adolescent is no longer the "typical" college student. Increasingly, traditional-aged students are finding themselves in classes with students closer to their parents' ages than their own. As Rimer points out, 25 percent of today's undergraduates are 30 years and older, as compared with 11 percent in 1972. The Smith College program written about here, which accepts mature women as full-time, residential students, is one of the more extraordinary approaches to what used to be called "adult education."*

A LOST MOMENT RECAPTURED

1   At 43, Sandy Colvard did not simply go back to college. She did something far more daring: she quit her job as a logistician with the United States Navy, packed up a U-Haul, drove from her home in Virginia to Smith College in Massachusetts and moved into a dormitory with 84 other undergraduates.

2   Her room measures all of 9 feet by 9 feet, big enough for a bed, desk and chair. She shares a bathroom with 14 women—and, on weekends, their boyfriends. Some of the women are messy. They leave hair in the sink. This fall, a chocolate bar landed in the dryer in the laundry. Dorm food is hardly haute cuisine, and dinner is served ridiculously early, at 5:30. Cutter House, four stories of cinder blocks unadorned by a single ivy vine, is considered one of the ugliest buildings on campus. Ms. Colvard, however, is not complaining.

3   Though her parents had been opposed to her going to college and had refused to fill out financial aid forms, she enrolled at the University of Maryland anyway after high school. But she had to quit within a year: she ran out of money and found herself homeless.

4   Twenty-four years later, Smith College accepted Ms. Colvard into its Ada Comstock Scholars Program, which was begun in 1975 to allow nontraditional-age students to complete their undergraduate degrees.

5   "When I got the letter that I had been accepted, I sat on the floor of my living room and I cried," said Ms. Colvard, whose stepfather was a sheet-metal worker and mother a bookkeeper. Neither went to college.

6   Ms. Colvard's story is not unusual, despite the advances women have made in higher education (8.4 million women versus 6.7 million men were enrolled in college in 1996, according to the Department of Education's latest statistics). Many of the "Adas," as they are known, have had families who discouraged their academic aspirations, said Eleanor Rothman, who shep-

herded hundreds of students through the program during her 23 years as its director. "I got a call once from a Hispanic woman in California whose 45-year-old daughter was here," Mrs. Rothman recalled. "She said, 'I don't know what you people are doing. What does she think she's going to do when she comes home with her fancy degree?'"

7   This year, there are 207 women in the program, which is named for Ada Comstock Notestein, who died in 1973 and had been a professor, dean and trustee of Smith and a president of Radcliffe College. While most Adas rent apartments off campus or commute, some prefer the cheaper option of a dorm. This fall, Cutter House is home to 14 older women.

8   In a way, the program demonstrates that it is possible to recapture a lost moment. "One of the missions of women's colleges has always been to allow women to think of themselves as individuals and not just in terms of social or familial roles," said Ellen Fitzpatrick, a historian at the University of New Hampshire in Durham, who has studied women in higher education.

9   "Young women are there to learn and to think about who they are and what they can contribute in an environment more free of gendered expectations. Older women who come back to college return with lives already shaped by these expectations, some of them low expectations. It's a situation of unusual freedom to strip away those expectations, to find out what they want to do, to explore different aspects of liberal education and to examine again their own sense of self. It can be, and often is, an exhilarating experience."

10   Kathi Legare got married at 19 and became a foster parent at 20. She worked as a waitress and helped run the office of her husband's plumbing business. She was 37 when she entered Smith. She and her husband, Brian, had seven children at home, six of them adopted. She hoped a degree

would help her find a career, and commuted two hours each day from Connecticut. She graduated in 1996, earned her master's degree from the Smith College School of Social Work, and is now a social worker.

11   "I went to Smith without a clear understanding of what anything in the world was about," Mrs. Legare said. "I knew reality from the blue-collar standpoint, but I had no idea about social policy—other than how it affected my children—about world politics, about local politics, the courts, the way others lived in general. My eyes opened wide when I got there. I was reading books I never knew existed."

12   Alyssa Mahoney, 36, a former hospice caregiver, is juggling her studies at Smith as a premed student with her responsibilities as the single parent of a 4-year-old boy. "One of the most common responses of Adas when they get into Smith is, 'They made a mistake,'" said Ms. Mahoney, who is from the Mission Hill neighborhood of Boston and, like most Adas, attended community college. "In your heart, you think, 'I'm here under false pretenses.'"

13   Smith is an intensely demanding college. On a recent night at Cutter House, the Adas and the trads, as traditional-age students are called, were mostly engaged in studying. Sandy Colvard was bent over precalculus textbooks in her room. On one wall was a poster with the Smith motto "Where Women's Minds Matter."

14   It was a half-hour before dinner, and Ms. Colvard was glad for the interruption when several young dormmates wandered by to admire her new short haircut and chat about the grueling workload. While dressed unremarkably in blue jeans and a Smith sweatshirt, Ms. Colvard did not wear the sweatshirt quite as casually as the younger students. On her, it held particular resonance; she had waited a quarter century to go to college, and a prestigious liberal arts one, no less.

15   To the trads, the Adas seem worldly. Shannon Friedrichs, a 21-year-old senior who hopes to work in the media, has become friendly with Kimberly B. Marlowe, 42, who came to Smith from *The Seattle Times*, where she was a staff writer. "Most of us have led very cloistered lives," Ms. Friedrichs said. "To have a woman who's been in the work force, who can give you advice about how to go about negotiating the work world, has been very helpful."

16   Occasionally, Ms. Friedrichs said, the older women can be dismissive. "They'll write us off because we're only 21, and we haven't had the life experience," she said.

17   Anne C. Martindell has had plenty of life experience. At 85, she is the oldest Ada on campus. She spent a year at Smith, from 1932 to '33, but was forced by her father to withdraw. "He wanted me to get married, and he thought it was a complete waste of time for me to be here," Mrs. Martindell said. "He thought I'd scare men off by being overeducated."

18   She did get married, and raised four children. But she also became active in New Jersey Democratic politics—as a state senator—and was appointed the first female ambassador to New Zealand, under President Jimmy Carter in 1979. Now Mrs. Martindell is back to finish her degree in American studies and write her memoirs.

19   Liz Land, 72, was a 16-year-old freshman when she arrived in Northampton from Manhattan in 1943. At the end of her sophomore year, she married a chemical engineer and graduate of the Massachusetts Institute of Technology. A week later, Smith returned her deposit for the next year; married women were not considered appropriate in the campus mix. Mrs. Land, who has four grown children, five grandchildren and two step-grandchildren, spends four days a week in Northampton and three days in Westport, Conn., with her husband, Gay.

20   While high-school seniors struggle to dredge up sufficient experiences to round out their admissions essays, midlife students have more than enough to write about. They often have trouble containing their complicated lives—husbands, children, jobs, volunteer work, setbacks, failures, illness, death—within the essay's allotted length. In hers, Mrs. Colvard wrote

how, at about the time she left college, someone informed her mother and stepfather that she was a lesbian.

21   "When my stepfather broke my jaw and threatened to kill me, I had to leave quickly," she wrote in her essay. "So, at 19 years of age, for about six months, I found myself homeless. I survived. I lived in my car, sleeping during the day and driving at night to stay warm."

22   During the next 10 years, she held a number of jobs—as part of a road construction crew, a delivery person, convenience-store clerk, truck driver, warehouse worker and secretary. She also described in the essay the all-women country rock band she started, Big Night Out.

23   Like many Ada scholars, Ms. Colvard received generous financial aid to attend Smith.

24   "We've had women who have overcome child abuse," Mrs. Rothman said. "They've overcome addictions. They've overcome serious mental illness and families that were hostile to the idea of college. We've had some women who, when they graduate, there is no one from their family to watch them graduate."

25   Many of the 1,375 Ada graduates have become social workers, teachers, school administrators and lawyers. They are more likely than younger graduates to choose the helping professions, according to Mrs. Rothman. "Many have had a hard time, and they want to help someone else," she said.

26   The Adas are part of a steadily growing trend of adults returning to college. The Census Bureau reports that more than 25 percent of today's undergraduates are age 30 or older, an increase of some 11 percent since 1972; 63 percent of those students are women. Half of nontraditional students study at community colleges, half at four-year colleges, and most attend near their homes, according to the Office of Adult Learning Services for the College Board.

27   While the majority of older students are seeking credentials and skills that can help their careers, those students at Smith and other elite women's colleges, like Mount Holyoke in South Hadley, Mass., and Bryn Mawr in Pennsylvania, seem more focused on gaining the knowledge that comes with a liberal arts degree.

28   "I with I could take at least one class in every subject," said Ms. Colvard, whose parents had pushed her to settle into a job as a legal secretary when she was in high school and earning straight A's. "I want to learn Latin and Greek. I always thought it would be so wonderful to read *The Odyssey* in Greek. I want to take a theater class, and more literature. There's nothing much I'm not interested in."

29   Ms. Colvard, who plans to major in religion with a minor in music, is still earning mostly A's. The Adas traditionally get higher grade point averages than undergraduates, and also graduate with a high rate of honors.

30   "Before, I would have been thrilled to get a B minus," said Ms. Marlowe, who is majoring in American studies, recalling the year she spent in college after high school. "Now, if I got a B minus, I'd hang myself."

31   Ms. Marlowe and other Adas—Mrs. Martindell, Mrs. Land, Roberta Jordan, 60, Cypriane Williams, 35—were sparkling recently in Daniel Horowitz's core class in American studies, an examination of methods of looking at American culture. With 27 students seated around him in a circle, Professor Horowitz was leading a discussion of the week's reading assignment, a book about African-American culture—dress, music, language—written by two Australians.

32   While younger students were hardly shy about expressing their opinions, the Adas could not contain their enthusiasm. Several commented that this sort of cultural study was relatively new. Mrs. Martindell, with her ambassador years in New Zealand, said that the Australian authors must have brought to their examination knowledge of Aborigines and their body painting. Ms. Williams questioned the legitimacy of two white men from Australia writing about African-Americans. Ms. Marlowe said the book should carry a disclaimer: Anyone reading it should have already studied slavery.

33   Adas always do the reading, turn in papers on time and have much to say. "Everyone talks about race, class, and gender, but

here you've got age, said Professor Horowitz, the author of a recent biography of a 1942 Smith graduate, Betty Friedan. "It really does add depth and perspective. I think of them as not unlike the men who came back to school on the G.I. Bill after World War II. They've been in battle, and boy, the education means something. That sets the tone for the discussion."

34 The Adas, of course, have had to make major adjustments to the rigors of academic life.

35 "My first semester, I was somewhat intimidated," said Ms. Jordan, whose father made it clear to her when she was a teenager that with seven brothers, she was not going to be the one to go to college. "There was a trad who sat next to me in Gothic literature last year who was 16, and she would speak right up. I was just intimidated. But I realized as the weeks went by that I had something to contribute that the trads didn't have."

36 Ms. Jordan raised two daughters mostly by herself—she was divorced—and helped put them through college partly by working her way up from secretary to vice president at a New Hampshire real-estate firm. She remarried in 1990; her husband, a landscape painter, died three years later.

37 "I didn't even know whether to use pen and paper in class," Mrs. Land said. "I didn't know how to prepare a paper. Should it be double-spaced? Where do you put your name?"

38 Campus life also has its uncertainties.

39 Adrienne McAlpine, 41, said she found dating a challenge, given her living situation at Cutter House. "What do you say to a guy? 'How would you like to come over to . . . my dorm?'"

40 She recalled: "I was in the bathroom brushing my teeth, and all of a sudden, there was a man coming out of the stall. I thought, 'Wow, when I was their age, I would have been petrified if that happened.'"

41 Last year, Ms. Jordan and Ms. Marlowe lived on the fifth floor of the Northrup House dormitory. Ms. Marlowe's room was 7 feet by 9 feet. There was no elevator. "It's like military service," she said. "I'm proud I

served, but I wasn't crazy enough to reup for another term."

42 "Half the time they're driving me crazy," Ms. Marlowe said, referring to the trads. "They have purple hair, their music is loud. But the other half I think, 'The country is in good hands.'"

43 As for the tattooing and piercing common among the trads, Mrs. Land said she barely notices that anymore. "It's a good learning experience," she said. "It's a lot like when we used to wear our sweaters backward, and my father never could understand."

44 This year, Ms. Jordan and Ms. Marlowe are sharing a spacious two-bedroom apartment just off campus. Mrs. Land and Mrs. Martindell have apartments in the same building.

45 Mrs. Land's sunny one-bedroom, filled with secondhand furniture—her husband's M.I.T. chair, her son Stephen's desk, her son David's chair. Most Thursdays, she collects her books, closes up the apartment and drives two hours home to Westport. There, she resumes her responsibilities as a wife, doing her husband's laundry and the grocery shopping and cooking. Since her husband stays in Manhattan while she is at Smith, she prepares food he can take back to the city in small containers, like chicken Parmesan, chicken salad, applesauce and hash.

46 She might go to a craft show with her daughter Ellie, or kayak with Stephen. It can be hard to find time to study.

47 Mrs. Land—who has been president of a P.T.A. and the Westport Young Women's League, served on the board of a regional mental health organization and worked with unmarried teenage mothers in Bridgeport, Conn.—made the dean's list last year. She will graduate this spring, three years after her granddaughter Elizabeth Humphries finished.

48 For Ms. Colvard, graduation is, thankfully, several years off. "If I had my druthers, I'd spend the next 10 years here," she said. "All the trads are talking about what they're going to do when they get out of here. I've been out of here. I've done out of here. I want to be in here for a while."

Source: Sara Rimer, "A Lost Moment Recaptured," in the *New York Times*, January 9, 2000, pp. 21–23 and 40.

DISCUSSION QUESTIONS

1. How would you classify this argument? What is the major claim (or claims) and by what kind of secondary arguments is it supported?

2. Isolate three examples of inductive reasoning used here. Using the criteria for sound induction presented in Chapter 5, evaluate the soundness of these claims and their support.

3. Much of the support for this argument consists of personally experienced facts—specifically, interviews Rimer conducted with individual Ada scholars. How does the author establish an image of credibility in her reporting of these interviews.

4. Use the World Wide Web to investigate Sara Rimer's professional credentials. What do you learn through this search about credibility?

5. Could the material in this article support an evaluative major claim? How might such a claim read?

SUGGESTIONS FOR WRITING (13.5)

1. According to the examples in this article, adults tend to be better students than 18–22 year olds. With a group of your classmates, brainstorm about possible reasons for this. What kind of evidence would you need to support these hypotheses?

2. Choose the most plausible and defensible of the hypotheses developed in Suggestion #1 as the working claim for a six- to eight-page causal argument and do the research necessary to support this claim, or a modified version of it (be careful to keep your claim limited, so you won't have to range too widely in the research stage). Hand your (probably revised) claim into your instructor with a bibliography.

3. Taking into consideration any comments made by your instructor about your claim from Suggestion #2, draft a six- to eight-page argument supporting the claim. What changes have you made to your original working claim through the drafting process?

4. After receiving input from a classmate on your draft argument, write a final version, complete with references (using the APA citation format).

STUDENTS BEHAVING BADLY

RICHARD FLACKS

Richard Flacks is a professor of sociology at the University of California, Santa Barbara. In this argument and in book-length studies, Flacks combines his interest in the students he teaches with his own expertise in the field of sociology in creating generalized profiles of "today's college student." Here, he focuses on the special attributes and successes of nontraditional students—those students who do not fit the mold of the middle-class, Caucasian, 18–22 year old. While his findings are similar to Sara Rimer's ("A Lost Moment Re-

captured") and, *in a way to Celeste Condit's ("Who Is a Teacher?"), the methods that lead him to his conclusions are quite different.*

1   Professors have been complaining about the lack of connection between faculty and students at least since the 1980's, with growing dismay at poor lecture attendance and attention, reading assignments that students suddenly find too onerous and courses that must be "dumbed down." Such disengagement, along with the binge-drinking party culture that predominates at many universities today, seems to be part of a broader pattern—a general decline in academic, intellectual and community life on campus.

2   I began to wonder several years ago about who these disconnected students were. My political-sociology class at the University of California, Santa Barbara, had turned in a particularly weak set of essays, yet there were a few papers of polished writing and obvious effort. Those papers had not come from the typical Santa Barbara student, who attends good schools and has high test scores and parents with advanced degrees. They had come from students with demanding and difficult personal lives—a single father of a young child who worked full time and commuted 40 miles a day, a single mother of two school-age children and an older student who had grown up in the inner city and entered college after serving time in prison.

3   In fact, the most active, responsive students in my classes fit this profile. Many were not admitted on the basis of their test scores but had managed to get here by shining in junior college or by dint of affirmative-action admissions policies.

4   In 1995, my colleague Scott Thomas and I began a study to explore whether there was a relationship between student disengagement and social background. We surveyed nearly 1,000 Santa Barbara students, about half white, a quarter Asian and 25 percent underrepresented minorities; 50 students provided diaries and were interviewed in depth.

5   At the extremes, 15 percent had family incomes below $25,000 and 15 percent above $125,000. The latter group's SAT scores averaged almost 200 points higher than those of the disadvantaged students. While their dismal scores would suggest the poor students were unprepared for the demands of college, their grade point averages were only slightly lower than those of the more privileged students: 2.80 versus 2.95.

6   The poor students reported studying 16 to 20 hours a week; students with household incomes of more than $125,000 said they studied fewer than 10 hours a week to maintain their higher grades. They also inhabited U.C.S.B.'s notorious social scene. For most of its 50-year history, the university has been labeled a party school. On any given weekend, music blares and drunken teenagers spill into the streets of the densely populated student enclave, Isla Vista.

7   About 75 percent of the high-income students reported binge drinking (five drinks in one sitting) at least once a month, and 40 percent imbibed excessively three to five times a month. At the same time, 70 percent of the poor students said they never binged. We found similar patterns whether adversity was defined by race, income or family educational levels.

8   In their spare time, the privileged students seemed to keep their distance from the intellectually challenging opportunities the campus offers. Instead, they worked out in the beautiful fitness facilities that were recently opened on campus or they watched television. A typical diary entry recounts a group of friends sitting on a couch watching sitcoms about a group of friends sitting on a couch.

9   Meanwhile, the students taking leadership roles in student government, tutoring in local high schools, attending the performance of a visiting theater troupe or a conference on the global economy were

disproportionately from working-class or minority backgrounds.

10   These highly motivated, striving students call to mind earlier moments in American higher education, when conventional assumptions about class, merit and intellectual passion were challenged.

11   From the 20's through the 50's, New York's city colleges ranked among the top in the nation as producers of future Ph.D.'s; City College was reputed to have one of the most intellectually vibrant student bodies in the country. Its students were overwhelmingly from working-class backgrounds, the first in their families to go to college and often first- and second-generation immigrants. In the 20's and 30's, the college's only admission requirement was a high school average of 60 percent (a C), and after World War II, 80 percent.

12   From 1945 through 1948, with the G.I. Bill of Rights luring students who would never have contemplated college before, two million veterans thronged the city system. A study by the Educational Testing Service in 1952 determined that veterans' college grades tended to be higher than non-veterans' when SAT scores were matched.

13   In the early 20th century, according to Nicholas Lemann's book *The Big Test: The Secret History of the American Meritocracy,* pioneers of testing thought they were creating a fairer basis for college admissions: if selection were based on test scores, working-class students could compete with graduates of prep schools, and colleges would have a solid way to measure the aptitudes of applicants.

14   But studies show that test scores are closely correlated to family income, which determines the quality of a student's schooling and a family's ability to pay for test preparation. There is also growing evidence that scores are affected by biases built into test content and by the emotional effect of the test-taking experience.

15   Conventional wisdom says that tests predict who will succeed in higher education. Accordingly, the best colleges recruit the highest scorers; to upgrade, they raise SAT requirements of the freshman class. Another prevailing assumption is that efforts to increase access and create a more diverse student body will result in admitting students who are unprepared for a college curriculum.

16   Such assumptions now pervade efforts for academic reform. Standardized testing has become the primary way to measure the achievement of individual students, schools and school systems. Teachers and administrators are driven by both sticks and carrots to set and fulfill test score targets. "Teaching to the test" is the newest look in pedagogy.

17   Preparation for college certainly entails mastery of subject matter and the discipline to study and learn; and standardized testing may be a useful tool for assessing educational outcomes. But to exploit the opportunities of higher education, students must be motivated not only to get the right test scores but also to test their values and assumptions, and to stretch their minds.

18   The students of sacrifice, the less-prepared but hungry students who have struggled to get and stay in college, see it as a precious opportunity for self-realization. They are the ones, at least at U.C.S.B., who are making the best use of what higher education has to offer, and at the same time invigorating the intellectual climate of the campus.

Source: Richard Flacks, "Students Behaving Badly," in the *New York Times*, January 9, 2000.

DISCUSSION QUESTIONS

1. In his first paragraph, Flacks offers a series of generalizations about faculty complaints about their students and then summarizes these complaints as "a general decline in academic, intellectual and community life on campus." Chapter 11 of this book tells you that generalizations can be effective intro-

ductory strategies. Discuss the effectiveness of Flacks's generalized introduction. Are the broad statements he makes supported elsewhere in the argument? Do they need to be? What effect does his opening paragraph have on his overall credibility?

2. Flacks's claim, which can be classified as a generalized evaluation, is explicitly stated in the last paragraph of the argument. It is supported by a series of narrower factual generalizations gleaned from a 1995 study of 1,000 Santa Barbara students. Discuss with your classmates and instructor the adequacy of the supporting evidence to the claim. You may want to review the section on "Supporting Factual Generalizations" in Chapter 6 of this book. Does Flacks's sample of 1,000 Santa Barbara students pass the three criteria identified there? Do you need more information about his survey to answer these questions? Is the movement from factual to evaluative generalization reasonable?

3. You know that Richard Flacks is a professor of sociology at UC Santa Barbara. Is this enough information to convince you of his authority and credibility? Where would you go to learn more about him and his reputation as a sociologist?

4. In terms of argument strategy, what purposes are served by the discussions of New York's City College (Par. 11), the G.I. Bill (Par. 12), and test scores (Par. 13–15)? Would Flacks's argument have been equally effective without this material? Why or why not?

5. Presumably, Flacks is summarizing the lengthier findings of his 1995 study. How would you go about finding the full-length study? Conduct your own search and then compare it with the process followed by a few of your classmates.

SUGGESTIONS FOR WRITING (13.6)

1. Using the observations of Flacks, Condit, Rimer, Levine and Cureton, as well as your own as support, write a five- to seven-page characterization of contemporary college students. Your claim will be some form of generalization (factual, causal, evaluative, etc.); given its breadth, you will need to provide adequate qualifiers (as Flacks does in the final sentence of his argument). Provide references using the APA format. (You might want to consult the Web site of the National Center for Education Statistics. You may need to include two or more groups in your characterization.)

2. Select a subpopulation of the student body at your institution—for example, students in a particular major, students in a particular class, students in a particular group—and conduct a series of interviews designed to gather information about their backgrounds, their goals, or their attitudes toward their college experience. Write a three-page summary of your findings (the summary will be a factual generalization).

3. Go to the UC Santa Barbara Web site (Hint: begin with *www.california.edu*). Based upon the information contained there, write a three-page description of the school to an audience of prospective students.

4. In your view, what does it take to be a successful college student? Write a fully supported causal argument answering this question, being sure to provide an extended definition of the term "successful student."

5. Interview one of your favorite professors. Based upon this interview and your own observations of the professor, write a description of "a day in the life of Professor X." Your argument will rely solely upon firsthand experience (your own observations) and the information obtained from the professor, so you will need to report this information carefully, accurately, and authoritatively (see Chapter 6).

14

The Internet

INTRODUCTION

When the idea for creating an anthology of readings featuring "everyday arguments" was conceived back in 1997, the original plan was to include a section of arguments on a variety of technologies informing contemporary life. Our intention was to find exemplary arguments on the familiar and often taken-for-granted devices that quietly influence our lives—from the microchip to the mechanical pencil.

But by the time I began selecting and organizing readings, the century's technological wonder—the Internet—had become at the same time so dominant, so "everyday," and so revolutionary that we scrapped the initial set of readings in favor of the following collection of diverse arguments revolving around that single topic. In looking for arguments on technologies simultaneously commonplace and extraordinary, I realized the 'Net' was made to order for my purposes. Everything about the Internet is breathtaking: the speed with which it has evolved from a novel toy to a dominating medium of human interaction; the grand scale on which those interactions are taking place; the variety of transactions conducted there—from e-commerce to matchmaking to education.

It was not that there was no Internet back in 1997. It existed, it was already powerful, and it was widely used. In 1994, then Vice President Al Gore had called for a "Global Information Infrastructure" built upon the Internet; that infrastructure is now well on its way to full development. But within the relatively short span of time since 1997 (although by Internet time, four years is a lifetime), what had arisen through "an accidental history" in which "the most important parts of the Net piggybacked on technologies that were created for very different purposes"[1]

---

[1]Howard Rheingold. *The Virtual Community: Homesteading on the Electronic Frontier.* Reading, MA: Addison Wesley (1983), 67.

had become a global phenomenon dominating the activities of information distribution, communication, and commerce. Overnight—or so it seemed—the Internet was everywhere and everyone was on the Internet. And they were on the Internet in multiple capacities: as users, producers, consumers, and merchants.

Given what you'll learn in other sections of this anthology about the susceptibility of all social phenomena to endless commentary, argument, and discussion, it should be no surprise to learn that the Internet and its attendant technologies and capabilities have become the occasion for what amounts to a new industry of publications. New magazines like *Wired* and *Internet World* are gaining impressive circulations; bookstore and library shelves are groaning with new tomes on the information superhighway; and, of course, the Internet itself is becoming the repository of countless commentaries on itself.

Some of this print material (both hard copy and electronic) falls within the category of "how-to" writing; but a good deal of it is interpretive, speculative, predictive, and evaluative. The Net is a controversial, complicated, and multifaceted phenomenon that has attracted the attention of countless thoughtful people who are excited, troubled, and disturbed by its endless implications. In short, as the following collection of readings demonstrates, the Net is the stuff of argument—good, bad, and indifferent. And while these readings represent only a miniscule slice of what people are writing and arguing on the subject, they do give some sense of the variety of perspectives that are out there. As with all the readings in this anthology section, you should read these arguments carefully and critically, analyzing each in terms of the principles and practices of effective argument.

DAEMON SEED

DAVID S. BENNAHUM

This argument about the accessibility of e-mail first appeared in the May 1999 issue of Wired *Magazine. Bennahum is a contributing editor to* Wired *as well as the author of a number of books on contemporary computer technology. You'll learn more about the author and the magazine in the following commentary.*

COMMENTARY

"Daemon Seed," by David S. Bennahum, appeared in the May 1999 issue of *Wired Magazine*. The essay is almost entirely a factual argument, and like all factual arguments, its success depends on the quality of the factual framework that supports it and on the reputation of the writer and the publisher.

So before analyzing the argument itself, let's do a little checking on the career and reputation of David Bennahum and on the history, advertisers, and circulation of *Wired Magazine*. As noted in Chapter 6 on Factual Arguments, these reputational issues can themselves operate as effective support for factual claims.

Given the topic of this section of the anthology, it seems appropriate to do these background checks on the Internet. It is a good guess that *Wired Magazine* has a Web site, and we know that it's a commercial journal, so its URL will end in ".com". Before using a Web search tool, I make a guess about the full URL and type in http://www.wired.com to see. This gets me to the Web site of Wired Digital, which is the company that owns *Wired Magazine*. There is a link on the home page to the magazine. If my guess had been incorrect, I could have used any of the search engines available through my university Internet server.

Here's some of what I learned about *Wired Magazine* from its Web site. The home page is a trove of information about the magazine, though of course the information will have a certain bias. But the list of awards is impressive. With a circulation of 425,000, *Wired* is directed at "high-tech professionals and the business savvy . . . the forward-looking, the culturally astute, and the simply curious." Translated, the typical *Wired* reader is intelligent, relatively young, professionally successful, creative, and innovative. I also take a close look at a hard copy of the magazine and learn that its advertisers are big-name, Internet-related computer and digital electronic companies like Cisco and Toshiba, and that the magazine itself is glossy and slick and full of visual distractions (much like the WWW).

According to the article itself, David Bennahum is a contributing editor to *Wired Magazine*. I don't find anything more about him on this Web site, so I use a search engine, which takes me first to the Amazon.com site, where I learn that David S. Bennahum has written a number of books on cybertechnology. Amazon has provided quotes from professional reviews of Bennahum's most recent book, *Extra Life: Coming of Age in Cyberspace,* and they are all positive (Amazon *does* include negative reviews of its books, by the way). There is also a good bit of information about Bennahum himself in the review section, all of which strongly suggests that he is an intelligent, reputable, responsible writer.

The bottom line of this "context check" is that we have no reason to suspect the reliability of the facts reported in "Daemon Seed." The essay appears in a reputable and respected magazine that has won a variety of awards, and the writer is an established voice in the field with the respect of his colleagues. Of course, the context check doesn't guarantee that the argument will be absolutely free of mistakes or untruths, but it does tell us that they are unlikely.

"Daemon Seed" opens with an anecdotal introduction that begins *in medias res*—in the middle of things: "It's almost impossible to hide your e-mail from John Jessen." With its casual implication that the reader is somehow a participant in the anecdote, the first paragraph successfully engages our attention. The next four paragraphs give the necessary background on John Jessen and his business, preparing us for the central claim—a factual generalization—in Par. 5: "Jessen's thriving business is a by-product of our growing dependency on e-mail in the workplace—e-mail that is increasingly important in civil lawsuits, criminal investigations, and libel law." This movement from the specific to the general is exactly the tactic presented in the example of an anecdotal introduction presented in Chapter 11. It is a favorite tactic of journalists, who, rarely blessed with captive audiences, must capture their readers' attention at the outset.

While the first part of the claim might appear to be causal ("Jessen's thriving business is a by-product of our growing dependency on e-mail in the workplace"), one thorough reading of the entire argument discovers that its focus is not on the cause-and-effect relationship between Jessen's business and our e-mail dependency, but on the legal liabilities of e-mail (the second part of the sentence). Bennahum is betting that we will accept the assumptions about the proliferation of workplace e-mail and its causal relationship between businesses like Jessen's as self-evident (later, in Par. 19, Bennahum does offer documentation of the growth of e-mail).

The success of a factual generalization depends upon both the quality and quantity of its supporting facts. Supporting facts must be recent, reliable, concrete, and verifiable; and they must be sufficient in number to warrant the generalization. Most extended factual arguments consist of a series of secondary factual claims in support of the central claim, with each of these secondary claims supported by more detailed and concrete facts. The *quantity* of supporting facts must be sufficient to warrant the generalization (see the section "Applying the Principles of Induction" in Chapter 6).

We won't put every factual support to the test in this analysis, but let's look at a sampling. In Par. 6–13, Bennahum offers concrete, directly quoted verification of the inductive factual claim that e-mail has increasing legal implications. He first cites the incriminating role played by Microsoft employee e-mail in the Microsoft antitrust case, then moves beyond this narrower but still general reference to supply the text of some of the actual e-mails (Par. 9–12).

The introduction of Joan Feldman in Par. 16 provides another example in support of the original generalization about the legal implications of e-mail. Here, Bennahum relies on summary rather than direct examples: "For more than 1,000 clients in six years, Feldman has turned to e-mail as an invaluable record of misdeeds, prevarication, plots, and sometimes tragedy." Since we have Feldman's name and the name of her company, we can assume the accuracy of the summary.

A third instance of e-mail's legal implications appears in Par. 21 with the reference to incriminating e-mail discovered by an ethics panel investigating the United States Olympic Committee in its attempt to bring the 2002 Winter Games to Salt Lake City.

Beginning in Par. 24, the argument turns to the legal history of e-mail. While this factual summary is not absolutely necessary to verify the central claim, it is useful in providing historical context for the claim. The background also serves to break up the marshalling of evidence for the central claim—not so much interrupting the train of supporting examples as offering some variation in the diet.

A similar tactic is employed in Par. 42 with the introduction of the film *You've Got Mail*. Here, Bennahum breaks away from the journalistic arrangement of facts to wax interpretive and philosophical about the film's meaning. He offers no support for his interpretation—his aim here seems to be merely to lend variety and rhythm to a rather long factual argument. This strategy reveals Bennahum's awareness of his audience, of the need to keep them interested as well as to convince them of his argument.

I have cited three of Bennahum's factual examples in support of his original claim, but there are many more. And since some of these examples themselves summarize literally hundreds of instances, we can conclude that the generalization is sufficiently supported. With the validity of the central claim established, Bennahum moves in the last part of his argument to coverage of possible solutions to the very real risks that employee e-mail poses to businesses. He reintroduces Jessen and Feldman and their recommendation of e-mail "centralization" (Par. 50), and cites at some length the e-mail containment strategies recommended by the Electronic Messaging Association (Par. 51–55). At this point, Bennahum is reporting recommendations, not supporting them, so he needn't launch into a full-blown argument of recommendation.

Bennahum skillfully concludes his argument with an implicit reference to its title—"Daemon Seed." While the analogy is never directly made, Bennahum is suggesting similarities between e-mail and this legendary seed that manages to sprout despite all attempts to contain it. There may be solutions out there for making employee e-mail less of a risk to companies, but the "seed" will grow in spite of the best precautions. And he supports this comparison by the final reference to Microsoft. Despite the legal damage done by Microsoft e-mail, employees continue to use it as they always have—indiscriminately and impulsively; e-mail at Microsoft remains "like a hallway conversation."

DAEMON SEED

1   It's almost impossible to hide your email from John Jessen. To him, the word *delete* is an invitation. Jessen can restore email from magnetic tapes that have been overwritten several times, resuscitating information off "deleted" files. He can read email and documents from obsolete computer systems. Jessen can capture phantoms; he understands the foibles of wordprocessing programs that leave undo lists and backups of old edits in hidden parts of files and disks.

2   "You see everything," he says, "from high and low comedy to human tragedy."

3   Jessen started reading email professionally out of his basement in 1988, when he launched a career as a "computer forensics" specialist, digging through disk drives to find incriminating words. Today, he's the president and CEO of Electronic Evidence Discovery in Seattle, a 50-person company whose additional offices include New York, Los Angeles, Chicago, and Washington, DC. Working with a team of computer programmers, behavioral scientists, and retired police detectives, Jessen ferrets out emails that people believe, mistakenly, are long gone.

4   "For every email system around, we've developed a piece of software that can find each hidden element and read it," he says, "like header and routing information. Our software goes in, finds it, strips it out with any attachments, and puts it into a searchable database."

5   Jessen's thriving business is a by-product of our growing dependency on email in the workplace—email that is increasingly important in civil lawsuits, criminal investigations, and libel law. In high-stakes corporate litigation, it has become routine to demand access to the company email dating back 10 to 20 years.

6   "If you're not prepared to deal with email, it's one of the most devastating liabilities in corporate America today," Jessen says. "Which is why everyone is so afraid of it."

7   Electronic Evidence's business is booming partly because of well-publicized email gaffes at neighboring Microsoft. Over the

past year, as internal Microsoft email has gone public in federal court, the shock value of intemperate messaging has sent many companies scurrying to Jessen for advice on protecting themselves. David Boies, the Justice Department's leading attorney in the antitrust trial, has shaken corporate America with his relentless digging for Microsoft messages, evidence that's been used to argue, with alarming specificity, that Gates & Co. tried to crush Netscape by forcing vendors to use Internet Explorer as the default browser on their systems.

8   The email trove has been ugly: "The threat to cancel MacOffice 97 is certainly the strongest bargaining point we have, as doing so will do a great deal of harm to Apple immediately," a senior Microsoft executive wrote in email to Bill Gates, allegedly hoping to force Apple to incorporate Internet Explorer. An internal mail from AOL, reportedly recounting a meeting with Gates, described him as saying, "How much do we need to pay you to screw Netscape?" Then there's the oft-quoted portion of an email from Gates to other Microsoft executives: "Do we have a clear plan on what we want Apple to do to undermine Sun?"

9   Over the years, Jessen has collected plenty of big-mouth emails, ones that very quickly settled the lawsuits involved. He sends me a few samples, with identifying characteristics blotted out. They read like parodies, but they're real:

```
    Yes  I  know  we  shipped
    100 barrels of [deleted],
    but  on  our  end,  steps
    have  been  taken  to  en-
    sure  that  no  record  ex-
    ists. Therefore it does-
    n't  exist.  If  you  know
    what  I  mean.  Remember,
    you  owe  me  a  golf  game
    next  time  I'm  in  town.

    Did  you  see  what  Dr.
    [deleted]  did  today?  If
    that   patient   survives
    it  will  be  a  miracle.
```

```
    Hi  David,  please  de-
    stroy  the  evidence  on
    the   [litigation]   you
    and  I  talked  about  to-
    day. Thx Laura
    ***Evidence Destroyed***
     Hi  Laura ack yr msg.
    and    taken    care    of.
    Aloha David.

    [National retail chain]
    would  like  2,500  free
    units  of  [our product]
    in  order  to  conduct  a
    test    marketing    study.
    If  the  study  goes  well,
    they  will  place  an  or-
    der  for  100,000  units.
    I  recommend  we  provide
    the  free  units  for  the
    following reasons:
     1.  2,500  free  units
    is  cheap  compared  with
    the  profit  from  an  or-
    der for 100,000 units.
     2.  They  will  provide
    the  names  and  addresses
    of  the  stores  involved
    in  the  study  so  that  we
    can  drop-ship  the  prod-
    uct.
     3.  Since  we  will  know
    where  the  product  will
    be,  I  will  send  someone
    around  to  buy  all  of
    it,  thereby  ensuring  a
    successful test.
```

What's most astonishing about these messages is, of course, their unequivocal honesty. Email is a truth serum. That's why it's scary—and why it's irresistible.

Every morning, I come to my computer, sit down, launch my email program. I'm an email pack rat, a compulsive saver and correspondent. I've kept every message —sent and received—since March 1994. My email folder contains 226 Mbytes of mail. That's around 14,811,136 characters, or approximately 300,000 words, lodged in more than 75,000 messages. I save them because I can

(I have an external drive connected to my PC for this sole purpose). My mail stays with me wherever I go, because endless possibility resides in the medium: An innocuous message might one day be exciting; an exciting message might become essential.

12   Joan Feldman, president of Computer Forensics in Seattle, and a colleague and competitor of Jessen's, tells me I am on the outer edge of compulsion. "Maybe 15 percent of the online population keeps as much as you do," she says.

13   From her office in Seattle, Feldman has a clear window on the collective psyche of the email nation, an exploding web of 96 million interconnected Americans. Where her forensic predecessors studies corpses, measuring time of death by the congealing of blood, Feldman studies the particularities of electromagnetic fields on digital media, gleaning the patterns that form words. "Dig deeper. Dig harder," she says with relish, describing her m.o. "When people are looking at me and lying, that gives me an extra incentive to look further." And look she has.

14   For more than 1,000 clients in six years, Feldman has turned to email as an invaluable record of misdeeds, prevarication, plots, and sometimes tragedy. In hundreds of lawsuits, Feldman has been called in to find hidden evidence, taking her to offices around the nation, people's homes, and vast warehouses where thousands of backup tapes containing millions of email messages are the digital equivalent of formaldehyde, a medium where nothing decays.

15   Meanwhile, the growth of email is relentless. In 1991, according to the Electronic Messaging Association, an industry trade group that helps corporations establish email policies, 8 million Americans had access to email. In 1997, the number grew to 67 million. Now, 96 million Americans use email. By next year, that number is expected to increase to 108 million, with office workers exchanging 25.2 billion messages daily. With nearly a third of the country sending messages to one another, hauls of electronic mail under subpoena have become more than a nuisance; they've exposed us all to the gnawing sense that anything we write may one day be held against us. It's led companies to want immunity from the human propensity to write what we think in electronic correspondence; a 1997 survey by the Society for Human Resource Management showed that 20 percent of US businesses reported they check employee email randomly.

16   "It's like insurance—people don't want to think about it until their house burns down. In the Microsoft case, they saw their neighbor's house burn down," says Feldman, who has seen demand for her preventive services—rules and procedures for systematically retaining or deleting company mail—increase by 50 percent over the last year.

17   The cost of uncontainable email is most obvious in the workplace. Daily, more revelations of email's truth-telling power are revealed; think of *The New York Times* headline about the Salt Lake City Olympics scandal: E-MAIL TRAIL ADDS DETAILS TO U.S.O.C.'S ROLE. The story reprinted emails sent among officials of the United States Olympic Committee who were angling to bring the 2002 Winter Games to Utah. An ethics panel dug up email describing, with casual nonchalance, the way votes were collected by granting favors to visiting representatives of the International Olympic Committee. Referring to a quid pro quo in which Sudanese votes were traded for airfare, room and board, and other amenities for their athletes, one official wrote simply: "A lot of promises were made to secure votes."

18   The technology of electronic communications is moving so quickly that it has outpaced both the law and our own sense of propriety. In a weird and still unclear turn, our vast pools of saved email have mutated into personal surveillance mechanisms. Big Brother isn't some dark figure of distant, central control. He's us: the decentralized record of all our thoughts and feelings, preserved in the electronic platters of hard disks on desktops and in archives across the country.

19   For companies, email's permanence and seductive call to intimacy means facing a question: How can it be contained?

20   Federal law says that all email sent or received using a company's mail system is company property. The law, the Electronic Communications Privacy Act, dating from 1986, made perfect sense when email was still a novelty, confined mainly to large corporations with expensive, time-shared mainframes. But it makes little sense today.

21   In 1986, electronic mail moved through one of three types of networks. In the forefront were corporate email systems running off proprietary mainframes and terminals. Companies like Xerox interconnected thousands of employees within a vast local-area network. Sending an electronic message from, say, Xerox to General Motors was impossible. The systems were closed off, separate. The Internet was another type. Though it was growing rapidly in the '80s—with several hundred thousand users, interconnecting universities, government agencies, and companies involved in federally funded research—it remained explicitly noncommercial until 1991, when restrictions were lifted and Internet email started becoming a mass phenomenon. The third type was for general communications use. Systems like CompuServe, MCI Mail, and FidoNet, which linked privately run bulletin board systems, also had thousands of users.

22   In this world of separate computer networks, the ECPA allowed for an easy distinction between "open" and "closed" systems. The former provided email to paying customers; the latter gave people access to email as part of their employment. In a closed system, it is permissible for an employer, the system's owner, to treat all electronic mail like any other form of property, no different from printed letters. In an open system, messages are considered personal property, and private. But what happens when the once "closed" system of corporate email becomes connected to the "open" Internet? In a strictly legal interpretation, the answer is: Nothing changes. Any email composed at work and sent to the Internet emanates from a closed system, and is therefore company property.

23   Tora Bikson, a researcher specializing in issues of access to electronic communications with the Rand organization, says that the ECPA approach doesn't add up anymore. "What do you mean by open or closed?" she asks. "There are no longer any closed systems, since with the Internet you can connect almost every system with any system. The real question is, How much privacy do you want to trade for connectivity?"

24   Complicating matters are services like Hotmail—which gives workers free Web-based email accounts—and the increasing use of freelancers in the workplace.

25   "Say a company has an email system, hires temporary employees, and gives them an email account because they'll be there for several months," says Jessen. "Now you have nonemployees using the system. Does that mean you've switched from being closed to open?" Jessen's solution is what he calls "the consent rule—you put consent language in employee contracts that says by using the system you agree to have your email read by the company."

26   That doesn't sound very appetizing, but employees have little recourse when it comes to keeping email private on the job. Courts have consistently upheld the idea that constitutional rights to freedom of speech end when an employee arrives at the office. "It's the employer's workplace, and he's master of his domain," explains Jeremy Gruber, an attorney with the American Civil Liberties Union in New Jersey. For the past two years, Gruber has worked on the ACLU's Workplace Rights Project. Every week, he receives six or seven calls from people upset about workplace monitoring of their email and Internet use. Typical cases involve workers exchanging personal messages disparaging the boss or their superiors. When the employer finds out, the underling can be fired.

27   The Workplace Rights Project supports legislation requiring employers to tell employees whether their electronic communications are being monitored. It's a modest ambition, yet in the current Congress no

legislation has been proposed. Gruber's ideal scenario is one where "employers would have no right to intrude on your Internet use or email without just cause," but that possibility seems remote. For now, at least, the employer's concerns are getting more attention, and employers are frantic—justifiably—that problematic emails might cause them trouble.

28   "There isn't a single case I have that does not deal with email," says Claude Stern, an attorney with Fenwick & West in Palo Alto, California. Stern specializes in representing high tech companies, including Symantec, Intuit, Electronic Arts, and Broderbund. "One hundred percent of my lawsuits now have significant amount of time focused on emails and Internet communications, like discussion boards and chat rooms." The first thing Stern does in a lawsuit is request the other side's electronic mail. "Emails tend to contain very candid, and not particularly socially sensitive, remarks. We see it time and time again, making email the Achilles' heel of every party in litigation."

29   In 1998, for instance, several players of *Ultima Online* sued Electronic Arts, claiming the game was defective. Stern succeeded in getting the case thrown out thanks partly to email he'd lassoed. "One of these people had contacted customer support by email and admitted they loved the game. They said the real problem was not with the game, but with another player who had killed them and stolen all their stuff."

30   In another case, a man filed a wrongful termination suit against one of Stern's clients, claiming he'd been unfairly fired because of his age. Stern obtained the plaintiff's computer and email, which he used to identify key witnesses and support the company's argument that the plaintiff was terminated based on performance. A California court threw out the suit.

31   Stern, trained to see email as a booby trap, sees potential trouble almost anywhere. For instance, he says companies that rely on email to communicate with customers are opening themselves up to whole new varieties of liability.

32   "One of the greatest vulnerabilities for companies is tech support and customer service," he explains. "When customers are mad, they send in very frank email. The tech-support people tend to be very candid in their replies." Thus, a company selling a defective product, while officially claiming the product works fine, might find its defense destroyed in email from an honest support employee. A canny attorney will eventually find those tech-support messages.

33   "We have a company where the tech-support person admitted the product had problems, that they knew it for six months, and wished someone would finally get around to fixing it. You would think they would want to filter that."

34   Newsrooms are especially vulnerable to the danger of frank email, since successful libel suits are based on the premise that a journalist knowingly produced a story that was false—that is, with malice going in. "With respect to newspapers, email is going to be a very key part of libel cases," says James Goodale, an attorney with Debevoise & Plimpton who has represented *The New York Times* in libel cases. To win, the plaintiff has to show the journalist's state of mind while reporting the story. "It's difficult for courts to decide what someone is thinking when they are looking at a story," says Goodale. "The chances of having someone say something out loud is very slim. The substitute for that will be email."

35   The first high-profile libel cases based on email are just now taking shape. Goodale expects email to play a key role in a suit by retired military officers against CNN. The news broadcaster aired a report on Operation Tailwind alleging that the US military used chemical weapons during the Vietnam War, a story CNN later retracted.

36   Newspapers, like other big corporations, aren't adequately prepared. "We don't really have an email policy," admits a senior executive for *The New York Times,* who requested anonymity. The *Times* policy is limited to controlling workplace atmospherics. In a recent internal memo, circulated by email to all *Times* employees, the staff was told that

sending "messages with sexual implications, or which reflect offensively on another's age, race, sex, sexual orientation, national origin or disability, among other things" would not be tolerated. Even though the paper is sued for libel a dozen times a year, the exec says, "most lawyers are not sophisticated enough to ask for email. I've never had to do a real comprehensive email search.

37   "We've just been lucky," he says. "Courts have no sympathy when you say, 'I have no way to search my system except by hand.'"

38   The subtext of *You've Got Mail,* Nora Ephron's recent movie, is that authenticity, stripped of the social conventions of everyday life, is revealed in the world of email. Somehow the medium permits the characters in the movie to share truths about themselves, to reveal parts of themselves, that in the physical world would remain hidden. When we see the characters as antagonists in physical space, we squirm, knowing that they are meant to be with each other—that in fact they are electronic soulmates. And that if they are to become lovers, they must transcend the identities they've ascribed meaning to in the real world.

39   When I emailed Ephron (who's been online since 1995) asking about her email, she wrote back, explaining, "What interests me about it—besides all the obvious things (it brings back letter-writing, et cetera)—is that it's a form of communication unlike any other and yet the second you start doing it you understand it." The conundrum of email is that it's a shortcut to self-expression, but it's also a language of its own. It invites both the mere passing of information and the sharing of secrets, longings, emotions. There's a certain permissiveness to it that real-world addresses on paper letters don't offer.

40   One thing everyone gets right away is flirting. "The main thing about email is that it's God's gift to the adulterer," a well-known writer tells me, adding, "It is a little delicate, because I am in the middle of a divorce." The author is afraid that his wife's lawyers could go after his emails. "The notion that everything you say on email can be subpoenaed ought to give pause to everybody," he says.

He may be relieved to know that truth   41 hunting can be expensive. "We were involved with a case with 300 people and all their email going back four years," Jessen says. "It was a live email system with 16 backup tapes. The final email count was a couple million messages." That's relatively small, yet because the company was unprepared for electronic discovery, management had to hire 60 temps to sit at 60 workstations and pick through each message; relevant messages were forwarded to one of 20 attorneys. Those were cataloged and delivered to the opposition, under court order. "In nine months they had looked through not even a fraction of the live mail, let along the backup tapes," Jessen says. "They had put in $700,000 at this point."

Jessen's solution was to copy all the mail   42 to a central server and have an algorithm sort and search the mail for keywords. He billed the company $200,000, pushing the total cost of making email available to the plaintiff to $900,000.

Jessen cites another case where the two   43 sides had a combined email volume of 1 *billion* messages. Each individual message had to be indexed and made available for either side in discovery. Putting that document count in perspective, Jessen says it dwarfs that of one of the largest litigations in US history—the Justice Department's 13-year antitrust suit against IBM—which involved 30 million documents.

"Think about a company with a volume   44 of 50 million emails a month," Jessen says. "It does not take very long to hit those astronomical numbers. So the bottom line is that it costs a heck of a lot to deal with email in litigation." This fact, he assets, can lead companies to consider a settlement. "If it costs less to settle, then you settle. A company that is not prepared is in an adverse settlement position."

Being prepared for electronic discovery   45 requires a radical restructuring of the email mind-set. Email use tends to be concentrated in personal computers—and personal computers invariably become perceived as "belonging" to an employee, even though the vast majority of messages may be stored on a central mail server. So companies under subpoena must retrieve files that contain all sorts of personal stuff that gets scooped up in the net, opening doors to potential embarrassment, or even more lawsuits, as new traces of malfeasance are discovered.

46   The solution Jessen and Feldman embrace is a move toward further centralization. They believe employees should not be allowed to save mail on workplace PCs. Messages would be saved on central servers and automatically deleted. (Jessen recommends deleting after 90 days at the most.) Rules on what mail should be saved indefinitely would be defined by specific corporate "retention policies."

47   The Electronic Messaging Association publishes a booklet, *Message Retention Toolkit,* that outlines the basics of what it considers a sound email-retention policy. At its simplest, the EMA recommends that companies identify all the different kinds of email employees write, identify how long various types of messages should be saved (say, seven years for tax-related emails, 50 years for certain SEC-related mails, et cetera), and save them in a central archive. All other mail should be deleted quickly, the recommendations say, and employees should be given a thorough briefing on the retention files. That way, when a company is sued, management can get to the relevant messages quickly and inexpensively.

48   A retention policy can't do anything about calling back sent mail once it's left the company. And erased internal email may linger for a while as ghost fragments that can be reconstructed by the likes of Feldman and Jessen. When it comes to using email in lawsuits, "deletion" has a special meaning. It doesn't mean gone forever. It means, "Not our problem anymore." Assuming that deleting mail is done as part of a long-standing set of rules—rather than in a last-minute, frantic all-night purge—retrieving deleted mail falls to the other side. The adversary has to hire the forensic specialists and convince the judge to allow a peek into the opponent's computers, something that's hard to do without just cause.

The EMA Toolkit was written by a committee with representatives from a who's-who of corporate America: Texaco, Boeing, Chevron, Citigroup, and Hewlett-Packard. Yet, when contacted, many of the booklets authors refused to comment. "It's just that the moment we hear the word 'litigation' we get very uncomfortable discussing email," says one of the Toolkit's writers. "It's just not a good idea."

One contributor to the EMA booklet, Marion Weiler, did agree to talk about it. Responsible for crafting Chevron's email-retention policy, Weiler is in the midst of a $1 million review of how this 35,000-person corporation should handle email. "We're creating a whole set of rules for how long email has to be saved," Weiler says. "There are entire classes of email we are required to keep, like taxes and contracts describing oil-field rights. Dealing with email retention goes beyond deleting things that are not needed. It goes into organizational issues and structures that may not even exist yet."

Weiler estimates that Chevron's new retention policy—storing mail in central archives and establishing clear rules about what mail should and should not be saved—will save the company 30 percent on related costs, including email retrieval, in future litigation, savings expected to exceed the cost of devising the policy. Harder to quantify are the savings from avoiding catastrophic litigation and multimillion-dollar settlements. "In the worst-case scenario, you find yourself in litigation that revolves around some electronic records, and because you can't find them, you lose the full judgment," Weiler says. "And if that judgment is high, it could be worse than dealing with Y2K bugs in terms of cost."

Helping companies decide how to centralize email is itself now a booming trade. One popular approach is server-based programs that specifically allow for high levels of email filtering and saving based on centralized, company-controlled rules. A firm called Worldtalk in Santa Clara, California, has seen sales of its email-retention software, WorldSecure, increase 524 percent from 1997 to 1998. The company expects sales to

49

50

51

52

double this year. "In the last six months demand has really exploded," says company spokesperson Dawn Harris, attributing the boom to "the Monica Lewinsky subpoena and the Bill Gates subpoena."

53   Worldtalk targets companies in the insurance, finance, health care, and legal industries. WorldSecure generates 80 percent of the company's revenues. It can be configured to force messages emanating from senior executives to be encrypted. (Encryption can prevent email impersonation and provide protection from snoopers; encrypted mail, under subpoena, must be decrypted and made available.) WorldSecure can screen outbound mail for keywords like "hot stock tip" or "insider trading." It can also screen for words the company decides are sexist or racist, halting the message's delivery. WorldSecure can also be configured to limit who in the company can use email.

54   "To reduce risk, not everyone needs access to Internet mail," Harris explains. "The people in the mail room do not need it." Worldtalk's customers include 25 of the 100 largest US law firms, as well as Nike, OppenheimerFunds, and Catholic Healthcare West, one of California's largest health care providers.

55   In January, Compaq released a product that competes with WorldSecure. Vault is designed to keep continuous email archives, seamlessly integrating new messages with old ones stored on backup media like CD-ROM. Using the AltaVista search engine, Vault lets companies search their old mail by subject, keyword, and author, and has viewing capabilities to handle attachments in formats that, inevitably, will be obsolete in a few years. Prices for Vault and WorldSecure vary, depending on the amount of mail to be stored or the number of users sending mail. Vault, for instance, charges a onetime fee of $325 for the initial gigabyte of archived mail, with prices declining as the gigabytes increase. Individual user licenses to access the stored mail cost $15 to $41, with discounts for increased usage. A hypothetical Vault customer with 10,000 employees and 6 Gbytes of mail daily might buy a license to store 20 terabytes, with the archive

accessible to all company employees. The total cost: $185,000.

56   But, Jessen argues, there is only so much these programs, with their keyword searches and retention rules, can do to keep email under control.

57   "The single biggest impediment to companies cutting down their risk is culture," Jessen explains. "More than money or anything else, it's a cultural issue."

58   Email has a tone of intimate candor that's hard to imagine appearing in a secret business memo. It's a long-noted phenomenon, going as far back as the earliest studies of how electronic mail affects us. What's really eerie is how little our behavior has changed, even though email has been around for years. We still seem stuck in the same cycle of naivete and seduction, willing ourselves to believe that because email is electronic it is also somehow impermanent, equivalent to the temporary vibrations of air molecules when we speak.

59   In 1985, Robert Anderson, an analyst at Rand, cowrote (with Norman Shapiro) a seminal study on the social effects of email, called "Towards an Ethics and Etiquette for Electronic Mail." Writing at a time when fewer than a million Americans were exchanging messages, Anderson described email's greatest "phenomenon" as its propensity to lead to "misinterpretation." He warned of "the strange permanency yet volatility of electronic messages," and issued cautionary statements that still sound applicable; "Never say anything . . . you wouldn't want appearing, and attributed to you, in tomorrow morning's front-page headline in *The New York Times*"; "Assume that any message you send is permanent"; "Avoid responding while emotional"; and the very prescient "Consider alternative media."

60   Anderson, still at Rand, is a bit dismayed at how few people followed his advice. "So much for what I write! No one pays attention." He is particularly fascinated by email's mutation into a corporate problem. "In 1985, we saw email largely as individual to individual. All of our cautions were about how an individual could be affected," he says. "I have been taken by the Microsoft

case—how much of the day-to-day business of the company is done by email. Thus the organization's history literally becomes only available through email. That puts companies in a dilemma. Either they keep the email, so it can all be discoverable and appear on the front page of the *Times* the next day, or they scrub the files so nothing can be discovered in court, at the expense of their own corporate history."

61   Scrubbing the files, of course, does not ensure that intrepid computer specialists won't discover readable fragments, or that the recipient's copy won't reemerge one day from another computer system.

62   What would Anderson do about it? His proposed solution is rather quaint. "I would have a rule that anyone who creates email with corporate interest print it out and put it in a folder," he says. The rest he would delete —at least the copies he still had access to.

63   Out of curiosity, I share Anderson's idea with a Microsoft employee who prefers to stay anonymous. "Ted" is proud to tell me that his current email volume is a modest 100 messages a day—down from 900 last year—and he laughs at Anderson's idea. Call in the dump trucks! I got a lotta mail to print out!" A Microsoft program manager, he has been at the company for several years. He remembers the days before Windows could handle email, when the entire company was networked through PCs running Xenix, a version of Unix. At every em-

ployee's desk was a diminutive terminal, generally a VT-52, with a monochrome screen and text-only interface.   64

Like most Microsoft employees, Ted now has two PCs: one for testing software, one for writing email and documents. Part of his job is serving as a human email filter, relaying messages between the programmers developing a product and the marketers selling it. Last year, he typically filtered 500 messages daily—We are tapping into the great collective mind of everybody."   65

Maybe it should come as no surprise that he's seen no impact, internally, on the way email is handled at Microsoft because of the antitrust suit. "I haven't noticed a chilling effect," he says. "I do not pay much attention to the outcomes of what I write. When you look at the number of messages we exchange here, it's like a hallway conversation—in a medium that's stored."   66

He says controlling Microsoft email would be impossible. With thousands of "alias" lists—the equivalent of internal mailing lists—everyone's life is lived on email. When asked if he knows Microsoft's official position on what's appropriate use of email, he says, "I think it's in the handbook." Has the company ever sent around a memo about the policy? No. "It would be pretty funny if they did," he adds. "Everyone would comment on it." By email, naturally.

Source: David S. Bennahum, "Daemon Seed," in *Wired Magazine*, May 1999, pp. 101–111.

DISCUSSION QUESTIONS

1. See if you can find a definition of the meaning and history of the term "daemon seed" through the Internet.

2. Did you find any other statements in this essay that might also qualify as the central claim? What are they?

3. The purpose of factual arguments is often to give useful information to an audience. In the case of "Daemon Seed," what is the information? How useful would it be to the audience inferred in the preceding Commentary?

4. What kind of relationship does Bennahum seem to assume with his readers? What is your evidence for your answer?

5. Could Bennahum's argument have been made as effectively in less space? If so, what could have been eliminated? If you were Bennahum's editor, would you recommend these deletions? Why or why not?

SUGGESTIONS FOR WRITING (14.1)

1. Adapting the *persona* of a department manager in a small business, write a memorandum cautioning your employees against indiscriminate use of e-mail. Use at least three facts from the Bennahum essay to support your recommendation.

2. Some think that the very nature of e-mail—its impersonality, its speed, its ease of use—encourages impulsive and thoughtless communication. In a three-page causal argument, support or challenge this view.

3. Write an e-mail evaluating the course in which this book (*Everyday Arguments*) is assigned to another student not currently taking the course. You needn't worry about support or evidence, but do be sure your evaluation is clear and helpful.

4. Write a two- to three-page letter to your instructor evaluating the course, using the e-mail from Suggestion #3 as a starting point. In this case, be sure all your points are adequately supported and that your evaluative term is clearly defined, if necessary.

STOP ME BEFORE I SHOP AGAIN

JAMES GLEICK

This argument appeared in the May 24, 1999 issue of The New Yorker *magazine. James Gleick, a frequent contributor to* The New Yorker *and a prolific commentator on emerging technologies, writes here about the Internet phenomenon of eBay—an enormously popular virtual auction site. If you haven't ever visited that site (www.ebay.com), you might want to do so before you read Gleick's essay.*

1 Stuff has been lying dormant in the world's attics and garages—stuff we might call "junk," like that Early American iron steam whistle, that 1938 Luzianne coffee tin (three inches tall and apparently used as a piggy bank), that 1962 Geiger counter, with its original yellow carrying strap, and all the rest of the detritus of our productive little species. Suddenly, this stuff is on the move. It's churning through the Internet's new auction bazaars like water through Hoover Dam, maybe just destined for future attics and garages but providing considerable entertainment along the way. Economists have used the concept of velocity, *V,* to measure the turnover of the money supply. Now our flotsam and jetsam seem to be acquiring a velocity of their own. Look at eBay, the biggest of the auction sites that have sprung up on line. This place, if it is a place, is a billion-acre garage sale. Two million sixty-nine thousand seven hundred and forty-three auctions are under way right now, in real time. More than eight hundred of them involve, specifically, Collectibles–Advertising–Candy–M&M—boxes, cards, molds, planters, and an orange die-cast Reese's Pieces airplane bank ("only 5,000 were made," way back in 1992, the seller assures us). Pass them on. Then pass them on again.

2 It's not just old stuff. New retail merchandise is flowing in along with the antiques and "collectibles," and it's easy to get

hooked. I'd never bought a laser pointer—I'd never even desired a laser pointer—but I suddenly couldn't resist. I found myself at a "Featured Auction," happening before my eyes. The flashing blue icon said "COOL." This laser pointer was made of metal, not plastic, and the seller, one selwine@ix.netcom.com, stressed that it has been banned in many urban school systems. Also, it is vital in business presentations. Also, if you have pets, "they love to chase the little dot." But mainly I felt a hankering to own one of the century's essential pieces of technology, a powerful, pulsating energy machine that would surely have cost a lot more a few years ago. The ineffable Selwine called for bids of at least $13.99. He promised that in six days, at precisely 8:19:17 A.M. P.D.T., he would award a laser to each of the four hundred highest bidders. So, what to bid? Being new to this auction thing, I decided to type in a crafty "$14."

3   Then I waited. And browsed a few of the other ongoing auctions, here in the land of exclamation points. The eBay Webmasters have organized and recognized this cornucopia into "1,627 categories now!"—a giant directory, always in flux. Anyone can sign up and list an item for sale, and then everyone else can start bidding. The process is meant to be easier than the average arcade game. You choose a suitably cute or mysterious User ID ("muscles" or "buygonetrading" or "lulu32"). You type in a few sentences of description and, if you wish, put digitized photographs of the merchandise on line. (This makes the Erotica categories especially popular for browsing.) For a two-dollar fee, you can add a boldface title to your listing. For $99.95, you can buy a place in the rotating list of featured auctions. (You didn't think eBay was choosing these on the basis of merit, did you?) Sellers specify a minimum bid, and the eBay computers handle the rest. So here is a Drop Dead!!! one-of-a-kind Art Nouveau bronze chandelier with floral detail and mermaid cutouts, acquired from a Bel Air estate. I could bid on any one of the two thousand seven hundred and sixty-five Furbys for sale today. Or

a car. Or a house. Or "Soul of a 15-year-old girl, somewhat depleted and abused but still in good shape! Comes in an attractive cigarette box!"

The people at eBay aren't scrutinizing the offerings. They stay away from shipping and handling, settling payment—that sort of thing. They're just lending us their virtual back yard for a vast, free-floating, never-ending tag sale. They estimate that they get eight million unique visitors a month. More than five hundred million dollars' worth of stuff got sold in the first quarter of this year, and the number has been almost doubling from quarter to quarter. Of course, eBay takes a piece of the action: from one and a quarter to five per cent of every deal. Pretty much the entire human experience seems to be for sale, at eBay or some other Internet bazaar. Did you need "Las Vegas Rms New Yrs Eve 1999 for 3 nights"? How about a tee time for next Sunday morning—the 8:50 at the Heritage Palms Golf Club, in Indio, California, is available. The current bid: ninety-one dollars.   4

The new, on-line retailers of books, recorded music, and computer equipment have invaded their respective business territories to much greater fanfare. And with reason: the flow of goods through the mercantile world has never before been rerouted so dramatically, so fast. The news that Amazon.com, formerly a bookstore, has bought chunks of Drugstore.com and Pets.com should make one wonder whether it was ever that much fun trudging to real-world shops to stand in line for vitamins, laxatives, condoms, or dog food. But these retail enterprises, powerful though they will grow, are not the truest harbingers of the economy of the twenty-first century. That role falls to an assortment of odd marketplaces—auction bazaars with names that drive copy editors mad. Besides eBay, there are uBid, Onsale, AuctionBuy, AuctionInc., Auction-Port, AuctionAddict.com, bid4it, Up4Sale, Bidaway, EZbid. Now Amazon, too, is starting an auction service and is buying a company called LiveBid. Just as the World Wide Web seems to be turning every computer   5 owner into a "content provider"—publisher, broadcaster, artist, commentator—the auction sites promise to make all of us merchants. "We have to partner with thousands of sellers, even millions of sellers, over time," says Amazon's sportive founder and C.E.O., Jeff Bezos. "Our customers in a way are now able to compete with us."

6   Call these outfits junkmongers or facilitators of electronic commerce. Either way, Wall Street is having trouble coming to grips with them. When eBay went public eight months ago, for eighteen dollars a share, *Forbes* warned investors to watch out for the hype, the outrageous ratio of price to earnings, and the scent of "a bogus bill of goods." This was fair. Three years earlier, eBay had been nothing more than a personal World Wide Web page belonging to a bearded, bespectacled software engineer named Pierre Omidyar, who had also written a free program for playing chess on line. Luckily for people who ignored *Forbes,* eBay not only has failed to collapse but has climbed tenfold. Now the financial markets assign to this little San Jose, California, company a value greater than the combined worth of K mart, United Airlines, Apple Computer, and U.S. Steel. Unlike some Internet companies, eBay actually makes a profit. Anyway, the people driving up the stock price aren't the pros; they're day traders, sitting at home computers, hopping in and out of the stock with an attention span measured in minutes. Their mental arithmetic goes, *Take all global commerce and multiply by one and a quarter to five percent.* . . . And when the market closes and they need to cool down, they point their computers to eBay and trade sports memorabilia: cards, autographed balls, Olympic hand-me-downs. Maybe someone, somewhere, will actually bid $9.99 for this "glass Snickers commemorative canister type candy jar" from the 1992 Olympic Games in Barcelona. It might have some kind of personal meaning.

7   The eBay people see their service as a counterforce to an overcommoditized world, with Gaps and Starbucks in every downtown. They talk about using technology in the cause of individualism—as though we were a race of people defined by our fetishes. Certainly the world has never before seemed so full of tchotchkes and curios. Omidyar, who is thirty-two, started the company because his girlfriend collected Pez dispensers and needed an on-line forum for trading them. One eBay vice-president collects Monopoly games and Depression glass; another collects hand-painted toy soldiers. "People are at a certain fundamental level prewired to love collecting things," Steve Westly, the v.p. with toy soldiers, says. "They want to return to their childhood or memories that have had a special meaning." Either that or we're bid dumb squirrels who can't stop gathering nuts.

8   Executives at eBay and Amazon alike say that they are really building communities, composed of people who could never before have found so many secret fellow-obsessives on the trail of Barbie shoes or Wonder Woman figurines. They have auction cheerleaders to egg people on. "Express Yourself," urge the managers of eBay's jewelry neighborhood. "If you could have any piece of jewelry that you wanted, money (and any other types of reality) being no object, what would it be and why? Click here to share your thoughts." Hundreds of people do click there: "I think it would be great to have a piece of jewelry from everyone in the world so that you could spend every day looking at different jewelry. Now, that isn't too much to ask, is it?"

9   No, it isn't too much to ask. People who care about nothing so much as jewelry can spend every day looking at different jewelry. They can buy, and sell, and buy, and sell, or, at least, bid on, or view pictures of, or dream of, something not too far short of "jewelry from everyone in the world." The same goes for people who prefer antique microscopes, Beanie Babies, camera lenses, duck stamps, erotic photographs, or French brocade pillow covers. Or guns: eBay, reacting to criticism, has stopped providing a venue for the trading of firearms, but scores of less fastidious sites have leaped in to perform this service.

10 For human beings as shoppers, barterers, traders, collectors, and hagglers, the on-line bazaars represent a rapid retreat of the horizon. In olden days, someone in need of a Teddy bear would, at most, explore for it as far as the handful of stores near home. The consumer's reach grew with mail-order catalogues and the Yellow Pages. We have telephone ordering and FedEx. Still, the options were limited. Suddenly, the marketplace for Teddy bears is truly global—not to mention the marketplace for Furbys. Not only buyers can reach farther; so can sellers.

11 Charles Chiarchiaro, a Maine antique dealer who has been obsessed with old steam whistles since he was a boy of seven, now trades them on eBay, simultaneously buying from and selling to a larger peer group than he had ever imagined possible. He's waiting to see if eleven hundred dollars will win him the variable-tone Crane Mockingbird fire whistle being auctioned. He sees it as a "technological icon, a representation of technology and industrial art." Even when he travels to real flea markets, as he still does, he brings his P.C. along and monitors his eBay auctions through his car phone. I know how he feels. It turns out that I could have called RadioShack or the Sharper Image and got a laser pointer for anywhere from thirty-nine to ninety-nine dollars, but that's a bit pricey. And, besides, I hadn't realized I wanted one. Meanwhile, U.S. Pawn Inc., an operator of old-fashioned pawnshops, is rushing to open its own global on-line pawnshop-cum-auction service.

12 The auction process is a loopy kind of entertainment that is even more hypnotic than the Home Shopping Network. It's a participant sport. Bonnie Burton, a compulsive shopper who has started an "eBay Weirdness Mailing List," says she is reliving her childhood in daily auctions of pop-culture toys— Little Miss No Name, Spirograph, Talking View-Master. She finds herself getting frenzied over a small, waiflike plastic doll: "I started at twenty-five dollars, but ten minutes before the auction ended I got outbid over and over again by some pesky old-man collector. I wanted to E-mail him during the bidding to ask him what the hell an old man needed a little dolly for? Was he a perv? Could I make him ashamed, so he'd let me win? Yeah, right. One thing you have to remember on eBay: no one has any shame, ever!" She hung in and won the doll, for sixty dollars. In theory, bidders can avoid this kind of undignified last-minute craziness. You can tell eBay what you are "really" willing to pay, and the computers will increment your bid for you as is necessary, keeping your bottom-line number secret from the other bidders. In reality, though, people seem to prefer making their own heat-of-the-moment decisions, costly though that can be. "You start thinking of different ways to outsmart other bidders so you can get that mint-condition Super Spirograph," Burton says. "It's sick, and we're all happy to be addicts."

13 The average sale price for an item at eBay is modest—under fifty dollars. If I want to get more serious about this, maybe I should look at the on-line auctions that are underway over at Butterfield & Butterfield, the venerable San Francisco auction house, which is now trying, as they put it, to "leverage our traditional model to the Internet world." Past meets present, and past keeps on meeting present. I could bid on first editions of Nabokov's "Lolita" and Madonna's "Sex" (the latter guaranteed to be unopened). Sotheby's is preparing to open a sothbys.com auction business this summer. Christies.com hopes to start Internet auctions in September, notwithstanding its scorn for certain unnamed "recent on-line auction initiatives." ("It is not surprising," Christie's C.E.O., Christopher Davidge, declared recently, "that these initiatives have come under considerable criticism and raise concerns of potential fraud.")

14 All these houses stress their old-line virtues. They appraise and authenticate and stand behind the merchandise that passes through their doors, even if the doors are virtual. George Noceti, Butterfield's senior vice-president for Internet strategy, says that the people who really know auctions are the old, old auction firms. Those mini-auctions

over at eBay just barely qualify as auctions. "They're glorified classified ads in most cases," Noceti says. "But the matching they do is the best I've ever seen—people who want to buy with people who want to sell. Everybody can participate: you can put something on sale for a dollar, you can put something on sale for a hundred dollars." Or a thousand, or a hundred thousand. It hardly needs to be added that after a hundred and thirty-four years in the business Butterfield & Butterfield filed for an I.P.O. this year. But they have already cancelled it. Instead, eBay is buying the whole company.

15   It's worth remembering that the auction and all its variants, including formal and informal haggling, predate fixed pricing in economic history. Academics have long argued about whether auctions—dynamic, raucous, and equilibrium-seeking as they are—lead to fair prices. Why shouldn't they, as long as they are open and honest? Because we humans aren't robots. Richard H. Thaler, a University of Chicago economist, argues in his provocative book "The Winner's Curse" that people who win auctions almost automatically overpay. If you take a jar of coins to a bar, he says, and auction it off to the assembled patrons, the average bid will probably be less than its real value but the winning bid will be greater—because everybody is guessing, and some people will guess too high. And if the online world is like a bar it's very, very big and very, very crowded. Then again, not everything has a "true" value. It's easier to put a rational price on a jar of coins than on a vintage Little Miss No Name. Our obsessions and irrationalities aside, the global on-line auction does seem to represent a leap forward in price-setting efficiency, if only because of the sheer volume of information now sloshing around the world at high speed. There are few secrets here. Thousands of laser pointers are up for sale on eBay at any given moment: *Liquidation! Blowout! Incredible closeout!* All these mercurial transactions establish a knowledge-driven marketplace. In another eBay auction, you can buy for a dollar a list of fifty wholesale laser-pointer distributors.

So sellers like on-line auctions because they get a flood of new bidders, and thus better prices for their merchandise. The bargain-crazed consumers who populate the auctions feel that they, too, are getting better prices. Can this be real? Kevin Kelly, the author of "New Rules for the New Economy: Ten Radical Strategies for a Connected World," sees a remarkable illusion of loaves-and-fishes happening here. "The miracle of both sellers' and buyers' doing better at once is really a statement about how clumsy and full of fat the usual way of buying something is," he says. "I don't think this paradoxical state where both buyer and seller gain together is sustainable in the long term. I think it is a sudden and temporary 'gift.' The techniques used in auctions will benefit ordinary retail outlets; the bidding for things and the taking of bids will become so routine that they disappear into the background, done mostly by programs."

One tiny detail: payment is still not quite frictionless. The people at eBay just don't get involved, so people have to fuss with checks and money orders. Amazon.com, by contrast, is setting up a system using credit cards. At the less well-organized end of the spectrum, some people will think that E-auctions will lead to E-barter. A person with, say, a surplus of Beanie Babies and a need for outdoor furniture could find ways to trade and cut out the middleman. "Barter, sufficiently lubricated by electrons," Kelly says, "bypasses the inefficiencies in money itself." Maybe the whole mercantile economics of the past few millennia will turn out to have been a passing phase. People find themselves as addicted to selling junk as to buying it.

What's really flowing freely, of course, is information. We see now that high profits all along the distribution chain from producer to consumer have depended on pockets of darkness—places where information failed to penetrate. That's why local realtors and car dealers guard their price lists so jealously. It is why retailers have been slow to sell directly on line, where they inevitably compete with their own distributors. It is why pure Information is a major eBay category: wholesale lists; how to make money on government C.D.s; best "Secret Info Sellers Don't Want U to See!" ($9.95); and plenty of vaporous get-rich-quick schemes. In the auction bazaars of the Internet, there will always be someone with a lower price. "The world as we know it today is going to change," says George Noceti, at Butterfield's. "I don't expect us to have new-car lots anymore. Everybody knows that you can get a better price on line than from a dealer." The auction model has begin to transform the business-to-business supply chain as well. Industrial procurement of coal, machine parts, plastic moldings, cosmetics ingredients, and specialty steel has all turned to real-time, interactive, on-line bidding, which saves money and cuts out middlemen.

19   Jeff Bezos, at Amazon.com, doesn't think electronic commerce means the end of stores, any more than television meant the end of cinema. He finds himself in the enviable position of being able to condescend to what we used to call reality. "The fact of the matter is, the physical world is the best medium ever," he says. "It's an amazing medium. You can do more in the physical world than you can do anywhere else. I love the physical world!" Hey, don't we all? But it's 8:19:17, and, lucky me, I have won a laser pointer. (In E-auction world, we don't buy things; we win them.)

20   Selwine@ix.netcom.com steps out from behind the curtain and reveals himself as Spencer Zink, a sometime wine salesman from Torrance, California. Only thirty-six people bid on this lot of several hundred laser pointers, so we all pay the same as the lowest winning bidder—in this case, the original $13.99. Plus shipping and handling, of course. We're inclined to trust Zink and cheerfully mail off our personal checks, because he rates well in eBay's feedback system, where users can both praise and slander our fellows, for all to see. Talk is cheap, and there are plenty of shady buyers and sellers trying out various scams on line. Consumer-fraud bureaus in many localities have been struggling to find a way of dealing with the eBay phenomenon, but it isn't easy, because, after all, they are in localities. Anyway, almost a thousand of Zink's past buyers have posted comments like "Great seller, excellent deal, superfast shipping— I'll bid again!" He started about a year ago, with some wine he happened to have on hand. Then he looked around, "did some homework," and found cheap sources of merchandise, like laser pointers, wholesale, from Taiwan. Sometimes he uses the more traditional auction style, starting off with a minimum bid as low as a dollar. He tries to double his money while undercutting the retailers by fifty percent or more. He has sold about seven thousand items in this manner, and he is just a piker.

So go back to eBay's home page. A genuine five-hundred-billion-dinar note from the former Yugoslavia can be yours for $9.95. (Eleven zeroes! Be a billionaire!) If you're an adult, or are willing to pretend you're an adult, you can bid on pornographic pictures from all eras, in all media, not to mention leather whips, chains, handcuffs, vinyl, and more mysterious technologies. Several dozen Internet users in the United States and Canada are vying for a few cases of military-surplus meals—chili with beans, chunky beef stew. They have a five-year shelf life, and are "a must for those preparing for Y2K." And, lo and behold, Spencer Zink has a new auction under way. It seems he has some pointers to sell.   21

Source: James Gleick, "Stop Me Before I Shop Again!" in the *New Yorker*, May 24, 1999, pp. 42–47.

DISCUSSION QUESTIONS

1. Identify the central claim(s) and its (their) argument class(es). Compare your answers with those of three of your classmates. If there is a discrepancy, can you reconcile it through discussion among you?

2. Characterize the tone of Gleick's argument.

3. How does the tone as you've described it in Question #2 work for or against the success of the argument? (Note: you will need to identify Gleick's intended audience to answer this question.)

4. Use the World Wide Web to get information about James Gleick. Record both your route to that information and a summary of the information itself. Then compare both with the search results of two students in your class.

5. What point does Gleick seem to be making in his final two sentences?

SUGGESTIONS FOR WRITING (14.2)

1. Spend some time on the eBay site and write your own one- to two-page description (first-person factual argument) of the experience.

2. Exchange descriptions from Suggestion #1 with a classmate and see if you can detect an implicit, non-factual claim within his/her argument. Your classmate will do the same. Then modify your initial description to an argument that clearly supports the claim your classmate has identified. (If your classmate has not found an implicit non-factual claim, convert your original description to an evaluation of the eBay site.)

3. Choose a particular phenomenon of the Internet and write a three- to five-page interpretation of it. (Possible topics: chat rooms; automobile "lots"; singles sites; newspages; travel agents.)

4. In Par. 18, George Noceti, Senior Vice President for Internet strategy at the venerable auction house Butterfield & Butterfield, is quoted as follows: "The world as we know it today is going to change." Specifically, he is referring to changes brought about by electronic commerce. Using Noceti's prediction as your central claim, write your own prediction (causal argument) of changes likely to evolve from the explosion of buying and selling over the Internet. You may cite several instances of probable change and support them briefly, or you may concentrate on one. (Note: if you have trouble coming up with focused examples of changes, see the section "Finding a Claim" in Chapter 3.)

5. Write an extended two-page definition of electronic commerce. The purpose of your definition is to clarify the term to readers not familiar with it.

LISTENING FOR THE SILENCE

STEPHEN E. TALBOTT

"Listening for the Silence" is a chapter in Stephen Talbott's book The Future Does Not Compute: Transcending the Machines in Our Midst *(1995). According to the book jacket, Talbott worked for 14 years in the computer industry, but "recently moved . . . from the Boston technology belt to rural New York, where his efforts to reach an accommodation with his computer continue."*

Notice as you read this argument the differences in tone between Talbott on the one hand and Gleick and Bennahum on the other.

1   The notorious sloppiness of computer-mediated communication is often attributed to its being more like conversational speech than like traditional writing. The idea seems to be that sloppiness works fine in conversation, so why shouldn't it work just as well in online communication? But perhaps the premise here sneaks within the gates just a bit too easily.

2   There are several elements of effective conversation:

3   *The ability to listen.* I mean an active sort of listening—the kind that enables and encourages, eliciting from the speaker an even better statement than he knew he was capable of producing. The kind that enters sympathetically into the gaps, the hesitations, the things left unsaid, so that the listener can state the speaker's position as effectively as his own. To listen productively is to nurture a receptive and energetic void within which a new word can take shape. Such listening is half of every good conversation, perhaps the most creative half.

4   Needless to say, listening expresses a deep selflessness. And, if my own experience is any guide, the discipline required is far from natural. In fact, it usually seems impossible. But this does not prevent our working toward it, as toward any ideal.

5   What about computer-mediated communication? Clearly, listening is still more difficult here. The speaker is no longer physically present. He no longer demands so insistently that I attend to his words, nor is my listening immediately evident to him. If I wish, I can more easily conceal my disinterest.

6   However, the situation is not hopeless. Even in face-to-face communication I must "overcome" the physically detached word if I would find my way to the mind of the speaker. So it's not as if the computer confronts me with an altogether new challenge. It's just that I must make a more conscious effort of attention, actively seeking out the speaker behind the words on my screen. When I do this well, my response can still convey a quality of listening. Listening is in any case more than a mere visible blankness. It is a receptive participation that colors all aspects of the conversation.

7   *Silence.* Silence is implied in listening, but also in speaking. It is the place where the right words can come together. Without silence, the torrent of words becomes coercive for both speaker and listener. The words are automatic, unconsidered, expressing thoughts and feelings the speaker himself is not fully aware of. They run in ruts, responding in the same old ways to the same old triggering remarks. Silence is the dark soil through which the seedleaves of a new understanding may push through to the light.

8   Silence is essential to the proper management of a conversation. Only when I am silent can another contribute in a balancing way. Only when the whole group regularly punctuates its discourse with silences is there a chance for the conversation to be formed consciously as a common work of art instead of running on wildly under its own power.

9   How does an electronic discussion group incorporate a discipline of silence? I'm not sure to what extent it is possible. But each contributor can at least exercise such a discipline within himself, weighing each remark before submitting it. The familiar advice about writing a response, then waiting a day before mailing it, is often appropriate. So, too, one can give place to silence in contemplating the shape of the conversation as a whole—as one would a painting before adding a new stroke. Admittedly, online discussions are so often utterly random and shapeless that it hardly seems worth the effort. This is not surprising, since creative silence is a rare thing even in our deeply personal conversations. Nevertheless, there is a goal we can work toward here.

10 *Respect for the word.* The word is the instrument of our *meanings.* Only with

words can a human being mean something. In this sense, every meaning-gesture is a "word." There is no activity we can properly call human that is not a kind of speaking—whether it occurs in a conversation, on a ballet stage, or in a sports stadium.

11   Our ability to convey meaning depends on two things. We need an established, shared vocabulary of some sort. And we need to employ that vocabulary in a distinctive way, impressing our meanings—which is to say, ourselves—upon it. To whatever extent this latter effort is superfluous, we are passing along empty information. For meanings are not simply given in our words, as if those words were containers; meaning arises dynamically in the gaps between the words—but does so in part because of the particular words we have used.

12   That is why machine translation only works (to some extent) with highly formalized (that is, relatively empty) vocabularies typical of certain sciences and scholarly disciplines. Such languages are designed to eliminate all meaning, to squeeze out every contaminant that might infect the spaces between the words.

13   Computers, so far as they act in their own right, are exchangers of information, not meaning. They do not learn from the gaps between words. So there is no need for a computer to apply the disciplines of listening and silence. There is nothing to listen for, no human meaning to take form in the silences. The transactions are automatic, given solely by what is "contained in" the words—which is a purely formal emptiness.

14   As we embrace the age of information and all the tools for processing information, it is well to keep asking: where in all this is the listening? Where is the silence and the meaning? In all the discussion of information, one rarely hears a clear distinction articulated between automatic processing and human conversation. The distinction matters.

15   *Attention to the larger human context.* Conversing is the way we are human. We are not machines exchanging data; rather,

we should expect that our every meeting is fated; that the way we handle ourselves may help someone else along the way, or else cause him to stumble; that we have something important to learn from the encounter—all the more so if we find ourselves irritated, angry, or otherwise derailed from constructive response.

16   Online flame wars have attracted much attention, leading some to ask whether electronic communication encourages undue emotional outbursts. The question is worth asking, but I wonder whether the more dangerous symptoms lie at the other end of the spectrum. Anger is at least an indication that there is something *personal* at stake, even if we are not fully conscious of it. What if we lose the personal altogether?

17   One can imagine businesslike networks of communication that verge increasingly upon the "ideal" of pure, automatic information exchange. One might even suspect that this is the required direction of movement, since, for reasons of efficiency, we must transfer responsibility for more and more of our business communication to software. We who must merge our own efforts with those of our machines cannot help feeling ourselves pulled toward the machines. How do we pay attention to the person on the other end when it's unclear who that person is—if he's anyone at all—amid the mechanisms?

18   To respond to a system as if it were a person becomes downright silly. (Do I apologize to the software for my mistakes?) We *can,* however, read every system as the human expression that it ultimately is, and then act accordingly. This could mean refusing to reply to a computerized suite of telephone recordings, opting instead for the human speaker. It could mean recognizing that a particular computer-based system expresses so fundamental a denial of the human being that the only acceptable response is to unplug one's connection—or even to carry out some strategy of "technological disobedience."

19   I am not being facetious here. Any such reactions will necessarily be highly personal—which is not another way of saying they are unimportant. Quite the contrary; from the sum total of such reactions we will

determine the future shape of technological society. And the more radical responses at least have this merit; they take the system *seriously,* rather as we must take people seriously. These responses are vivid testimony to the presence of a human being at some point in the system. Our need for such reminders may become acute.

Filtering out the human being

20 Such, then, are a few features of conversation: listening, silence, respect for the words that make communication possible, and attention to the larger human context of all meaningful communication. Of course, the contrast between "good practice" and reality can be painful. I have lately been asking myself about the effects of the peculiar *scanning* mode I find myself reverting to when perusing a much-too-full electronic mailbox or discussion folder. Not only is it uncomfortable to eyes and head, but it reminds me of the state I can fall into when listening to a rather dull lecture: I drowsily follow the words and phrases at a certain superficial level (so that I would immediately perk up if the lecturer interjected a wholly absurd sentence), and yet engage in no creative interaction with the speaker's *meaning* at all. I just track along with the surfaces of the words—behaving rather like an electronic search tool, paying attention to mere word sequences rather than meanings.

21 Can I even make it an *ideal* to listen attentively when, as happens so often, I must sift through masses of half-considered words on my computer screen—many of them uninvited, of little interest, and from unknown sources? Full attention would sap my energies and prevent "getting the job done." And yet, this habit pretty well encompasses a denial of every principle discussed above. To receive *any* language this superficially damages us, I suspect. Penetrating the thought of another requires an active ability to recreate within one's own consciousness the inner life of the other. It's an ability employing the utmost in attention and conscious effort, and can only be learned over a lifetime. Every time I attend to someone's words in a merely

mechanical fashion, I degrade what is most fully human in both of us.

22 Could it be that the "necessity" I feel for superficial scanning tells me something important about what I have allowed my job to become? Isn't it really under my control? Why do I call down upon myself so much "half-important" material, if not to satisfy some sort of profitless information greed? These questions lead directly to one of today's hottest topics on the Net: information filtering.

23 *Fading conversations.* The information glut is not new. Long before the Net's burgeoning it was impossible to keep up with more than a tiny fraction of the journals, books, conferences, and discussions bearing on one's professional field, let alone those relating to avocational interests. No one with any sense tried to take in *everything,* for that could lead only to the intellectual shallows. Far more important was deep interaction with those colleagues one did encounter in person or in writing.

24 Now, however, there is almost a frenzy of concern for "filtering." Software tools for selecting, categorizing, filing, and analyzing information—and even for responding automatically to personal messages—are under intense development. A primary reason for this, quite evidently, is that computers give us our first automatic scanning and processing abilities. Somehow it seems that we can "get at" much more information than we could in the old-fashioned library.

25 This is no doubt true in some sense. But two cautions seem necessary. First, no more today than yesterday does breadth of acquaintance substitute for depth of contemplation—even if the available tools make the temptation to spread wide almost irresistible. And second, we need to realize the subtle nudges these new information-processing tools administer to us. Just consider: in conversation with a friend or colleague you would most definitely *not* apply a rigidly pre-set filter to his remarks—not, at least, if you were interested in learning from him rather than imposing your biases upon him.

26   Tools for filtering make it clear that human exchange is becoming less conversational. The human context of the word is ever less important, which is to say that what the words mean is defined within a relative vacuum. This necessarily leads to our taking them more abstractly, for concreteness derives from a particular human milieu. Without such a milieu, we can only talk about what the words might mean "in general."

27   Half of every conversation consists of what meets me unpredictably from the other side. Half of learning is achieved by the world, working upon me at its own initiative. The aim of the filter is, at one level, to eliminate unpredictability—to select my "input" according to criteria *I* can fully control. Of course, it's also true in direct conversation that I can choose my partners, but certain human constraints prevent my simply walking away as soon as a "wrong" turn is taken or one of my "filter this out" keywords is spoken. I have to deal with the person, whose presence alone grants him a certain claim upon me.

28   The frightening prospect is that cyberspace will fade into a mere disjunction of subjective universes as each of us encases himself within a solipsistic cocoon. The paradox here is that reduction of knowledge to "objective" information is precisely what prepares the way for this triumph of subjectivity. But, then, in all things a perverse subjectivity is the unavoidable correlation of perverse objectivity.

29   Am I advising you to avoid all use of software filters? No. The only thing I would state in such absolute terms is the most general principle: we must do whatever we find necessary to preserve our fullest humanity in the presence of our machines. But it does seem to me that the comparison between online communication and conversation proves useful in focusing our thinking about the choices. Certainly it is true—to retrieve our starting point—that if we take the requirements for conversation seriously, then the demands placed upon us by the "orality" of computer-mediated communication are at least as stringent as the demands embodied in traditional standards of writing, even if they are somewhat different.

Source: Stephen E. Talbott, "Listening for the Silence," in *The Future Does Not Compute: Transcending the Machines in Our Midst*, Sebastopol, CA: O'Reilly & Associates, 1995, pp. 227–234.

DISCUSSION QUESTIONS

1. This argument relies heavily on abstract claims. With a small group of your classmates, create concrete examples for the following abstractions:

   a. "Only when the whole group regularly punctuates its discourse with silences is there a chance for the conversation to be formed consciously as a communal work of art instead of running on wildly under its own power." (Par. 7)

   b. "The human context of the word is ever less important, which is to say that what the words mean is defined within a relative vacuum." (Par. 25)

   c. "Half of learning is achieved by the world, working upon me at its own initiative." (Par. 27)

   How different were your understandings of these statements?

2. Do you find any unsupported claims in this argument? Is the lack of support acceptable? That is, are the claims self-evident? Why do you suppose Talbott has included these in his argument?

3. Discuss in a small group the effectiveness of the extended definition of "conversation (Par. 1–18). Which of the techniques of definition presented in Chapter 4 are used by Talbott? Which of these are the most effective and why? Is this an extended *stipulative* definition?

4. Select four adjectives to characterize the tone of this argument. Then, in a class discussion, consider the appropriateness of your characterization to the purpose, subject, audience, and claims of the argument.

SUGGESTIONS FOR WRITING (14.3)

1. With two classmates, participate in a "conversation" (according to Talbott's use of the term) about the dehumanizing effect of on-line communication. Try to include in your conversation all the defining elements of the term offered by Talbott. Did you find the discussion more valuable than typical small-group discussions because of your attention to Talbott's definition?

2. Exchange e-mails with a classmate on the subject of oral versus electronic conversation (two e-mails apiece). Then write a one- to two-page formal argument comparing the two forms of conversation, using any material from the e-mail exchange.

3. In a two-page evaluative argument, compare the two preceding experiences. Be very clear about the meaning of your evaluative term(s).

4. Talbott writes in Par. 28, "we must do whatever we find necessary to preserve our fullest humanity in the presence of our machines." Using this statement as your central claim, write a three- to four-page recommendation emphasizing the future. On the title page, briefly describe your audience.

5. Write an extended definition of one of the following, modeled on Talbott's definition of "conversation": communication; reading; sharing; debate; discussion.

WOMEN AND CHILDREN FIRST
Gender and the Settling of the Electronic Frontier

LAURA MILLER

"Women and Children First" first appeared in a collection of essays about the Internet entitled Resisting the Virtual Life: The Culture and Politics of Information *(ed. James Brook and Iain A. Boal, 1995). According to the back cover, the collection is one in which "Scholars, writers, and activists gauge the impact of the new video, computer, and networked communications on our ways of life in a restructured world."*

The editors of this collection (Brook and Boal) are, respectively, a poet and an Irish social historian of science and technics.

1   When *Newsweek* (May 16, 1994) ran an article entitled "Men, Women and Computers," all hell broke out on the Net, particularly on the on-line service I've participated in for six years, The Well (Whole Earth 'Lectronic Link). "Cyberspace, it turns out," declared *Newsweek*'s Nancy Kantrowitz, "isn't much of an Eden after all. It's marred by just as many sexist ruts and gender conflicts as the Real World. . . . Women often feel about as welcome as a system crash." "It was horrible. Awful, poorly researched, unsubstantiated drivel," one member wrote, a sentiment echoed throughout some 480 postings.

2   However egregious the errors in the article (some sources maintain that they were incorrectly quoted), it's only one of several mainstream media depictions of the Net as an environment hostile to women. Even women who had been complaining about on-line gender relations found themselves increasingly annoyed by what one Well member termed the "cyberbabe harassment" angle that seems to typify media coverage of the issue. Reified in the pages of *Newsweek* and other journals, what had once been the topic of discussions by insiders—on-line commentary is informal, conversational, and often spontaneous—became a journalistic "fact" about the Net known by complete strangers and novices. In a matter of months, the airy stuff of bitch sessions became widespread, hardened stereotypes.

3   At the same time, the Internet has come under increasing scrutiny as it mutates from an obscure, freewheeling web of computer networks used by a small elite of academics, scientists, and hobbyists to . . . well, nobody seems to know exactly what. But the business press prints vague, fevered prophecies of fabulous wealth, and a bonanza mentality has blossomed. With it comes big business and the government, intent on regulating this amorphous medium into a manageable and profitable industry. The Net's history of informal self-regulation and its wide libertarian streak guarantee that battles like the one over the Clipper chip (a mandatory decoding device that would make all encrypted data readable by federal agents) will be only the first among many.

4   Yet the threat of regulation is built into the very mythos used to conceptualize the Net by its defenders—and gender plays a crucial role in that threat. However revolutionary the technologized interactions of on-line communities may seem, we understand them by deploying a set of very familiar metaphors from the rich figurative soup of American culture. Would different metaphors have allowed the Net a different, better historical trajectory? Perhaps not, but the way we choose to describe the Net now encourages us to see regulation as its inevitable fate.

And, by examining how gender roles provide a foundation for the intensification of such social controls, we can illuminate the way those roles proscribe the freedoms of men as well as women.

5   For months I mistakenly referred to the EFF (an organization founded by John Perry Barlow and Lotus 1-2-3 designer Mitch Kapor to foster access to, and further the discursive freedom of, on-line communications) as "The Electronic Freedom Foundation," instead of by its actual name, "The Electronic Frontier Foundation." Once corrected, I was struck by how intimately related the ideas "frontier" and "freedom" are in the Western mythos. The *frontier,* as a realm of limitless possibilities and few social controls, hovers, grail-like, in the American psyche, the dream our national identity is based on, but a dream that's always, somehow, just vanishing away.

6   Once made, the choice to see the Net as a frontier feels unavoidable, but it's actually quite problematic. The word "frontier" has traditionally described a place, if not land then the limitless "final frontier" of space. The Net on the other hand, occupies precisely no physical space (although the computers and phone lines that make it possible do). It is a completely bodiless, symbolic thing with no discernable boundaries or location. The land of the American frontier did not become a "frontier" until Europeans determined to conquer it, but the continent existed before the intention to settle it. Unlike land, the Net was created by its pioneers.

7   Most peculiar, then, is the choice of the word "frontier" to describe an artifact so humanly constructed that it only exists as ideas or information. For central to the idea of the frontier is that it contains no (or very few) other people —fewer than two per square mile according to the nineteenth-century historian Frederick Turner. The freedom the frontier promises is a liberation from the demands of society, while the Net (I'm thinking now of Usenet) has nothing but society to offer. Without other people, news groups, mailing lists, and files simply wouldn't exist and e-mail would be purposeless. Unlike real space, cyberspace must be shared.

8   Nevertheless, the choice of a spatial metaphor (credited to the science-fiction novelist William Gibson, who coined the term "cyberspace"), however awkward, isn't surprising. Psychologist Julian Jaynes has pointed out that geographical analogies have long predominated humanity's efforts to conceptualize—map out—consciousness. Unfortunately, these analogies bring with them a heavy load of baggage comparable to Pandora's box: open it and a complex series of problems have come to stay.

9   The frontier exists beyond the edge of settled or owned land. As that land that doesn't belong to anybody (or to people who "don't count," like Native Americans), it is on the verge of being acquired; currently unowned, but still ownable. Just as the ideal of chastity makes virginity sexually provocative, so does the unclaimed territory invite settlers, irresistibly so. Americans regard the lost geographic frontier with a melancholy, voluptuous fatalism— we had no choice but to advance upon it and it had no alternative but to submit. When an EFF member compares the Clipper chip to barbed wire encroaching on the prairie, doesn't he realize the surrender implied in his metaphor?

10   The psychosexual undercurrents (if anyone still thinks of them as "under") in the idea of civilization's phallic intrusion into nature's passive, feminine space have been observed, exhaustively, elsewhere. The classic Western narrative is actually far more concerned with social relationships than conflicts between man and nature. In these stories, the frontier is a lawless society of men, a milieu in which physical strength, courage, and personal charisma supplant institutional authority and violent conflict is the accepted means of settling disputes. The Western narrative connects pleasurably with the American romance of individualistic masculinity; small wonder that the predominantly male founders of the Net's culture found it so appealing.

11   When civilization arrives on the frontier, it comes dressed in skirts and short pants. In the archetypal 1939 movie *Dodge City,* Wade Hatton (Errol Flynn) refuses to accept the position of marshal because he prefers the footloose life of a trail driver. Abbie Irving (Olivia De Havilland), a recent arrival from the civilized East, scolds him for his unwillingness to accept and advance the cause of law; she can't function (in her job as crusading journalist) in a town governed by brute force. It takes the accidental killing of a child in a street brawl for Hatton to realize that he must pin on the badge and clean up Dodge City.

12   In the Western mythos, civilization is necessary because women and children are victimized in conditions of freedom. Introduce women and children into a frontier town and the law must follow because women and children must be protected. Women, in fact, are usually the most vocal proponents of the conversion from frontier justice to civil society.

13   The imperiled women and children of the Western narrative make their appearance today in newspaper and magazine articles that focus on the intimidation and sexual harassment of women on line and reports of pedophiles trolling for victims in computerized chat rooms. If on-line women successfully contest these attempts to depict them as the beleaguered prey of brutish men, expect the pedophile to assume a larger profile in arguments that the Net is out of control.

14   In the meantime, the media prefer to cast women as the victims, probably because many women actively participate in the call for greater regulation of on-line interactions, just as Abbie Irving urges Wade Hatton to bring the rule of law to Dodge City. These requests have a long cultural tradition, based on the idea that women, like children, constitute a peculiarly vulnerable class of people who require special protection from the elements of society men are expected to confront alone. In an insufficiently civilized society like the frontier, women, by virtue of this childlike vulnerability, are thought to live under the constant threat of kidnap, abuse, murder, and especially rape.

15   Women, who have every right to expect that crimes against their person will be rigorously prosecuted, should nevertheless regard the notion of special protections (chivalry, by another name) with suspicion. Based as it is on the idea that women are inherently weak and incapable of self-defense and that men are innately predatory, it actually reinforces the power imbalance between the sexes, with its roots in the concept of women as property, constantly under siege and requiring the vigilant protection of their male owners. If the romance of the frontier arises from the promise of vast stretches of unowned land, an escape from the restrictions of a society based on private property, the introduction of women spoils that dream by reintroducing the imperative of property in their own persons.

16   How does any of this relate to on-line interactions, which occur not on a desert landscape but in a complex, technological society where women are supposed to command equal status with men? It accompanies us as a set of unexamined assumptions that we believe are rooted in the imperatives of our bodies. These assumptions follow us into the bodiless realm of cyberspace, a forum where, as one scholar put it "participants are washed clean of the stigmata of their real 'selves' and are free to invent new ones to their tastes." Perhaps some observers feel that the replication of gender roles in a context where the absence of bodies supposedly makes them superfluous proves exactly how innate those roles are. Instead, I see in the relentless attempts to interpret on-line interactions as highly gendered, an intimation of just how artificial, how created, our gender system is. If it comes "naturally," why does it need to be perpetually defended and reasserted?

17   Complaints about the treatment of women on line fall into three categories: that women are subjected to excessive, unwanted sexual attention, that the prevailing style of on-line discussion turns women off, and that women are singled out by male participants for exceptionally dismissive or hostile treatment. In making these assertions, the *Newsweek* article and other stories on the issue do echo grievances that some on-line women have made for years. And, without a doubt, people have encountered sexual come-ons, aggressive debating tactics, and ad hominem attacks on the Net. However, individual users interpret such events in widely different ways, and to generalize from those interpretations to describe the experiences of women and men as a whole is a rash leap indeed.

18   I am one of many women who don't recognize their own experience of the Net in the misogynist gauntlet described above. In researching this essay, I joined America Online and spent an hour or two "hanging out" in the real-time chat rooms reputed to be rife with sexual harassment. I received several "instant messages" from men, initiating private conversations with innocuous questions about my hometown and tenure on the service. One man politely inquired if I was interested in "hot phone talk" and just as politely bowed out when I declined. At no point did I feel harassed or treated with disrespect. If I ever want to find a phone-sex partner, I know where to look but until then I probably won't frequent certain chat rooms.

19   Other women may experience a request for phone sex or even those tame instant messages as both intrusive and insulting (while still others maintain that they have received much more explicit messages and inquiries completely out of the blue). My point isn't that my reactions are the more correct, but rather that both are the reactions of women, and no journalist has any reason to believe that mine are the exception rather than the rule.

20   For me, the menace in sexual harassment comes from the underlying threat of rape or physical violence. I see my body as the site of my heightened vulnerability as a woman. But on line—where I have no body and neither does anyone else—I consider rape to be impossible. Not everyone agrees. Julian Dibble, in an article for *The Village Voice,* describes the repercussions of a "rape" in a multiuser dimension, or MUD, in which one user employed a subprogram called a "voodoo doll" to cause the personae of other users to perform sexual acts. Citing

the "conflation of speech and act that's inevitable in any computer-mediated world," he moved toward the conclusion that "since rape can occur without any physical pain or damage, then it must be classified as a crime against the mind." Therefore, the offending user had committed something on the same "conceptual continuum" as rape. Tellingly, the incident led to the formation of the first governmental entity on the MUD.

21 No doubt the cyber-rapist (who went by the nom de guerre Mr. Bungle) appreciated the elevation of his mischief-making to the rank of virtual felony: all of the outlaw glamour and none of the prison time (he was exiled from the MUD). Mr. Bungle limited his victims to personae created by women users, a choice that, in its obedience to prevailing gender roles, shaped the debate that followed his crimes. For, in accordance with the real-world understanding that women's smaller, physically weaker bodies and lower social status make them subject to violation by men, there's a troubling notion in the real and virtual worlds that women's minds are also more vulnerable to invasion, degradation, and abuse.

22 This sense of fragility extends beyond interactions with sexual overtones. The *Newsweek* article reports that women participants can't tolerate the harsh, contentious quality of on-line discussions, that they prefer mutual support to heated debate, and are retreating wholesale to women-only conferences and newsgroups. As someone who values on-line forums precisely because they mandate equal time for each user who chooses to take it and forestall various "alpha male" rhetorical tactics like interrupting, loudness, or exploiting the psychosocial advantages of greater size or a deeper voice, I find this perplexing and disturbing. In these laments I hear the reluctance of women to enter into the kind of robust debate that characterizes healthy public life, a willingness to let men bully us even when they've been relieved of most of their traditional advantages. Withdrawing into an electronic purdah where one will never be challenged or provoked, allowing the ludicrous ritual chest-thumping of

some users to intimidate us into silence— surely women can come up with a more spirited response than this.

23 And of course they can, because besides being riddled with reductive stereotypes, media analyses like *Newsweek*'s simply aren't accurate. While the on-line population is predominantly male, a significant and vocal minority of women contribute regularly and more than manage to hold their own. Some of The Well's most bombastic participants are women, just as there are many tactful and conciliatory men. At least, I think there are, because, ultimately, it's impossible to be sure of anyone's biological gender on line. "Transpostites," people who pose as a member of the opposite gender, are an established element of Net society, most famous a man who, pretending to be a disabled lesbian, built warm and intimate friendships with women on several CompuServe forums.

24 Perhaps what we should be examining is not the triumph of gender differences on the Net, but their potential blurring. In this light, *Newsweek*'s stout assertion that in cyberspace "the gender gap is real" begins to seem less objective than defensive, an insistence that on-line culture is "the same" as real life because the idea that it might be different, when it comes to gender, is too scary. If gender roles can be cast off so easily, they may be less deeply rooted, less "natural" than we believe. There may not actually be a "masculine" or "feminine" mind or outlook, but simply a conventional way of interpreting individuals that recognizes behavior seen as in accordance with their biological gender and ignores behavior that isn't.

25 For example, John Seabury wrote in the *New Yorker* (June 6, 1994) of his stricken reaction to his first "flame," a colorful slice of adolescent invective sent to him by an unnamed technology journalist. Reading it, he begins to "shiver" like a burn victim, an effect that worsens with repeated readings. He writes that "the technology greased the words . . . with a kind of immediacy that allowed them to slide easily into my brain." He tells his friends, his coworkers, his partner—even his mother—and, predictably, appeals to CompuServe's management for recourse—to

no avail. Soon enough, he's talking about civilization and anarchy, how the liberating "lack of social barriers is also what is appalling about the Net," and calling for regulation.

26   As a newcomer, Seabury was chided for brooding over a missive that most Net veterans would have dismissed and forgotten as the crude potshot of an envious jerk. (I can't help wondering if my fellow journalist never received hate mail in response to his other writings; this bit of e-mail seems comparable, par for the course when one assumes a public profile.) What nobody did was observe that Seabury's reaction—the shock, the feelings of violation, the appeals to his family and support network, the bootless complaints to the authorities—reads exactly like many horror stories about women's trials on the Net. Yet, because Seabury is a man, no one attributes the attack to his gender or suggests that the Net has proven an environment hostile to men. Furthermore, the idea that the Net must be more strictly governed to prevent the abuse of guys who write for the *New Yorker* seems laughable—though who's to say that Seabury's pain is less than any woman's? Who can doubt that, were he a woman, his tribulations would be seen as compelling evidence of Internet sexism?

27   The idea that women merit special protections in an environment as incorporeal as the Net is intimately bound up with the idea that women's minds are weak, fragile, and unsuited to the rough and tumble of public discourse. It's an argument that women should recognize with profound mistrust and resist,

especially when we are used as rhetorical pawns in a battle to regulate a rare (if elite) space of gender ambiguity. When the mainstream media generalize about women's experiences on line in ways that just happen to uphold the most conventional and pernicious gender stereotypes, they can expect to be greeted with howls of disapproval from women who refuse to acquiesce in these roles and pass them on to other women.

And there are plenty of us, as The Well's response to the *Newsweek* article indicates. 28 Women have always participated in on-line communications, women whose chosen careers in technology and the sciences have already marked them as gender-role resisters. As the schoolmarms arrive on the electronic frontier, their female predecessors find themselves cast in the role of saloon girls, their willingness to engage in "masculine" activities like verbal aggression, debate, or sexual experimentation marking them as insufficiently feminine, or "bad" women. "If that's what women on line are like, I must be a Martian," one Well woman wrote in response to the shrinking female technophobes depicted in the *Newsweek* article. Rather than relegating so many people to the status of gender aliens, we ought to reconsider how adequate those roles are to the task of describing real human beings.

Laura Miller, "Women and Children First: Gender and the Settling of the Electronic Frontier," in *Resisting the Virtual Life: The Culture and Politics of Information*, ed. James Brook and Iain A. Boal. San Francisco: City Lights, 1995, pp. 49–57.

DISCUSSION QUESTIONS

1. Using at least three different Internet sources, write a professional biography of Laura Miller.

   Based on this biography, discuss with a classmate what biases on Miller's part a reader might expect.

2. Create an outline for this essay, indicating central and supporting claims. Be sure to identify the class of each claim and its support.

3. Does the outline created in Question #2 reveal an awareness on Miller's part of the structural principles of written argument?

4. How does the "frontier" analogy contribute to the argument's effectiveness? Could Miller's points have been made equally well without this extended analogy?

SUGGESTIONS FOR WRITING (14.4)

1. Based upon careful attention to this argument's references, tone, and level of diction, create a one-page description of Miller's intended audience. Support your description with specific references to the text of the argument.
2. Read the May 16, 1994 *Newsweek* article referred to by Miller. Form a small discussion group in which each member shares his/her reactions to the *Newsweek* article. Record the views of the group members and write a two- to three-page factual argument summarizing the discussion.
3. Spend some time in a chat room of your choice, and then write a first-person factual argument reporting the experience.
4. Literature about the Internet is filled with predictions of gloom and glory about its effects on virtually every facet of human experience. Using only electronic resources, write a five page causal argument predicting the Internet's impact on one of the following (or on an area supplied by your instructor):

> gender equity
> consumer greed
> recreational time
> relationships
> children's values

Include a bibliography of sources, following the Internet-citation format suggested by MLA or APA.

INFORMATION LITERACY: THE WEB IS NOT AN ENCYCLOPEDIA

This page from The University of Maryland's Web site serves a dual purpose in this book. First, it exemplifies an argument of recommendation. Second, its content—the cautions and recommendations regarding the World Wide Web—are valuable to anyone who uses the Web as a research tool.

1   In this Information Age it is important to pay attention to issues of information literacy in traditional, media, and computing arenas. I use the term information literacy to mean the ability of people to:

- know when they need information
- find information
- evaluate information
- process information
- use information to make appropriate decisions in their lives

2   The Internet has added a new dimension to traditional information literacy issues—especially in the exploding growth of the World Wide Web. Nearly a mix between all other media, the Web democratizes information ownership, provision, and retrieval. The federal government is leading the way in publishing its vast array of information on the Web. On many campuses every student may publish a webpage.

3   The Web allows us to speak directly to the purveyors of information in every imaginable field. Few reference librarians, teachers, publishers, or other mediating forces stand between us and information on the Internet, and specifically, the Web. While this does have great advantages in expanding our

information base and providing more accurate and timely information at the "click of a mouse," it also means, perhaps, more intellectual effort on the part of the information consumer to develop valuable critical thinking skills and to evaluate the sources, quality, and quantity of that information. It also means serious attention should be paid to intellectual property and appropriate use issues.

4   The Web is **not** a huge book written by multiple authors. There is no definitive table of contents for the Web and no definitive index. To some it seems more like a giant reference collection.

5   While it is true that many fine reference materials are available on the Web, it is **not** an encyclopedia. Encyclopedias have subject experts writing refereed articles that pass through editors and style guides before publication. The Web has these same experts, and many non-experts, creating non-refereed webpages on a vast array of topics at a vast range of quality and depth. Some people consider the Web to be a digital library full of materials of varying quality and format.

6   The Web is **not** one large digital library. Libraries have trained professionals who carefully evaluate, select, organize, and index materials from credible sources.

7   The Web **IS** an electronic repository for books, data collections, encyclopedias, libraries, **AND** any disparate piece of text, graphic, or sound byte that someone chose to put on-line. And some of it is inaccurate, biased, out-of-date, shallow, and inappropriate for academic use.

8   In evaluating information on the Internet, one should consider many of the same elements that would be considered when selecting resource material in other formats, and a new one: permanence. As when judging any kind of publication, much is subjective. However, keeping the following elements in mind will assist users to identify resources of value to meet their information needs.

- Scope
- Authority and Bias
- Accuracy
- Timeliness
- Permanence

- Value Added Features
- Presentation

Information Literacy Issues: Content Scope

Evaluate the scope of the site

Identifying the scope of material presented is   9
the basic breadth and depth question of **what's covered** and in **what detail.** The scope should reflect the purpose of the site and its intended audience. Evaluating scope includes reviewing topical aspects of a subject on which the site is focused and noting if there are any key omissions from the subject area.

Many Web sites have abstract levels of   10
current information but no archives or information in depth. Users should look for specific information included on the web site that describes the intended scope and audience. If this information is not available, and it usually is not, one can look for clues in key headings and follow links to estimate the scope of the material.

Things to look for: 11

- Is there a stated purpose of the site
- Who is the intended audience for the site
- Are there statements of scope and any limitations which may apply
- What is the site comprehensiveness

Authority and Bias

Evaluate the authority and bias of the Internet site

Sometimes it is very difficult to discover   12
who actually provided the information available at a Web site. One can always check if the site is officially mandated by an organization or institution. Is it an individual's page or is it institutionally supported? Was it created by a subject area expert or by an undergraduate student doing a class project?

Checking the publisher of the informa-   13
tion may be helpful. Sites in the .edu (education) or .gov (government) domains have often built important databases in specific topic areas and/or have public information and services available on-line. Sites in the .com (commercial) and .org (organization)

domains are usually selling something—a product or a point of view.

14   Bias can be introduced in any Web site furthering a political or social philosophy and in any domain, however, it is most prevalent in organization Web sites (.org).

15   Email, web chats, threaded conversations, provide special cases for consideration. Electronic communication in these formats may provide valuable archives of conversations between or from experts, but does the informal nature lessen its value as an authoritative reference?

16   Things to look for:

- Who provided the information and why
- What credentials do they have
- Is the provider affiliated with a known organization
- Is a point of view being "sold" to the user
- Can you find explicit statements of authority—such as a statement of institutional support
- For "advocacy" pages see *Checklist for an Advocacy Web Page* from Widener University.

Information Literacy Issues: Accuracy

Evaluate the accuracy of the site

17   Unless you already have a base knowledge of a particular field and its experts, how do you tell if information is "good"? One way is to measure it against information on the same topic in other formats. Or you may have found a rich source of information on your chosen topic by following a link from a page you judge to contain accurate information.

18   It is helpful to know if you are at a site that is referenced by other sites for its content. It may not be a citation in a printed bibliography, but it *may* mean that someone thought well enough of it to provide a link to it. Not many institutional sites provide links to badly constructed websites with inaccurate information.

19   Things to look for:

- Is the topic appropriate for the site
- Is the source of the information clearly posted

- Who is the author/creator/publisher and what are his/her/their credentials
- Are there references from other resources on the same or related topics
- Has the site been reviewed by a professional organization or your peers

Information Literacy Issues: Timeliness

Evaluate the timeliness of the site

20   Printed media is often considered to be out of date before it reaches its audience. Some data gathered by electronic means can be displayed immediately on the Internet while other information was translated from printed materials that already fit the "out of date" description. If a government manual is on-line, it can be edited within minutes of new policy implementation, but was it?

21   With the exception of archival information, all sources should be checked for currency. Email sent to a Listserv is dated. Many websites post the date and, sometimes, the time of the last modification to the information. This may be included in a stated policy for the site or be given on individual files. Sometimes you will find relevant information in a document header or footer. This may help you determine if you revisit the site in the future for additional or newer information.

22   Things to look for:

- Posting and revision dates
- Policy statements for information maintenance
- Link maintenance—do the hyperlinks work?

Information Literacy Issues: Permanence

Evaluate the permanence of the site

23   Here today and gone tomorrow! There is no guarantee that a particular file of information will reside in the same location today that it did yesterday. On the Internet, files move from server to server, undergo on-line editing or deletion, and otherwise change their form and/or their location routinely. It is important to note the date and time that a

site is visited if one plans to use the information and a citation is taken. In some cases, the researcher may wish to download, or otherwise capture the file or the section of the file being cited, for on-site reference.

24   Things to look for:

- Explicit statements of temporary or changing location of servers or files
- Author's relationship to the server infrastructure
- Impermanent or transitory nature of the information

Information Literacy Issues: Value Added Features

Evaluate any 'Value Add' service of the site

25   What can be considered a valuable addition to a Web site? Generally, anything that helps the user find the information needed. Here are some examples: Web sites moderated by trained professionals who receive and respond to feedback; evaluation or rating of informational content or presentation on this or other sites; provision of text-only formats, search engines, navigational and help tools.

26   Things to look for:

- Evidence of a content manager with appropriate credentials
- Clear navigation bars
- Index and/or search facilities
- Descriptions of site structure beyond the table of contents (site maps)

- About or help information
- Summaries or abstracts
- Ratings and/or evaluations
- Feedback mechanisms

Information Literacy Issues: Presentation and Organization

Evaluate the presentation and organization of the site

Presentation issues include page or site **lay-** 27 **out,** clarity or intuitiveness of the site's organizational design, and help/example sections. Presentation issues may, or may not, impact the information provided. If a citation of the source means that others will visit the site, the citation should be annotated to include information about the site presentation and organization. If a site is very difficult to use, it might be better to not use it as a reference.

Things to look for: 28

- Intuitive site organization for the appropriate audience
- Clear headings and textual references
- Appropriate use of graphics and multimedia
- Help and example sections appropriately placed
- Navigational links provided back to starting points or table of content pages

Source: "Information Literacy: The Web Is Not
An Enclyclopedia."
http://www.inform.umd.edu/LibInfo/literacy/

DISCUSSION QUESTIONS

1. The URL for this Web site is http://www.inform.umd.edu/LibInfo/literacy/. Find the site and determine, based upon the cautions and recommendations contained in the article, the reliability of the source.

2. What is the purpose of the initial bulleted definition? To clarify? To introduce? To interpret? To argue? What in the rest of the article leads you to this conclusion?

3. This Web site is essentially a set of recommendations for getting the most out of the World Wide Web as an information resource. Working from what you learned in Chapter 9 on writing arguments of recommendation, discuss, with two or three of your classmates, the effectiveness of the recommendations.

4. Find three or four other college or university Web sites with similar pages on using the WWW (Hint: check your school's library link). How similar are the principles and recommendations included in these sites to those presented here?

SUGGESTIONS FOR WRITING (14.5)

1. Using three different search tools, search for information on a single topic of your or your instructor's choice. For each tool, note the usefulness of the search tips, the number of "hits" for your topic, the range of hits, the reliability of sites, and so on. Then, in a three- to four-page argument, recommend one of these tools (comparing all three) to a first-time Internet user doing research on your topic.
2. Select two of the criteria discussed in this site (i.e., Scope, Authority and Bias, Accuracy, etc.). For each, study one of the linked sites (on the Web site itself) and write a brief, bulleted evaluation of the site in terms of the criterion.
3. Write a one-page extended definition of "information," using at least three of the definitional strategies in Chapter 4.
4. Write a one-page extended definition of "knowledge," in which you contrast it with "information."

POLITICS ON THE INTERNET

DOUG BAILEY

"Politics on the Internet" appeared in the August/September 1999 issue of the Library of Congress magazine Civilization. *According to its site on the Web (www.civmag.com),* "Civilization *covers the life of the mind, literature, history, culture and social issues. The magazine is not a political journal, but it encourages strong opinions. Taking its inspiration from the vast holdings of the Library [of Congress],* Civilization *uses the past to increase understanding of the present."*

Doug Bailey is particularly well-suited to write on the subject of politics on the Internet, as he is the founder and publisher of National Journal's The Hotline, *an Internet service offering daily on-line briefings on American politics.*

1 The jukebox classically embodies a corollary to the general law of supply and demand: When the people pick the music, they're much more likely to listen to it.

2 So while some of us may dread the prospective democratization of democracy via the Internet—and some may cringe at the thought that an on-line campaign by core supporters helped lift Jesse Ventura off the mat and into the Minnesota governor's chair—make no mistake: The full interactive potential of the Internet offers a real chance to restore some purpose to our politics by restoring some power to our people.

3 Of course, there already have been a number of well-publicized abuses of democracy on-line—and there will be plenty more. E-mail campaigns organized by interest groups will clog congressional computers. Politicians will scarcely be in a position to restrain themselves from spewing e-mail spam—it being as free as the franking privilege. Phony sites will fool the gullible. Some members of congress will even use the web to raise campaign contributions the night before a big floor vote. All that, and more, is inevitable.

4 Individual empowerment, of course, is most likely to give advantage to those who seek it—including relatively small-scale but highly motivated, true-believing interests. And even the most ubiquitous availability of technology is unlikely to empower those on the bottom rungs in a free-enterprise economy. It's a new millennium, not nirvana.

5   But the convergence of television and on-line capability is opening up extraordinary new opportunities in entertainment, communications, and education, and it will likely also mean a welcome fresh start for our politics. Interactive video-on-demand will not just let you instantly replay Leno one-liners, choose optional database reports to accompany the news, and view a ball game from the camera angle of your choice. It will also enable voters to dial up candidates they want to hear from—on issues they want to hear about—all at times they choose themselves.

6   Even in the absence of a fully two-way conversation, it will be the voters who ask the questions and control the conversation. The voters in control! Hmmmm. What a revolutionary idea.

7   The contrast with today's world of 30-second TV spots could not be greater. No one watches TV for the ads; the challenge to admakers, both commercial and political, is to be entertaining enough or confrontational enough or bizarre enough to keep the viewer from clicking elsewhere or going for a beer. For the most part, only negative ads make contact—so that's what we get.

8   And for any TV audience, even on today's niche channels, the demographics are still broad enough that a campaign risks boring the public, or worse, by making ads issue-specific instead of taking up the character issue or other emotionally charged themes. There's a reason why elevator music bores its captive audience: Muzak doesn't connect because it's for everyone and thus for no one.

9   That has been the politics OF passive television. Everything changes in the Wurlitzer world of video-on-demand, in which the subject is chosen by the voters themselves—not by candidates, consultants, or admakers. When you click to see candidate Giuliani's position on police brutality, you want Giuliani, not marching bands. And you want his comments on police brutality, not on Hillary Rodham Clinton's role in Whitewater. And if you don't get what you want, you and your vote may just go elsewhere.

10   Video-on-demand is just another example of people on-line taking charge of their lives. They trade the stocks they want; the middleman is out. They order their own airline tickets; the middleman is out. They deliver their own mail; the middleman is out. With video-on-demand, the voters will set the agenda, the candidates will respond, and the middleman consultant will be out—or at least humbled.

11   Is it a panacea? Of course not. Will it change things? Count on it.

12   The 30-second television ad won't disappear. Not a chance. But pretaped direct answers to FAQs (that's e-speak for "frequently asked questions") on the issues will be more important. Fundraising may still be a crucial part of most campaigns, but when it comes to financing, the on-line playing field is as level as they come. There are few lower overheads in campaign strategy than the cost of going on-line.

13   Voting may even increase a little. When we can pick the music, we're also more likely to dance. At the very least, those who vote are likely to know more about who they are voting for, and why.

14   Every day, more Americans are on-line, and most who are on-line vote. Every day, each computer sold has greater capacity for video streaming. Every day, more broadband options are available for quicker and clearer video images on-line. This convergence is about to rock our world with a cultural change nearly as great as television itself.

15   And video-on-demand will be only the beginning. Video e-mail is around the next corner. And users will become their own Peter Jenningses, downloading their own nightly news reports directly to their computers, uniquely tailored to their own interests, needs, and whims. On-line registration and on-line voting, each with video-imprint safeguards, seem inevitable.

16   There's enough time—and good reason—to ponder and worry about all that. But video-on-demand in simple forms is already with us now, and is sure to produce some winners in 2000.

17   And politics so loves a winner that by the campaign of 2004, it seems certain to be dancing to an interactive beat—with the people calling the tune.

Source: Doug Bailey, "Politics on the Internet," in *Civilization:* Library of Congress. August/September 1999, p. 71.

DISCUSSION QUESTIONS

1. In this causal argument predicting the effect of the Internet on political campaigns and voting behavior, what is the behavioral principle linking cause and effect? Is the principle a plausible one that can be accepted without support?
2. This argument does not contain much in the way of concrete factual support. Does this weaken its effectiveness? Why or why not?
3. With two or three classmates, discuss the effectiveness of the supporting comparisons in Par. 10.
4. Make a list of characteristics you think apply to the intended audience of this argument (e.g., income, education, computer literacy, gender, political persuasion, ethnic background, etc.).
5. What purpose(s) does the extended analogy comparing the Internet with a jukebox serve? What are the similarities between the Internet and the jukebox? The differences? Do the differences undermine the effectiveness of the analogy? (See Chapter 10 for a discussion of the strengths and limitations of analogy in written argument.)

SUGGESTIONS FOR WRITING (14.6)

1. In Par. 15, Bailey predicts a number of Internet-based innovations. Research and write a four-page causal argument demonstrating the likelihood or unlikelihood of one of these innovations.
2. Every argument in this section on The Internet contains metaphor and/or analogy. Brainstorm with a classmate about the possible reasons for such heavy reliance on figurative language in arguments on this subject. Then write a two-page causal argument that speculates on the reasons for this tendency.
3. In a four- to five-page argument, compare the impact that television and the Internet have had on your life. Your instructor will specify the audience for this argument.
4. In a two-page factual argument, describe the Internet to someone who has never used it. Use at least two analogies in your description.

15

Sports

INTRODUCTION

Last year on a Sunday evening in January, my daughter and I made our customary weekly trip to the nearby frozen yogurt shop for dessert. When we arrived at the little strip mall where the shop—part of a national chain—is located, we were surprised to find it closed. It took us a minute to figure out the reason, and when we did, we were both amused and appalled: it was Super Bowl Sunday. As we drove home on a normally busy suburban artery, we realized the streets were as empty as if it had been 8:00 on Christmas morning. A football game some 3,000 miles away had effectively closed down a large eastern city.

This personal anecdote demonstrates a fact that few Americans could argue: sports are a dominant force in American culture, regularly touching the lives of even those most determinedly uninterested in them. From nursery schools to nursing homes, sports saturate our lives, defining our language, our values, our image of ourselves and others, and the patterns of our days and nights.

The term "sports" is a broad one. To define it for the purposes of this reading unit, I borrow from Norbert Elias, an early sociologist of sport. According to Elias, sports are those "leisure activities demanding bodily exertion . . . with a framework of rules, including those providing for 'fairness,' for equal chances to win for all contestants."[1] Elias's definition makes no distinction regarding the participants of sports; children playing stickball in the street are engaging in sports, as are Michael Jordan and Mia Hamm.

If you need evidence of the ubiquity of sports in our lives, consider how fully its language has been incorporated into all our vocabularies. Unruly toddlers are required by parents and caretakers to take "time-outs," with adults who have

[1]Norbert Elias, "An Essay on Sport and Violence." *Quest for Excitement: Sport and Leisure in the Civilizing Process*. Ed. Elias, Norbert and Eric Dunning. Oxford: Blackwell (1986), p. 151.

never watched a football or basketball game using the referee's hand signal; contemporary businesses are requiring all their employees to work as "teams"; more and more of us are joining life in "the fast lane"; an uncontested victory of any kind is a "slam dunk"; criminals are discouraged by a "three strikes and you're out" policy. In 10 minutes, even the least athletic-minded of you could come up with your own lengthy list of examples.

Or, if you need further proof of the high profile of sports, look at the front page of any newspaper on any day—not the sports page, but the front page. A recent Wednesday morning edition of my local paper proclaimed on the front page in underscored red letters above the paper's masthead, "Notre Dame thumps Syracuse." Well below the basketball headline was the headline "Bush lays out school reforms."

Explanations for the omnipresence of sports in modern life abound, from the economic (sports is a multi-billion dollar industry) to the sociological (sports is a social microcosm) to the political (sports is an empire built upon an intricate power structure). But however you account for its dominant position, whatever perspective you view the phenomenon of modern sport from, there is no denying that it is an infinitely rich and instructive subject from which we can learn a great deal more than rules, records, wins, and losses.

We often think of sports as a mindless activity reserved for those times when we need to let down. This is equally true for the television jock who "veges out" in front of Sunday afternoon football and for the overloaded student who runs five miles at the end of a full day to clear her head. But the arguments in this unit—while varying widely in subject and argument class—share an implicit claim about another, very different appeal of sports: to a thoughtful, reasonable mind, sports are an uncommonly rich and provocative field of inquiry. The arguments you will read here cover a variety of athletic subjects from a variety of angles, but they all discover considerable meaning and resonance within the seemingly simple, "mindless" domain of sports. Like all of the topics in this readings section, sports contain as much meaning and as many implications as the eye of their observer is inclined to discover there.

LITTLE GIRLS IN PRETTY BOXES

JOAN RYAN

By the author's own admission, Joan Ryan's book Little Girls in Pretty Boxes *emerged from an experience of powerful dissonance. A reporter for the* San Francisco Examiner, *Ryan initially intended to write a single newspaper article about female gymnasts and figure skaters. But as she says, "I couldn't close my notebook." Her discovery of the painful sacrifices made by these young girls was disturbing enough to prompt her to take a year's leave from the newspaper to continue her investigation. The product of this dissonance is the much discussed book* Little Girls in Pretty Boxes: The Making and Breaking of Elite Gymnasts and Figure Skaters *(1995). The following is the full "Introduction" to the book.*

COMMENTARY

Joan Ryan's "Introduction" to her *Little Girls in Pretty Boxes* models a successful introduction to a lengthy—in this case, book-length—argument. As discussed in Chapter 11, the goals for such introductions are at least two: 1) to engage the reader, to draw him or her into reading the entire book; and 2) to clearly represent the content of the full argument. This second goal can be especially tricky, as introductory summaries can become tedious, causing the reader to skip them altogether, or worse, to put the book aside permanently. While introductions such as this one might best be classified as hybrid arguments that represent the many claims of the book, they also contain an implicit argument, which could be stated as "You will find this book compelling and clearly organized."

The opening paragraphs of Ryan's introduction skillfully engage the reader's interest and attention. The essay begins with two detailed anecdotes—brief but vivid narratives of a gymnastic and a figure skating competition. In the third paragraph, this concrete detail gives way to a more general claim about the popularity of the two sports, which includes both familiar and startling evidence. Finally, the fourth paragraph applies the "hook": "Yet while gymnastics and figure skating are among the most-watched sports in the country, the least is known about the lives of their athletes." Few readers who have read this far are likely to put the book down; they have, in effect, been drawn into a mystery and will stay the course until they know more.

Having engaged her reader's interest and attention, Ryan now moves to her second introductory task: previewing the content of the book. Paragraph 7 serves as a summary (albeit a rather sensationalistic one) of all the worst discoveries Ryan encountered in her research on elite gymnasts and figure skaters: broken bodies, sexual abuse, anorexia, self-mutilation, parental ambition, and sadistic coaches. These discoveries will become the major claims of the book; each will have a chapter dedicated to it. (The subtitles of the chapters are as follows: 1) Injuries; 2) Eating Disorders; 3) Image; 4) Pressure; 5) Parents; 6) Politics and Money; and 7) Coaches.)

The strategy of the rest of the introduction is to pick up each one of these subjects and provide more, but still tantalizing, detail about them. While the introduction reads as a self-contained argument in its own right, it is also successful in beckoning the reader to the succeeding chapters that will provide still further details about the plight of these young female athletes.

While it may seem unlikely that you will ever be writing a complete book requiring an introduction of such length and completeness, many undergraduate college students end up writing senior and/or honors theses in their majors. These theses can be as many as 50 to 75 pages in length, and will require thorough and strategic introductions.

LITTLE GIRLS IN PRETTY BOXES

1   The little girls marched into the Atlanta arena in single file, heads high, shoulders back, bare toes pointed. Under hair ribbons and rouged cheeks, their balletic bodies flowed past bleachers where expectant fathers craned forward with videocameras.

Small and pretty in their shimmery leotards, the girls looked like trinkets from a Tiffany box. They lined up facing the crowd, and when the announcer summoned the winners of the Peachtree Classic, the gymnasts stepped forward and bowed their heads as soberly as Nobel laureates to receive their medals. Mothers with scoresheets tucked under their arms clapped until their hands hurt, shooting hopeful glances at the ESPN cameras roving among the girls. Along velvet ropes strung across the base of the bleachers, awestruck seven- and eight-year-olds stretched toward the winning gymnasts clutching programs and gym bags for them to sign.

2   On the opposite coast, at a skating rink in Redwood City, California, one fifteen-year-old skater—in a ponytail, braces and baby-blue sequins—stood at the edge of the rink, eyes wide, listening to her coach's last-minute instructions as her parents held hands in the bleachers, packed solid for the Pacific Coast Sectional Championships. She glided to the center of the ice. Then, as her music began, she spun like a jewel-box ballerina, executing the intricate choreography of leaps and footwork she had practiced nearly every day for as long as she could remember. On her ¼-inch skate blades rode her hopes of qualifying for the U.S. Figure Skating Championships, moving her one step closer to the Winter Olympic Games.

3   In gyms and rinks across the country, the air is thick with the scent of the Olympics. And the parents, coaches and young athletes chase it like hounds, impatient for the rewards of the sports that captivate American audiences as no others do. Gymnasts and figure skaters hold a unique and cherished place among American athletes. Gymnasts are the darlings of the Summer Games, figure skaters the ice princesses of the Winter Games. Every four years they keep us glued to our televisions for two weeks with their grace, agility, youth and beauty. They land on magazine covers, Wheaties boxes, the "Today" show. Television ratings for Olympic gymnastics and figure skating events rank among the highest for any sport on television. Helped by the Tonya Harding–Nancy Kerrigan saga, the women's technical program at the 1994 Winter Games drew the fourth-highest rating of any show in the history of television, placing it up there with the final episode of "M*A*S*H." But even at the controversy-free 1992 Winter Games, women's figure skating attracted a larger television audience than either the final game of the 1992 World Series or the 1992 National Collegiate Athletic Association basketball championship game between Michigan and Duke. Americans are so enchanted by gymnasts and figure skaters that in a 1991 survey they chose gymnast Mary Lou Retton and skater Dorothy Hamill—both long retired—as their favorite athletes, beating out the likes of Chris Evert, Michael Jordan and Magic Johnson.

4   Yet while gymnastics and figure skating are among the most-watched sports in the country, the least is known about the lives of their athletes (with the exceptions, of course, of Harding and Kerrigan). We watched thirteen-year-old Michelle Kwan, an eighth grader, land six triple jumps to finish second at the 1994 U.S. Figure Skating championships. We see sixteen-year-old Shannon Miller soar above the balance beam as if it were a trampoline to win a silver medal at the 1992 Olympics. But we know little about how they achieve so much at such a young age or what becomes of them when they leave their sport.

5   Unlike women's tennis, a sport in which teenage girls rise to the highest echelon year after year in highly televised championships, gymnastics and figure skating flutter across our screens as ephemerally as butterflies. We know about tennis burnout, about Tracy Austin, Andrea Jaeger, Mary Pierce and, more recently, about Jennifer Capriati, who turned pro with $5 million in endorsement contracts at age thirteen and ended up four years later in a Florida motel room, blank-eyed and disheveled, sharing drugs with runaways. But we hear precious little about the young female gymnasts and figure skaters who perform magnificent feats of physical strength and agility, and

even less about their casualties. How do the extraordinary demands of their training shape these young girls? What price do their bodies and psyches pay?

6   I set out to answer some of these questions during three months of research for an article that ran in the *San Francisco Examiner*, but when I finished I couldn't close my notebook. I took a year's leave to continue my research, focusing this time on the girls who never made it, not just on the champions.

7   What I found was a story about legal, even celebrated, child abuse. In the dark troughs along the road to the Olympics lay the bodies of the girls who stumbled on the way, broken by the work, pressure and humiliation. I found a girl whose father left the family when she quit gymnastics at age thirteen, who scraped her arms and legs with razors to dull her emotional pain and who needed a two-hour pass from a psychiatric hospital to attend her high school graduation. Girls who broke their necks and backs. One who so desperately sought the perfect, weightless gymnastics body that she starved herself to death. Others—many—who became so obsessive about controlling their weight that they lost control of themselves instead, falling into the potentially fatal cycle of bingeing on food, then purging by vomiting or taking laxatives. One who was sexually abused by her coach and one who was sodomized for four years by the father of a teammate. I found a girl who felt such shame at not making the Olympic team that she slit her wrists. A skater who underwent plastic surgery when a judge said her nose was distracting. A father who handed custody of his daughter over to her coach so she could keep skating. A coach who fed his gymnasts so little that federation officials had to smuggle food into their hotel rooms. A mother who hid her child's chicken pox with makeup so she could compete. Coaches who motivated their athletes by calling them imbeciles, idiots, pigs, cows.

8   I am not suggesting that gymnastics and figure skating in and of themselves are destructive. On the contrary, both sports are potentially wonderful and enriching, providing an arena of competition in which the average child can develop a sense of mastery, self-esteem and healthy athleticism. But this book isn't about recreational sports or the average child. It's about the elite child athlete and the American obsession with winning that has produced a training environment wherein results are bought at any cost, no matter how devastating. It's about how our cultural fixation on beauty and weight and youth has shaped both sports and driven the athletes into a sphere beyond the quest for physical performance.

9   The well-known story of Tonya Harding and Nancy Kerrigan did not happen in a vacuum; it symbolizes perfectly the stakes now involved in elite competition—itself a reflection of our national character. We created Tonya and Nancy not only by our hunger for winning but by our criterion for winning, an exaggeration of the code that applies to ambitious young women everywhere: Talent counts, but so do beauty, class, weight, clothes and politics. The anachronistic lack of ambivalence about femininity in both sports is part of their attraction, hearkening back to a simpler time when girls were girls, when women were girls for that matter: coquettish, malleable, eager to please. In figure skating especially, we want our athletes thin, graceful, deferential and cover-girl pretty. We want eyeliner, lipstick and hair ribbons. Makeup artists are fixtures backstage at figure skating competitions, primping and polishing. In figure skating, costumes can actually affect a score. They are so important that skaters spend $1500 and up on one dress—more than they spend on their skates. Nancy Kerrigan's dresses by designer Vera Wang cost upward of $5000 each.

10   Indeed, the costumes fueled the national fairy tale of Tonya and Nancy. Nancy wore virginal white. She was the perfect heroine, a good girl with perfect white teeth, a 24-inch waist and a smile that suggested both pluck and vulnerability. She remained safely within skating's pristine circle of grace and feminin-

ity. Tonya, on the other hand, crossed all the lines. She wore bordello red-and-gold. She was the perfect villainess, a bad girl with truckstop manners, a racy past and chunky thighs. When she became convinced Nancy's grace would always win out over her own explosive strength, Tonya crossed the final line, helping to eliminate Nancy from competition. The media frenzy tapped into our own inner wranglings about the good girl/bad girl paradox, about how women should behave, about how they should look and what they should say. The story touched a cultural nerve about women crossing societal boundaries—of power, achievement, violence, taste, appearance—and being ensnared by them. In the end, both skaters were trapped, Tonya by her ambition and Nancy by the good-girl image she created for the ice—an image she couldn't live up to. The public turned on Nancy when foolish comments and graceless interviews made it clear she wasn't Snow White after all.

11   Both sports embody the contradiction of modern womanhood. Society has allowed women to aspire higher, but to do so a woman must often reject that which makes her female, including motherhood. Similarly, gymnastics and figure skating remove the limits of a girl's body, teaching it to soar beyond what seems possible. Yet they also imprison it, binding it like the tiny Victorian waist or the Chinese woman's foot. The girls aren't allowed passage into adulthood. To survive in the sports, they beat back puberty, desperate to stay small and thin, refusing to let their bodies grow up. In this way the sports pervert the very femininity they hold so dear. The physical skills have become so demanding that only a body shaped like a missile—in other words, a body shaped like a boy's—can excel. Breasts and hips slow the spins, lower the leaps and disrupt the clean, lean body lines that judges reward. "Woman's gymnastics" and "ladies' figure skating" are misnomers today. Once the athletes become women, their elite careers wither.

12   In the meantime, their childhoods are gone. But they trade more than their childhoods for a shot at glory. They risk serious physical and psychological problems that can linger long after the public has turned its attention to the next phenom in pigtails. The intensive training and pressure heaped on by coaches, parents and federation officials—the very people who should be protecting the children—often result in eating disorders, weakened bones, stunted growth, debilitating injuries and damaged psyches. In the last six years two U.S. Olympic hopefuls have died as a result of their participation in elite gymnastics.

13   Because they excel at such a young age, girls in these sports are unlike other elite athletes. They are world champions before they can drive. They are the Michael Jordans and Joe Montanas of their sports before they learn algebra. Unlike male athletes their age, who are playing quarterback in high school or running track for the local club, these girls are competing on a worldwide stage. If an elite gymnast or figure skater fails, she fails globally. She sees her mistake replayed in slow motion on TV and captured in bold headlines in the newspaper. Adult reporters crowd around, asking what she has to say to a country that had hung its hopes on her thin shoulders. Tiffany Chin was seventeen when she entered the 1985 U.S. Figure Skating Championships as the favorite. She was asked at the time how she would feel if she didn't win. She paused, as if trying not to consider the possibility. "Devastated," she said quietly. "I don't know. I'd probably die."

14   Chin recalled recently that when she did win, "I didn't feel happiness. I felt relief. Which was disappointing." Three months before the 1988 Olympics, Chin retired when her legs began to break down. Some, however, say she left because she could no longer tolerate the pressure and unrelenting drive of her stern mother. "I feel I'm lucky to have gotten through it," she said of skating. "I don't think many people are that lucky. There's a tremendous strain on people who don't make it. The money, the sacrifices, the time. I know people emotionally damaged by it. I've seen nervous breakdowns, psychological imbalances."

15   An elite gymnast or figure skater knows she takes more than her own ambitions into a competition. Her parents have invested tens of thousands of dollars in her training, sometimes hundreds of thousands. Her coach's reputation rides on her performance. And she knows she might have only one shot. By the next Olympics she might be too old. By the next *year* she might be too old. Girls in these sports are under pressure not only to win but to win quickly. They're running against a clock that eventually marks the lives of all women, warning them they'd better hurry up and get married and have children before it's too late. These girls hear the clock early. They're racing against puberty.

16   Boys, on the other hand, welcome the changes that puberty brings. They reach their athletic peak after puberty when their bodies grow and their muscles strengthen. In recent years Michael Chang and Boris Becker won the French Open and Wimbledon tennis titles, respectively, before age eighteen, but in virtually every male sport the top athletes are men, not boys. Male gymnastics and figure skating champions are usually in their early to mid twenties; female champions are usually fourteen to seventeen years old in gymnastics and sixteen to early twenties in figure skating.

17   In staving off puberty to maintain the "ideal" body shape, girls risk their health in ways their male counterparts never do. They starve themselves, for one, often in response to their coaches' belittling insults about their bodies. Starving shuts down the menstrual cycle—the starving body knows it cannot support a fetus—and thus blocks the onset of puberty. It's a dangerous strategy to save a career. If a girl isn't menstruating, she isn't producing estrogen. Without estrogen, her bones weaken. She risks stunting her growth. She risks premature osteoporosis. She risks fractures in all bones, including her vertebrae, and she risks curvature of the spine. In several studies over the last decade, young female athletes who didn't menstruate were found to have the bone densities of postmenopausal women in their fifties, six-

ties and seventies. Most elite gymnasts don't begin to menstruate until they retire. Kathy Johnson, a medalist in the 1984 Olympics, didn't begin until she quit the sport at age twenty-five.

18   Our national obsession with weight, our glorification of thinness, have gone completely unchecked in gymnastics and figure skating. The cultural forces that have produced extravagantly bony fashion models have taken their toll on gymnasts and skaters already insecure about their bodies. Not surprisingly, eating disorders are common in both sports, and in gymnastics they're rampant. Studies of female college gymnasts show that most practice some kind of disordered eating. In a 1994 University of Utah study of elite gymnasts—those training for the Olympics—59 percent admitted to some form of disordered eating. And in interviewing elites for this book, I found only a handful who had not tried starving, throwing up or taking laxatives or diuretics to control their weight. Several left the sport because of eating disorders. One died. Eating disorders among male athletes, as in the general male population, are virtually unknown.

19   "Everyone goes through it, but nobody talks about it, because they're embarrassed," gymnast Kristie Phillips told me. "But I don't put the fault on us. It's the pressures that are put on us to be so skinny. It's mental cruelty. It's not fair that all these pressures are put on us at such a young age and we don't realize it until we get older and we suffer from it."

20   Phillips took laxatives, thyroid pills and diuretics to lose weight. She had been the hottest gymnast in the mid-1980s, the heir apparent to 1984 Olympic superstar Mary Lou Retton. But she not only didn't win a medal at the 1988 Summer Games, she didn't even make the U.S. team. She left the sport feeling like a failure. She gained weight, then became bulimic, caught in a cycle of bingeing and vomiting. Distraught, she took scissors to her wrists in a botched attempt to kill herself. "I weighed ninety-eight pounds and I was being called [by her

coach] an overstuffed Christmas turkey," Phillips said in our interview. "I was told I was never going to make it in life because I was going to be fat. I mean, in *life*. Things I'll never forget."

21   Much of the direct blame for the young athletes' problems falls on the coaches and parents. Obviously, no parent wakes up in the morning and plots how to ruin his or her child's life. But the money, the fame and the promise of great achievement can turn a parent's head. Ambition gets perverted. The boundaries of parents and coaches bloat and mutate, with the parent becoming the ruthless coach and coach becoming the controlling parent. One father put gymnastics equipment in his living room and for every mistake his daughter made at the gym she had to repeat the skill hundreds of times at home. He moved the girl to three gyms around the country, pushing her in the sport she came to loathe. He said he did it because he wanted the best for her.

22   Coaches push because they are paid to produce great gymnasts. They are relentless about weight because physically round gymnasts and skaters don't win. Coaches are intolerant of injuries because in the race against puberty, time off is death. Their job is not to turn out happy, well-adjusted young women; it is to turn out champions. If they scream, belittle or ignore, if they prod an injured girl to forget her pain, if they push her to drop out of school, they are only doing what the parents have paid them to do. So, sorting out the blame when a girl falls apart is a messy proposition; everyone claims he was just doing his job.

23   The sports' national governing bodies, for their part, are mostly impotent. They try to do well by the athletes, but they, too, often lose their way in a tangle of ambition and politics. They're like small-town governments: personal, despotic, paternalistic and absolutely without teeth. The federations do not have the power that the commissioners' offices in professional baseball, football and basketball do. They cannot revoke a coach's or an athlete's membership for anything less than criminal activity.

(Tonya Harding was charged and sentenced by the courts before the United States Figure Skating Association expelled her.) They cannot fine or suspend a coach whose athletes regularly leave the sport on stretchers.

24   There simply is no safety net protecting these children. Not the parents, the coaches or the federations.

25   Child labor laws prohibit a thirteen-year-old from punching a cash register for forty hours a week, but that same child can labor for forty hours or more inside a gym or an ice skating rink without drawing the slightest glance from the government. The U.S. government requires the licensing of plumbers. It demands that even the tiniest coffee shop adhere to a fastidious health code. It scrutinizes the advertising claims on packages of low-fat snack food. But it never asks a coach, who holds the lives of his young pupils in his hands, to pass a minimum safety and skills test. Coaches in this country need no license to train children, even in a high-injury sport like elite gymnastics. The government that forbids a child from buying a pack of cigarettes because of health concerns never checks on the child athlete who trains until her hands bleed or her knees buckle, who stops eating to achieve the perfect body, who takes eight Advils a day and offers herself up for another shot of cortisone to dull the pain, who drinks a bottle of Ex-Lax because her coach is going to weigh her in the morning. The government never takes a look inside the gym or the rink to make sure these children are not being exploited or abused or worked too hard. Even college athletes—virtually all of whom are adults—are restricted by the NCAA to just twenty hours per week of formal training. But no laws, no agencies, put limits on the number of hours a child can train or the methods a coach can use.

26   Some argue that extraordinary children should be allowed to follow extraordinary paths to realize their potential. They argue that a child's wants are no less important than an adult's and thus she should not be denied her dreams just because she is still a child. If pursuing her dream means training

eight hours a day in a gym, withstanding abusive language and tolerating great pain, and if the child wants to do it and the parents believe it will build character, why not let her? Who are we to tell a child what she can and cannot do with her life?

27   In fact, we tell children all the time what they can and cannot do with their lives. Restricting children from certain activities is hardly a revolutionary concept. Laws prohibit children from driving before sixteen and drinking before twenty-one. They prohibit children from dropping out of school before fifteen and working full-time before sixteen. In our society we put great value on protecting our children from physical harm and exploitation, and sometimes that means protecting them from their own poor judgment and their parents' poor judgment. No one questions the wisdom of the government in forbidding a child to work full-time, so why is it all right for her to train full-time with no rules to ensure her well-being? Child labor laws should address all labor, even that which is technically nonpaid, though top gymnasts and figure skaters *do* labor for money.

28   In recent years the federations have begun to pay their top athletes a stipend based on their competition results. The girls can earn bonuses by representing the United States in certain designated events. Skaters who compete in the World Figure Skating Championships and the Olympic Games, for example, receive $15,000. They earn lesser amounts for international competitions such as Skate America. They also earn money from corporate sponsors and exhibitions. The money might not cover much more than their training expenses, which can run $75,000 for a top skater and $20,000 to $30,000 per year for a top gymnast, but it's money—money that is paid specifically for the work the athletes do in the gym and the skating rink.

29   The real payoff for their hard work, however, waits at the end of the road. That's what the parents and athletes hope anyway. When Mary Lou Retton made millions on Madison Avenue after winning the gold medal at the 1984 Olympics, she changed gymnastics forever. "Kids have agents now before they even

make it into their teens," Retton says. Now the dream is no longer just about medals but about Wheaties boxes and appearance fees, about paying off mom and dad's home equity loans and trading in the Toyota for a Mercedes. It doesn't seem to matter that only six girls every four years reach the Olympics and that winning the gold once they get there is the longest of long shots. Even world champion Shannon Miller didn't win the all-around Olympic gold in 1992.

30   Figure skating, even more than gymnastics, blinds parents and athletes with the glittering possibilities, and for good reason. Peggy Fleming and Dorothy Hamill are still living off gold medals won decades ago. Nancy Kerrigan landed endorsements with Reebok, Evian, Seiko and Campbell's soup with only a bronze medal in 1992. With glamorous and feminine stars like Kerrigan and Kristi Yamaguchi to lead the way, the United States Figure Skating Association has seen the influx of corporate sponsorship climb 2000 percent in just five years. Money that used to go to tennis is now being shifted to figure skating and gymnastics as their popularity grows. The payoff in money and fame now looms large enough to be seen from a distance, sparkling like the Emerald City, driving parents and children to extremes to reach its doors.

31   I'm not suggesting that all elite gymnasts and figure skaters emerge from their sports unhealthy and poorly adjusted. Many prove that they can thrive under intense pressure and physical demands and thus are stronger for the experience. But too many can't. There are no studies that establish what percentage of elite gymnasts and figure skaters are damaged by their sports and in what ways. So the evidence I've gathered for this book is anecdotal, the result of nearly a hundred interviews and more than a decade of covering both sports as a journalist.

32   The bottom line is clear. There have been enough suicide attempts, enough eating disorders, enough broken bodies, enough regretful parents and enough bitter young women to warrant a serious reevaluation of what we're doing in this country to produce Olympic champions. Those who work in

these sports know this. They know the tragedies all too well. If the federations and coaches truly care about the athletes and not simply about the fame and prestige that come from trotting tough little champions up to the medal stand, they know it is past time to lay the problems on the table, examine them and figure out a way to keep their sports from damaging so many young lives. But since those charged with protecting young athletes so often fail in their responsibility, it is time the government drops the fantasy that certain sports are merely games and takes a hard look at legislation aimed at protecting elite child athletes.

It is also my hope that by dramatizing the particularly intense subculture of female gymnastics and figure skating, we can better understand something of our own nature as a country bent on adulating, and in some cases sacrificing, girls and young women in a quest to fit them into our pretty little boxes. 33

Source: Joan Ryan, *Little Girls in Pretty Boxes*, New York: Time Warner, 1995, pp. 1–15.

DISCUSSION QUESTIONS

1. Is the implicit claim identified in the "Commentary" on this argument ("You will find this book compelling and clearly organized") amply supported in the essay? By what methods? Give specific examples.

2. Ryan makes frequent use of metaphors, similes, and analogies to stress her points. Identify some of these and discuss their effectiveness in terms of argument.

3. Ryan makes a number of factual generalizations in her essay. Identify three or four of them and consider whether they are adequately supported by specific examples. In an introduction of this type, is full support necessary?

4. Describe Ryan's implied audience; what does Ryan assume to be their needs and values? Where does she appeal to these?

SUGGESTIONS FOR WRITING (15.1)

1. Ryan is writing about what she calls "elite" athletes, whose training and goals are very different from those of the average high school or even college varsity athlete. Yet the abuses Ryan exposes are not limited to the elite level. Write a factual argument exposing training abuses you have experienced or witnessed in high school, college, or amateur athletics.

2. Based on this introduction, which faithfully represents the contents of the book, write a 250-word abstract of the book.

3. In Par. 18, Ryan refers to "our national obsession with weight, our glorification of thinness." Based upon your own personal observations, compose an inductive argument that supports one of the following, more modest generalizations: "My own experience and observations lead me to conclude that at least among my acquaintances, there is (or is not) an obsession with weight, a glorification of thinness." You may adapt the suggested conclusion, but be sure to qualify it and support it with an appropriate number of specific examples.

4. Participate in a discussion with three or four of your classmates in which you brainstorm about the advantages and/or disadvantages of the participation of girls and young women in organized (not professional) athletics. Based upon the discussion, create your own list of advantages or your own list of disadvantages. Then write a working claim that would introduce an evaluation of this participation.

WHERE HAVE ALL THE HEROES GONE?

STEPHEN D. MOSHER

This article was first published in the Ithaca College Quarterly *(Winter 1998). The head note to the article reads as follows:*

Racism. Sexual assault. Biting an opponent's ear. These are the actions of our "national heroes"? Why do we make sports figures into heroes, anyway? Do athletes have any responsibility to act as role models? We asked associate professor of exercise and sport sciences Stephen D. Mosher to give us a little background on sport in the United States, so we can make up our own minds.

If you want to find out more about Stephen Mosher, visit his Web page on the Ithaca College site at http://www.ithaca.com.

1   In the opening scenes of Robert Redford's *The Natural*, Roy Hobbs's father teaches his son how to pitch a baseball but also warns him, "You have a gift, Roy. But if you rely too much on your gift, you'll fail."

2   During one of the endless bus rides through the North Carolina League in Bull Durham, veteran catcher Crash Davis tells rookie Nuke Lalouche, "You don't respect yourself, which is your problem; but you don't respect the game, and that's my problem."

3   When we survey the contemporary American sport landscape, we are struck by the almost never-ending displays of immaturity (the frustrated American Olympic men's ice hockey team trashing their hotel rooms in Nagano), shameless self-promotion (the NBA/WNBA's two-ball fiasco during the 1998 all-star weekend), blatant profit taking (Wayne Huizenga's dismantling of the Florida Marlins less than two weeks after they won the 1997 World Series), elitist protectionism (the PGA, trying to prevent Casey Martin from joining its ranks by claiming that walking is integral to golf), overtly racist slurs (Fuzzy Zoeller's comments on Tiger Woods's eating habits, John Rocker's condemnation of virtually all non-white New Yorkers, Payne Stewart's tasteless imitation of "Chinese" Ryder Cup golfers), and personal violence (Latrell Sprewell's attack on Golden State coach P.J. Carlesimo), never ending streams of drug abuse (Darryl Strawberry's tragic addiction to cocaine), and even participation in deadly street fights (the Baltimore Ravens' Ray Lewis on Superbowl night 1999) or, perhaps the most disturbing example, North Carolina Panthers' Ray Carruth's hiring hit men to commit murder.

4   We ask ourselves: Where have all the heroes gone? Where is the nobility of the sport? Who holds true to the ideals of the game? Who cares about sportsmanship and playing fair? Is it all just about winning?

5   The best athletes we can come up with to be role models for our children are those like Cal Ripken Jr. and Tara Lipinski. What exactly does Ripken do to have earned his hero status? Go to work every day and do his job just like countless other citizens? What advice for living life can come from the mouth of Lipinksi? She's not even 19, has spent over half her life skating, and already she's written *two* autobiographies?

6   They are, however, reminders that celebrity is not fame. Moreover, the most honest athlete today may be Charles Barkley, who insists, "I am not a role model!"

7   Wherever did we come up with the belief that sport builds character or that it

teaches us teamwork and how to be "good sports," how to be modest in victory and gracious in defeat? We must understand this before we can even ask our athletes to be our heroes.

8 Sport has not always been considered a good thing in American life. The Puritans, in their attempt to reform the Church of England, sought to squelch virtually all forms of organized rituals, holy days, pageantry, symbols, and play associated with the Roman Catholic church. Sporting pastimes in early America involved gambling (horse racing, bowling), violence (gouging, cockfighting), or both (boxing); all those directly connected with Catholic holidays were discouraged. However, the Puritans did approve "lawful" sport that could "refresh the spirit" or better prepare people to fulfill their religious duties. Lawful sports included fishing, hunting, and swimming. Children's play was also tolerated.

9 Nonetheless, the sporting traditions of the citizenry remained impossible to fully regulate. These activities were the province of the poor, the working class, children, and single, young men. But starting in the 1850s, as an outgrowth of the Second Great Awakening, social reformers again sought to govern the recreation of the greater society. Catharine Beecher's concept of womanhood—the "cult of domesticity"—and Thomas Higginson's concept of manhood—"muscular Christianity"—were the first sports-specific manifestations of this movement. The ideas gained momentum because advances in science, medicine, and technology, as well as the move away from an active agrarian lifestyle, meant that people no longer had physical activity, with its side perks of endurance and stamina, built into their daily lives. People were becoming sedentary.

10 For the first time in modern history, sport was seen to serve a purpose in developing the character of both boys and girls. Sport and physical exercise would assist girls in becoming healthy homemakers and nurturers and would prepare boys to enter the professional world. Basketball itself was invented by Dr. James Naismith, who'd been charged with creating a game that could be played indoors during the winter and would embrace all of the ideals of the Muscular Christian movement regarding teamwork, self-sacrifice, obedience, self-control, and loyalty.

11 The mottoes of the play movement organizations reveal volumes about their underlying purpose: "Mind, Body, Spirit" (YMCA), "Wohelo"—Work, Health, Love (Campfire), "Be Prepared" (Girl and Boy Scouts), "Head, Heart, Hands, Health" (4-H). The pledges of these movements are even more revealing. 4-H's pledge is *I pledge/My Head to clearer thinking,/My heart to greater loyalty,/My Hands to larger service, and/My Health to better living,/for my club, my community, my country, and my world.* Even Little League Baseball has its own reformist pledge and motto: "Character, Courage, Loyalty."

12 Perhaps the most important key to understanding the problem of asking athletes to be role models is found in the modern Olympic movement. There is no doubt that the ideals of amateurism established in Britain at the end of the 19th century and promulgated through the Olympic Games served to separate people by social class. Many people fondly talk of the nobility of the "taking part," the "inclusion of all" in the Olympics. But the amateur code actually sought to prevent the working class from corrupting the sporting diversions of the wealthy. Simply put, the requirement that competitors be amateurs meant those who had to work for a living could not compete. Consequently, the "civilized gentlemen" of the ruling elite were able to exclude from sport virtually anyone they wanted.

13 In America, the self-described classless society, amateurism was met with some initial resistance (the early days of college sport were full of paid players and pseudostudents), but slowly took hold in the middle class. The morality of privilege, however, had little influence among those who were born to poverty and struggle or were immigrants; sport soon took on the looks of its

new practitioners and was no longer cloaked simply in hunting suits and riding boots.

14   To expect sports as they exist today to teach children to play games, become physically healthy, and also build character may be unrealistic. In fact, the results of sport participation fall far short of these expectations. Competitive sports actually have little effect on the development of positive social characteristics. Research shows that competitive team sports are more likely to teach children that "winning is the *only* thing" and that "the end justifies the means" rather than that hard work, dedication, and self-sacrifice are the true payoffs. There are no convincing data to support the belief that sport prevents juvenile delinquency or reduces drug abuse. There are, however, data that suggest that male athletes develop a view of gender superiority that may explain their higher rates of promiscuity and sexual abuse than those of nonathletes. (There is also ample research showing that athletes are significantly less altruistic than nonathletes.) It is certainly quite clear that in most high schools varsity athletes enjoy higher status than those students who excel in art, music, and even academics.

15   We are quick to condemn the behavior of Mike Tyson, as if we can separate the champion boxer from the street thug. We are disgusted by Latrell Sprewell's assault on an authority figure, as if P. J. Carlesimo's long history of bullying players is irrelevant. We are horrified by Ray Lewis's and Ray Carruth's crimes and countless incidents of domestic violence, but overlook the fact that the teams in the National Football League actually scout for players in prisons and deliberately seek out personnel with violent tendencies. On the other hand, Arthur Ashe was certainly a hero, but it wasn't tennis that led him to fight for greater awareness of HIV/AIDS, write *A Hard Road to Glory*, or protest the racist government in South Africa. Muhammad Ali was certainly a warrior king, but it wasn't boxing that prompted him to sacrifice his career when he said, "I ain't got no quarrel with them Viet Cong."

16   The heroism found in sports is powerful, legitimate, and sometimes even magical, but it is a heroism that is quite different from that of everyday people. When Gatorade urges us to "Be like Mike," are they talking about Michael Jordan the basketball player, the husband and father, or the endorser of a company that has been accused of exploiting child labor in the third world? Are we really supposed to believe Andre Agassi when he says for Canon cameras, "Image is everything"? Earl Woods has said that his son is literally capable of *saving the world*. Isn't it enough to simply marvel at Tiger's heroic golfing ability? Why do we insist on turning this young man's good manners into heroism? In recent years, as Woods replaces Michael Jordan as America's version of the global sporting icon, his political actions become eligible for public scrutiny. In the summer of 2000, Woods, a member of the Screen Actors Guild, crossed the strike line by filming Buick commercials in Canada for telecast during the Sydney Olympic Games. And like Jordan, his predecessor as Nike's dominant global spokesperson, Woods has yet to follow through on his promise to examine in person the working conditions at Nike's alleged sweatshops in southeast Asia.

17   One of the most tragic figures in recent American sport is Pete Rose. The ultimate symbol of hard work and determination overcoming a perceived lack of talent, Rose nonetheless remains the disgraced and fallen hero, clueless as to why he can't get into baseball's hall of fame on the basis of his heroic diamond feats alone. Rose's hubris really knows no limits. He would be well served to heed Crash Davis's advice: "You have to play this game with fear and arrogance." Rose, like so many of our celebrity athletes, has the arrogance but lacks the fear. Like those celebrities who refer to themselves in the third person, Rose—the self-proclaimed "Hit King"—places himself above the game. Also known as "Charlie Hustle," Rose betrayed those who depended on him when, as manager of the Cincinnati Reds, he gambled on baseball. Rose's greatest "hustle" was trying to convince the public he loved the game more than he loved himself. Rose still does not recognize that heroes must fear letting us down.

18   The responses of public grief to the tragic deaths of Payne Stewart and Dale Earnhardt reveal a nation starving for people to admire. But is the nation looking in the wrong direction? Stewart's blatantly conservative racial politics of exclusion, his reputation as an out of control youth sport parent, and his dedication to consumer capitalism is somehow overwhelmed by the images of a "WWJD" (What would Jesus do?) bracelet and the ghost plane crashed in the South Dakota farmland. Dale Earnhardt's death in the 2001 Daytona 500 received unprecedented media attention, but through it all there was never a mention that his nickname—"The Intimidator"— was earned through a career of *deliberately* running his NASCAR opponents off the race track, putting them at death's door.

19   Roy Hobbs's home run at the end of *The Natural* brings us joy and hope, not because he saves the world but because he saves himself. Ray Kinsella eases our pain at the end of *Field of Dreams*, not because he demonstrates the moral superiority of baseball but because he finally has the chance to tell his father he's sorry.

20   Perhaps Cal Ripken Jr., Tiger Woods, and Sammy Sosa are heroes. They are certainly marvelous athletes. But to ask them—or any other athletes—to be the fathers of the nation is unfair. They have enough of a burden being fathers to their own children or children who can make their parents proud. For us to get anything more than that from them is simply a blessing.

Source: Stephen D. Mosher, "Where Have All the Heroes Gone," *Ithaca College Quarterly*, Winter 1998.

DISCUSSION QUESTIONS

1. Go to Stephen Mosher's Web page on the Ithaca College site at http://www.ithaca.com. Without clicking on any links, what do you learn about Mosher from the contents, design, and graphics of the Web site? How are these clues borne out by the article itself?

2. Mosher uses the third person plural pronoun, "we," throughout his argument (for example, "When we survey the contemporary American sport landscape, we are struck by the almost never-ending displays of immaturity," Par. 3). What effect do you think Mosher was trying to achieve through this rhetorical strategy? In considering this, you might think of how different the argument might have been if Mosher had used "I" or "one" or "you" instead of "we."

3. Par. 15 claims that "Competitive sports actually have little effect on the development of positive social characteristics." How convincingly is this generalization supported? Given what you know about Mosher's credentials and the nature of the publication for which his argument is written, is the support sufficient? Why or why not?

4. In which category of argument would you place "Where Have All the Heroes Gone?"? Where do you find the best statement of the central claim?

5. How does Mosher's detour into the history of sport (Par. 10–13) contribute to his argument? Is this historical survey necessary to the success of the argument?

SUGGESTIONS FOR WRITING (15.2)

1. Write an outline for a four- to five-page direct refutation of Mosher's argument. (To do this, you must be very clear about the answers to Question #4.) You may use any of the other arguments in this section as support for your counter-argument.

2. Exchange outlines with a fellow student and review the structure of each other's outline. Is the central claim clear? Will it be supported by appropriate secondary claims and support? Will there be adequate support for each claim? Is the order of the argument sensible? Write a one-page set of comments and recommendations for your partner.

3. With the comments from Question #2 in mind, draft your counterargument and hand it in to your instructor, who will hold it for two days, then return it to you for revision.

4. Write a final draft of your argument including an introduction and conclusion. Try to follow Mosher's use of introductory and closing anecdotes.

THE CHOSEN ONE

GARY SMITH

Gary Smith is a senior writer for Sports Illustrated *and has won the National Magazine Award for feature writing, an honor not often conferred upon sports journalists.*

This essay on Tiger Woods first appeared in Sports Illustrated *in December of 1996, before Woods won his first major tournament, the Masters. "The Chosen One" was included in the prestigious anthology* The Best American Sports Writing *(1997), an annual collection of each year's finest sports writing.*

1   It was ordinary. It was oh so ordinary. It was a salad, a dinner roll, a steak, a half potato, a slice of cake, a clinking fork, a podium joke, a ballroom full of white-linen-tablecloth conversation. Then a thick man with tufts of white hair rose from the head table. His voice trembled and his eyes teared and his throat gulped down sobs between words, and everything ordinary was cast out of the room.

2   He said, "Please forgive me ... but sometimes I get very emotional ... when I talk about my son.... My heart ... fills with so ... much ... joy ... when I realize ... that this young man ... is going to be able ... to help so many people.... He will transcend this game ... and bring to the world ... a humanitarianism ... which has never been known before. The world will be a better place to live in ... by virtue of his existence ... and his presence.... I acknowledge only a small part in that ... in that I know that I was personally selected by God himself ... to nurture this young man ... and bring him to the point were he

can make his contribution to humanity.... This is my treasure.... Please accept it ... and use it wisely.... Thank you."

3   Blinking tears, the man found himself inside the arms of his son and the applause of the people, all up on their feet. In the history of American celebrity, no father has ever spoken this way. Too many dads have deserted or died before their offspring reached this realm, but mostly they have fallen mute, the father's vision exceeded by the child's, leaving the child to wander, lost, through the sad and silly wilderness of modern fame.

4   So let us stand amidst this audience at last month's Fred Haskins Award dinner to honor America's outstanding college golfer of 1996, and take note as Tiger and Earl Woods embrace, for a new manner of celebrity is taking form before our eyes. Regard the 64-year-old African-American father, arm upon the superstar's shoulder, right where the chip is so often found, declaring that this boy will do more good for

the world than any man who ever walked it. Gaze at the 20-year-old son, with the blood of four races in his veins, not flinching an inch from the yoke of his father's prophecy but already beginning to scent the complications. The son who stormed from behind to win a record third straight U.S. Amateur last August, turned pro and rang up scores in the 60s in 21 of his first 27 rounds, winning two PGA Tour events as he doubled and tripled the usual crowds and dramatically changed their look and age.

5 Now turn. Turn and look at us, the audience, standing in anticipation of something different, something pure. Quiet. Just below the applause, or within it, can you hear the grinding? That's the relentless chewing mechanism of fame, girding to grind the purity and the promise to dust. Not the promise of talent, but the bigger promise, the father's promise, the one that stakes everything on the boy's not becoming separated from his own humanity and from all the humanity crowding around him.

6 It's a fitting moment, while he's up there at the head table with the audience on its feet, to anoint Eldrick (Tiger) Woods—the rare athlete to establish himself immediately as the dominant figure in his sport— as Sports Illustrated's 1996 Sportsman of the Year. And to pose a question: Who will win? The machine . . . or the youth who had just entered its maw?

7 Tiger Woods will win. He'll fulfill his father's vision because of his mind, one that grows more still, more willful, more efficient, the greater the pressure upon him grows.

8 The machine will win because it has no mind. It flattens even as it lifts, trivializes even as it exalts, spreads a man so wide and thin that he becomes margarine soon enough.

9 Tiger will win because of God's mind. Can't you see the pattern? Earl Woods asks. Can't you see the signs? "Tiger will do more than any other man in history to change the course of humanity," Earl says.

10 Sports history, Mr. Woods? Do you mean more than Joe Louis and Jackie Robinson, more than Muhammad Ali and Arthur Ashe? "More than any of them because he's more charismatic, more educated, more prepared for this than anyone."

11 Anyone, Mr. Woods? Your son will have more impact than Nelson Mandela, more than Gandhi, more than Buddha?

12 "Yes, because he has a larger forum than any of them. Because he's playing a sport that's international. Because he's qualified through his ethnicity to accomplish miracles. He's the bridge between the East and the West. There is no limit because he has the guidance. I don't know yet exactly what form this will take. But he is the Chosen One. He'll have the power to impact nations. Not people. Nations. The world is just getting a taste of his power."

13 Surely this is lunacy. Or are we just too myopic to see? One thing is certain: we are witnessing the first volley of an epic encounter, the machine at its mightiest confronting the individual groomed all his life to conquer it and turn it to his use. The youth who has been exposed to its power since he toddled onto The Mike Douglas Show at 3, the set of That's Incredible! at 5, the boy who has been steeled against the silky seduction to which so many before him have succumbed. The one who, by all appearances, brings more psychological balance, more sense of self, more consciousness of possibility to the battlefield than any of his predecessors.

14 This is war, so let's start with war. Remove the images of pretty putting greens from the movie screen standing near the ballroom's head table. Jungle is what's needed here, foliage up to a man's armpits, sweat trickling down his thighs, leeches crawling up them. Lieut. Col. Earl Woods, moving through the night with his rifle ready, wondering why a U.S. Army public information officer stationed in Brooklyn decided in his mid-30s that he belonged in the Green Berets and ended up doing two tours of duty in Vietnam. Wondering why his first marriage has died and why the three children from it have ended up without a dad around when it's dark like this and it's time for bed—just as Earl ended up

as a boy after his own father died. Wondering why he keeps plotting ways to return to the line of fire—"creative soldiering," he calls it—to eyeball death once more. To learn once again about his dark and cold side, the side that enables Earl, as Tiger will remark years later, "to slit your throat and then sit down and eat his dinner."

15   Oh, yes, Earl is one hell of a cocktail. A little Chinese, a little Cherokee, a few shots of African-American; don't get finicky about measurements, we're making a vat here. Pour in some gruffness and a little intimidation, then some tenderness and some warmth and a few jiggers of old anger. Don't hold back on intelligence. And stoicism. Add lots of stoicism, and even more of responsibility—"the most responsible son of a bitch you've ever seen in your life" is how Earl himself puts it. Top it all with "a bucket of whiskey," which is what he has been known to order when he saunters into a bar and he's in the mood. Add a dash of hyperbole, maybe two, and to hell with the ice, just whir. This is one of those concoctions you're going to remember when morning comes.

16   Somewhere in there, until a good fifteen years ago, there was one other ingredient, the existential Tabasco, the smoldering why? The Thai secretary in the U.S. Army office in Bangkok smelled it soon after she met Earl, in 1967. "He couldn't relax," says Kultida (Tida) Woods. "Searching for something, always searching, never satisfied. I think because both his parents died when he was young, and he didn't have Mom and Dad to make him warm. Sometimes he stayed awake till three or four in the morning, just thinking."

17   In a man so accustomed to exuding command and control, in a Green Beret lieutenant colonel, *why?* has a way of building up power like a river dammed. Why did the Vietcong sniper bracket him that day (first bullet a few inches left of one ear, second bullet a few inches right of the other) but never fire the third bullet? Why did Earl's South Vietnamese combat buddy, Nguyen Phong—the one Earl nicknamed Tiger, and in whose memory he would nick-

name his son—stir one night just in time to awaken Earl and warn him not to budge because a viper was poised inches from his right eye? What about that road Earl's jeep rolled down one night, the same road on which two friends had just been mutilated, the road that took him through a village so silent and dark that his scalp tingled, and then, just beyond it . . . hell turned inside-out over his shoulder, the sky lighting up and all the huts he had just passed spewing Vietcong machine-gun and artillery fire? He never understands what is the purpose of Lieutenant Colonel Woods's surviving again and again. He never quite comprehends what is the point of his life, until . . .

18   Until the boy is born. He will get all the time that Earl was unable to devote to the three children from his first marriage. He will be the only child from Earl's second marriage, to the Thai woman he brought back to America, and right away there are signs. What other 6-month-old, Earl asks, has the balance to stand in the palm of his father's hand and remain there even as Daddy strolls around the house? Was there another 11-month-old, ever, who could pick up a sawed-off club, imitate his father's golf swing so fluidly, and drive the ball so wickedly into the nylon net across the garage? Another 4-year-old who could be dropped off at the golf course at 9 A.M. on a Saturday and picked up at 5 P.M., pockets bulging with money he had won from disbelievers ten and twenty years older, until Pop said, "Tiger, you can't do that"? Earl starts to get a glimmer. He is to be the father of the world's most gifted golfer.

19   But why? What for? Not long after Tiger's birth, when Earl has left the military to become a purchaser for McDonnell Douglas, he finds himself in a long discussion with a woman he knows. She senses the power pooling inside him, the friction. "You have so much to give," she tells him, "but you're not giving it. You haven't even scratched the surface of your potential." She suggests he try EST, Erhard Seminars Training, an intensive self-discovery and self-actualizing technique, and it hits Earl hard, direct mor-

tar fire to the heart. What he learns is that his overmuscular sense of responsibility for others has choked his potential.

20 "To the point," says Earl, "that I wouldn't even buy a handkerchief for myself. It went all the way back to the day my father died, when I was 11, and my mother put her arm around me after the funeral and said, 'You're the man of the house now.' I became the father that young, looking out for everyone else, and then she died two years later.

21 "What I learned through EST was that by doing more for myself, I could do much more for others. Yes, be responsible, but love life, and give people the space to be in your life, and allow yourself room to give to others. That caring and sharing is what's most important, not being responsible for everyone else. Which is where Tiger comes in. What I learned led me to give so much time to Tiger, and to give him the space to be himself, and not to smother him with dos and don'ts. I took out the authority aspect and turned into companionship. I made myself vulnerable as a parent. When you have to earn respect from your child, rather than demanding it because it's owed to you as the father, miracles happen. I realized that, through him, the giving could take a quantum leap. What I could do on a limited scale, he could do on a global scale."

22 At last, the river is undammed, and Earl's whole life makes sense. At last, he sees what he was searching for, a pattern. No more volunteering for missions—he has his. Not simply to be a great golfer's father. To be destiny's father. His son will change the world.

23 "What the hell had I been doing in public information in the army, posted in Brooklyn?" he asks. "Why, of course, what greater training can there be than three years of dealing with the New York media to prepare me to teach Tiger the importance of public relations and how to handle the media?"

Father: Where were you born, Tiger?

Son, age 3: I was born on December 30, 1975, in Long Beach, California.

Father: No, Tiger, only answer the question you were asked. It's important to prepare yourself for this. Try again.

Son: I was born in Long Beach, California.

Father: Good, Tiger, good.

The late leap into the Green Berets? "What the hell was that for?" Earl says. "Of course, to prepare me to teach Tiger mental toughness."

24 The three children by the first marriage? "Not just one boy the first time," says Earl, "but two, along with a girl, as if God was saying, 'I want this son of a bitch to really have previous training.'"

25 The Buddhist wife, the one who grew up in a boarding school after her parents separated when she was 5, the girl who then vowed that her child would know nothing but love and attention? The one who will preach inner calm to Tiger simply by turning to him with that face—still awaiting its first wrinkle at 52? Whose eyes close when she speaks, so he can almost see her gathering and sifting the thoughts? The mother who will walk every hole and keep score for Tiger at children's tournaments, adding a stroke or two if his calm cracks? "Look at this stuff!" cries Earl. "Over and over you can see the plan being orchestrated by someone other than me because I'm not this damn good! I tried to get out of that combat assignment to Thailand. But Tida was meant to bring in the influence of the Orient, to introduce Tiger to Buddhism and inner peace, so he would have the best of two different worlds. And so he would have the knowledge that there were two people whose lives were totally committed to him."

26 What of the heart attack Earl suffered when Tiger was 10 and the way the retired lieutenant colonel felt himself floating down the gray tunnel toward the light before he was wrenched back? "To prepare me to teach Tiger that life is short," Earl says, "and to live each day to the maximum, and not to worry about the future. There's only now. You must understand that time is just

a linear measurement of successive increments of now. Anyplace you go on that line is now, and that's how you have to live it."

27   No need to wonder about the appearance of the perfect childhood coach, John Anselmo; the perfect sports psychologist, Jay Brunza; the perfect agent, Hughes Norton; the perfect attorney, John Merchant; and the perfect pro swing instructor, Butch Harmon. Or about the great tangle of fate that leads them all to Tiger at just the right junctures in his development. "Everything," says Earl, "right there when he needs it. Everything. There can't be this much coincidence in the world. This is a directed scenario, and none of us involved in the scenario has failed to accept the responsibility. This is all destined to be."

28   His wife ratifies this, in her own way. She takes the boy's astrological chart to a Buddhist temple in Los Angeles and to another in Bangkok and is told by the monks at both places that the child has wondrous powers. "If he becomes a politician, he will be either a president or a prime minister," she is told. "If he enters the military, he will be a general."

29   Tida comes to a conclusion. "Tiger has Thai, African, Chinese, American Indian, and European blood," she says. "He can hold everyone together. He is the Universal Child."

30   This is in the air the boy breathes for twenty years, and it becomes bone fact for him, marrow knowledge. When asked about it, he merely nods in acknowledgment of it, assents to it; of course he believes it's true. So failure, in the rare visits it pays him, is not failure. It's just life pausing to teach him a lesson he needs in order to go where he's inevitably going. And success, no matter how much sooner than expected it comes to the door, always finds him dressed and ready to welcome it. "Did you ever see yourself doing this so soon?" a commentator breathlessly asks him seconds after his first pro victory, on October 6 in Las Vegas, trying to elicit wonder and awe on live TV. "Yeah," Tiger responds. "I kind of did." And sleep comes to him so easily: in the midst of conversation, in a car, in a plane, off he goes, into the slumber of the destined. "I

don't see any of this as scary or a burden," Tiger says. "I see it as fortunate. I've always known where I wanted to go in life. I've never let anything deter me. This is my purpose. It will unfold."

31   No sports star in the history of American celebrity has spoken this way. Maybe, somehow, Tiger can win.

32   The machine will win. It must win because it too is destiny, 5 billion destinies leaning against one. There are ways to keep the hordes back, a media expert at Nike tells Tiger. Make broad gestures when you speak. Keep a club in your hands and take practice swings, or stand with one foot well out in front of the other, in almost a karate stance. That will give you room to breathe. Two weeks later, surrounded by a pen-wielding mob in La Quinta, California, in late November, just before the Skins Game, the instruction fails. Tiger survives, but his shirt and slacks are ruined, felt-tip-dotted to death.

33   The machine will win because it will wear the young man down, cloud his judgment, steal his sweetness, the way it does just before the Buick Challenge in Pine Mountain, Georgia, at the end of September. It will make his eyes drop when the fans' gaze reaches for his, his voice growl at their clawing hands, his body sag onto a sofa after a practice round and then rise and walk across the room and suddenly stop in bewilderment. "I couldn't even remember what I'd just gotten off the couch for, two seconds before," he says. "I was like mashed potatoes. Total mush."

34   So he walks. Pulls out on the eve of the Buick Challenge, pulls out of the Fred Haskins Award dinner to honor him, and goes home. See, maybe Tiger can win. He can just turn his back on the machine and walk. Awards? Awards to Tiger are like echoes, voices bouncing off the walls, repeating what a truly confident man has already heard inside his own head. The Jack Nicklaus Award, the one Jack himself was supposed to present to Tiger live on ABC during the Memorial tournament last spring? Tiger would have blown it off if Wally Goodwin, his coach at Stanford during the two years

he played there before turning pro, hadn't insisted that he show up.

35   The instant Tiger walks away from the Buick Challenge and the Haskins dinner, the hounds start yapping. See, that's why the machine will win. It's got all those damn heel-nippers. Little mutts on the PGA Tour resenting how swiftly the 20-year-old was ordained, how hastily he was invited to play practice rounds with Nicklaus and Arnold Palmer, with Greg Norman and Ray Floyd and Nick Faldo and Fred Couples. And big dogs snapping too. Tom Kite quoted as saying, "I can't ever remember being tired when I was twenty," and Peter Jacobsen quoted, "You can't compare Tiger to Nicklaus and Palmer anymore because they never [walked out]."

36   He rests for a week, stunned by the criticism—"I thought those people were my friends," he says. He never second-guesses his decision to turn pro, but he sees what he surrendered. "I miss college," he says. "I miss hanging out with my friends, getting in a little trouble. I have to be so guarded now. I miss sitting around drinking beer and talking half the night. There's no one my own age to hang out with anymore because almost everyone my age is in college. I'm a target for everybody now, and there's nothing I can do about it. My mother was right when she said that turning pro would take away my youth. But golfwise, there was nothing left for me in college."

37   He reemerges after the week's rest and rushes from four shots off the lead on the final day to win the Las Vegas Invitational in sudden death. The world's waiting for him again, this time with reinforcements. Letterman and Leno want him as a guest; *GQ* calls about a cover; Cosby, along with almost every other sitcom you can think of, offers to write an episode revolving around Tiger, if only he'll appear. Kids dress up as Tiger for Halloween—did anyone ever dress up as Arnie or Jack?—and Michael Jordan declares that his only hero on earth is Tiger Woods. Pepsi is dying to have him cut a commercial for one of its soft drinks aimed at Generation Xers; Nike and Titleist call in chits for the

$40 million and $20 million contracts he signed; money managers are eager to know how he wants his millions invested; women walk onto the course during a practice round and ask for his hand in marriage; kids stampede over and under ropes and chase him from the 18th hole to the clubhouse; piles of phone messages await him when he returns to his hotel room. "Why," Tiger asks, "do so many people want a part of me?"

38   Because something deeper than conventional stardom is at work here, something so spontaneous and subconscious that words have trouble going there. It's a communal craving, a public aching for a superstar free of anger and arrogance and obsession with self. It's a hollow place that chimes each time Tiger and his parents strike the theme of father and mother and child love, each time Tiger stands at a press conference and declares, "They have raised me well, and I truly believe they have taught me to accept full responsibility for all aspects of my life." During the making of a Titleist commercial in November, a makeup woman is so moved listening to Earl describe his bond with Tiger that she decides to contact her long-estranged father. "See what I mean?" cried Earl. "Did you affect someone that way today? Did anyone else there? It's destiny, man. It's something bigger than me."

39   What makes it so vivid is context. The white canvas that the colors are being painted on—the moneyed, mature, and almost minority-less world of golf—makes Tiger an emblem of youth overcoming age, have-not overcoming have, outsider overcoming insider, to the delight not only of the 18-year-olds in the gallery wearing nose rings and cornrows, but also—of all people—of the aging insider haves.

40   So Tiger finds himself, just a few weeks after turning pro at the end of August, trying to clutch a bolt of lightning with one hand and steer an all-at-once corporation—himself—with the other, and before this he has never worked a day in his life. Never mowed a neighbor's lawn, never flung a folded newspaper, never stocked a grocery shelf; Mozarts just don't, you know. And he has to act as if

none of this is new or vexing because he has this characteristic—perhaps from all those years of hanging out with his dad at tournaments, all those years of mixing with and mauling golfers five, ten, twenty, thirty years older than he is—of never permitting himself to appear confused, surprised, or just generally a little squirt. "His favorite expression," Earl says, "is, 'I knew that.'" Of course Pop, who is just as irreverent with Tiger as he is reverent, can say, "No, you didn't know that, you little s—." But Earl, who has always been the filter for Tiger, decides to take a few steps back during his son's first few months as a pro because he wishes to encourage Tiger's independence and because he is uncertain of his own role now that the International Management Group (IMG) is managing Tiger's career.

41   Nobody notices it, but the inner calm is beginning to dissolve. Earl enters Tiger's hotel room during the Texas Open in mid-October to ask him about his schedule, and Tiger does something he has never done in his twenty years. He bites the old man's head off.

42   Earl blinks. "I understand how you must feel," he says.

43   "No, you don't," snaps Tiger.

44   "And I realized," Earl says later, "that I'd spent twenty years planning for this, but the one thing I didn't do was educate Tiger to be the boss of a corporation. There was just no vehicle for that, and I thought it would develop more slowly. I wasn't presumptuous enough to anticipate this. For the first time in his life, the training was behind the reality. I could see on his face that he was going through hell."

45   The kid is fluid, though. Just watch him walk. He's quick to flow into the new form, to fit the contour of necessity. A few hours after the outburst he's apologizing to his father and hugging him. A few days later he's giving Pop the O.K. to call a meeting of the key members of Tiger's new corporation and establish a system, Lieutenant Colonel Woods in command, chairing a two-and-a-half-hour teleconference with the team each week to sift through all the demands, weed

out all the chaff, and present Tiger five decisions to make instead of five hundred. A few days after that, the weight forklifted off his shoulders, at least temporarily, Tiger wins the Walt Disney World/Oldsmobile Classic. And a few weeks later, at the Fred Haskins Award dinner, which has been rescheduled at his request, Tiger stands at the podium and says, "I should've attended the dinner [the first time]. I admit I was wrong, and I'm sorry for any inconvenience I may have caused. But I have learned from that, and I will never make that mistake again. I'm very honored to be part of this select group, and I'll always remember, for both good and bad, this Haskins Award; for what I did and what I learned, for the company I'm now in and I'll always be in. Thank you very much." The crowd surges to its feet, cheering once more.

46   See, maybe Tiger can win. He's got the touch. He's got the feel. He never writes down a word before he gives a speech. When he needs to remember a phone number, he doesn't search his memory or a little black book; he picks up a phone and watches what number his fingers go to. When he needs a 120-yard shot to go under an oak branch and over a pond, he doesn't visualize the shot, as most golfers would. He looks at the flag and pulls everything from the hole back, back, back . . . not back into his mind's eye, but into his hands and forearms and hips, so they'll do it by feel. Explain how he made that preposterous shot? He can't. Better you interview his knuckles and metacarpals.

47   "His handicap," says Earl, "is that he has such a powerful creative mind. His imagination is too vivid. If he uses visualization, the ball goes nuts. So we piped into his creative side even deeper, into his incredible sense of feel."

48   "I've learned to trust the subconscious," says Tiger. "My instincts have never lied to me."

49   The mother radiates this: the Eastern proclivity to let life happen, rather than the Western one to make it happen. The father comes to it in his own way, through fire. To kill a man, to conduct oneself calmly and efficiently when one's own death is immi-

nent—a skill Earl learns in Green Beret psychological training and then again and again in jungles and rice paddies—one removes the conscious mind from the task and yields to the subconscious. "It's the more powerful of the two minds," Earl says. "It works faster than the conscious mind, yet it's patterned enough to handle routine tasks over and over, like driving a car or making a putt. It knows what to do.

50   "Allow yourself the freedom of emotion and feeling. Don't try to control them and trap them. Acknowledge them and become the beneficiary of them. Let it all outflow."

51   Let it all because it's all there: the stability, almost freakish for a close-of-the-millennium California child—same two parents, same house all his twenty years, same best friends, one since second grade, one since eighth. The kid, for god's sake, never once had a baby-sitter. The conditioning is there as well, the two years of psychological boot camp during which Earl dropped golf bags and pumped cart brakes during Tiger's backswings, jingled change and rolled balls across his line of vision to test his nerves, promising him at the outset that he only had to say "Enough" and Earl would cut off the blowtorch, but promising too that if Tiger graduated, no man he ever faced would be mentally stronger than he. "I am the toughest golfer mentally," Tiger says.

52   The bedrock is so wide that opposites can dance upon it: the cautious man can be instinctive, the careful man can be carefree. The bedrock is so wide that it has enticed Tiger into the habit of falling behind—as he did in the final matches of all three U.S. Junior Amateur and all three U.S. Amateur victories—knowing in his tissue and bones that danger will unleash his greatest power. "Allow success and fame to happen," the old man says. "Let the legend grow."

53   To hell with the Tao. The machine will win, it has to win, because it makes everything happen before a man knows it. Before he knows it, a veil descends over his eyes when another stranger approaches. Before he knows it, he's living in a walled community with an electronic gate and a security guard, where the children trick-or-treat in golf carts, a place like the one Tiger just moved into in Orlando to preserve some scrap of sanity. Each day there, even with all the best intentions, how can he help but be a little more removed from the world he's supposed to change, and from his truest self?

54   Which is ... who? The poised, polite, opaque sage we see on TV? No, no, no; his friends hoot and haze him when they see that Tiger on the screen, and he can barely help grinning himself. The Tiger they know is perfectly a fast-food freak who never remembers to ask if anyone else is hungry before he bolts to Taco Bell or McDonald's for the tenth time of the week. The one who loves riding roller coasters, spinning out golf carts, and winning at cards no matter how often his father accuses him of "reckless eyeballing." The one who loves delivering the dirty joke, who owns a salty barracks tongue just a rank or two beneath his father's. The one who's flip, who's downright cocky. When a suit walks up to him before the Haskins Award dinner and says, "I think you're going to be the next great one, but those are mighty big shoes to fill," Tiger replies, "Got big feet."

55   A typical exchange between Tiger and his agent, Norton:

> "Tiger, they want to know when you can do that interview."
> "Tell them to kiss my ass!"
> "All right, and after that, what should I tell them?"
> "Tell them to kiss my ass again!"
> "O.K., and after that ... "

56   But it's a cockiness cut with humility, the paradox pounded into his skull by a father who in one breath speaks of his son with religious awe and in the next grunts, "You weren't s— then, Tiger. You ain't s— now. You ain't never gonna be s—."

57   "That's why I know I can handle all this," Tiger says, "no matter how big it gets. I grew up in the media's eye, but I was taught never to lose sight of where I came from. Athletes aren't as gentlemanly as they used to be. I

don't like that change. I like the idea of being a role model. It's an honor. People took the time to help me as a kid, and they impacted my life. I want to do the same for kids."

58   So, if it's a clinic for children instead of an interview or an endorsement for adults, the cynic in Tiger gives way to the child who grew up immersed in this father's vision of an earth-altering compassion, the 7-year-old boy who watched scenes from the Ethiopian famine on the evening news, went right to his bedroom and returned with a $20 bill to contribute from his piggy bank. Last spring busloads of inner-city kids would arrive at golf courses where Tiger was playing for Stanford, spilling out to watch the Earl and Tiger show in wonder. Earl would talk about the dangers of drugs, then proclaim, "Here's Tiger Woods on drugs," and Tiger would stagger to the tee, topping the ball so it bounced crazily to the side. And then, presto, with a wave of his arms Earl would remove the drugs from Tiger's body, and his son would stride to the ball and launch a 330-yard rocket across the sky. Then Earl would talk about respect and trust and hard work and demonstrate what they can all lead to by standing ten feet in front of his son, raising his arms and telling Tiger to smash the ball between them— and, *whoosh,* Tiger would part not only the old man's arms but his haircut too.

59   They've got plans, the two of them, big plans, for a Tiger Woods Foundation that will fund scholarships across the country, set up clinics and coaches and access to golf courses for inner-city children. "I throw those visions out there in front of him," Earl says, "and it's like reeling in a fish. He goes for the bait, takes it, and away he goes. This is nothing new. It's been working this way for a long time."

60   "That's the difference," says Merchant, Tiger's attorney and a family friend. "Other athletes who have risen to this level just didn't have this kind of guidance. With a father and mother like Tiger's, he has to be real. It's such a rare quality in celebrities nowadays. There hasn't been a politician

since John Kennedy whom people have wanted to touch. But watch Tiger. He has it. He actually listens to people when they stop him in an airport. He looks them in the eye. I can't ever envision Tiger Woods selling his autograph."

See, maybe Tiger can win.   61

Let's be honest. The machine will win because you can't work both sides of this street.   62
The machine will win because you can't transcend wearing sixteen Nike swooshes, you can't move human hearts while you're busy pushing sneakers. Gandhi didn't hawk golf balls, did he? Jackie Robinson was spared that fate because he came and went while Madison Avenue was still teething. Ali became a symbol instead of a logo because of boxing's disrepute and because of the attrition of cells in the basal ganglia of his brain. Who or what will save Tiger Woods?

Did someone say Buddha?   63

Every year near his birthday, Tiger goes with his mother to a Buddhist temple and makes a gift of rice, sugar, and salt to the monks there who have renounced all material goods. A mother-of-pearl Buddha given to Tiger by his Thai grandfather watches over him while he sleeps, and a god Buddha hangs from the chain on his neck. "I like Buddhism because it's a whole way of being and living," Tiger says. "It's based on discipline and respect and personal responsibility. I like Asian culture better than ours because of that. Asians are much more disciplined than we are. Look how well behaved their children are. It's how my mother raised me. You can question, but talk back? Never. In Thailand, once you've earned people's respect, you have it for life. Here it's, What have you done for me lately? So here you can never rest easy. In this country I have to be very careful. I'm easygoing, but I won't let you in completely. There, I'm Thai, and it feels very different. In many ways I consider that home.   64

"I believe in Buddhism. Not every aspect, but most of it. So I take bits and pieces. I don't believe that human beings can achieve ultimate enlightenment, because humans   65 have flaws. I don't want to get rid of all my wants and desires. I can enjoy material things, but that doesn't mean I need them. It doesn't matter to me whether I live in a place like this"—the golf club in his hand makes a sweep of the Orlando villa—"or in a shack. I'd be fine in a shack, as long as I could play some golf. I'll do the commercials for Nike and for Titleist, but there won't be much more than that. I have no desire to be the king of endorsement money."

66   On the morning after he decides to turn pro, there's a knock on his hotel room door. It's Norton, bleary-eyed but exhilarated after a late-night round of negotiations with Nike. He explains to Tiger and Earl that the benchmark for contract endorsements in golf is Norman's reported $2 ½ million-a-year deal with Reebok. Then, gulping down hard on the yabba-dabba-doo rising up his throat, Norton announces Nike's offer: $40 million for five years, 8 mil a year. "Over three times what Norman gets!" Norton exults.

67   Silence.

68   "Guys, do you realize this is more than Nike pays any athlete in salary, even Jordan?"

69   Silence.

70   "Finally," Norton says now, recalling that morning, "Tiger says, 'Mmmm-hmmm,' and I say, 'That's it? Mmmm-hmmm?' No 'Omigod.' No slapping five or 'Ya-hooo!' So I say, 'Let me go through this again, guys.' Finally Tiger says, 'Guess that's pretty amazing.' That's it. When I made the deal with Titleist a day later, I went back to them saying, 'I'm almost embarrassed to tell you this one. Titleist is offering a little more than $20 million over five years.'"

71   On the Monday morning after his first pro tournament, a week after the two megadeals, Tiger scans the tiny print on the sports page under Milwaukee Open money earnings and finds his name. Tiger Woods: $2,544. "That's my money," he exclaims. "I earned this!"

72   See, maybe Tiger can win.

73   How? How can he win when there are so many insects under so many rocks? Several more death threats arrive just before the Skins Game, prompting an increase in his plainclothes security force, which is already larger than anyone knows. His agent's first instinct is to trash every piece of hate mail delivered to IMG, but Tiger won't permit it. Every piece of racist filth must be saved and given to him. At Stanford he kept one letter taped to his wall. Fuel comes from the oddest forms.

74   The audience, in its hunger for goodness, swallows hard over the Nike ad that heralds Tiger's entrance into the professional ranks. The words that flash on the screen over images of Tiger—"There are still courses in the United States I am not allowed to play because of the color of my skin. I've heard I'm not ready for you. Are you ready for me?"—ooze the very attitude from which many in the audience are seeking relief. The media backlash is swift: the Tiger Woods who used to tell the press "The only time I think about race is when the media ask me"—whoa, what happened to him?

75   What happened to him was a steady accretion of experiences, also known as life. What happened, just weeks before he was born, was a fusillade of limes and BBs rattling the Woods house in Cypress, California, one of the limes shattering the kitchen window, splashing glass all around the pregnant Tida, to welcome the middle-class subdivision's first non-Caucasian family.

76   What happened was a gang of older kids seizing Tiger on his first day of kindergarten, tying him to a tree, hurling rocks at him, calling him monkey and nigger. And Tiger, at age 5, telling no one what happened for several days, trying to absorb what this meant about himself and his world.

77   What happened was the Look, as Tiger and Earl came to call it, the uneasy, silent stare they received in countless country-club locker rooms and restaurants. "Something a white person could never understand," says Tiger, "unless he went to Africa and suddenly found himself in the middle of a tribe." What happened was Tiger's feeling pressured to leave a driving range just two years ago, not far from his family's California home, because a resident watching Tiger's drives

rocket into the nearby protective netting reported that a black teenager was trying to bombard his house.

78   What happened was the cold shoulder Earl got when he took his tyke to play at the Navy Golf Course in Cypress—"a club," Earl says, "composed mostly of retired naval personnel who knew blacks only as cooks and servers, and along comes me, a retired lieutenant colonel outranking 99 percent of them, and I have the nerve to take up golf at 42 and immediately become a low handicap and beat them, and then I have the audacity to have this kid. Well, they had to do something. They took away Tiger's playing privileges twice, said he was too young, even though there were other kids too young who they let play. The second time it happened, I went up to the pro who had done it and made a bet. I said, 'If you'll spot my 3-year-old just one stroke a hole, nine holes, playing off the same tees, and he beats you, will you certify him?' The pro started laughing and said, 'Sure.' Tiger beat him by two strokes, got certified, then the members went over the pro's head and kicked him out again. That's when we switched him to another course."

79   Beat them. That was his parents' solution for each banishment, each Look. Hold your tongue, hew to every rule, and beat them. Tiger Woods is the son of the first black baseball player in the Big Seven, a catcher back in the early '50s, before the conference became the Big Eight. A man who had to leave his Kansas State teammates on road trips and travel miles to stay in motels for blacks; who had to go to the back door of restaurant kitchens to be fed while his teammates dined inside; who says, "This is the most racist society in the world—I know that." A man who learned neither to extinguish his anger nor spray it but to quietly convert it into animus, the determination to enter the system and overcome it by turning its own tools against it. A Green Beret explosives expert whose mind naturally ran that way, whose response, upon hearing Tiger rave about the security in his new walled community, was, "I could get in. I could blow up the clubhouse and be gone before they ever knew what hit them." A

father who saw his son, from the beginning, as the one who would enter one of America's last Caucasian bastions, the PGA Tour, and overthrow it from within in a manner that would make it smile and ask for more. "Been planning that one for twenty years," says Earl. "See, you don't turn it into hatred. You turn it into something positive. So many athletes who reach the top now had things happen to them as children that created hostility, and they bring that hostility with them. But that hostility uses up energy. If you can do it without the chip on the shoulder, it frees up all that energy to create."

80   It's not until Stanford, where Tiger takes an African-American history course and stays up half the night in dormitories talking with people of every shade of skin, that his experiences begin to crystallize. "What I realized is that even though I'm mathematically Asian—if anything—if you have one drop of black blood in the United States, you're black," says Tiger. "And how important it is for this country to talk about this subject. It's not me to blow my horn, the way I come across in that Nike ad, or to say things quite that way. But I felt it was worth it because the message needed to be said. You can't say something like that in a polite way. Golf has shied away from this for too long. Some clubs have brought in tokens, but nothing has really changed. I hope what I'm doing can change that."

81   But don't overestimate race's proportion in the fuel that propels Tiger Woods. Don't look for traces of race in the astonishing rubble at his feet on the Sunday after he lost the Texas Open by two strokes and returned to his hotel room and snapped a putter in two with one violent lift of his knee. Then another putter. And another. And another and another—eight in all before his rage was spent and he was ready to begin considering the loss's philosophical lesson. "That volcano of competitive fire, that comes from me," says Earl. A volcano that's mostly an elite athlete's need to win, a need far more immediate than that of changing the world.

82   No, don't overestimate race, but don't overlook it, either. When Tiger is asked

about racism, about the effect it has on him when he senses it in the air, he has a golf club in his hands. He takes the club by the neck, his eyes flashing hot and cold at once, and gives it a short upward thrust. He says, "It makes me want to stick it right up their asses." Pause. "On the golf course."

83   The machine will win because there is so much of the old man's breath in the boy . . . and how long can the old man keep breathing? At 2 A.M., hours before the second round of the Tour Championship in Tulsa on October 25, the phone rings in Tiger's hotel room. It's Mom. Pop's in an ambulance, on his way to a Tulsa hospital. He's just had his second heart attack.

84   The Tour Championship? The future of humanity? The hell with 'em. Tiger's at the old man's bedside in no time, awake most of the night. Tiger's out of contention in the Tour Championship by dinnertime, with a second-round 78, his worst till then as a pro. "There are things more important than golf," he says.

85   The old man survives—and sees the pattern at work, of course. He's got to throw away the cigarettes. He's got to quit ordering the cholesterol special for breakfast. "I've got to shape up now, God's telling me," Earl says, "or I won't be around for the last push, the last lesson." The one about how to ride the tsunami of runaway fame.

86   The machine will win because no matter how complicated it all seems now, it is simpler than it will ever be. The boy will marry one day, and the happiness of two people will lie in his hands. Children will follow, and it will become his job to protect three or four or five people from the molars of the machine. Imagine the din of the grinding in five, ten, fifteen years, when the boy reaches his golfing prime.

87   The machine will win because the whole notion is so ludicrous to begin with, a kid clutching an eight-iron changing the course of humanity. No, of course not, there won't be thousands of people sitting in front of tanks because of Tiger Woods. He won't bring about the overthrow of a tyranny or spawn a religion that one day will number 300 million devotees.

88   But maybe Pop is onto something without quite seeing what it is. Maybe it has to do with timing: the appearance of his son when America is turning the corner to a century in which the country's faces of color will nearly equal those that are white. Maybe, every now and then, a man gets swallowed by the machine, but the machine is changed more than he is.

89   For when we swallow Tiger Woods, the yellow-black-red-white man, we swallow something much more significant than Jordan or Charles Barkley. We swallow hope in the American experiment, in the pell-mell jumbling of genes. We swallow the belief that the face of the future is not necessarily a bitter or bewildered face; that it might even, one day, be something like Tiger Woods's face: handsome and smiling and ready to kick all comers' asses.

90   We see a woman, 50-ish and Caucasian, well-coiffed and tailored—the woman we see at every country club—walk up to Tiger Woods before he receives the Haskins Award and say, "When I watch you taking on all those other players, Tiger, I feel like I'm watching my own son" . . . and we feel the quivering of the cosmic compass that occurs when human beings look into the eyes of someone of another color and see their own flesh and blood.

Source: Gary Smith, "The Chosen One," in *The Best American Sports Writing*, ed. George Plimpton. Boston: Houghton-Mifflin, 1997, pp. 297–316.

DISCUSSION QUESTIONS

1. Smith develops a number of metaphors to express his views on Tiger Woods. Of these, the most extended is the metaphor of the "machine." What, exactly, does the "machine" stand for? How appropriate is this metaphor for Smith's

purposes? How effective do you find his repeated references to the machine? Identify other examples of extended metaphors in this argument and discuss their effectiveness.

2. From what point of view does Smith write—that is, personal, impersonal, first person or third person, formal or familiar, and so on? Do you think this choice of perspective was strategic on Smith's part, intended to create a particular effect or support a particular position? Discuss.

3. Summarize Smith's major claim in a sentence or two. To what class of argument does this claim belong?

4. Smith makes a number of secondary causal arguments—some indicating why the "machine" will win, others, why Tiger will win. Identify three or four of these secondary arguments and discuss with your classmates the adequacy of their support.

5. Characterize the overall tone of Smith's writing. Then, conduct a World Wide Web search for other writing by Smith and obtain two or three other samples. Is the tone similar in all the pieces? If not, why do you think he has adopted this particular tone to write about "The Chosen One"?

SUGGESTIONS FOR WRITING (15.3)

1. You are a senior editor of *Sports Illustrated* submitting Gary Smith's "The Chosen One" to George Plimpton, editor of *The Best American Sports Writing*, for inclusion into the annual collection. Selection is highly competitive, and, as Smith's editor, you have to point out the merits of his article. Write a one-page cover letter to Plimpton evaluating Smith's writing and recommending it for inclusion.

2. Earl Woods, Tiger's father, claims that his son "is the Chosen One. He'll have the power to impact nations. Not people. Nations." Construct an outline for a causal argument (an argument of effect) claiming that "Tiger Woods will impact nations." Indicate in your outline the kind of information and support you would need to argue this claim effectively. Don't forget Mill's tests for causality as possible support (see Chapter 7).

3. Smith has created an interesting device for presenting argument and counterargument ("The machine will win . . . . Tiger will win."). Write your own argument of effect about the future of a young person you know or know about, using Smith's model for presenting the counterargument. Note: your claim need not be as ambitious as Smith's. For example, you could claim that a sibling will be a varsity athlete or that a popular movie star will be a flash in the pan.

4. Do you think that the particular sport a person plays can tell us something about that person? For example, is Tiger Woods's choice of golf or Michael Jordan's choice of basketball (or, briefly, baseball, for that matter) significant in our attempt to understand each? Select an athlete you know or know about (professional, amateur, or recreational) and write a two- to three-page argument demonstrating what we learn about this person through his or her athletic activity. Your argument may be interpretive or causal. Be sure you are clear which it is before you begin supporting it.

Because this assignment is relatively sophisticated, you should show a draft to your instructor to make sure you're on the right track.

PUBLIC USE OF NATIVE AMERICAN NAMES, SYMBOLS, AND MASCOTS

RICHARD P. MILLS

Richard Mills is the Commissioner of Education for the State of New York. This argument was written in the form of a memorandum to presidents of boards of education and superintendents of public schools in New York state.

According to the N.Y. State Education Web site, "As Commissioner of Education, Mills serves as chief executive officer of the Board of Regents, which has jurisdiction over the most comprehensive state educational system in the nation. The system encompasses every education endeavor in the State, including public and non-public elementary, middle, and secondary education; public and independent colleges and universities; museums, libraries, historical societies, and archives; the vocational rehabilitation system; and responsibility for the licensing, practicing, and oversight of 38 professions."

April 5, 2001
TO: Presidents of Boards of Education and Superintendents of Public Schools
FROM: Richard P. Mills
SUBJECT: Public Schools Use of Native American Names, Symbols, and Mascots

1   Some time ago, I directed Department staff to study the use of Native American mascots by public schools. I would like to share with you the results of that work.

What I conclude:

2   Our review confirmed that the use of Native American symbols is part of time-honored traditions in some of our communities, and that there are deeply felt, albeit conflicting, ideas about them. Some members of these communities believe that the mascots honor or pay tribute to Native Americans and their culture. However, most Native Americans appear to find the portrayal by others of their treasured cultural and religious symbols disparaging and disrespectful. Many [others] who have looked at this issue concur.

3   After careful [thought] and consideration, I have concluded that the use of Native American symbols or depictions as mascots can become a barrier to building a safe and nurturing school community and improving academic achievement for all students. I ask the superintendents and presidents of school boards to lead their communities to a new understanding of this matter. I ask boards to end the use of Native American mascots as soon as practical. Some communities have thought about this and are ready to act. Others already have acted and I commend them. Yet, in others, more reflection and listening is needed, and so I ask that these [discussions] begin now. I believe that local leaders can find the right way to inquire into this matter and resolve it locally. Next year I will formally evaluate the progress on this issue.

4   Here is my reasoning.

What we found:

5   There has already been extensive statewide discussion of this issue. Some of it is eloquent. We sought the views of local superintendents. Many wrote directly and many others expressed their thoughts through District Superintendents. I have had extended conversations with a few of them. We contacted representatives of Native American communities. We also asked the counsel of District Superintendents. We researched the literature on this subject and read legal documents from other states. We examined New York law, regulation, and

Regents policy. In addition, many citizens wrote to us.

6   The use of Native American names, symbols, and mascots is such a significant issue that it is being looked at in other states, in professional sports, at the collegiate level, as well as at the local level in some New York school districts. The Society of the Indian Psychologists of the Americas has raised the concern that the use of these mascots and symbols creates an "unwelcome academic environment" for Native American students. Organizations such as the NAACP, and the NEA have issued statements calling for an end to the use of mascots. The U.S. Census 2000 issued a resolution stating that it would not include teams that used these symbols as part of its promotional program. over the last 30 years, more than 600 colleges, universities and high schools have changed or eliminated their use of Native American mascots. For example, the Los Angeles school board required its junior high and high schools to drop Native American-themed names and mascots, and 20 high schools in Wisconsin followed suit. Collegiate institutions such as Miami University of Ohio, St. John's University, Siena College and Stanford University have changed their school logos. In the professional sports world, objections have also arisen, and it is clear that recent expansion teams in professional baseball, hockey, football and basketball have avoided the use of Indian-themed names or mascots.

7   In 1999, the United States Department of Justice Civil Rights Division investigated a North Carolina school district to determine if the high school's mascot and nicknames violated Federal Civil Rights Law by creating a racially hostile environment. That investigation was closed after the school district's board of education decided to eliminate the use of Native American religious symbols.

8   In August 2000, Attorney General Elliot Spitzer [reviewed] this issue as it related to a New York State school district. The Attorney General raised serious concerns that certain uses of Native American mascots and symbols could violate the Federal Civil Rights Act of 1964. His opinion identified many factors that school districts should consider in examining their use of these symbols and mascots, particularly areas such as stereotypical nicknames, images, gestures and use of historical and religious symbols such as feather headdress, face-paint, or totem poles.

9   Clearly, many of those who are thinking deeply about this issue are concerned that the use of these symbols should end.

The argument:

10   Schools must provide a safe and supportive environment that promotes achievement of the standards for all children. The use of Native American mascots by some schools can make that school environment seem less safe and supportive to some children, and may send an inappropriate message to children about what is or is not respectful behavior toward others. For that reason we must question the use of such mascots. If children and parents in the school committee are offended or made to feel diminished by the school mascot, what school leader or board would not want to know that and correct the situation? School mascots are intended to make a statement about what the school values. School leaders and communities may not be aware that the statement heard can be contrary to the one intended.

11   Here are some thoughts from a student: "Today this school promotes respect, responsibility, compassion, [honesty,] and tolerance. When you use words like these, you need to teach by example. The resigning of this mascot would be a great example of these character education words. I would like to see my brother, sister, and cousins go to a school that shows respect and tolerance for other cultures. I don't want them to feel the confusion that I have felt going to this school. It has taken me a couple of years to come to understand Native American stereotypes and their effects on me. By keeping [this] mascot the principal lesson the students, staff, and community learn is how to tolerate stereotypes."

12   Some argue that such mascots honor Native Americans. Most Native American representatives do not share that view.

13   Some would argue that mascots that are problematic could be made dignified through some state review process. It is difficult to imagine how to craft criteria to make such a judgment process feasible on a statewide basis. Most people would recognize and deplore mocking, distorted representations of minority group members. However, fair-minded people might view these mascots as respectful without realizing that the representation included religious symbols that Native American observers would find distressing when used in that manner.

14   Some urge keeping the status quo. That is not realistic either. Collegiate sports and newer professional teams have recognized changing public attitudes and decided not to use Native American mascots. The same changes that affected them will eventually overtake schools. It would be better [to] resolve the matter now. The central role of sports in this issue is advantageous. Few areas of American life are as concerned about fairness and respect for individual value and achievement as is the world of sport. We can turn to those values as we think about mascots.

15   Some call for an immediate and statewide halt to the use of these mascots. That approach is not advisable. People in many communities haven't had an opportunity to talk about this and listen to one another. There are cherished traditions surrounding many of the mascots. There are even significant costs involved: consider mascots on team uniforms and gymnasium floors, to cite obvious examples. In any case, local remedies should be exhausted first. Many communities have engaged the issue and made changes. Many other communities will now do so.

16   Still others believe this is a local matter. I cannot agree that it is *only* a local matter. There is state interest in providing a safe and supportive learning environment for every child. The use of Native American mascots involves a state responsibility as well.

17   Here are some questions that might help local communities consider how to approach the issue. I have adapted them from ideas suggested by a New York School Superintendent and they seem like a good place to begin.

- Do Native Americans and non-Native Americans perceive the mascot differently?
- Is there a significant difference between how the mascot may have been intended and how it is interpreted?
- How should an organization respond if its well-intentioned actions unintentionally offend a member of the group's [religious] or ethnic beliefs?
- Are there other symbols that represent the school's values that could be used in place of the existing mascot?

18   I call upon school leaders in communities that use Native American symbols, names, or mascots to pose these questions to their communities and lead them in a discussion of the right path to take. It is important that our students learn about the diversity of our communities so that they will understand and respect our differences and draw strength from them in becoming good citizens and productive adults. School administrators, staff, parents, and community members play a critical role in modeling behavior that celebrates and honors traditions and beliefs of our fellow citizens. As educators, we have an obligation to inform communities so that they might come to understand the pain, however unintentionally inflicted, these symbols cause.

Source: Richard P. Mills, "Public Schools Use of Native American Names, Symbols, and Mascots," http://earnestman.tripod.com/ fr.2001nysed.htm

DISCUSSION QUESTIONS

1. Under the heading *"What we found,"* Mills concludes "Clearly, many of those who are thinking deeply about this issue are concerned that the use of these symbols should end." Is this an example of the *ad populum* fallacy?

2. Is the factual support Mills introduces to support his argument adequate? Why or why not?

3. Discuss with two or three of your classmates how appropriate Mills's diction, tone, references, etc. are to his intended audience?

4. Place the claims made in the first paragraph under the heading *"The argument"* into the syllogistic model. With a group of your classmates, consider whether each element of the syllogism is adequately supported.

5. Mills makes a number of inductive conclusions that lack support through individual examples. Identify two or three of these and consider whether they weaken his overall argument.

SUGGESTIONS FOR WRITING (15.4)

1. Create an analogy to the use of Indian mascot names that might be used in an argument supporting their discontinuance—e.e., "Using mascot names like 'the Braves' or 'the Redskins' would be like calling a team xxx or xxx." Make sure your analogy satisfies the criteria of a reasonable comparison.

2. Regardless of your own views on this topic, write a three-page argument supporting the use of team mascots with Indian names. Be sure to identify the type of claim you are making and to support it as reasonably as possible.

3. Assume you are the principal of a high school with a long tradition of using a "Redskin" mascot. Write a one-page letter to your athletic teams supporting your decision to discontinue use of this mascot. You may use Commissioner Mills's memo as support.

4. Write a three– to four-page causal argument speculating on the reasons for the widespread adoption of Indian mascot names for sports teams.

RUNNER'S STORY: WHY DID KATHY ORMSBY JUMP OFF THAT BRIDGE?

SHARON ROBB

This article first appeared in the Fort Lauderdale Sun-Sentinel *in June of 1986. Sharon Robb is an experienced sports journalist who has covered football and basketball for the* Sun-Sentinel *as well as three Olympics. As with Joan Ryan, another female sports journalist, this article evolved from an experience of dissonance occasioned by the seemingly unaccountable tragedy of Kathy Ormsby.*

1   On the surface, Kathy Orsmby had it all. The adoration of her hometown, a straight-A average in pre-med and the respect of her peers as one of the premier female distance runners.

But something must have been torturing Kathy Ormsby. On the evening of June 4 in Indianapolis, she dropped out of a race, ran to a bridge and jumped, an apparent suicide attempt. Today she lies in the Duke

University Medical Center, paralyzed from the waist down. There is little hope she will walk again.

3   Only Ormsby knows why she jumped. And for now, friends, relatives and teammates are trying to figure out why the 21-year-old record-setting junior from North Carolina State, who seemed to have everything, would want to throw it all away.

4   "It's going to take a while for me to get a handle on this," said N.C. State women's track coach Rollie Geiger, who found Ormsby crumpled in the grassy field below the bridge. "How can I tell you what I felt when I found her? I love her. We all do. She was—still is—a very caring and loving person. She was a true reflection of our program.

5   "If I were going to pick an athlete to be in our program, it would be Kathy. If I were going to pick an individual to be my daughter, it would be Kathy."

6   "I will never accept that it was a suicide attempt in the classical sense," said Ralph Robertson, principal of Richmond County Senior High School, where Ormsby was valedictorian and a hero to the townspeople. "I don't think she was Kathy Ormsby at that point—not the Kathy Ormsby we know. I am convinced she made no conscious decision to do this."

7   In Rockingham, Ormsby won friends with her selfless devotion, but at the same time worried them with her drive for perfection.

8   "You get a Kathy Ormsby but once in a lifetime," Robertson said. "She was the classic overachiever, doing nothing but the best. Track just seemed to be a sidelight from her studies, we thought."

9   On the night of June 4, Ormsby was competing in the 10,000 meters of the NCAA Outdoor Track and Field Championships at Indiana University's stadium. She was in fourth place and within a step of third with 3,500 meters to go in the race when she broke away from the pack.

10   Said Harley Lewis, NCAA track rules committee member and former Oregon track coach: "She was in a position where she could have won the race. She apparently just felt she was no longer able to continue at that pace and quit. Usually when they quit, they drop off to the inside of the track and walk. She didn't. She walked to the outside and disappeared."

11   Ormsby slowed her pace to duck under a railing and ran past Wisconsin coach Peter Tegen. She picked up speed again and ran up a set of steps into the stands and vanished. Geiger had seen Ormsby leave the race and had gone outside to look for her.

12   According to witnesses, she ran across a softball field, scaled a 7-foot chain-link fence and then ran west for two blocks alongside New York Street, a main thoroughfare, toward the bridge.

13   When she reached the steel bridge over the White River, she apparently climbed a four-foot guard rail and jumped. Instead of landing in the water, she fell onto a hard field beside the river.

14   Geiger went looking for her. About 10 minutes after she ran off the track, Geiger spotted Ormsby on the river bank, flagged down a motorist to call an ambulance and then climbed down the bank to her side and waited for help.

15   When a campus policeman, Bill Abston, questioned the coach, Geiger replied, "She said she jumped."

16   Police called it a suicide attempt.

17   The cost of success is sometimes a price runners are too willing to pay. In Ormsby's case, the price was too high. Ormsby probably never realized the social and psychological aspects of her growing period were sometimes more strenuous than the endless workouts that she demanded of herself.

18   She earned a partial track scholarship to North Carolina State and enrolled in a premed program with hopes of becoming a medical missionary. Although she made the dean's list every semester, running came first. She found herself on a team full of high school champions. Overcome by anxiety to do well, Ormsby started blacking out and dropping out of big races. At Geiger's

suggestion, she started seeing a sports psychologist a month ago.

19   Ormsby blacked out her freshman year in a meet at Lehigh and again last fall in Milwaukee at the NCAA cross country championships. She would faint during the race and after a minute or two get up on her own and take herself out of the race. Most other times she ran well.

20   She was becoming a star collegiate runner her junior year. She set a U.S. collegiate women's record for 10,000 meters (32:36.2) at the Penn Relays April 24. In her first 10,000-meter race on the track, she broke another record.

21   "It was great," Geiger said. "We had just wanted to find out how fast she could run the event."

22   "That's why she ran so well, she was relaxed," said teammate and close friend Connie Jo Robinson. "It was her first time running the distance and she was an unknown. No one expected her to win."

23   After her Penn Relays performance, Ormsby told *Track and Field News*, "One thing that has helped me is not placing so much importance on my performances and trying to please other people. I just have to learn to do my best for myself and for God, and to turn everything over to Him. It seems like I have been able to do that better this track season than ever."

24   She was selected a track All-American.

25   A week after the Penn Relays, at the Twilight Track Invitational in Raleigh, she blacked out again. "She was seeing a sports psychologist. But who knows if she opened up to him?" Robinson said.

26   Stanford's Brooks Johnson, 1984 U.S. Olympic Women's track coach, cited the fine line between pressure, impulse and chemical imbalance when dealing with runners, especially women. He said the pressure at national athletic championships leads runners to levels of frustration and identity crises beyond the norm.

27   "I think what people have to realize is what happened to Kathy Ormsby could have happened to any runner," Johnson said. "She was operating in a state of diminished capacity. The heat conditions were severe. The mind could no longer control what was going on. She was pushed to the brink.

28   "She was embarrassed because she thought she wasn't doing well. She was hurt and distraught when she ran off the track. The bridge happened to be there. How many times have you and I thought about committing suicide but never did because the opportunity wasn't there? Well, this time the opportunity presented itself. The impulse was there, and so was the bridge. Here was a girl who always needed to overcompensate in athletics. People just don't realize how much pressure these runners put on themselves."

29   For Geiger and his runners, the agonizing began the day after the tragedy.

30   "I feel like I missed something along the way, but I had no indication whatsoever something like this would happen," Geiger said. "When we talked just before the race, she seemed to be looking forward to it—not only that race, but other things this summer."

31   Robert Phillips, a Charlotte sports psychologist, said athletes tend to define their whole reality around that one thing they do and "When you combine total mental, emotional and physical involvement, it's not hard to define your world as being totally good or bad at that moment.

32   "When you're running in that race, you don't look ahead to next week or back at last week. There is potential for distortion of reality to a high degree. During the running experience, with chemical reactions going on and with natural opiates released causing a high, inhibitions are greatly reduced. Seeds of depression or stress could come out."

33   Geiger was unprepared for what happened: "Either I missed the signs or there were no signs. Maybe it was something that had been building up through the years. All I know is, if you were to walk into that hospital room, meet and talk with her, you

wouldn't know what to write. She's the sweetest person you'd ever want to know."

34   Robinson said there were no signals that she would do anything so drastic. "She never mentioned the pressure. She believed her record was a gift from God," she said. "A lot of new things were happening to her. She had stepped up from being a 5:02 high school miler. She was elite. She was on TV and in the newspapers. Anytime a person excels the way she did, there's obviously a lot more pressure. When you get better, you are expected to do more, and there's just no way out. I don't think she saw a way out."

35   "Running and school are her life," said teammate Wendy McLees. "She's always been a pusher, very dedicated to both."

36   Kathy Love Ormsby, born Nov. 1, 1964, grew up in Rockingham, a textile town of 8,284, a quiet place of sandy hills that was the perfect training ground for a long-distance runner.

37   She was a shy, Baptist girl with little time for socializing, an overachiever whose motivation was not to glorify herself but God. She loved to win, but was embarrassed by the adulation. She loved to run, but at times would become so lost in her exhilaration at workouts that her coach would have to hold her back.

38   She was dedicated to making good grades: She brought her notes to track practice and studied in the car on trips to track meets. She ran at 5 a.m. Sunday mornings so she could get back in time for services at the First Baptist Church, where she was a youth co-pastor and sang in the choir.

39   She lived with her parents in a two-story colonial brick house on tree-lined Curtis Street in a middle-class neighborhood. There were no tragic overtones to her background.

40   "Even though she's been a high achiever most of her life, you would never know it because she is so unassuming," said First Baptist's pastor, William W. Leathers.

41   Ormsby began running in junior high. She ran the 100- and 200-yard dashes. Those who saw her race the first few times knew she was special.

42   "You don't have to know her very long to know she is a very conscientious and dedicated person," said Rockingham Junior High track coach Charlie Bishop, who converted her from sprinting to distance running.

43   The rewards were many for the state high school champion middle-distance runner. Her sophomore year she won the state championship in the 1,600 meters. Her senior year she set state high school records at 800, 1,600 and 3,200 meters. Her only disappointing race was a cross country championship her junior year when she finished second. After the race, her coach found out she had run with a stress fracture in one leg.

44   She was as brilliant in the classroom as on the track: No. 1 in her high school class of 600, never making below an A. She was the only student honored by the 12-year-old school with her own day, Kathy Ormsby Day, May 26, 1983. There was an assembly in her honor and a proclamation to hang on her bedroom wall.

45   Although pro athletes Franklin Stubbs of the Los Angeles Dodgers, Mike Quick of the Philadelphia Eagles and Perry Williams of the New York Giants graduated from Richmond County Senior High, only Ormsby had her jersey retired.

46   She was under great pressure to succeed, not from her parents, coaches or teammates but from within, according to her high school track coach, Pete Pittman.

47   "During the three years she ran here, she never once left practice without saying, 'Coach, is there anything else I need to do?'" Pittman said. "She was that way in the classroom, too. She kept her mind on business."

48   There is a clearly defined peak for the academic perfectionist—a perfect score of 100 or straight A's. But for the runner, there is no ultimate time.

49   "As far as who worked hard to be better than anybody else, I've never seen anybody like her," said Richmond Athletic Director George Whitfield.

50   Kathy's mother, Sallie, 49, a nurse at Richmond Memorial Hospital, once told a training mate of Kathy's, Rockingham

marathoner Jackie Tanner, that she wished her daughter would relax a little—ease up.

51   Her father, Dale, 58, a Burlington Industries Inc. textile plant manager in Cordova, said his daughter was under great pressure to succeed.

52   "Kathy has always tended to be an overachiever and puts a tremendous amount of pressure on herself," Dale Ormsby said. "I believe it had something to do with the pressure put on young people to succeed.

53   "It's a question of pressure, pressure to succeed. It was physical, and maybe it was mental, and it blotted out the ability to think rationally. I know she wanted to do well, it was important to her."

54   Ormsby told her father she doesn't remember exactly what happened. According to a team of physicians, she probably will have significant lapses in her memory for some time.

55   Her parents have kept a prayerful vigil by her bedside. Only her two brothers, Dale Jr. and John, sister Donna Freshwater, and close friends have been allowed to visit her, first at the Wishard Memorial Hospital in Indianapolis and now at Duke, where she was moved to be closer to home.

56   Robinson said the hardest part of the ordeal was seeing her in the hospital, on a respirator, unable to talk. "I told her I loved her and that God would love her," Robinson said. Ormsby squeezed her hand.

57   Johnson said it is ironic one of Geiger's runners would attempt suicide. Geiger is nationally respected and known for sensitivity toward his athletes.

58   Ormsby wasn't the first runner Geiger dealt with who had a personal crisis. In 1981, former Hollywood McArthur High state champion Sue Overbey Molloy had a 15-month struggle with anorexia nervosa, a psychological disorder characterized by self-starvation. At one point, she dropped to 86 pounds, having lost 29. After coming to grips with her problems, she recovered. Today the newlywed is an electrician's apprentice, lives in Lake Worth and no longer races competitively.

59   "His kind of program is not one that lends itself to that kind of thing," Johnson said.

60   Upgraded from serious to stable condition June 9, Ormsby underwent an operation June 19 to stabilize the spine. A second operation will remove fragments from the spinal canal—before her six-week rehabilitation period begins and she can go home.

61   She suffered a broken rib, a collapsed lung and a fractured vertebra, which injured her spinal cord in her middle back. The paralysis has been diagnosed as permanent. She has complete use of her arms.

62   "About everybody who goes through this will experience some depression, usually a few weeks down the road," said Dr. Peter Hall, chief of neurosurgery, who supervised her treatment at Wishard Memorial.

63   "Kathy has been told this and has kind of accepted it, and so have her mother and I," Dale Ormsby said. "We can only hope that something good will come out of it."

64   Kathy Ormsby's day of reckoning may have been inevitable; she had lived on the fringes for some time.

65   World-class runner Mary Decker Slaney said she "can't see running becoming an obsession—not to the point of hurting yourself or taking your life." But she cites the fine line between dedication and obsession.

66   One of Ormsby's closest friends, Alex Wallace, said he often wanted to tell her she worked too hard. He said when they last talked, two weeks before Ormsby jumped, she seemed happy.

67   "I can't imagine what was going through her mind," said Wallace, who went to high school with her and is on a baseball scholarship at N.C. State. "To me, everybody looked up to her. She was my hero, even though she was my peer."

68   Missouri women's track coach Rick McGuire, who has a doctorate in sports psychology, has been working with elite athletes, preparing them for the Olympics. McGuire was going to see Ormsby, but scheduling conflicts set it back.

69   "We assume it was a sports-related crisis, and it may not be that at all," McGuire

said. "Maybe things had happened so that she couldn't handle a highly visible failure."

70   None of her teammates had to ask why.

71   "They didn't need to know why," Robinson said. They know why. We're all in the same boat. We feel the same pressure."

72   Honors student and national age-group and high school state champion Mary Wazeter of Wilkes-Barre, Pennsylvania, felt the same pressure when she tried to kill herself by leaping from a bridge in February 1982. Wazeter, 22, now a paraplegic living with her parents and writing a book, said their stories are similar.

73   "You think you're going to find happiness in setting goals, and you think if you win this race, you'll be happy," Wazeter said. "So you try to compensate for that with achievement and please people by winning.

74   "I would like to talk with Kathy someday. The most important word of encouragement I could offer is to be patient with herself and learn not to be driven and not to be hard on herself. You can't expect to be superhuman."

Source: Sharon Robb, "Why Did Kathy Ormsby Jump Off That Bridge?" *Fort Lauderdale Sun-Sentinel*, June 1986.

DISCUSSION QUESTIONS

1. Sharon Robb reports a number of different theories about the reasons for Ormsby's jump. What are they and to whom is each attributed? Which seems the most plausible to you?

2. After carefully reading this article at least twice, can you identify an implicit claim suggested by Robb? If so, what is it and what are the concrete references that led you to this conclusion?

3. What do you see as the overall purpose or goal of this article?

4. Robb has gathered a considerable amount of information and a number of direct quotes from people associated with Ormsby in one way or another. Indeed, direct quotations constitute the majority of the text. Can you detect any strategy behind Robb's organization of her material? Would a different arrangement of the material leave a very different impression in the reader's mind?

5. With a small group of your classmates, compare the styles of Joan Ryan and Sharon Robb.

SUGGESTIONS FOR WRITING (15.5)

1. Working from the discussion elicited by Question #1, select one of the explanations for Ormsby's jump reported by Sharon Robb. In a page or two, write down additional information you would need in order to create a convincing causal argument around this explanation.

2. Using at least three authoritative sources, write a three-page causal argument identifying the kind of mental characteristics that are necessary in a successful runner (you will probably have to specify sprinter, middle- or long-distance runner). If you like, you may substitute another sport for running.

3. After attending a live sporting event on your campus, write a one- to two-page report of the event, being very careful to be objective. Give your report to a classmate to see if he or she detects any implicit claims or bias in your writing.

4. Using the same sporting event, write a two-page interpretation or causal argument. An interpretation might point out the significance of the win/loss # of the event; a causal argument might explain the win or loss.

BIZBALL

HARVEY ARATON

This argument was the feature story in a Sunday New York Times Magazine *issue devoted entirely to sports (October 1998). Harvey Araton is a sports columnist for the* New York Times. *The cover of this issue of the magazine carried the following teaser/abstract: "For the Murdochs and the Disneys, sports is no game. It's a hot, global entertainment product—and that's changing all the rules."*

1   Once every spring, I get a telephone call from my friend Michelle, who informs me she has received her invoice for Knicks season tickets and will be faxing news of the latest increase in the price of her two seats in the front row, directly behind the team's bench. This year, despite the lockout that threatens to delay the start of the National Basketball Association's season, the markup is $20 per ticket. That's the lowest since Pat Riley began modeling Armani at Madison Square Garden in 1991, at the expense of Michelle's once-perfect sight lines. The other good news is that Jeff Van Gundy—considerably shorter than his predecessor, with much less hair and given to the occasional midgame squat—remains the coach.

2   For the amount she is sacrificing to support her decades-old basketball habit, Michelle Musler prefers to see for herself why her beloved Knicks haven't won the championship in a quarter-century. On the other hand, she can no longer afford the unobstructed view she had when the Knicks' bench was across the way, where Spike Lee holds court, in a camera-friendly seat that will cost the he's-gotta-have-it filmmaker $1,350 per game this year, or $116,100 for his two season tickets. Comparatively, at $220 a pop, or $9,460 per season ticket, Michelle is in the cheap seats.

3   She also sends me the welcome-back letter that annually accompanies the bill and is signed by David W. Checketts, the Garden's chief executive officer. For years, Michelle has indignantly scrawled in the margin, "No

reference to price increase!" Lo and behold, a corporate conscience emerged last spring, albeit one line's worth, near the bottom of a cheerful, go-team epistle. "In such a competitive marketplace," Checketts wrote, "please be aware that you will notice an increase in your 1998–99 ticket renewal package."

4   Her five adult children were typically trenchant when their mother's tickets went up again. (The cost was a Broadway bargain at $45 as recently as 1991.) When, they wondered, would she outgrow this draining obsession and pay more attention to her retirement savings? A single woman in her early 60's, Michelle loves basketball, though, from the pregame buzz to the fourth-quarter buzzer. She holds stubbornly to the illusion of the extended team family, despite evidence all around her that the big sports daddies are more concerned with the construction of intricate global networks and taxpayer-financed stadiums that feature club seats and luxury suites, set conveniently apart from the rabid riffraff.

5   I have known few, if any, more involved fans during my sportswriting career than Michelle, who, to me, represents the endangered spirit of an industry that keeps getting bigger and, admittedly, better in many qualitative ways. When Riley's Knicks went to Houston in June 1994 with a chance to win that elusive championship, Michelle procured a ticket, booked a flight, ditched a client and went down with the ship. Now she wonders where many of the other committed loyalists from her Section 15 have gone.

6   "So many people I knew dropped out," she says ruefully. Like Dennis, the postal worker who brought priests from his community, and Danny, who though legally blind knew more about basketball than anyone Michelle has known. Her friends from down the row, the Coplands and the Tamans, were told by the man who'd sold them tickets for 20 years to get lost when he realized he could extract a lot more from brokers than he could from them.

7   "I'm embarrassed to tell people what I pay for basketball tickets," says Michelle, a professional coach herself, of corporate executives, who lives comfortably, not luxuriously, in Stamford, Conn. "They think you're rich or crazy."

8   Sometimes, it does seem as if the world has gone, well, sports crazy. Like the runaway cost of Michelle Musler's tickets, there appears to be no stopping this locomotive industry, as it has merged with the entertainment game to create a television-fueled explosion of expansion and wealth. Who could have imagined a decade ago that a single player, even one as breathtaking as Michael Jordan, could reel in a reported $80 million in salary and endorsements in a single year? That a media and entertainment baron would bid $1 billion to own a single team, as Rupert Murdoch offered recently for England's world-famous Manchester United soccer club? A year ago, Murdoch paid $311 million for the Los Angeles Dodgers, after *Financial World* magazine estimated the value of the team and its assets at about $180 million. That all-time-high price for a sports team had little of the endurance of Roger Maris's home run record. Compared with the $530 million Alfred Lerner recently agreed to pay for football's expansionist Cleveland Browns, it's a bargain.

9   Once derided as an Australian interloper and muckraker, Murdoch is now the most influential man in sports. He has made himself the face on the corporate invasion, steering his Fox Sports tank across the American landscape, removing competitors from his path by shooting off serious denominations of cash. "Murdoch and Fox changed the economics of sports when he took football away from CBS five years ago," says Robert M. Gutkowski, Checketts's predecessor at the Garden and now C.E.O. of the Marquee Group, a New York-based sports-marketing company.

10   When Fox lifted rights to the National Football Conference from CBS for $1.58 billion in 1993, Murdoch recognized the heightened appeal of live programming in a saturated market of taped family entertainment. If a sports deal lost money, it could nonetheless pull strong demographic groups to a network's mainstream programming. According to a report in *Barron's*, the Fox Network is worth about $4 billion more than it was when it struck its original N.F.L. deal, on which it lost $350 million.

11   By the time CBS paid $4 billion to regain a share of N.F.L. rights this season, some media analysts said it was banking its very future on football's power to draw male viewers back to the slumping network. Early in the fall TV season, it's looking like a good bet: CBS won the ratings race the opening two weeks, the first time it had led in any week since—take a guess—1993.

12   "Sports at the highest level is what people want to see," says Chet Simmons, who was the first president of ESPN and is currently a consultant for the Marquee Group. "And it's no different anywhere you go." The beauty of sports is that you don't have to go anywhere. Images of the games, bouncing off satellites, cross not only cultures but also continents. The world has become a playground for the media conglomerates as they pursue live, unscripted programming that is more valuable than ever on an increasingly crowded dial.

13   As a result, television money is pouring into the mainstream leagues as never before. The turn-of-the-century deals for national rights are staggering. N.F.L.: $17.6 billion over eight years in various network and cable deals. N.B.A.: $2.4 billion over four years. Even the National Hockey League, a sport with limited American appeal and a television audience that has been in sobering retreat, reeled in a five-year, $600 million deal

from ABC/ESPN—more than four times its previous Fox deal.

14   "Twenty years ago, we all thought the numbers couldn't get any higher," Simmons says. "There was a time in my career when I recommended the company not spend more than the previous year. I don't think that way anymore."

15   Given recent developments, it is no wonder that men like Checketts find it difficult to imagine a ceiling to this expanding universe, particularly as long as people wait on lists for Michelle Musler to follow her old friends out the Garden door.

16   "People have warned me and warned me that anger was building over the Knicks tickets and that the real fans were gone," Checketts says. "I have to tell you that I used to feel stronger about this than I do now. We raised Knicks prices 11 percent after a year when we got trounced in the second round, haven't been able to make any moves to significantly better the team and had a season-threatening lockout all summer. And guess what? We had a 96 percent season-ticket renewal rate, an all-time high."

17   Back in the early 1980's, when there were nights Michelle couldn't give her tickets away, I was an eager young beat reporter for *The New York Post*, dispatched on my Murdochian mission to search and distort. We were both drawn to the sport by the Knicks' 1970 and 1973 championship teams of Willis Reed and Walt Frazier. Sportswriters not much younger than myself look at me as if I'm 100 when I tell them how the Knick's mid-1980's star, Bernard King, would playfully punch a computer key as he strolled by me to his seat on the plane, or how the coaches might look up from a Robert Ludlum novel to recommend the chicken over the steak. Today's coaches might be more inclined to allow a terrorist aboard the private jet than a reporter.

18   It wasn't that long ago that we could all feel closer to sports, more in touch, less likely to be shooed away by an executive bodyguard or a player's entourage. The players are richer, the arenas are nicer and the telecasts are better, but the financial

and ideological divide has grown. Michelle has waiter service at her seat but rare is the player or coach who will turn around and chat, as their predecessors did not long ago.

19   This distancing process began decades ago with the rise of the sports unions. But the perception of professional athletes as Our Guys was forever shattered when the sports agent David Falk walked into Nike headquarters one day in the mid-1980's and soon after Michael Jordan evolved from basketball icon to global marketing superman with a dollar sign on his chest. The old-school consensus was that such power handed to the players—though obviously extreme in Jordan's case—would be the death knell of professional sports. Free agency for players granted by the courts in the 1970's would damage fan loyalties, curtail interest. It sounded logical, but failed to foretell fundamental social and technological changes that transformed the way information is received.

20   Detailed reports of athletes who use drugs, commit acts of violence or father children out of wedlock are finally making corporate America more circumspect in choosing its jock-celebrity pitchmen, though it wasn't as if the public had begun looking elsewhere for action heroes. A dozen Chris Webbers, players pathologically drawn to trouble, are obscured by one Jordan, who is treated by the media and the public as Presidents once were.

21   By and large, the young channel surfers don't look at sports through a boys-of-summer prism. They have learned to define change as a way of life, and in a nation of so many single-parent homes, what's the big deal, anyway, of having a sports hero walk out after a championship season when Daddy has already traded in Mom? The bottom line: The more players have moved, the more off-season rumors have flowed, the more there has been to gossip about on another relatively new phenomenon, all-sports talk radio. Murdoch's formula has become the industry model. Stretch the story. Inflate the value. Cross the promotion.

22   Aging Americans may bristle at the manufactured noise and rank commercialism at sporting events and mourn the dearth of affordable seats and free autographs. But there is actually something right with this picture. Today's young sports fan has a much more sophisticated menu of options from which to choose—and learn. In the new world order, there are no more cold-war collisions between the Patriots and the Reds. The once-hated Russians skate on our fancy capitalist ponds and Europeans drop routinely into the N.B.A. Our football gladiators rumble in Europe, and you're no true baseball fan unless you can match the Hispanic superstar with his Caribbean home. There are competing professional women's basketball leagues. The ice hockey women were a bigger story at the Nagano Olympics last winter than the men. The world's hottest young tennis players are named Martina and Venus and Anna. The good old days may be gone for Michelle Musler, but there is no argument about this being a far better time for women and girls to get in the game.

23   And no matter how many overhyped jocks curse the adoring multitudes and spit on umpires, there seems no end to the fans' appetite for the games. As Mark McGwire and Sammy Sosa sprayed record-setting home-run balls around the nation's bleachers, we opened our hearts to baseball after years of watching it stumble into foul territory. The national media celebrated baseball's return to its pastime pedestal, while a recent *USA Today*/Gallup poll gave the game its highest approval ratings since before the 1994 season-ending strike.

24   The breaking of Maris's 37-year-old record was the equivalent of a large dose of Prozac, temporarily lifting the country from depressing developments in the capital. McGwire and Sosa, day after day, were an example of sports in all its galvanizing splendor, its knack for unifying a society polarized by politics, by gender, by religion and by race. And we saw it all, every at-bat, every pitch, shown live and a hundred times more on 24-hour sports networks and Internet sites by the end of the night.

25   Some have speculated that declining television ratings—even the near-monolithic National Football League is down 22 percent over the past decade—is an ominous message that working- and middle-class families and fans are less frequently able to afford the games and are gradually losing interest in watching them. An equally plausible generalization is that lower ratings are resulting from the far greater number of choices available today than a decade ago. Satellite dishes provide more games in a year than most could watch in a lifetime, while the more conventional airwaves are saturated with pro and college games and a variety of events for the most eclectic tastes. The sports cable networks never sleep, and when they run short of viable programming, they can always make something up, as ESPN has done with its Extreme, or X, Games, a virtual Olympics "R" Us.

26   "It's quite successful, how's that?" the ABC/ESPN sports president, Steven Bornstein, said when I recently asked how much money the Extreme Games make.

27   It is the unpredictable nature of sports that makes it unique to the television audience. But maintaining that quality requires a delicate competitive balance, or at least the sense of a level playing field. More and more, the immediate future of sports looks like a half-dozen media titans bulking up in the gym for interminable rounds of corporate chess, with the same player sometimes controlling competing pieces on the board. For instance, under an umbrella Murdoch has walked with John Malone's TeleCommunications, Fox-Liberty has what Checketts calls "direct equity interest" in the Cablevision-owned Garden and its basketball and hockey teams. Murdoch this year has also acquired part ownership in a new Los Angeles arena, along with options to purchase minority shares of basketball's Lakers and hockey's Kings, in addition to their television rights. Given Murdoch's dual involvement, how can the Lakers ever make a trade with the Knicks without raising the issue of impropriety?

28   The trend of the elite sports teams and television rights being bought up by the

many-headed media conglomerates like Fox, Turner and Disney is creating a nightmare of hidden agendas and potential conflicts. Several major-market teams reportedly opposed the lockout orchestrated by the N.B.A. commissioner, David Stern, last June because it was designed to protect smaller, poorer teams. "We may be getting $150 for a club ticket, but we have to have compelling teams coming in on a Tuesday night," Checketts says.

29   In other words, he is saying that sports has a class crisis in ownership that mirrors the one in the stands. There must be room for the smaller market within the process, if not necessarily the little guy inside Madison Square Garden.

30   Recently, Paul Allen, the Portland Trail Blazers' owner, went against the inflationary grain and slashed season-ticket prices an average of 14 percent, a kickback to his most loyal fans. As television and other revenues increase, this is the formula that would seem to be the most prudent long-term strategy to protect a team's fan base. Yet the big-market teams have habitually driven up player salaries (and forced once-thriving small-market teams to atrophy) by overspending. Then they pass this payroll burden on to ticket holders. On and on it has gone, with the average player salary now more than $2.6 million in basketball, $1.4 million in baseball and $1.2 million in hockey. Meanwhile, *Team Marketing Report* estimates the cost of basketball, football and hockey games for a family of four at between $214 and $245.

31   I recently commented to Checketts that my own family of four had attended just one major-league game last summer but a dozen games at Yogi Berra Stadium (ticket price: $4 to $8) on the campus of Montclair State University in New Jersey, one of the many minor-league operations that have flourished in recent years on the periphery of major-league markets. We also made a couple of summer visits to the Garden to see the Liberty of the Women's National Basketball Association, which was more affordable, family-oriented and, to our pleasant surprise, far more integrated than any Knicks' game of the past decade I have been to.

32   Checketts said he understood what I was getting at, but added that this was not distressing news. No matter which events my young children are taken to, he said, they are being turned into sports fans. They will, before long, spend their own money at the ball parks and arenas. Or they will ante up to watch on pay TV, another unavoidable 21st-century revenue stream that men like Murdoch and Cablevision's Charles Dolan and Disney's Michael Eisner are factoring into their expansion outlay. As long as there is a next generation, Checketts was saying, there will be a game.

33   "I'm not trying to defend sports as untouchable," he said. "But sometimes it seems as if there's an insatiable appetite for more."

34   And in such a competitive marketplace, please be aware that you will notice an increase in your bill, because it is generally assumed that you are crazy for sports—or rich.

Source: Harvey Araton, "Bizball," in the *New York Times Sunday Magazine*, Oct. 18, 1998.

DISCUSSION QUESTIONS

1. Araton embeds his explicit central claim within his lengthy introductory narrative regarding sports fan Michelle: "I have known few, if any, more involved fans during my sportswriting career than Michelle, who, to me, represents the endangered spirit of an industry that keeps getting bigger and, admittedly, better in many qualitative ways." But these introductory paragraphs (Par. 1–7) also implicitly reflect a considerable amount of information about Araton's position. What elements of style, tone, diction, and figurative language are clues to this position?

2. In Par. 15–21, Araton provides a thumbnail survey of how sports have changed in recent decades. One of his examples concerns the changing attitudes toward sports heroes among young fans. In Par. 21, Araton writes of these fans ("the young channel surfers"): "They have learned to define change as a way of life, and in a nation of so many single-parent homes, what's the big deal, anyway, of having a sports hero walk out after a championship season when Daddy has already traded in Mom?"
As support to the secondary factual argument that sports have changed, how reasonable and effective is this statement? Do you find the lack of evidence acceptable? Are there other examples in the argument of similarly supported statements?

3. Discuss with some classmates the effectiveness of Araton's reference to himself, his friends, his family. How does this affect your response to the argument? If Araton had written from the "we" point of view (as Mosher does in "Where Have All the Heroes Gone?"), would the effect have been different?

4. In Par. 25, Araton offers two causal explanations to the ratings decline in televised sports. What are the two explanations? How would both of these speculations need to be supported in order to be reasonable causal arguments?

5. What do you think are the strongest parts of this argument? The weakest?

SUGGESTIONS FOR WRITING (15.6)

1. Choose a sports event that was particularly memorable to you—as a spectator or participant. Write a two-page argument (probably interpretive, evaluative, or causal) explaining its significance to you. Your argument should include a factual description of the event.

2. Using the steps included in Suggestion #2 of "Finding a Claim" in Chapter 3, derive a focused working claim regarding the differences between professional and amateur sports. Submit your list of increasingly narrowed claims to your instructor.

3. Write a one-paragraph description of the audience Araton seems to have addressed.
   Then write a one-paragraph description of an audience different in every regard (age, gender, education level, etc.). Make a list of the changes you would make in Araton's argument for this audience (keeping the central claim the same).

4. Do you think the huge salaries in mainstream professional sports make it easier or harder for sports stars to be true heroes? Beginning with a stipulative definition of "hero," write a causal argument answering this question.

16

Work

INTRODUCTION

Of all the subjects treated in this reader, perhaps the one that you take least for granted is the subject of work—particularly as it applies to your future. In fact, most of you are in college and even taking this course in order to prepare for your full-time entry into the world of work. Some people know from an early age what they're going to do when they grow up; others graduate from college and even graduate school still uncertain about what line of work they are going to commit some 80,000 hours of their waking lives to. It's one of the most difficult decisions we make in our lives, and in this new millennium, the decision is getting harder and harder. Now more than ever in history, with breathtaking changes in technology, the global economy, and knowledge in general, it is almost impossible to predict with certainty what and where the jobs of the future will be.

Which is not to say that pundits aren't making these predictions liberally. As always at times of momentous transition (in this case, the turn of a century and a millennium), would-be prophets abound, with analysts of every ilk forecasting dramatic transformations in every quarter of life. And a favorite theme of the current crop of fortune tellers is the future of work. However different their crystal balls may look, there is consensus about one thing: the current landscape of work—the nature of jobs, the pay and prestige associated with them, the places where they're done—is going to be completely redrawn within a relatively short period of time.

The first three arguments in this section take three very different positions about what work will look like, where the jobs will be, and who will be doing them in this new century. Reading them may not give you clear-cut answers about the future and how you may fit into it, but it will help you take the long view on the subject, which can be useful when you're stuck in the personal and specific.

And as an antidote to the long view, this unit also contains essays about the actual jobs that some individuals have selected—about the frustrations and satisfactions of these jobs, as well as about the process by which they were chosen. While it is important to make a career choice with some understanding of the likely trends and patterns in technology and the economy, sometimes, as this second group of essays demonstrates, the best career choices are not the result of careful, conscious planning, but the ones we seem to fall into accidentally. However we get there, the most successful career choices are always those that allow us to express ourselves and to do the work with dignity, care, and self-respect.

THE THREE JOBS OF THE FUTURE

ROBERT B. REICH

"The Three Jobs of the Future" is the last chapter of Robert Reich's book The Work of Nations: Preparing Ourselves for 21st Century Capitalism. *As the book's title suggests, Reich's argument is concerned with predicting the future. Briefly, the book claims that the current trend toward economic and social globalization will completely reconfigure the landscape of work in the next century. Reich, formerly President Clinton's Secretary of Labor, is one of a growing number of analysts seeking to predict the long-term effects of today's economic and technological forces.*

COMMENTARY

Reich's identification of "the three jobs of the future" is essentially a factual argument, though it is predicated upon an argument of effect. That argument of effect claims that the emerging "transnational" economy (cause) requires that we redefine "the work that Americans do in terms of categories that reflect their real competitive positions in the global economy" (effect). This argument of effect, while clearly stated, lacks the development and support that you have learned to expect from effective causal arguments. Note that Reich does little to establish the existence of his cause through factual support, and that he does not articulate the link between cause and effect. However, this causal claim is not the center of his argument, but rather a way of moving him to the central claim, which is the factual claim that "Three broad categories of work are emerging, corresponding to the three different competitive positions in which Americans find themselves" (Par. 9).

Reich develops this factual argument in two ways. First, he offers extended definitions of each of these three categories of work; second, he demonstrates that specific kinds of jobs do fit within the categories he defines. This demonstration takes the form of the classical syllogism (see Chapter 5), in which

Category 1 = X (the definition of the category)
Jobs 1, 2, 3 . . . = X
therefore Jobs 1, 2, 3 . . . = Category 1

Reich's definitions of each category (Par. 9, 16, and 20) constitute the major premises; the enumerations of the different jobs that match with that definition are the minor premises (Par. 10–12, 17–10, and 20–27, respectively); and, as is often the case in syllogistic reasoning, the conclusions of each syllogism are implied.

Chapter 5 tells you that for a syllogism to be true, it must contain true premises (i.e., factual assertions). In this case, the major premise is a stipulative definition. But it differs from the kind of stipulative definition discussed in Chapter 5, in that Reich is stipulating, or coining, both the term (category) and its definition. It is as if he were saying, "Let this new breed of daffodils be known as *splzzytum.*" Generally, such stipulative definitions are accepted for the sake of argument. Here, there is no reason to object to Reich's claim that the first category, "routine production services," will stand for those tasks that are done "over and over—one step in a sequence of steps for producing finished products tradable in world commerce" (Par. 10).

We can now proceed to evaluate the minor premise. What we're looking for here is correspondence between the jobs Reich enumerates ("traditional blue-collar jobs" and "routine supervisory jobs performed by low- and mid-level managers . . . involving repetitive checks on subordinates' work and the enforcement of standard operating procedures") (Par. 10) and his definition of "routine production services." An example of Reich's development of the minor premise occurs in paragraph 12, where he describes the job of data processors in such a way that it corresponds perfectly with the definition of "routine production services" offered in paragraph 10 and following.

Reich repeats this syllogistic pattern with his next two categories—"in-person services" and "symbolic analytic services"—offering as well certain exceptions to the categories and instances of overlap between them.

THE THREE JOBS OF THE FUTURE

1 The usual discussion about the future of the American economy focuses on topics like the competitiveness of General Motors, or of the American automobile industry, or, more broadly, of American manufacturing, or, more broadly still, of the American economy. But, as has been observed, these categories are becoming irrelevant. They assume the continued existence of an American economy in which jobs associated with a particular firm, industry, or sector are somehow connected within the borders of the nation, so that American workers face a common fate; and a common enemy as well: The battle-fields of world trade pit our corporations and our workers unambiguously against theirs.

2 No longer. In the emerging international economy, few American companies and industries compete against foreign companies and industries—if by *American* we mean where the work is done and the value is added. Becoming more typical is the global web, perhaps headquartered in and receiving much of its financial capital from the United States, but with research, design, and production facilities spread over Japan, Europe, and North America; additional production facilities in Southeast Asia and Latin

America; marketing and distribution centers on every continent; and lenders and investors in Taiwan, Japan, and West Germany as well as the United States. This ecumenical company competes with similarly ecumenical companies headquartered in other nations. Battle lines no longer correspond with national borders.

3   So, when an "American" company like General Motors shows healthy profits, this is good news for its strategic brokers in Detroit and its American investors. It is also good news for other GM executives worldwide and for GM's global employees, subcontractors, and investors. But it is not necessarily good news for a lot of routine assembly-line workers in Detroit, because there are not likely to be many of them left in Detroit, or anywhere else in America. Nor is it necessarily good news for the few Americans who are still working on assembly lines in the United States, who increasingly receive their paychecks from corporations based in Tokyo or Bonn.

4   The point is that Americans are becoming part of an international labor market, encompassing Asia, Africa, Latin America, Western Europe, and, increasingly, Eastern Europe and the Soviet Union. The competitiveness of Americans in this global market is coming to depend, not on the fortunes of any American corporation or on American industry, but on the functions that Americans perform—the value they add—within the global economy. Other nations are undergoing precisely the same transformation, some more slowly than the United States, but all participating in essentially the same transnational trend. Barriers to cross-border flows of knowledge, money, and tangible products are crumbling; groups of people in every nation are joining global webs. In a very few years, there will be virtually no way to distinguish one national economy from another except by the exchange rates of their currencies—and even this distinction may be on the wane.

5   Americans thus confront global competition ever more directly, unmediated by national institutions. As we discard vestigial notions of the competitiveness of American corporations, American industry, and the American economy, and recast them in terms of the competitiveness of the American work force, it becomes apparent that successes or failures will not be shared equally by all our citizens.

6   Some Americans, whose contributions to the global economy are more highly valued in world markets, will succeed, while others, whose contributions are deemed far less valuable, fail. GM's American executives may become more competitive even as GM's American production workers become less so, because the functions performed by the former group are more highly valued in the world market than those of the latter. So when we speak of the "competitiveness" of Americans in general, we are talking only about how much the world is prepared to spend, *on average,* for services performed by Americans. Some Americans may command much higher rewards; others, far lower. No longer are Americans rising or falling together, as if in one large national boat. We are, increasingly, in different, smaller boats.

2

7   In order to see in greater detail what is happening to American jobs and to understand why the economic fates of Americans are beginning to diverge, it is first necessary to view the work that Americans do in terms of categories that reflect their real competitive positions in the global economy.

8   Official data about American jobs are organized by categories that are not very helpful in this regard. The U.S. Bureau of the Census began inquiring about American jobs in 1820, and developed a systematic way of categorizing them in 1870. Beginning in 1943, the Census came up with a way of dividing these categories into different levels of "social-economic status," depending upon, among other things, the prestige and income associated with each job. In order to determine the appropriate groupings, the Census first divided all American jobs into either business class or working class—the same two overarching categories the Lynns had devised for their study of Middletown— and then divided each of these, in turn, into

subcategories.[1] In 1950, the Census added the category of "service workers" and called the resulting scheme America's "Major Occupational Groups," which it has remained ever since. All subsequent surveys have been based on this same set of categories. Thus, even by 1990, in the eyes of the Census, you were either in a "managerial and professional specialty," in a "technical, sales, and administrative support" role, in a "service occupation," an "operator, fabricator, and laborer," or "transportation and material moving" occupation.

9   This set of classifications made sense when the economy was focused on high-volume, standardized production, in which almost every job fit into, or around, the core American corporation, and when status and income depended on one's ranking in the standard corporate bureaucracy. But these categories have little bearing upon the competitive positions of Americans worldwide, now that America's core corporations are transforming into finely spun global webs. Someone whose job falls officially into a "technical" or "sales" subcategory may, in fact, be among the best-paid and most influential people in such a web. To understand the real competitive positions of Americans in the global economy, it is necessary to devise new categories.[2]

10   Essentially, three broad categories of work are emerging, corresponding to the three different competitive positions in which Americans find themselves. The same three categories are taking shape in other nations. Call them *routine production services, in-person services,* and *symbolic-analytic services.*

Routine production services entail the   11
kinds of repetitive tasks performed by the old foot soldiers of American capitalism in the high-volume enterprise. They are done over and over—one step in a sequence of steps for producing finished products tradeable in world commerce. Although often thought of as traditional blue-collar jobs, they also include routine supervisory jobs performed by low- and mid-level managers—foremen, line managers, clerical supervisors, and section chiefs—involving repetitive checks on subordinates' work and the enforcement of standard operating procedures.

Routine production services are found   12
in many places within a modern economy apart from older, heavy industries (which, like elderly citizens, have been given the more delicate, and less terminal, appellation: "mature"). They are found even amid the glitter and glitz of high technology. Few tasks are more tedious and repetitive, for example, than stuffing computer circuit boards or devising routine coding for computer software programs.

Indeed, contrary to prophets of the "in-   13
formation age" who buoyantly predicted an abundance of high-paying jobs even for people with the most basic of skills, the sobering truth is that many information-processing jobs fit easily into this category. The foot soldiers of the information economy are hordes of data processors stationed in "back offices" at computer terminals linked to worldwide information banks. They routinely enter data into computers or take it out again—records of credit card purchases and payments, credit reports,

[1]   See Alba M. Edwards, *U.S. Census of Population, 1940: Comparative Occupation Statistics, 1870–1940* (Washington, D.C.: U.S. Government Printing Office, 1943).

[2]   Because much of the information about the American work force must be gleaned from the old categories, however, the only way to discover who fits into which new category is to decompose the government's data into the smallest subcategories in which they are collected, then reorder the subcategories according to which new functional group they appear to belong in. For a similar methodology, see Steven A. Sass, "The U.S. Professional Sector: 1950 to 1988," *New England Economic Review,* January–February 1990, pp. 37–55.

checks that have cleared, customer ac-counts, customer correspondence, payroll, hospital billings, patient records, medical claims, court decisions, subscriber lists, personnel, library catalogues, and so forth. The "information revolution" may have rendered some of us more productive, but it has also produced huge piles of raw data which must be processed in much the same monotonous way that assembly-line work-ers and, before them, textile workers processed piles of other raw materials.

14   Routine producers typically work in the company of many other people who do the same thing, usually within large enclosed spaces. They are guided on the job by stan-dard procedures and codified rules, and even their overseers are overseen, in turn, by people who routinely monitor—often with the aid of computers—how much they do and how accurately they do it. Their wages are based either on the amount of time they put in or on the amount of work they do.

15   Routine producers usually must be able to read and to perform simple computa-tions. But their cardinal virtues are reliabil-ity, loyalty, and the capacity to take direc-tion. Thus does a standard American education, based on the traditional premises of American education, normally suffice.

16   By 1990, routine production work com-prised about one-quarter of the jobs per-formed by Americans, and the number was declining. Those who dealt with metal were mostly white and male; those who dealt with fabrics, circuit boards, or information were mostly black or Hispanic, and female; their supervisors, white males.[3]

17   *In-person services,* the second kind of work that Americans do, also entail simple and repetitive tasks. And like routine pro-duction services, the pay of in-person servers is a function of hours worked or amount of work performed; they are closely supervised (as are their supervisors), and they need not have acquired much educa-tion (at most, a high school diploma, or its equivalent, and some vocational training).

18   The big difference between in-person servers and routine producers in that *these* services must be provided person-to-person, and thus are not sold worldwide. (In-person servers might, of course, work for global cor-porations. Two examples: In 1988, Britain's Blue Arrow PLC acquired Manpower Inc., which provides custodial services through-out the United States. Meanwhile, Den-mark's ISS-AS already employed over 16,000 Americans to clean office buildings in most major American cities.) In-person servers are in direct contact with the ultimate beneficiaries of their work; their immediate objects are specific customers rather than streams of metal, fabric, or data. In-person servers work alone or in small teams. In-cluded in this category are retail sales work-ers, waiters and waitresses, hotel workers, janitors, cashiers, hospital attendants and orderlies, nursing-home aides, child-care workers, house cleaners, home health-care aides, taxi drivers, secretaries, hairdressers, auto mechanics, sellers of residential real es-tate, flight attendants, physical therapists, and—among the fastest growing of all—security guards.

19   In-person servers are supposed to be as punctual, reliable, and tractable as routine production workers. But many in-person servers share one additional requirement: They must also have a pleasant demeanor. They must smile and exude confidence and good cheer, even when they feel morose. They must be courteous and helpful, even to the most obnoxious of patrons. Above all, they must make others feel happy and at ease. It should come as no surprise that, tra-ditionally, most in-person servers have been women. The cultural stereotype of women

---

[3] For an illuminating discussion of routine jobs in a high-technology industry, see D. O'Connor, "Women Workers in the Changing International Division of Labor in Microelectronics," in L. Benerici and C. Stimpson (eds.), *Women, Households, and the Economy* (New Brunswick, N.J.: Rutgers University Press, 1987).

as nurturers—as mommies—has opened countless in-person service jobs to them.[4]

20   By 1990, in-person services accounted for about 30 percent of the jobs performed by Americans, and their numbers were growing rapidly. For example, Beverly Enterprises, a single nursing-home chain operating throughout the United States, employed about the same number of Americans as the entire Chrysler Corporation (115,174 and 116,250, respectively)—although most Americans were far more knowledgeable about the latter, including the opinions of its chairman. In the United States during the 1980s, well over 3 million *new* in-person service jobs were created in fast-food outlets, bars, and restaurants. This was more than the *total* number of routine production jobs still existing in America by the end of the decade in the automobile, steelmaking, and textile industries combined.[5]

21   *Symbolic-analytic services,* the third job category, include all the problem-solving, problem-identifying, and strategic-brokering activities we have examined in previous chapters. Like routine production services (but *unlike* in-person services), symbolic-analytic services can be traded worldwide and thus must compete with foreign providers even in the American market. But they do not enter world commerce as standardized things. Traded instead are the manipulations of symbols—data, words, oral and visual representations.

22   Included in this category are the problem-solving, identifying, and brokering of many people who call themselves research scientists, design engineers, software engineers, civil engineers, biotechnology engineers, sound engineers, public relations executives, investment bankers, lawyers, real estate developers, and even a few creative accountants. Also included is much of the work done by management consultants, financial consultants, tax consultants, energy consultants, agricultural consultants, armaments consultants, architectural consultants, management information specialists, organization development specialists, strategic planners, corporate headhunters, and systems analysts. Also: advertising executives and marketing strategists, art directors, architects, cinematographers, film editors, production designers, publishers, writers and editors, journalists, musicians, television and film producers, and even university professors.

23   Symbolic analysts solve, identify, and broker problems by manipulating symbols. They simplify reality into abstract images that can be rearranged, juggled, experimented with, communicated to other specialists, and then, eventually, transformed back into reality. The manipulations are done with analytic tools, sharpened by experience. The tools may be mathematical algorithms, legal arguments, financial gimmicks, scientific principles, psychological insights about how to persuade or to amuse, systems of induction or deduction, or any other set of techniques for doing conceptual puzzles.

24   Some of these manipulations reveal how to more efficiently deploy resources or shift financial assets, or otherwise save time and energy. Other manipulations yield new inventions—technological marvels, innovative legal arguments, new advertising ploys for convincing people that certain amusements have become life necessities. Still other manipulations—of sounds, words, pictures— serve to entertain their recipients, or cause them to reflect more deeply on their lives or on the human condition. Others grab money from people too slow or naïve to protect themselves by manipulating in response.

25   Like routine producers, symbolic analysts rarely come into direct contact with

---

[4] On this point, see Arlie Russell Hochschild, *The Managed Heart: The Commercialization of Human Feeling* (Berkeley: University of California Press, 1983).

[5] U.S. Department of Commerce, Bureau of Labor Statistics, various issues.

the ultimate beneficiaries of their work. But other aspects of their work life are quite different from that experienced by routine producers. Symbolic analysts often have partners or associates rather than bosses or supervisors. Their incomes may vary from time to time, but are not directly related to how much time they put in or the quantity of work they put out. Income depends, rather, on the quality, originality, cleverness, and, occasionally, speed with which they solve, identify, or broker new problems. Their careers are not linear or hierarchical; they rarely proceed along well-defined paths to progressively higher levels of responsibilities and income. In fact, symbolic analysts may take on vast responsibilities and command inordinate wealth at rather young ages. Correspondingly, they may lose authority and income if they are no longer able to innovate by building on their cumulative experience, even if they are quite senior.

26   Symbolic analysts often work alone or in small teams, which may be connected to larger organizations, including worldwide webs. Teamwork is often critical. Since neither problems nor solutions can be defined in advance, frequent and informal conversations help ensure that insights and discoveries are put to their best uses and subjected to quick, critical evaluation.[6]

27   When not conversing with their teammates, symbolic analysts sit before computer terminals—examining words and numbers, moving them, altering them, trying out new words and numbers, formulating and testing hypotheses, designing or strategizing. They also spend long hours in meetings or on the telephone, and even longer hours in jet planes and hotels—advising, making presentations, giving briefings, doing deals. Periodically, they issue reports, plans, designs, drafts, memoranda, layouts, renderings, scripts, or projections—which, in turn, precipitate more meetings to clarify what has been proposed and to get agreement on how it will be implemented, by whom, and for how much money. Final production is often the easiest part. The bulk of the time and cost (and, thus, real value) comes in conceptualizing the problem, devising a solution, and planning its execution.

28   Most symbolic analysts have graduated from four-year colleges or universities; many have graduate degrees as well. The vast majority are white males, but the proportion of white females is growing, and there is a small, but slowly increasing, number of blacks and Hispanics among them. All told, symbolic analysis currently accounts for no more than 20 percent of American jobs. The proportion of American workers who fit this category has increased substantially since the 1950s (by my calculation, no more than 8 percent of American workers could be classified as symbolic analysts at midcentury), but the pace slowed considerably in the 1980s—even though certain symbolic-analytic jobs, like law and investment banking, mushroomed. (I will return to this point later.)[7]

3

29   These three functional categories cover more than three out of four American jobs. Among the remainder are farmers, miners, and other extractors of natural resources,

---

[6] The physical environments in which symbolic analysts work are substantially different from those in which routing producers or in-person servers work. Symbolic analysts usually labor within spaces that are quiet and tastefully decorated. Soft lights, wall-to-wall carpeting, beige and puce colors are preferred. Such calm surroundings typically are encased within tall steel-and-glass buildings or within long, low, postmodernist-structures carved into hillsides and encircled by expanses of well-manicured lawn.

[7] Sass's definition of "professional worker" overlaps significantly with my definition of symbolic analyst (although, as I will explain, not all symbolic analysts are professionals, and not all professionals are symbolic analysts). Sass finds that by 1988 professional workers comprised 20 percent of the American labor force. See Sass, op. cit.

who together comprise less than 5 percent of American workers. The rest are mainly government employees (including public school teachers), employees in regulated industries (like utility workers), and government-financed workers (American engineers working on defense weapons systems and physicians working off Medicaid and Medicare), almost all of whom are also sheltered from global competition.

Some traditional job categories—managerial, secretarial, sales, and so on—overlap with more than one of these functional categories. The traditional categories, it should be emphasized, date from an era in which most jobs were as standardized as the products they helped create. Such categories are no longer very helpful for determining what a person actually does on the job and how much that person is likely to earn for doing it. Only some of the people who are classified as "secretaries," for example, perform strictly routine production work, such as entering and retrieving data from computers. Other "secretaries" provide in-person services, like making appointments and fetching coffee. A third group of "secretaries" perform symbolic-analytic work closely allied to what their bosses do. To classify them all as "secretaries" glosses over their very different functions in the economy. Similarly, "sales" jobs can fall within any one of the three functional groups: some salespeople simply fill quotas and orders; others spend much of their time performing in-person services, like maintaining machinery; and some are sophisticated problem-identifiers no different from high-priced management consultants. "Computer programmers" (one of the more recent additions to the standard list of occupations) are as varied: They might be doing routine coding, in-person troubleshooting for particular clients, or translating complex functional specifications into software.

That a job category is officially classified "professional" or "managerial" likewise has little bearing upon the function its occupant actually performs in the world economy. Not all professionals, that is, are symbolic analysts. Some lawyers spend their entire working lives doing things that normal people would find unbearably monotonous—cranking out the same old wills, contracts, and divorces, over and over, with only the names changed. Some accountants do routine audits without the active involvement of their cerebral cortices. Some managers take no more responsibility than noting who shows up for work in the morning, making sure they stay put, and locking the place up at night. (I have even heard tell of university professors who deliver the same lectures for thirty years, long after their brains have atrophied, but I do not believe such stories.) None of these professionals is a symbolic analyst.[8]

Nor are all symbolic analysts professionals. In the older, high-volume economy, a "professional" was one who had mastered a particular domain of knowledge. The knowledge existed in advance, ready to be mastered. It had been recorded in dusty tomes or codified in precise rules and formulae. Once the novitiate had dutifully absorbed the knowledge and had passed an examination attesting to its absorption, professional status was automatically conferred—usually through a ceremony of appropriately medieval pageantry and costume. The professional was then authorized to place a few extra letters after his or her name, mount a diploma on the office wall, join the professional association and attend

---

[8] In the remainder of this book when discussing symbolic analysts, I shall, on occasion, illustrate my point by referring to lawyers, management consultants, software engineers, and other professionals, but the reader should understand that this is a shorthand method of describing only the symbolic and analytic work undertaken by such professionals.

its yearly tax-deductible meeting in Palm Springs, and pursue clients with a minimum of overt avarice.

33   But in the new economy—replete with unidentified problems, unknown solutions, and untried means of putting them together—mastery of old domains of knowledge isn't nearly enough to guarantee a good income. Nor, importantly, is it even necessary. Symbolic analysts often can draw upon established bodies of knowledge with the flick of a computer key. Facts, codes, formulae, and rules are easily accessible. What is much more valuable is the capacity to effectively and creatively *use* the knowledge. Possessing a professional credential is no guarantee of such capacity. Indeed, a professional education which has emphasized the rote acquisition of such knowledge over original thought may retard such capacity in later life.

Source: Robert B. Reich, "The Three Jobs of the Future," in *The Work of Nations: Preparing Ourselves for 21st Century Capitalism.* New York: Knopf, 1991 pp. 171–182.

DISCUSSION QUESTIONS

1. Make a list of the definition strategies Reich uses for each of his three definitions. Can you think of any other strategies (see Chapter 4) that he might have used?

2. Using specific examples, characterize the tone of the argument. Is the tone uniform throughout? Does it make Reich's argument more or less effective?

3. To what extent is Reich's argument weakened by its failure to develop its initial argument of effect? Is this an instance where the truth of the causal claim is so obvious that it doesn't require support?

4. With a group of your classmates, prepare a list of approximately 30 jobs. Does each one of these jobs fit neatly within one of Reich's three categories? If not, is this evidence that Reich's argument is faulty?

5. Reich goes to considerable lengths to recategorize the jobs that we do. With a group of your classmates, discuss the reasons for the recategorization. What purposes are served by this new classification system? How might it change the way we think about work, the way we reward certain jobs more than others?

SUGGESTIONS FOR WRITING (16.1)

1. Write a four- to five-page argument that classifies a particular group into three categories (you could categorize the students in this class, the music you listen to, clothing styles on your campus). Include extended definitions of each category and the kind of syllogistic reasoning that Reich uses.

2. After you have written the argument in Suggestion #1, and before you hand it in to your instructor, trade papers with a classmate and write a two- to three-page analysis of his or her argument, using the commentary before Reich's essay as a model.

3. Write a two-page argument based on electronically conducted research claiming that Reich is or is not a credible authority on the subjects of the economy and the labor force.

4. As a college student soon to embark on a full-time career, you may have found Reich's essay to be of particular interest. Write a three-page causal argument describing how this argument could influence your choice of career.

THE END OF WORK

JEREMY RIFKIN

"The End of Work" is the first chapter of Jeremy Rifkin's 1996 book The End of Work: the Decline of the Global Labor Force and the Dawn of the Post-Market Era. *Like Robert Reich, Rifkin writes about the dramatic changes occurring in the nature of work. While Reich's redrawing of the categories of American workers is comparatively optimistic, Rifkin paints a bleaker picture of the future of work: technology may eliminate work altogether for millions of workers worldwide.*

Jeremy Rifkin is an economist, philosopher, and activist with a long list of books to his credit on such wide-ranging topics as the beef industry, biotechnology, and entropy.

1   From the beginning, civilization has been structured, in large part, around the concept of work. From the Paleolithic hunter/gatherer and Neolithic farmer to the medieval craftsman and assembly line worker of the current century, work has been an integral part of daily existence. Now, for the first time, human labor is being systematically eliminated from the production process. Within less than a century, "mass" work in the market sector is likely to be phased out in virtually all of the industrialized nations of the world. A new generation of sophisticated information and communication technologies is being hurried into a wide variety of work situations. Intelligent machines are replacing human beings in countless tasks, forcing millions of blue and white collar workers into unemployment lines, or worse still, breadlines.

2   Our corporate leaders and mainstream economists tell us that the rising unemployment figures represent short-term "adjustments" to powerful market-driven forces that are speeding the global economy into a Third Industrial Revolution. They hold out the promise of an exciting new world of high-tech automated production, booming global commerce, and unprecedented material abundance.

3   Millions of working people remain skeptical. Every week more employees learn they are being let go. In offices and factories around the world, people wait, in fear, hoping to be spared one more day. Like a deadly epidemic, inexorably working its way through the marketplace, the strange, seemingly inexplicable new economic disease spreads, destroying lives and destabilizing whole communities in its wake. In the United States, corporations are eliminating more than 2 million jobs annually.[1] In Los Angeles, the First Interstate Bankcorp, the nation's thirteenth-largest bank holding company, recently restructured its operations, eliminating 9,000 jobs, more than 25 percent of its workforce. In Columbus, Indiana, Arvin Industries streamlined its automotive components factory and gave out pink slips to nearly 10 percent of its employees. In Danbury, Connecticut, Union Carbide re-engineered its production, administration, and distribution systems to trim excess fat and save $575 million in costs by 1995. In the process, more than 13,900 workers, nearly 22 percent of its labor force, were cut from the company payroll. The company is expected to cut an additional 25 percent of its employees before it finishes "re-inventing" itself in the next two years.[2]

[1] "When Will the Layoffs End?" *Fortune*, September 20, 1993, p. 40.

4   Hundreds of other companies have also announced layoffs. GTE recently cut 17,000 employees. NYNEX Corp said it was eliminating 16,800 workers. Pacific Telesis has riffed more than 10,000. "Most of the cuts," reports *The Wall Street Journal*, "are facilitated, one way or another, by new software programs, better computer networks and more powerful hardware" that allow companies to do more work with fewer workers.[3]

5   While some new jobs are being created in the U.S. economy, they are in the low-paying sectors and generally temporary employment. In April of 1994, two thirds of the new jobs created in the country were at the bottom of the wage pyramid. Meanwhile, the outplacement firm of Challenger, Gray and Christmas reported that in the first quarter of 1994, layoffs from big corporations were running 13 percent over 1993, with industry analysts predicting even steeper cuts in payrolls in the coming months and years.[4]

6   The loss of well-paying jobs is not unique to the American economy. In Germany, Siemens, the electronics and engineering giant, has flattened its corporate management structure, cut costs by 20 to 30 percent in just three years, and eliminated more than 16,000 employees around the world. In Sweden, the $7.9 billion Stockholm-based food cooperative, ICA, re-engineered its operations, installing a state-of-the-art computer inventory system. The new laborsaving technology allowed the food company to shut down a third of its warehouses and distribution centers, cutting its overall costs in half. In the process, ICA was able to eliminate more than 5,000 employees, or 30 percent of its wholesale workforce, in just three years,

while revenues grew by more than 15 percent. In Japan, the telecommunications company NTT announced its intentions to cut 10,000 employees in 1993, and said that, as part of its restructuring program, staff would eventually be cut by 30,000—15 percent of its workforce.[5]

7   The ranks of the unemployed and underemployed are growing daily in North America, Europe, and Japan. Even developing nations are facing increasing technological unemployment as transnational companies build state-of-the-art high-tech production facilities all over the world, letting go millions of laborers who can no longer compete with the cost efficiency, quality control, and speed of delivery achieved by automated manufacturing. In more and more countries the news is filled with talk about lean production, re-engineering, total quality management, post-Fordism, decruiting, and downsizing. Everywhere men and women are worried about their future. The young are beginning to vent their frustration and rage in increasing antisocial behavior. Older workers, caught between a prosperous past and a bleak future, seem resigned, feeling increasingly trapped by social forces over which they have little or no control. Throughout the world there is a sense of momentous change taking place—change so vast in scale that we are barely able to fathom its ultimate impact. Life as we know it is being altered in fundamental ways.

Substituting Software for Employees

8   While earlier industrial technologies replaced the physical power of human labor, substituting machines for body and brawn, the new computer-based technologies

[2] Ibid., pp. 54–56.

[3] "Retooling Lives: Technological Gains Are Cutting Costs, and Jobs, in Services," *Wall Street Journal*, February 24, 1994, p. A1.

[4] "Strong Employment Gains Spur Inflation Worries," *Washington Post*, May 7, 1994, pp. A1, A9.

[5] "Siemens Plans New Job Cuts as Part of Cost Reductions," *New York Times*, July 6, 1993, p. D4; "On the Continent, a New Era Is Also Dawning," *Business Week*, June 14, 1993, p. 41; "NT T's Cut of 10,000 Jobs Could Pave Way for Others," *Financial Times*, September 1, 1993, p. 5.

promise a replacement of the human mind itself, substituting thinking machines for human beings across the entire gamut of economic activity. The implications are profound and far-reaching. To begin with, more than 75 percent of the labor force in most industrial nations engage in work that is little more than simple repetitive tasks. Automated machinery, robots, and increasingly sophisticated computers can perform many if not most of these jobs. In the United States alone, that means that in the years ahead more than 90 million jobs in a labor force of 124 million are potentially vulnerable to replacement by machines. With current surveys showing that less than 5 percent of companies around the world have even begun to make the transaction to the new machine culture, massive unemployment of a kind never before experienced seems all but inevitable in the coming decades.[6] Reflecting on the significance of the transition taking place, the distinguished Nobel laureate economist Wassily Leontief has warned that with the introduction of increasingly sophisticated computers, "the role of humans as the most important factor of production is bound to diminish in the same way that the role of horses in agricultural production was first diminished and then eliminated by the introduction of tractors."[7]

9   Caught in the throes of increasing global competition and rising costs of labor, multinational corporations seem determined to hasten the transition from human workers to machine surrogates. Their revolutionary ardor has been fanned, of late, by compelling bottom-line considerations. In Europe, where rising labor costs are blamed for a stagnating economy and a loss of competitiveness in world markets, companies are hurrying to replace their workforce with the new information and telecommunication technologies. In the United States, labor costs in the past eight years have more than

tripled relative to the cost of capital equipment. (Although real wages have failed to keep up with inflation and in fact have been dropping, employment benefits, especially health-care costs, have been rising sharply.) Anxious to cut costs and improve profit margins, companies have been substituting machines for human labor at an accelerating rate. Typical is Lincoln Electric, a manufacturer of industrial motors in Cleveland, which announced plans to increase its capital expenditures in 1993 by 30 percent over its 1992 level. Lincoln's assistant to the CEO, Richard Sobow, reflects the thinking of many others in the business community when he says, "We tend to make a capital investment before hiring a new worker."[8]

10   Although corporations spent more than a trillion dollars in the 1980s on computers, robots, and other automated equipment, it has been only in the past few years that these massive expenditures have begun to pay off in terms of increased productivity, reduced labor costs, and greater profits. As long as management attempted to graft the new technologies onto traditional organizational structures and processes, the state-of-the-art computer and information tools were stymied, unable to perform effectively and to their full capacity. Recently, however, corporations have begun to restructure the workplace to make it compatible with the high-tech machine culture.

Re-engineering

11   "Re-engineering" is sweeping through the corporate community, making true believers out of even the most recalcitrant CEOs. Companies are quickly restructuring their organizations to make them computer friendly. In the process, they are eliminating layers of traditional management, compressing job categories, creating work teams, training employees in multilevel skills, shortening and simplifying produc-

[6] "Stanching the Loss of Good Jobs," *New York Times*, January 31, 1993, p. C1.

[7] Leontief, Wassily, *National Perspective: Definition of Problems and Opportunities*, paper presented at the National Academy of Engineering Symposium, June 30, 1983, p. 3.

[8] "Businesses Prefer Buying Equipment to Hiring New Staff," *Wall Street Journal*, September 3, 1993.

tion and distribution processes, and streamlining administration. The results have been impressive. In the United States, overall productivity jumped 2.8 percent in 1992, the largest rise in two decades.[9] The giant strides in productivity have meant wholesale reductions in the workforce. Michael Hammer, a former MIT professor and prime mover in the restructuring of the workplace, says that re-engineering typically results in the loss of more than 40 percent of the jobs in a company and can lead to as much as a 75 percent reduction in a given company's workforce. Middle management is particularly vulnerable to job loss from re-engineering. Hammer estimates that up to 80 percent of those engaged in middle-management tasks are susceptible to elimination.[10]

Across the entire U.S. economy, corporate re-engineering could eliminate between 1 million and 2.5 million jobs a year "for the foreseeable future," according to *The Wall Street Journal*.[11] By the time the first stage of re-engineering runs its course, some studies predict a loss of up to 25 million jobs in a private sector labor force that currently totals around 90 million workers. In Europe and Asia, where corporate restructuring and technology displacement is beginning to have an equally profound impact, industry analysts expect comparable job losses in the years ahead. Business consultants like John C. Skerritt worry about the economic and social consequences of re-engineering. "We can see many, many ways that jobs can be destroyed," says Skerritt, "but we can't see where they will be created." Others, like

John Sculley, formerly of Apple Computer, believe that the "reorganization of work" could be as massive and destabilizing as the advent of the Industrial Revolution. "This may be the biggest social issue of the next 20 years," says Sculley.[12] Hans Olaf Henkel, the CEO of IBM Deutschland, warns, "There is a revolution underway."[13]

Nowhere is the effect of the computer revolution and re-engineering of the workplace more pronounced than in the manufacturing sector. One hundred and forty-seven years after Karl Marx urged the workers of the world to unite, Jacques Attali, a French minister and technology consultant to socialist president François Mitterrand, confidently proclaimed the end of the era of the working man and woman. "Machines are the new proletariat," proclaimed Attali. "The working class is being given its walking papers."[14]

The quickening pace of automation is fast moving the global economy to the day of the workerless factory. Between 1981 and 1991, more than 1.8 million manufacturing jobs disappeared in the U.S.[15] In Germany, manufacturers have been shedding workers even faster, eliminating more than 500,000 jobs in a single twelve-month period between early 1992 and 1993.[16] The decline in manufacturing jobs is part of a long-term trend that has seen the increasing replacement of human beings by machines at the workplace. In the 1950s, 33 percent of all U.S. workers were employed in manufacturing. By the 1960s, the number of manufacturing jobs had dropped to 30 percent, and by the 1980s to 20 percent. Today, less than

[9] "Price of Progress: Re-engineering Gives Firms New Efficiency, Workers the Pink Slip," *Wall Street Journal,* March 16, 1993, p. 1.

[10] "Conference Stresses Job Innovation," *Washington Post*, July 21, 1993, p. D5.; "A Rage to Re-engineer," *Washington Post*, July 25, 1993, p. H1.

[11] Cited in "Into the Dark: Rough Ride Ahead for American Workers," *Training*, July 1993, p. 23.

[12] "Price of Progress."

[13] "Germany Fights Back," *Business Week*, May 31, 1993, p. 48.

[14] Attali, Jacques, *Millennium: Winners and Losers in the Coming World Order* (New York: Random House, 1991), p. 101.

[15] Barlett, Donald L., and Steele, James B., *America: What Went Wrong?* (Kansas City: Andrews and McMeel, 1992), p. xi.

[16] "Germany Fights Back," p. 49.

17 percent of the workforce is engaged in blue collar work. Management consultant Peter Drucker estimates that employment in manufacturing is going to continue dropping to less than 12 percent of the U.S. workforce in the next decade.[17]

15   For most of the 1980s it was fashionable to blame the loss of manufacturing jobs in the United States on foreign competition and cheap labor markets abroad. Recently, however, economists have begun to revise their views in light of new in-depth studies of the U.S. manufacturing sector. Noted economists Paul R. Krugman of MIT and Robert L. Lawrence of Harvard University suggest, on the basis of extensive data, that "the concern, widely voiced during the 1950s and 1960s, that industrial workers would lose their jobs because of automation, is closer to the truth than the current preoccupation with a presumed loss of manufacturing jobs because of foreign competition."[18]

16   Although the number of blue collar workers continues to decline, manufacturing productivity is soaring. In the United States, annual productivity, which was growing at slightly over 1 percent per year in the early 1980s, has climbed to over 3 percent in the wake of the new advances in computer automation and the restructuring of the workplace. From 1979 to 1992, productivity increased by 35 percent in the manufacturing sector while the workforce shrank by 15 percent.[19]

17   William Winpisinger, past president of the International Association of Machinists, a union whose membership has shrunk nearly in half as a result of advances in automation, cites a study by the International Metalworkers Federation in Geneva forecasting that within thirty years, as little as 2 percent of the world's current labor force "will be needed to produce all the goods necessary for total demand."[20] Yoneji Masuda, a principal architect of the Japanese plan to become the first fully computerized information based society, says that "in the near future complete automation of entire plants will come into being, and during the next twenty to thirty years there will probably emerge . . . factories that require no manual labor at all."[21]

18   While the industrial worker is being phased out of the economic process, many economists and elected officials continue to hold out hope that the service sector and white collar work will be able to absorb the millions of unemployed laborers in search of work. Their hopes are likely to be dashed. Automation and re-engineering are already replacing human labor across a wide swath of service related fields. The new "thinking machines" are capable of performing many of the mental tasks now performed by human beings, and at greater speeds. Andersen Consulting Company, one of the world's largest corporate restructuring firms, estimates that in just one service industry, commercial banking and thrift institutions, re-engineering will mean a loss of 30 to 40 percent of the jobs over the next seven years. That translates into nearly 700,000 jobs eliminated.[22]

19   Over the past ten years more than 3 million white collar jobs were eliminated in the United States. Some of these losses, no doubt, were casualties of increased international competition. But as David Churbuck and Jeffrey Young observed in *Forbes*,

[17] Barlett and Steele, p. 18; Drucker, Peter F., *Post-Capitalist Society* (New York: Harper-Collins, 1993), p. 68.

[18] Krugman, Paul, and Lawrence, Robert, "Trade, Jobs and Wages," *Scientific American*, April 1994, pp. 46, 47.

[19] "The Myth of Manufacturing's Decline," *Forbes*, January 18, 1993, p. 40; Judis, John, "The Jobless Recovery," *The New Republic*, March 15, 1993, p. 22.

[20] Winpisinger, William W., *Reclaiming Our Future* (Boulder: Westview Press, 1989), pp. 150–151.

[21] Masuda, Yoneji, *The Information Society as Post-Industrial Society* (Washington, D.C.: World Future Society, 1980), p. 60.

[22] "Price of Progress."

"Technology helped in a big way to make them redundant." Even as the economy rebounded in 1992 with a respectable 2.6 percent growth rate, more than 500,000 additional clerical and technical jobs simply disappeared.[23] Rapid advances in computer technology, including parallel processing and artificial intelligence, are likely to make large numbers of white collar workers redundant by the early decades of the next century.

Many policy analysts acknowledge that large businesses are shedding record numbers of workers but argue that small companies are taking up the slack by hiring on more people. David Birch, a research associate at MIT, was among the first to suggest that new economic growth in the high-tech era is being led by very small firms—companies with under 100 employees. At one point Birch opined that more than 88 percent of all the new job creation was taking place in small businesses, many of whom were on the cutting edge of the new technology revolution. His data were cited by conservative economists during the Reagan-Bush era as proof positive that new technology innovations were creating as many jobs as were being lost to technological displacement. More recent studies, however, have exploded the myth that small businesses are powerful engines of job growth in the high-tech era. Political economist Bennett Harrison, of the H. J. Heinz III School of Public Policy and Management at Carnegie-Mellon University, using statistics garnered from a wide variety of sources, including the International Labor Organization of the United Nations and the U.S. Bureau of the Census, says that in the United States "the propor-

tion of Americans working for small companies and for individual establishments . . . has barely changed at all since at least the early 1960s." The same holds true, according to Harrison, for both Japan and West Germany, the other two major economic superpowers.[24]

The fact is that while less than 1 percent of all U.S. companies employ 500 or more workers, these big firms still employed more than 41 percent of all the workers in the private sector at the end of the last decade. And it is these corporate giants that are re-engineering their operations and letting go a record number of employees.[25]

The current wave of job cuts takes on even greater political significance in light of the tendency among economists continually to revise upward the notion of what is an "acceptable" level of unemployment. As with so many other things in life, we often adjust our expectations for the future, on the basis of the shifting present circumstances we find ourselves in. In the case of jobs, economists have come to play a dangerous game of accommodation with steadily rising unemployment figures, sweeping under the rug the implications of an historical curve that is leading inexorably to a world with fewer and fewer workers.

A survey of the past half-century of economic activity discloses a disturbing trend. In the 1950s the average unemployment for the decade stood at 4.5 percent. In the 1960s unemployment rose to an average of 4.8 percent. In the 1970s it rose again to 6.2 percent, and in the 1980s it increased again, averaging 7.3 percent for the decade. In the first three years of the 1990s, unemployment has averaged 6.6 percent.[26]

[23] Churbuck, David, and Young, Jeffrey, "The Virtual Workplace," *Forbes*, November 23, 1992, p. 186; "New Hiring Should Follow Productivity Gains," *Business Week*, June 14, 1993.

[24] Harrison, Bennett, *Lean and Mean: The Changing Landscape of Corporate Power in the Age of Flexibility* (New York: Basic Books, 1994), pp. 45–47, 51.

[25] U.S. Bureau of Census, 1987 Enterprise Statistics, Company Summary (Washington, D.C.: U.S. Government Printing Office, June 1991), Table 3.

[26] U.S. Department of Labor, Bureau of Labor Statistics, *Employment and Earnings*, January 1994, p. 182; Mishel Lawrence, and Bernstein, Jared, *The Joyless Recovery: Deteriorating Wages and Job Quality in the 1990s* (Washington, D.C.: Economic Policy Institute, Briefing Paper).

24   As the percentage of unemployed workers edged ever higher over the postwar period, economists have changed their assumptions of what constitutes full employment. In the 1950s, 3 percent unemployment was widely regarded as full employment. By the 1960s, the Kennedy and Johnson administrations were touting 4 percent as a full employment goal. In the 1980s, many mainstream economists considered 5 or even 5.5 percent unemployment as near full employment.[27] Now, in the mid-1990s, a growing number of economists and business leaders are once again revising their ideas on what they regard as "natural levels" of unemployment. While they are reluctant to use the term "full employment," many Wall Street analysts argue that unemployment levels should not dip below 6 percent, lest the economy risk a new era of inflation.[28]

25   The steady upward climb in unemployment, in each decade, becomes even more troubling when we add the growing number of part-time workers who are in search of full-time employment and the number of discouraged workers who are no longer looking for a job. In 1993, more than 8.7 million people were unemployed, 6.1 million were working part-time but wanted full-time employment, and more than a million were so discouraged they stopped looking for a job altogether. In total, nearly 16 million American workers, or 13 percent of the labor force, were unemployed or underemployed in 1993.[29]

26   The point that needs to be emphasized is that, even allowing for short-term dips in the unemployment rate, the long-term trend is toward ever higher rates of unemployment. The introduction of more sophisticated technologies, with the accompanying gains in productivity, means that the global economy can produce more and more goods and services employing an ever smaller percentage of the available workforce.

A World Without Workers

27   When the first wave of automation hit the industrial sector in the late 1950s and early 1960s, labor leaders, civil rights activists, and a chorus of social critics were quick to sound the alarm. Their concerns, however, were little shared by business leaders at the time who continued to believe that increases in productivity brought about by the new automated technology would only enhance economic growth and promote increased employment and purchasing power. Today, however, a small but growing number of business executives are beginning to worry about where the new high-technology revolution is leading us. Percy Barnevik is the chief executive officer of Asea Brown Boveri, a 29-billion-dollar-a-year Swiss-Swedish builder of electric generators and transportation systems, and one of the largest engineering firms in the world. Like other global companies, ABB has recently re-engineered its operations, cutting nearly 50,000 workers from the payroll, while increasing turnover 60 percent in the same time period. Barnevik asks, "Where will all these [unemployed] people go?" He predicts that the pro-portion of Europe's labor force employed in manufacturing and business services will decline from 35 percent today to 25 percent in ten years from now, with a further decline to 15 percent twenty years down the road. Barnevik is deeply pessimistic about Europe's future: "If anybody tells me, wait two or three years and there will be a hell of a demand for labor, I say, tell me where? What jobs? In what cities? Which companies? When I add it all together, I find a clear risk that the 10% unemployed or underemployed today could easily become 20 to 25%."[30]

[27] Peterson, Wallace C., *Silent Depression: The Fate of the American Dream* (New York: W. W. Norton & Co., 1994), p. 33.

[28] "The Puzzle of New Jobs: How Many How Fast?" *New York Times*, May 24, 1994, p. D1.

[29] U.S. Bureau of Labor Statistics, *Current Population Survey*, 1993.

[30] "Apocalypse—But Not Just Now," *Financial Times*, January 4, 1993, p. D1.

28   Peter Drucker, whose many books and articles over the years have helped facilitate the new economic reality, says quite bluntly that "the disappearance of labor as a key factor of production" is going to emerge as the critical "unfinished business of capitalist society."[31]

29   For some, particularly the scientists, engineers, and employers, a world without work will signal the beginning of a new era in history in which human beings are liberated, at long last, from a life of backbreaking toil and mindless repetitive tasks. For others, the workerless society conjures up the notion of a grim future of mass unemployment and global destitution, punctuated by increasing social unrest and upheaval. On one point virtually all of the contending parties agree. We are, indeed, entering into a new period in history—one in which machines increasingly replace human beings in the process of making and moving goods and providing services. This realization led the editors of *Newsweek* to ponder the unthinkable in a recent issue dedicated to technological unemployment. "What if there were really no more jobs?" asked *Newsweek*.[32] The idea of a society not based on work is so utterly alien to any notion we have about how to organize large numbers of people into a social whole, that we are faced with the prospect of having to rethink the very basis of the social contract.

30   Most workers feel completely unprepared to cope with the enormity of the transition taking place. The rash of current technological breakthroughs and economic restructuring initiatives seem to have descended on us with little warning. Suddenly, all over the world, men and women are asking if there is a role for them in the new future unfolding across the global economy. Workers with years of education, skills, and experience face the very real prospect of being made redundant by the new forces of automation and information. What just a few short years ago was a rather esoteric debate among intellectuals and a small number of social writers around the role of technology in society is now the topic of heated conversation among millions of working people. They wonder if they will be the next to be replaced by the new thinking machines. In a 1994 survey conducted by *The New York Times,* two out of every five American workers expressed worry that they might be laid off, required to work reduced hours, or be forced to take pay cuts during the next two years. Seventy-seven percent of the respondents said they personally knew of someone who had lost his or her job in the last few years, while 67 percent said that joblessness was having a substantial effect on their communities.[33]

31   In Europe, fear over rising unemployment is leading to widespread social unrest and the emergence of neo-fascist political movements. Frightened, angry voters have expressed their frustration at the ballot box, boosting the electoral fortunes of extreme-right-wing parties in Germany, Italy, and Russia. In Japan, rising concern over unemployment is forcing the major political parties to address the jobs issue for the first time in decades.

32   We are being swept up into a powerful new technology revolution that offers the promise of a great social transformation, unlike any in history. The new high-technology revolution could mean fewer hours of work and greater benefits for millions. For the first time in modern history, large numbers of human beings could be liberated from long hours of labor in the formal marketplace, to be free to pursue leisure-time activities. The same technological forces could, however, as easily lead to growing unemployment and a global depression. Whether a utopian or dystopian future awaits us depends, to a great

---

[31] Drucker, p. 68.

[32] "Life on the Leisure Track," *Newsweek*, June 14, 1993, p. 48.

[33] "From Coast to Coast, from Affluent to Poor, Poll Shows Anxiety Over Jobs," *New York Times*, March 11, 1994, p. A1.

measure, on how the productivity gains of the Information Age are distributed. A fair and equitable distribution of the productivity gains would require a shortening of the workweek around the world and a concerted effort by central governments to provide alternative employment in the third sector—the social economy—for those whose labor is no longer required in the marketplace. If, however, the dramatic productivity gains of the high-tech revolution are not shared, but rather used primarily to enhance corporate profit, to the exclusive benefit of stockholders, top corporate managers, and the emerging elite of high-tech knowledge workers, chances are that the growing gap between the haves and the have-nots will lead to social and political upheaval on a global scale.

33   All around us today, we see the introduction of breathtaking new technologies capable of extraordinary feats. We have been led to believe that the marvels of modern technology would be our salvation. Millions placed their hopes for a better tomorrow on the liberating potential of the computer revolution. Yet the economic fortunes of most working people continue to deteriorate amid the embarrassment of technological riches. In every industrial country, people are beginning to ask why the age-old dream of abundance and leisure, so anticipated by generations of hardworking human beings, seems further away now, at the dawn of the Information Age, than at any time in the past half century. The answer lies in understanding a little-known but important economic concept that has long dominated the thinking of both business and government leaders around the world.

Source: Jeremy Rifkin, *The End of Work: The Decline of the Global Labor Force and the Dawn of the Post-Market Era.* New York: G.P. Putnam's Sons, 1995, pp. 3–14.

DISCUSSION QUESTIONS

1. Do you know what the following words mean: "inexorably" (Par. 3), "recalcitrant" (Par. 11), "enormity" (Par. 28), "redundant" (Par. 17). After looking up any that are unfamiliar to you, discuss, with two or three of your classmates, the *connotations* of these words. Which have particularly negative or positive connotations? Does Rifkin's use of these words constitute *slanting*?

2. In a class discussion, consider the effectiveness of Rifkin's introduction and conclusion. What tactics (as identified in Chapter 11) are used? Are they appropriate to this kind of argument? If you were Rifkin's editor, what alternative tactics might you suggest?

3. The central claim of this essay is an argument of effect. As Chapter 8 demonstrates, an important step in these arguments is to establish the existence of the causal factors through a secondary factual argument. What are the causes that Rifkin identifies and how effectively are they argued? Consider the reliability of the facts chosen to support these factual claims. Are their sources authoritative and current? Are there enough supporting facts? What further kinds of facts might have strengthened the secondary argument further?

4. Through what methods does Rifkin establish the causal link between the causes he cites and the effects he predicts (See Chapter 8)?

5. What image does Rifkin present of himself throughout the argument? Does he come across as credible, authoritative, and objective? Or is the image projected less favorable? Try to put your finger on exactly what features of his writing create this impression.

SUGGESTIONS FOR WRITING (16.2)

1. As a college student preparing to enter the workforce, you must have read Rifkin's prediction of the "end of work" with some alarm. Write a two- to three-page essay describing your personal response to Rifkin's argument (Your essay will be a *causal* argument, with Rifkin's predictions the cause, and your response the effect. In presenting the effect (a secondary factual argument), follow the suggestions made in Chapter 6 regarding personally experienced facts.

2. Both "The Three Jobs of the Future" and "The End of Work" rely heavily on factual support. Write a comparative evaluation of the two essays in terms of the credibility of their factual support. Your claim statement might read something like "Reich's [or Rifkin's] is the stronger argument because its factual support is more effective." (Note: make sure to define your evaluative term.)

3. In the last decade, how has the technological revolution affected the career field that you are interested in pursuing? Research and write a five-page causal argument answering this question. Feel free to use personal interviews as support for your argument.

4. Based upon your reading of Rifkin's argument, do you think Reich has overlooked the effects of technology on the future of work? Would his argument have reached different conclusions if he had included some of Rifkin's facts about technology? After discussion with your classmates, write a two- to three-page answer to these questions. Base your answer on the material within the two essays; you do not have to do outside research.

THE AGE OF SOCIAL TRANSFORMATION

PETER F. DRUCKER

The following argument by Peter Drucker appeared in the November 1994 issue of the magazine Atlantic Monthly. *After examining the dramatic transformations the world's workforce has undergone in the twentieth century, Drucker goes on, in the section printed here, to identify the challenges and opportunities posed by the latest generation of workers: knowledge workers.*

Peter Drucker is a noted advisor and consultant on long-range trends. He is currently the Clark Professor of Social Science at Claremont Graduate School in California.

1   The emerging society, the one based on knowledge and knowledge workers, is the first society in which ordinary people—and that means most people—do not earn their daily bread by the sweat of their brow. It is the first society in which "honest work" does not mean a callused hand. It is also the first society in which not everybody does the same work, as was the case when the huge majority were farmers or, as seemed likely only forty or thirty years ago, were going to be machine operators.

2   This is far more than social change. It is a change in the human condition. What it means—what are the values, the commitments, the problems, of the new society—we do not know. But we do know that much will be different.

3   Knowledge workers will not be the majority in the knowledge society but in many if not most developed societies they will be the largest single population and work-force group. And even where outnumbered by other groups, knowledge workers will give the emerging knowledge society its character, its leadership, its social profile. They may not be the ruling class of the knowledge society, but they are already its leading class. And in their characteristics, social position, values, and expectations, they differ fundamentally from any group in history that has ever occupied the leading position.

4   In the first place, knowledge workers gain access to jobs and social position through formal education. A great deal of knowledge work requires highly developed manual skill and involves substantial work with one's hands. An extreme example is neurosurgery. The neurosurgeon's performance capacity rests on formal education and theoretical knowledge. An absence of manual skill disqualifies one for work as a neurosurgeon. But manual skill alone, no matter how advanced, will never enable anyone to be a neurosurgeon. The education that is required for neurosurgery and other kinds of knowledge work can be acquired only through formal schooling. It cannot be acquired through apprenticeship.

5   Knowledge work varies tremendously in the amount and kind of formal knowledge required. Some jobs have fairly low requirements, and others require the kind of knowledge the neurosurgeon possesses. But even if the knowledge itself is quite primitive, only formal education can provide it.

6   Education will become the center of the knowledge society, and the school its key institution. What knowledge must everybody have? What is "quality" in learning and teaching? These will of necessity become central concerns of the knowledge society, and central political issues. In fact, the acquisition and distribution of formal knowledge may come to occupy the place in the politics of the knowledge society which the acquisition and distribution of property and income have occupied in our politics over the two or three centuries that we have come to call the Age of Capitalism.

7   In the knowledge society, clearly more and more knowledge, and especially advanced knowledge, will be acquired well past the age of formal schooling and increasingly, perhaps, through educational processes that do not center on the traditional school. But at the same time, the performance of the schools and the basic values of the schools will be of increasing concern to society as a whole, rather than being considered professional matters that can safely be left to "educators."

8   We can also predict with confidence that we will redefine what it means to be an educated person. Traditionally, and especially during the past 300 years (perhaps since 1700 or so, at least in the West, and since about that time in Japan as well), an educated person was somebody who had a prescribed stock of formal knowledge. The Germans called this knowledge *allgemeine Bildung,* and the English (and, following them, the nineteenth-century Americans) called it the liberal arts. Increasingly, an educated person will be somebody who has learned how to learn, and who continues learning, especially by formal education, throughout his or her lifetime.

9   There are obvious dangers to this. For instance, society could easily degenerate into emphasizing formal degrees rather than performance capacity. It could fall prey to sterile Confucian mandarins—a danger to which the American university is singularly susceptible. On the other hand, it could overvalue immediately usable, "practical" knowledge and underrate the importance of fundamentals, and of wisdom altogether.

10   A society in which knowledge workers dominate is under threat from a new class conflict: between the large minority of knowledge workers and the majority of people, who will make their living traditionally, either by manual work, whether skilled or unskilled, or by work in services, whether skilled or unskilled. The productivity of knowledge work—still abysmally low—will become the economic challenge of the knowledge society. On it will depend the competitive position of

every single country, every single industry, every single institution within society. The productivity of the non-knowledge, services worker will become the social challenge of the knowledge society. On it will depend the ability of the knowledge society to give decent incomes, and with them dignity and status, to non-knowledge workers.

11 No society in history has faced these challenges. But equally new are the opportunities of the knowledge society. In the knowledge society, for the first time in history, the possibility of leadership will be open to all. Also, the possibility of acquiring knowledge will no longer depend on obtaining a prescribed education at a given age. Learning will become the tool of the individual—available to him or her at any age—if only because so much skill and knowledge can be acquired by means of the new learning technologies.

Another implication is that how well an 12 individual, an organization, an industry, a country, does in acquiring and applying knowledge will become the key competitive factor. The knowledge society will inevitably become far more competitive than any society we have yet known—for the simple reason that with knowledge being universally accessible, there will be no excuses for nonperformance. There will be no "poor" countries. There will only be ignorant countries. And the same will be true for companies, industries, and organizations of all kinds. It will be true for individuals, too. In fact, developed societies have already become infinitely more competitive for individuals than were the societies of the beginning of this century, let alone earlier ones.

Source: Peter F. Drucker, "The Age of Social Transformation." *The Atlantic Monthly,* 1994, Vol. 274, No. 5, pp. 53–80.

DISCUSSION QUESTIONS

1. What is the class (or classes) of Drucker's argument? Identify the claim(s).

2. Through what methods are these claims supported? Do you find the support adequate? If not, make a list of additional methods or material that would strengthen the argument.

3. Drucker does not define the term "knowledge worker" anywhere in his essay (though he cites his original use of the term in an earlier work). Does this absence of definition weaken the argument, or is it clear from the context what he means by the term? Based upon Drucker's use of the term, write a formal sentence definition of "knowledge worker" and compare it with definitions written by two or three of your classmates. Into which of Reich's categories of workers would you place Drucker's knowledge workers?

4. What kind of image does Drucker project? Write a paragraph describing that image. Discuss with your classmates whether the image adds to or detracts from the effectiveness of the argument.

SUGGESTIONS FOR WRITING (16.3)

1. Write a two- to three-page comparison of Drucker's knowledge worker with Reich's symbolic analyst. Write a working claim first, and think carefully about the class of that claim (i.e., evaluative, causal, etc.). Then proceed according to the strategies associated with that class of argument.

2. Write a five-page letter to Drucker, Reich, or Rifkin. In that letter, state and support your disagreements with the recipient based upon your reading of the

other two. Since this is a letter, you do not need to provide notes and a bibliography, but you should include exact quotations from the other two writers where appropriate. (Note: this assignment requires a very careful reading of all three arguments.)

3. In Par. 6, Drucker states that "increasingly, an educated person will be somebody who has learned how to learn." Colleges and universities are claiming that they are teaching students "how to learn." Write an extended definition of the term "learning to learn," including concrete examples as one of your definition strategies.

LESSONS FROM 2 GHOSTS

SCOTT M. FISHER

In this causal argument, Scott Fisher, an instructor of English at Rock Valley College, identifies the reasons for his career choice. Fisher assumes that his readers are familiar with the political situation of the late 1960s, when the Vietnam war was raging and young American men lived in the shadow of the military draft. This was a time when the war in Vietnam was the preoccupation of all young men, many of whom went to incredible and often self-destructive lengths to avoid the "1-A" draft status that guaranteed a military stint in the dangerous Vietnam conflict. Throughout America's involvement in the war (1965–1972), full-time undergraduate students were automatically exempted from the draft.

This essay first apeared in June of 1996 in the Chronicle of Higher Education, *a weekly publication covering higher education issues for college and university faculty, administrators, and graduate students.*

1   I know many educators who, like me, spend scores of extra hours planning, developing, and evaluating ideas and materials for their courses. I admire my colleagues for being so dedicated to their students and their profession. I wish I could say my reasons for my long hours were as altruistic. In fact, I often wish I had more time to read for pleasure, hike in the mountains, or go to more baseball games.

2   The truth is that there are ghosts in my office that force me to stay there and work, even when I'd rather be somewhere else. Oh, they let me go home and get enough rest and nourishment to sustain my body. But they know I'll be back, and they're always waiting for me when I unlock the door to my office. As Poe would have asked: "You think me mad?" Maybe I am.

3   I've known these ghosts—there are two of them—for about 25 years. That's longer than I've been teaching, although they really only started haunting me on my first day as a student teacher. Every day since then, they've been standing right behind or on either side of me. Heck, I knew them before they were ghosts. They were young men once, as I was.

4   Their names are (were) Pritchard and Simplett. We were classmates—freshmen—in the late '60s at a teachers' college in the Midwest. Pritchard was the kicker on our football team. He could make field goals from any angle, off any surface, in any temperature, in rain, snow, or high winds. If the ball was inside the 30-yard line, Pritch could nail it dead center every time. He didn't miss a single field goal or extra point all

season. I can testify to that, because I was his holder (I was too small and slow to start in any other position). We weren't a power-house team, by any means, but Pritchard's foot made the difference in some of our games.

5   Simplett and I were on the baseball team that year. He was an outstanding shortstop, with a rifle arm (excuse the cliche). He could go into the hole, drop to his knees, and fling a runner out at first base by two steps. I was a fourth-string catcher, used almost exclusively when the game was not in doubt and the coach didn't want to risk injury to any of his "good" players. That was also when Simp got his chance to pitch. He was magnificent—about one-third of the time. The other two-thirds, his blazing fastball had a mind of its own. Also, Simp had a little trouble reading his catcher's signs. He couldn't see too well from 60 feet away. That's why no-body wanted to catch for him. I tried every-thing—flashing the signs very slowly, wrapping white adhesive tape around my fingertips—but nothing worked. We finally agreed that he would just "throw 'em," and I'd try to "catch 'em," which worked out about as well as anything else. We didn't win many games, but we had fun.

6   Pritch, Simp, and I had a couple of other things in common besides sports. For one thing, we all liked to write. I liked research and writing historical narrative—essays on the Old West, sports teams of the 1930s, classic airplanes, that kind of thing.

7   Pritch was into fantasy. He could weave a wonderful tale, gripping readers with his spellbinding tales of planets and sorcerers, which he illustrated deftly with bizarre, in-triguing drawings.

8   Simp was a poet. His mind worked in metaphor; even in the dugout he would call umpires the "traffic cops of the basepaths" and the pain of a batter's hands when the bat connected on a cold day "the sweet sting of spring." And he loved all kinds of music. He lived across the hall from me in the dorm, and on Thursday nights ("rave" nights, when it was okay to make a little

more noise), he'd bring over his Country Joe McDonald records, and we'd sing along at the top of our off-key voices. "And it's one, two, three, what're we fightin' for? Don't ask me, I don't give a damn; next stop is Vietnam."

9   Just as I admired their athletic ability, I was in awe of my friends' talents and cre-ativity, both in writing and in living. While I had to work for each ounce of strength, both on the athletic field and at the type-writer, Pritch and Simp had natural gifts. I was envious, but also proud to know them. Their talents inspired me to work harder to improve myself.

10   It may sound corny now, but those guys were preparing themselves to be skilled ed-ucators in every activity they pursued. They often helped out in the tutoring lab in the evenings and volunteered to coach elementary-school teams on weekends. They loved taking kids from the town on field trips to nearby farms or sporting events. I was amazed at how both of them could motivate even the shyest youngster. They were natural leaders and role mod-els. Kids seemed to be drawn to them instinctively.

11   The only time all three of us were together regularly was in "Old Man" Rivers's (Professor Rivers, that is) English-composition class. Now, in retrospect, I can corroborate what we thought then: He was a complete jerk. He seems to be about 160 years old, wore black suits, starched white shirts, bow ties, black wingtip shoes, and white socks. He was a fanatical Freudian and expected all our writing to reflect Freud's theories. Even though I did my best to work them into my narrative essays, short-story analyses, and research thesis, my papers al-ways came back with a C, if I was lucky. Al-though I had been praised as a clear and insightful writer in high school, Old Man Rivers made it clear to me that I had no writing talent and that perhaps I should con-sider hiring a tutor or retaking the class in the summer.

12   I was too immature and unclear about my role as a future teacher to care all that

much about what an eccentric English professor thought of me. But for Simp and Pritch it was different. They saw Professor Rivers for what he really was—a "scholarly bully," Simp called him. (Pritch's description was more profane, as I recall.) They often challenged (respectfully, at first) his weird interpretations of the stories, poems, and essays that we discussed in class. Of course, this did not please Rivers one bit, although their arguments made perfect sense to me.

13   Some of the more "intellectually needy" members of the class, including me, often tried to get some extra help from the old duffer, but he always was too busy to bother with "ignorant freshmen," especially if he was working on his latest textbook. He was particularly cool to us athletes, because he thought college sports were a waste of time and didn't like the fact that we had permission to miss classes when we had games at other colleges.

14   Most of us decided just to go with the flow, earn our solid C's, and get on with our lives. But Pritchard and Simplett were not about to go that route. They each spent hours preparing for the essays we had to write in class, looking up literary critical analysis that even doctoral candidates wouldn't want to read, just so they could prove their points with logic that Rivers couldn't refute. Yet Rivers was such a pedant that my two friends didn't stand a chance.

15   Those two guys spent all year—freshmen were stuck with Rivers for both semesters—trying to show him up. They each received D's the first semester, which threatened to put them on academic probation. By April, the situation had deteriorated to the point that they no longer even tried to suppress their snide comments in class. Pritch drew some hilarious, obscene sketches of Rivers expounding on Freudian aspects of fiction. And Simp concocted a tune about what a dirty old man Rivers was. Both of these creative scholarly works were published in the local forum—the men's bathroom in the athletic building.

16   Pritch and Simp each were called in by the dean at various times and told to knock it off. They were reminded that we "boys" were all 1-A in the eyes of Uncle Sam, and that without their educational deferments, they would quickly find themselves in the military.

17   But that wasn't enough of a threat for them, because they had very different ideas of what education was supposed to be. They continued to rebel against Old Man Rivers, and they continued to be reprimanded. In they end, they both failed Rivers's class the second semester and were placed on academic probation, with the understanding that they could make up the credits during summer session. But guess who taught all the summer composition classes?

18   There was a lot I didn't quite grasp back then. I couldn't understand how a teacher at the college to which we were paying such high tuition could be so aloof and arrogant. I also couldn't understand how a published author of English textbooks could fail to recognize the talents of two gifted writers, right under his own nose. But neither could I understand why two intelligent guys would keep trying to buck the system when they knew Rivers wasn't going to change. Didn't they get it? They could just get through the class and pursue their own ideas after they graduated, with their own students.

19   But they just laughed in disgust at any notion of compromise. Each of them, separately, refused to take the summer-school makeup course from Rivers and decided to head back to their respective hometowns. They planned to take their chances with the draft, maybe start again at another college the following year or when they got out of the service, should they be drafted.

20   Within 18 months, Pritchard and Simplett were dead. Pritch was blown apart by a land mine during an infantry patrol. A few months later, the Army helicopter in which Simp was riding crashed and burned, leaving no survivors.

21   Of course, it's really not Old Man Rivers's fault that my friends died. It was just a cruel trick of timing. Still, I can't help thinking that by sticking around my

office after hours, I might help some student stay on track. I feel the presence of my two old friends, and I see traits of theirs, such as their eagerness to ask challenging questions and explore opposing viewpoints, in a lot of my students. Some of them may go on to make a difference in young people's lives in a way in which my ghostly friends cannot. I hope they do.

So I just keep plugging away, like a 22 fourth-string catcher, giving extra help where I can. It's not because I'm a great humanitarian, or that I'm gifted or even dedicated.

I'm just haunted.   23

Source: Scott M. Fisher, "Lessons From 2 Ghosts," *The Chronicle of Higher Education.* June 14, 1996. pp. A56.

DISCUSSION QUESTIONS

1. "Lessons From 2 Ghosts" proceeds through retrospective narrative, with the author describing his two friends and their eventual fates. Yet it also qualifies as a causal argument, in which a given effect (the author's own dedication to his teaching job) is accounted for by an identified cause (the influence of his two friends). Assuming that one of Fisher's main purposes here is to demonstrate cause, consider the level of narrative detail in the essay. For example, are the stories about the pair's athletic talents necessary (Par. 3–4)? Do we need to know about their literary talents (Par. 5–7) and other "natural gifts" (Par. 8–9)? In other words, from the point of view of argument, how necessary are these details?
2. Identify the unstated motivational link between cause and effect in this essay.
3. What does Fisher mean when he claims that he is "haunted" by the ghosts of his friends?
4. Describe the image of the writer that comes through in this essay. How does that image affect your response to the essay?

SUGGESTIONS FOR WRITING (16.4)

1. Interview one of your professors about his or her reasons for choosing a career in teaching. Then write a three-page causal argument on the subject. Before the interview, think carefully about the questions you want to ask, and prepare them in such a way that they don't determine the answers.
2. If you were one of these two "ghosts," what advice might you have for today's young college students? Write a three-page recommendation from Pritchard's or Simplett's point of view that makes use of their own experience during and after college.
3. Write your own two- to three-page personal narrative about a high school friendship that taught you something important. After providing background information about your friend and the relationship, relate one important thing you learned from that friend. In effect, this will be a factual argument based upon personal experience. Your challenge will be to make the narrative engaging, but also credible and realistic.

CAREER TRANSITIONS

NANCY KOLLAMER

"Career Transitions" is an advice column for women in career transition and a regular feature of the Web site "Oxygen" (http://www.oxygen.com). The site describes itself as follows: "A blend of Web sites and TV that's designed to serve women better than they've ever been served before. More important than what we are though, is what we hope to mean to you. We'd like to create a new kind of relationship with you—one based on honesty, humor and heart."

1   **Q.** I am a nurse but I'm thinking about making a career change into finance. How can I get the experience I need without quitting my job and living on savings for the next three years?

2   **A.** There are four tried-and-true ways to get experience—three of which you can do without quitting your job. The simplest step is to attend continuing-education classes at your local community college or high school. This is an inexpensive, low-risk alternative for testing out your interest and skill level. While taking the class, talk with the teacher and other students to find out their recommendations for employment options, degree programs and growth opportunities within the world of finance. If you really enjoy the classes and decide you're ready to get the needed credentials for success, then investigate the possibility of enrolling in a degree or certificate program at an accredited college. Most programs offer weekend or evening classes to accommodate older students. Don't forget to investigate finance courses and degree programs taught online as well.

3   Once you get some basic financial skills under your belt, then it's time to polish your skills by doing some financially related volunteer work. Consider working as the treasurer for a fund-raising event at your church or synagogue. Or volunteer to prepare some budgets for your favorite local nonprofit agency. A good volunteer job can be time consuming, but you should be able to work your hours around your paid work commitments.

4   Working as an intern on a part-time basis is another wonderful way to get those needed skills. Try to find degree programs that offer internship opportunities. If that can't be arranged through the school, you might be able to arrange an internship with a local CPA or financial planner in private practice. Many interns are ultimately offered permanent employment by their internship supervisors.

5   After you have completed your classes and polished your skills through volunteer work and/or internships, you should be ready to commence a job search. But, if you find the job hunt tough going, it may behoove you to work on a temporary basis to further enhance your portfolio of skills and "real-world" job experience. Of course, working as a temp will mean that you'll have to abandon your day job, but the experience and networking contacts you'll gain should help pave the way to a successful job search.

6   Making the transition into a new career takes time, so be patient but persistent. Develop a plan, stay focused on learning new skills, earn the necessary credentials and before you know it, you'll be well on your way to a more satisfying career.

Source: http://www.oxygen.com

DISCUSSION QUESTIONS

1. Nancy Kollamer's answer to the woman contemplating a career change exemplifies just how broad the definition of "argument" is. Discuss with your classmates how this reading fits into the definition of argument offered in Chapter 1. What features qualify Kollamer's response as an argument? Are there features that disqualify it?

2. Into what class of argument does Kollamer's response best fit? Is the support sufficient and appropriate to that class?

3. After looking at more of the "Career Transitions" columns on this Web site, discuss with your classmates their assumed audience. Are the content, diction, and tone of Kollamer's responses appropriate to the audience you identify? Give examples.

4. Using the Oxygen Web site as a starting point, investigate the background and credentials of Nancy Kollamer. Record all the steps in your investigation process. Then, with two of your classmates, compare both what you've learned about Kollamer and how.

5. Discuss with your class the image projected by the home page of the Oxygen Web site. To what audience do the visuals appeal? How representative is the home page of the entire Web site? Why would a person who happens on the Web site explore it further?

SUGGESTIONS FOR WRITING (16.5)

1. Create a request for advice on any general topic that might be submitted to an advice column such as this one. Exchange letters with a classmate and write a one-page response, making sure that you follow the principles of sound recommendations.

2. Based upon the investigation about Kollamer you did for Question #4, write a one-page evaluation of her qualifications as a "Career Transition" expert.

3. Create a detailed outline from Kollamer's response, including an identification of central claim, supporting claims, and strategies of support. Be sure to include the class of each claim. Compare your outline with that of your classmates. Is it possible, through discussion, to reconcile any significant differences in your outlines?

4. Write a two- to three-page factual argument (based upon first- or secondhand experience) describing a career transition made by you or someone you know. Before writing, review the section in Chapter 6 on "Supporting Personally Experienced Facts."

5. Find a recent advice column from a magazine or newspaper and write a one-page letter to the columnist evaluating the quality of his/her recommendations.

ON DUMPSTER DIVING

LARS EIGHNER

Lars Eighner is a graduate of the University of Texas at Austin. He began writing soon after college, publishing articles and a volume of short stories. In 1988, he became homeless, a three-year experience that he wrote about in his book Travels with Lizbeth *(1993). After publishing his first novel,* Pawn to Queen Four *in 1995, Eighner became homeless again.*

1   I began Dumpster diving about a year before I became homeless. I prefer the term *scavenging.* I have heard people, evidently meaning to be polite, use the word *foraging,* but I prefer to reserve that word for gathering nuts and berries and such, which I also do, according to the season and opportunity.

2   I like the frankness of the word *scavenging.* I live from the refuse of others. I am a scavenger. I think it a sound and honorable niche, although if I could I would naturally prefer to live the comfortable consumer life, perhaps—and only perhaps—as a slightly less wasteful consumer owing to what I have learned as a scavenger.

3   Except for jeans, all my clothes come from Dumpsters. Boom boxes, candles, bedding, toilet paper, medicine, books, a typewriter, a virgin male love doll, coins sometimes amounting to many dollars: all came from Dumpsters. And, yes, I eat from Dumpsters, too.

4   There is a predictable series of stages that a person goes through in learning to scavenge. At first the new scavenger is filled with disgust and self-loathing. He is ashamed of being seen.

5   This stage passes with experience. The scavenger finds a pair of running shoes that fit and look and smell brand-new. He finds a pocket calculator in perfect working order. He finds pristine ice cream, still frozen, more than he can eat or keep. He begins to understand: people do throw away perfectly good stuff, a lot of perfectly good stuff.

6   At this stage he may become lost and never recover. All the Dumpster divers I have known come to the point of trying to acquire everything they touch. Why not take it, they reason, it is all free. This is, of course, hopeless, and most divers come to realize that they must restrict themselves to items of relatively immediate utility.

7   The finding of objects is becoming something of an urban art. Even respectable, employed people will sometimes find something tempting sticking out of a Dumpster or standing beside one. Quite a number of people, not all of them of the bohemian type, are willing to brag that they found this or that piece in the trash.

8   But eating from Dumpsters is the thing that separates the dilettanti from the professionals. Eating safely involves three principles: using the senses and common sense to evaluate the condition of the found materials; knowing the Dumpsters of a given area and checking them regularly; and seeking always to answer the question "Why was this discarded?"

9   Yet perfectly good food can be found in Dumpsters. Canned goods, for example, turn up fairly often in the Dumpsters I frequent. I also have few qualms about dry foods such as crackers, cookies, cereal, chips, and pasta if they are free of visible contaminants and still dry and crisp. Raw fruits and vegetables with intact skins seem perfectly safe to me, excluding, of course, the obviously rotten. Many are discarded for minor imperfections that can be pared away.

10   A typical discard is a half jar of peanut butter—though nonorganic peanut butter does not require refrigeration and is unlikely to spoil in any reasonable time. One

of my favorite finds is yogurt—often discarded, still sealed, when the expiration date has passed—because it will keep for several days, even in warm weather.

11   No matter how careful I am I still get dysentery at least once a month, often in warm weather. I do not want to paint too romantic a picture. Dumpster diving has serious drawbacks as a way of life.

12   I find from the experience of scavenging two rather deep lessons. The first is to take what I can use and let the rest go. I have come to think that there is no value in the abstract. A thing I cannot use or make useful, perhaps by trading, has no value, however fine or rare it may be.

13   The second lesson is the transience of material being. I do not suppose that ideas are immortal, but certainly they are longer-lived than material objects.

14   The things I find in Dumpsters, the love letters and rag dolls of so many lives, remind me of this lesson. Now I hardly pick up a thing without envisioning the time I will cast it away. This, I think, is a healthy state of mind. Almost everything I have now has already been cast out at least once, proving that what I own is valueless to someone.

15   I find that my desire to grab for the gaudy bauble has been largely sated. I think this is an attitude I share with the very wealthy—we both know there is plenty more where whatever we have came from. Between us are the rat-race millions who have confounded their selves with the objects they grasp and who nightly scavenge the cable channels for they know not what.

16   I am sorry for them.

Source: From *Models for Writers: Short Essays for Composition*, 6th ed. Alfred Rosa and Paul Eschholz, New York: St. Martin's, 1998. pp. 531–533.

DISCUSSION QUESTIONS

1. With a group of your classmates, make a list of adjectives that describe the tone of this essay. For each adjective, attach an example quoted from the text. Is there consensus within the group about the essay's tone? If not, how do you account for the different responses?

2. What are Eighner's definitions of the terms *scavenging* (Par. 1) and *foraging* (Par. 2)? Are the definitions complete and clear? What do you think about their placement in an essay that describes finding a living from garbage Dumpsters?

3. What is the central claim here. Is it explicit or implicit?

4. Based upon your careful reading of this essay, compose, with a few of your classmates, a character portrait of Eighner. What kind of man does he seem to be? Does he have a sense of humor or is he very serious? Is he intelligent? Would you like to know him? Be sure to point to those parts of the essay that lead you to your portrait.

5. Do you think Eighner finds satisfaction in his work? What evidence do you have for your answer?

6. Is Eighner's essay just about Dumpster diving, or can you attach further significance to it? Participate in a full class discussion of this question.

SUGGESTIONS FOR WRITING (16.6)

1. Write a "how-to" essay on an activity that most people would find very unappealing.

2. In a half page, characterize the tone of your "how-to" essay.

3. Write a two-page argument of any type about a job you've had. Do not state the claim explicitly, but make sure that it is clear to your readers. After you've written the essay, give it to two or three of your classmates and ask them to state the implicit claim.

4. Write a factual argument describing how your preconceptions about the homeless have changed (or stayed the same) based on Eighner's essay.

17

Diet

INTRODUCTION

Of all the subject units in this anthology of arguments, this one on "Diet" may seem the most curious.

The term "diet," which derives from the Latin *dies,* or "days," means simply "daily fare"—the combination of food and drink that we consume from day to day. More specifically, we use the term "diet" to refer to habits of food consumption directed toward a particular goal. One can be on a diet for weight gain, a diet for improved memory, a diet for increased energy. But as members of a culture that prizes thinness above all body shapes, many of us immediately associate the term "diet" with weight loss strategies—with calorie counting, low-fat food, and self-imposed hunger. It is largely with this use of the word diet that this unit is concerned.

If at this point you're wondering what the literature of diet, with its preoccupation with calorie counting and fat reduction, could possibly teach about writing reasonable and effective arguments, consider the following.

First, the very *dailiness* of diet qualifies it for the attention of this book. Like every other unit in this reader—popular culture, the Internet, work, sports, and so on—diet, in all senses of the word, is everywhere. It has spawned numerous industries that barrage us daily with their marketing ploys; it requires constant decisions that consume huge amounts of our time, whether we are counting fat grams or picking a restaurant; and it is the occasion of countless conversations (try counting the number of conversations you overhear or participate in, in a single day that revolve around eating—you'll be amazed). In other words, diet has become a kind of ever-present, ambient noise that we hear but don't always listen to. We need to pay attention to the noise once in a while, to analyze those claims and conclusions that too often we unthinkingly accept.

Second, as you will see in some of the following readings, arguments concerning diet seem to be particularly susceptible to flawed reasoning. One can hypothesize a number of explanations for this susceptibility. For one, when it comes to body-sculpting through diet, our own credulity, fueled by our desperation to emulate those impossible models in magazines, probably encourages advertisers to indulge in careless reasoning (not that advertising in any area is distinguished by reason).

Third, the universality of diet—the fact that it is something all of us engage in on a daily basis—tends to make us behave like experts on the subject. Just as we are all doctors when it comes to the common cold, we are dietitians when it comes to eating. Though we often lack rigorous scientific studies to back up our claims, experience, and intuitions, few of us can resist adding to the abundant supply of unwarranted pronouncements about diet. When was the last time you contributed to this store of "common knowledge" about diet?

And finally, arguments about diet are unreliable because the subject is anything but an exact science. Even the experts—the nutritionists, dieticians, and physiologists—disagree about the facts. Look at the parade of claims, revisions, and counterclaims that regularly come out of medical center laboratories and double-blind studies. When publications as prestigious as the *New England Journal of Medicine* and the *Journal of the American Medical Association* come out with directly contradictory claims about diet—as they did, for example, about the disputable benefits of oat bran in the 1980s[1], how can we expect lucidity and reason in the popular literature about diet?

But not all the readings in this section are examples of argument gone awry. For while the subject of diet may tempt misguided and misguiding reasoning, it is also, like all the topics represented in this reader, a fascinating and provocative phenomenon that, when given our (unaccustomed) attention, yields a wealth of information about who we are, what we value and why, where we locate our identities, and how we construct meaning. Diet, it turns out, is a remarkably rich site at which to extend your understanding of argument, readily offering cautionary examples of faulty argument and worthy instances of original, well-reasoned thinking.

THE DIET BIZ

DONALD JACKSON

Reading Donald Jackson's "The Diet Biz" may give you a jaundiced view of the "diet industry" of the last century. This survey of the history of dieting, which originally appeared in the Smithsonian *magazine in November 1994, highlights some of the more crackpot diet plans in a business not noted for following scientific principles.*

---

[1] Kinosian, Bruce P., M.D. and John M. Eisenberg, M.D. M.B.A. "Cutting Into Cholesterol." *Journal of the American Medical Association,* April 15, 1988, Vol. 259, No. 15. Swain, Rouse, Curley, Sacks. "Comparison of the Effects of Oat Bran on Serum Lipoprotein Levels and Blood Pressure." *New England Journal of Medicine,* Jan. 18, 1990, Vol. 322, No.3.

COMMENTARY

The essay's claim, which appears at the outset in large bold and italicized print, is a factual generalization: "The art of wishful shrinking has made a lot of people rich. But it has not made many thin—or at least not for long. Diet sensations come and go but excess weight seems to hang on forever." The body of the essay consists of a series of factual examples that support the opening generalization.

The organization of the many examples is chronological. Paragraphs 3–16 provide numerous examples of diet conjurers, beginning with William Banting in the mid-nineteenth century and ending with Gayelord Hauser in the 1930s. Paragraphs 17–22 offer examples of diet devices. Finally, paragraphs 23–24 detail examples of the development of diet organizations like Weight Watchers and dieting "methods" like Atkins and Scarsdale.

Writing an exclusively factual survey of the bizarre history of dieting would challenge even the most objective and humorless writer. Jackson is not at all reluctant to offer his evaluative take on the subject matter, though his evaluations are not argued at any length. Rather, they are expressed through the use of strongly connotative language and a consistently ridiculing tone. Terms like "diet hustling" (Par. 3), "dietmeister-showman-mogul" (Par. 14), "glop" (Par. 24), and "talkaholic" (Par. 27) reveal pretty clearly what the author thinks of this "diet roadshow" (Par. 12). As Chapter 10 cautions, connotative language, slanting, and sarcasm do not make arguments, though they can certainly influence a careless reader. In the case of this essay, however, the silliness and deceit of the diet industry is sufficiently obvious (a diet, for example, that claims thorough chewing causes weight loss) to warrant Jackson's shorthand judgments.

THE DIET BIZ

1   Any day now it's coming, you can bank on it—the ultimate no-pain, no-sacrifice, no-hunger, eat-all-you-want diet, guaranteed medically and nutritionally sound, effortless, and did I say *guaranteed,* that's right, and all in a book for a mere $24.95, your money back if not delighted and transformed into a new, wonderful, slimmer you in, oh, three weeks tops. Listen—hear that tapping in the far reaches of the doctor's office? He's finishing it now, publication is a couple of months off; they're just buttoning up paperback rights.

2   The author-promoter of the next diet sensation will take his or her place in a long, gaudy and intermittently felonious procession of gurus and messiahs who have lived well while dispensing weight-loss wisdom, more or less. Happily for them, there has ever been a huge reservoir of pudgy people ready and willing to snap up the latest offerings. As the apostles of slenderness know full well, rare is the overweight individual who will not do almost anything to improve his or her appearance—and, of course, the less a diet requires one to do, the more likely one is to try it. This is why dieting has become such a big business. In 1993, Americans spent around $30 billion on books, video tapes, nutritional aides, reducing salons and other diet-related goods and services. If some would-be dieters are hanging back

now because of the latest scientific reservations about the long-term value of self-denial, just wait until the new book comes out. They'll find it impossible to resist.

3 Doctors have been the most conspicuous promoters, especially in recent years, but diet hustling is an equal-opportunity field. Tycoons and housewives have had a go at it, as have self-styled "nutritionists" of a dozen different shadings, preachers and writers and actors and a few with no credentials whatever, people who seemed to wander in off the street to conjure up a diet plan. One of the first such savants in the historical record, as it happens, was a mid-19th-century London undertaker.

4 His name was William Banting, and his problem was that at age 65 he had 14 stone 6 (202 pounds) of lard lumpily distributed on his 5-foot-5 frame. He couldn't tie his shoes or descend a staircase frontally, and he was going deaf. Banting tried rowing and horseback riding, purgatives and diuretics and Turkish baths, but nothing worked until his doctor prescribed a diet free from sugar and starch. When he dropped 52 pounds on a regimen of lean meat, vegetables, dry toast and soft-boiled eggs (with a daily alcoholic toddy), when his hearing improved and he could again navigate a stairway with dignity, Banting the pioneer dieter became Banting the promoter, producing a book that had sold 58,000 copies by the time he died in 1878.

5 In this country, Horace Fletcher attained early dietary eminence as "The Great Masticator." Fletcher parlayed a fanatical dedication to the act of chewing, a serene self-assurance and some remarkable physical exploits into a career as a self-taught expert on diet and health just after the turn of the century. Fletcher was a cosmopolitan businessman who made a fortune in ink and imports only to find himself at age 40 unable to buy life insurance because he was a white-haired, 217-pound blob.

6 The turning point came when a friend told him about former British prime minister William Gladstone's conviction that proper and prolonged chewing precluded

overeating and led to good health. It was not a totally novel notion, since vigorous chewing had been viewed as an aid to digestion for years, but Fletcher embraced it like a sinner saved. Gladstone had counseled 32 chews per morsel, one for each tooth in a normal mouth, but Fletcher, soon known as "the chew chew man," raised the dental ante and urged that all food be munched until it turned to liquid. Never mind if it was liquid already—soup and milk were to be "chewed" as well. Fletcher argued further that any food that did not liquefy under such relentless mastication should be spit out. That eliminated roughage and thus made constipation a problem to be reckoned with.

7 Fletcher, by now 65 pounds lighter and down to one noisy, drawn-out meal a day, did what all diet mavens do: he wrote a book. *The AB-Z of Our Own Nutrition.* He dressed in white suits, bought a house in Venice and churned out articles claiming that 200,000 families in the United States lived by his precepts. Students at Yale and West Point "fletcherized" their meals. The faithful in Britain had "munching parties"; John D. Rockefeller solemnly fletcherized. Fletcher's own weight fluctuated—one professor described him at 55 as "rather plump than otherwise"—but he now appeared to be mostly muscle. At 58 he performed the astonishing feat (or so he claimed) of lifting 300 pounds dead weight 350 times with his right leg, double a previous record.

8 Fletcher eschewed meat, alcohol, coffee and tea. His meals ran to potatoes, cornbread, beans, sometimes eggs and toast, and the occasional stewed tomato. His guidelines were light on specific food groups but heavy on the attitude the eater brought to the table. Rule No. 1 was "wait for a true, earned appetite." A diner could eat what he wanted as long as he chewed till the food "swallowed itself," and no "depressing or diverting feelings" were to intrude at mealtime. The consequences would be complete and easy digestion, perfect health, and a farewell to eczema, headaches, pimples, boils and "that foggy feeling."

9   In his sunset years, the man once denounced as a food crank became a venerated figure, but the Great Masticator's star eventually faded. Early adherents like Dr. John Harvey Kellogg, of the Battle Creek, Michigan, cereal Kelloggs, defected over the roughage issue, adding the gratuitous observation that Fletcher's breath was "highly malodorous."

10   A little book printed a year before Fletcher's death at 70 in 1919 showed that in dieting, as in other difficult but rewarding pastimes, the best advice is not always the latest word. Dr. Lulu Hunt Peters, who wrote *Diet and Health, with a Key to the Calories,* had a precocious grasp of the awful truth that millions would ultimately spend billions to avoid: successful dieting was a hard, demanding, lifelong commitment. Having pared her own weight from 200 to 150, she told her readers that "no matter how hard I work—no matter how much I exercise, no matter what I suffer, I will always have to watch my weight, I will always have to count my calories."

11   Calorie-counting was still a novelty when Dr. Peters, a physician in Los Angeles who wrote a syndicated health column, introduced it in her book. (A calorie is a unit of measurement representing the energy-producing value of food.) Addressing herself mainly to women, then as now the foot soldiers in the diet forces, she instructed them to use the word "calorie" as routinely as they used "pound," "gallon" or "yard." "Hereafter you are going to eat calories of food," she wrote. "Instead of saying one slice of bread or a piece of pie, you will say 100 calories of bread, 350 calories of pie."

12   Her diet began with a fast to show the body who was boss, then imposed a 1,200-calorie daily limit, followed by a more relaxed but permanent—as in *forever*—maintenance plan. The Peters preachments of self-denial and self-discipline won the endorsement of government agencies while selling two million books, making hers the first and one of the best in a long and often odious line of American diet-book best-sellers.

13   Two other leading lights of the diet roadshow in the 1920s and '30s took a different approach. Dr. William Howard Hay and Gayelord Hauser were forerunners of what was waiting down the road in the wide-open, largely unregulated diet biz. Promoters of soft, semiscientific hustles that defied the medical establishment while profiting from Americans' nutritional gullibility, they were early masters of the art of wishful shrinking.

14   Hay, who operated out of a resort he called Pocono Hay-ven, Pennsylvania, decreed that proteins, starches and fruits had to be eaten separately to avoid acidosis, which drained vitality and led to fat. One food category per meal was the best way—plus a daily enema to flush out the poison. Henry Ford obediently chomped down on fruit at breakfast, carbohydrates for lunch and proteins at dinner. Critics churlishly pointed out that nature had already mixed proteins and carbohydrates in many foods, and that the digestive system handles the mix with minimal difficulty, but Hay diets still lured millions.

15   Hauser was one of the earliest dietmeister-showman-moguls, a suave, charismatic European with a vaguely academic background. (He was an N.D., or doctor of naturopathy, a system of treatment that uses natural substances to help the body heal itself.) He enjoyed showy cars and the company of film stars like Greta Garbo and Paulette Goddard. He lectured, wrote best-sellers (*Look Younger, Live Longer*), developed his own lucrative line of special foods and supplements, and for a time indulged a Fletcher-like preference for white suits.

16   His 10- and 28-day diets stressed his five vitamin-B-heavy "wonder foods"—brewer's yeast, wheat germ, yogurt, powdered skim milk and blackstrap molasses. Hauser agitated medical hackles with pronouncements like his claim that we all have both an "appestat," which he defined as an acquired appetite for the wrong stuff, and a "hungerstat," or craving for nutritionally correct foods. He and Garbo sometimes shared hungerstat-driven lunches of wild-rice burgers and broiled grapefruit.

17   By the time Hay and Hauser bestrode the diet whirlwind, the public was beginning to flinch under a baffling bombardment of confusing claims. One expert, for example, plumped for a breakfast of whole-wheat pancakes with maple syrup, another advised vegetable soup, and a third urged melon, peaches or berries, a baked potato and broiled fish. Special combinations of foods, "magic pairs" like lamb chops and pineapple, were touted as bearers of unique "fat-burning" properties, a notion debunked by two generations of scientists.

From belts to creams to salts to ...

18   In such an atmosphere it was little wonder that almost any device, instrument or lotion that promised weight loss without the bother of stress or sacrifice found a ready market. As far back as the 1890s, a Boston druggist had peddled a corsetlike "obesity belt" bearing electrically charged disks that purportedly dispelled intestinal gas, disintegrated fat and dispersed tumors. By the 1930s, dieters could rub away flab with "reducing creams," melt it away with bath salts, or jiggle it away on a "Slendro Massager Table" or "the magic couch."

19   Slenderella reducing salons, which first appeared in 1950, invited women into curtained booths where they listened to piped-in music and quivered fully clothed on a specially designed vibrating table. They remained clad because of founder Larry Mack's belief that the "only place a respectable woman ever took her clothes off was her bedroom." Customers were given low-calorie diets disingenuously labeled "menu adjustments" to preserve the illusion that nothing so taxing as a diet was called for. By 1955, more than 16,000 women were shimmying daily in more than 100 Slenderella salons and shelling out $2 for each of the 30 to 150 sessions. Despite a Food and Drug Administration (FDA) warning that no device was effective for "spot reducing, melting away fat or breaking up fatty deposits," it was the Internal Revenue Service and not customer discontent that

brought Slenderella down in 1959. The name was later sold to a company that made low-cal jelly.

20   Dieting, the American Medical Association (AMA) declared in the mid-1950s, had become a national neurosis. Thinner was better—more attractive, more youthful, healthier, more productive. And if a product could deliver thinness in a reasonably palatable form, the possibilities were limitless. At least that's how it looked for the Mead Johnson drug company and the product Metrecal—short for "metered calories"—in 1960.

21   Metrecal came as a powder made from milk, soya flour, starch, corn oil, yeast, vitamins, coconut oil and chocolate, vanilla or butterscotch flavoring. A $1.59 can contained 900 calories and when mixed with four glasses of water provided a day's nourishment. (Metrecal was also sold in a premixed, liquid form.) It satisfied hunger, and it seemed to satisfy the medical establishment, which detected no nutritional Achilles heel. A dieter didn't even have to count calories and commonly dropped about ten pounds in two to three weeks. All of this accompanied by a smooth advertising campaign produced a bonanza: Mead Johnson's profits rocketed from $5.5 million to $13.3 million in a year.

22   Then, suddenly, consumers stopped buying. Nothing happened—no revelation, no assault in the courts. People simply got tired of swilling the same stuff meal after meal. Profits went south in 1962 and '63 while the company scrambled up a Metrecal cookie that failed to halt the plunge. Somebody suggested that Metrecal palled because people missed chewing; the Great Masticator may have been on to something after all.

23   Metrecal's boom and bust, like the profusion of exercise salons and the swelling numbers of diet books (from 60 in the 1960s to 260 in the '70s), diet foods, diet doctors and especially diet pills, was another sign that the diet biz was now a big-ticket enterprise. A 25-cent calorie-counter book that first appeared in 1951 had sold 17 million

copies by 1973. Diet pills in one form or another had been around for decades. A pamphlet one drug company distributed to doctors illuminated the ethics of the diet-pill trade: recommend NO diet or exercise, the company advised, prescribe plenty of tablets and demand payment in cash.

Take these whether you need 'em or not

24 In 1968, when *Life* magazine dispatched reporter Susanna McBee to visit ten "fat doctors" as an undercover patient, the FDA estimated that as many as 7,000 such practitioners were doling out more than two billion diet pills annually, including diuretics, barbiturates, amphetamines, thyroid tablets and laxatives. McBee, at about 5-feet-6 and 125 pounds, was anything but obese. Every one of her ten doctors prescribed pills, most after only a cursory examination and conversation; one saw her for three minutes and gave her 150 capsules. Her total haul from the ten healers was 1,479 pills.

25 The vilest potion concocted in the name of weight reduction was doubtless the liquid protein mixture popularized by Dr. Robert Linn in his 1970s book *The Last Chance Diet*. Like Banting and Fletcher in dieting's more innocent era, Linn presented himself as an ex-portly advertisement, claiming he had dropped 83 pounds while subsisting on his syrup. It was a loathsome blend of crushed animal horns, hooves and hides mixed with enzymes, tenderizers—one would hope so—and fruit flavoring. The idea was that 300 to 400 calories a day of this glop would sustain a person who was otherwise fasting. The AMA warned of side effects like renal and coronary disease. The FDA and the Centers for Disease Control investigated several dozen deaths among liquid protein consumers, but an estimated two million to four million hard-core dieters tried it anyway.

26 Esther Manz of Milwaukee became a diet-club pioneer after learning about the Alcoholics Anonymous network. She had no product or plan to hustle, just a consignment of fat to shed and the belief that it would be more pleasant to lose it amid an agreeable, mutually supportive group. She nourished the idea during a year of therapeutic weekly meetings with a few friends, lost 45 pounds and emerged with TOPS—for Take Off Pounds Sensibly (some called it Tomorrow Or Pretty Soon)—the first national dieting organization.

27 The TOPS clubs that blossomed around the country gave themselves good-natured names like Button Busters, Zipper Rippers, Thick 'n Tired and InvisiBelles. Members followed individual diets under the supervision of their doctors and met regularly to fuss over one another when they lost and shame one another when they gained. Backsliders were tried at a "Court of Weights and Measures" and deposited fines in piggy banks; the worst offender in one club was crowned "Queen Pig" and honored with a bouquet of weeds. By the late 1950s, the 60,000 members were losing an average of 15 pounds a year, but studies suggested that group dieters were not much more successful than solo, unsupervised reducers in keeping lost weight off.

28 Jean Nidetch, the Brooklyn-born talkaholic who founded Weight Watchers in 1963, was another overextended housewife who couldn't jettison pounds in solitude and, like Manz, she found Nirvana in a support group. Initially Weight Watchers differed from TOPS in that its members all followed the same diet, which involved no calorie-counting. Treating overeating almost as an addiction ("I used to hide chocolate cake in the laundry hamper," Nidetch confessed), it permitted unlimited gnoshing of certain vegetables while banning other foods altogether. Weight Watchers also differed from TOPS in that it was a profit-making business, and the proceeds from such products as frozen foods, desserts, cookbooks, scales and other goods were so rich that the company was gobbled up by the H. J. Heinz Company 16 years ago.

29 The somewhat startling truth about dieting is that, for all its up-and-down, cash-and-carry history, nothing much changes.

Elizabeth Sharon Hayenga puts it this way in her doctoral dissertation titled "Dieting Through the Decades": "Virtually everything . . . cottage cheese diets, low-carbohydrate diets, diet pills, diet clubs, fasting, liquid diets—is reincarnated with a new title, author or brand name decade after decade. And each new incarnation produces new sales records."

30 In the 1960s and '70s, the boffo diets came attached to doctors' names but most owed their high-protein, low-carbohydrate regimen to William Banting, the London undertaker who had beaten that old devil corpulence with a low-carbohydrate diet in the 1860s. One after another the white-coated savants appeared in the center ring clutching nutritional salvation between hard covers—Dr. Herman Taller with *Calories Don't Count* in 1961, Dr. Irwin Stillman with *The Doctor's Quick Weight-Loss Diet* in 1967, Dr. Robert Atkins with *Dr. Atkins' Diet Revolution* in 1972, and Dr. Herman Tarnower with *The Complete Scarsdale Medical Diet* in 1978.

High-fat fraud, extra-light fine

31 The Romanian-born Taller, a gynecologist, contended that his book reflected "new knowledge" that polyunsaturated fats "softened" body fat, which then melted away quicker. He promoted a high-fat diet supplemented with vegetable oil capsules, but he veered into trouble when he mentioned a particular mail-order company as a source for the capsules. To federal prosecutors, this sounded like an advertisement and, when it turned out that the doctor owned an interest in the capsule company, they indicted him for mail fraud, conspiracy and mislabeling. Convicted of 12 counts in 1967, Taller was given a suspended sentence and fined $7,000, probably far short of a month's royalties for his book.

32 Stillman, who was a medical consultant at Coney Island Hospital, advocated a regimen similar to Taller's but lower in fat and cholesterol, in deference to evidence linking high cholesterol to heart disease. He urged lean meats, cottage cheese, hard-boiled eggs and eight ten-ounce glasses of water a day. Atkins' diet was another spin of the same tune, spiced with the identification of a previously (and still) unknown substance he called FMH (for "fat mobilizing hormone"), which he said "moves fat around the body." His tolerance of high-cholesterol bacon, cream and mayonnaise appalled the medical establishment—one critic called it "planned malnutrition"—but went over big with dieters.

33 Tarnower's Scarsdale diet marked a return to the traditional low-calorie, low-fat, low-carbohydrate discipline, with meals precisely spelled out in a 14-day plan. But Tarnower, too, was prone to gild biology a bit, declaring on no particular authority that the food combination in his plan stimulated a unique metabolic change that diminished fat. He had little time to enjoy his celebrity as a diet maven. He was shot to death by a jealous lover in 1980—but that's another story.

34 Not until the late 1980s did disaffection with the received wisdom that thinner was better begin to simmer beneath a surface still littered with diet books (300 were in print in 1984). Researchers commenced taking potshots at long-accepted theories (SMITHSONIAN, January 1986): heredity and metabolism might have more to do with rotundity, they suggested, than overeating: "yo-yo" dieting, the chronic swings endured by many dieters, could do more long-run harm than good; some scientists contended that each of us has a "set point" weight that the body finds ways to maintain, diet or no. Was dietmania, after booming for a century or so, on the wane? Probably not, but last year *Consumer Reports* concluded an article on weight-loss methods with these heretical words: "The majority of dieters would probably do better to forget about cutting calories, focus on exercising and eating a healthful diet, and let the pounds fall where they may."

35 Let them fall where they may? You mean all those diets, all that self-denial

and self-discipline, all that ingenuity and imagination and hustle and con—all that was in vain? No more belts, rainbow pills or diet books? No more salons, clubs and obnoxious concoctions? That can't be right. Don't forget: I still hear somebody tapping away out there, cranking up yet another best-seller. This expert is laying the foundation of the diet revolution of all time. Really. It's the next big thing.

Notes: *Never Satisfied: A Cultural History of Diets, Fantasies and Fat* by Hillel Schwartz, Macmillan, 1986.

"Losing Weight: What Works, What Doesn't," *Consumer Reports*, June 1993.

"The Diet Biz" by Bonnie Blodgett, *Glamour*, January 1991.

Source: Donald Dale Jackson, The Art of Wishful Shrinking Has Made a Lot of People Rich, *Smithsonian*, November 1994.

DISCUSSION QUESTIONS

1. Do you agree with the commentary's appraisal of Jackson's use of connotative language? Is his use of language warranted by the evidence, or is it a sleight-of-hand tactic that should be avoided?

2. How different would the essay's effect be if the author had avoided all connotative language? You might want to rewrite one or two of the paragraphs that are especially slanted, using the most impartial, objective language.

3. Reread the section in Chapter 6 on "Supporting Facts Reported by Second- and Third-Party Sources." With a classmate or two, divide up the sources cited at the end of the article and investigate the expertise of the authors cited and the reputation of the publication. Consider whether these sources pass the tests of reliability, impartiality, and currency. Is the number of sources cited adequate? If not, what further kinds of sources would be useful?

4. Has this essay influenced your thinking on the subject? What features of the argument do you think are responsible for that (e.g., the number of examples, the sources cited, the organization of support, the connotative language, etc.)?

SUGGESTIONS FOR WRITING (17.1)

1. Write a three- to four-page causal argument speculating on the reasons for the public's willingness to believe the impossible when it comes to one of the following: dieting; get-rich-quick-schemes; exercise equipment; age-defying potions.

2. Conduct research for a five- to seven-page factual survey of a pastime that you find silly or a waste of time or senseless (e.g., gambling, bridge, golf, computer games, etc.). Including at least four sources you located, write an objective factual argument laying the background and evolution of this activity. In your argument, do not follow Jackson's example: avoid slanted, evaluative language. Use the APA form for your notes and bibliography.

3. Write an evaluation of one of the activities suggested in the preceding question. You may use slanted or connotative language, provided it is supported. Be sure to define your audience carefully so you can appeal to appropriate needs and values. Also, if necessary, define your evaluative term carefully.

INTUITIVE EATING

EVELYN TRIBOLE AND ELYSE RESCH

Intuitive Eating, *by Evelyn Tribole and Elyse Resch, is one of the many dieting "how to" books available on bookstore shelves. The book as a whole is an extended recommendation claiming that those who want to lose weight should* not *diet ("lose the diet mentality"). Instead, would-be dieters should rely on their own nutritional intuition to tell them when and what to eat.*

Tribole and Resch are registered dietitians. Both are regular contributors to the growing literature of dieting.

Step I: Recognize and Acknowledge the Damage That Dieting Causes

1   There is a substantial amount of research on the harm that dieting causes. Acknowledge that the harm is real, and that continued dieting will only perpetuate your problems. Some of the key side effects gleaned from major studies are described below in two categories, biological and emotional. As you read, take a personal inventory and ask yourself which of the problems you are already experiencing. Recognizing that dieting is the problem will help you break through the cultural myth that diets work. Remember, *if dieting is the problem, how can it be part of the solution?*

Damage from Dieting: Biological and Health

2   In every century, famine and human starvation has existed. Sadly, this is true even today. Survival of the fittest in the past meant survival of the fattest—only those with adequate energy stores (fat) could survive a famine. Consequently, our bodies are still equipped in this modern age to combat starvation at the cellular level. As far as the body is concerned, dieting is a form of starvation, even though it's voluntary.

3   Chronic dieting has been shown to:

- *Teach the body to retain more fat when you start eating again.* Low-calorie diets double the enzymes that make and store fat in the body. This is a form of biological compensation to help the body store more energy, or fat, after dieting.

- *Slow the rate of weight loss* with each successive attempt to diet. This has been shown to be true in both rat and human studies.

- *Decrease metabolism.* Dieting triggers the body to become more efficient at utilizing calories by lowering the body's need for energy.

- *Increase binges and cravings.* Both humans and rats have been shown to overeat after chronic food restriction. Food restriction stimulates the brain to launch a cascade of cravings to eat *more.* After substantial weight loss, studies show that rats prefer eating more fat, while people have been shown to prefer foods both high in fat and sugar.

- *Increase risk of premature death and heart disease.* A thirty-two-year study of more than 3,000 men and women in the Framingham Heart Study has shown that *regardless of initial weight,* people whose weight repeatedly goes up and down—known as weight cycling or yo-yo dieting—have a higher overall death rate and twice the normal risk of dying from heart disease. These results were independent of cardiovascular risk factors, and held true regardless if a person was thin or obese. The harm from yo-yo dieting may be equal to the risks of staying obese.

Similarly, results of the Harvard Alumni Health Study show that people who lose and gain at least eleven pounds within a decade or so, don't live as long as those who maintain a stable weight.

- *Cause satiety cues to atrophy.* Dieters usually stop eating due to a self-imposed limit rather than inner cues of fullness. This, combined with skipping meals, can condition you to eat meals of increasingly larger size.
- *Cause body shape to change.* Yo-yo dieters who continually regain the lost weight tend to regain weight in the abdominal area. This type of fat storage increases the risk of heart disease.

4   Other documented side effects include headaches, menstrual irregularities, fatigue, dry skin, and hair loss.

Damage from Dieting: Psychological and Emotional

5   Psychological experts reported the following adverse effects at the landmark 1992 National Institutes of Health, Weight Loss and Control Conference:

- Dieting is linked to eating disorders
- Dieting may cause stress or make the dieter more vulnerable to its effects.
- Independent of body weight itself, dieting is correlated with feelings of failure, lowered self-esteem, and social anxiety.
- The dieter is often vulnerable to loss of control over eating when violating "the rules" of the diet, whether there was an actual or *perceived* transgression of the diet! The mere perception of eating a forbidden food, regardless of actual calorie content, is enough to trigger overeating.

6   In a separate report, psychologists David Garner and Susan Wooley make a compelling case against the high cost of false hope from dieting. They conclude that:

- Dieting gradually erodes confidence and self-trust
- Many obese individuals assume they could not have become obese unless they possessed some *fundamental character deficit.* Garner and Wooley argue

that while many obese individuals may experience binge eating and depression, these psychological and behavioral symptoms are the *result of dieting.* But these overweight individuals easily interpret these symptoms as further evidence of an underlying problem. Yet, obese people do not have inordinate psychological disturbances compared to normal weight people.

Step 2: Be Aware of Diet-Mentality Traits and Thinking

The diet mentality surfaces in subtle forms,   7
even when you decide to reject dieting. It's important to recognize common characteristics of the diet mentality; it will let you know if you are still playing the dieting game. Forget about willpower, being obedient, and failing. The general difference in the ways the dieter versus the nondieter views eating, exercise, and progress are summarized by a chart at the end of this chapter.

Forget Willpower.   While no doctor would   8
expect a patient to "will" blood pressure to normal levels, physicians frequently expect their overweight patients to "will" their weight loss by restricting their food, according to Susan Z. Yanovski, M.D. This is also a prevailing attitude among our clients and many Americans—all you need is willpower and a little self-control. In a 1993 Gallup poll, the most common obstacle to losing weight cited by women was willpower.

For example, Marilyn is a highly suc-   9
cessful lawyer who climbed to the top of the corporate ladder. She credits determination, willpower, and self-discipline as being responsible for her success. Yet, when she tried to use these exemplary principles in her dieting attempts, she always failed. Whatever success she had achieved in her professional life was dulled by her sense of failure with eating.

Why was Marilyn able to be so disci-   10
plined in one area of her life but not in the other? The word "discipline" derives from the word "disciple." According to Stephen Covey's work, if you are a disciple to your

own deep values that have an overriding purpose, it's likely that you'll have the *will* to carry them out. Marilyn believed deeply that writing exacting contracts and keeping immaculate records were requisites to building confidence with her clients and her law firm. But, somehow, hearing that bread was wrong on one diet and anything with sugar was wrong on another, did not engender the same kind of deep beliefs. Try as she might, she couldn't really believe that chocolate chip cookies were that evil!

11   *Willpower* can be defined as an attempt to counter natural desires and replace them with proscriptive rules. The desire for sweets is natural, normal, and quite pleasant! Any diet that tells you you can't have sweets, is going against your natural desire. The diet becomes a set of rigid rules, and these kinds of rules can only trigger rebellion.

12   *Willpower does not belong in Intuitive Eating.* As Marilyn became an Intuitive Eater, she found that listening to her personal signals reinforced her natural instincts, rather than fighting them. She had no one else's proscriptive rules to follow or to rebel against. Marilyn has stopped fighting the phantom willpower battle and she has lost all the weight with which she had been struggling.

13   ***Forget Being Obedient.*** A well meaning suggestion by a spouse or significant other, such as: "Honey, you should have the broiled chicken . . ." or "You shouldn't eat those fries . . ." can set off an inner food rebellion. In this type of food combat, your only weapon to fight back becomes a double order of fries. Our clients call this *forget-you eating.*

14   In physics, resistance always occurs as a reaction to force. We see this principle in action in society as riots often erupt when the force of authority becomes too great. Similarly, the *simple act of being told what to do* (even if it's something you want to do) can trigger a rebellious chain reaction. Just like "terrible two year olds," or teenagers who revolt to prove they are independent, dieters can initiate rebellious eating in response to the act of dieting, with its set of rigid rules dictating what to eat. And so, it's not sur-

prising to hear from our clients that breaking the rules of a diet makes them feel just like they did when they were defiant teens.

15   But take heart, rebellion is a normal act of self-preservation—protecting your space or personal boundaries.

16   Think of a personal boundary as a tall brick fence surrounding you, with only one gate. Only you can open that gate, if you choose. Therefore, no one is allowed inside, unless you invite the person in. Within your fence reside private feelings, thoughts, and biological signals. People who *assume* they know what you need and tell you what to do are picking the lock to your gate, or invading your boundaries. No one could possibly know what's inside unless you tell him, by inviting him in.

17   What diet or diet counselor can possibly know when you are hungry or how much food it will take to satisfy you? How can anyone but you know what texture and taste sensations will be pleasing to your palate? In the world of dieting, personal boundaries are crossed at many levels. For example, you are told what to eat, how much of it to eat, and when to eat it. These decisions should be personal choices, with respect for individual autonomy and body signals. While food guidance may come from elsewhere, *you* should ultimately be responsible for the *when, what,* and *how much* of eating.

18   When a diet doctor or a diet plan invades your boundaries, it's normal to feel powerless. The longer you follow the food restrictions, the greater the assault to your autonomy. Here is where the paradox lies. When dieting, you will likely rebel by eating more—to restore your autonomy and protect your boundaries. But the act of rebelling can make you feel as out of control as a city riot. Instead, you have an inner food fight on your hands. But once the food rebellion is unleashed, its intensity reinforces feelings of lack of control and the belief that you don't possess willpower. Ultimately you begin to drown in a sea of self-doubt and shame. *What begins as a psychologically healthy behavior, ends in disaster.* Ultimately, weight loss is sabotaged as a result of personal boundary protection. With Intu-

itive Eating, there is no need to rebel, because you become the one in charge!

19   Boundaries are also invaded when someone makes comments about your weight or how you should look. Again, you are bound to rebel by overeating. It's a way of saying "forget you" once again; "You have no right to tell me what to weigh."

20   Rachel is an artist who had dieted all of her life. She was married to a successful lawyer who wanted to show off his beautiful *slim* wife to all of his colleagues. He'd continually make subtle remarks that she wasn't as thin as she could be. He would even go so far as to give her dirty looks when she reached for a rich dessert at a party. Rachel rebelled against her husband by sneaking foods behind his back (free from his evil eye). While going through the Intuitive Eating process, Rachel discovered that she was actually keeping extra weight on as the ultimate form of rebellion toward her husband.

21   But instead of feeling strong and powerful from her rebellion, she found that she actually felt weak, out of control, and miserable. She knew that she would feel better at her natural, lower weight, but "something" kept making her turn to the hidden extra foods. Rachel had been trapped in a game of control, boundary invasion, and rebellion all her life. Her husband and the world of dieting had been trying to control this free spirited woman. To protect her boundaries, she would fight the diets by overeating and fight her husband's inappropriate demands by staying overweight.

22   Eventually, Rachel stood up to her well meaning husband and told him that he had no right to make comments about her food or her weight. Although initially resistant, he began to respect her boundaries. She also made a firm commitment to give up dieting. As a result, Rachel was shocked to find that her secret eating disappeared, as did her self doubt, and she began to lose weight without a struggle.

23   ***Forget About Failure.*** All of our chronic dieters walk into our offices feeling as if they are failures. Whether they are highly placed executives, prominent celebrities, or straight A students, they all talk about their food experiences shamefully, and they doubt whether they'll ever be able to feel successful in the area of eating. The diet mentality reinforces feelings of success or failure. You can't fail at Intuitive Eating—it's a learning process at every point along the way. What used to be thought of as a setback, will instead be seen as a growth experience. You'll get right back on track when you see this as progress, not failure.

Step 3: Get Rid of the Dieter's Tools

24   The dieter relies on external forces to regulate his eating, sticking to a regimented food plan, eating because it's time, or eating only a specified (and measured) amount, whether hungry or not. The dieter also validates progress by external forces, primarily the scale, asking "How many pounds have I lost? Is my weight up or down?" It's time to throw out your dieting tools. Get rid of the meal plans and the bathroom scales. If all it took was a good "sensible" calorie-restricted meal plan to lose weight, we'd be a nation of thin people—free meal plans are readily available from magazines, newspapers, and even some food companies.

25   *The Scale As False Idol.* "Please, please, let the number be . . ." This wishful number prayer is not occurring in the casinos of Las Vegas, but in private homes throughout the country. But just like the desperate gambler waiting for his lucky number to come in, so is it futile for the dieter to pay homage to the "scale god." In one sweep of the scale roulette, hopes and desperation create a daily drama that will ultimately shape what mood you'll be in for the day. Ironically, "good" and "bad" scale numbers can *both* trigger overeating—whether it's a congratulatory eating celebration or a consolation party.

26   The scale ritual sabotages body and mind efforts; it can in one moment devalue days, weeks, and even months of progress, as illustrated with Connie.

27   Connie had been working very hard at Intuitive Eating and refrained from weighing herself, which in itself was a feat since she originally weighed in daily, and sometimes

even twice a day at home. But Connie felt she had made so much progress in three months that she was certain she had lost a significant amount of weight. To "confirm" her progress, Connie stepped on the scale. But the number of pounds she had lost was disappointing, compared to how great she felt. The momentary brush with the scale boomeranged Connie right back to the diet mentality. That week, Connie cut back on her food intake, which resulted in a large binge. Stepping on the scale was a step back into the diet mentality. It was no surprise that Connie countered her scale experience with a dieting approach. She also thought, "I must be doing something wrong." Her newfound trust began to erode—all with a single trip to the scale.

28   So much power is given to the almighty scale that it ultimately sabotages our efforts. But in the case of Sherry, she found the weighing process to be so humiliating that she had postponed going to doctors for fifteen years! At the age of fifty-five, Sherry had not had a mammogram or other essential physical exams because she did not want to be weighed at the doctor's office (although she weighed in at home daily). In this case, the scale was getting in the way of Sherry's health. She was at risk for breast cancer because it ran in her family. Getting the mammogram was more important than any number on the scale, but Sherry couldn't face the routine admonishments from the nursing staff. It was standard procedure—weigh the patient regardless of the reason for the appointment. Sherry did not realize that she had the right to refuse to be weighed. She finally got the courage after our work together. She made a doctor's appointment and refused to be weighed since it was not an essential component of her medical care at the moment. Fortunately her physical exam results were healthy.

29   We have found that the "weigh-in" factor usually detracts from a person's progress. In the "old days" when we used to weigh all patients, we found that sessions were often spent on why the weight went up or did not move at all, and they became scale-counseling sessions. Our patients also dreaded the weighing-in part as much as we did.

When a Pound Is Not a Pound.   Many factors can influence a person's weight which do not reflect that person's body fat. For example, two cups of water weigh one pound. If you tend to retain water or bloat, the scale can easily rise a few pounds without a change in what you have eaten. But for the oft guilt-ridden dieter, the consequences of water weight can seem severe. For example, we have had many patients feel bad about eating an extra dessert over the weekend and weigh themselves on the following Monday. The scale shoots up five pounds—and they *believe* they gained five pounds of *fat*. Since many dieter-clients are quick with the calorie calculator, we ask, "Did you eat an *extra* 17,500 calories over the weekend?" Of course not, would be their retort. Yet to make five pounds of fat requires a calorie *excess* of 17,500 calories above normal eating (one pound of fat is equivalent to 3,500 calories).

31   So how do you explain the weight gain? Water weight. Any time the scale suddenly rises or falls, it is usually because of a fluid shift in the body. Eating high-sodium foods can also provoke water retention (not fat retention) in salt-sensitive individuals. Yet how easily chronic dieters believe they did something wrong; they must have single-handedly gobbled five pounds worth of food! No! No! No!

32   Similarly, losing two pounds immediately from an hour of aerobics is not a two pound fat loss. Rather, it's mostly water loss from sweat.

33   Jubilant dieters who think that they have lost ten pounds in a week may be in for an unwanted surprise. While it may be true that the scale indicated ten pounds less than when they weighed one week ago, the question is, what *kind* of weight did they lose? To lose ten pounds of fat in one week requires an energy deficit of 35,000 calories, or a deficit of 5,000 calories each day! The average woman only eats about 1,500 to 1,600 calories per day. The sad reality is that this

Summary: The Diet Mentality Versus the
Nondiet Mentality

Issue	Diet Mentality	Nondiet Mentality
Eating/Food Choices	• Do I deserve it? • If I eat a heavy food, I try to find a way to make up for it. • I feel guilty when I eat heavy foods. • I usually describe a day of eating as either good or bad. • I view food as the enemy.	• Am I hungry • Do I want it? • Will I be deprived if I don't eat it? • Will it be satisfying? • Does it taste good? • I deserve to enjoy eating without guilt.
Exercise Benefits	• I focus primarily on the calories burned. • I feel guilty if I miss a designated exercise day.	• I focus primarily on how exercise makes me feel, especially the energizing and stress-relieving factors.
View of Progress	• How many pounds did I lose? • How do I look? • What do other people think of my weight? • I have good willpower.	• While I'm concerned with my weight, it is not my primary goal or indicator of progress. • I have increased trust with myself and food. • I am able to let go of "eating indiscretions." • I recognize inner body cues.

person is losing a lot of water weight, usually at the expense of their muscles, due to the process of *muscle-wasting*. Muscle is made up mainly of water (about 70 percent).

When a hungry body is not given enough calories, the body cannibalizes itself for an energy source. The prime directive of the body is that it must have energy, at any cost—it's part of the survival mechanism. The protein in muscles is converted to valuable energy for the body. When a muscle cell is destroyed, water is released and eventually excreted—there's your precious weight loss. The whittled-away muscle contributes to lowering your metabolism. Muscles are metabolically active tissue—generally the more muscle we have, the higher our metabolic rate. That's one of the reasons men burn more calories than women—they have more muscle mass.

Increased muscle mass, while metabolically more active and desirable, weighs more than fat. Muscle also takes up less space than fat. While this is certainly beneficial, a chronic dieter often gets frustrated by the rising, or unchanging, scale number. *The scale does not reflect body composition*—just like weighing a piece of steak at the butcher's does not tell you how lean the meat is.

Weighing in on the scale only serves to keep you focused on your weight, it doesn't help with the process of getting back in touch with Intuitive Eating. Constant weigh-ins can leave you frustrated and impede your progress. Best bet—stop weighing yourself.

Works Cited: Associated Press (Washington). Vitamin retailer to pay fine. *AP Online*, April 29, 1994.

Berdanier, C.D., and McIntosh, M.K. Weight loss—weight regain: A vicious cycle. *Nutrition Today* 26, 5(1991):6.

Berg, F.M. *The Health Risks of Weight Loss*. Hettinger, N.D.: Healthy Living Institute, 1993.

Blackburn, G.L., et al. Weight cycling: The experience of human dieters. *American Journal of Clinical Nutrition* 49(1989):1105.

———. Why and how to stop weight cycling in overweight adults. *Eating Disorders Review* 4, 1(1993):1.

Ciliska, D. *Beyond Dieting*. New York, N.Y.: Brunner/Mazel, 1990.

Foreyt, J.P., and Goodrick, G.K. *Living Without Dieting*. Houston, TX.: Harrison, 1992.

———. Weight Management Without Dieting. *Nutrition Today* March/April (1993):4.

Gallup Organization. Women's Knowledge and Behavior Regarding Health and Fitness. Conducted for American Dietetic Association and Weight Watchers, June 1993.

Garrow, J.S. Treatment of obesity. *Lancet* 340(1992):409–13.

Goodrick, G.K., and Foreyt, J.P. Why treatments for obesity don't last. *Journal of the American Dietetic Association* 91, 10(1991):1243

Grodner, M. Forever dieting: Chronic dieting syndrome. *Journal of Nutrition Education* 24, 4(1992):207–10.

Hartmann, E. *Boundaries in the Mind. A New Psychology of Personality*. New York, N.Y.: Basic Books, 1991.

Hill, A.J., and Robinson, A. Dieting concerns have a functional effect on the behaviour of nine-year-old girls. *British Journal of Clinical Psychology* 30(1991):265–67.

Katherine, A. *Boundaries—Where You End and I Begin*. Park Ridge, Ill. Parkside Publishing, 1991.

Kern, P.A., et al. The effects of weight loss on the activity and expression of adipose-tissue lipoprotein lipase in very obese humans. *New England Journal of Medicine* 322,15(1990):1053–59.

National Research Council *Diet and Health* National Academy Press, Washington, D.C., 1989.

Polivy, J., and Herman, C.P. Undieting: A program to help people stop dieting. *International Journal of Eating Disorders* 11, 3(1992) 261–68.

Rodin, J., et al. Weight cycling and fat distribution *International Journal of Obesity* 14(1990): 303–10.

Wilson, G.T. Short-Term Psychological Benefits and Adverse Effects of Weight Loss. NIH Technology Assessment Conference: Methods for Voluntary Weight Loss and Control, March 30–April 1, 1992.

Wooley, S.C., and Garner, D.M. Obesity treatment. The high cost of false hope. *Journal of the American Dietetic Association* 91, 10(1991) 1248.

Yanovski, S.Z. Are anorectic agents the magic bullet for obesity? Editorial *Arch Family Medicine* 2(1993)1025–27.

Source: Evelyn Tribole, *Intuitive Eating: A Recovery Book for the Chronic Dieter*. M.S., R.D. & Elyse Resch, M. S., R. D, New York: St. Martin's Press, 1995. pp. 49–60.

DISCUSSION QUESTIONS

1. This argument of recommendation emphasizes the future. After reviewing Chapter 10 on writing recommendations, identify and evaluate the effectiveness of the argument's support.

2. What are the needs and values being appealed to in this set of recommendations? (Hint: the list will be considerably longer than the obvious value of thinness.)

3. The authors present a number of brief case studies to illustrate their arguments about the negative effects of dieting. Discuss with your class the effectiveness of these examples. What, if anything, do they add to the argument?

4. Discuss the reliability of facts in this essay (be sure to study the references listed at the end). As a reader, are you confident that the third-party facts supporting this recommendation are authoritative, sufficiently recent, and reasonably objective?

5. Do you find the chart on p. 355 to be a helpful summary of the argument's content? Would the argument be as effective without this chart?

SUGGESTIONS FOR WRITING (17.2)

1. Write your own set of recommendations for losing weight, based upon your own experience or that of someone you know. Your audience will be a group of your peers who have struggled with their weight. Be sure that the causal connection between your recommendation and the future effect is plausible.

2. With a group of your classmates, discuss possible reasons for our worship of thinness. Then, using the best ideas generated by this discussion, write a three-page causal argument speculating on the causes of the high value we place on thinness.

3. Select a popular fashion magazine (e.g., *Vogue, GQ, Mademoiselle*). After studying the photographs carefully, write an inductive factual argument describing the body type prized by this magazine.

4. Write a one- to two-page letter to a friend recommending the argument by Tribole and Resch. Be sure to identify to yourself the emphasis of your recommendation (present, future, or combination). Your argument should include a secondary evaluative argument.

PUBLIC EATING

MICHELLE STACEY

"Public Eating" first appeared as a chapter in Michelle Stacey's book, Consumed: Why Americans Love, Hate, and Fear Food *(1994). A professional writer and editor, Stacey claims no particular expertise in the subject of the American diet. She has written on a variety of subjects for various publications, including* The New Yorker; *she has also been an editor for such magazines as* Mademoiselle, Savvy, *and* Outside.

1   The big wall clock in the cramped, steamy kitchen of the Blue Ribbon restaurant was inching toward eight on a Friday evening, and things were beginning to accelerate. Escargots simmered with bacon and apples in a reduction of veal stock and red wine (soon to be enhanced by a sizable hunk of butter mixed with herbs and garlic), salmon and steak sizzled over a grill, huge pots of gravy and broth issued wisps of steam, a whole trout bubbled in a deep fryer. The three chefs in charge of all this—Eric and Bruce Bromberg, brothers and co-owners of the restaurant (with Eric's wife, Ellen), and sous-chef Kris Polak—moved among the various pots and sauté pans with a frenzy that seemed partly balletic and always on the verge of dangerously chaotic. Bruce flipped and salted the contents of several frying pans in one swift movement; Eric slathered grilled vegetables with oil, then spun around to pare delicate slices from a fat-topped hunk of duck breast; Kris deposited pieces of steaming-hot fried chicken on a plate with bare fingers, wincing with each one. Shawn Sant Amour, the waiter who served as liaison between the dining room staff and the kitchen, emerged

slightly breathless at the window—the counter between the kitchen and the waiters' station—and shouted "Ordering!," slapping down two written orders. "And fire tables ten and twelve," he added. "Firing" is the kitchen's signal to put the entrees on to cook; a sign that the customers at that table are winding down on their appetizers. "Okay," Eric called out to the other two chefs, "we're going to go on it all now. You ready? Stay with the program. Want me to call them one more time? Okay: two paella, one London broil, one tofu ravioli, one turkey, two catfish, one rack of lamb." Bruce and Kris responded silently, spinning for new pans, reaching for another clump of butter.

2   At Blue Ribbon, a small (sixteen-table) restaurant in the heart of SoHo, New York's hip, downtown neighborhood, the kitchen is located at the bottom of a steep flight of stairs. This setup can appear a little Biblical at times: upstairs all is calm and cool, in a dining room bathed in a warm yellow light and decorated in rose tints and wood, small enough to be intimate and not too loud; downstairs is a cramped, harshly lit, steaming room easily twenty degrees hotter, filled with clangs and shouts and crashes, a seeming hell of cookery. But in another sense the atmosphere, on that Friday night the week before Christmas, 1992, was positively jubilant. Blue Ribbon had opened barely more than a month before, on November 3, and the restaurant was already packing people in. That very Friday Blue Ribbon had received a short but positive review in the *New York Times,* in the newspaper's "$25 and Under" slot, and the night before they had served dinner to a table hosted by Gael Greene, restaurant critic for *New York* magazine. In a business renowned for its brutality and its many failed establishments, Blue Ribbon was enjoying a very promising start.

3   But beneath the jokes exchanged between the kitchen and waitstaff, most of them about the fact that many people were ordering exactly what was mentioned in the *Times* re-

view (potato pancakes, escargots, beef marrow with oxtail marmalade, paella, salmon) ran a very serious concern: How were people liking their food? Plates that were completely cleaned were displayed proudly to the chefs; one half-eaten plate of paella prompted a somber postmortem. Eric Bromberg, at thirty-one an experienced, Cordon-Bleu-educated chef and spiritual head of the Blue Ribbon kitchen (its name is the English translation of Cordon Bleu, where Bruce also took his degree), wants people to like the food he makes for them, and in pursuit of that goal he will cook whatever his customers want to eat. That is not to suggest that he does not have a point of view about food. He has, in fact, very strong opinions about what he likes, but they are matched by a strong opinion about service and the notion that people who are paying for their food deserve to get exactly what they ask for.

Bromberg has attempted to serve both   4 himself and his customers by, quite simply, cooking for others the food that he likes to eat himself. He first got a chance to create a menu that truly reflected that at a New York restaurant right across the street from Blue Ribbon called Nick and Eddie, where he was a co-owner. (Before that he had worked at several high-profile New York restaurants, including three years at the American Hotel in Sag Harbor, a resort community on Long Island.) Nick and Eddie, which opened in 1990, was one of the best of a miniboom in "new American" restaurants that found interesting, sometimes European-inspired ways to present some classic American foods—catfish, hamburgers, mashed potatoes, leg of lamb, pork loin, hot fudge sundaes. Opening when Americans were becoming ever more concerned about meats and fats, Nick and Eddie bucked the trend and served food that just happened to be deliciously sinful to capacity crowds.

Blue Ribbon opened to an even more   5 diet-concerned clientele, in an age when meat-and-potatoes are considered déclassé and many restaurants feel compelled to offer at least some "spa cuisine" or "heart-healthy" entrées (even Nick and Eddie had, by this time, added two dishes adorned with a heart motif on the menu to signify low-fat and low-salt). Bromberg's concession to such societal pressure was to offer tofu ravioli on a plate heaped high with glistening grilled and steamed vegetables, his single vegetarian entrée among twenty-two others that included beef stew, fried chicken, sesame-glazed catfish, rib steak, swordfish, leg of lamb, chocroute garni, hamburgers and turkey burgers, and a paella filled with clams, shrimp, salmon, sweet peppers, turkey sausage, and saffron rice. He soon sensed the need for another nonmeat dish and added vegetable fried rice; both the rice and the ravioli became good sellers.

6   Bromberg seems completely sanguine about offering such a full-bodied menu, and part of his unconcern may derive from this knowledge: Some people are going to ask him to make changes in what he cooks, no matter what he offers. If this era is diet-obsessed, it is also unashamedly activist. Almost every magazine article or book about changing one's diet includes advice about eating out: Request your food cooked without oils, sauces on the side, balsamic vinegar in place of mayonnaise, salt banished. Eating out is no longer automatically an occasion for indulging, eating something you wouldn't cook at home, or even trusting a chef to prepare his or her dishes in the best possible way. Paying for one's food to be prepared by others now rivals home-cooking—in 1990 Americans spent 42.5 percent of their food dollars on meals away from home—and the result is a new tradition: second-guessing the chef. Why go off your diet, runs the reasoning behind this, simply because you're in a restaurant? This attitude has brought a new, perhaps not too inviting, day for chefs. It also means that chefs have a unique insight into the way Americans truly eat: they see how people request their food (and therefore how they imagine or idealize it), and they see what actually gets eaten. There is often a sizable gap between the two.

7   Bromberg has a layered reaction to the new wave in restaurant ordering: While he professes himself happy to make any changes his customers desire, he regards many of those changes as misinformed and rather silly. He described these particular culinary trials to me on a sunny October day about a month before Blue Ribbon opened. Because the restaurant was in the midst of renovation (all accomplished by Eric, Bruce, and a few core members of the staff) and choked with plaster dust, we sat in a nearby park. It was an unseasonably warm day and Bromberg wore roomy California-surfer shorts and a T-shirt. He is slightly heavy-set (he confessed to being on a diet himself), with dark, longish hair just beginning to be touched with premature gray, and a face that can look a little cherubic, especially when flushed pink with the heat of a kitchen. His manner is brisk and straightforward; when he talks about food and how people eat, opinions and judgments come flowing out. "I got into this business because I love to cook," he said, "and I love to make stuff that people like. And if that means putting fish and one piece of broccoli in the steamer and the person that eats that says, 'That was fantastic,' I'm just as happy about that as I would be to make foie gras with filet mignon in some very fancy French preparation."

8   But, Bromberg has found, there is a recurring problem with that scenario: People don't always like what they think they *ought* to eat. "Why do you go to a restaurant in the first place?" he asked. "Because people have said the food is good, in one way or another. Now, some people go to that restaurant and then say, 'I want my fish steamed, I want my vegetables steamed, I want my sauce on the side or no sauce at all, I want a side of balsamic vinegar'—all of these are common orders. But then when the food gets there, some people end up saying, 'This was bland and really not very good. I don't know why everybody thinks this restaurant's so good.' There's a real

contradiction here. I do think customers should have exactly what they want. But when people get too aggressive and too picky, it affects the flavors. I wouldn't suggest that a piece of steamed fish and some steamed vegetables isn't delicious, because I think it is, and it's natural flavors. But many people are bored with those flavors they've grown up eating food that's been seasoned, that has salt and pepper, that has herbs, cooked in butter or oil, and then they order something with none of those ingredients and say, 'This doesn't taste great to me.' And I think another thing that occurs to them is that they could go to the supermarket, get some vegetables, go home, put them in a dish with a little water, plastic-wrap it, put it in the steamer or microwave, and have the whole thing for two dollars instead of seventeen dollars."

9   While Bromberg professed an unending willingness to rearrange his menu for customers with special requests—"demanding customers is what the business is all about," he said—several aspects of the current rage for such rearrangement clearly stick in his craw (in addition to the one he just described, being judged as a chef on food that he prepared to someone else's specifications). One is the irritating habit some customers have of making menu changes and not recognizing that the kitchen will need extra time to accommodate them. "If someone wants their mashed potatoes with skim milk or olive oil, that's fine," said Bromberg, "but it's going to take an extra fifteen minutes or so to cook the potatoes, get a new thing going. Most customers understand that, but a reasonable amount would also say, 'Where the hell is my food?' That's kind of a dangerous trend in terms of where restaurants are going."

10   Then, too, he is annoyed—but also sometimes amused—by the huge volume of misinformation that permeates his customers' desires. "We get some pretty strange orders," he said. "Like: I'm on a diet so I don't want mashed potatoes, I want french fries.' Or, 'I'd like my burger with no bread, and a double order of mashed pota-

toes.' Or people don't understand that while olive oil has no cholesterol, it has just as much fat as butter, just as many calories. So someone will say they're on a diet and they don't want butter but they do want olive oil. Or they ask for their salad dressing on the side, or just oil and vinegar on the side, and then they end up putting three or four or five tablespoons of oil on their salad and think they're eating healthy. The American public gets fixated on words and specifics. We see it immediately in the kitchen, an absolutely up-to-the-minute response to health news. There could be a report on the 'Channel Seven News' about polluted waters at six o'clock, and at eight o'clock people are asking us, 'Is this polluted fish? Where does this fish come from?' Every health item in the *New York Times* has an instant response, too. As a chef you either stay up-to-date or you don't know what you're talking about."

Bromberg felt that health concerns were   11 so central to his work that in the fall of 1991 he spent several weeks at the Duke Fitness Center at Duke University in Durham, North Carolina, one of the nation's leading diet and nutrition centers. "I studied heart disease and cholesterol and obesity and every other issue pertaining to food and human beings," Bromberg said. "I learned that going over the edge—like no fat, no meat, limiting your diet completely to vegetables—is less beneficial than moderating. Now, I'm sure I'd get a pretty good argument about that from macrobiotic people, but this program said that for healthy eating you should have a balanced intake." Bromberg has translated that idea of moderation into a theory of restaurant eating based on twin notions of enjoyment and self-control. "Once you get into a good, high-quality restaurant," he said, "I think health concerns are so apparent now that, even if you get a cream sauce on a fish dish, you're talking about maybe an ounce or so of sauce. Now, an ounce of cream—I don't know the exact number of calories, but it's not a lot. It's on your fish and you eat your fish, and usually there's some sauce left on the plate when you're done. Now, you have the option of sopping that up with your bread or leaving it on the plate. Or, for instance, take the mashed potatoes we make; they have cream and butter in them, but realistically in a single serving the amount you're getting may be a teaspoon of cream and a teaspoon of butter. Not an enormous amount. I think moderating your intake is the key. If you like bacon and you want to have it, have a piece—about seventy calories, not a big deal. If you eat twelve pieces of bacon every morning, you're probably running some kind of risk. But I think substituting your taste sensations and enjoyment from food now, so that you'll sustain yourself for another year and a half or two years down the road . . . well, I think it would be nice to have enjoyed your meals along the way."

12   What seems to Eric Bromberg a simple matter of moderate self-knowledge and self-control—leaving a little rich sauce on the plate if one is concerned about fats, for instance—seems to constitute a significant challenge to many restaurant patrons, however. Restaurants seem to be, in fact, the ground upon which Americans duel most fiercely with their conflicted impulses toward renunciation and indulgence. Part of the reason for this may lie in the very public nature of restaurants—where else does one have to speak aloud one's choices for a meal? These days the social pressure is on to show one's nutritional correctness, which can be indicated not only by opting for seafood or salad but by specifying "sauce on the side" or "no oil used in preparation." And yet this choice is made especially difficult by the immediate juxtaposition of the tempting and forbidden: steak au poivre and fettuccini Alfredo offer themselves up right next to the grilled scallops on a bed of radicchio and the boneless, skinless breast of chicken. An increasing number of people split the difference; many chefs tell of serving meals that begin with a light salad, dressing on the side, and end with the double-chocolate mousse surrounded by raspberry crème sauce. If this schizophrenic response threatens to dull

the pleasure of the chef's job—which has traditionally been defined as serving others the tastiest dishes one could devise—it could also be perceived as a challenge to be more inventive and more flexible. But even those chefs, like Eric Bromberg, who strive most of the time to treat their patrons' food-health sensitivities as an opportunity to be more creative find themselves losing patience when customers' zeal outpaces logic, when the perception of what is healthiest or most abstemious overshadows the reality of what a meal is all about.

13   When the National Restaurant Association conducted a nationwide survey of restaurant-goers in late 1989 that would assess "consumer attitudes toward nutrition in restaurants," the researchers found that almost everyone fell naturally into one of three categories. First there were the "unconcerned patrons"—self-described "meat-and-potatoes" types who eat whatever they feel like eating and whose most frequent orders in restaurants include steak or roast beef, fried chicken or fish, premium ice creams, and rich, gooey or chocolate desserts. At the other extreme were the "committed patrons," who believe that diet plays a role in the prevention of illness and whose restaurant food choices reflect that belief; their favorite orders are broiled or baked seafood, poultry without skin, raw-vegetable appetizers, fresh fruit, vegetables seasoned with only herbs or lemon juice, whole-grain muffins, and low-fat frozen yogurt. Between these two groups an almost equally large eating-type emerged: "vacillating patrons." The vacillators are concerned about health and nutrition, but when they eat out they are what the survey calls "taste-and-occasion-driven." Their restaurant choices are all over the map: they're likely to specify lean meats, food cooked without salt, and caffeine-free coffee, but they also favor steak or roast beef, fried chicken or fish, premium ice creams, and, like the unconcerned eaters, "rich, gooey or chocolate desserts." They are also much more likely to eat differently in a restaurant than they do at home.

14   These groups divided the population almost exactly into thirds, although the committed patrons are on the rise (moving from 35 percent in 1986 to 39 percent in 1989) and the unconcerned eaters are waning (from 38 percent in 1986 to 32 percent in 1989). All of this means that two-thirds of all restaurant-goers—the committed plus the vacillating—make at least some of their food choices based on nutritional concerns. That's why the National Restaurant Association also offers a nutrition guide to restaurateurs to help them modify recipes and menus to meet the demands of the concerned eaters, as well as offering a nutrient-analysis service that uses computer software to calculate the nutritional content of recipes.[1] That's also why when the *Zagat* restaurant-review guides conducted a survey in 1990 of 8,500 of their participants, that asked, What will be the food trends of the nineties?, two suggestions that came up were "The No's—no salt, no fat, no cholesterol, no oil, no butter . . ." and "The Free's—bacteria-free, additive-free, hormone-free, nitrate-free, pesticide-free . . ." (along with other such items as nonfat ice cream, macrobiotic African dishes, seaweed, rice bran, "listing nutritional contents on menus," and "appetizer-dessert meals—no entrees").[2]

15   These numbers and lists and predictions all point to the same unassailable fact: restaurant eating is undergoing a metamorphosis. Two changes have coincided—people eat out more often, and they are more concerned about what is in the food they eat. The result is a lessening of the distance between chef and customer and an almost unconscious effort to make eating out more like eating at home, where one's meal is not a special occasion and where one has complete control over what goes into the pan. Consider, for instance, this restaurant ordering advice from *Dr. Dean Ornish's Program for Reversing Heart Disease:* "If you eat out frequently, get to know the chef and maitre d' at two or three favorite restaurants. . . . Spend a few minutes with them at an off-peak time and explain the guidelines of your dietary preferences. . . . When you eat at a new restaurant, call ahead if possible and explain your dietary requests to the chef or maitre d'. Is the food made to order or is it a 'we heat 'em, you eat 'em' place? Baking, steaming, boiling, and poaching don't require the addition of oil—can the chef prepare something for you in this way? Will he or she cook something for you without butter and oil? Will they put the sauce on the side? Does the restaurant offer fruit for dessert? Or a fruit sorbet? . . . If you see an interesting item on the menu, ask if the chef could modify it for you. For example, if the restaurant serves mushrooms sautéed in butter, ask if the chef could sauté the mushrooms in wine instead. . . . In almost every fine restaurant, the chef will prepare for you a vegetable plate, fruit plate, or a special salad, even if these are not on the menu. If you order a vegetable plate, ask the chef to steam, boil, bake, or grill the vegetables and specify that he or she not use any oil or butter in preparing them."[3] One chef commented to *Allure* magazine in 1992: "You think, my God, why do these people come to a restaurant?"[4]

16   Mark Miller, an anthropologist by training who is now owner and chef of three high-profile Southwestern-style restaurants (Red Sage, in Washington, D.C., and two Coyote Cafes, in Santa Fe and Las Vegas), is, like Eric Bromberg and most other chefs, happy to give people what they ask for in the name of service. But he sees in the restaurant-worries of eaters a serious misperception not only of nutrition but of the fundamental meaning of food. "People in America have dietary problems not because of what's done in restaurants," he said recently, "but because they continue to consume junk, and too much animal protein. There really isn't a good understanding of nutrition in the United States. Someone in one of my

[1] "Consumer Commitment to Nutrition Increases," *Restaurants USA*, Mar. 1990, 36–38.
[2] *Zagat Survey*, Dec. 1990, 4.
[3] Dean Ornish, *Program for Reversing Heart Disease*, 297–98.
[4] Regina Schrambling, "Chefs Bite Back," *Allure*, Dec. 1992, 56.

restaurants will tell me, 'I'm on a diet,' and then sit there lapping up olive oil, which is one hundred percent fat. And then I make them a tamale with one teaspoon of lard, and they say, "Oh, I can't have that.' But, for instance, one tablespoon of duck fat in a sauce that gets spread out among twenty people, that's inconsequential. These people aren't fat or having health problems because they ate one-twentieth of a tablespoon of duck fat in one dish two weeks ago. And they don't have a respect for what one tablespoon of duck fat can give to a sauce."

17 The lack of understanding and, especially, respect is, to Miller, a key to American problems with food. "People are not taking food seriously in America," he said. "We need to take ourselves and our culinary history seriously, but instead we're caught up in misconceptions, in convenient eating, and in placing blame on the wrong things. Lard is not the problem. Too many of our food choices are being driven by psychological perceptions of what the food is about, and ideas of status. People feel that olive oil has a higher status than lard, so it's okay. But what's happened is that we don't have rituals with food, we don't understand the importance of food, we've lost the connection with farms, the connection of food with the land and the sea. People don't really want to discuss food. We don't have a food culture. It goes back to the Puritan days when people were put in the stocks for having spices in their kitchens. It's turning away from life. Food would make you sensual, it would make you real, it would make you alive." Here is where Miller draws upon his earlier training: he can't help but see his customers from the point of view of a psychological anthropologist.

18 "Food also feeds the soul," he continued. "But we are isolating ourselves from those 'soft issues' of food. Living longer doesn't make any difference. Anthropologists rank societies based on their aesthetic levels, not on science—not on how long they live and their health programs. Do you fulfill your human potential by living longer, or by being more creative and more experiential? Food is part of the availability of richness in life, richness that adds to enjoyment and

pleasure in life. Most cultures have nurtured that sense of the value of experience, but what we're doing is denying that. We've got a scientific way of looking at things, and it's not a qualitative, cultural, experiential way of looking at things. If you feed the body and starve the soul, you still have a dead spirit."

19 This way of looking at food—coldly, with distance and distrust—becomes self-perpetuating, according to Miller. "Our current situation is not going to lead to furthering the enjoyment and experience of food. And that's a real problem, because the experience and acknowledgment of food brings you more self-awareness, and self-awareness will bring self-control. With self-control you will basically be able to have a correct diet. The moment people stop buying potato chips is when the potato chips will disappear from the supermarket." He gives as an example dietary traditions in Japan, where he has served as a restaurant consultant. The exquisite, marbled Japanese beef that floors Americans by costing fifty to one hundred dollars per pound is enjoyed—every mouthful—in serving sizes of one to three ounces. In fact, the average Japanese serving size in general is three ounces; the average American serving is at least eight. (Miller feels that we should all be "reverting back to the historical diets that were nutritionally and culturally correct." He includes in these the Mediterranean and Asian diets. "The new food pyramid doesn't tell us anything that these societies didn't know and practice. And that didn't happen randomly.")

20 Miller's prognosis is not promising for the American diet. "We're not developing a food culture that is rational and sensible and that can create a nutritionally balanced diet while also being part of the great enjoyment of life. We're cutting ourselves off from food experience, which is worse for our soul upkeep. For instance, most chefs I know are probably a little overweight. Do they have stressful lives? Yes. But do they enjoy life? Have they had more experiences? If you added all the experiences and enjoyment they've had out of life, they've had seven or eight lifetimes. I think more people should pay more attention to their psychological

health than their physical health. But instead we're starving ourselves for real experiences. I feel that there's this whole existential starving going on out there."

21   In the steamy, sticky belly of a restaurant kitchen, one fact is quickly evident: oils and sauces and salt are the essential glues and flavor-conductors of cooking—especially fast cooking that places a premium on taste. Over a high flame, oil in the pan is almost a necessity, barring a few foods that can cook in their own juices. But there is one thing about oil that nervous restaurant-goers overlook: a well-trained chef can use just enough to coax the most pungent flavors out of a dish without drowning it. Eric Bromberg explained this process on another evening in the Blue Ribbon kitchen, this one in early January, after the holiday rush. "If things are cooked well, and you cook them in oil," he said, "the amount of oil absorbed by the food is very low. Maybe a tablespoon here or there, and in the context of an entire dish and an entire meal, it's not a dangerous thing." His sesame-glazed catfish was a case in point; while it appeared to be sautéeing in a considerable amount of oil, when the fish was cooked he threw most of the oil away. And although he makes a habit of brushing olive oil on meat that he is about to grill, most of it, he pointed out, drips off into the flames. "Now, that doesn't happen with vegetables," Bromberg continued, pointing out the mushrooms and peppers, burnished with olive oil, that sat on the grill. "Vegetables just soak up oil like crazy, especially mushrooms, eggplant—like a sponge. Most people don't realize this, but I bet you get *more* oil with grilled vegetables than with a lot of other dishes. They think they're ordering healthy."

22   Oil and herbed butter and cream, even on the lightest dishes in this enlightened kitchen, are constant presences. The butter finishes the sauce on the shrimps Provençale and the escargots; the oil annoints everything that alights on the grill, soaking the leeks thoroughly before and after cooking; the cream enriches the mashed potatoes, acorn squash, and mussel soup. According to any government study, this is not the way one should eat every night of the week. But once you begin to try to shift the balance that is created by knowledgeable chefs, you run into instant contradictions. "Post-holidays, a lot of people have been asking for sauce on the side," said Eric Bromberg, working over the grill. "It's like that's the thing they know to ask for: sauce on the side. Well, it annoys the hell out of us. You know why? Because normally we put about an ounce of sauce on, say, a piece of fish. But when you put it on the side, you have to give them about four ounces, because one ounce looks skimpy sitting in a dish. Well, every time, they eat the whole four ounces! And we go through a lot more sauce." It's a truth universally acknowledged by chefs: Put anything on the side, and customers will eat a lot more of it.

23   The orders on that January night were subtly different from the ones coming in before Christmas. Many more listed only entrees, with no appetizers—what the waiters and kitchen staff call "o.p.u." for "order pick up." "What is all this o.p.u. stuff tonight?" someone called out in some irritation; making meals without "aps" throws off the kitchen rhythm somewhat. More customers were also trying their hand at rehabilitating the recipes. One man requested a change in the collard-green brochettes that accompany the grilled swordfish—little packets that look like stuffed grape leaves but are instead collard-green leaves wrapped around a mixture of goat cheese and camembert, grilled on skewers with mushrooms and onions. He wanted the brochettes, but without the camembert. Eric got to work constructing new brochettes from scratch (Bruce and Eric Bromberg had already noticed an interesting fact about the camembert: when they had recently rewritten the menu to list only the camembert in the brochettes, orders for that dish had fallen off; when they added the mention of goat cheese back in, orders rebounded. Goat cheese, it seemed had a better image than camembert, perhaps because it is perceived as less rich.)

24   Another table ordered the pu-pu platter appetizer—an eclectic mixture of international morsels that includes fried chicken wings, potato pancakes, barbecued ribs, piero-

gies, and grilled shrimp—but wanted to "stay on the light side." Thus, they specified no wings and ribs, "nothing fried," but wanted to keep the potato pancakes and pierogies, both deep-fried. This occasioned a brief conference in the kitchen, complete with a few ironic comments. "Oh, I get it—nothing fried, except for the fried stuff," said Bruce. "Maybe I should send it up like this," said Kris, holding up the wooden pu-pu platter decorated with a bed of shredded lettuce and nothing else. After some discussion, they decided on making special grilled skewers with mushrooms and scallops to replace the offending items. Those, of course, as with anything grilled, were coated first with oil. The same customer who had ordered the pu-pu restrictions had as a main course the swordfish with plain couscous, without the collard-green-camembert brochettes. Little patterns in the special ordering were discernible to the chefs. Bruce, for instance, noted that "sauce on the side" was almost always for salads and fish; almost no one made that request for the sauces on the London broil or duck. (The latter orders come, perhaps, from the "unconcerned patrons.") All of the special requests were knit somehow into the controlled chaos that peaked at about 8:45: "Ordering three times!" "Rack of lamb on the board." "I need sesame and scallions—now!" "Vegetables, looking for rice." "Firing tables fourteen and eleven." "Picking up a duck and a London on the super-fly." "Let's get some of this stuff out here—are you listening?—we're going with fifteen, thirteen, thirty." "Scallops looking for greens!" "Bruce, I need that London. All the other food is up at the table." "Twenty, twenty-two, and ten, as fast as humanly possible."

25   Dessert, it seems, calls up its own second-guessing. Just deciding to indulge doesn't end the matter: control can still be exerted. "Ordering a Chocolate Bruno, but without the ice cream." (The dish, named in honor of a French chef who trained both Eric and Bruce, consists of a little ramekin of something akin to chocolate mousse, surrounded by three scoops of ice cream and a drizzle of chocolate sauce.) This order occasioned another conference: how to make the dish look inviting when it had only the ramekin marooned on a plate? Another order came in: "A very thin piece of cheesecake." Another discussion: What's very thin? Kris cut one and it looked too thin; he made another pass at it. The very thin slice of cheesecake lined up in the window next to a huge sundae drenched in chocolate sauce, strawberries, nuts, and whipped cream.

All of these special orders are not simply   26
verbal; they are translated into an arcane code on the written orders, which come down to the kitchen looking like hieroglyphics. Several years ago Eric designed an order-writing system for the waiters to accommodate the growing numbers of special requests, and he now hands out an instruction sheet several pages long that outlines the rules. Every possible variation is provided for: Two people order the same dish and both want to delete, or "86," the mashed potatoes but each asks for a different substitution; or, both want lamb, one medium, one medium-rare, one wants a substitution, one wants sauce on the side ("SOS"). A strong distinction is made between "no butter," "no oil," and "no fat." If the customer asks for no butter, the waiter must ask: "Is oil OK?" If so, he writes "no butter." If not, "no fat." Sometimes even this complex code fails to fully enlighten the chefs. "What is this about the artichoke?" Kris asked one of the waiters. "Oh, with balsamic vinegar on the side. Okay."

"It's been my mission to get the waiters to   27
absorb as much information from the customers as possible," Eric explained as he turned brochettes and scallops on the grill and whipped open the oven door to bring out a pan holding a duck breast sizzling in its own fat. "If the customer has requested something special, I'm going to make it the best I can with those restrictions, but I don't feel compromised by that. In fact, a lot of times I come up with new things because of special requests. Five or six years ago someone wanted salmon cooked with absolutely no butter, no oil, anything. All I could think of to do was put it in a nonstick pan without any fat at all, and it cooked perfectly—you get a beautiful crisp skin. It was a neater way to cook it. I started cooking it that way all the

time. I grew up with a grandmother who doesn't eat anything and my mother who doesn't cook or eat anything, and friends who were picky about one thing or another, and my brother who wouldn't eat tomatoes—I'm used to it, it seems completely normal. I don't feel, as a chef, that my job is to force anyone to do something they don't want to do. That's not the reason I got into this business; I didn't do it to flex my muscles or prove to anyone how great or cool I am. No matter what kind of cultural era you're in, no matter what the issues are, you have the customer to please and the ingredients to concoct." He began to slice precise, thin pieces of duck, topped with a beautifully browned ridge of fat, and lay them gently on a plate.

28   The next time I was at the Blue Ribbon, it was to eat. It was a frosty Wednesday night in late January—not prime restaurant time— but we got the last available table for two. The dining room at Blue Ribbon is small, essentially a storefront, and the sense of intimacy is enhanced by the colors: brick walls painted rose, yellow wall lights, a wooden mirrored bar. There was something of the sense of being at a small cocktail party; undefinable, slightly abstract rock music played just loud enough to raise everyone's voice one level, wine corks popped, candles flickered, the bartender occasionally rattled a glass cocktail shaker and poured mysterious drinks, the scene at the bar shifted as those waiting were seated and others scanned the menu, deciding whether to stay. At the tables people leaned to converse across trays of raw oysters, sampled

each other's foie gras and steak tartare appetizers, smoked cigarettes, sipped wine.

I knew my apple-and-leek potato pancake   29
appetizer achieved its delicious light crust in the deep fryer, and on the plate the pancakes were topped with a good-sized dollop of sour cream, but I also knew I had nothing else from a deep fryer in recent memory. Then my sesame-glazed catfish arrived, lightly browned and glistening on its bed of mashed potatoes. I could picture exactly how it had looked going into the pan—soaked in olive oil, enhanced by a sizable blob of herbed butter toward the end of cooking—and I had seen much of that oil go into the garbage pail after the catfish was lifted out of the pan. The toasted, almost burnt, sesame coating contrasted beautifully with the fresh, light taste of the fish itself. I ate every bite. And I remember Eric Bromberg describing his personal feelings about food—not just cooking it but living with it. "One of the greatest pleasures I know is eating," he said. "And I don't mean just eating indiscriminately, I mean the flavors and the tastes and the enjoyment that that can bring you. To deprive yourself of that for some future benefit—I can understand the thinking, but I think we've gone too far over the edge of restricting. I'm not saying everybody should just sit down and gorge themselves until they die; I'm not suggesting a solely hedonistic approach to life. But taste is one of your greatest senses, and you should allow yourself to taste, and to appreciate."

Source: Michelle Stacey, *Consumed: Why Americans Love, Hate & Fear Food,* New York: Simon & Schuster, 1994.

DISCUSSION QUESTIONS

1. The first three paragraphs of this essay are a good example of an introduction by anecdote (see Chapter 10). But as well as engaging the reader through the specificity of narrative, Stacey's introduction also makes a certain point about the activity that goes on in the Blue Ribbon kitchen. After studying the imagery, figures of speech, and references used by Stacey in her opening, describe the implicit claim that she is making about this activity.

2. Why do you think Stacey has presented the activity of restaurant cooking in this way? How does it serve her overall argument?

3. Create an outline of Stacey's essay that identifies the major claim(s), the secondary supporting claims, and the support (including the type of support) for

each claim. Compare your outline with a classmate's. If there are major differences, are these a reflection of a structural weakness in Stacey's argument or careless reading on the part of you or your classmate?

4. Stacey makes extended use of the views of two restaurateurs, Eric Bromberg and Mark Miller. Discuss the effectiveness of this strategy, as opposed to one that would cite the expert views of a number of authorities on restaurant cooking. Does the fact that Stacey invites readers to develop a familiarity with Bromberg and Miller make them more or less credible as experts?

5. Analyze the conclusion (the last two paragraphs) of this argument. Consider the purpose and effectiveness of Stacey's self-references, the careful physical description, the concluding quote from Eric Bromberg. Is the conclusion appropriate to the tone and length of the argument? Does it satisfy the requirements of a conclusion (see Chapter 10)?

SUGGESTIONS FOR WRITING (17.3)

1. In Par. 15, Stacey concludes (from a survey by the National Restaurant Association) that "people eat out more often." Using the time period 1986–1989, brainstorm a list of possible explanations for this increase. Select three or four of the most plausible explanations and determine, through secondary sources, whether these possible causes actually occurred (i.e., document their factuality). Finally, write a two- to three-page draft of a causal argument identifying the reasons for the increase in eating out. In your draft, you should support the argument by explicitly citing your application of one or more of Mill's methods for determining cause (Chapter 7).

2. Rewrite the introduction of Stacey's essay (the first three paragraphs), eliminating all slanted and/or connotative language. Make the rewrite as objective and dispassionate as possible.

3. Write a one-page interpretation of Mark Miller's statement that "Food also feeds the soul" (Par. 18).

4. In a one-page factual argument based upon personally experienced facts, describe the eating habits of a friend or acquaintance who is a particularly eccentric eater. Keep your language as objective as possible.

In a second one-page argument, describe the eating habits of the same person, this time using as much connotative language and "loaded" figures of speech as you like.

DIETING DIALOGUE

SIDE PANEL "SPECIAL K" BOX

Cereal boxes have provided breakfast table reading for generations. A closer reading than you are accustomed to giving them will reveal all the rudiments of argument on a single side panel.

YOUR A.M. DIET PLAN

Take a look at what the *Kellogg's®* *Special K®* Breakfast can bring to your table: fresh fruit, hot coffee, skim milk and lightly toasted, delicious flakes of *Kellogg's®* *Special K®* cereal. It's a breakfast loaded with taste—with less than one gram of fat! The *Kellogg's®* *Special K®* Breakfast . . . a great-tasting way to start a healthy day.

The *Kellogg's®* *Special K®* Breakfast

The *Kellogg's®* *Special K®* cereal	1 cup
skim milk,	1/2 cup
fresh strawberries,	1/2 cup
black coffee or tea,	6 oz.
TOTAL CALORIES	less than 200
TOTAL FAT	less than 1 gram

See other side panel for nutrition facts.

Ctn. No. K-0162G

DIETING DIALOGUE

MYTH vs. FACT

DO Got an on-again, off-again relationship with exercise?

YOU One of the biggest exercise roadblocks is insufficient motivation.

YO Wanting to lose weight is a good start, but think about it this way:

YO? you've got a lot to gain— self-esteem, energy, good mood, and fun!

MYTH: Carbohydrates are fattening.

FACT: Often, it's the calories from fat, rather than carbohydrates, that can pack on the extra pounds. One gram of fat provides nine calories; one gram of carbohydrate or protein provides only four calories.

MYTH: To lose weight, just watch what you eat—no need to exercise.

FACT: If you want to lose weight faster and steadier, there's no better way than the right combination: reduced calorie diet and exercise!

MYTH: You can eat and drink all the "diet" foods and beverages you want!

FACT: "Low-calorie" or "no fat" does not mean "all you can eat," especially if you're having a diet soda with chocolate cake!

DISCUSSION QUESTIONS

1. To what class of argument does this selection belong?
2. Is the central claim stated or unstated?
3. Through what secondary claims is the central claim supported?
4. Are the second-party facts reliably presented? Are their sources recent, objective, authoritative?
5. What would it take to strengthen this argument?
6. Why would a manufacturer place information like this on its cereal box?

SUGGESTIONS FOR WRITING (17.4)

1. The design of cereal boxes has an interesting history that reveals a good bit about our culture. Research and write a seven-page factual and interpretive study of the evolution and significance of cereal box design. (You may want to check newspapers and magazines from the summer of 1996 to get information about the suspense over the Wheaties pictures.)
2. Conduct your own research to determine the accuracy, reliability, and objectivity of the facts listed on the Special K box. Are any of these "facts" contradicted in the literature you consult? Stated significantly differently? Qualified?

MY STORY: BOB

DANIEL SLOSBERG

While the vast majority of those who suffer from eating disorders (anorexia nervosa, bulimia nervosa, binge eating) are female, these disorders can afflict men as well, as Bob's story illustrates. This reading was found within a World Wide Web site titled "Males and Eating Disorders" (http://www.primenet.com/~danslos/males/story.html). The site was copyrighted by Daniel Slosberg in 1998. Slosberg's Web site contains a number of sections, including one called "Stories," which consists of first-person accounts by males with eating disorders.

1 When I was about fifteen, a freshman in High School, and slightly overweight, I went on a diet so that, ostensibly, I wouldn't have to move from the "C" division to the "B" division on my swimming and water polo teams. I alternately starved myself (in a relative sense—I ate, but not nearly enough to sustain my activity level) and binged (donuts and halvah were favorites at the time).

2 Thus began about ten years of bulimia during which I exercised more and more so that I could eat as much as I wanted. No one ever knew I had a problem; people just thought that I was a good athlete. I eventually became one of only five people ever to complete a double-crossing of the Catalina Channel (Catalina's an island off the coast of California), and I became one of the first

people to compete in the Iron-Man Triathlon in Hawaii. And I did it all out of fear: I couldn't stop or I'd get *fat*, a fate worse than death or having to live far from the beach.

3   My sister, a year and a half younger than I, began her own eating disorder about the time I did, maybe a little earlier. She binged and purged for about fourteen years. After many attempts to deal with her eating disorder, including residential treatment and different drug therapies, she committed suicide. This happened about seven years ago.

4   I got into short-term therapy after a close friend died. I had previously felt like something was wrong, but I couldn't put my finger on it. I couldn't have said, "I have an eating disorder," or, "I've been depressed," even though I clearly was both. Opening up about my eating disorder (and other stuff) seemed to begin the process of sloughing it off.

5   I have since been to two other therapists, the most current one I began seeing shortly after we adopted my first son four years ago.

After my son's birth, I went into the deepest depression I'd ever experienced, kind of a fear-of-fatherhood crisis. Perhaps this occurred because I didn't have the food to hide behind; perhaps the depression was, in a sense, a more constructive coping mechanism. Anyway, I found a therapist who's been very helpful, and I've been dealing with the issues which led to the eating problems (and the depression) in the first place. These issues include both familial and cultural issues which left me empty and unable to cope.

I figure that something must be working   6 because, when our twins arrived two years after my son, I didn't get depressed—just exhausted. The twins turned two in May, five months after the birth of our fourth child, Noah. Though I remain exhausted, I never cease feeling incredibly lucky to be part of my family.

Source: Daniel M. Slosberg, *My Story*.
http://www.primenet.com/~danslos/
males/story.html

DISCUSSION QUESTIONS

1. Does Bob's narrative account qualify as argument? If so, what kind? If not, how would you describe or categorize it?

2. What do you think Bob wanted to accomplish by writing this account and posting it on the Web site? Do you have any evidence for your theory? Identify Bob's intended audience. Again, cite any evidence you find within the text.

3. What image of the author is projected within this account? What evidence can you cite for this image?

4. Do your own Web search on males and eating disorders. List the sites you discover and compare your list with the lists of a few of your classmates.

SUGGESTIONS FOR WRITING (17.5)

1. Write a one-page personal account of a "condition" you have suffered from (the condition can be as mild as laryngitis or as severe as Bob's eating disorder). Before you write, identify to yourself your motive for writing the paper (other than that your instructor has assigned it)—that is, to instruct, to confess, to vent, to sympathize. At the end of the paper, identify the motive for your instructor.

2. We all know that females are particularly susceptible to eating disorders. The subject has received so much public attention lately that most of us know the most frequently cited hypotheses for this susceptibility: the pressure to conform to fashion norms; a search for control; a reluctance to grow up. Given the scant public attention paid to the subject of males and eating disorders, we are more at a loss to explain this phenomenon. In a two-page speculative argument, identify two or three possible causes for eating disorders in men. Concentrate on establishing a probable motivational link between the causes you identify and their effect.

3. Write a two-page review (i.e., evaluation) of one of the Web sites you identified in Question #4. Consider such factors as visual layout, content, expertise of Web site owner, accessibility of links, and so on.

BED CONFESSIONS

K.D. ELLIOTT

The "BED" in the title of this reading doesn't refer to the place you sleep at night; it is an acronym for a condition known as Binge Eating Disorder. This argument was found on the Healthgate Web site, one of the many sites devoted to physical and mental health issues.

While "My Story" (the preceding reading), is a painful personal confession of an eating disorder victim, "BED Confessions" is an objective and dispassionate description of a related disorder.

1 BED. It's something shared by men and women in more ways than one. BED, or Binge Eating Disorder, has become an emotional and health concern for men across the United States. This eating disorder, which affects more than 1 million men in America, has only recently been recognized by the American Psychiatric Association as a disorder of its own, that needs further study.

2 Ninety-five percent of the U.S. population has cravings for "pleasure" or "comfort" foods. The other five percent crave alcohol, cigarettes, or some other addictive substance. Having cravings, and fulfilling them, is natural human instinct.

3 But BED is more than an occasional craving for a sweet snack. At first, eating may satisfy cravings. But eventually the eating becomes more and more frequent, and higher in calories and fat. This overeating leads to feelings of self-disgust and guilt, which may cause a person to eat even more.

4 A typical binge may include eating anywhere from 1000 to 15,000 calories at a time. In fact, it is not uncommon to actually have a "food hangover" the day following an especially large binge. The foods consumed are usually high in fat and are eaten in a relatively short period of time, putting an enormous amount of stress on the digestive and endocrine systems. BED is different from the two other characteristic eating disorders, anorexia and bulimia. Anorexia is a condition of slow, self starvation; bulimia is a binging and vomiting syndrome.

5 BED is formally characterized by the American Psychiatric Association in the Diagnostic and Statistical Manual for Mental Disorders (DSM-IV) according to the following five criteria:

1. Recurring binge eating episodes. An episode of binge eating is characterized by both of the following:

- eating an amount of food that is definitely larger than most people would eat in a similar amount of time under similar circumstances
- a sense of lack of control over eating during the episode

2. The binge eating episodes are associated with three or more of the following:

- eating much more rapidly than you usually would
- eating until you feel uncomfortably full
- eating large amounts of food when you don't physically feel hungry
- eating alone because of embarrassment at how much you are eating
- feeling disgusted with yourself, depressed, or very guilty after overeating

3. Binge eating causes emotional and physical stress or remorse.
4. The binge eating occurs, on average, at least two days a week for six months or more.
5. The binge eating is not followed by other inappropriate behaviors such as purging, fasting, excessive exercise and does not occur exclusively during episodes of other eating disorders, such as anorexia nervosa or bulimia nervosa.

6   BED is a unique eating disorder, especially when it comes to men. While only 5% to 10% of people with anorexia and bulimia nervosa are male, it is estimated that BED affects a much greater proportion of men. According to Dr. Anne Becker of the Harvard Eating Disorders Center, "The ratio of females to males with this disorder is about 1.5 to 1.0 or about 40% men." Dr. Becker adds, "Binge eating disorder has become more recognizable by doctors as more attention is given to weight control in the clinical setting."

7   There are some underlying common characteristics of men who have BED. Most are overweight, with a history of depression, low assertiveness, and poor self-esteem. Similar to all people with eating disorders, men with BED view themselves in a negative light and allow food to control their lives in order to compensate for their lack of control in other areas such as work or family matters.

8   Another common characteristic of men with BED is that they fail to address their own personal needs, and instead, turn to food. For these men, food can be a great sedative and a means of suppressing feelings of anger, guilt, despondency, and sadness. Men with eating disorders tend to eat in private, not wanting to alert others to their habit. This increases the feelings of isolation and sadness, and creates another vicious cycle.

9   Unlike bulimia, where people eat and then purge, there is no counteraction to bingeing. Therefore, weight gain is a likely effect. As noted above, men with BED are often overweight to begin with. The effects of BED on health include all the possible consequences of overweight or obesity— diabetes, hypertension, and heart disease.

10   An ever more serious consequence is death. According to Dr. Ken Stephenson, a psychotherapist who specializes in treating males with eating disorders, "People with eating disorders have the highest mortality rate of all psychiatric patients." Isn't that a good enough reason to seek help now?

11   Men with symptoms of BED need to seek treatment as soon as possible. The longer a person waits, the greater the risk to their health. Treatment of the disorder generally includes cognitive-behavioral or interpersonal therapy performed by a licensed clinician. Cognitive-behavioral therapy teaches patients techniques to monitor and change their eating habits as well as to change the way they respond to difficult situations. Interpersonal psychotherapy helps people examine their relationships with friends and family and to make changes in problem areas.

12   Treatment with medications such as antidepressants may be helpful for some individuals. Self-help groups also may be a source of support. Researchers are still trying to determine which method or combination of

methods is the most effective in controlling binge eating disorder. The type of treatment that is best for an individual is a matter for discussion between the patient and his or her health care provider.

13 Professional and confidential treatment and information can be sought through the following organizations:

The National Eating Disorders Organization
6655 South Yale Avenue
Tulsa, OK 74136
918-481-4044
http://www.laureate.com/

Overeaters Anonymous
PO Box 44020
Roe Ranchero, New Mexico 87174
505-891-2664
http://www.overeatersanonymous.org/

Other resources

Males and Eating Disorders
http://www.primenet.com/~
danslos/males/links.html

Source: K.D. Elliot, Bed Confessions.
http://www.healthgate.com/

DISCUSSION QUESTIONS

1. Using the guidelines contained in the reading "Information Literacy" in the "Internet" section of these readings, evaluate the reliability of the Healthgate Web site (http//www3.healthgate.com). Do you find any reason not to trust the material on this site as accurate and authoritative?

2. The first part of this article is an extended definition of Binge Eating Disorder. How many strategies of definition are used here (see Chapter 4 of this book for a list of possible strategies)? Compare your findings with those of two classmates.

3. Discuss with your classmates what the overall purpose of this argument is. Is that purpose fulfilled? Support your answer.

4. The final two paragraphs contain a recommendation. What is the emphasis of this recommendation? Present or future? Can you place the recommendation into the Toulmin model presented in Chapter 9?

5. Discuss the overall tone of this article. Do you find any evidence of slanted or connotative language? Is the tone appropriate to the apparent purpose of the article? How do you think it would affect someone suffering from the disorder?

SUGGESTIONS FOR WRITING (17.6)

1. With a classmate, draw up a list of speculations about why men are more afflicted with BED than any other eating disorder. Choose two of the most plausible explanations and brainstorm together how you would go about turning this speculation into an effective causal argument.

2. While men are not generally assumed to be preoccupied with how their bodies look to others, ten minutes in the weight room of any gym might contradict this assumption. After going through the necessary preliminary steps outlined in Chapters 2 and 3, write an argument comparing male interest in muscle-building with female interest in thinness. Your comparison can be evaluative, interpretive, causal, or a hybrid of two classes.

3. Most of us have friends who engage in worrisome behavior—for example, unhealthy eating or drinking habits, too much time on the computer, poor relationship choices. Write a three-page recommendation to a friend that attempts to modify such risky behavior. Your recommendation can be in letter form, but it must follow the principles of effective recommendations presented in Chapter 9. Be sure that you can document any of the physical or mental consequences of your friend's risky behavior.

4. Identify with a group of classmates some of the most prevalent risky behaviors on your campus. Pick one of these and compose a formal proposal for reducing that behavior that would be submitted to administrators on your campus. Be sure that the behavior you choose is something you are actually concerned about. Follow the model of the computer facility proposal presented in Chapter 9.

18

Reading Popular Culture

INTRODUCTION

For most of you, formal reading lessons began in first grade, when you were launched on an elementary school curriculum that taught you what words say. By fifth or sixth grade, as primers and readers give way to "real" literature, reading became more complicated; you were expected not only to understand what the words *said,* but also what they *meant.* At this point, you learned that writers have all sorts of tricks for meaning more than they appear to say—tricks like symbols, imagery, and setting. Throughout high school, especially in your English classes, you probably became skilled at interpreting these literary techniques, at discovering and unpacking the multiple meanings they allow. By the time you entered college, you knew perfectly well that the kind of reading assigned in an English course would be entirely different from the reading you do for recreation in your increasingly limited spare time. The first requires energy, creativity, and active, alert thought; the second, not much more than passive, relaxed attention.

At this point in your education, you also know that the skills of careful reading you've been practicing for at least the last 12 years are not exclusive to written texts. If you've taken a course in art history, film studies, or music appreciation, you're aware that other art forms contain rich and diverse meaning that, like literature, reveals itself to students with the right analytical tools.

The following unit of essays, entitled "Reading Popular Culture," contains arguments that extend the practice of close reading from the productions of what some call "high" culture (Rembrandt's paintings, Shakespeare's plays) to those of popular culture (television shows, horror movies, even clothing fashion—any artifact with mass appeal). In recent years, the activity of reading or interpreting popular culture has grown in popularity and legitimacy within academic circles. Indeed, your college or university probably offers courses in popular culture, possibly even a minor or a major. There are also academic associations and conferences in this new area, and it's even possible to receive a Ph.D. in Popular Culture.

But why, just when you might think your lessons in reading are behind you, should you worry about the subtle meanings contained in television sitcoms and trashy novels? And what does reading popular culture have to do with writing arguments?

Let's look at the first question: why study popular culture? For one thing, "reading" a popular artifact, uncovering subtle messages and patterns of meaning in a magazine ad or a soap opera, is like looking into a cultural mirror—one that reflects the often unadmitted values and priorities of its audience. There is a good deal to be learned about a culture with a seemingly insatiable taste for war movies, or a generation glued to a Thursday night television line-up featuring shallow, sex-based relationships.

But there is more than knowledge about ourselves and others to be gained from seriously attending to popular culture; we also can become conscious of the ways in which the brokers of popular culture use cultural productions to manipulate their audience. As college student Kevin Maloney says in his argument reproduced in Chapter 8, "Being unable to recognize the sometimes hidden messages of . . . [popular culture] is like being in a foreign country where you don't speak the language. In both cases, you can easily fall prey to individuals eager to take advantage of your ignorance, to manipulate you into doing what they want you to do." Close readers of popular culture are agents capable of forming their own opinions and withstanding the powerful but often unreasonable suasions of the popular culture industry. The essays included in this unit model this kind of reading for you.

And finally, why include readings of popular culture in a textbook on argument? Because multiple layers of arguments, both explicit and implicit, faulty and reasonable, reside in every production of contemporary popular culture. And all the essays in this unit are in the business of revealing and evaluating these arguments. By reading these "readings," by learning through them to detect hidden as well as manifest arguments, you will become that much more effective in your own creation of reasonable, ethical arguments.

POPULAR CULTURE AND THE FAMILY: HOW MASS-MEDIATED CULTURE WEAKENS THE TIES THAT BIND

KENNETH A. MYERS

Kenneth Myers is a former producer of National Public Radio's "All Things Considered." He currently produces "Mars Hill Tapes," a bimonthly audio magazine. Myers is also the author of All God's Children and Blue Suede Shoes: Christians and Popular Culture *(Crossway).*

The journal Family Policy, *where this essay first appeared, is published bimonthly by the Family Research Council, a tax-exempt social policy research, educational, and advocacy organization chartered in 1983.*

COMMENTARY

As its subtitle suggests, "Popular Culture and the Family" is primarily a generalized causal argument linking the phenomenon of popular culture with a dissolution of communal values. As a causal argument, the essay combines organizational and stylistic strengths with a number of those same weaknesses in reasoning and strategy you've been cautioned against in the first part of this book.

Following an engaging, albeit highly slanted anecdotal introduction that takes us on a tour of contemporary magazine stands, Myers introduces his central claim in Par. 7: "popular culture as known today is a complete novelty in human history. Its very nature, not simply its content, coupled with its role in American life pose great challenges to the work of families in shaping the moral character of children."

Immediately following the claim, Myers proceeds with a survey of the decline of traditional culture—from the pre-Freudian age when, Myers attests, culture was a force of moral guidance largely in the hands of the family and its immediate community, to contemporary society, ruled by mass-distributed, liberationist popular culture. The historical survey consists of factual generalizations supported by appeals to authority—a wide range of individuals whom Myers presumes his readers will recognize as distinguished experts on the subject of culture and morality (T.S. Eliot, Philip Rieff, Allan Carlson, etc.). The brief references to the experts are Myers's only support for generalizations about entire eras—generalizations like the one found in Par. 12: "Empowering people to be all that they can be, to express all that they feel, and to obtain all that they desire is now seen to be the proper function of cultural institutions, including the family."

Myers then enlists this unsupported characterization of the post-Freudian decline in values to serve as the "factual" foundation of the succeeding causal argument. This is an example of how arguments can be built on sand, with unsupported generalizations being treated as justified conclusions that are then promoted to serve as springboards for new claims.

The next four sections of the argument identify the many losses brought about by popular culture—the losses of "the local," of "moral authority," of "tradition," and of "moral seriousness." These sections constitute the heart of the causal argument, identifying popular culture as the cause of a number of deficiencies in contemporary life. Yet the plausibility of the causal argument is extremely hard to measure because of the vagueness of the primary causal agent: popular culture itself. The failure to offer a clear definition of the term, which is the very subject of the essay, is probably its gravest flaw. In Par. 9, Myers borrows from T.S. Eliot and David Wells to offer a definition of culture as "the outward discipline in which inherited meanings and morality, beliefs and ways of behaving are preserved." Yet no such succinct definition of "popular culture" is ever offered, and though Myers implies a certain understanding of the term, he never defines it clearly, and we are left at the mercy of inference and speculation. Is popular culture the same as "culture," but popular? Is popular culture "mass mediated culture," as he says in Par. 13? Is popular culture really just television, as paragraphs 15 and following seem to imply?

As Chapter 7 of this book demonstrates, reasonable causal arguments link two clearly established phenomena through any number of causal principles. Forgetting for a moment that the causal agent (popular culture) lacks a clear definition, let's take a look at the manner in which Myers links cause and effect. In the section "The Loss of Moral Seriousness," he tells us that popular culture, or "the forms in which it is presented," "discourage depth, reflection, and moral seriousness." He then quotes media critic Todd Gitlin's characterization of television's glib, superficial conversational style as an instance of one example of popular culture. While Gitlin's quote does help us to understand one of the "forms in which [popular culture] is presented" (i.e., television), it does nothing to warrant the causal connection between popular culture and a lack of moral seriousness. Presumably, we are to assume that those who watch superficial television become superficial. Myers is using an implied linking principle here to connect his cause and effect. This strategy works fine as long as the linking principle—in this case the principle of "monkey see, monkey do"—is universally accepted. But in this case, the linking principle hardly qualifies as universally accepted: volumes have been written about the effects of television on behavior and no definitive conclusion on the topic has yet been reached.

Myers's argument is a causal generalization, and causal generalizations are two-step arguments. First, the claim that A causes B must be established according to principles of causality; and second, the generalization that A causes B on a large scale must be established through principles of inductive reasoning. As you learned in Chapter 5, inductive claims—which tend to be most convincing when they are qualified—are best supported through the citing of numerous specific examples. Yet Myers does very little in the way of offering specific instances of his generalizations. Look, for example, at the following paragraph:

> The frame of mind encouraged by modern entertainment is one which is suspicious of any legacy or inheritance, and which is committed to the assertion of the sovereignty of the self. It is a mentality that evokes a mood of restlessness and blocks out the reflection necessary for acknowledging its disease and then seeking a remedy. It is a sensibility rooted only in the present, ignoring the past, indifferent to the future.

How many specific supporting examples for these sweeping generalizations do you find?

In sum, while Myers makes a number of fascinating and provocative claims in this argument, his failure to clarify critical terms of the argument, to apply the principles of causality, and to support his generalized claims seriously undermine the plausibility of those claims.

POPULAR CULTURE AND THE FAMILY: HOW MASS-MEDIATED CULTURE WEAKENS THE TIES THAT BIND

KENNETH A. MYERS

1   On a recent visit to a local grocery store, I passed by the magazine rack. Such a place is not the source of most of my reading material, but I stopped long enough to check out some titles. I noticed that *Jane,* a magazine pitched to adolescents, carried a feature on "summer clothes sexier than going naked." Another teen publication, *ym* ("young and modern"), was

distributed with a free booklet: "your 8-page school-year love horoscope." The issue also ran an article "love at first sight—what makes him fall?" Though I did not even glance at the articles in question, I doubt the girls who purchase such magazines are likely to gain wisdom about love or about their own identities.

2 Meanwhile, *American Woman,* a periodical for older but not necessarily more mature readers, teased shoppers seeking fresh produce or ginger snaps: "Discover his private pleasure zones and drive him wild with desire! SEXUAL ECSTASY: naughty tricks that *always* work." The magazine also contained a QUIZ: "How do you rate in bed?" Then there were the fan magazines, one carrying a cover shot of gender nightmare Marilyn Manson; the computer game magazines, several extolling heavy doses of virtual violence and imaginary sex; and the venerable *Rolling Stone*—once the saucy bad boy of newsstands—now, given the raucous competition, looking rather conservative, with a cover photograph of Madonna less provocative than most celebrity photographs from the 1940s.

3 At the checkout counter, I was greeted with the usual assembly of lurid tabloids and soap-opera magazines, each with promises of predictably provocative and pitifully tawdry trash. The cover of *Redbook* featured a photograph of Harrison Ford juxtaposed with screaming headlines in large type heralding an inside feature revealing "46 things to do to a naked man." One might safely assume that "Tell him to get dressed or get out" is not numbered among the suggestions.

4 These may not be the worst examples of magazine covers parents and children see regularly in public; most city newsstands and bookstores display magazines even more blatant in their commitment to radical liberation. But the matter-of-factness of such display in a family neighborhood *grocery* store, for all passing eyes to see, is a profoundly disturbing fact of life in late twentieth-century America. Certainly *ym* or *Jane* are nowhere near 2 Live

Crew in morally destructive megatonnage. Nor does *Redbook* and its ilk rate with the disgusting lyrics in rap music, degrading dialogue in television shows, and detestable violence in movies. Yet the question arises: does not our culture invite the extremities of celebrity vulgarists and blasphemers because it is so blasé about the everyday desensitizing by enticements such as "naughty tricks that *always* work" and "summer clothes sexier than going naked" displayed in the same aisle as Betty Crocker and Mrs. Butterworth?

5 Whatever the connection between the two, Protestant theologian David F. Wells pulls no punches in his astute assessment of our cultural situation:

> The moral hedges that surrounded our collective life have been trampled down. That is the paramount truth. What once was sublimated is now, in all of its raw and often violent nature, spewed forth in the name of liberty or self-expression. What once had to be private is now paraded publicly for the gallery of voyeurs. The virtues of the old privacy, such as reticence and modesty, are looked upon today as maladies. What was once unseemly is now commonplace.[1]

6 Perhaps no class of American citizens feels the consequences of cultural regress more forcefully than parents, many of whom believe that popular culture is the most powerful carrier of this decline. A 1995 *New York Times* poll indicated that Americans blame television more than any single factor for teenage sex and violence.[2] So parents and other authority figures, quite naturally, try to restrict children's access or exposure to some "artifacts" of popular culture. Or they may patronize only "sanitized" artifacts of popular culture, whether G-rated movies and television programming or rock music whose lyrics have been cleaned-up or attached to a good cause.

---

[1] David F. Wells, *No Place for Truth, or, Whatever Happened to Evangelical Theology?* (Grand Rapids: Wm. B. Eerdmans Publishing Co., 1993), p. 168.

[2] Elizabeth Kolbert, "American Despair of Popular Culture," *New York Times,* August 20, 1995, Section 2.

7   Consider how schools—public and private—have within a generation moved from virtually ignoring popular culture to blessing it. Dana Mack, in *The Assault on Parenthood: How Our Culture Undermines the Family,* writes:

> In a misguided effort to make school "relevant" to children's lives outside of school, educators often bring popular culture into the classroom in the form of literature, music and social instruction. In fourth grade, for example, my own child was assigned to write a "rap" poem as part of her language-arts program. Not surprisingly, children take this emphasis on popular culture as an endorsement and end up clinging to the tastes of the marketplace rather than expanding their horizons toward more sophisticated work with a longer shelf life.[3]

8   Mack notes that "even in affluent suburban schools, art education is based far more on contemporary models taken from popular culture than on historical models of high art or folk culture.[4]

9   With blessings from schools, churches, and other historically normative institutions, popular culture is assumed to be a perfectly normal attribute of life. But let the buyer (or parent) beware: popular culture as known today is a complete novelty in human history. Its very nature, not simply its content, coupled with its role in American life, pose great challenges to the work of families in shaping the moral character of children.

The Function of Culture

10   Historically, culture has had an intrinsically moral dimension. Borrowing from T. S.

Eliot, David F. Wells defines culture as "the set of values, the network of beliefs that are institutionalized in a people's collective life and that govern their behavior. Culture, then, is the outward discipline in which inherited meanings and morality, beliefs and ways of behaving are preserved.[5]

11   Since they communicate moral content from one generation to the next, and because human beings are inherently in need of correction and guidance, cultures have always been mechanisms of restraint. Cultural institutions, traditions, and artifacts developed as means of encouraging members of a society to respect its taboos, to obey its laws, and to become the sort of persons whose characters served the common good by conforming to a view of the good that the society held in common. In theological terms, cultures are thus instruments of common grace or natural law that keep people from doing everything that they want to do. Cultures are by nature communal—not individualistic—and deliberately intergenerational; cultural artifacts are ways of handing down to the coming generation the commitments and beliefs of the passing generation. Culture by its nature transmits morals, and families by their nature transmit culture. Those two laws of social life seem to be at work throughout history around the world.

12   The family, of course, has been the key. As T. S. Eliot has argued "the primary vehicle for the transmission of culture is the family."[6] Even as forces seek to redefine it, the family remains "a constant expectation for all humanity, past, present, and future," according to Allan C. Carlson.[7] Families, with the aid and support of other cultural institutions, such as church and school, have the primary responsibility of teaching moral principles to the young, not only by

---

[3] Dana Mack, *The Assault on Parenthood: How Our Culture Undermines the Family* (New York: Simon and Shuster, 1997), p. 218.

[4] Ibid.

[5] Ibid., p. 167.

[6] T.S. Eliot, "Notes towards the Definition of Culture," *Christianity and Culture* (New York: Harcourt Brace Jovanovich, 1968), p. 121.

[7] Allan C. Carlson, *From Cottage to Workstation: The Family's Search for Social Harmony in the Industrial Age* (San Francisco: Ignatius Press, 1993), p. 5.

establishing the content of morality in their minds, but by instilling a love for the true and the good in their hearts. This affective role, a critical component of moral instruction, explains why stories and songs are central cultural expressions. The stories we love, and the songs we delight in singing and hearing, are the mechanisms whereby we, as parents and children, commit ourselves to virtue.

13   Since the time of Sigmund Freud, however, the normative and restraining role of culture has been turned inside out. As sociologist Philip Rieff documents in *The Triumph of the Therapeutic,* cultures and specifically cultural institutions in the West have increasingly been redefined as instruments of *liberation* rather than restraint. Since repression is now presumed to be a bad thing, the commonweal is best served, ironically, without any notion of the common good that cultural institutions formerly enforced. Empowering people to be all that they can be, to express all that they feel, and to obtain all that they desire is now seen to be the proper function of cultural institutions, including the family. As Wells puts it: "The external discipline of the culture is now denied in the name of the emancipated self."[8] This helps explain why unprecedented allusions to orgasms greet customers at the supermarket checkout line.

14   The transition from culture to its complete opposite, what some have termed anti-culture or postculturalism, has not happened overnight, but has been reinforced in the latter half of the twentieth century by all forms of popular culture, whether sanitized or not. The net result has reaped a far weaker family unit, particularly in its historic role as preserver and transmitter of morals.

The Loss of the Local

15   Some critics and historians argue that popular culture is nothing new, that Shakespeare was the popular culture of his day. That is not quite true. Prior to the invention of modern technologies of communications and travel, all culture was *local* culture. Music, dances, stories, visual representation, and sports all originated from and were sustained by people who were neighbors, who shared large enough amounts of time and small enough amounts of space to build some kind of knowledge of and affection for each other. Since culture was "produced and consumed" locally, the values communicated through cultural forms were values of the local community. Moral notions that did not fit "community standards" were not publicly tolerated.

16   In contrast, most of our cultural life is now defined by distant strangers; today's popular culture is *mass mediated culture.* As such, the moral dynamic of cultural activity has changed radically. We have moved from being creators and participants in culture to being simply consumers of culture. Culture is now a commodity, something we buy, "put on," or appropriate—a matter of fashion or taste, surely not something we receive, a legacy with permanent worth.

17   The extent to which mass mediators of culture were able to disturb the local mediation of culture was restrained until the 1960s. Neighborhoods still maintained their own standards, churches did not feel compelled to emulate television and popular music, and ethnic groups still transmitted some notion of identity that predated the products of mass media. But that local, religious, and ethnic independence is rapidly waning. Partly because of aggressive efforts in the name of free speech and partly because of the carelessness of a generation raised on television, the centrality of local life in the shaping of culture has given way to mass produced culture from Hollywood, New York, and Nashville.

18   Television, the dominant medium of popular culture, has been central to the transition from local to mass-mediated culture. By weaning children from local (specifically parental) authority, television

[8] Eliot, "Notes towards the Definition of Culture," p. 121.

reflects the dynamics of mass-mediated culture in general.

19   Prior to the advent of television, parents were the principal agents in establishing a trajectory for their children's intellectual and moral development. Writing in 1964, sociologists Oscar Ritchie and Marvin Koller argued that the home is the child's "small world" where the "family serves as a screen to the culture of its society and selects only those portions that it deems worthy of attention."[9] In this traditional pattern, the family is supplemented in its role by friends of the family, whose visits bring reports from the outside world that have different perspectives, but which are likely to be consonant with that of the parents. "As a person who lives outside the child's home, the guest functions as a transmitter, bringing into the world of the child new ideas and information, and new and different opportunities for vicarious participation in the outside world."[10]

20   This gentle and sensitive portrait of childhood seems painfully anachronistic today. The family is not the dominant "screen" in the lives of many children, who are given huge daily doses of television almost from birth. Rather than interacting with parents, extended family members, and neighbors, children increasingly interact with one-hundred-thousand watts of whatever network executives and cable companies think can make children buy more candy, toys, or designer clothes.

21   *That* children watch television in such quantity may be more significant than *what* they see. As Joshua Meyrowitz argues, television profoundly alters the moral relationship between parents and children:

> Children who have television sets now have outside perspectives from which to judge and evaluate family rituals, beliefs, and religious practices. Parents could once easily mold their young children's upbringing by speaking and reading to children only about those things they wished their children to be exposed to, but today's parents must battle with thousands of competing images and ideas over which they have little direct control. . . . Unable to read, very young children were once limited to the few sources of information available to them within and around the home: paintings, illustrations, views from a window, and what adults said and read to them. Television, however, now escorts children across the globe even before they have permission to cross the street.[11]

22   Whether or not the worldview children receive from television conforms to their parents' worldview does not really matter. Parents are simply no longer the dominant sources of moral instruction, thereby weakening their role and changing the perception that children have of parental authority long before they are even able to think about such things.

23   A subtle way television weakens parental authority, according to Meyrowitz, is by exposing "the backstage life" of adults to children. Even family-oriented shows like *Father Knows Best* or *Leave It To Beaver* reveal the behavior of adults when children are not around, including ways parents talk about their children. Meyrowitz says its *content* is less significant than the revelation of the backstage's very *existence*:

> As a result of such views of adulthood, children may become suspicious of adults and more unwilling to accept all that adults do or say at face value. Conversely, adults may feel 'exposed' by television and, in the long run, it may

[9] Oscar Ritchie and Marvin Koller, *Sociology of Childhood* (New York: Appleton-Century-Crofts, 1964), p. 86, 109.
[10] Ibid., p. 103.
[11] Joshua Meyrowitz, *No Sense of Place: The Impact of Electronic Media on Social Behavior* (New York: Oxford University Press, 1985), p. 238.

no longer seem to make as much sense to try to keep certain things hidden from children.[12]

24   In addition, popular culture has been able to interfere with local culture and the moral unity of communities by exploiting generational differences. By creating product lines that are intended to define adolescent identity as a deliberate rejection of parental expectations, the producers of popular culture have successfully entrenched the notion of a relatively new concept, youth culture. Our system of education does not help either, segregating young people from adults as well as from children outside a narrow age range, not to mention from infants and the elderly. This tendency is even unwittingly encouraged by many churches—the very institutions that should be the most vigilant in demonstrating that all ages dwell in unity, but which often celebrate the idea of youth culture as something divinely ordained.

25   Given that culture rightly understood is an intergenerational system of communicating moral convictions, the very phrase "youth culture" should be seen as a contradiction in terms. Not only does age segregation weaken the family's ability to pursue the cultural task of moral transmission, the glorification of the present at the expense of honoring the past and preparing for the future all work against the task of sustaining a rich idea of what family is. Among other things, it weakens the understanding of the family as an intergenerational entity that T. S. Eliot believed played a vital culture-shaping role:

> When I speak of the family, I have in mind a bond which embraces a longer period of time than this [that is, the living members of a nuclear family]: a piety toward the dead, however obscure, and a solicitude for the unborn, however remote. Unless this reverence for past and future is cultivated in the home, it can never be more than a verbal convention in the community.[13]

The Loss of Moral Authority

26   Another way popular culture interferes with the local and family mediation of culture is by undercutting the very notion of any properly recognized authority. Children have always challenged parental authority with the time-honored complaint: "But Johnny's mom lets him do it." While a child may not understand the moral reasoning, he is essentially arguing that since other authority figures have looser standards, more stringent standards cannot be justified. On the other hand, a common and worthy parental response is: "I'm not Johnny's mom." That response presumes the parent is the duly constituted authority here, giving her the right to establish local or family standards.

27   Another way of responding is to observe: "*We* don't do that sort of thing." The first person plural pronoun in the subject of that sentence suggests that the child belongs to a moral community, at least as large as the family, with certain received standards. To the degree parents are able to help children identify with that *we,* they can effectively transmit moral convictions, enabling a child to know he should not do such-and-such because it would not be fitting with his religious identity, or because it would give his family a bad name, or because it would poorly represent his hometown. Without this sense of "binding address," moral identity is left undefined and open; moral authority does not seem compelling.

28   By encouraging young people to become fans of whatever is regarded as trendy or hip each week, popular culture makes a morally recognizable *we* especially difficult to maintain. Television, in particular, undermines efforts of parents or other authority figures to establish terms of propriety in several ways. The immediacy of the medium and the easygoing, chumminess of television personalities make formalities of any kind seem alien; everyone is on a first-name basis.

[12] Ibid., p. 249.
[13] Eliot, "Notes towards the Definition of Culture," p. 116.

Its programming is equally problematic. By publicly displaying private behavior, television implicitly legitimizes virtually any behavior in any setting. Joshua Meyrowitz believes this leads to the elimination of the idea of moral and social taboos:

> Any topic on any popular situation comedy, talk shows, news program, or advertisement—be it death, homosexuality, abortion, male strippers, sex-change operations, political scandals, incest, rape, jock itch, or bras that "lift and separate"—can be spoken about the next day in school, over dinner, or on a date, not only because everyone knows about such subjects, but also because everyone knows that everyone knows, and everyone knows that everyone knows that everyone knows. In fact, it almost seems strange *not* to talk and write about such things. The public and all-inclusive nature of television has a tendency to collapse formerly distinct situations into one. In a society shaped by the segregated situations of print, people may secretly discuss taboo topics, but with television, the very notion of the "taboo" is lost.[14]

29   Television, of course, is not really all-inclusive. It actually presents a rather narrow range of experiences and personalities. But it gives the impression of being "all things considered," with the result that those aspects of existence not explored by television come to be regarded as more marginal to human experience than they might be otherwise.

30   Nor does television communicate moral accountability the way literature does. According to Meyrowitz,

A child's book is, in a sense, a "guest" in the house. It makes a "social entrance," that is, it comes through the door and remains under at least nominal parental authority. As a physical object it must be stored somewhere in the house and it can be discarded. The child's television set, in contrast, is like a new doorway [in]to the home. Through it come many welcome and unwelcome visitors: schoolteachers, Presidents, salesmen, police officers, prostitutes, friends, and strangers.[15]

31   All these factors profoundly affect the ability of families to be schools of character. By weakening the consciousness of moral accountability of children to parents and by distressing the prescriptive power of parents, popular culture establishes its own artifacts and celebrities as sources of moral understanding—a moral system that has only one commandment: Fulfill thyself.

The Loss of Tradition

32   The shift from understanding culture as a legacy to be received (on its terms) to a titillation to be consumed (on my terms) has another consequence: the loss of tradition. That may not initially sound so bad; Americans love innovation, change, and progress. Yet cultural conservatives may need to consider to what extent the traditional values they covet can be sustained without tradition, and especially without a more conscious effort to connect with the past. As Edward Shils, a prominent sociologist, wisely warns: "A family which incorporates into itself little of the past, and, of that which it does incorporate, little of high quality—not all of the past was of equal quality—deadens its offspring; it leaves them with a scanty set of categories and beliefs which are not easily extended or elaborated."[16]

[14] Meyrowitz, *No Sense of Place*, p. 92.
[15] Ibid., p. 245.
[16] Edward Shils, *Tradition* (Chicago: University of Chicago Press, 1981), p. 172f.

33   While he does not mention popular culture explicitly, Shils believes the family's ability to connect with the past has been weakened by parents who are reluctant to impose their beliefs on their children and who neglect the hard work of mediating tradition to their children because of other preoccupations. Cultural transmission is further weakened among single-parents who lack a needed spouse to reinforce family standards. All these factors "make the stream of tradition narrower and shallower." The phenomenon, writes Shils, resembles the aftermath of war which displaces parents from each other and their children: "The offspring are left to define their own standards; this means the acceptance of the norms of their most imposing coevals."[17]

34   By eliminating a sense of cultural legacy, popular culture weakens or destroys the sense of a permanent moral order in creation. One function of traditional culture is to transmit this sense of moral order, with the implication that each person is obligated to discern and obey the laws of Nature and of Nature's God. The modern sensibility, embodied so fully in popular culture, is that reality is something each individual invents. No moral order exists in the nature of things, only *my* will and *my* desires.

35   Traditional cultures work by a sense of prescription. The traditional order is given the benefit of the doubt, not the burden of proof. Living with the habit of submitting to the received order (unless it is perceived to be in violation of some natural law) cultivates a much greater sympathy to belief in moral absolutes. On the other hand, the regime of popular culture—in which one *must* do one's *own* thing—makes relativism much more plausible. In fact, the sort of aculturalism that popular culture encourages seems to prescribe relativism.

36   Not only does it prescribe a state of flux, but popular culture ends up filling the vacuum left by the abandonment of old ways. According to sociologist Daniel Bell:

A society in rapid change inevitably produces confusions about appropriate modes of behavior, taste, and dress. A socially mobile person has no ready guide for acquiring new knowledge on how to live 'better' than before, and his guides become the movies, television, and advertising. In this respect, advertising begins to play a more subtle role in changing habits than in stimulating wants. . . . Though at first the changes were primarily in manners, dress, taste, and food habits, sooner or later they begin to affect more basic patterns: the structure of authority in the family, the role of children and young adults as independent consumers in the society, the pattern of morals, and the different meanings of achievement in the society."[18]

The Loss of Moral Seriousness

37   A final criticism of popular culture is its superficiality. Not only is the content of popular culture often trite, but the forms in which it is presented discourage depth, reflection, and moral seriousness. As media critic Todd Gitlin describes it, television encourages the sensibility of being "flat and happy." Because the pace of television is relentless and because slick production values are more important than content, glibness rules:

On TV both children and adults speak with unprecedented glibness. Thanks to the wonders of editing, no one on television is ever at a loss for words or photogenic signs of emotion. . . . Hesitancy, silence, awkwardness are absent from TV's repertory of behaviors, except in sitcoms or made-for-TV movies where boy meets girl. Yet outside TV, awkwardness and hesitancy often characterize the beginning, and

---

[17] Ibid.

[18] Daniel Bell, *The Cultural Contradictions of Capitalism* (New York: Basic Books, 1996), p. 68f.

each further development, of inte-
riority, of a person's internal life.
On TV, however, speech is stripped
down, designed to move. The one-
liner, developed for ads, is the premium style. TV's common currency consists of slogans and
mockery. Situation comedies and
morning shows are in particular
obsessed with the jokey comeback.
The put-down is the universal
linkage among television's cast of
live and recorded characters. A
free-floating hostility mirrors, and
also inspires, the equivalent conversational style among the young
who grow up in this habitat.[19]

38   Gitlin quotes fellow critic Mark Crispin
Miller who has observed that this knowingly
snide attitude is so widespread and automatic
that it deserves to be called "the hipness unto
death." Earnestness is out, attitude is all, and
the development of character that was once
the proper goal of cultural life is thus stunted
if not exterminated. What remains stands in
vivid contrast to the kind of moral imagination that Russell Kirk claims is an essential
prerequisite to cultural health:

> One thing we can do is this: to re-
> frain from choking up the springs
> of the moral imagination. If we
> stifle the sense of wonder, no
> wonders will occur among us; and
> if wondrous remedies are lacking,
> then indeed the words of doom
> written on the sky will become as
> the laws of the Medes and the Per-
> sians, ineluctable.[20]

True Entertainment

39   In the 1950s, Martha Wolfenstein foresaw the
cumulative effect of popular culture: entire
generations who have a need to be constantly

entertained. In her telling essay, "The Emergence of a Fun Morality," the sociologist dis-
cerned signs of a new morality displacing an
emphasis on goodness. A preoccupation with
goodness was, after all, demanding, and in-
terfered with self-fulfillment. Fun morality
makes its own demands, since not having fun
becomes an occasion for anxiety. Wolfenstein
writes: "Whereas gratification of forbidden
impulses traditionally aroused guilt, failure
to have fun now lowers one's self-esteem."[21]
Ironically, many parents, teachers, and religious leaders who today might share Wolfenstein's concerns at face value often appear
more worried about being a fun person than
about being a good person. As products of
this new cultural climate, they assume their
roles of moral authority with the same in-
verted sense of what is moral.

40   For these reasons, the moral condition of
American society under the regime of popular culture is a serious and radical problem
for which no simple solutions exist. One step
in addressing the problem might be to define
the proper role of entertainment in society,
in the family, and in the life of the individual.
The Oxford English Dictionary lists the root
meaning of the verb *entertain* as: "To keep in
a certain state or condition; to keep in a certain frame of mind; to maintain a state of
things; to maintain in existence." That original meaning remains surprisingly accurate,
as in the television program, *Entertainment
Tonight*. The only difference is the state, condition, or frame of mind being sustained by
modern entertainment.

41   The condition of our times is one of disorder and relentless, boundless change.
Most entertainment serves to render Americans sympathetic to that condition, undisturbed by the losses, and impressed by the
pomp and show of bogus "progress." The
frame of mind encouraged by modern entertainment is one which is suspicious of any
legacy or inheritance, and which is commit-

[19] Todd Gitlin, "Flat and Happy," *The Wilson Quarterly* (Autumn 1993), p. 53.

[20] Russell Kirk, *The Wise Men Know What Wicked Things Are Written on the Sky* (Washington,
D.C.: Regnery Gateway, 1987), p. 128.

[21] Martha Wolfenstein, "The Emergence of Fun Morality," in *Mass Leisure*, ed. Eric
Larrabee and Rolf Meyerson (Glencoe, Ill: The Free Press, 1958), p.86.

ted to the assertion of the sovereignty of the self. It is a mentality that evokes a mood of restlessness and blocks out the reflection necessary for acknowledging its disease and then seeking a remedy. It is a sensibility rooted only in the present, ignoring the past, indifferent to the future.

42 In the Christian tradition, the Church (the bride of the One who Was and Is and Shall Be) is called to entertain herself with past and future matters: with millennia-long memories of her sovereign and suffering Lord and of her own rich history of loving and obeying him; and with visions of a distant yet certain glory in a time beyond time. The present is where people of faith are called to obey, but it only makes sense when triangulated within the history and future of redemption, from Creation to Consummation.

43 Conversely, the forms of worldly entertainment are marvelously suited to its content. Thanks to mass media, we are sovereign and isolated consumers of entertainment, seeking temporary amnesia from the unhappiness and disappointment of reality. To imagine entertainment that is radically different, truer to its root sense, and engages participants in a mutually edifying service of sustaining love is possible. But that sort of entertainment requires serious attention to the recovery of local culture and how the shape of shared life together might recover a richer sort of entertainment.

44 Poet-farmer Wendell Berry's description of families entertaining one another in his essay, "The Work of Local Culture," describes entertainment in the root sense of the word. In Berry's view, the sharing of memories, not the pursuit of forgetting, maintains a people in its existence. Cultural conservatives therefore should be as concerned about the *form* of entertainment as its content. Our social and cultural disorder does not simply spring from the fact that R-rated movies outnumber G-rated movies. It issues equally from parents who are more likely to take or send their children to the movies than tell them stories. Our society suffers not from being over-entertained, but from not being *truly* entertained. Whether we can recover depends to the extent we attend, not just to the words, but to the way the song is being sung.

Source: Kenneth Myers, "Popular Culture and the Family." *Family Policy,* Family Research Council. Sept. 15, 1998. http.//www/frc.org/papers

DISCUSSION QUESTIONS

1. What examples of slanted language can you find in the introductory section of "Popular Culture and the Family"?

2. Throughout his argument, Myers supports his various claims through appeals to authority. Using the World Wide Web, find information on three of the authorities Myers cites. Based upon what you've learned, discuss with classmates the degree of authority these references lend to the argument.

3. Identify a secondary causal claim in the essay (other than the one analyzed in the preceding commentary). Write a brief summary of the strategies used to support this argument.

4. Select two or three of the generalized claims in the essay and consider how many and what kind of specific examples would have supported the generalization adequately.

5. Select another generalized claim and list three or four counterexamples.

SUGGESTIONS FOR WRITING (18.1)

1. Try writing a one-paragraph definition of the term "popular culture" based upon Myers's apparent understanding of the term.

2. Without consulting any outside sources, write an extended definition of "popular culture" that reflects your personal understanding of the term.

3. Using the definition you wrote for Suggestion #2, write a three- to four-page evaluative argument defending or attacking popular culture. You will probably support your evaluation of the concept through causal arguments that demonstrate its positive or negative effects.

4. Trying to be as engaging as possible, write your own three-or four-paragraph description of the magazine rack in a grocery store, using no slanted language at all. Exchange descriptions with a classmate and discuss how successfully each engaged the reader's interest.

LISTENING TO KHAKIS

MALCOLM GLADWELL

The New Yorker's *Web site describes this venerated magazine as follows:*

The New Yorker *is a weekly magazine dedicated to ideas. It is timeless and immediate, energetic and thoughtful, serious and funny. The* New Yorker *is about good writing, a point of view, and a deeper understanding of the world. . . . Contributors to the* New Yorker *include both recognized talents of long standing and newly discovered voices*

Malcolm Gladwell, the author of this 1997 New Yorker *article, belongs in the first category of "recognized talents of long standing." Gladwell writes for a number of magazines and journals and is a regular contributor to the* New Yorker.

LISTENING TO KHAKIS

What America's most popular pants tell us about the way guys think

1   In the fall of 1987, Levi Strauss & Co. began running a series of national television commercials to promote Dockers, its new brand of men's khakis. All the spots—and there were twenty-eight—had the same basic structure. A handheld camera would follow a group of men as they sat around a living room or office or bar. The men were in their late thirties, but it was hard to tell, because the camera caught faces only fleetingly. It was trained instead on the men from the waist down—on the seats of their pants, on the pleats of their khakis, on their hands going in and out of their pockets. As the camera jumped in quick cuts from Docker to Docker, the men chatted in loose, overlapping non sequiturs—guy-talk fragments that, when they are rendered on the page,

achieve a certain Dadaist poetry. Here is the entire transcript of "Poolman," one of the first—and, perhaps, best—ads in the series:

"She was a redhead about five foot six inches tall."

"And all of a sudden this thing starts spinning, and it's going round and round."

"Is that Nelson?"

"And that makes me safe, because with my wife, I'll never be that way."

"It's like your career, and you're frustrated. I mean that— that's—what you want."

"Of course, that's just my opinion."

"So money's no object."

"Yeah, money's no object."

"What are we going to do with our lives, now?"

"Well . . ."

"Best of all . . ."

[Voice-over] "Levi's one-hundred-per-cent-cotton Dockers. If you're not wearing Dockers, you're just wearing pants."

"And I'm still paying the loans off."

"You've got all the money in the world."

"I'd like to at least be your poolman."

2   By the time the campaign was over, at the beginning of the nineties, Dockers had grown into a six-hundred-million-dollar business— a brand that if it had spun off from Levi's would have been (and would still be) the fourth-largest clothing brand in the world. Today, seventy per cent of American men between the ages of twenty-five and forty-five own a pair of Dockers, and khakis are expected to be as popular as blue jeans by the beginning of the next century. It is no exaggeration to call the original Dockers ads one of the most successful fashion-advertising campaigns in history.

3   This is a remarkable fact for a number of reasons, not the least of which is that the Dockers campaign was aimed at men, and no one had ever thought you could hit a home run like that by trying to sell fashion to the American male. Not long ago, two psychologists at York University, in Toronto—Irwin Silverman and Marion Eals—conducted an experiment in which they had men and women sit in an office for two minutes, without any reading material or distraction, while they ostensibly waited to take part in some kind of academic study. Then they were taken from the office and given the real reason for the experiment: to find out how many of the objects in the office they could remember. This was not a test of memory so much as it was a test of awareness—of the kind and quality of unconscious attention that people pay to the particulars of their environment. If you think about it, it was really a test of fashion sense, because, at its root, this is what fashion sense really is—the ability to register and appreciate and remember the details of the way those around you look and dress, and then reinterpret those details and memories yourself.

4   When the results of the experiment were tabulated, it was found that the women were able to recall the name and the placement of seventy per cent more objects than the men, which makes perfect sense. Women's fashion, after all, consists of an endless number of subtle combinations and variations—of skirt, dress, pants, blouse, T-shirt, hose, pumps, flats, heels, necklace, bracelet, cleavage, collar, curl, and on and on—all driven by the fact that when a woman walks down the street she knows that other women, consciously or otherwise, will notice the name and the placement of what she is wearing. Fashion works for women because women can appreciate its complexity. But when it comes to men what's the point? How on earth do you sell fashion to someone who has no appreciation for detail whatsoever?

5   The Dockers campaign, however, proved that you could sell fashion to men. But that was only the first of its remarkable implications. The second—which remains as weird and mysterious and relevant to the fashion business today as it was ten years ago—was

that you could do this by training a camera on a man's butt and having him talk in yuppie gibberish.

6   I watched "Poolman" with three members of the new team handling the Dockers account at Foote, Cone & Belding (F.C.B.), Levi's ad agency. We were in a conference room at Levi's Plaza, in downtown San Francisco, a redbrick building decorated (appropriately enough) in khaki like earth tones, with the team members—Chris Shipman, Iwan Thomis, and Tanyia Kandohla—forming an impromptu critical panel. Shipman, who had thick black glasses and spoke in an almost inaudible laid-back drawl, put a videocassette of the first campaign into a VCR—stopping, starting, and rewinding—as the group analyzed what made the spots so special.

7   "Remember, this is from 1987," he said, pointing to the screen, as the camera began its jerky dance. "Although this style of film making looks everyday now, that kind of handheld stuff was very fresh when these were made."

8   "They taped real conversations," Kandohla chimed in. "Then the footage was cut together afterward. They were thrown areas to talk about. It was very natural, not at all scripted. People were encouraged to go off on tangents."

9   After "Poolman," we watched several of the other spots in the original group—"Scorekeeper" and "Dad's Chair," "Flag Football" and "The Meaning of Life"—and I asked about the headlessness of the commercials, because if you watch too many in a row all those anonymous body parts begin to get annoying. But Thomis maintained that the headlessness was crucial, because it was the absence of faces that gave the dialogue its freedom. "They didn't show anyone's head because if they did the message would have too much weight," he said. "It would be too pretentious. You know, people talking about their hopes and dreams. It seems more genuine, as opposed to something stylized."

10   The most striking aspect of the spots is how different they are from typical fashion advertising. If you look at men's fashion magazines, for example, at the advertisements for the suits of Ralph Lauren or Valentino or Hugo Boss, they almost always consist of a beautiful man, with something interesting done to his hair, wearing a gorgeous outfit. At the most, the man may be gesturing discreetly, or smiling in the demure way that a man like that might smile after, say, telling the supermodel at the next table no thanks he has to catch an early-morning flight to Milan. But that's all. The beautiful face and the clothes tell the whole story. The Dockers ads, though, are almost exactly the opposite. There's no face. The camera is jumping around so much that it's tough to concentrate on the clothes. And instead of stark simplicity, the fashion image is overlaid with a constant, confusing patter. It's almost as if the Dockers ads weren't primarily concerned with clothes at all—and in fact that's exactly what Levi's intended. What the company had discovered, in its research, was that babyboomer men felt that the chief thing missing from their lives was male friendship. Caught between the demands of the families that many of them had started in the eighties and career considerations that had grown more onerous, they felt they had lost touch with other men. The purpose of the ads—the chatter, the lounging around, the quick cuts—was simply to conjure up a place where men could put on one-hundred-percent-cotton khakis and reconnect with one another. In the original advertising brief, that imaginary place was dubbed Dockers World.

11   This may seem like an awfully roundabout way to sell a man a pair of pants. But that was the genius of the campaign. One of the truisms of advertising is that it's always easier to sell at the extremes than in the middle, which is why the advertisements for Valentino and Hugo Boss are so simple. The man in the market for a thousand-dollar suit doesn't need to be convinced of the value of nice clothes. The man in the middle, though—the man in the market for a fortydollar pair of khakis—does. In fact, he probably isn't comfortable buying clothes at all. To sell him a pair of pants you have to take him somewhere he is comfortable, and that was the point of Dockers World. Even the apparent gibberish of lines like "'She was a red-

head about five foot six inches tall.' / 'And all of a sudden this thing starts spinning, and it's going round and round.' / 'Is that Nelson?'" have, if you listen closely enough, a certain quintessentially guy-friendly feel. It's the narrative equivalent of the sports-highlight reel—the sequence of five-second film clips of the best plays from the day's basketball or football or baseball games, which millions of American men watch every night on television. This nifty couplet from "Scorekeeper," for instance—"'Who remembers their actual first girlfriend?' / 'I would have done better, but I was bald then, too'"—is not nonsense but a twenty-minute conversation edited down to two lines. A man schooled in the highlight reel no more needs the other nineteen minutes and fifty-eight seconds of that exchange than he needs to see the intervening catch and throw to make sense of a sinking liner to left and a close play at the plate.

12   "Men connected to the underpinnings of what was being said," Robert Hanson, the vice-president of marketing for Dockers, told me. "These guys were really being honest and genuine and real with each other, and talking about their lives. It may not have been the truth, but it was the fantasy of what a lot of customers wanted, which was not just to be work-focused but to have the opportunity to express how you feel about your family and friends and lives. The content was very important. The thing that built this brand was that we absolutely nailed the emotional underpinnings of what motivates baby boomers."

13   Hanson is a tall, striking man in his early thirties. He's what Jeff Bridges would look like if he had gone to finishing school. Hanson said that when he goes out on research trips to the focus groups that Dockers holds around the country he often deliberately stays in the background, because if the men in the group see him "they won't necessarily respond as positively or as openly." When he said this, he was wearing a pair of stone-white Dockers, a deep-blue shirt, a navy blazer, and a brilliant-orange patterned tie, and these worked so well together that it was obvious what he meant. When someone like Hanson dresses up that

fabulously in Dockers, he makes it clear just how many variations and combinations are possible with a pair of khakis—but that, of course, defeats the purpose of the carefully crafted Dockers World message, which is to appeal to the man who wants nothing to do with fashion's variations and combinations. It's no coincidence that every man in every one of the group settings profiled in each commercial is wearing—albeit in different shades—exactly the same kind of pants. Most fashion advertising sells distinctiveness. (Can you imagine, say, an Ann Taylor commercial where a bunch of thirtyish girlfriends are lounging around chatting, all decked out in matching sweater sets?) Dockers was selling conformity.

"We would never do anything with our   14
pants that would frighten anyone away," Gareth Morris, a senior designer for the brand, told me. "We'd never do too many belt loops, or an unusual base cloth. Our customers like one-hundred-per-cent-cotton fabrics. We would never do a synthetic. That's definitely in the market, but it's not where we need to be. Styling-wise, we would never do a wide, wide leg. We would never do a peg-legged style. Our customers seem to have a definite idea of what they want. They don't like tricky openings or zips or a lot of pocket flaps and details on the back. We've done button-through flaps, to push it a little bit. But we usually do a welt pocket—that's a pocket with a button-through. It's funny. We have focus groups in New York, Chicago, and San Francisco, and whenever we show them a pocket with a flap—it's a simple thing—they hate it. They won't buy the pants. They complain, 'How do I get my wallet?' So we compromise and do a welt. That's as far as they'll go. And there's another thing. They go, 'My butt's big enough. I don't want flaps hanging off of it, too.' They like inseam pockets. They like to know where they put their hands." He gestured to the pair of experimental prototype Dockers he was wearing, which had pockets that ran almost parallel to the waistband of the pants. "This is a stretch for us," he said. "If you start putting more stuff on than we have on our product, you're asking for trouble."

15   The apotheosis of the notion of khakis as nonfashion-guy fashion came several years after the original Dockers campaign, when Haggar Clothing Co. hired the Goodby, Silverstein & Partners ad agency, in San Francisco, to challenge Dockers' khaki dominance. In retrospect, it was an inspired choice, since Goodby, Silverstein is Guy Central. It does Porsche ("Kills Bugs Fast") and Isuzu and the recent "Got Milk?" campaign and a big chunk of the Nike business, and it operates out of a gutted turn-of-the-century building downtown, refurbished in what is best described as neo-Erector set. The campaign that it came up with featured voice-overs by Roseanne's television husband, John Goodman. In the best of the ads, entitled "I Am," a thirtyish man wakes up, his hair all mussed, pulls on a pair of white khakis, and half sleepwalks outside to get the paper. "I am not what I wear. I'm not a pair of pants, or a shirt," Goodman intones. The man walks by his wife, handing her the front sections of the paper. "I'm not in touch with my inner child. I don't read poetry, and I'm not politically correct." He heads away from the kitchen, down a hallway, and his kid grabs the comics from him. "I'm just a guy, and I don't have time to think about what I wear, because I've got a lot of important guy things to do." All he has left now is the sports section and, gripping it purposefully, he heads for the bathroom.   "One-hundred-per-cent-cotton wrinkle-free khaki pants that don't require a lot of thought. Haggar. Stuff you can wear."

16   "We softened it," Richard Silverstein told me as we chatted in his office, perched on chairs in the midst of—among other things—a lacrosse stick, a bike stand, a gym bag full of yesterday's clothing, three toy Porsches, and a giant model of a Second World War Spitfire hanging from the ceiling. "We didn't say 'Haggar Apparel' or 'Haggar Clothing.' We said, 'Hey, listen, guys, don't worry. It's just stuff. Don't worry about it.' The concept was 'Make it approachable.'" The difference between this and the Dockers ad is humor. F.C.B. assiduously documented men's inner lives. Goodby, Silverstein made fun of them. But

it's essentially the same message. It's instructive, in this light, to think about the Casual Friday phenomenon of the past decade, the loosening of corporate dress codes that was spawned by the rise of khakis. Casual Fridays are commonly thought to be about men rejecting the uniform of the suit. But surely that's backward. Men started wearing khakis to work because Dockers and Haggar made it sound as if khakis were going to be even easier than a suit. The khaki-makers realized that men didn't want to get rid of uniforms; they just wanted a better uniform.

17   The irony, of course, is that this idea of nonfashion—of khakis as the choice that diminishes, rather than enhances, the demands of fashion—turned out to be a white lie. Once you buy even the plainest pair of khakis, you invariably also buy a sports jacket and a belt and a whole series of shirts to go with it—maybe a polo knit for the weekends, something in plaid for casual, and a button-down for a dressier look—and before long your closet is thick with just the kinds of details and options that you thought you were avoiding. You may not add these details as brilliantly or as consciously as, say, Hanson does, but you end up doing it nonetheless. In the past seven years, sales of men's clothing in the United States have risen as astonishing twenty-one per cent, in large part because of this very fact—that khakis, even as they have simplified the bottom half of the male wardrobe, have forced a steady revision of the top. At the same time, even khakis themselves—within the narrow constraints of khakidom—have quietly expanded their range. When Dockers were launched, in the fall of 1986, there were just three basic styles: the double-pleated Docker in khaki, olive, navy, and black; the Steamer, in cotton canvas; and the more casual flat-fronted Docker. Now there are twenty-four. Dockers and Haggar and everyone else has been playing a game of bait and switch: lure men in with the promise of a uniform and then slip them, bit by bit, fashion. Put them in an empty room and then, ever so slowly, so as not to scare them, fill the room with objects.

18 There is a puzzle in psychology known as the canned-laughter problem, which has a deeper and more complex set of implications about men and women and fashion and why the Dockers ads were so successful. Over the years, several studies have been devoted to this problem, but perhaps the most instructive was done by two psychologists at the University of Wisconsin, Gerald Cupchik and Howard Leventhal. Cupchik and Leventhal took a stack of cartoons (including many from the *New Yorker*), half of which an independent panel had rated as very funny and half of which it had rated as mediocre. They put the cartoons on slides, had a voice-over read the captions, and presented the slide show to groups of men and women. As you might expect, both sexes reacted pretty much the same way. Then Cupchik and Leventhal added a laugh track to the voice-over—the subjects were told that it was actual laughter from people who were in the room during the taping—and repeated the experiment. This time, however, things got strange. The canned laughter made the women laugh a little harder and rate the cartoons as a little funnier than they had before. But not the men. They laughed a bit more at the good cartoons but much more at the bad cartoons. The canned laughter also made them rate the bad cartoons as much funnier than they had rated them before, but it had little or no effect on their ratings of the good cartoons. In fact, the men found a bad cartoon with a laugh track to be almost as funny as a good cartoon without one. What was going in?

19 The guru of male-female differences in the ad world is Joan Meyers-Levy, a professor at the University of Chicago business school. In a groundbreaking series of articles written over the past decade, Meyers-Levy has explained the canned-laughter problem and other gender anomalies by arguing that men and women use fundamentally different methods of processing information. Given two pieces of evidence about how funny something is—their own opinion and the opinion of others (the laugh track)—the women came up with a higher score than before because they added the two clues together: they integrated the information before them. The men, on the other hand, picked one piece of evidence and ignored the other. For the bad cartoons, they got carried away by the laugh track and gave out hugely generous scores for funniness. For the good cartoons, however, they were so wedded to their own opinion that suddenly the laugh track didn't matter at all.

20 This idea—that men eliminate and women integrate—is called by Meyers-Levy the "selectivity hypothesis." Men are looking for a way to simplify the route to a conclusion, so they seize on the most obvious evidence and ignore the rest, while women, by contrast, try to process information comprehensively. So-called bandwidth research, for example, has consistently shown that if you ask a group of people to sort a series of objects or ideas into categories, the men will create fewer and larger categories than the women will. They use bigger mental bandwidth. Why? Because the bigger the bandwidth the less time and attention you have to pay to each individual object. Or consider what is called the invisibility question. If a woman is being asked a series of personal questions by another woman, she'll say more if she's facing the woman she's talking to than she will if her listener is invisible. With men, it's the opposite. When they can't see the person who's asking them questions, they suddenly and substantially open up. This, of course, is a condition of male communication which has been remarked on by women for millennia. But the selectivity hypothesis suggests that the cause of it has been misdiagnosed. It's not that men necessarily have trouble expressing their feelings; it's that in a face-to-face conversation they experience emotional overload. A man can't process nonverbal information (the expression and body language of the person asking him questions) and verbal information (the personal question being asked) at the same time any better than he can process other people's laughter and his own laughter at the same time. He has to select, and it is Meyers-Levy's contention that this pattern of behavior suggests significant differences in the way men and women respond to advertising.

21   Joan Meyers-Levy is a petite woman in her late thirties, with a dark pageboy haircut and a soft voice. She met me in the downtown office of the University of Chicago with three large folders full of magazine advertisements under one arm, and after chatting about the origins and the implications of her research she handed me an ad from several years ago for Evian bottled water. It has a beautiful picture of the French Alps and, below that, in large type, "Our factory." The text ran for several paragraphs, beginning:

22   You're not just looking at the French Alps. You're looking at one of the most pristine places on earth. And the origin of Evian Natural Spring Water.

23   Here, it takes no less than fifteen years for nature to purify every drop of Evian as it flows through mineral-rich glacial formations deep within the mountains. And it is here that Evian acquires its unique balance of minerals.

24   "Now, is that a male or a female ad?" she asked. I looked at it again. The picture baffled me. But the word "factory" seemed masculine, so I guessed male.

25   She shook her head. "It's female. Look at the picture. It's just the Alps, and then they label it 'Our factory.' They're using a metaphor. To understand this, you're going to have to engage in a fair amount of processing. And look at all the imagery they're encouraging you to build up. You're not just looking at the French Alps. It's 'one of the most pristine places on earth' and it will take nature 'no less than fifteen years' to purify." Her point was that this is an ad that works only if the viewer appreciates all its elements—if the viewer integrates, not selects. A man, for example, glancing at the ad for a fraction of a second, might focus only on the words "Our factory" and screen out the picture of the Alps entirely, the same way he might have screened out the canned laughter. Then he wouldn't get the visual metaphor. In fact, he might end up equating Evian with a factory, and that would be a disaster. Anyway, why bother going into such detail about the glaciers if it's just going to get lost in the big male bandwidth?

26   Meyers-Levy handed me another Evian advertisement. It showed a man—the Olym-pic Gold Medal swimmer Matt Biondi—by a pool drinking Evian, with the caption "Revival of the fittest." The women's ad had a hundred and nineteen words of text. This ad had just twenty-nine words: "No other water has the unique, natural balance of minerals that Evian achieves during its fifteen year journey deep within the French Alps. To be the best takes time." Needless to say, it came from a men's magazine. "With men, you don't want the fluff," she said. "Women, though, participate a lot more in whatever they are processing. By giving them more cues, you give them something to work with. You don't have to be so literal. With women you can be more allusive, so you can draw them in. They will engage in elaboration, and the more associations they make the easier it is to remember and retrieve later on."

27   Meyers-Levy took a third ad from her pile, this one for the 1997 Mercury Mountaineer four-wheel-drive sport-utility vehicle. It covers two pages, has the heading "Take the Rough with the Smooth," and shows four pictures—one of the vehicle itself, one of a mother and her child, one of a city skyline, and a large one of the interior of the car, over which the ad's text is superimposed. Around the border of the ad are forty-four separate, tiny photographs of roadways and buildings and construction sites and manhole covers. Female. Next to it on the table she put another ad—this one a single page, with a picture of the Mountaineer's interior, fifteen lines of text, a picture of the car's exterior, and, at the top, the heading: "When the Going Gets Tough, the Tough Get Comfortable." Male. "It's details, details. They're saying lots of different stuff," she said, pointing to the female version. "With men, instead of trying to cover everything in a single execution, you'd probably want to have a whole series of ads, each making a different point."

28   After a while, the game got very easy—if a bit humiliating. Meyers-Levy said that her observations were not antimale—that both the male and the female strategies have their strengths and their weaknesses—and, of course, she's right. On the other hand, reading the gender of ads makes it painfully obvious how much the advertising world—

consciously or not—talks down to men. Before I met Meyers-Levy, I thought that the genius of the famous first set of Dockers ads was their psychological complexity, their ability to capture the many layers of eighties guyness. But when I thought about them again after meeting Meyers-Levy, I began to think that their real genius lay in their heroic simplicity—in the fact that F.C.B. had the self-discipline to fill the allotted thirty seconds with as little as possible. Why no heads? The invisibility rule. Guys would never listen to that Dadaist extemporizing if they had to process nonverbal cues, too. Why were the ads set in people's living rooms and at the office? Bandwidth. The message was that khakis were wide-bandwidth pants. And why were all the ads shot in almost exactly the same way, and why did all the dialogue run together in one genial, faux-philosophical stretch of highlight reel? Because of canned laughter. Because if there were more than one message to be extracted men would get confused.

29   In the early nineties, Dockers began to falter. In 1992, the company sold sixty-six million pairs of khakis, but in 1993, as competition from Haggar and the Gap and other brands grew fiercer, that number slipped to fifty-nine million six hundred thousand, and by 1994 it had fallen to forty-seven million. In marketing-speak, user reality was encroaching on brand personality; that is, Dockers were being defined by the kind of middle-aged men who wore them, and not by the hipper, younger men in the original advertisements. The brand needed a fresh image, and the result was the "Nice Pants" campaign currently being shown on national television—a campaign widely credited with the resurgence of Dockers' fortunes.

30   In one of the spots, "Vive la France," a scruffy young man in his early twenties, wearing Dockers, is sitting in a café; in Paris. He's obviously a tourist. He glances up and sees a beautiful woman (actually, the supermodel Tatjana Patitz) looking right at him. He's in heaven. She starts walking directly toward him, and as she passes by she says, "Beau pantalon." As he looks frantically through his French phrase book for a translation, the waiter comes by and cuffs him on the head: "Hey, she says, 'Nice pants.'" Another spot in the series, "Subway Love," takes place on a subway car in Chicago. He (a nice young man wearing Dockers) spots her (a total babe), and their eyes lock. Romantic music swells. He moves toward her, but somehow, in a sudden burst of pushing and shoving, they get separated. Last shot: she's inside the car, her face pushed up against the glass. He's outside the car, his face pushed up against the glass. As the train slowly pulls away, she mouths two words: "Nice pants."

    It may not seem like it, but "Nice Pants"   31 is as radical a campaign as the original Dockers series. If you look back at the way that Sansabelt pants, say, were sold in the sixties, each ad was what advertisers would call a pure "head" message: the pants were comfortable, durable, good value. The genius of the first Dockers campaign was the way it combined head and heart: these were all-purpose, no-nonsense pants that connected to the emotional needs of baby boomers. What happened to Dockers in the nineties, though, was that everyone started to do head and heart for khakis. Haggar pants were wrinkle-free (head) and John Goodman-guy (heart). The Gap, with its brilliant billboard campaign of the early nineties—"James Dean wore khakis," "Frank Lloyd Wright wore khakis"—perfected the heart message by forging an emotional connection between khakis and a particular nostalgic, glamorous all-Americanness. To reassert itself, Dockers needed to go an extra step. Hence "Nice Pants," a campaign that for the first time in Dockers history raises the subject of sex.

    "It's always been acceptable for a man to   32 be a success in business," Hanson said, explaining the rationale behind "Nice Pants." "It's always been expected of a man to be a good provider. The new thing that men are dealing with is that it's O.K. for men to have a sense of personal style, and that it's O.K. to be seen as sexy. It's less about the head than about the combination of the head, the heart, and the groin. It's those three things. That's the complete man."

33   The radical part about this, about adding the groin to the list, is that almost no other subject for men is as perilous as the issue of sexuality and fashion. What "Nice Pants" had to do was talk about sex the same way that "Poolman" talked about fashion, which was to talk about it by not talking about it—or, at least, to talk about it in such a coded, cautious way that no man would ever think Dockers was suggesting that he wear khakis in order to look pretty. When I took a videotape of the "Nice Pants" campaign to several of the top agencies in New York and Los Angeles, virtually everyone agreed that the spots were superb, meaning that somehow F.C.B. had managed to pull off this balancing act.

34   What David Altschiller, at Hill, Holliday/Altschiller, in Manhattan, liked about the spots, for example, was that the hero was naïve: in neither case did he know that he had on nice pants until a gorgeous woman told him so. Naïveté, Altschiller stressed, is critical. Several years ago, he did a spot for Claiborne for Men cologne in which a great-looking guy in a bar, wearing a gorgeous suit, was obsessing neurotically about a beautiful woman at the other end of the room: "I see this woman. She's perfect. She's looking at me. She's smiling. But wait. Is she smiling at me? Or laughing at me? . . . Or looking at someone else?" You'd never do this in an ad for women's cologne. Can you imagine? "I see this guy. He's perfect. Ohmigod. Is he looking at me?" In women's advertising, self-confidence is sexy. But if a man is self-confident—if he knows he is attractive and is beautifully dressed—then he's not a man anymore. He's a fop. He's effeminate. The cologne guy had to be neurotic or the ad wouldn't work. "Men are still abashed about acknowledging that clothing is important," Altschiller said. "Fashion can't be important to me as a man. Even when, in the first commercial, the waiter says 'Nice pants,' it doesn't compute to the guy wearing the nice pants. He's thinking, What do you mean, 'Nice pants'?" Altschiller was looking at a videotape of the Dockers ad as he talked—standing at a forty-five-degree angle to the screen, with one hand on the top of the monitor, one hand on his hip, and a small bemused smile on his lips. "The world may think they are nice, but so long as he doesn't think so he doesn't have to be self-conscious about it, and the lack of self-consciousness is very important to men. Because 'I don't care.' Or 'Maybe I care, but I can't be seen to care.'" For the same reason, Altschiller liked the relative understatement of the phrase "nice pants," as opposed to something like "great pants," since somewhere between "nice" and "great" a guy goes from just happening to look good to the unacceptable position of actually trying to look good. "In focus groups, men said that to be told you had 'nice pants' was one of the highest compliments a man could wish for," Tanyia Kandohla told me later, when I asked about the slogan. "They wouldn't want more attention drawn to them than that."

35   In many ways, the "Nice Pants" campaign is a direct descendant of the hugely successful campaign that Rubin-Postaer & Associates, in Santa Monica, did for Bugle Boy Jeans in the early nineties. In the most famous of those spots, the camera opens on an attractive but slightly goofy-looking man in a pair of jeans who is hitchhiking by the side of a desert highway. Then a black Ferrari with a fabulous babe at the wheel drives by, stops, and backs up. The babe rolls down the window and says, "Excuse me. Are those Bugle Boy Jeans that you're wearing?" The goofy guy leans over and pokes his head in the window, a surprised half smile on his face: "Why, yes, they are Bugle Boy Jeans."

36   "Thank you," the babe says, and she rolls up the window and drives away.

37   This is really the same ad as "Nice Pants"—the babe, the naïve hero, the punch line. The two ads have something else in common. In the Bugle Boy spot, the hero wasn't some stunning male model. "I think he was actually a box boy at Vons in Huntington Beach," Larry Postaer, the creative director of Rubin-Postaer & Associates, told me. "I guess someone"—at Bugle Boy—"liked him." He's O.K.-looking, but not nearly in the same class as the babe in the Ferrari. In "Subway Love," by the same token, the Dockers man is medium-sized, almost small, and gets pushed

around by much tougher people in the tussle on the train. He's cute, but he's a little bit of a wimp. Kandohla says that F.C.B. tried very hard to find someone with that look—someone who was, in her words, "aspirational real," not some "buff, muscle-bound jock." In a fashion ad for women, you can use Claudia Schiffer to sell a cheap pair of pants. But not in a fashion ad for men. The guy has to be believable. "A woman cannot be too gorgeous," Postaer explained. "A man, however, can be too gorgeous, because then he's not a man anymore. It's pretty rudimentary. Yet there are people who don't buy that, and have gorgeous men in their ads. I don't get it. Talk to Barneys about how well that's working. It couldn't stay in business trying to sell that high-end swagger to a mass market. The general public wouldn't accept it. Look at beer commercials. They always have these gorgeous girls—even now, after all the heat—and the guys are always just guys. That's the way it is. We only reflect what's happening out there, we're not creating it. Those guys who run the real high-end fashion ads—they don't understand that. They're trying to remold how people think about gender. I can't explain it, though I have my theories. It's like a Grecian ideal. But you can't be successful at advertising by trying to re-create the human condition. You can't alter men's minds, particularly on subjects like sexuality. It'll never happen."

38   Postaer is a gruff, rangy guy, with a Midwestern accent and a gravelly voice, who did Budweiser commercials in Chicago before moving West fifteen years ago. When he wasn't making fun of the pretentious style of East Coast fashion advertising, he was making fun of the pretentious questions of East Coast writers. When, for example, I earnestly asked him to explain the logic behind having the goofy guy screw up his face in such a—well, goofy—way when he says, "Why, yes, they are Bugle Boy Jeans," Postear took his tennis shoes off his desk, leaned forward bemusedly in his chair, and looked at me as if my head came to a small point. "Because that's the only way he could say it," he said. "I suppose we might have had him say it a little differently if he could actually act."

39   Incredibly, Postaer said, the people at Bugle Boy wanted the babe to invite the goofy guy into the car, despite the fact that this would have violated the most important rule that governs this new style of groin messages in men's-fashion advertising, which is that the guy absolutely cannot ever get the girl. It's not just that if he got the girl the joke wouldn't work anymore; it's that if he got the girl it might look as if he had deliberately dressed to get the girl, and although at the back of every man's mind as he's dressing in the morning there is the thought of getting the girl, any open admission that that's what he's actually trying to do would undermine the whole unself-conscious, antifashion statement that men's advertising is about. If Tatjana Patitz were to say "Beau garçon" to the guy in "Vive la France," or the babe on the subway were to give the wimp her number, Dockers would suddenly become terrifyingly conspicuous—the long-pants equivalent of wearing a tight little Speedo to the beach. And if the Vons box boy should actually get a ride from the Ferrari babe, the ad would suddenly become believable only to that thin stratum of manhood which thinks that women in Ferraris find twenty-four-dollar jeans irresistible. "We fought that tooth and nail," Postaer said. "And it more or less cost us the account, even though the ad was wildly successful." He put his tennis shoes back up on the desk. "But that's what makes this business fun—trying to prove to clients how wrong they are."

40   The one ad in the "Nice Pants" campaign which isn't like the Bugle Boy spots is called "Motorcycle." In it a nice young man happens upon a gleaming Harley on a dark back street of what looks like downtown Manhattan. He strokes the seat and then, unable to contain himself, climbs aboard the bike and bounces up and down, showing off his Dockers (the "product shot") but accidentally breaking a mirror on the handlebar. He looks up. The Harley's owner—a huge, leather-clad biker—is looking down at him. The biker glowers, looking him up and down, and says, "Nice pants." Last shot: the biker rides away,

leaving the guy standing on the sidewalk in just his underwear.

41   What's surprising about this ad is that, unlike "Vive la France" and "Subway Love," it does seem to cross the boundaries of acceptable sex talk. The rules of guy advertising so carefully observed in those spots—the fact that the hero has to be naïve, that he can't be too good-looking, that he can't get the girl, and that he can't be told anything stronger than "Nice pants"—are all, in some sense, reactions to the male fear of appearing too concerned with fashion, of being too pretty, of not being masculine. But what is "Motorcycle"? It's an ad about a sweet-looking guy down in the Village somewhere who loses his pants to a butch-looking biker in leather. "I got so much feedback at the time of 'Well, God, that's kind of gay, don't you think?'" Robert Hanson said. "People were saying, 'This buff guy comes along and he rides off with the guy's pants. I mean, what the hell were they doing?' It came from so many different people within the industry. It came from some of our most conservative retailers. But do you know what? If you put these three spots up—'Vive la France,' 'Subway Love,' and 'Motorcycle'—which one do you think men will talk about ad nauseam?

'Motorcycle.' It's No. 1. It's because he's really cool. He's in a really cool environment, and it's every guy's fantasy to have a really cool, tricked-out fancy motorcycle."

Hanson paused, as if he recognized that 42 what he was saying was quite sensitive. He didn't want to say that men failed to pick up the gay implications of the ad because they're stupid, because they aren't stupid. And he didn't want to sound condescending, because Dockers didn't build a six-hundred-million-dollar business in five years by sounding condescending. All he was trying to do was point out the fundamental exegetical error in calling this a gay ad, because the only way for a Dockers man to be offended by "Motorcycle" would be if he thought about it with a little imagination, if he picked up on some fairly subtle cues, if he integrated an awful lot of detail. In other words, a Dockers man could only be offended if he did precisely what, according to Meyers-Levy, men don't do. It's not a gay ad because it's a guy ad. "The fact is," Hanson said, "that most men's interpretation of that spot is: You know what? Those pants must be really cool, because they prevented him from getting the shit kicked out of him."

Source: Malcolm Gladwell, "Listening to Khakis," the *New Yorker*. July 28, 1997.

DISCUSSION QUESTIONS

1. Like most of Malcolm Gladwell's pieces, this article is (at least for a magazine), long, thoughtful, and fairly complex. It is also typical of *New Yorker* features. Using this article and the *New Yorker* Web site description cited earlier, create a speculative description of a typical *New Yorker* reader. Include in your description level of education, type of employment, salary level, marital status, geographical location, and any other descriptors you can think of.

2. After reading the article carefully at least twice, prepare an outline of its structure, making sure to indicate the logical relationships among the parts.

3. Gladwell refers to polls, focus groups, studies, and experiments. In some cases, he cites the specific sources within the text; in others, he does not. He does not provide (and this is standard for the *New Yorker*) a bibliography or list of works cited. Discuss with a group of your classmates whether these omissions detract from the writer's overall credibility. Why do you think the magazine has adopted this editorial policy?

4. Discuss with your classmates the usefulness of an argument such as this. What, if anything, is to be gained by the reader of such an argument? Why would it interest a *New Yorker* reader? Does it go too far in analyzing cultural artifacts?

SUGGESTIONS FOR WRITING (18.2)

1. Select an item of clothing commonly worn on your campus (blue jeans, T-shirts, baseball caps, for example), and write a parody of Gladwell's Dockers interpretation.

2. According to one of Gladwell's sources, "baby-boomer men felt that the chief thing missing from their lives was male friendship." Create a set of interview questions for a group of your male peers designed to identify the chief thing missing from their lives.

3. Gladwell concludes in Par. 28 that "the advertising world—consciously or not—talks down to men." Using this conclusion as your central claim, write a four- to five-page interpretation of three magazine ads clearly designed for men. To be sure you've chosen appropriate ads, look through publications that are clearly male-oriented (e.g., *Sports Illustrated, Field and Stream,* etc.).

4. Many believe that our clothes reveal a great deal about us. Using two or three of your closest friends or family members as supporting examples, write a factual argument that agrees or disagrees with this maxim.

THE CONTENTS OF WOMEN'S PURSES: AN ACCESSORY IN CRISIS

DANIEL HARRIS

This "reading" of women's purses and their contents appeared in 1997 in the quarterly journal Salmagundi. *Daniel Harris is a writer whose most recent book is* The Rise and Fall of Gay Culture. Salmagundi *is a decidedly upscale periodical published by Skidmore College. Its contents include original poetry and fiction, book reviews, literary criticism, and cultural reflections like this one by Harris.*

THE CONTENTS OF WOMEN'S PURSES: AN ACCESSORY IN CRISIS

1   Before the twentieth century, when housewives began to spend more time away from home than they had ever spent before, the purse had not yet evolved into the bottomless pit of the contemporary woman's seemingly infinite handbag whose unplumped depths are full of business cards, subway passes, grocery lists, and ATM receipts. Instead, it was a largely optional accessory designed to carry a few basic items for brief excursions to church, the opera, the theater, or other women's houses, places where they could survive quite comfortably on the contents of a draw-string pouch slung around their wrists containing such things as a fan, mirror, handkerchief, smelling salts, pad of paper, pencil, and powder puff. The collection of objects that women carried during the nineteenth century was far less complex than the odd assortment of

mismatched articles that many women now carry in their pocketbooks, which overflow with used Kleenexes, aspirin, hair spray, lip balm, dental floss, peppermint Altoids, charge cards, Lifesavers, gum wrappers, loose jelly beans, parking validations, expired bus transfers, good luck stones, and Walgreen's receipts.

2   As women began to join the work force in ever larger numbers during World War I and dramatically increased the scope of their activities to everything from lobbying for suffrage to engaging in competitive sports, the purse slowly began to bulge with a surfeit of inessentials. Today's working woman needs countless provisions to survive for the prolonged periods of time she is now stranded in public, marooned in anonymous spaces far away from the luxuries of the vanity table and the medicine cabinet. The modern woman's psychologically complicated relationship with her purse is thus directly linked to the enormous improvement in her political and economic status in the course of the struggle for women's rights which freed her from the captivity of her own home, a realm she nonetheless nostalgically clings to by carrying around with her a seemingly inexhaustible stockpile of tweezers, Rolaids, mangled Tampax, eye pencil sharpeners, and hair "thingeys." The purse's own intense and carefully guarded privacy embodies the extreme loss of privacy that occurred in women's lives as they exchanged one role for another, an upheaval whose consequences they have attempted to soften by creating on their own person a microcosm of "home," a cache of talismanic articles suggestive of the domestic world's intimacy and security.

3   The transition from the kitchen to the office was made easier by the revolution in packaging that occurred in the early part of the twentieth century which suddenly miniaturized cosmetics and hygienic products, shrinking them into the minute squeeze tubes and dainty roll-on sticks that could be used anywhere, in a public rest room or even out in the open at the worker's desk. Ironically, however, while consumerism subtly enhanced women's mobility by allowing them to move about more freely and remain in public for longer periods of time it also, until very recently, as we shall see, increased their dependence on their purses, which became reassuring surrogates for the bathroom. These psychological crutches made them more vulnerable to the panaceas of the beauty industry. The modern makeup bag's light-weight, space-saving cover sticks and lip glosses stretched, but carefully refrained from cutting, the now endlessly elastic umbilical cord that tied women to their houses. Although the packaging revolution contributed in a small but important way to the confidence they needed to escape from the shackles of domestic life (as the automobile was later to do on a much larger scale for women living in the suburbs), such products as Wash and Dry hand wipes or tiny tubes of toothpaste ultimately didn't liberate the housewife from the house so much as they did the house from its foundations; in enabling women to venture out into public equipped with a portable comfort station, the tricks of consumerism turned them into white-collar pack rats who carted around with them wherever they went a rudimentary drug store of eye brow pluckers, curling irons, breath fresheners, and "herbal flower rescue remedies." As women became more independent, they paradoxically became more burdened with things, so that in the course of their emancipation they acquired a new and very literal kind of ball and chain, albeit one with a lining of satin and the ebony sheen of a Tignanolla.

4   Women's almost atavistic memory of the anxiety they once experienced in public, far away from the things that they were accustomed to having immediately at hand, surfaces in a recurrent feminine fantasy in which the modern purse plays a central role. When women discuss their pocketbooks, they frequently boast of the readiness with which they could face unforeseen disasters, claiming that "I could

survive for 24 hours out of my purse," "it contains enough stuff that if I were trapped somewhere overnight, I could still get by," or "I carry all the emergency supplies I would need if something were to happen." Such statements reveal that, in comparison with men, many women have a more complex attitude towards being in public, a realm in which they experience a vague sense of aggravation, even fear, a feeling that emerges in the rhetoric of crisis with which they often describe their purses. Even the youngest and most confident of professional women express concern about being trapped in public during an emergency, unable to get home, stranded in the corporate wilderness where their purses, like sofas that fold out into beds or airplane seats that also function as "flotation devices," would magically become survival kits rigged out with flashlights, matches, Swiss Army knives, and other essentials necessary for subsisting under difficult conditions. In every woman's purse, there lurks a hidden survivalist, a crazed Mormon busily stocking her pantry for the coming apocalypse. When women venture out-of-doors, they remain on a permanent state of high alert, of Girl Scout "preparedness" that by now is an important part of the purse's mythology as a bulwark against a hostile world. The psychological roots of this ill-defined feeling of defenselessness are the conditions of insecurity that arose during the difficult transition from the home to the office.

5   As deceptively commonplace as purses might seem, they are in fact mausoleums in which anachronistic feminine roles have been preserved for all time. When women sought out new opportunities in the workplace, they took with them attitudes towards their possessions that had been developed specifically for a pre-industrialized culture but that are irrelevant in the fast-paced environment of corporate America. One of the most distinctive features of the modern purse is the way in which many women unthinkingly stash away in it, with absurd yet affectionate loyalty, all of the

refuse of consumerism, which they are strangely reluctant to part with, whether it be ratty Kleenexes, crumpled drinking straw wrappers, or the six dead chapsticks of the physical therapist from North Carolina who admits to having what she calls a "chapstick security issue." In the worst cases, purses become ambulatory compost heaps in whose dark and unfathomable recesses women squirrel away the rubbish of an over-packaged society whose commodities are designed to be used once and then discarded. Just as the purse still retains, in the conspicuous uselessness of its vast collection of accessories, the faint image of the nineteenth-century housewife unaccustomed to remaining in public for sustained periods of time, so it also preserves another sort of archaic woman. The habits of possessiveness of this strange figure were established in a culture of durable goods immune to obsolescence, things that were meant to be treasured and cared for for an entire life. In this older America, one did not throw out one's embroidered handkerchief, as one does one's dirty Kleenexes, nor did one throw out one's fountain pen, as one does one's empty Bic. Try as she might, this quaint Victorian ghost, who still haunts the modern purse, jealously guarding empty Maalox bottles and Trident sugarless gum wrappers, cannot fully overcome her indoctrination as the overprotective curator of her cherished belongings. Having failed to adapt to a culture of instant trash, she cannot throw away the old hotel room key given to her several years ago by a friend visiting from out of town nor can she get rid of the moist towelette she acquired at a barbecue in 1988 or in the lint-covered cough drop from last season's cold.

Women also hoard items like broken   6 eye-glass frames, tarnished belt buckles, gloves without mates, pieces of string, extra curtain rings, mechanical pencils without lead, and shoes with torn straps in the mistaken belief that these things might come in handy at some point in the future. The modern purse is an almost tragic collection of the good intentions of the efficient homemaker who, while she dreams of mending and recycling the avalanche of clutter she carries, simply does not have the time, ingenuity, or will power to carry out the aborted projects and stillborn ideas contained in a bag that, however stylish, frequently amounts to little more than a traveling lost-and-found. Side by side with the pocketbook's resident survivalist and curator is yet another ghost, a figure that the woman aspires to be but whose high standards of organization and resourcefulness she is helpless to attain: the shrewd economizer and conscientious domestic engineer who dutifully tucks away for a rainy day a small arsenal of damaged odds and ends and dilapidated knickknacks, from the stray button, the mystery key, and the broken watchband to the unmatched earring, the bracelet with the missing clasp, and the things-to-remember book that is "empty because I never remember to use it." The purse is thus the crash site in which two roles collided, that of the perfect fifties housewife who found a use for every pencil stub and broken zipper she encountered and that of the busy professional perpetually on the run, dashing from the dry cleaners to the staff meeting to the day-care center, all the while leaving in her wake a path strewn with the wreckage of the ingenious but forever unfinished schemes of a woman she no longer has the time to be. Because her instinct for efficiency is at war with the very conditions of her life, the purse is full of frustrated efforts to reclaim the mythic past of the contemporary career woman's maddeningly competent alter ego whose farsighted practicality and daunting skills in exploiting her limited resources were the first casualties of the modern professional's stressful life as both a mother and a member of the work force.

7   A strange amnesia comes over women when they review the contents of their purses, an inability to remember why they placed things in an accessory that, in the cases of the most absent-minded women, begins to resemble the Freudian subconscious, the psychic realm of forgetfulness in whose darkness objects—like painful memories—are swallowed up, never to appear again. Shaking their heads in disbelief as they sort through their things, they pluck out items they hadn't even realized were there or that they misplaced months ago, from the pair of earrings they removed at a dance ("so that's where those were!") to the mysterious business card of a lawyer with the note "call Sunday" scrawled in pencil (I haven't the slightest idea who this guy is!"). Many women unpack their purses with a sense of amazement and lack of recognition, totally unable to explain the inclusion of articles they stash away almost unconsciously, as if the purse were not exclusively their own but were held in joint custody with a split personality whose existence they become aware of only in the course of these periodic spring cleanings, which function almost like rites of confession, psychoanalytic unmaskings of the inner-most secrets of their purse's hidden pockets. The irrationality of what ultimately ends up in the purse is highly significant. The decision to incorporate something into one's permanent collection is often determined, less by the needs of the particular individual, than by reflexive and involuntary requirements of archaic social roles. The three abandoned personae that women have largely forgotten, the survivalist, the curator, and the homemaker, have never completely disappeared from the scene but are holed up in her bag where they continue to operate like underground fugitives, leading her to collect things that serve no discernible purpose. Her amnesia is therefore indicative, not just of her inability to remember the reason for a particular object, but of her inability to remember former stages in the evolution of women's roles, which still linger in the purse's collective unconscious like past lives.

The proverbial rat's nest of the purse, which sometimes looks like the lair of a slovenly nocturnal creature, is also the result of a strong psychological need for mess, which women use as a form of rebellion

8

against the oppressive feminine mandate for tidiness. The disorder of the purse is the result of the self-inflicted vandalism of the disgruntled saboteur, the slob, the slattern, who has declared civil war on the meticulously neat supermodels that women's magazines hold up as icons of effortless perfection. The filth of the modern purse, which is especially noticeable in the pocketbooks of older women, resembles the binge of the bulimic, the spotless little lady who is as persecuted by self-punishing expectations of cleanliness and organization as the victim of an eating disorder is by our society's sadistic vision of feminine gauntness. The purse is thus full of aggression and hostility against the suffocating chic of the fashion plate. The pocketbook is the place on her own body where the perfectly manicured office worker makes a kind of mud pie, indulging in an infantile act of liberating self-desecration.

9   Although most women continue to carry purses, we are in fact entering a period of transition in which these once mandatory accessories are shriveling up into fanny packs, assuming the unisex disguises of briefcases or book bags, or vanishing altogether into the pockets of jackets and blue jeans. But while it is safe to say that the heyday of the purse is over, it is difficult to predict if its imminent disappearance will be permanent, since this most mercurial of accessories has always been subject to the whims of changing fashions. Throughout the centuries, it has gone in and out of style according to how much room was available inside of any given type of dress for hidden pockets that could be camouflaged in such a way that they did not ruin an elegantly tapered figure by adding to it unsightly lumps and disfiguring bulges. Whereas the hoops and farthingales that prevailed from the late sixteenth century to the early nineteenth provided cavernous tents in which various articles could be stored in large pockets easily concealed under billowing layers of flounces and petticoats, the classical Greek and Roman costumes worn after the French Revolution were much more form-fitting and therefore resurrected the need for the

purse, which had languished for centuries in the complicated folds of bloomers, slips, and crinolines.

Today, however, it is not the tightness or   10
looseness of clothing that is once again contributing to the demise of the accessory but changes in women's perceived dependence on the private world of domestic life. The waning of the pocketbook's importance in the modern outfit is the direct outcome of the growing confidence that women below the age of 40 feel as self-sufficient and autonomous individuals who no longer need to carry their houses on their backs in order to survive in the work place. Younger women are now fully acclimated to living in public, and their purses are accordingly dwindling into empty conventions, outmoded status symbols that, like reliquaries, contain the fossilized remnants of a more tranquil and secluded type of life. The modern purse was created, not only by the absence of pockets in relatively tight twentieth-century dresses, but by women's emancipation, by their need to be out-of-doors; paradoxically, it will be rendered obsolete by a later stage of this same process of political and emotional enfranchisement as women finally sever the umbilical cord that linked them to the protective realm of privacy.

The modern worker's growing detach-   11
ment from the purse can be seen in the very language she uses to characterize its contents, which some women refer to as "basics," "necessities," or "essentials" but others disparage as "junk," "crap," "stuff," "shit," "debris," "litter," and "garbage." Such words denote items that, far from needing to be handled with care and gently deposited in their proper compartments, are "shoved," "crammed," "dumped," "tossed," "pushed," and "thrown" into a receptacle that is so jam-packed that it must be squeezed shut like the crushing jaws of a trash compactor. When they describe the contents of their purses, many women bristle with irritation at the sheer weight of their "crap," which they deride in a way that would have been unthinkable for the proudly accessorized, early-twentieth-century female, who would

never have used such caustic and unladylike terminology for articles she cherished and depended on. An element of self-mockery, even self-contempt, has crept into the language with which women belittle an accessory they are saddled with like overburdened pack mules lumbering under an enormous cargo of superfluous provisions.

12   The precipitous decline of the purse is also evident in the way that younger women, who often carry pocketbooks to work, use more convenient fanny packs on the weekends or dispense with handbags altogether on a date, where they reduce their possessions to a bare minimum—a credit card, their keys, and some cash, items they stuff into their pockets or carry in small coin purses. This conscious effort to lighten the load when they go out to a party, bar, or restaurant is partly the result of the burden the purse imposes on their mobility, specifically on their freedom to dance, which is inhibited by their fear of leaving their pocketbooks unattended. But it is not only the physical burden of the handbag that makes it an unwanted third party on the modern date. It is the mental burden of the purse that the woman leaves behind when she goes out to meet a man, the psychological burden of the purse's negative associations with a certain sort of over-dressed, uptight, priggish woman who still inhabits the purse in all of the clunky old-maidishness and thus inevitably gets parked right on the table like a boxy lunch pail, where she detracts from the image of youthfulness and hedonism that many women now attempt to project. Erotic encounters like dates involve the meeting of sexual equals in which women wear clothing that enhances their accessibility and their readiness to engage in the rough-and-tumble of flirtation. The somewhat off-putting panoply of accessories in which the proper, middle-aged matron is clad like protective armor would interfere with the spirit of the evening's playfulness and spontaneity. Women's sexual independence is thus in a certain sense linked in their minds with their indepen-

dence from their purses, from the respectable world of "home," from the three weird sisters of the survivalist, the curator, and the homemaker who, like Macbeth's witches, continue to use the purse as a caldron of spinsterly reservations, taboos, pruderies, and fears.

The purse is thus the battlefield of an-   13
other conflict of roles, of another set of contradictory images of women, the disparate personae who are waging war in the seemingly untroubled darkness of the pocketbook. But whereas the conflict between the industrious homemaker and the ambitious professional created in the purse a crash site strewn with broken-down gadgets, no such record exists of the conflict between the dowdy matriarch in her support hose and sensible shoes, clutching her pocketbook like an anxious mother hen, and the modern and independent professional who jettisons unnecessary feminine baggage so that she doesn't have to baby-sit her purse like a safety-deposit box. The contemporary woman, who can go anywhere she pleases and do anything she wants with her own body, wins this particular civil war handsdown by leaving her purse, and all of its associations, at home and presenting to the world the sleek new minimalism of a non-consumerized body that is rapidly undermining the over-accessorized ideals of a fussy, old-fashioned kind of sexual attractiveness.

This spirit of simplification, this desire   14
to cut oneself free from the purse's ball and chain, must be seen as part of a widespread reassessment of the whole concept of sufficiency. Women are reevaluating what they actually need to survive in public, a phenomenon largely fueled by the accomplishments of feminism. In the course of the twentieth century, consumerism insinuated itself into the woman's very understanding of her own body, which manufacturers coopted and commercialized, integrating their products into her sense of her physical well-being, so that she became literally "attached" to her provisions, ad-

dicted to the false safety they provided. Items that were meant to make her feel more relaxed, at home, at ease, shielded from all foreseeable emergencies, paradoxically eroded her sense of self-containment. Like sedatives that ultimately induce anxiety and then panic, the contents of her purse made her feel more unprotected, more defenseless, and therefore in desperate need of such deceptively reassuring "essentials" as her lipliner, lipliner brush, lip gloss, lip balm, lip stick, and lip pencil. As the female body was transformed into a playground of market forces, women's perception of their own self-sufficiency was so thoroughly impaired, so compromised, that they began to talk about their "faces" as if they were a detachable mask, an accessory like any other. Many women still describe their faces in an eerily dehumanized way that seems to suggest that their eyes and mouths are components of a do-it-yourself kit, a Mr. Potato Head that they remove from their purses, put together, and later pack away again, as can be seen in such statements as "I can never leave the house without my face" or "I need to put my face on at least twice a day."

As feminism increases women's awareness of the trumped-up "neediness" that was foisted upon them by the beauty and health-care industries, which exploited for financial gain their anxiety about leaving the house, the purse is increasingly becoming a source of nagging irritation, of insecurity rather than comfort. The cat is literally out of the bag, and women are turning against their purses and reclaiming territory they have lost to the forces of commercialism, which rushed through the breach that emancipation inadvertently created on their very person, the foothold, the point of entry, through which manufacturers launched their intimate invasions of the consumer's body.

Source: Daniel Harris, "The Contents of Women's Purses," *Salmagundi: A Quarterly of the Humanities & Social Sciences.* 1997. pp. 122–131.

DISCUSSION QUESTIONS

1. Identify the following: the essay's main claim; the type of argument; the apparent audience.

2. Read Harris's essay carefully in order to identify his implicit and/or explicit attitude towards women. Describe this attitude in writing, including specific examples. Then compare your characterization with two of your classmates'.

3. Chapter 6, "Arguing Facts," points out the essential role to all argument of supported facts. Comment on Harris's use of facts; do they tend to be first-, second-, or third-party facts? Are they specific or generalized? Are they adequately supported?

4. Engage in a discussion with your classmates about the rather unusual topic of this essay. What purpose do you believe the author intended it to serve? Do you find the essay useful and/or interesting? Have you learned anything from reading it?

SUGGESTIONS FOR WRITING (18.3)

1. Write, for an audience of males, a causal argument identifying the reasons that the majority of men do not carry purses.

2. Write, for an audience of females, a causal essay identifying the reasons that the majority of men do not carry purses.

3. Evaluate, in a two- to three-page argument, the reasonableness, logic, and credibility of Harris's essay.

4. Using the Internet, your library catalogue, and electronic or printed biographical resources, gather information on Daniel Harris. Then write a carefully referenced two-page factual argument about him, using MLA style citation.

WHAT DOES THIS INDIAN SYMBOL MEAN?

This article was found on the World Wide Web at the following url: http://www. collectorsguide.com/fa/fa040.shtml. According to the Web site, the piece originally appeared in The Wingspread Collector's Guide to Albuquerque Metro Area, *Volume 8. The endnote to the article reads "Thanks to* **Barton Wright** *of Phoenix, Arizona for contributing this information and these drawings." Whether Mr. Wright was the original author or merely the supplier of the article is unclear.*

WHAT DOES THIS INDIAN SYMBOL MEAN?

Decorative and symbolic, these designs are seen frequently.

1   Visitors to the Southwest are often intrigued by the variety and aesthetic appeal of the design elements used in Native American arts and crafts. The designs on Indian pottery, weavings, baskets and silver and stone jewelry are so intricate and carefully constructed, it is inconceivable they are not configurations holding some deeper meaning, shaped from a forgotten age, relics of an arcane language, or symbols of some old and secret religion.

2   In all cultures, symbols borrow from experience, vision, and religion and become individualized through the creative process of the artist/symbol-maker. The designs used in the Southwest are from varied sources and they have been adapted and used by divergent tribes. Some have sifted in slowly as different groups arrived bringing their own inventory of designs; others have arrived with new technologies; still others have origins and, therefore, meanings, that will never be deciphered. The designs may be decorative, symbolic or combinations of both. Meanings may change from tribe to tribe. In one location a symbol may have meaning and in an adjacent tribe be used entirely as a decorative element. In short, every variation is possible.

3   If a symbol is produced by one culture and interpreted by another, its meaning is far more often obscured than clarified. So it is with the symbols and designs of the Indian people of the Southwest. Over the years, both Native American designs (merely decorative forms) and symbols (a sign representing an idea, a quality or an association) have been subject to "interpretation" by non-Indian dealers and traders. Often, these interpretations are explained in terms of Anglo-European concepts that were nonexistent to the Native American. The result frequently bears little or no relationship to the true meaning of the symbols.

4   Designs and symbols used in the Southwest actually have come from many places.

Some design elements emerge out of the nature of the craft. The warp and weft of baskets or blankets produce a preponderance of geometrics, stars, swastikas and whirlwind designs. One of the most controversial of Native American designs is the swastika.

Swastika   Whirling Log

5   While the swastika immediately brings to mind Nazi Germany, it is not only a native Southwestern design, it can be called a native design almost *anywhere in the world*. It is the result of basket weaving where the ends of a simple cross design are turned either to the right or left, depending on the direction of the weaving, to form a swastika. Its meanings are as diverse as its worldwide origins.

6   Other designs also have been introduced with the technology of a craft. For example, a host of designs appear in metal dies which were derived from much older stamps used to decorate leather.

Decorative Leather Stamps

7   These designs have been called by such fanciful names as rattlesnake jaws, Thunderbird tracks or a medicine man's eye. Others bear more prosaic names such as fence, tipi, mountain range, hogan, sun's rays, headdress or running water. However, in most instances they are purely decorative

and their presence may be noted far back in history as elements of cultures other than that of the Native American.

Thunderbird   Zuni Knife-Wing

8   In the craft of silversmithing, the Thunderbird is used lavishly on stamped jewelry. The Thunderbird came to the Southwest via industrial dies furnished to Indian artists.

Navajo   Moorish   Roman

9   While it is a symbol of importance among the Plains Indians, this immense bird is neither characterized by the Southwestern Indians, nor do their myths offer explanations. Rather, the bird symbols of importance in the Southwest are the giant Knife-wing of the Zuni or the vulture, Kwatoko, of the Hopi. Nonetheless, the unknown individuals who supplied the dies for the silver felt that the Thunderbird was a "good Indian design" and so it appears on Southwestern jewelry and even on the beams of the Great Hall in the Albuquerque International Airport.

10   The form of the silver *naja,* or pendant, at the end of the squash blossom necklace is traceable to Moorish Spain and even farther back in time to a device used to ward off the evil eye.

11   Earlier still, it was found as boar's tusks hanging point-to-point decorating a Roman legionnaire's staff. In the same way, the squash blossom bead emerges from the pomegranate blossoms of Spain.

Pomegranate

Squash Blossom

12   Despite the multiple origins and mistaken interpretations of designs and symbols used in the Southwest, it is possible to recognize the meanings of many representations used in Native American works. The simplest of all representations is that which characterizes some element of the environment (bird, man, flower, horse, etc.) and is clearly distinguishable. Almost always it is used as a decorative device and nothing more, although its form may vary from tribe to tribe.

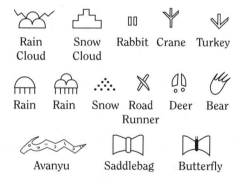

Rain   Snow   Rabbit Crane   Turkey
Cloud   Cloud

Rain   Rain   Snow   Road   Deer   Bear
                          Runner

Avanyu   Saddlebag   Butterfly

13   These symbols are frequently seen on the pottery, weavings and jewelry made by Native Americans of the Southwest and generally can be interpreted as indicated. Several other symbols that arise from Native American cultures have become unrecognizable in their new "interpretations" including the butterfly.

Parrot

Snakes & Lightning   Macaw

The snake and lightning or lightning arrow are considered by the native Southwesterner to be a single element as they are the same visual form. The snake does not symbolize "defiance" except possibly in New England, nor is its meaning "wisdom." Lightning is used by Anglo-Europeans indoctrinated in Greek mythology to denote swiftness, but among the Pueblo Indians snakes and lightning are equated with and symbolize *rain,* hence, *fertility.* These bird signs are often listed by traders as meaning "carefree or light-hearted," but the symbol is the macaw, a Zuni symbol for *summer.*

This is but a glimpse of the rich inventory of Native American designs and symbols which are an integral part of antique and contemporary arts and crafts of this area and, in the form of petroglyphs throughout the Southwest, on the ancient rocks of this ancient land.

Source: Barton Wright.
http://www.collectorsguide.com

DISCUSSION QUESTIONS

1. How would you classify this argument?

2. Identify four secondary factual claims that support the argument's central claim. What is the support for these claims? Is the support adequate? Why or why not?

3. What indications about the argument's reliability does this Web site give you?

4. Discuss with your classmates whether you would be comfortable using the material in this argument as a source for your own argument on a related topic.

5. How helpful are the graphics in illustrating points made in the argument? How might they be more helpful?

SUGGESTIONS FOR WRITING (18.4)

1. Using any of the hints given on this Web site, conduct your own research to determine the reliability of this source. Then write a 250-word evaluation of its reliability.

2. Write a two-page extended definition of the term "symbol." Do not consult any outside sources for this definition.

3. The third paragraph begins "If a symbol is produced by one culture and interpreted by another, its meaning is far more often obscured than clarified." Discuss this statement with a classmate, brainstorming until you have a two symbols in mind that would confirm or contradict its claim. (Examples: the peace symbol popularized in the 1960s and '70s; a manual gesture; a corporate logo.)

4. Write a three- to four-page argument based upon your discussion in Suggestion #3 and additional research on the topic. Be sure you know the category of your working claim and that you qualify it sufficiently.

5. Think of a personal experience in which you or someone you were with misinterpreted a symbol. Write a two-page factual description of the event, implying your own reliability as suggested in Chapter 6.

WHY WE CRAVE HORROR MOVIES

STEPHEN KING

*Our culture's taste for murder and mayhem has made Stephen King a rich man. As the twentieth century's premiere writer of horror fiction, King knows better than anyone where this taste comes from and how to exploit it. A writer by trade, King also has sure cinematic instincts: many of his books—*Carrie *(1974),* The Shining *(1977), and* Pet Sematary *(1983), for example, have been made into blockbuster movies.*

This piece was written in 1981, and first appeared in Playboy *magazine. As an explanation of our tastes for the terrifying, this causal argument also offers a "reading" of the cultural genres of horror stories and films.*

1   I think we're all mentally ill; those of us outside the asylums only hide it a little better—and maybe not all that much better, after all. We've all known people who talk to themselves, people who sometimes squinch their faces into horrible grimaces when they believe no one is watching, people who have some hysterical fear—of snakes, the dark, the tight place, the long drop . . . and, of course, those final worms and grubs that are waiting so patiently underground.

2   When we pay our four or five bucks and seat ourselves at tenth-row center in a theater showing a horror movie, we are daring the nightmare.

3   Why? Some of the reasons are simple and obvious. To show that we can, that we are not afraid, that we can ride this roller coaster. Which is not to say that a really good horror movie may not surprise a scream out of us at some point, the way we may scream when the roller coaster twists through a complete 360 or plows through a lake at the bottom of the drop. And horror movies, like roller coasters, have always been the special province of the young; by the time one turns 40 or 50, one's appetite for double twists or 360-degree loops may be considerably depleted.

4   We also go to re-establish our feelings of essential normality; the horror movie is innately conservative, even reactionary. Freda Jackson as the horrible melting woman in *Die, Monster, Die!* confirms for us that no matter how far we may be removed from the beauty of a Robert Redford or a Diana Ross, we are still light-years from the true ugliness.

5   And we go to have fun.

6   Ah, but this is where the ground starts to slope away, isn't it? Because this is a very peculiar sort of fun, indeed. The fun comes from seeing others menaced—sometimes killed. One critic has suggested that if pro football has become the voyeur's version of combat, then the horror film has become the modern version of the public lynching.

7   It is true that the mythic, "fairy-tale" horror film intends to take away the shades of gray. . . . It urges us to put away our more civilized and adult penchant for analysis and to become children again, seeing things in pure blacks and whites. It may be that horror movies provide psychic relief on this level because this invitation to lapse into simplicity, irrationality and even outright madness is extended so rarely. We are told we may allow our emotions a free rein . . . or no rein at all.

8   If we are all insane, then sanity becomes a matter of degree. If your insanity leads you to carve up women like Jack the Ripper or the Cleveland Torso Murderer, we clap you away in the funny farm (but neither of those two amateur-night surgeons was ever caught, heh-heh-heh); if, on the other hand, your insanity leads you only to talk to yourself when you're under stress or to pick your nose on your morning bus, then you are left alone to go about your business . . . though it is doubtful that you will ever be invited to the best parties.

9   The potential lyncher is in almost all of us (excluding saints, past and present; but then, most saints have been crazy in their own ways), and every now and then, he has to be let loose to scream and roll around in the grass. Our emotions and our fears form their own body, and we recognize that it demands its own exercise to maintain proper muscle tone. Certain of these emotional muscles are accepted—even exalted—in civilized society; they are, of course, the emotions that tend to maintain the status quo of civilization itself. Love, friendship, loyalty, kindness—these are all the emotions that we applaud, emotions that have been immortalized in the couplets of Hallmark cards and in the verses (I don't dare call it poetry) of Leonard Nimoy.

10   When we exhibit these emotions, society showers us with positive reinforcement; we learn this even before we get out of diapers. When, as children, we hug our rotten little puke of a sister and give her a kiss, all the aunts and uncles smile and twit and cry, "Isn't he the sweetest little thing?" Such coveted treats as chocolate-covered graham crackers often follow. But if we deliberately slam the rotten little puke of a sister's fingers in the door, sanctions follow—angry remonstrance from parents, aunts, and uncles, instead of a chocolate-covered graham cracker, a spanking.

11   But anticivilization emotions don't go away, and they demand periodic exercise. We have such "sick" jokes as, "What's the difference between a truckload of bowling balls and a truckload of dead babies? (You can't unload a truckload of bowling balls with a pitchfork . . . a joke, by the way, that I heard originally from a ten-year-old). Such a joke may surprise a laugh or a grin out of us even as we recoil, a possibility that confirms the thesis: If we share a brotherhood

of man, then we also share an insanity of man. None of which is intended as a defense of either the sick joke or insanity but merely as an explanation of why the best horror films, like the best fairy tales, manage to be reactionary, anarchistic, and revolutionary all at the same time.

12   The mythic horror movie, like the sick joke, has a dirty job to do. It deliberately appeals to all that is worst in us. It is morbidity unchained, our most base instincts let free, our nastiest fantasies realized . . . and it happens, fittingly enough, in the dark. For those reasons, good liberals often shy away from horror films. For myself, I like to see the most aggressive of them—*Dawn of the Dead,* for instance—as lifting a trap door in the civilized forebrain and throwing a basket of raw meat to the hungry alligators swimming around in that subterranean river beneath.

13   Why bother? Because it keeps them from getting out, man. It keeps them down there and me up here. It was Lennon and McCartney who said that all you need is love, and I would agree with that.

14   As long as you keep the gators fed.

Source: Stephen King, "Why We Crave Horror Movies," *Playboy* magazine, Dec. 1981.

DISCUSSION QUESTIONS

1. With a small group of your classmates who have read this essay, analyze and discuss the effectiveness of the image projected by King. Consider such questions as King's authority and how it is projected, the audience he appears to be addressing, the relationship he assumes between himself and this audience, and the overall tone of his argument. Cite specific examples of the elements you analyze.

2. The essay begins with an attention-grabbing generalization: "I think that we're all mentally ill." Is this the argument's central claim? If so, how is it supported throughout the argument? If not, what is its logical relationship to the central claim?

3. What does King mean by "mentally ill"? Is the definition implicit or explicit? Is the behavior he cites in all of us coincident with this definition?

4. King makes liberal use of analogy and other figures of speech. Two of the most important are 1) the analogy between watching horror movies and riding roller coasters (Par. 3); and 2) the concluding alligator metaphor (Par. 12–14). Discuss with your class the effectiveness of these figures of speech; do they further the argument? Do they take shortcuts that are not warranted by the argument? Are they useful or distracting?

SUGGESTIONS FOR WRITING (18.5)

1. Write an interpretation of a horror movie you have seen recently and focus on messages that may lurk behind its portrayal of a particular group—for example, children, animals, old people, women. Your argument should be approximately five pages long.

2. Horror movies are not the only genre of entertainment we seem to crave; others are romance novels, detective novels, sitcoms, war movies. Choosing one, brainstorm on a piece of paper about the reasons for its popularity. Then share your list with a small group of your classmates, adding any of their ideas you like. Based upon the final set of explanations you come up with, draft an argument of about the same length as King's accounting for the popularity of the genre you have chosen.

Have a classmate read the draft, providing comments about the ideas, the effectiveness of the argument, the writing style, and so on. Based upon these comments and your own further thinking, prepare a final draft of the argument.

3. King compares the experiences of watching horror movies and riding roller coasters. Create another extended analogy that helps to describe what it's like to sit in a dark theater, scared to death.

4. What reasons besides the ones King cites could account for the popularity of horror films? Write your own causal argument, citing two or three reasons other than the ones King addresses.

ALLY MCBEAL'S YOUNGER SISTERS

JANE ROSENZWEIG

"Ally McBeal's Younger Sisters" appeared in the November 23, 1999 issue of the magazine The American Prospect. *(I found this article on the Web simply by doing a search on "popular culture" with a search engine.)* The American Prospect *is a print periodical, but it has a comprehensive Web site on which most of its archived issues are available.*

According to The American Prospect *Web site, "Jane Rosenzweig teaches writing at Yale University. Formerly a staff editor at the* Atlantic Monthly, *Ms. Rosenzweig covers television regularly for the Prospect and is the only TAP writer able to list 99 Brady Bunch episodes from memory."*

ALLY MCBEAL'S YOUNGER SISTERS

1   In the premiere of Wasteland, ABC's new prime-time soap by the creator of the WB Network's Dawson's Creek and the film Scream, 26-year-old Dawnie theorizes that her generation is experiencing a "second coming of age" in which twenty- and thirty-somethings face uncertainties of growing up that used to be the exclusive province of adolescents.

2   "Look at me," she says. "I've spent my entire life in school, my parents still support me, human relationships baffle me, and I am acutely self-aware—to the point where I am clueless and slightly suicidal." (She is also, in an interesting twist on tele-vision's conventional mores, a virgin.) Whether or not Dawnie's hypothesis is applicable to real people—and with any luck for ABC, this will be a subject of fervent water-cooler debate around the country—it certainly applies to the young women of prime time, who are trapped in the most protracted adolescence in television history.

3   It is perhaps no accident that at a time when youth sells (advertising slots for shows about teenagers, like Dawson's Creek, can command more money than those for the consistently top-10 rated Touched by an Angel), American pop culture has become preoccupied with our col-

lective inability to grow up. People are staying single longer, and the beauty industry is constantly coaxing us to make ourselves look younger if we want to stay in romantic business.

4 But the proliferation of teen shows is one thing; the packaging of female adulthood as an extended adolescence is something else altogether. Indeed, what's most interesting about this infantilization of twenty- and thirty-something women—a trend started by David Kelley's Ally McBeal and perpetuated by the women of Wasteland, Providence, and to varying degrees a number of new fall programs—is that it coincides with a flood of shows about teenage girl characters who are more assertive, more independent, and more interesting than their adult counterparts. I'd say Ally McBeal ought to grow up—except the real problem seems to be that she already has and is still less mature than the average television teenager.

Q: What makes your problems bigger than everyone else's?

A: They're mine.

–Ally McBeal

Most of the people here have been saved by you or helped by you at one time or another.

–A classmate speaking to Buffy Summers, Buffy the Vampire Slayer

5 The preoccupations of young women are not new to television; women have always been the key audience for advertisers. A teenage girl in 1963 could flip on the TV to look for facsimiles of herself on The Patty Duke Show and Gidget. Young adult women, of course, have a long history of television "role models": think of June Cleaver, Donna Reed, and Laura Petrie—or more recently, Mary Tyler Moore. And the history of television is rife with ambiguous portrayals of women: Are they empowered or trapped in traditional roles (think of I Dream of Jeannie and Charlie's Angels)?

Can brains and femininity be reconciled in a single character, or must they always be dichotomized into either Cagney and Lacey or Baywatch? Or if they can be reconciled, must the result be Xena: Warrior Princess? But for all this history of mixed messages, there has never been a time when the girls were more like women and the women more like girls than right now.

6 True, the conventional wisdom these days is that the line between adolescence and adulthood is blurring: the young are getting older, the old younger. Though if that's the case, shouldn't our television counterparts be meeting in the middle? Why, instead, do television teenagers have more mature relationships with men than the thirty-somethings do? Why are Buffy the vampire slayer, Felicity, and the girls of Party of Five and Dawson's Creek so much more emotionally intelligent than the grown-ups on other shows? Harvard psychologist Carol Gilligan and others have observed that the confidence and self-esteem of young girls diminish when they reach adolescence, at which point girls start downplaying their intellects and compromising their personalities in order to adapt to society's expectations—and to be attractive to boys. If current television is any indication, the cultural manifestation of this trend now occurs twice (Wasteland's Dawnie may be onto something bigger than she knows): if girls go ditzy when they reach adolescence, they seem to be going ditzier still as they pass into young adulthood.

7 This phenomenon, I think, can be explained at least in part by our cultural preoccupation with women's biological clocks, a preoccupation that has clearly constrained the imaginations of today's television writers. Can't they conceive of any other kinds of lives for women? If we succumb to the creative failure represented by the latest crop of television shows, the danger is that we, as viewers, will find ourselves accepting these same constraints in our own lives.

I want to save the world. I just want to get married first.

–Ally McBeal

8   It has become fashionable to loathe Ally McBeal. Her contribution to the putative death of feminism, her diminutive cuteness, her short skirts, and her perky pouts all combine to make her an insult to any actual Harvard law graduate—or any graduate of any school in any field, for that matter. While the show is still at times clever and even resonant in its focus on the lonely search for a soul mate, Ally is a hard character to sympathize with. It may be kind of funny when she says, "I'm tempted to become a street person cut off from society, but then I wouldn't get to wear my outfits," but it's also pathetic. By the end of last season, when she schemed to win back her boyfriend by hiring a gigolo to make him jealous and then propositioned the gigolo, she'd lost all credibility as an adult character. Mary Tyler Moore wouldn't be caught dead messing up her life like this.

9   While originally hailed as a whimsical and imaginative, and even as it continues to garner accolades (most recently, in September, an Emmy for Best Comedy Series), Ally McBeal is well on its way to being the biggest failure of the imagination in prime time. But because of its early critical and ongoing ratings success, Ally has basically created a new category of women on television: pretty young things who, in the guise of successful career women, are actually completely defined by an inability to find a husband and have children. Ally is stalked by a holographic dancing baby meant to remind her (and us) that her biological clock is ticking. While there are women in her age group on television who do care about their careers in some workplace-centered shows—most notably Carol Hathaway on ER—most of the dramas and comedy-dramas that focus on personal lives feature immature women who share more with Ally McBeal than with the people we know in real life. Lindsay Dole on Kelley's The Practice throws tantrums in court; her unhappy housemate, played by Lara Flynn Boyle, appears more anorexic than Calista Flockhart's Ally and seems even more ill-equipped to handle her personal life. It's as

though you're supposed to look at Boyle and think, If only she had a nice husband to take care of her, maybe she would eat.

10   Perhaps the worst example of TV's confused conception of the single woman is Dr. Sydney Hansen of NBC's Providence, which debuted last season. After coming home to find her boyfriend in the shower with another man, she left her lucrative job as an L.A. plastic surgeon and moved home to practice medicine at a free clinic in Providence. Sleeping once again in the room she grew up in, she regularly wakes, sweating, from dreams in which her dead mother is chastising her about her inability to find a man. Syd consistently makes dating decisions more worthy of a teenager than a smart, adult woman, which is what she is theoretically supposed to be. And her skirts are as short as Ally McBeal's; most real doctors and lawyers, it's safe to say, don't dress like that.

11   Unfortunately, the new fall season offers more of the same. In addition to Dawnie on Wasteland, there are the women of NBC's Cold Feet, one of whom strikes a blow to sexism by marching into her husband's business meeting to demand, for once and for all, a nanny. (And never mind that the husband appears to have no interest in either wife or child.) Another of the main characters in Cold Feet runs off to sulk at her mother's house when she argues with her husband. These characters are like early adolescents who relate to one another by screaming, pouting, and stamping their feet.

12   Funny thing is, turn the channel to the WB Network, which has made the strongest effort to stake out the youth market, and you find that the characters who actually are adolescent girls do not stamp their feet. They are calm and collected, surprisingly analytical. Television's message: only when they're not worrying about their biological clocks can women have fully developed characters. Is it really the case that only women who are still in high school have the luxury of thinking about things other than themselves without constantly being inter-

rupted by thoughts of their own reproductive limits?

> I need to find out if I'm capable of being a whole person without you.
>
> –15-year-old Joey Potter to her boyfriend Dawson on the WB's Dawson's Creek

13 Don't get me wrong: teenage girls on television are not ideal role models. They all have clear skin and shiny hair and don't seem afflicted by any of the maladies of girlhood described by experts. It's not hard to see how some critics would assert that these characters are the primary contributors to body image problems of ordinary girls. (The actress who plays Buffy, Sarah Michelle Gellar, is a spokesmodel for Maybelline cosmetics, whose ads run throughout the show.) And some characters are perhaps more sexually active earlier than we would like the role models for our children to be. But I would rather have my girls watch Dawson's Creek or Buffy than Ally McBeal.

14 Say what you will about the fanciful premise of Buffy, in which Buffy Summers fights the evil denizens of hell in order to save her town. But Buffy is neither man obsessed nor self-absorbed, and she refuses to see her problems, like Ally McBeal does, as bigger than everyone else's. In fact, she balances her personal life quite elegantly with her responsibility to protect her community from evil vampires (okay, so that sounds ridiculous on its face; nevertheless, the lesson it conveys is a worthy one.) The problems are of a different scale. She misses out on her own prom in order to make school safe for her friends; she gives up something but earns loyalty and respect in return. Also, her best friend Willow is intelligent, sensitive, principled, and the least stereotypical Jewish woman on television.

15 Similarly, peel away the music-video veneer from Dawson's Creek or Party of Five and you'll find some young women who clearly have their feet planted firmly on the ground, even in the context of formulaic television plots. Joey Potter, for example, in spite of having a dead mother and a jailed father, has enough self-awareness to realize that there is an asymmetry between her boyfriend Dawson's passion for filmmaking and her own passion for Dawson. After some initial sadness, she pulls herself together enough to think about what she really wants out of life—and to realize the folly of a self-definition that requires always having a man. Ally McBeal never shows this kind of independence. The tragedy is that, assuming television convention holds, if Joey graduates from college without having landed a husband, she'll be reduced to jabbering preadolescence. (The self-reliant title character of the WB Network's Felicity suggests that college women still have their own identities and therefore that it is sometime after college that life begins to be about having babies.)

16 Sometimes the divide between adolescent maturity and post-adolescent immaturity is starkly evident even within a single show. Party of Five, for instance, depicts both teenage girls and twenty-something women. The differences are striking. (Originally about a family of orphans trying to raise themselves, the show has turned into a fairly formulaic soap about adolescents and young adults coexisting in an adult-free San Francisco universe.) Sarah—whose character, now 19, is spinning off this season to a new show called Time of Your Life—was one of the first TV characters I saw with the self-awareness to realize that her coquettish attempts to win her boyfriend's heart (in a batch of episodes a few years ago) were not only a waste of her time but also a challenge to her self-esteem, and that she shouldn't have to compromise her intelligence to win love. In an episode at the end of last season, Sarah, now older, attempted to teach this lesson to 16-year-old Claudia while at the same time struggling to maintain her own interests as her life was increasingly overtaken by her boyfriend's responsibilities.

17 In contrast, twenty-something Kirsten, the girlfriend of the show's oldest sibling, is a unidimensional character painted almost entirely in terms of her inability to

have children. The chain of events that followed her learning this fact was over the top: she plagiarized her Ph.D. thesis, had a nervous breakdown, married a man she didn't love, and spent several seasons obsessing about how she would hold onto a man if she couldn't bear children. Meanwhile, the only other twenty-something women on this show have been a stripper who doesn't love her child, an alcoholic who depends on a 19-year-old man to take care of her, and a hard-edged and independent—but, alas, unlovable and unappealing—social worker.

18   What is it in the logic of television that demands that self-possessed girls full of possibility must evolve into women who are defined entirely by their marriage status and act like spoiled children? To the extent that television reflects or defines many of our central preoccupations as a society, this is a question to take seriously. Mightn't television capture some more complex way of thinking about the role of women in society? Or must television continue to make women into one-issue vessels when they reach childbearing age? The women I know lead richly textured lives, and the ones who do feel the loneliness of being single do not deal with it by throwing tantrums in court or moving home of live with their parents; surely it's the same for the women you know, too. But that's not the impression your daughters would get—or your sons, for that matter—from watching TV.

Sadly, shows featuring teen girls are becoming more and more formulaic, their lead characters more and more flat and conventional. Television producers are like sheep; thus a few dramas about teenagers from the last two seasons have generated a trend that will feature as many as 10 such shows this season, not counting the returning sitcoms Moesha and Sabrina the Teenage Witch, or the Moesha spinoff The Parkers. As the new season starts, it will be worth watching to see which of these teen girls can sustain their level of maturity as they age and which will become ditzy stereotypes. We can only hope the girls don't lose character definition as these shows become the norm. One thing is certain: if Buffy Summers grows up to be Ally McBeal, there will be hell to pay. Literally.

Source: Jane Rosenzweig, "Ally McBeal's Younger Sisters, *American Prospect*, Volume II, Number 1, November 23, 1999.

DISCUSSION QUESTIONS

1. This article argues a variety of claims. Identify and classify each of them. Be sure to distinguish between primary claims and secondary, supporting claims.

2. Rosenzweig's argument relies heavily on descriptive/interpretive summaries of a handful of television shows. Based upon your experience viewing any of these shows, do you find her summaries fair and representative?

3. For what audience do you think this argument was written? What audience do you think would likely be most opposed to the views presented here? Most receptive? How would the argument's approach need to change in order to convince the opposing audience you identify?

4. Like most readings of popular culture, this essay includes interpretive arguments. Identify one or two and evaluate their effectiveness in terms of the principles and practices presented in Chapter 8 of this book.

SUGGESTIONS FOR WRITING (18.6)

1. Select a popular television series with which you are familiar. Write a two-page interpretation of the role of women in that series. Assume that your audience is not familiar with the show.

2. Rosenzweig's subject is female roles in television. What about the role of men? Select one of the shows she writes about and write a companion argument about the roles of men.

3. Rosenzweig appears to accept implicitly Kenneth Myers's view that television influences the behavior of the young people who watch it. Using your own experience as a television viewer, write a three- to four-page causal argument agreeing or disagreeing with this view. Your factual support will consist of personally experienced facts, so be sure to present yourself and your experience as credibly and reasonably as possible.

4. Select a recent full-length film that has been extremely popular. Do some research on that film to determine the demographics of the viewers. Then write a combination interpretive/causal argument that accounts for the popularity of the film with its viewers. As with all causal arguments, your claim will be speculative; the more carefully you establish the factuality of cause and effect and link the two through a universal principle or principles of behavior, the more convincing your argument will be.

Text Credits

page 45   "Letter from Birmingham Jail" by Martin Luther King Jr. Reprinted by arrangement with the Estate of Martin Luther King Jr., c/o Writers House as agent for the proprietor. Copyright © 1963 Martin Luther King Jr., copyright renewed 1991 Coretta Scott King.

page 70   "Eating Disorders in Males" by Leslie Knowlton, *Psychiatric Times,* XII, September 1995. Reprinted by permission of the author.

page 91   "'Vonnegut Speech' Circulates on Net" by Dan Mitchell from *Wired* (on-line), August 4, 1997.

page 113   "I, Too, Am a Good Parent" by Dorsett Bennett. From *Newsweek,* July 4, 1994. All rights reserved. Reprinted by permission.

page 127   "From Sweet Anarchy to Stupid Pet Tricks" by Mark Edmundson as appeared in *Civilization,* December 1996/January 1997, Vol. 3, No. 6.

page 136   Excerpt from "Hawaii Judge Ends Ban on Gay Marriages" as appeared in the *Los Angeles Times* (Rpt. in *The Plain Dealer*), December 4, 1996, pp. la, 28a.

page 164   "The Side Effects of Affirmative Action" by Pamela J. Hsu from *The Detroit News,* May 22, 1994. Reprinted with permission from *The Detroit News.*

page 171   From "History as Mirror" by Barbara W. Tuchman. Reprinted by permission of Russell & Volkening as agents for the author. Copyright © 1973 by Barbara Tuchman.

page 179   From "Medicine and the Media: A Case Study" by David Brown. Copyright © 1984 by Alpha Omega Honor Medical Society, reprinted by permission from *The Pharos,* Vol. 47, Number 3.

page 183   "Particle Accelerators Test Cosmological Theory" by David N. Schramm and Gary Steigman, New York: *Scientific American,* June 1988, Vol. 258, #6.

page 186   From "Cutting into Cholesterol" by Bruce P. Kinosian and John M. Eisenberg, *Journal of American Medical Association,* April 15, 1988, 259; 2249–54. Reprinted by permission of the American Medical Association.

page 186   Reprinted by permission of the Modern Language Association of America from "Don't Tell: Imposed Silences in 'The Color Purple'" by King-Kok Cheung, *PMLA,* 1983.

page 206   From *When Hope and Fear Collide* by Arthur Levine and Jeannette S. Cureton, 1998. Reprinted by permission of Jossey-Bass, Inc., a subsidiary of John Wiley & Sons, Inc.

Index